Serious Pursuits

The Collected Essays of Asa Briggs
Volume I: Words, Numbers, Places, People
Volume II: Images, Problems, Standpoints, Forecasts

Serious Pursuits
Communications
and Education

Asa Briggs

Volume III
The Collected Essays of Asa Briggs

University of Illinois Press
Urbana and Chicago

Published simultaneously in Great Britain by Harvester Wheatsheaf
under the title *The Collected Essays of Asa Briggs: Volume III:
Serious Pursuits: Communications and Education*

Manufactured in Great Britain

Cataloging in Publication Data available on request from the
Library of Congress

ISBN 0–252–01872–9

In Memory of My Friend and Colleague
Eddi Ploman

The air is full of ideas – bubbles, as it were – which float in the ether to be dispelled by reason of their tender structure, or to be expanded and thoroughly worked out in the progress of time and the interests of science.

(Invention, 25 April 1896)

Contents

1 Foreword: Convergences and Coincidences

This volume of articles, essays and lectures on communications and education is the sequel to two previous volumes published in 1985. These included many of my academic articles on different aspects of history that had particularly interested me. *Words, Numbers, Places, People* was the very broad title of the first volume, *Images, Problems, Standpoints, Forecasts* the equally broad title of the second. The essays had been written at different times and had been published in different places, but they were all concerned with social and cultural change and how it was perceived.

The preparation of a third volume was always part of my plan, since I knew that any selection from my published work that did not include articles – and lectures – on communications and education would be bound to be incomplete. In this volume the lectures are as significant as the articles, for lectures remain a central feature not only of the university year but of the media year. The Granada Lectures, for example, have stimulated as much interest as the BBC's Reith Lectures. Perhaps there are echoes of the pulpit in this. There are other echoes, however. My own Granada Lecture was called 'University Challenge': the title was taken from the television programme.

The media figure prominently in this volume, testimony to the fact that I have spent a great deal of my time and energy in writing the history of broadcasting in the United Kingdom, sometimes to the expressed regret of several of my historian colleagues who have argued that I might have been better employed elsewhere. Certainly I myself did not appreciate that I was giving myself a life sentence when in 1958 I accepted an invitation from General Sir Ian Jacob, the then Director-General of the BBC, to write its history. Yet I have never regretted taking on the commission. It has kept me regularly in touch with a national institution that has sometimes seemed to be in the process of perpetual change. Still more important, it has kept me in touch also with the social and cultural changes, national and international, that broadcasting both registers and influences. In what ways and how profoundly have almost always been subjects of controversy.

1

While broadcasting is a topic that until a few years ago had engaged few historians, this, I am sure, was a mistake. Apart from its inherent interest – and this includes the controversy – the history of broadcasting leads naturally into general social and cultural history. To try to write the history of broadcasting in the twentieth century is in a sense to try to write the history of everything else.

Whatever may be said of the pleasures and perils of the time that I have devoted to writing broadcasting history, it has sometimes been to my own regret as a historian, although in this case not necessarily to the regret of others, that I have spent far more of my time in educational management than I have done in writing the history of broadcasting – or, for that matter, of any other kind of history. 'Cares of office' have frequently kept me completely away from my study, often to my considerable frustration. In the last resort, however, I have no lasting regrets about this either. Over the years I have derived great satisfaction out of my educational activities. They have seldom been a complete diversion. Drawn irresistibly as I have been – and still am – towards writing, I would never have been satisfied only to write – or to carry out research.

I have long been interested in 'management', a word that I choose deliberately instead of the word 'office', although it is only recently that it has begun to be widely used – and then controversially – in educational circles. Without good management of people, the most important task of all, and of resources – a task that has recently involved private money-raising on a large scale – educational plans can be discussed, but they can never be implemented. When the resources were largely public and relatively – only relatively *pace* Lord Annan – plentiful, as they were during the 1960s – there was just as great a need for their good management. Indeed, good management was as essential in a period of university expansion as it has been in a period of university cuts.

There have been changes in the background and style of 'university managers' since the exciting, if contentious, 1960s. I am strongly of the opinion, however, that in present circumstances, as in past, the best managers, if they are not 'academics' themselves, must be completely familiar with academic matters. They cannot delegate that task to others. For myself it has undoubtedly been a great advantage to me in university management that I have been able to do some teaching as well as a great deal of research. Both the teaching and the research have kept me in close touch with individual undergraduate students, without whom there would be no universities, and with individual postgraduate students, without whom there would be no future for universities as teaching institutions.

In retrospect, I see my very varied work as being of one piece, at its best, I hope, 'balanced', not lopsided; and this third volume sets out some of the considerations that have shaped it. I am aware above all else that I myself have benefited personally from the new educational opportunities of the twentieth century. Without them I would never have become a professional historian. I have always maintained – and for me it follows directly from my own experience – that such opportunities should be available to everyone who wishes to take advantage of them – in the interests of the community as much as in their personal interests. Because my belief is a strong one, I have always felt, too, that I should do something about it. I have set out to act as well as to communicate. Education for me has always been a serious pursuit.

The pursuit has not been without its own frustrations, of course, and there have been many times when I have noted that educational management encompasses the trivial as well as the serious. Because of this, indeed, the bigger purposes of education can all too easily be obscured. So, too, of course, can the bigger purposes of broadcasting, since in broadcasting there are even more obvious trivialities – so many, indeed, that some critics of television in particular, have focused entirely on the triviality of by far the largest part of its output. I have never concluded from this, however, that broadcasting should be dismissed as a trivial pursuit. Even when it is concerned not with 'education' and 'information' but with 'entertainment', the third item in a trinity, it goes far beyond the 'quiz'.

Like Huw Weldon, who was the most eloquent spokesman of the merits of television, not least as a medium of entertainment, I believe that 'being able to go bald-headed for the difficult as well as the popular and for serious programmes as well as for laughter is a privilege and an achievement in the world of television'. Like him, too, I have never ignored entertainment, including sport, as more than one of the papers in this volume shows. It is fascinating that over the last twenty years historians have moved increasingly into this territory. There are now specialised journals as well as learned monographs dealing with the history of sport and with many other aspects of 'leisure', a term that should not be left to the sociologists.

I recognise clearly that my own historical writing, including several of the republished essays in my first two volumes – for example my essay in the first volume on 'The Language of "Mass" and "Masses" in Nineteenth-century England' – has been profoundly affected both by my studies of twentieth-century communications and by my involvement over the same period in education, most particularly, perhaps, in 'continuing education'. Having studied the first impact of television, I was drawn to studying the first impact of the printing press and in the nineteenth century to the cartoons in *Punch*. Having looked at correspondence courses for adults, I turned to videos. And the other way round.

It may well be that the most important influences on my work as a historian have been my place of birth and my family background, and these are discussed in one of the papers, a new one, that I have included – as the last – in this collection. Yet it is through my experience both in communications and education that I changed myself first from being an economic, or primarily an economic, historian into becoming a social historian and, second, from being a social historian into becoming a cultural historian. By comparison, I have been relatively uninfluenced by ideology, and in this I am sharply different from some of my contemporaries, including some of those with whom I have often worked extremely closely, particularly in labour history, in business history, and in the history of popular culture, where the ideology is seldom inconspicuous.

If it is solely through examining twentieth-century communications history that I have gained new insights into the history of communications in previous centuries before the term 'media' had come into use, it is largely, though not entirely, through my experience in policy-making in higher education and in educational management that I have moved far outside history to other disciplines, related and unrelated. Through practical encounters within the university context, such as those with specialist colleagues in the life sciences or in technology, the latter another subject, itself sometimes ideological, that greatly interests me, I have been forced to consider their serious pursuits as well as my own.

While I was a young Fellow in Worcester College in 1954, I put on with the help of a colleague – a former student – a pioneering comparative seminar on concepts and methods in the natural and social sciences; and my interest in such matters moved from the seminar stage to the practical stage at Leeds. I was able to take the initiative then in the appointment of a lecturer in the history of technology and in the introduction into the history syllabus of optional subjects on the history of science, an option set against what was by then the traditional 'history of political thought', and the novel history of economic thought. At the University of Sussex, we were able to go further, and I spent more time in discussions concerning a School of Biological Sciences and a School of Applied Sciences than I did in discussions on the history curriculum.

As a result of this experience, I have spent much of life reflecting on 'interdisciplinarity', a term from which some scholars still shrink. I devoted a large part of a volume devoted to it that was published by OECD in English and French, in 1972. I also became deeply involved in the practical implications of the 'two cultures' debate, when I inaugurated an 'arts/science' programme at Sussex. Indeed, there were times when I was more preoccupied in Sussex with trying to get this right than with anything else.

The fact that the terms 'interdisciplinary' and 'interdisciplinarity' still need to be put between inverted commas is unfortunate. When we try to tackle so-called 'real life' problems – in business, in industrial relations, in economic development, in the organisation of government, in the care of the environment, in communications and, not least, in education itself – we cannot make progress without a convergence of disciplinary insights and concepts.

When I have tried myself to tackle problems of communications and education, I have often found that I have had more in common with people from outside my own discipline than I have had with people inside it. For example, Colin Cherry, Professor of Engineering at Imperial College, London, who studied as a laboratory assistant, working his way 'upwards' through evening classes, eventually approached communications issues in much the same way as I did, although by a totally different route; and after his untimely death I was proud to be allowed to deliver an address at his Memorial Service and to write an introduction to his posthumous paper *The Age of Access: Information Technology and the Social Revolution* (1985). Cherry's *Pulse and Transients in Communications Circuits*, a thoroughly disciplinary study, preceded his *World Communication: Threat or Promise* (1971) by more than twenty years, but as early as 1957 he had written his major study *On Human Communication* (1957). We had a common friend in Sir Willis Jackson with whom I always felt to be on the same wavelength.

In describing the origins of my interest in interdisciplinarity, I added the qualification 'largely, though not entirely', since, long before my experiences as an educational policy-maker and manager had begun, I had already taken first degrees both in history and in economics, a combination that in itself determined my own initial research. I found the combination of empirical and theoretical studies appealing and rewarding, as I did when I turned in 1945 to the teaching of PPE, Modern Greats, in Worcester College, often to pupils older than myself.

I have always had my own map of learning, and history and economics were the first two territories on that map. Literature was already there, however, thanks largely to one dedicated schoolmaster, and I have never wanted to leave it off my map. I believe that history can best be studied either along with literature or with the social sciences, preferably with both. In PPE I taught both economics and politics, and while I was a young Fellow I was invited to chair the Faculty of Geography, Anthropology and Archaeology, I fear largely because the members of the Faculty could not agree on a chairman from their own ranks. The fact that many of my metaphors are geographical shows how much importance I have always attached to geography – and to travel.

At least since Rousseau, most statements on education have been essentially autobiographical, and the papers included in this volume, particularly this foreword, unlike many of the papers in my first two volumes, reflect this obviously. It is both through learning from and dealing with particular people and with particular institutions – and what extraordinary institutions the BBC and the University of Oxford, in particular, are – that I have forged my own sense of interdisciplinarity. It is through life as much as through 'thought', therefore, that I have become deeply interested both in 'convergences' and in 'coincidences'.

I almost chose 'convergences and coincidences' as the title of this volume, but I discarded it eventually in favour of the less cryptic and more evocative title – *Serious Pursuits*. None the less, the convergence between education and communications in this century is one of the main recurring themes in the papers in this volume, and I have dedicated my book to my Swedish friend Eddi Ploman, who died, alas, in the last stages of its preparation, because he was one of the first people to realise this. With his initial experience in Swedish broadcasting and in the European Broadcasting Union, he moved to London to become Director of the International Broadcast Institute and later to Tokyo to become a Vice-President of the United Nations University on the Council of which I had served myself for six years.

Decades ago, communication and computer technologies converged to produce what Americans called 'compunications', and in 1976 the International Broadcasting Institute, more fully described below, changed its name to the International Institute of Communications. More recently, as my friend Everett Dennis, the Director of the Gannett Center for Media Studies at Columbia University in New York, has put it, convergence has become even broader – 'at the level of media functions and product development, at the level of ownership and control, in management and supervision, and with regard to individuals in the workplace'.

Dennis rightly draws out the wide-ranging educational implications of such convergences. So, too, do I. Historians can miss them. So, too, can those 'educationists' who stick firm to the old ways. Dennis writes from a good address – from inside the solid building of the School of Journalism in Columbia, a pioneering institution with no English parallel. I myself owe a considerable debt to the Gannett Foundation, where I spent an all-too-brief, but extremely constructive, period as a Senior Fellow in 1987. Away from action, I had time to reflect on bigger issues in the company of others who were sharing the same privilege. This book might never have appeared had I not enjoyed this spell in New York.

Dates matter in private history at least as much as in public history, and after surveying dates in my own life for the purposes of this volume, I put together the two sets of dates, private and public, that are equally relevant in relation to the material in this book. My own life – and my family's life – were influenced by communications long before 1958, when I decided to write the history of the BBC. I was born one year before the British Broadcasting Company, not then a Corporation, was founded, and I was brought up within a radio age, the contours of which have been enticingly explored by my wife in *Those Radio Times* (1982). The oldest of my four children, Katharine, was born in 1956, one year after the BBC monopoly was broken in what was already a 'television age'.

I had an early acquaintance with computers too, although they were not then known as such, at Bletchley, where I was a cryptographer in the Ultra team during the War; and I was moved more than he can have realized when Richard Shannon chose 'Decoding and Communicating' as the title of his review in *The Times Literary Supplement* of the first two volumes of my essays. Bletchley was my second university.

As far as university education is concerned, I would never have met my wife in any previous century, for, like me, she was the first person from her own family to go to university, and it was in Oxford that our paths converged. We had been 'selected', a term that is referred to in several of my essays. The University of Sussex I selected myself, although I might never have gone there – and this, as the papers in this volume reveal, was the most important decision of my life – had I not attended the 1960 annual conference in Brighton of the Workers' Educational Association of which I was then President. Knowing that I was going to be there, John Fulton, Principal-elect of the planned new University College of Sussex, as it was then called, invited me to go around the site with him and learn of his plans. We had an absorbing afternoon together, and as I left Brighton by train, he called out to me to ask me to join him as his deputy. The convergence, like so many convergences, rested on a coincidence. It took me several months, however, to make up my mind.

It has been a great advantage to me as a historian of broadcasting that I have been a participant in, rather than an observer of, 'the golden age of wireless', as I called the second volume of my *History*, and 'the age of television'. I first broadcast in 1944 in Forces Education programmes, the scripts of which I had written myself while I was still in uniform, and I took part in my first television programme (with G. M. Young, the historian, whom I greatly admired, as a fellow participant) in 1953. Forces Education programmes were serious enough, although there was great fun in doing them, but nothing could have been more trivial than that first television programme, which was called 'The Balloon Game'.

Trivial pursuits can themselves be testing, and neither Young nor I was made to feel complacent when we read in a newspaper gossip column announcing the programme that, given the people in the balloon, it would be extremely unlikely to take off. Fortunately, it was not a one-and-only event in my television career, even as far as television entertainment was concerned. I was glad to appear occasionally in *'That Was the Week that Was'* and in several other explicitly 'entertainment' programmes.

The experience taught me at least as much about broadcasting as my experience in a far larger number of 'serious' interviews and discussion programmes with characters as different as Lord Beeching, Frank Cousins, Dick Crossman, and Alastair Horne. Boundaries, however, are no more easy to draw in broadcasting then they are between academic disciplines, and if I were asked whether or not my appearance in *'Desert Island Discs'* – and in a number of other well-known programmes – was entirely 'entertainment' I would be forced to reply no. I know, too, that competition for resources can produce just as much departmentalisation in broadcasting as there is in universities.

Broadcasting for me has been a continuing education, if fortunately not a continuous education, for it can spoil people or use them up. I have had my high points, including the chairing of one of the last mass audience radio discussion programmes, 'Our Present Discontents', the preparation with others and the writing of scripts for one major and highly imaginative radio series, 'The Long March of Everyman', and the writing of scripts and presentation for one major television series, 'The Legacy of Marx', produced in 1983 on the occasion of the centenary of Marx's death.

Each of these ventures deserves an essay. In all of them I worked with a team, as I have often worked with teams in universities, and working with camera teams is above all an illuminating task. *Experientia docet.* Scriptwriting requires great patience as well as imagination.

Most of my pursuit of broadcasting has been scriptless, however, although on more than one occasion in presenting a programme I have had to learn by heart the words of a script which I myself had written – and to repeat every word of it even when on the spot I had found a better way – or so I thought – of expressing myself.

By a coincidence, I became a member of the University Grants Committee (UGC) in 1958, the same year that I began to write the history of the BBC, and that, in days of 'visitations' – an awe-ful word – took me round all the universities of the country. There were no scripts then, but we were overwhelmed with paper. I joined the UGC three years after I had moved by choice from a Fellowship in Worcester College, Oxford, and a Readership in the University of Oxford in Recent Social and Economic History – the word 'recent' had been carefully chosen – to the Professorship of Modern History at Leeds. I wanted not only to return to the North of England, where I was born, but to acquire the new experience of directing a large department in a great civic university.

The history department was called 'a School', and my co-director, Professor John Le Patourel, a mediaevalist, was rightly proud of this. It carried with it echoes of great continental schools of history. And we tried to behave like a School, producing, after fascinating discussions, what we thought was the best history syllabus in any university, in Britain or abroad. Once we had produced it, however, we were as aware of constraints as we were of opportunities, for when we dealt with other professors – for example, in organising joint degrees (History + x) – we were always conscious of the fact that they were Heads of Departments (with capital letters) and that some of them did not like discussions of any kind: these, they felt, lowered their status. If we wanted to make progress, we had, none the less, to sign bilateral treaties with them. It was then that my dislike of 'departmentalisation' began.

I am 'Oxbridge' on paper – a hybrid noun or adjective that I dislike as much as the with-it hybrid noun 'compunications' or the pompous non-hybrid noun 'visitations' – since I began my university education as a Scholar of Sidney Sussex College, Cambridge, and became a Fellow of Worcester College, Oxford while I was still in uniform in 1944 and just before I gave my first Forces Education broadcast. Formal letters, some of which I never saw, had to be exchanged between the two institutions, and I was invited to return to Cambridge before I had really settled down in Oxford. By the early 1950s, however, I had decided that I did not want my life and work to be confined either within an Oxford or a Cambridge context. I was ready to 'get out', although I turned down one offer of the Chair in Leeds before I accepted a second offer – due again to a series of coincidences – in 1955. I was to hesitate longer about leaving Leeds in 1961 to become the first Professor appointed to Sussex than I had done when I left Oxford for Leeds or – and there were certainly hesitations then – when I left Cambridge for Oxford.

My six happy years at Leeds were the most creative years in the pursuit of my historical interests. It was then that I wrote *The Age of Improvement* (1959) and prepared the ground, literally, for my book *Victorian Cities* (1963), the sequel to *Victorian People* (1954), which I had written while still in Oxford. Before I left Leeds for Sussex there was a short, stimulating break in Australia as Visiting Professor at the Australian National University in 1959, at least as stimulating as my later period at the Gannett Foundation. Canberra did not then have a lake. But it had a superb outback. And it had people who wanted to talk – and not just to listen. Several of the papers in this book have an Australian provenance. It is reflected too in my chapter on Melbourne in *Victorian Cities*.

It was Sussex, a county which in 1961 I knew less well than Australia, that drew me into the vortex of national education change, and much else. Indeed, it was there that I became more directly involved than I ever had been before in the communication as well as the educational scene, partly because at last universities were ceasing to be remote institutions, little-known to most of the public. It was partly, however, because my academic home, in particular, was, from its creation, of great interest to the media. There were social and cultural reasons for this – why otherwise would *Vogue* have been attracted to devote a large part of one number to it, or *Reader's Digest*? – but an obvious reason was that Brighton was the home of many of the people who worked in the media and a magnet, not far from London, for those who did not.

I was to stay in Sussex until 1976, for fifteen years in all, nearly ten of them as Vice-Chancellor. And at no time were we ever free of the media. By the time that I left, there was another reason for this. The media, including publishing, now employed large numbers of graduates of the University. Some of them were to keep in regular touch with me, and collectively they were to entertain me years later at a wonderful party given in the headquarters of the Independent Broadcasting Authority.

I wish in retrospect, as I wished at the time, that it would have been possible while I was at Sussex to set up a School of Communications there. I tried hard, with the invaluable help at one time of Tom Hopkinson, whose name will always be associated with *Picture Post*, but who believed passionately in education in communications, particularly for communicators.

Brighton would have been – and still would be – the perfect location as it has proved to be for Tom Harrisson's Mass Observation collection under Dorothy Sheridan's tender care. Tom, my second Tom, whom I first met by coincidence rather than by design, was a good friend, and for a time housed himself in a back office of my own building, complete with stacks of photographs and Asian masks and weapons. He was applying mass observation techniques to Sussex undergraduates and Brightonians on the beach. His tragic death in an accident near Bangkok was a great blow, and I was the first person to be telephoned with the news from the Foreign Office.

If Brighton brought new experiences, it was my earlier experience of tutorial teaching in Oxford and of the departmental lecture system in Leeds that influenced much that I tried to do at the University of Sussex. I was interested, above all else, in what kind of education we were offering to our students, most of whom had made a deliberate choice to get into Sussex if they possibly could, and I had my eye on what kind of society we would possibly be living in during their lifetimes after graduation.

I wanted Sussex to be a university without departments, with a very special interest in the development of the individual undergraduate – and the individual postgraduate. The emphasis was on learning, and at first this was completely in line with what the University Grants Committee wanted to do. Quantitative expansion was not deemed enough. There had to be qualitative change, and it had to affect the sciences – and technology – as much as the humanities. You did not have to be a Marxist to realise that quantity and quality were related. We said little at Sussex about lectures, much about tutorials and seminars. I should add that I felt (rightly) that, given the academic calibre of the early staff, the lectures – and, indeed, the research – would look after themselves, at least during the early years.

This was the most creative period of my public life, if not of my life as a historian, and I was to stay in Sussex for fifteen years, nearly ten of these as Vice-Chancellor. When in 1966, therefore, I was asked to serve on the Planning Committee of the new Open University, of which I was to become Chancellor in 1979, I carried with me my Sussex preoccupations, as did my Sussex colleague, Norman McKenzie, whom I had met in Australia and who had become involved with the preparation for an Open University through a Parliamentary Committee even before I did. I felt from the start that the Open University should be more than a 'University of the Air', dependent primarily on television. Indeed, I was convinced that if it were to succeed it would have to employ a whole battery of learning devices, including print and radio, and, above all that it would have to make the most of each student's individual experience through personalised supervision.

My attitude towards the Open University was strongly influenced not only by Oxford or Leeds or Sussex but by aspects of my own experience that had little to do with my role either as a Professor or as a Vice-Chancellor. Because of my background, I have never taken university education for granted. Nor have I ever inflated its significance. People who have been 'rejected' – by school or by university – may have more impressive qualities, including intelligence, than those who have been 'selected'. For me, education is a life-long process – I stress the word 'process' – in which I myself am still a learner. My interest in what has come to be called 'open learning' is, therefore, another of the main recurring themes in this volume. People should be able to learn when they want, and the universities of the future will have to be learning resources centres for a far larger section of the population than their own teenage undergraduates.

I was drawn by choice into adult education when I was a young historian, several years before I gave a keynote address at the Workers' Educational Association Jubilee Conference in Harrogate in 1953. There, I looked forwards rather than backwards, as I did five years later when I become national President of the WEA. My nine years of presidential office – and in this case 'office' is the right word – taught me much that I would never have learnt from undergraduates within the conventional age group, so that it seemed a natural move later to become involved in the planning of the Open University.

Long before I became President of the WEA, however, I had come to admire the way in which men and women were pursuing or had pursued education under difficulties, people of our own time and deprived people in the eighteenth and nineteenth centuries who struggled to become literate. There were still many of them left in the Keighley of my boyhood. Theirs was indeed a serious pursuit, far more serious than mine has ever been, for at times everything for them was at stake – for me, seldom, if ever. When I confer Open University degrees at ceremonies which are attended not just by those receiving degrees but by whole families, I am deeply affected when I learn of the experience of some of the graduates. They have obtained their degrees in the hardest way possible. Some are handicapped, and this is the only way that they could have obtained a degree.

The WEA was uninterested in qualifications and pursued 'liberal education' for its own sake. I learned much from it not only about teaching and learning, but about the strengths and weaknesses of voluntary organisations and about the importance of national policy-making in education, education at every level. Indeed, it was just because I was interested in adult education that I became increasingly interested in school education also – and in vocational education – and one of the most forceful articles that I ever wrote was called 'Education to Improve Education': it appeared in the WEA's magazine *Highway* in 1958. Much of the adult education that I first encountered was remedial education designed to make up for the deficiencies, largely social in origin, of school education. And this led me to press for public action both to improve 'State education' for the great majority of the population and to broaden access to higher education.

It also led me to re-evaluate – the right word – what could and could not be done in the school classroom. I had been fortunate to have the opportunity of teaching for a short time in a secondary modern school in my home town of Keighley before I put on uniform. I greatly enjoyed the experience and learned much from it. It is impossible to carry through any educational reforms, radical or conservative, without recognising that their success depends on the quality of teachers, on their motivations and on their sense of involvement. In the Keighley of my boyhood their quality had varied, as had their motivations, but the best of them were in touch with families as well as with pupils and they did much to encourage parents as well as children to believe that education mattered. They had an accepted place in the community. My own headmaster, Neville Hind, was a formidable local presence. I owe much to him.

I went through a second protracted period of re-evaluation of school education in the ten years from 1975 to 1985, a very different period, when I was Chairman of the Heritage Education Group, a group that, not coincidentally, received a small annual grant not from the Department of Education and Science but from the Department of the Environment. The Group was founded at my instigation – and at the instigation of our energetic and imaginative secretary, Keith Eggleston – at the end of European Architectural Heritage Year. It would have been even more absurd to conclude that the remarkable work carried out in that year – under the energetic general auspices of Raine Dartmouth, now Lady Spencer – was once-and-for-all work than it would have been to conclude that education stops with a degree – or with a General Certificate of Education. Fortunately, Lady Birk, then Minister in the Department of Environment, clearly saw the logic of this – and acted accordingly. The year 1975, therefore, was not an end but a beginning.

My work with the Group was concerned essentially with 'visual education'. I wanted everyone to learn how to judge new buildings and new environments as well as old ones. The word 'heritage' was not intended to inhibit. Our scope was deliberately wide – 'all environments' (not just individual buildings); 'all disciplines' (not just history or architecture); all 'levels' of education (not just secondary schooling). Our work, well recorded in *Heritage Education News*, which was circulated in every school in the country, took me personally into all kinds of schools, in some of which the quality of teaching was quite exceptionally high. So, too – and they went together – was the commitment of the teachers, not least the head teachers. Unfortunately, when the heads changed, the schools often changed. That is the major reason why 'management' matters.

It was the primary schools that interested me most, for it was there more than anywhere else that the best teachers were encouraging the desire of very young Children to explore. Such exploration, based on curiosity, the key to all learning, is even more important at the beginning of the learning process than it is at university. Yet I myself see a great arc linking the two. It is never wise, except for convenience, to separate the educational process into entirely distinct phases; and as we went to places just off the tourist map, like Bridgwater or Daventry, or Wareham or Wyndham, I began to feel an affinity with teachers working in entirely different circumstances from myself with pupils of a very different age range.

I learned also from my experience with the Heritage Education Group, if I still needed to be taught the lesson, that imagination and effective communication is at the heart of education. There has to be interaction. Our own Group included teachers and planners (and people involved in the committee work and administration of teaching and planning), people who usually communicate far too little in local government, but it also included representatives of the media, whose professional job is communication. Whatever our experience, we all learned a great deal from schoolchildren. We saw through their eyes – not just at exhibitions but on 'town trails', a term that I liked, perhaps because it is geographical in character.

To me 'visual communication', of which 'design' was a part, was particularly important in all our work. I was aware from the start how visual education had long been neglected in this country – more, for example, than musical education, which has also increasingly interested me. It was John Ruskin who observed in the nineteenth century that 'hundreds of people can talk for one who can think. But thousands can think for one who can see. To see clearly is poetry, prophecy and religion all in one.'

In an 'age of television' the message is surely more important than ever, even for those who believe, in my view innocently, that the medium is the message. 'Visual literacy' is an unsatisfactory phrase, but what lies behind it is plain enough. Unfortunately, those enthusiasts who are interested in visual aspects of the heritage – and there are now more of them than there ever have been before – are not necessarily interested in what we see on our television screens, and how we should judge it – nor for that matter in design, where belatedly our late-twentieth-century record has at last improved.

I gave a lecture in Tokyo for the International Institute of Communications on 'Visual Literacy' in 1976, where I was very conscious of the distinctive Japanese experience of a large part of my audience, and eight years earlier, when I knew less about the subject, I felt that I had been especially privileged to deliver the Design Oration to the Society of Industrial Artists and Designers in London. For a short time I was a member, too, of the Design Council in London, and undoubtedly all this experience influenced me in writing *Victorian Things* (1988), a book that, above all others, I was determined to write. In 1981 I felt that I was still in a small minority, however, when I drew attention to the links between different aspects of visual communication in an Open University Chancellor's lecture, delivered at Milton Keynes and televised throughout the country. My title was 'Learning to Look'.

From my personal research as well as from my experience, the usually neglected links between communications, including visual communications, and education, had become clear to me, and I have now traced them back far beyond the nineteenth century, Ruskin's century and the century of William Morris – a century which neither of them admired, but the century on which much of my research as a historian has been concentrated. I am convinced, however, that there is need for still further research, and with this in mind, I have chosen as the theme of my six Ford Lectures in Oxford in 1991 'Communications and Culture in Victorian England'. I shall include both the visual arts and music within the scope of my survey and analysis, though I shall prove no more willing than T. S. Eliot was to define 'culture'.

I recognise that in our own century, at least from the 1920s onwards, it has been argued, in part correctly, that the influence of 'mass communications', a term that I have always treated critically, has run directly counter, through the Press and through publishing as much as through the 'electronic media', to the influence of school education. In particular, during the 'age of television', it has often been asserted that what is achieved in the classroom is abandoned in the home. The screen defeats the teacher. And teachers' trade unions, in particular, often used to say this regularly.

Such a view has always seemed to me to be as inadequate as are general dismissals of television as 'merely trivial' or condemnations of computers as being 'anti-human'. In my own view, it would be unjust also to see radio or the Press entirely within such a perspective. Many factors have to be taken into the reckoning in studying the media and their impact; and only a few of them have received much attention. For example, the common characteristics of educational systems and of communication systems in different countries have been studied far too little, even by historians of the media. There has been a gap here, for with significant exceptions, like Richard Hoggart, whose Reith Lectures of 1971 'Only Connect' were explicitly concerned with 'culture and communication', few scholars were interested in both. Fewer still have been involved, as he has, in policy-making in both. Another who has is Lord Annan.

The fact that in this country we have developed a communications system which through the evolution of public broadcasting policy has emphasised the importance of information and education as well as of entertainment is historically significant. When the Open University took in its first students in 1971, the year Hoggart was broadcasting, there was an obvious convergence between communications developments and educational developments, and it seemed natural that the new institution should rely on the BBC, which had always attached great importance, if seldom with unanimous backing from inside it, to its educational activity. That activity was, of course, not restricted to universities. Kenneth Fawdry's *Everything but Alf Garnett: A personal view of BBC school broadcasting* (1974) makes that plain. And this well-titled book should be read alongside Josephine Langham's less catchily titled but equally illuminating *Teachers and Television: A history of the IBA's educational fellowship scheme* (1990).

Not all countries have shared the British approach to radio and television education, and for this reason alone I have always urged the need for comparative studies designed to explain why different countries, using what is essentially the same communications technology, have made such different social and cultural uses of it. For this reason, the International Institute of Communications commissioned a series of 'case studies', which I edited, on broadcasting in different countries in different continents. Generous research support came from Hoso Bunka, a Japanese Foundation linked to the Japanese public broadcasting organisation, NHK. Significantly there has been more public and media interest in this subject in Japan than there has been in Britain, and I was asked to contribute an item for the first day on which Japanese satellite television broadcast to the rest of the world.

The International Institute of Communications, in its origins the

International Broadcast Institute, founded in 1968, was primarily concerned with the quality of programming, and, more recently, following its change of name, has an impressive record of involvement in the study of telecommunications policy. For many years I was privileged to be its Honorary Research Projects Chairman, first with Eddi Ploman as Director, and next with John Howkins, who before becoming Director had been editor of *Intermedia*, a communications magazine which set out to serve many of the purposes, including the pursuit of interdisciplinarity, to which I am committed. I loved the title. My closest colleague in IIC was Joanna Spicer, who was joint author with me of *The Franchise Affair* (1986) which exposed some of the limitations in the procedures of the Independent Broadcasting Authority, not my favourite body. As a member for many years of the Board of Southern Television I had learnt much of the operations of the 'other sector'. There were problems in Southampton – but there was also friendship and – above all – creativity.

The main thrust of the research of the Institute, most of which was policy-orientated, was incorporated in an 'action' programme; and this included not only national case studies but an on-going study of changes in communications structures and technologies – and their influence on attitudes – and a large-scale study of the global and regional 'flow' of information, ideas and entertainment from one country to others. Geography was a key subject in the last of these studies which set out, over-ambitiously perhaps, to prepare an 'atlas of flow'.

Education has not been a main element in 'flow' – entertainment has – and in the future it may not always be considered as one of three objects of domestic broadcasting. Moreover, even if it will be, there will be an increasing tendency to segregate it – as classical music will also be segregated – in a separate channel. The 'balanced broadcasting' element, offering the possibility of changing tastes and not simply accepting them as they now are, will be lost. The word 'channel' is an attractive word with a long history; the word 'ghetto' with an equally long history is not. And I am concerned that if we force particular broadcast material into rigidly determined channels, whether we accept the fact or not we shall be creating ghettos.

I realise that if the whole public broadcasting system changes in Britain, as it seems likely to do, the future pattern of educational provision may become completely different from that which has evolved since the 1920s, and that many of the essays in this volume, concerned mainly, as they are, with the record as it was, will have only an historical interest as evidence of 'a world that we have lost'. There is still time, none the less, to point to some of the illusions associated with philosophy of choice – one being that with more choice there is necessarily more variety. I pondered on all these questions when I was privileged to receive – or share – the Marconi Medal in 1975. Giaia Marconi and Walter Roberts made this possible, and I am still pondering.

In our age of multiple channels, cables, satellites and videos, all of which claim to offer more choice, there is scope for initiatives, and one with which I have been particularly concerned is the Commonwealth of Learning, created by Commonwealth Prime Ministers to bring the different distance learning systems of the Commonwealth into a network. Other international educational networks are being created, too, including networks in Europe, some of them organised not by governments but by business, international business that has for long transcended frontiers. The essay on the 'Commonwealth of Learning' that I have included in this volume is based on lectures that I gave in 1990 as part of the fortieth anniversary celebrations of the University of the West Indies.

In sorting out my old papers while preparing this volume, I came across the script of a forgotten broadcast which I had written and 'narrated' as long ago as 1963 with the same title – 'The Commonwealth of Learning'. In it I had interviewed a number of Commonwealth academic figures on the occasion of the Jubilee Conference of the Association of Commonwealth Universities held in London in that year. The last word was not mine, but that of Dr Davidson Nicol, then Principal of Fourah Bay College in Sierra Leone:

> The emphasis which we want to put in our universities in Africa is that of [producing] an individual who may not be bent on scholarship, but simply because he has had the advantage of university education will be able, wherever he is, to make original observations and think things out afresh. . . .

Obviously Dr Nicol was concerned with more than an education designed to increase human adaptability at work and to enrich human leisure, serious though these concerns were even when he spoke.

Others long before Dr Nicol had more fundamental concerns in mind also. I have always been drawn to a passage about Henry Brougham, founder of the University of London – and of much else – in an early book by F. D. Maurice, written in 1828. Maurice complained, in my view correctly, that in all his talk about education and his policy-making Brougham had not 'proposed any plan for cultivating more wisely and carefully the better feelings of mankind'. He had seemed to imagine that 'universal justice may be obtained by chemical analysis, and that benevolence will be the product of a quadratic equation'. Twentieth-century experience reinforces early nineteenth-century experience, and in my view Maurice was right.

Serious as are the concerns expressed in this book, I have no doubt, therefore, that there are still more serious pursuits than education and communications. As Maurice added,

> Inquiries, arts and inventions [are] instruments, not the standards, of good. [There is] more of precious influence in one kindly feeling, one generous sacrifice, than in all the riches of colleges, the shadowy limbos of libraries and museums, the quarrels of the religions about 'the letter that killeth', and the contempt of worldly men for 'the spirit that giveth life'.

There was more than a touch of rhetoric here, a quality that Maurice admired rather than condemned in Brougham, but it was rhetoric that called for contemplation – contemplation about dispositions, desires and acts – rather than for speculation – speculation about ideas and problems. Brougham, always restless, never stopped thinking, but he would have had little time for contemplation which he never really understood. By contrast, I do not believe, although some did, that it was just rhetoric when John Fulton, always busy, always on the move, chose as the motto of Sussex University 'Be still and know'.

Brougham rightly figures in the very first essay in this volume, which originally – and Brougham would have approved – took the form of a lecture, and the index will show that he figures elsewhere, too, sometimes in unlikely places. He figures prominently, too, in just the right place on a plaque inside Birkbeck College, London, where the lecture was delivered. The plaque was first unveiled in 1824, one year after the London Mechanics Institute, a precursor of Birkbeck, had been founded in 1824. I am fond of Birkbeck, and always look at the plaque when I visit it.

Quite deliberately, I have included next in my volume, by way of contrast, an essay on the rise of mass entertainment. It was originally a lecture, delivered far away from London in Adelaide in 1960, and I have printed it just as it was delivered – with no additions and few subtractions – to show what the state of the historical study of mass entertainment was at that time. Since then, like the study of 'leisure', it has broadened and deepened.

The order in which the other papers appear in this volume is not strictly chronological, that is to say it does not follow the order in which the papers originally appeared. It rather reflects my own present sense of the connections between them, connections that often have a feel of coincidence – or apparent coincidence – about them. Thus, my piece on the television pioneer, John Logie Baird, is based on a lecture originally given at the University of Strathclyde, the precursor of which, the Andersonian Institution, had appointed George Birkbeck as a Professor of Chemistry and Natural Philosophy in 1799.

I hope, therefore, that the general reader will feel that there is continuity as well as connection in my book, particularly since the Andersonian Institution was founded 'for the good of mankind and the improvement of science'. I hope also that some of my papers will provide useful source material for future historians both of twentieth-century education and of twentieth-century communications. For this reason, throughout the volume I have seldom tampered with the content of the items as originally published, and where I have made significant changes I have said so. The lectures, papers and essays stand as they originally did, although for reasons of space I have omitted the footnotes.

I have also omitted some essays that might have been relevant for readers wanting source material. Thus, my views on 'the map of learning' were foreshadowed in an article that I wrote on 'The New Learning' in *Highway* in February 1956, only a few months after I had arrived in Leeds, and the most recent statement of my views on the new universities of the 1960s was a lecture I gave this year not at the University of Sussex but at the University of Kent, which is celebrating its silver jubilee. I called it 'A Slice of History'.

Some of the essays inevitably look different – and read differently – in the light of what has come afterwards. As more than one of them points out, everything in history depends on the vantage point. It has been a shifting one, not least in recent months, and we still cannot catch the shape of our century which is drawing to its close. Indeed, there is more uncertainty about the shape of the 1990s than there was about the shape of the 1970s at the same relative point in time.

For the historian, old statements that with hindsight are dated, incomplete or even manifestly wrong can acquire their own historic significance. Incomplete statements can point to what was being thought before dies were cast: they draw attention both to origins and to trends. Statements that are wrong call for analysis in the light of what actually happened or what has been said since. The measurement of the angle of divergence between what is 'forecast' and what is 'actualised' is of much interest to the futurologist also. He figured prominently in the second volume of my essays, and he is seldom absent from this volume also. Of course, the most that he can do is to plot 'alternative futures'. As one of the essays in this volume suggests, history is often a tale of the unexpected.

In looking back, we have to understand without always wishing to score points. The Open University, a great success story, has not developed in quite the same way as the Planning Committee thought that it would, but that does not render invalid the conclusions the Planning Committee reached. It makes them more interesting. Nor do the contrasting careers of Reith and Baird deserve to be treated as 'prehistory'. The Commonwealth of Learning, still in its earliest stage, may have a different future from that envisaged in the Memorandum of Understanding which was signed by Heads of Governments at Vancouver in 1988.

Continuity, perhaps, should be the last word in this book, provided that it is recognised that it covers burdens as well as traditions and problems as well as achievements. I certainly do not use it in a 'whiggish' sense. In many of the most recent essays on education in this book there is a note not of uncertainty but of *déja vu*. None of the problems currently being identified is entirely new, as the very last essay in the book reveals. I return there to my native town. It has changed almost out of recognition in my own life-time. Yet, as I suggest in my last essay, which also brings in coincidences, educational problems – and problems of social communication – were identified in the nineteenth-century with an even greater sense of urgency than they are being identified today. There certainly has been no 'final edit'. This would have made a perfect title not for my thirteenth essay but for my last, had we been in a position to rule anything off. We are not.

Asa Briggs
Worcester College, Oxford

2 Communications and Culture, 1823–1973: A Tale of Two Centuries*

Historians were once described by the late G. M. Young as 'the high priests of continuity'. It is a description which requires qualification, particularly in an age of revolutionary change and particularly, per-haps, for a historian like myself who has been deeply concerned with sharp breaks in human experience. Yet I count it a very special privilege as a historian to be invited to give the Foundation Oration in this College one hundred and fifty years and two days after the meeting at which, following a vote, it was decided to found the London Mechanics' Institution from which this College has derived.

The meeting took place, of course, not in a college but in a tavern, the famous Crown and Anchor Tavern at the junction of the Strand and Arundel Street, a centre of many of the most radical and some of the least radical meetings in London during the late eighteenth and early nineteenth centuries. If you like contrasts as well as continuities – and my sub-title 'A Tale of Two Centuries' should make it clear that I do – you should not jump too easily to the conclusion that the contrast between a tavern and a college as an educational *rendez-vous* marks the social distance between communications and culture in 1823 and communications and culture now. In my own University of Sussex, before there were any university buildings the first meetings of our Planning Committee were held in the Old Ship Inn in Brighton.

James Mill, who was one of the most enthusiastic supporters of the London Mechanics' Institution in 1823 – he subscribed £5 to the initial appeal fund – had written a few years earlier to Francis Place, the radical tailor and another keen supporter, that if he had time to write a book he would 'make the human mind as plain as the road from Charing Cross to St. Paul's'. Even if I had far more time available to me today than one lecture, I could not hope to make the story of culture and communication anywhere near as plain as that.

Some of the big contrasts between the nineteenth and twentieth centuries are obvious enough – the contrasts in wealth, in population, in scale, in social relationships, in the sense of time and space, and,

*'An Oration delivered at Birkbeck College, London, in celebration of the 150th Anniversary of the Foundation of the College', 4 December 1973.

22

above all, in human expectations. Yet the actual processes of cultural transformation, the shifts, sometimes subtle, from one generation to another, and the development of new means of communication, usually gradual, sometimes sudden, always uncertain in their consequences, are complex, difficult to understand, and controversial. The whole idea of 'culture', a relatively new and unformed idea in 1823, has itself evolved, not least since specialists in different discliplines took it over, while it is only during the course of the last fifteen years that we have become accustomed to thinking in terms of 'communication'. Phrases like 'mass communication', 'the media', and 'the communications revolution' are all far more recent than we tend to assume.

Yet it is not necessary to chart the history of the terminology or the ideas and experience that lie behind it to grasp the difficulty both in dating and in interpreting cultural change. Even James Mill, pursuing his own topographical simile, would have been surprised to see all the changes on the way from Charing Cross to St Paul's by the end of the nineteenth century, not to speak of the more drastic changes of the Second World War which dramatically destroyed most remaining continuities.

There was already much demolition between 1823 and 1900, including houses in the Strand with overshot windows suggesting the age of Chaucer at the beginning of the first 'communications revolution', the revolution in print. The Crown and Anchor was one of the later landmarks to go: it had ceased to be a tavern and had turned into a club before it was destroyed by fire in 1854, and it soon ceased to be a club. As old buildings disappeared, new buildings transformed the view, particularly the Law Courts, where Mill might have lingered impatiently: there were bitter arguments before it was decided to build them, and strikes while they were being built. Foreign labourers had to be imported to finish them.

What would have surprised Mill most would have been Fleet Street, symbol of a cultural change, not so much the buildings of Fleet Street as the power they represented. The new Press, perhaps the biggest transformation in the nineteenth-century communications set-up, linked Fleet Street by telegraph, a new miracle of electrical communication, with the world. Alfred Harmsworth had moved his magazine *Answers* to Fleet Street in 1889 – from Paternoster Square, for long a centre of the book trade. 'We were fond of the quaint old premises', he told his readers, 'but *Answers* went up, up, up in the world until we have been obliged to make a departure. . . . We hope to make the new premises a model of what the home of a journal should be.'

So much changed on the road from Charing Cross to St Paul's

between the time of Mill and the time of Harmsworth that Justin McCarthy, the Irish Member of Parliament and historian, wrote a whole book on what the changed vistas looked like in 1893. He dwelt mainly on the events of his own life-time, but in his last few pages went back further in time and drew a somewhat fanciful contrast between St Paul's and Westminster Abbey. St Paul's had been built and rebuilt and rebuilt again: it had been fashioned to be new. It, too, was a symbol of change, large-scale change, and it took 'fresh and eager notice of everything it saw' around it. Westminster Abbey was indubitably old: it had grown with history and was, above all, a part of it: 'each day makes its slight and almost imperceptible change, and the cathedral changes with the day, and is all unconscious of it'.

Birkbeck was always nearer to McCarthy's St Paul's than to the gothic Westminster Abbey, though it was explicitly set aside from the start from traditional religious culture. It was part of a great city which was never still and of an exciting century which was always on the move. I want to focus attention on it mainly at three points in time – first in its beginnings, second in the last three decades of the nineteenth century, and third in what can be loosely called 'our own time', and I want to try to show how at each of these three points its cultural bearings were different and must be explained in different terms.

In the beginning – when it was called an Institution – with a capital I – it had little in common with older institutions. It was, indeed, highly controversial. In 1825 the *St James's Chronicle* talked of it 'scattering the seeds of evil the extent of which the wisest amongst us cannot anticipate'. Moreover, attacked as it was from outside, it was also torn by dissension from within. Men like George Birkbeck himself and Mill and Place were on one side, and early socialist theorists, like Thomas Hodgskin and J. C. Robertson, editors of the *Mechanics' Magazine*, were on the other. Mill was just as uneasy about the content and impact of Hodgskin's views as was the *St James's Magazine*, and a few years later was to depict them as 'worse than the overwhelming deluge of Huns and Tartars'. He was afraid that the Press, still an infant Press and still a controlled Press, would devote too much attention to them and give them undue publicity. Charles Knight, popular publisher, apostle of cheap literature and one of the most prominent figures in the Society for the Diffusion of Useful Knowledge, which was founded three years after the London Mechanics' Institution (and under the same impulses), pointed eloquently not to the theories themselves, but to the dangers of students of Hodgskin actually trying to put his wicked ideas into practice. 'Such doctrines may begin in the lecture room, and there look harmless enough as abstract propositions; but they end in the maddening passion; the drunken frenzy, the unappeasable tumult – the plunder, the fire and the blood.'

There was fear in the 1820s, therefore, as well as hope. The hope, spotlighted by Brougham, was in Knowledge itself, and in the very idea of diffusion – reaching larger and larger numbers – a key idea, as we shall see, in the evolution of both nineteenth- and twentieth-century communication. The fear was twofold. Brougham's enemies were, in his view at least, afraid of knowledge itself, of the 'March of Mind'. It could not have been otherwise during the 1820s, the final address of the Society for the Diffusion of Useful Knowledge put it in 1846, 'when the opinion that there was danger to religion and to government in the spread of knowledge was avowed by many, acted on by more, and generally supposed, whether justly or not, to be at least not discouraged by those at the head of State'. That was one kind of fear, fear buttressed by tradition and often expressed in ridicule. What is remarkable is that the Society for the Diffusion of Useful Knowledge thought that this particular fear had been exorcised as early as 1845. In consequence, it decided in that year, appropriately enough the year of the repeal of the corn laws and the triumph of free trade, to disband itself.

The other fear, fear in the heart of the March of Mind group, as well as in the heart of their opponents, was that of an alternative political economy which would lead to 'the subversion of civilised society'. This second fear was sometimes expressed, however, in less dramatic language than this. 'Working men have so much to learn that may be of *real use* to them in their journey through life', it was argued, 'and such ample employment for every minute they can spare in acquiring this sort of learning, that it is sheer folly in them to trouble their heads about anything else.'

What was 'the sort of learning' recommended? – recommended specifically for 'working men'? We get a very good idea from the literature of the Society for the Diffusion of Useful Knowledge and (in a very few pages) from the last disconnected parts of Francis Place's recently published *Autobiography*. The poet Thomas Campbell, who in February 1825 wrote a letter to Brougham recommending the establishment of a University in London (a project closely related to that of the London Mechanics' Institution, as the biographies of Brougham show), cited self-taught Francis Place as 'one of the best informed men in the kingdom': 'that highly laudable person, and others who could be mentioned, shew that a man may rise to fortune even amidst unintellectual pursuits'. It was a lesson which was to be cited time and time again in the subsequent history of the London Mechanics' Institution and Birkbeck College, even though the word 'fortune' was very broadly interpreted.

Place himself, however, was not content with what Campbell said about him and wrote his own self-assessment.

> I do not know several languages, nor indeed any one language to which the word *know* can be properly applied. I regret I do not . . . Of science I really know very little. Chemistry. I know as much as is necessary to keep me from committing gross errors . . . Geology, my knowledge of this science is very general and superficial [he added a note in 1838 'I have since attended a good deal to this science']. Natural history the same – Botany much less, or rather none at all. Mathematics, here again my knowledge is very limited . . . Machinery – I have a competent share of knowledge of the construction and uses of machinery . . . Law. This has never been with me a 'dry subject'. I have read much for an 'unlearned' man . . . I have taken every opportunity I could to obtain information respecting Jurisprudence. I have pursued it as far as I could . . . Political economy. I read Adam Smith when I was very young . . . [and] since 1817 this subject has engaged much of my attention . . . I believe that I now understand as much of this 'science' as almost anyone . . . Metaphysics was for some years my most important study, other subjects were read of and thought of in a more desultory way, but this was studied as assiduously as any my avocations permitted. I attribute much of the knowledge and utility I possess to this science. It has taught me nearly all the knowledge I have of myself . . . It has made me understand my own ignorance by enabling me to understand more correctly the actual boundaries of knowledge, and kept me from wasting my time in speculative enquiries where nothing could be learned. Many years since it put me at ease on subjects which annoy and distress, and corrupt and destroy mankind – the vain enquiries engendered in the imagination and then reasoned upon and acted upon as realities.

That was not the end of Place's curriculum:

> I have been and am now intimately acquainted with several painters [he went on] and have known two or three sculptors and several architects . . . I can model a head indifferently, can sketch a simple object, and know the outlines of perspective . . . [Of] Astronomy as a science I know nothing – I however understand as much popular astronomy as most men who have not pursued it as a science. Geography. I have a very competent knowledge of geography . . . I have all along attended to it. . . . Physiology. I know as much respecting the sciences which may be classed under this head as can be necessary to be known by a non-professional man. . . This [Place concluded quietly], is I believe a fair, and as clear as I can make it, account of what I do and what I do not know, in Arts and Sciences and Language.

This fascinating student self-assessment deserves to be quoted at length because it shows how wide-ranging was 'the sort of learning' which the sponsors of the London Mechanics' Institution had in mind. It was not the kind of specialised learning which would be covered in a single subject honours degree, nor would it have been easy to have tested it in an examination or series of examinations. Utilitarian views of education have often been criticised for leaving things out – and some of the things which John Stuart Mill regretted had been left out in his own education are missing from Place's list, too, particularly poetry. None the less, Place's statement shows just how much was put in. The cultural ideal, if it can be put in that way, spanned arts and sciences, the verbal and the visual, factual information and speculation. No wonder that Brougham thought that it was 'sheer folly' for working men faced with so much to learn to waste their time about anything else. Note, too, how Place in his statement, which lacks the sense of order and hierarchy which characterised formal utilitarian curricula and syllabuses of the same period, covered under the heading 'metaphysics' and not under the heading 'political economy' those 'speculative enquiries where nothing may be learned'. He added a rider, however, to his account, a rider which mattered most to him then and most to many other people in his time and since. 'The subject on which without pretension I have prided myself most, is the power I have possessed of influencing or governing other men individually and in bodies . . . This has always been to me a test of the information I had acquired.' Knowledge was power. It was for the world, even if it was acquired in the study. Culture had to be related to politics, and politics was always related to economics. This was a different cultural ideal from that of Coleridge or Newman or later of Arnold. It was a ideal which in 1903 was to inspire the newly formed Workers' Educational Association.

Comparing Place's self-assessment with an early syllabus of the Society for the Diffusion of Useful Knowledge as set out in the *Quarterly Journal of Education*, published by Charles Knight in 1831, we can note what happened when self-education began to be systematised according to plan. Diffusion meant the publication of books and treatises:

> Each Scientific Treatise will contain an Exposition of the Fundamental Principles of some Branch of Science – their proofs and illustrations – their application to practical uses, and to the explanation of facts and appearances. For this purpose, the greater Divisions of Knowledge will be subdivided into Branches; and if one of these Subdivisions or Branches cannot be taught in a single Treatise, it will be continued in a second.

Under the heading 'Natural Philosophy', 'dialling' and 'mill work' figure along with 'elementary astronomy' and 'hydrostatics' and 'hop planting' and 'sheep farming' alongside 'chemical apparatus' and 'meteorology'. A last great sub-division was called 'History of Individuals'. The individuals came in seven varieties – patriots, warriors, discoverers, self-exalted men, moral philosophers, navigators and statesmen, and all in all, appropriately enough, there were fifty-seven names. Literature did not figure on the list, and whether or not to buy novels, poems or plays was a matter of fierce contention in many provincial Mechanics' Institutes.

The Society for the Diffusion of Useful Knowledge was only one, if perhaps the most important, of the agencies which tried through the supply of books and treatises to assist the self-education of people who may or may not have belonged to Mechanics' Institutes scattered around the country. The London Mechanics' Institution could employ well-known and often extremely competent tutors. Elsewhere working men often had to depend either on themselves – engaging in 'the pursuit of knowledge under difficulties' – or on each other in mutual improvement classes, which were described later in the century by Samuel Smiles, who had himself organised such a class, as 'the educational Methodism of our day'. In Birkbeck itself there could be lectures and scientific demonstrations, some of them so educationally successful that the Royal Commission on Oxford University, reporting in 1852, could fear that unless Oxford undergraduates took up the sciences they could find themselves 'placed below persons in many respects inferior, . . . a large proportion of the middle and even of the labouring classes'. The elevation of the role of science in the promotion of general culture in London provided a model for some of the keenest advocates of educational change. Yet there was music also at the London Mechanics' Institution, and B. R. Haydon's classes on art. Haydon had said in 1823 that he had only two wishes left in life – to be able to pay all he owed and to see 'the government practically, by purchase, encourage painting'.

Outside London, not least in the industrial provinces, where economic change was most obvious and where the conflicts implicit in early industrialisation were generating whole new views of society, books were the main instrument of communication, although the mastery of them was often used, as in the case of Place, to 'influence or govern other men individually or in bodies'. And one other medium of communication then became relevant as well as books – the Press. It is only in recent years, as a result of the work of historians like Patricia Hollis and Joel Wiener, that the relationship between the attack on the 'taxes on knowledge' by working-class reformers and the other great political movements of the 1830s and 1840s has been fully explored. Cultural history, mainly the cultural history of the metropolis, has thereby been brought into the heart of the radical story. Birkbeck himself stated that 'newspapers were of great use in spreading the habit of reading, which was the first great step in human improvement'. Others of his contemporaries would have stood this judgment on its head and argued that reading was dangerous just because it enabled people who had started with the Bible to graduate to newspapers, some of them working-class newspapers with articles in them by working men themselves. There were some of the ambiguities in this issue as there were in the early history of the London Mechanics' Institution itself. Nor would everyone have agreed with the general comment of John Stuart Mill that the age through which they were passing was one in which 'mankind have outgrown old institutions and old doctrines and have not yet acquired new ones'. For some, the 'new doctrines', seminal doctrines Mill would have called them, were already there.

It is remarkable how many of the terms used in the discussions of the nineteenth-century processes I have been describing had their origins not in the city but in the country, not in industry but in agriculture – the word 'seminal' – like the word 'culture' itself – and the associated word 'cultivation'; the memorable phrase 'scattering the seeds of evil'; even the word 'education', which, as classicists were wont to point out, was derived from the word *educare*, to rear, which could be used to refer to the growing of crops. Surprisingly, perhaps, the first new twentieth-century 'medium of communication', though it took a long time to describe it as such – broadcasting – also was to have an agricultural name. Broadcast seed was seed scattered freely, not in drills or rows.

There was much in common between the underlying conception of broadcasting and that of 'diffusion' with which we have so far been concerned, although perhaps significantly the word 'diffusion', so much favoured by Brougham, Mill and Knight, did not have an agricultural derivation. Like the 'steam engine', it was part of a new vocabulary, the vocabulary of 'technology', a word which was first used in the 1770s on the eve of the great economic changes. The relationship of technology both to economics and to culture was to be debated in every generation – as it is being debated today – in the age of coal, iron and steam, 'carboniferous capitalism'; in the age of steel and electricity; and in the age of atomic power, economic planning and nationalisation. So far in my story, however, the impact of technology on the means of communication had been limited, even if *The Times* had begun to be printed on steam presses in 1814 and in 1823, the year the London Mechanics' Institution was founded, Charles Babbage had begun the construction of his famous calculating machine, the primitive ancestor of the modern computer.

There were many twists in the story between Babbage and the computer and between steam presses in *The Times* and McLuhan's electronic circuitry. And the first of them were all concerned with the social dimensions of culture. What happened to the London Mechanics'

Institution after the 1830s and 1840s, years of more dramatic change than the 1820s, change both in the social landscape and in the mind of individuals, when the railway brought steam technology to its triumphant, though still controversial climax? First of all, it survived the death of George Birkbeck in 1842, though only just, when many of the other Mechanics' Institutes in the provinces were withering away or revising their objects. Indeed, the London Mechanics' Institution, which changed its name in 1866 to the Birkbeck Literary and Scientific Institution – with an educational council to supervise its teaching – was able then to hitch itself to the new examinations complex of the University of London.

This was a quite new phase in nineteenth-century history during which culture was less important than qualifications, a vantage point in time where I would like to hover. To understand it we need no longer turn to the autobiographies of working men: we can turn very simply to examination syllabuses. The London University Charter of 1858 had, in effect, converted the University into an examining board. A more complex society, more dependent on the exploitation of individual ability than pre-industrial societies, found it necessary to lay down standard tests, and examinations were the necessary instrument to ensure competence while at the same time guaranteeing competition. There were only residual links with the philosophies of the 1820s. Thus, when in 1879 London University reported on the possibility of instituting university examinations in education, it was stated confidently that examinations would be 'the means of creating a class of teachers of higher intelligence and of superior culture, and better qualified to discharge the several duties of their profession'. The phrase 'superior culture' suggests little more than a social gloss: what really mattered was the last phrase – 'better qualified to discharge the several duties of their profession'.

More has been written about the effects of the examination system in schools in the nineteenth century – particularly in relation to the system of 'payment by results' introduced after 1862 – than about the development of the system in universities. In London they were most far-reaching, for, as a recent historian has put it, 'it was deemed no business of the University to enquire how a student got his education'. The anonymity was like the anonymity of the growing city itself, Henry James's 'complete compendium of the world'. If they wanted, students could rely on books, the new textbooks which were the market response to new needs. So, too, could teachers in training, to such an extent that one inspector wrote during the 1890s that 'salvation is . . . supposed to be found in a study of the textbook – and that alone'. Many students, however, including practising teachers, particularly if they lived in

London – whatever their social background – turned to a whole range of institutions some good, some bad, of which the Birkbeck Literary and Scientific Institution was one. It was described in 1873, fifty years after its foundation, as a 'knowledge hive', and twelve years later, when it moved to Fetter Lane, more than 4000 students were attending its lectures, art classes (still a lively feature) and science demonstrations. It was obviously a place that mattered.

I quoted Francis Place to show how broad the conception of working-class culture could be in the 1820s. Undoubtedly it was narrower during the 1870s and 1880s (despite the excitement of evolution) when academic knowledge was becoming more specialized and academic disciplines more professionally organised and controlled. For the 1870s let me quote Annie Besant, Birkbeck science student, to show how narrow conceptions of culture could then be. And I hasten to add – this is the reason why I have chosen Annie Besant – that she was one of the least narrow people in nineteenth-and twentieth-century cultural history. Her biographer has given her nine lives, and she ended her days in an Indian culture very different from that known either to John Stuart Mill or Cardinal Newman. In February 1879 Charles Bradlaugh, the freethinking radical with whom Annie Besant was then notoriously associated, inserted a prominent announcement in his magazine the *National Reformer*:

> Mrs Besant, thinking that it may add to her usefulness to the cause, intends to try to take advantage of the opportunity afforded for women obtaining degrees in the London University. [The opportunity had just been afforded in a supplemental Charter in 1878.] The necessary studies in preparation for the very severe examinations will occupy so much of her time that for many months to come she will be able to lecture only on Saturday and Sunday. Miss Hypatia Bradlaugh is studying with Mrs. Besant for the same object.

I have no time to tell the detailed story of what happened to Annie Besant afterwards. She not only attended Birkbeck classes but was tutored privately by Edward Aveling – a fascinating character in late nineteenth-century cultural history. He was the lover of one of Karl Marx's daughters and the prototype of Dubedat in George Bernard Shaw's *The Doctor's Dilemma*, but for all his romanticism he first appeared in the pages of the *National Reformer* very starkly as 'E. D. (D.Sc., Lond.)'.

Annie was rated first-class in her first London University examinations in inorganic chemistry, mathematics, theoretic mechanics, magnetism and electricity, botany, general biology, animal physiology and acoustics, light and heat, but she never graduated. Nominally, practical chemistry was her undoing. But, in the full glare of the Press, she had in fact, stirred up as much controversy as Hodgskin had done during the 1820s. Birkbeck omitted her name from the list of its successful candidates at the South Kensington examinations, and after she asked why, she was told that members of a committee who were collecting money for their building fund feared that some of their contributors would withdraw their contributions if they realised she had been allowed to attend a Birkbeck class. Very properly she quickly printed and published a circular drawing the attention of the world to this injustice, a circular which was given great publicity.

The story of Annie Besant is important, of course, not only because of its rich incidentals, but because of the fact that she was a woman. This was the heroic age in the fight for women's rights, just as the 1820s and the 1830s had been the heroic age in the fight for the freedom of the Press. There had been no better judge of the texture of the culture of the 1860s and 1870s than Marian Evans, *alias* George Eliot, who, significantly, apart from a few visits to Oxford and Cambridge, one brilliantly recorded by a Cambridge don, F. W. H. Myers, was largely outside the university life of her age. She showed, incidentally, in those few visits just how superior she was to most of the dons with whom she was drawn into conversation. Here is one comment by a barrister don on an after-dinner talk in Oxford in 1877. 'Spottiswoode began to talk to her of a Frenchman who had solved theoretically the problem of turning up and down motion into circular, the usual method in vogue being only an approximation to the theoretically perfect way . . . They (then) got on to 'spiral vortices', and then 'imaginary geometry', after which I understood not one word.' Had he understood before?

Throughout the nineteenth century, university culture, whether of the Oxford or of the London variety – and there were links between them mainly, perhaps, through the literary more than the scientific world – was by its nature exclusive, and it was not only women who were left out or kept at the margins. 'Popular culture', as it would now be called, was something apart – whether didactic or diverting – and for long it expressed itself less in a national version (commercialised or otherwise) than through local sub-cultures, strongly influenced by social class. Only a few sensitive or very exuberant observers were able to understand it rather than to moralise about it, and of these the most sensitive were more aware of their limitations than of their insights. Yet popular culture, too, was changing during the 1880s and 1890s, the period of Harmsworth's *Answers*, the necessary precursor of the *Daily Mail*. The opportunity of profiting from the national exploitation of a growing market directly or indirectly through advertising – and it was thought of more and more as a 'market' and not as a 'public' – was greater than it had been earlier in the century, given improved transport, greater urbanisation and rising disposable incomes, and the men who profited most from it had little formal education and little access to 'high culture'. It was then increasingly that the word 'mass' began to be used in place of the word 'class' to describe cultural phenomena, some of them supported by new technology – 'mass entertainment', 'mass culture', and last of all, much later, 'mass communication'. What had been done 'by' now began to be done 'for'. Voluntary organisation, on which both working-class and middle-class mid-Victorian life had depended, by no means disappeared, but its organisation was challenged, remoulded or subverted.

During this period Birkbeck College moved in a different direction both from 'mass culture' and 'high culture', within the complex of the City Polytechnic, a loose cluster of diverse institutions with different pedigrees, designed as a whole, it was claimed, to 'promote the industrial skill, general knowledge, health and well-being of young men and women belonging to the poorer classes of London'. I should add that this comprehensive, even picturesque, statement of social purposes did not accurately reflect the actual role of Birkbeck which was at once narrower and broader, although many kinds of education were lopped off the Birkbeck syllabus during the long and distinguished Principal-ship of George Armitage-Smith which began in 1896. At least in retro-spect, the year of his retirement was a hinge year between the cultures of the nineteenth and the twentieth centuries. (See below, p. 42.)

To revert to agricultural metaphor, it took a long time for most of the new social phenomena, like cinema and wireless, to 'mature' – for many of them it took until the 1920s and 1930s – yet here undoubtedly was the beginning of a new time. And to complete the picture there were far-reaching parallel changes in organised education. In 1904 the Principal of the London Working Men's College remarked at the time of the College's fiftieth anniversary celebrations that

> the spread of education . . . and its supply at the expense of the State is an outward and visible sign of a revolution in public opinion. In 1854 reformers laid unlimited stress upon the virtues of self-help (the features we have already noted in 1823) . . . In 1904 the tendency of opinion is to lay immense, some may think, excessive, emphasis on the duty of society to help its individual members.

Birkbeck, dependent on funds from the London County Council, would scarcely have thought the emphasis excessive, as did the remark-able, but somewhat unlikely, Principal of the London Working Men's College, Professor A. V. Dicey, the lawyer/historian. In retrospect, indeed, the shift to State or local authority provision in education, which fascinated him, seems to have been remarkably slow and faltering, if primary education, is left out – as most people concerned with higher education at the time chose to leave out. The Universities with increasingly specialised syllabuses were thought of then as institutions for a few, the privileged in Oxford and Cambridge, the others outside in institutions, more open of access. In 1900 only 0.8 per cent of the age group was at university – 20,000 people in all out of a total population of over 40 millions – and only 0.4 per cent in teacher training. Nor was this situation exceptional. Thirty years later, after a period of immense social change, including the first of the world wars, the proportions were still only 1.7 (50,000 students) and 0.7 per cent respectively, with a further 0.3 per cent engaged in miscellaneous versions of 'further education', the kind of education which Birkbeck had lopped off.

The statistics of secondary education reveal the same slowness of development. The tiny minority of children enjoying any kind of post-primary education in 1900 was still a minority during the late 1930s, though by now a substantial one of over half a million. Attitudes towards scale of provision remained cautious. In 1901 Sir John Gorst, who genuinely believed in education through public provision and had fought hard for it, stated plainly that while in his view 'every boy and girl showing capacities above average should be caught [note the word 'caught', a metaphor derived from fishing and not from agriculture] and given the best opportunities for developing those capacities', it would not be right 'to scatter broadcast [note again the word in this context] a huge system of higher instruction for any one who chooses to take advantage of it, however unfit to receive it'. Thirty years on, R. H. Tawney was complaining that secondary education was being rationed 'like bread in a famine, under stringent precautions, as though, were it made too accessible, the world would end – as it is possible, indeed, that one sort of world might'.

It is only recently after a second world war that 'a huge system of higher education' has been created, and although it looks less huge when compared with that of some other countries, particularly that of the United States, and its scale is less impressive than the scale of many other social features of contemporary Britain – the scale of newspaper readership, for example, or of television ownership or even of attendance at or concern for spectator sports – it is none the less a powerful element in our culture that was missing in the nineteenth century.

Birkbeck College has been incorporated within the developing new system as inexorably – some would say as naturally – as it was hitched to the late-Victorian complex of a different kind. In 1900 eight of its teachers had been nominated as 'recognised teachers of the University' – a badge of assured status – and thirteen years later the Royal

Commission on the University of London under the powerful chairmanship of R. B. Haldane affirmed without hesitation that 'the original purpose of the Founder of Birkbeck College and the excellent work that the Institution has done for the education of evening students who desire a University training mark it out as the natural seat of the constituent college for evening or other part-time students'. Seven years later, after the War, it was admitted – under Haldane's presidency – as a School of the University, and six years later still it was granted a Royal Charter as a full University College. There was direct continuity between then and now – although during the Second World War there were complex problems, and it was not until 1951 that the move was made to Malet Street. The college was now within the purview of the University Grants Committee, an organisation which could not have taken institutional shape as early as 1900.

Before reaching the end of a journey, which has far more twists and turns than the road from Charing Cross to St Paul's, one other feature of educational development – adult education – must be related to the story and a few further characteristics of contemporary culture must be identified and contrasted with those of the past. It is significant that the Birkbeck themes of the 1820s were re-enacted in the early twentieth century not within the context of the public education system but within the context of the rise of the university extension movement and the Workers' Educational Association which I have already mentioned. And in the late twentieth century they are not extinct themes. Albert Mansbridge, founder of the Workers' Educational Association in 1903, believed in what he called 'the glory of education', a phrase plucked out of a different tradition from that of James Mill, but very soon the new Association, which was not concerned with examinations or qualifications, was entangled in exactly the same complex of issues as the London Mechanics' Institution had been in its infancy.

> It was not unnatural [wrote one of Mansbridge's university allies, J. A. R. Marriott] that some working-class students themselves tending towards Socialism, should come to regard me with suspicion as an obscurantist and a reactionary. Our University Extension methods were not 'democratic' enough for them; they would fain, if not tune the pulpits, at least choose the preachers . . . above all, they revolted against what it became fashionable to describe as 'middle class economics'.

We are back in 1823, reminded as G. M. Young put it – and he was the first Birkbeck Orator after the Second World War – that 'culture . . . is constantly swerving back to gather up something which the grandfathers had dropped and the sons left lying by the course'. Whatever may be said of the United States as a 'post-industrial society', we are still caught in this country in the mesh of industrialism – in issues of conflict, centred on coal and railways, and in ways of thinking and feeling which stretch further back still.

More recently, adult education has come into the picture again in a different way. The Academic Advisory Committee of 1966 on the future of the College was headed by Sir Eric (later Lord) Ashby, who had already produced important recommendations on the finance of adult education and who later on was to produce one of the few challenging academic statements about the role of examinations in a university. The Committee's report talked not only of meeting the needs of 'traditional Birkbeck students' but of assisting in a process of continuing education through renewal and, when necessary, re-equipment. The experience of the student outside the university was seen as an asset. Similarly, in last year's Oration Sir Kenneth Berrill chose to talk about 'lifetime education'. He used no agricultural metaphors, but he did say that 'if one limits the instruction in new knowledge and new techniques to today's young people then it will be forty years before all the working population acquire this advance, and at today's rate of change of knowledge that is just not acceptable'.

There are, of course, many other ways of learning in the twentieth century besides learning in institutions, old or new. For the first time in my story books have had powerful competitors (besides newspapers and magazines). Cinema, radio and television have developed as media – the term is a relatively new one – and have raised separately or together basic questions not only about the context of what is being communicated – or not communicated – or the patterns of control, but about the relationship between the actual techniques of communication through images and words and ways of thinking and feeling. The histories of the different media in this country were for long distinct – press, radio and cinema, for example – and there were different guiding philosophies and distinct forms of organisation. Recently, however, they have converged with a massing of economic power and a relentless socio-psychological pressure unknown to the nineteenth century. There is talk now of a 'leisure industry' as well as of a continuing 'communications revolution' of which so far we have merely gone through the first phases. Both have had their prophets, major and minor, some of whom suggest that we are passing through a period of such unprecedented change that there is little point in looking back at all at the record of the past. The twenty-first century is already here.

There is no time further to expound such prophecies or to question the prophets, except to say that the activities of the formal 'education system' are often curiously remote from the common concerns of our contemporary culture. We have separated the arts and sciences at school and university and have created separate institutions for our tech-nologists, and we are still far from clear – for all the educational 'expansion', the twentieth-century equivalent of 'diffusion' – just what are the crucial relationships between the different 'disciplines' that we have carved out and the problems of society . . . the kind of problems, sometimes recurring, sometimes cumulative, which a historian can place firmly within the specific time framework of this lecture.

Within this framework books are not yet dead. More of them are being read than ever before. Nor, so long as these Orations continue to be delivered, are lectures dead. As early as 1946, when there were only 20,000 television sets in the country, Douglas Woodruff was complain-ing that one of the most significant differences between the twentieth and the nineteenth century was that now we are too impatient and will not listen.

> In the age of the great preachers . . . an hour was the normal time for a sermon, as it still is in the universities for a lecture. No doubt we shall see that change, and twenty-five bright and pithy minutes will be found to suit better the convenience both of the undergraduates and the lecturers. So the newspapers have gradually reduced the favourite length for an article till it is now under rather than over one thousand words.

We may have different opinions about the merits of particular times and lengths, but Woodruff's conclusion would have received assent – sometimes reluctant assent – not only from Francis Place but from successive generations of students at Birkbeck over one hundred and fifty years: 'Of a great many subjects, particularly in the great fields of philosophy, theology, politics and economics, the very first truth that has to be accepted is that the business will take some time to unfold.' It is still unfinished business.

3 Mass Entertainment: The Origins of a Modern Industry*

The provision of entertainment has never been a subject of great interest either to economists or to economic historians – at least in their working hours. Nor is the word 'industry' universally applied to it. Yet in twentieth-century conditions it is proper to talk of a highly organised and often highly lucrative entertainment industry, to distinguish within it between production and distribution, to examine forces making for competition, integration, concentration and control, and to relate such study to the central economic concept of the market which in the twentieth century is as much concerned with leisure as it is with work. There is a public dimension, too, since entertainment is provided in part by public broadcasting organisations and other institutions.

It is possible in addition to pursue a statistical investigation, relating a number of business indices, including those of advertising, to movements of national income and output; and since the industry straddles national boundaries – and has done to an increasing extent in this century – it is necessary to compare its impact in one country with another.

How far back is it necessary to go to understand the story of how and why a so-called 'mass entertainment industry' emerged? Some people would say to the fall of the Roman Empire or before. In the sixth century, it has been pointed out, the barbarians closed the Roman theatres, amphitheatres and circuses, and dispossessed entertainers became, in consequence, 'wanderers on the face of the earth'. Thereafter, entertainment was decentralised and the status of the full-time entertainer was undermined. The travelling fair became the main institution. Although the entertainment of the few might on occasion be sophisticated and expensive, for centuries the entertainment of the many – with the exception of self-entertainment, later home entertainment – was local, intermittent, boisterous and cheap. It was associated above all else with festivals, later called holidays: they were specially set apart in a religious calendar.

*The 29th Joseph Fisher Lecture in Commerce, delivered at the University of Adelaide, 19 October 1960.

38

During the 1830s and 1840s, at the beginning of the period covered in this lecture, the biggest of the London pleasure fairs, Bartholomew Fair in Smithfield, was still going strong, as it had done in Ben Jonson's day. For one penny you could see the Black Wild Indian Woman and Child, the White Indian Youth and the Welsh Dwarf. You could join a thousand other spectators in visiting Richardson's Theatre with a twenty-five minute show of melodrama, pantomime, comic songs and incidental music (Dickens described it). You could take your pick of two menageries – one of them, Wombwell's Menagerie, collected £1700 in sixpences from satisfied clients in the three days of the Fair in 1828 – or, if you preferred, you could restrict your spending to one halfpenny and see real Chinese jugglers. The sponsor of these jugglers collected £50 in halfpennies in 1828.

Such figures give a fleeting but vivid glimpse of the limited economic dimensions of show business at what was then one of the biggest fairs in the world. The businessmen behind the scenes were obviously far from being tycoons. They were still wanderers: some of them, as in Jonson's times, were hucksters and tricksters, adept in judging the levels of popular credulity. But there was plenty of subsidiary and lucrative commerce at the Fair – in transport, accommodation, ballad selling (one of the biggest scale sectors of nineteenth-century entertainment), and, probably the most important of all, in the supply of food and drink. The retailing of commodities and the provision of entertainment were already associated.

Bartholomew Fair disappeared before the rise of modern mass entertainment. It was too rowdy for the respectable mid-Victorians and was held for the last time in 1855. In most other parts of the country also, as a very shrewd observer noted just over twenty years later, fairs were becoming institutions which in their old form were 'almost out of date'. So, too, were showmen's vans packed with wares. Big changes had also taken place during the middle nineteenth century in the provision of other kinds of metropolitan entertainment. Vauxhall Gardens, the great seventeenth- and eighteenth-century centre of outdoor entertainment in London, closed its gates for the last time in 1850 after a lavish fireworks display. A year later the Great Exhibition of 1851, housed in the Crystal Palace was a triumphant landmark in the new history both of 'improvement' and entertainment, attended by over six million people drawn by cheap transport not only from London but from all parts of the country and overseas. The road to the Crystal Palace was full of stalls and sidesows, and the incidental business carried on in connection with the Exhibition was prodigious. The earnestness of the so-called lessons of 1851 should not eclipse the incidental fun surrounding the event.

There was no doubt about the fun in the biggest single development in entertainment during the next thirty years – the rise of the music halls. The first buildings specifically erected for this purpose were the Canterbury in Lambeth and the Oxford in Oxford Street. Charles Morton, their proprietor, had acquired his initial capital from receipts from so-called 'free-and-easies' in a London tavern. During the next thirty years the growth of music halls destroyed the hold of the old elaborate pantomime on the London audience. Meanwhile, the Crystal Palace, moved to Sydenham, offered new and old diversions.

In sport there were big changes, too, as the rough, crude and often dangerous sports of earlier centuries gave way to more highly organised, more precisely regulated games. Football was one of these. Eight years after the death of Bartholomew Fair the Football Association was founded – a small enough association in all conscience, with an income in its first year of only £5, but a portent of the shape of things to come. The first admission charges to football games were made in Britain in 1870: the Aston Villa Club in Birmingham, founded as a Sunday School team, took 5s. 3d. at its first game when spectators were called upon to pay in 1874. Gates remained small throughout the 1870s and professionalism was not legalised until 1885, but journalists were beginning to see the possibilities of sport appealing to spectators – or even mere readers – as much as to players. The participants would be few: the spectators and readers would be many. In 1867 Routledge's *Handbook of Football* was the first important publisher's response to the new developments.

Publishers were usually in the vanguard of the mass entertainment business. I have already mentioned the sale of ballads. An early nineteenth-century publisher, James Catnach, specialised in sensational cheap books, ballads and broadsides to bewitch and titillate 'the masses' of his age. In 1828, the same year for which the statistics of Bartholomew Fair are available, he is said to have sold over 1,100,000 copies of the 'Last Dying Speech and Confession' of William Corder, the murderer of Maria Marten in the Red Barn. In 1837 he sold 1,650,000 copies (with illustrations) of the last thoughts before execution of another murderer, James Greenacre. That was the pinnacle of his success, for another spectacular murder took place just too soon afterwards for success to be repeated. There is a modern ring in a Victorian comment on his inability to make good use of the second of the two murders. 'That took the beauty off him. Two murders together is no good to anybody.' Catnach operated from the heart of London. He employed a team of helpers known as 'the Seven Bards of Seven Dials' who knew their public and composed fluently to order. During the middle years of Victorian England – a very different age from that described in most nineteenth-century history books or even in the pages of Lytton Strachey – there was a regular sale of 'penny dreadfuls', and at least one publisher 'pre-tested' his manuscripts by having them read first by a servant or a machine-boy.

At the same time, the Sunday newspapers first came into their own. They still lack a serious historian. A. P. Wadsworth, the economic historian and late-editor of the *Manchester Guardian*, described them briefly in a lecture that he gave to the Manchester Statistical Society in 1955. He pointed out that as early as 1812, when eighteen Sunday newspapers were being published in London, they were as renowned for their ribaldry as for their radicalism and they devoted large sections to sport and crime. The *Observer*, for instance, specialised in woodcuts of murders, Edward Lloyd's newspaper named after him (1842) and G. W. M. Reynolds's *Reynolds Weekly News* (1850) were pioneers of 'sensationalism', a new, mid-Victorian term, and the *News of the World* (1843) was selling 109,000 copies a week by 1854. These Sunday papers were the real precursors of the mass circulation papers of today.

In the United States of America as early as 1833 Benjamin Day, with a few associates, started a paper specifically intended – in his own words – for 'mechanics and the masses generally'. The price of this paper – the *Sun* – was only one cent at a time when the other New York papers were selling for six cents. The publishers in what is now a familiar fashion expected to make up by larger circulation and by advertising the loss sustained by the lower price. This was the same successful formula later applied by Joseph Pulitzer and James Gordon Bennett, the publisher of the *New York Herald*, in New York and by Alfred Harmsworth, later Lord Northcliffe, in London. The founding of the *Daily Mail* in 1896 should be seen against this background and not simply, as it far too often is, against the cultural background of the so-called new reading public created by the British Education Act of 1870. *Titbits* and *Answers*, the weekly papers that provided a cultural and a business prelude to the *Daily Mail* were part of an earlier tradition which linked reading and entertainment. The *Daily Mail* and Northcliffe's later venture the *Daily Mirror* were attacked as earlier publications had been attacked – the first as the paper for people who could not think, the second (the pioneer of the tabloids) as the paper for people who could not read – but they survived. During the first twelve months of its existence the average daily sale of the *Daily Mail* was over 200,000: three years later it was well over half-a-million. The *Mirror*, designed at first as a women's paper, had a more shaky start and passed through a number of business hands. In time, however, it became the daily paper with the biggest circulation in the world, appealing as much through the picture as through the word.

The year 1896 is an important date in the history of mass entertainment, a vantage point from which to look backwards and forwards. In the same year as Harmsworth created the *Daily Mail*, a young Italian inventor, Guglielmo Marconi, arrived in London to demonstrate for the British Post Office how he could send signals by wireless for a hundred yards. Later in the year, he filed his first wireless patent. Also in the same year, the first moving picture show was presented in London. A February showing at the Regent Street Polytechnic was so successful that the cinema show was transferred to the Empire Music Hall, Leicester Square, where it subsequently ran for eighteen months.

The economic conditions for the development of a mass entertainment industry were all there in 1896. Five conditions stood out. First, a large and concentrated urban population had come into existence in the course of the nineteenth century: the citizens of the towns and cities, provided for half a century with only limited means of entertainment, made up the first segment of what has since been called 'the great audience'. Second, the incomes in real terms of large sections of this urban population had risen sufficiently during the previous fifty years to enable people to afford to buy regular, cheap entertainment. Third, an increase in the amount of available leisure time had prepared the way for its commercial exploitation. Fourth, urban public transport systems had improved sufficiently during the 1880s and early 1890s to permit late night travel from city centres to residential suburbs; trams (and in London underground railways) were the latest instruments of this transport revolution. Fifth, technology was being applied to entertainment, sometimes falteringly and uncertainly, but, in retrospect at least, decisively.

Each of these five economic conditions – and particularly the first four – were also essential to the development of the retail trade in the 1880s and 1890s, and it is not an accident that the merchandising of entertainment and the large-scale mass merchandising of branded retail products lead back to the same initial historical situation.

The term 'mass market' precedes the terms 'mass communications' and 'mass culture': the department store preceded the cinema. Advertising provides an additional link between retailing and entertainment. Advertising and showmanship were closely associated in the 1880s, and the successful proprietor of a departmental store had to have some of the qualities of a successful showman. Like his predecessors in the fairs and his contemporaries in the development of patent medicines, he had to understand and, if need be, tap human credulity.

P. T. Barnum (1810–91) was the classic figure in this context: a second was W. F. Cody, 'Buffalo Bill', whose Wild West Show, 'the show of shows', netted one million dollars in receipts in a year and profits of $100,000. Queen Victoria described the show as a 'very extraordinary and interesting sight'. In 1841, Barnum took over Scudder's American Museum, which had been started in the year of his birth and had become New York's greatest storehouse of 'curiosities'. It was at Barnum's American Museum that Tom Thumb first made his public appearance: it was this Museum which toured parts of Europe in 1844, Barnum having boldly announced that he intended to take over Buckingham Palace as his headquarters. Barnum's later ventures were sometimes more sophisticated. For instance, he sponsored the American tour of Jenny Lind, 'the Swedish Nightingale', in 1849, paying her 1000 dollars a time for her one-hundred-and-fifty appearances, along with one-fifth of the net profits. This, incidentally, was an early example of the 'star system', but Barnum did not invent it: in London in 1847 the crowds were so thick in the Haymarket where Jenny Lind was appearing at Her Majesty's Theatre that the crush was later called 'the Jenny Lind crush'.

Barnum went on later in 1871 to develop the circus, which in the now familiar language of superlatives was proudly called 'the greatest show on earth'. He remained in close touch with retailers and advertisers: he had met the great Boucicaut in Paris in the 1840s, and in the 1880s at least one pioneer English retailer, David Lewis of Liverpool, deliberately set out to imitate Barnum's methods in his departmental store. Although Barnum's career had its ups-and-downs (bankruptcy, for example, in 1856), he achieved a hitherto unparalleled success in mass entertainment. He tried to tell his public the secret in books, including *A Life of P. T. Barnum Written by Himself*, which went through several editions, and *Dollars and Sense or How to get on: The Whole Secret in a Nutshell*, published in the last year of his life with a touch of Samuel Smiles as well as of the showman in its title. The subtitle was even more Smilesian – 'Sketches of the Lives of Successful Men who "rose from the Ranks" and from the most Humble Starting Point achieved Honourable Fame'.

The didactic side even of entertainment was never overlooked by the Victorians. Advertising, too, a superb mirror of social history, reflects the same features. And advertising was more than an historical link between developments in the expansion of the retail market and in entertainment. From the start it entered into calculations about the financing of mass entertainment, providing a hidden or overt subsidy from various forms of business to one particular business, the entertainment business. Newspaper history brings out this point very clearly, as does the later history of commercial radio. That it was not lost sight of even in the early days of the mass entertainment industry is shown by an incident in the history of the gramophone. In 1894 the United States Gramophone Company offered as a 'novel form of advertising' to record any musical selection along with a sponsor's advertisement. 'Nobody would refuse', the Company claimed, 'to listen free to a fine song or concert piece or an oration – even if it is interrupted by a modest remark, "Tartar's Baking Powder is Best".'

Of the five economic conditions, the fifth – the application of technology to entertainment – is in some ways most interesting. A characteristic cluster of inventions was developed in the last quarter of the nineteenth century. They were as basic to new ways of life in the twentieth century as were the inventions of the last quarter of the eighteenth century in textiles, iron and power to the new industrial pattern of the nineteenth century. The difference between them is that the eighteenth-century inventions transformed the material standard of living and the nineteenth-century inventions the forms of culture. Critics of the first talked of 'exploitation', critics of the second have already talked of 'manipulation'. Yet both clusters of inventions are related to each other. Without the existence of the first cluster there could not have been the second. One point of special interest, which must be elaborated later, is that the social consequences of the second cluster were not clearly foreseen: there was a great gulf between prediction and prophecy on the one hand and what has actually happened on the other.

It is amazing how many of the inventions came out of the American laboratory of Thomas A. Edison, born one year after Buffalo Bill, in 1847. Edison's formal education was limited to three months in a public school. At the age of twelve he had his first taste of communications – as a railroad newsboy – and at the age of fifteen he became a telegraph operator. He took out his first patent in 1868 for an electrical vote recorder. Later, among the thousand patents he took out, he devised telephones, gramophones, electric lamps and kinetoscope cameras. He lived until 1931, when all these key objects of the twentieth century were already taken for granted. He still lacks a good up to date biographer, but it is clear from the Edison papers that he was the James Watt and Richard Arkwright (rolled into one) of the modern mass entertainment revolution. He had little directly to do with the early development of wireless before and after Marconi's patent of 1896, but the invention of the thermionic valve, without which subsequent wireless history in the pre-transistor phase would have been very different, owed much to his work with electric lamps, the one invention of the four I mentioned above which, at first sight, seems out of place in the list.

Paradoxically the telephone, which also may seem a little out of place, was associated by contemporaries with entertainment as well as with work, while wireless was at first thought of entirely as a means of point-to-point communication – a substitute for line telegraphy – rather than a possible medium of entertainment. It was certainly in relation to the telephone not in relation to wireless that the idea of scattering 'sound-at-a-distance' was first mooted. A short story of October 1878 published in a Sydney magazine, *The Australian*, includes this passage:

> The telephone wire was laid on between Abney Hall and the village church of Mortham, so that the Hall people could have the benefit of Mr. Earle's pulpit oratory without going outside their own doors.

Frank Gill, in later years a leading figure in the 1922 talks leading up to the inauguration of broadcasting in Britain, wrote that 'telephony has some of the properties both of the letter and of the newspaper: it can be clothed with privacy, given to one individual only, or it can be broadcast to millions simultaneously'.

In some towns and cities of Britain the practicability of the telephone as a technical instrument was first demonstrated by the transmission of music, frequently organ music, from a 'distant source', and in 1892 performances at the Lyric Theatre in London and theatres and concerts in Birmingham, Liverpool, Manchester and other places were successfully transmitted 'with entire success' to an Electrical Exhibition at the Crystal Palace. Ten years before this experiment, a Hungarian, Theodore Puskas, had demonstrated a 'telephoned newspaper' at an Electrical Exhibition in Paris. In 1894 an Electrophone Company was formed in London to provide 'listening facilities', including four pairs of headphones and an answering-back 'hand microphone' for every subscriber. Musical performances, public lectures and addresses, and church services were 'electrophoned'. The service was neither a technical nor a business success: after twelve years of activity sounds were still distorted and there were only six hundred subscribers. In its restricted way, however, it pointed to the existence not only of a potential demand for diffused entertainment but of a wide range of available 'programmes'.

It took longer for Edison to realise the possibilities for organised entertainment of either the gramophone or the motion picture camera, the first of which he invented (in simple form as a phonograph or speaking machine) in 1877, the latter in 1889. Both of them were thought of as ingenious 'novelties' rather than as instruments of mass entertainment, while Edison himself, the prototype of what David Riesman would call an 'inner directed man', attached chief importance to the 'serious' rather than to the frivolous use of both, the first as an 'aid to the businessman', the second as an aid to educators.

The showmen of the day were more percipient in relation to their immediate interests if not to an extended vision of the future. The early phonograph would 'speak' in Dutch, German, French, Spanish and Hebrew and 'imitate the barking of dogs and the crowing of cocks'. Showmen could collect as much as $1800 a week by playing it at exhibitions. Edison was very annoyed in 1891 when some of his salesmen went further and offered to lease phonographs to cafes and stores for coin-in-the-slot playing. 'The coin-in-the-slot', he wrote in *The Phonogram* in January 1891, with a sublime ignorance of the future of the juke box, 'is calculated to injure the phonograph in the opinion of those seeing it only in that form, as it has the appearance of being nothing more than a mere toy.' It was not until three years later – after competitors, notably Emile Berliner and the Pathé brothers in Paris, had entered the field – that Edison began to see the future of the gramophone in terms of entertainment.

He was more dilatory still with the kinetoscope, so much so that Gilbert Seldes, one of the first serious writers on mass entertainment, has suggested in his fascinating book *The Movies come from America* (1931) that the history of the motion picture industry should be called 'The Mistakes of Edison'. Edison himself thought of the kinetoscope as a toy, developed it slowly, and, even after he had seen a moving picture, stated that he thought the basic inventions (the camera and the so-called peep-show machine) would be useful only because they made possible photographic reproduction of scenes from natural life, operas or plays. He saw no future in the projector. His reasoning was as follows: if hundreds of people could see a picture at one time, the public would be very quickly exhausted. In other words, he failed to see the existence of either a potential mass or a market. As Seldes goes on, 'The moving picture had to be taken away from its inventors by aggressive and ignorant men without taste or tradition, but with a highly developed sense of business, before it could be transformed from a mechanical toy into the medium of the first popular art.'

It was certainly humble men who first took up the new invention, men already in the entertainment business. The first films were made in single rolls, fifty feet long, and were shown in 'peep-show machines'. Peep shows had always been popular at Bartholomew Fair – one of the most popular of the last of them was the Murder in the Red Barn – and as early as the 1820s sequences of pictures could be manipulated through the peep hole. Edison applied the invention of the motion picture camera to the peep show, offering pictures of a performing dog, a trained bear and a strong man, and the first cinema peep show was opened in Broadway, New York, in 1894. The business was thought to be so disreputable that even after the peep show had been replaced by the more respectable-sounding nickelodeon, David Warfield, a well-known actor, kept secret his investment in one of these enterprises for fear that publication would ruin his stage reputation. The title of one of the first peep-show films of 1894 – 'Dolorita in the Passion Dance' – suggests that he may have been right.

The first full screening of a motion picture took place in New York in 1896, the year when motion pictures began to be regularly screened in London. In both cases the *rendezvous* was a music hall – Koster and Bial's in New York and, as we have seen, the Empire Music Hall in London. The men responsible for developing the new medium – although it could not be so described at that stage – were men associated with old forms of entertainment. The first American films were offered to the public for ten years in the composite package 'Vaudeville and Pictures': it was only after ten years that the label was changed to 'Pictures and Vaudeville'. The first show at the Empire consisted of an overture, a ten minute programme of Tyrolean singers and dancers, a ballet, a trio, a group of Russian dancers ('first performance in England'), a display by Cinquevalli, the great juggler, then – and only then – the films, very modestly placed, to be followed by acrobats, a singer, an hour's performance of *Faust* and, to close the four-hour show, a pair of 'eccentrics'. There were four films – *The Arrival of the Paris Express*, *A Practical Joke on the Governess*, *The Fall of a Wall* and *Boating in the Mediterranean*.

The most numerous of the first British distributors of films were music hall proprietors and showmen who put up their booths at fair grounds. From 1904 onwards they were able to hire films as well as buy them. A third type of distributor, however, the real innovators, held the key to the future. A number of more specialised dealers travelled round the country with films, booking a local hall and giving shows at 2d, or 3d, a time for as long as they could hold an audience. The dealers were sometimes known as 'town hall' showmen because town halls were frequently the most convenient places to show the films. Other places chosen were shops, theatres, music halls or even skating rinks. It was not until 1908 that the first building specially built for film shows was opened at Colne in Lancashire. By then there were three exhibiting companies in Britain with a total capital of £110,000: one of them was controlled by Albany Ward, a 'town hall' showman, who by 1914 owned twenty-nine cinemas, a second in Scotland was controlled by George Green, whose first activities had been in the fair grounds. The word 'bioscope' had now passed into the language, as the name of a journal as well as a cinema. It was not until 1909, however, that bigger business entered the field of film distribution, and Provincial Cinematograph Theatres Ltd was set up with a nominal capital of £100,000 and a leading British financier, Sir William Bass, as its chairman. Progress was rapid – to use a film phrase 'spectacular' – in the years immediately before the First World War. In 1914 there were at least 3500 cinemas in Britain, and 1833 companies were in existence with a combined capital of £11,304,500.

At this stage the United States did not completely dominate either distribution or production. Demand for films was greatly in excess of supply, and A. C. Bromhead, who was later to become the Chairman of the Gaumont–British Picture Corporation, has reported how in the early days of the cinema 'American showmen, unable to find enough films on their own side, visited England and the Continent seeking films.' France was a main source of supply, as it was also in the gramophone business. Yet by 1914 the United States came second in the world export market and during the first two years of the First World War American exports almost doubled. In the already large American overseas market in 1918 Britain was the most important customer, Canada the second and Australia the third. American pictures by then had acquired something like 80 per cent of the world's screen time. As in so many other sectors of twentieth-century economic life, war has favoured the position of the United States in the world economy.

Having started the story of technical invention in the laboratory of Edison, it is important to qualify the claim that technical change was primarily dependent on his personal contribution. He was no more the only inventor of the new entertainment devices than most of the eighteenth-century inventors were sole inventors of new industrial devices. Like them, he was engaged in fierce patent battles which dominated the early years of business exploitation. It is possible to understand the early development of the mass entertainment industry only if two kinds of conflict associated with the business side of the story are unravelled. The first kind of conflict was that between one form of entertainment and another. This conflict did not always end in the supplanting of one kind of entertainment by another but more frequently by their commercial integration. The second kind of conflict was between different contestants seeking to provide the same kind of entertainment. This conflict centred on patent rights and invoked frequent litigation. Again, it was more likely to end in integration – mergers, trusts and the erection of a network of holding companies – than in complete victory or defeat. The details are frequently intricate and difficult; the pattern, however, is plain and straightforward.

The early history of the cinema illustrates both kinds of conflict. E. V. Lucas visited Barnet Fair in 1906, nearly two years before Barnet's first cinema opened. He noted that 'many of the old shows had given place to animated pictures, and at the Fêtes of the Invalides in Paris a few weeks later I observed the same development . . . Instead of taking the place of the illustrated paper, as the cinematograph did at first almost exclusively, it was taking the place of the theatre.' A year later a writer in *Encore*, the music hall journal, claimed that as early as 1900 he had

> pointed out to the profession that the greatest enemies the artistes had were the film merchants. The kinematograph picture shows have come here to stay was my argument, and each time an operator is employed two or three single items are ousted. How thoroughly my predictions were borne out by events is patent to everyone today, although at the time I was being accused of being alarmist and pessimistic.

There was some truth in these verdicts, particularly as far as music halls and vaudeville were concerned, but there was a real element of pessimism, too. The truth was twofold. First there was inevitable technological unemployment of a number of people in the old entertainment business, and second there were unprecedented and dazzling prospects for the artist who could adapt himself or be adapted to the new medium. Thus, a French film starring Sarah Bernhardt was a transatlantic success in 1912. Charlie Chaplin is by far the best early example of the financial effects of the development of mass entertainment on the financial prospects of the mass entertainer. In the summer of 1913 he was appearing in vaudeville and refused an offer to appear in films for $75 a week. The offer was doubled and Chaplin accepted. His first feature-length comedy *Tillie's Punctured Romance* was so successful that other companies began to bid for his services, and he soon signed for another company at $1250 a week. It is said that in the course of the negotiations he was offered $1000 a week and in reply asked for $1075. When asked why he wanted so much, he said he had to have $75 a week to live on. A year after receiving $1250 a week, he signed a contract in 1915 for $10,000 a week with a bonus of $150,000.

The immediate consequences were first that Mary Pickford, working for a rival concern, had to have her salary put up, too, and second that the company producing Chaplin recouped its heavy costs at once by selling the British Empire rights of Chaplin's comedies for $670,000. The size of these transactions emphasises an element of caution and pessimism amid all the excitement. Just as important as the stars to the success of the cinema were the 'fans': indeed, it goes without saying that without fans there could have been no stars.

Over a long period the cinema did not so much divert an older audience from other kinds of entertainment as create an enormous new one. From its first beginnings until the end of the First World War the cinema attracted a steadily increasing international audience, including a large number of people who were regular habitués, neither of theatres nor music halls, and a very high proportion of young people (up to 30 per cent. of the total cinema audiences below the age of 17) for whom the local cinema was the first institution of entertainment they had ever encountered. From 1918 to 1926–7 the attendance rate appears to have fluctuated within narrow limits until in 1926–7, when there was a definite slump and the cinema appeared to be losing its hold.* This slump was overcome first by the development of a new invention, the 'talkie' – the first talking picture being shown in 1926 – and second by a re-styling of cinemas and their amenities until they became 'luxury palaces' for the masses of the population, the Granadas, Rialtos, Eldorados and Ritzes of modern urban life.

From 1929 onwards film attendances increased until in Britain they had reached 19 millions a week in 1939. The peak of over 31 millions came in 1946, the year also of the American peak, 98 millions; and since then – in a period which lies outside the scope of today's lecture – they have fallen very sharply indeed. In Britain, for example, they fell by 16 per cent during the twelve months ending in March this year. All in all since 1945 more than a quarter of Britain's cinemas have closed. In the United States average weekly attendances dropped from 98 millions in 1946 to 41 millions in 1953. They are still falling.

These statistics measure the rise and fall of the greatest public audience ever collected. The facts of the fall, however, should not eclipse the facts of the rise. Superlatives are strictly appropriate in this context. The British public in the five years after the Second World War was spending twice as much (£105 million a year) on attendance at cinemas as on going to theatres, concert halls, music halls, dance halls, skating rinks, sporting events (including football and racing) and all other places of public entertainment. Comparative American figures – they run into much bigger aggregates – are not easy to come by, but before the Second World War, in 1937, motion picture corporations in America, constituting 44 per cent of all so-called amusement corporations,

---

* The 1926–7 slump is an interesting phenomenon. The threat to the cinema was due partly to the poor quality of films, partly to the competition of radio. One response to it was the provision of additional attractions (e.g., double features, cinema organs, orchestras). Another was 'give-aways' (dishes, refrigerators, etc.). Higher admission prices, the consequences of such policies, aggravated the problem. The popular press also developed highly competitive 'give-away' strategies.

accounted for 78 per cent of the gross income and 92 per cent of the total net income of the group. The people who were afraid of the competition of films in 1906 and 1907 had no conception of the dimensions of the future demand for entertainment. They saw only the shadows of conflict between different entertainment interests and were afraid, just as established film interests, saddled by high capital costs, feared the future during the 1950s.

The established film interests were the product of bitter and prolonged internal conflicts within the rapidly growing industry. Edison's patents were challenged. Other inventors in several different countries were responsible either for parallel inventions or basic improvements, and it is historically accurate to say of most cinema inventions as of radio and gramophone inventions that they were products not of one particular man but of an epoch. Since in any case Edison's patents were not international, there were always foreign competitors in the early days as well as domestic American developers of thinly disguised Edison discoveries. The issue of monopoly became important long before it did in broadcasting. An attempt in 1908 by the ten leading American producing and supplying companies of equipment and films – all using Edison patents on the basis of an agreement with Edison – to monopolise the industry through a Motion Picture Patents Company failed. The so-called 'Independents', who opposed the Patents Company, moved far away from New York, the Company's headquarters, to what Billie Burke has described as 'a pepper-tree-lined village which had begun a few years before as a suburb (of Los Angeles) for retired Iowans'. The suburb was Hollywood, and some of the 'Independents' were men who subsequently became the moguls of the growing international industry. The Motion Picture Patents Company was finally broken up in 1915 as a monopoly by order of the Federal Court.

Zukor, the chief of the Independents, changed from rebel into mogul between 1911 and 1921. With the destruction of his enemy, he turned to integration himself, passing from production to distribution and then into exhibition. In 1919 he raised funds through a $10 million issue of preferred stock, the first major attempt to finance cinema development from capital raised on the market. By 1921 he controlled over 300 cinemas. It was his turn now to be accused of the same monopolistic tendencies which he had condemned in the Motion Picture Patents Company. 'It is made difficult,' ran a complaint made to the Federal Trade Commission in 1921, 'for small and independent producers or distributors of films to enter into or remain in the moving picture industry or market, or to lease individual pictures on merit . . . By the said methods Famous Players–Lasky Corporation (Zukor's group) has unduly hindered, and is unduly hindering competitors, lessening competition, and restraining trade in the motion picture industry.'

Zukor's group was not the only menace to the new Independents, and by 1923 it was clear that they were fighting an inevitable losing battle. The American industry had taken on the shape which it was to retain until 1950 – throughout the whole golden age of the cinema. There were several large completely integrated units, including Paramount, Loew's and Fox (with unequal strength, however, in production, distribution and exhibition); a number of powerful unaffiliated chains of cinemas, dominated by the so-called 'first-run' cinemas; and more numerous but less powerful individual cinema proprietors competing with the chains for 'product and patronage'.

The most important shift in power after 1923 was the rise of Warner Brothers, who had grown from nickelodeon operators to a medium-scale enterprise, and who became one of the giants, the so-called 'Big-Five', because they were the first concern to exploit the commercial development of sound. Other companies were conservative in technical matters, concentrating, as is so often the case in economic history, on commercial rather than technical development. They were really impressed only when Warner Brothers' first all-sound feature *The Jazz Singer*, which cost $500,000 to make, netted $2,500,000 in box-office receipts. Warner Brothers converted earlier business losses into a profit of $17 million in 1929. In 1928 they were a corporation with capital assets of only $16 million; in 1930 – with the financial crash of 1929 intervening – their assets totalled $230 milion. Their stupendous progress was a measure not only of their own initiative and drive but of business acceptance of the film industry as a profitable field of activity.

The most revealing expression of overseas alarm at the dominance of Hollywood in economic – and indirectly of cultural life – was the British Cinematograph Films Act of December, 1927. When the British film industry (producers and exhibitors) failed to agree voluntarily on measures to preserve itself from threatened extinction, the government intervened directly in the industry. It controlled advance and block booking of films, established a quota system and created a Cinematograph Films Advisory Committee to advise the Board of Trade on the administration of the Act. Hitherto the government's only measure of control over the industry was an Act of 1909 which regulated the licensing of cinemas and the censorship of films: it now maintained that while it saw no reason to give financial assistance to the British film industry, as one section of the trade wished, it had the right to intervene in the industry because of the magnitude of what were described by Lord Newton as 'the industrial, commercial, education, and Imperial interests involved'. 'Should we be content,' the President of the Board of Trade asked, 'if we depended upon foreign literature or upon a foreign Press in this country?' At this point questions of mass entertainment were bound up with questions of propaganda and prestige. From a strictly business point of view, however, the Act had important consequences. With the prospect of quotas and a guaranteed market, a new company, British International Pictures, founded a few months before the Films Act, quickly raised £1 million from outsiders. Production increased, large-scale vertical integration took place in the industry, and a decade of investment in the British film industry began.

The history of the film industry deserves detailed and protracted attention because during the twentieth century it became by far the biggest element in the provision of mass entertainment. The story of the gramophone industry, however, has many features in common with the story of the cinema, while the story of radio touches the history of the cinema at several points and at the same time provides illuminating contrasts as well as comparisons.

In the early years of the gramophone industry there were fierce struggles between the Bell and the Edison interests – a continuation of the telephone struggle – the rapid bankruptcy in 1890 of a businessman outsider, J. H. Lippincott, who for a brief spell of two years secured control of both Edison and Bell inventions, the successful challenge of gramophone records to the discs which Edison employed on his early phonographs, and an agreement about the pooling of patents in 1902 – the same year as the famous American steel merger – of two of the biggest gramophone interests in America – the Victor and Gramophone Companies. Together they achieved a dominance in the American gramophone industry which endured for more than half a century. At the end of the First World War, the Victor Company's capital assets amounted to nearly $38 million. By 1921 a hundred million records were sold in the United States, four times as many as in 1914.

Like the cinema industry, the gramophone record industry faced troubles in the mid 1920s, a little earlier than the cinema industry, particularly during the period from 1921 to 1925, but unlike the cinema industry it also faced a major crisis from 1929 to 1932. Only six million records were sold in the United States in 1932, 6 per cent of the total sales in 1927. Immediate recovery was not spectacular, yet during the difficult 1930s it was a highly integrated industry on both sides of the Atlantic that faced the continued depression. Technical progress was not rapid, and it was not until much later in 1947–8 that magnetic tape recording and long-playing records introduced a new technical phase associated also with very substantial commercial expansion. The 'battle of the speeds' was reserved for a later post-war generation, as was the golden age of the disc (and the disc jockey), coinciding with the dramatic expansion of the teenager market. In the meantime, however, the 'hit parade' established itself during the 1930s, and by 1939 there were 225,000 juke boxes in the United States.

Integration on the business side led to many mergers and the formation in 1931 of one new company which was later to be of international importance – the Electrical and Musical Industries Ltd. EMI was a merger of the Columbia Gramophone Company and the Gramophone Company: it was to be the first company to produce cathode-ray tubes for television sets. This is to point to the future. A fascinating side glance at the past is that in 1929, the year of another huge American merger, that between the Victor Company and the Radio Corporation of America – a merger facilitated by the development of the radio gramophone – the Edison Company completely suspended the building of gramophones. Edison himself was then aged 82. It might be very revealing to have a record from that date of his impressions of fifty years of the mass entertainment industry.

Mention of the Radio Corporation of America (RCA) and earlier of the British Cinematograph Act directs attention to the place of wireless in this story. RCA, founded in 1919, was the biggest of the American radio interests, while on 1 January 1927, the same year as the Cinematograph Act, the British Broadcasting Corporation came into existence, an experiment in public control which went much further than public control over the film industry. The British Cinematopgraph Act reflected British fear of American economic dominance in the film industry; the foundation of RCA eight years earlier reflected American fear of British dominance – through the Marconi Company network – of the international wireless business. From its foundation in 1898 to the end of the First World War the Marconi Company with its subsidiaries had controlled a number of key wireless patents. The big American electrical companies, such as Westinghouse and American Telephone and Telegraph, could not exploit radio fully unless they used Marconi-controlled patents in addition to the patents in their own possession.

In 1919, therefore, the three biggest American electric firms, with substantial United States government backing, agreed to pool their resources, buy out American Marconi and, following a suggestion of Owen D. Young, Chairman of the Board of General Electric, form a new company, the Radio Corporation of America. The corporation or consortium, as it is more properly regarded, was less concerned with the manufacture of radio sets than with their distribution, and far less concerned with broadcasting matter than with business expansion. The Corporation was drawn during the course of the 1920s both into the gramophone business and after the advent of 'talkies' into films: the Radio-Keith-Orpheum (RKO) Film Corporation, founded in 1929 was an offshoot of the Radio Corporation of America (RCA) and soon became 'an active, aggressive force in production, distribution and exhibition'. The Chairman of its Board was a Vice-President of RCA. Films and radio were thus brought directly into relation with each other.

Broadcasting developed as a by-product of business pressure, not as an end in itself. Of all the new inventions of the late nineteenth century which were to transform twentieth-century social life, radio inventions were least clearly appreciated as potential agents of social transformation. Wireless was thought of, as we have seen, as a substitute for telegraphic communication by wire, and it was not until the First World War that the possibility of broadcasting regular programmes was recognised. Paradoxically, it was believed in the early days that broadcasting was a disadvantage of wireless, not an advantage: confidential messages designed for one person or place could be picked up indiscriminately by other people. Moreover, because free transmission of radio messages from individual to individual was known to involve a great deal of 'mutual interference', it was wrongly assumed that radio could not be fully exploited in populous areas. 'Wireless telegraphy', a witness told a British Select Committee of the House of Commons in 1906, 'can only be used in lines removed from each other's disturbing influences, as in sparsely populated countries and underdeveloped regions.' To have restricted the use of radio to underdeveloped regions, lighthouses and ships at sea would have been like using the telephone only as an internal instrument within the house. Yet the use of radio in the *Titanic* disaster and the arrest of Dr Crippen was what interested people most before 1914, not its possible use as an instrument of instruction or entertainment. The idea of a radio audience was stumbled upon, not deliberately planned.

Two young prophets saw more clearly than their contemporaries during the First World War that wireless could transform society. The first was David Sarnoff, later the first Vice-President of RCA; the second was Arthur Burrows, later the first Programmes Director of the BBC. In 1906, the same year that an American, R. A. Fessenden, made a pioneer broadcast of music and the human voice from Brant Rock, Massachusetts – the technical break-through from wireless telegraphy to wireless telephony – Sarnoff, then fifteen years old, became an office boy on the staff of the Marconi Wireless Telegraph Company of America at a salary of five and a half dollars a week. He grew up with radio till he became the commanding figure in the American radio business.

It was in 1916 that Sarnoff made his first striking prophecy about the future of radio.

> A radio telephone transmitter [he wrote] having a range of say twenty-five to fifty miles can be installed at a fixed point where instrumental or vocal music or both are produced. The problem of transmitting music has already been solved in principle and therefore all the receivers attuned to the transmitting wave length shall be capable of receiving such music. The receiver can be disguised in the form of a simple 'Radio Music Box' and arranged for several different wave lengths, which should be changeable with the throwing of a single switch or pressing of a single button.

Sarnoff did not stop at what came to be called the 'wireless set'. He went on to describe the potential radio audience, a large number of people all receiving simultaneously from a single transmitter. He even forecast the kind of programmes which would attract this new audience – broadcasting of events of national importance, concerts, lectures and baseball scores. Modestly he added that 'there are numerous other fields to which the principle can be extended'.

On this side of the Atlantic, Arthur Burrows was also successful in peering even further into the future.

> There appears to be no serious reason [he wrote] why before we are many years older, politicians speaking, say, in Parliament, should not be heard simultaneously by wireless in the reporting room of every newspaper office in the United Kingdom. The same idea might be extended to make possible the concert reproduction in all private residences of Albert Hall or Queen's Hall concerts, or the important recitals at the lesser *rendezvous* of the music world . . . Such departures would expose us, of course, to all sorts of logical but unwelcome developments. There would be no technical difficulty in the way of an enterprising advertisement agency arranging for intervals in the musical programme to be filled with audible advertisements, pathetic or forcible appeals – in appropriate tones – on behalf of somebody's soap or tomato ketchup.

Burrows in Britain looked further into the future than Sarnoff in the United States, for Sarnoff did not reconcile himself to the arguments for commercial broadcasting until the late 1920s. In looking forward, however, Burrows was also looking back. Given the transition from radio to broadcasting, he realised that a prophet had to take into account not only technical but social forces. Broadcasting would never be left to the scientists and engineers alone. He turned back to the previous thirty or forty years of history and selected a number of elements in British history which would help to shape the use of the new invention. Today we can see them more clearly still – the attitude of government; the power of the Press; the strength of business –

particularly business in so-called 'consumer goods', those which were bought over the counter and, as the market was extended, were advertised for all the world to buy; the organisation of entertainment, both local and national; and, not least in importance, the level of education of the potential radio audience. Given the transition from radio to broadcasting, all these became factors to take into the reckoning.

On both sides of the Atlantic, the radio audience grew rapidly during the ealry 1920s, America leading the way in the boom of 1922 and 1923. There were only three American radio stations in 1920; by the spring of 1923 there were nearly 600, and the number of radio retail dealers had risen to 15,000; 60,000 radios were in use in the United States at the beginning of 1922: 2,850,000 by the end of 1925. In Britain, where a licensing system was in operation, 35,744 licences had been issued by the end of 1922, 1,645,207 by the end of 1925, and 2,178,259 by the end of 1926.

American broadcasting was provided by a welter of stations, relying increasingly – against Sarnoff's own personal predilections – on commercial advertising for their revenue. There was no Federal direction either of financial control or the allocation of wavelengths until the Federal Radio Commission was set up in 1927.

The 'chaos of the ether' in the United States served as a warning in the United Kingdom, where, with the approval of the Post Office, broadcasting was established as a monopoly by a consortium of business interests in December, 1922. Six manufacturing companies subscribed the bulk of the original £100,000 capital of the British Broadcasting Company. Revenue was to be raised from royalties on the sale of receiving sets and from a share (50 per cent) of the licence fee which was to be exacted from everyone who bought a receiving set in Britain. Profits on the working of the Company were to be restricted to 7½ per cent per annum, and there was to be no opportunity for windfall capital gains.

There were thus two completely different kinds of broadcasting systems in operation in Britain and the United States by the mid-1920s – the American system resting on advertising subsidies and suggesting to the listener that radio broadcasting was like 'manna from heaven' coming to them 'without money and without price, entertainment that was as free as air', the British system directed as a public service but compelling the listener (sometimes against his will) to pay for benefits which he did not always appreciate. The gap between the two systems was further widened – formally at least – when on 1 January 1927, the British Broadcasting Company was converted into the British Broadcasting Corporation. All direct links with the British radio and electrical trade were broken, and under the continued régime of John

Reith, who had been General Manager and Managing Director of the old Company and became Director General of the new Corporation, emphasis on the public service aspect of broadcasting continued to dominate all discussion of policy.

In the meantime, the volume and cost of American radio advertising sharply increased, following the same kind of formulae which had been followed successfully in relation to the Press, though with greater sophistication and complexity. It is impossible to give exact figures for the early years or to trace in detail the history of the great advertising agencies, one of the most important of which – the A. C. Nielson Company – was founded in 1923. Again, however, the main outlines of the story are clear. Down to about 1930 the big American networks, the products of difficult and often complicated business mergers, of which the National Broadcasting Company of 1926 (NBC), a subsidiary of RCA, was the first and the Columbia Broadcasting System (CBA) of 1927 the second, looked for attractive broadcast programmes and then sought advertisers 'who would take a fling at broadcasting'. After 1930 the agencies came in direct. By 1935, the net incomes of NBC and CBS had soared to $3,656,907 and $3,228,194 respectively.

The linking of entertainment interests was pushed still further in 1938 when CBS purchased from Consolidated Film Industries Inc. the capital stock of the American Record Company and its subsidiaries, changing the name to the Columbia Recording Corporation.

When television developed as a natural growth within the radio and broadcasting business, the income (and profits) from advertising moved up sharply, and Britain itself eventually succumbed in 1955 to commercial television as part of the national pattern. To give some idea of the change of economic scale in the age of television, network advertisers in the United States were by then spending approximately $320 million for television time along with $137 million for radio advertising. One advertiser alone, the Procter and Gamble Company, spent over $36 million on both.

These figures are far removed from the figures of receipts of Bartholomew Fair in 1828. Mass entertainment had become big business, and the bigger and more organised it grew, the higher the costs of entry became. When J. G. Bennett started the *New York Herald* as a mass paper he had a capital of 500 dollars: today to launch a metropolitan paper would take at least ten million dollars. Press power has become increasingly concentrated in the hands of a small number of interests: it has also become increasingly concerned with entertainment, even in its own particular domain. The comic strip, for example, is the substitute for (or perhaps complement to) the image on the screen. But the mutual influence is not limited to cultural forms. After feuding with new agencies, particularly radio, the press has in some cases, as in Australia, penetrated them. There has also been marked economic interpenetration of sport by the different entertainment agencies – press, television, cinema and so on.

Sport is a subject I have only briefly touched on in this survey, but it is common knowledge that there are many signs in the middle of the twentieth century that the small business of sport (leaving on one side amateur sport) is giving way to big business. Contemporary trends already have their history: by the late 1940s there were 14 million people in Britain betting regularly on football pools and spending more than £60 million a year on them. Taxation introduced in 1948 meant that a share of this sum passed into the hands of the State. By the outbreak of the Second World War, the annual turnover of the football pools in Britain was at least ten times as great as the annual turnover of all the football clubs put together. Yet it was not until a recent court action in Britain (1959) that it was laid down that a share of football pool revenue should also pass directly to the Football League.

Television, as the newest and most aggressive of the new entertainment interests, has already made an impact (still a controversial impact) on the organisation of sport. British television companies, for example, have recently acquired a controlling interest in the Wembley Stadium, Britain's greatest sports arena, while the televising of football matches has begun to revolutionise football finance. Advertising and business sponsorship cement the complex. All this is far removed from what at the time was a prophetic cartoon in the *Strand Magazine* of 1898 showing a silk-hatted pedestrian at a rugby match equipped with a kind of walky-talky set listening to the half-time scores, which he was about to pass on to a distant friend.

To an economic historian pausing briefly after surveying the vast field described in this lecture, the main conclusion must be that the chief theme of the story is the way in which massive market interests have come to dominate an area of life which until recently was dominated by individuals themselves (or groups of individuals in voluntary association) with the intermittent help of showmen and the more regular help of two groups scarcely mentioned in this lecture – innkeepers and bookmakers. The massiveness of the control is certainly more revealing than the often dubious statements made by the controllers about the character of the 'masses' whose wants they claim they are satisfying. For the sake of simplification, I have referred throughout to 'mass entertainment', a now common term like a score of other terms beginning with mass like 'mass media', 'mass communication' and 'mass culture'. I must end, however, by querying the use of the term 'masses' in this context since it begs more questions than almost any term which is used in business or society today. To see people as 'masses' is not to know them as individuals or to think of them in terms of a market formula. To talk of 'mass communications' is to mislead: the agencies of so-called 'mass communication' are really agencies of mass or multiple transmission.

These points have been well made by Raymond Williams in Britain and by Max Lerner in the United States in his *America as a Civilisation* (1958). Let me quote Max Lerner's comment on the idea of the 'masses' applied to mass entertainment.

> The editors of the big papers and magazines, the producers of movie, radio and TV shows, the publishers of paperbacks and comic books, and of popular records fall into the habit of abstracting some common denominator from all these audiences. I suppose they have to in order to keep themselves from going crazy. Yet the hardheaded, sharp-featured men must know that those whom they have thus abstracted continue to be individuals with a variety of tastes. If they forget this they forget it at their peril, for an audience whose varied and changing taste is neglected will dissolve into thin air. Hence the continuing search for 'fresh ideas', new 'formulas' and 'formats'. If the 'mass' of the 'mass media' were uniform, passive and plastic, there would be no need to woo it by novelties or to watch the fever chart of the changes and chances.

In judgements of this kind we cross what I described at the beginning of this lecture as the fascinating but formidable frontier between problems of commerce and problems of taste; and we must remember, of course, that minority audiences as well as mass audiences have grown in the twentieth century. Even briefly to discuss the issues raised by this would take not one lecture but a dozen.

Yet 'mass' is not the only theme in the story I have been telling. On the technical side scattered developments have led to the creation of an international electronics industry with a top tier, interested in a large number of fields, producing a wide range of products and maintaining (sometimes with limited business results) large and impressive research laboratories. On the industrial relations side, not only has a group of trade unions and employers associations been created – of which the American Society of Composers, Authors and Publishers (ASCAP) and the Musicians' Union in the United States have been the most militant – but a huge network of agency organisations is now interspersed between the artist and his employer. On the social side, institutions of entertainment have come and gone in peaks and troughs of acceptance and rejection. The music hall, for example, has almost completely gone, while other new institutions – the bowling alley in the United States, for example – are on the way in. Paradoxically some of the changes have reinforced the position of the home. Before the rise of radio and television, the revolution in mass entertainment was a revolution outside the home; now it is a revolution from within. Given the sequence and the pattern, there is need for greater public knowledge and discussion of what is going on and what has already gone on. The want of entertainment is basically a simple want which we all share: 'show business' and 'sporting business' are news. They are also history.

4   The Communications Revolution*

The word 'revolution' is one of the most overworked words of our age. We used to apply it to great events, the culminating points of relentless social pressures, and to the sequences of further and far-reaching episodes or phases, some of them violent, during which old conceptions of authority were overturned and new forms of action, most of them fiercely contested, were tried out. More recently, however, we have freely applied the word revolution to economic, technological, social and cultural changes which have carried with them few direct political implications, certainly not in the short run. Many of these changes we can plausibly call silent revolutions, for they have, indeed, long-term implications in relation either to power or to culture, perhaps to both. Thus fortified, we set the retail revolution against the Russian Revolution or the revolution in education against the revolution in Cuba. It is a measure of our imaginative response to the enormous changes of our own lifetimes in our own still partly traditional society that we do not find it too difficult to persuade ourselves that we are living in an age of revolution or that while the world is torn by violent political revolution there are further and bigger revolutions round the corner in this country, concerned with such issues as modernisation or automation.

I make no apologies, however, for using the word revolution – stale though it may already be beginning to be – to describe the communications revolution, a genuinely international revolution. I do not know who first invented the phrase, but it has had particularly wide currency in the headlines this year with the centenary of the International Telecommunications Union. At the centre of the revolution, as scientists see it at the present time, is the control of *information*. The electronics industry is the main agent of technical transformation, a new and expanding industry, with a compound annual rate of growth of over 10 per cent (at constant prices) since 1935, an industry dependent for its development on ever more sophisticated mathematical techniques and insights. The implications of the term *information*, however, are wide

* The Third Mansbridge Memorial Lecture, delivered at Leeds University, 1966.

enough to cover the classification and transmission of scientific or business knowledge at one end of the scale and the presentation of popular entertainment at the other; computer programmes or the Light Programme. Recent developments in the electronics industry obliterate all kinds of old industrial dividing lines, covering as they do, big electronics concerns, programmed learning and film production. Data transmission is likely to transform hospital or office management as much as mass media of communication transform leisure patterns.

There are psychological dimensions to all these questions also, like the relationship between *information* and *persuasion*, along with difficult border problems where aesthetics and economics converge or where education and entertainment overlap. A whole new environment distinctive to the electronic age is being created; it is an environment of instant circuitry transforming our sense of perception and our use of time. This is a revolution indeed.

The origins of the mass media of communication – one side of the communications revolution and the side with which I shall mainly be concerned in this lecture – go back in time, as we shall see, to Victorian England, to an age when men were so preoccupied with production and distribution, particularly production, that they were not fully aware of how one aspect of communication was or could be related to another. Now, at last, we are beginning to pull together, to relate, to generalize, and to find new patterns. Accepting the existence of communications technology, a distinctive as well as a sophisticated technology, dealing with brain rather than body, we are turning to the problems of human relationships in a period of rapid communications development. We are becoming aware of effects on society and culture which force us to ask questions. A small but mixed group of writers in this country, as outside, have tried to see what is happening in perspective.

Some writers have turned to biological analogies and referred to changes in our collective nervous system, while Professor Colin Cherry, the first professor of communications in this country, has compared the rapid development of modern communications with the introduction of money into the medieval economy.

> These inventions of communications systems, which now enmesh the globe, are systems of *exchange*, and are very similar to the invention of money. The effects upon our societies are rather as though we had invented money for the first time. Going further with this analogy – the invention of money as a system of exchange led to power residing in accumulation of these tokens. It seems conceivable then that the ownership of the means of communicating and storing information may lead to a totally new form of organization. Information may become the token of power.

Raymond Williams has detected whole new ways of thinking in terms of communications not only about power but about ourselves. In his writing, indeed, the technology is pushed into the background, and it is the language that is scanned and interpreted.

> We are used to descriptions of our whole common life in political and economic terms. The emphasis on communications asserts, as a matter of experience, that men and societies are not confined to relationships of power, property and production. Their relationships in describing, learning, persuading and exchanging experiences are seen as equally fundamental.

The kind of issues raised by Cherry and Williams are the issues which I want to discuss briefly in this lecture, which, at best, will be an attempt to provide some sense of perspective for further study. They seem to me to be issues particularly relevant to a Mansbridge Memorial Lecture, which it is a great privilege to deliver in my old university, since Mansbridge was always more concerned with that brand of adult education which raised difficult issues than with that which simply provided facts. He was far more confident in his assessment of the relationship between tradition, innovation and purpose than I would care to be, but he admired imaginative boldness. 'Knowledge is not education; it is but the fuel burnt in a flame which comes from the heart of the world and which makes all things new.' Does the kind of mass communications complex about which I shall be talking make Mansbridge completely out-of-date?

We shall not escape questions of this kind by evading them. They are part of a range of bigger questions about the social use, private and public, that we can make of the new media, and, equally important, about the effects of the media on our consciousness. At a very simple level, the new means of communication enable us to travel widely, to talk to our friends and relatives miles away, to take photographs of each other, to share in great audiences scattered in town and country, to see and hear in our own homes people who are making history, even to have the sense of participating in great events. At a deeper level, they rearrange the pattern of impressions and relationships, and modify all historical notions of scale (more people could watch a television Shakespeare cycle than had ever watched Shakespeare before, etc.) and of time (through our sense of both today and yesterday, even of tomorrow). They are ubiquitous in their effects here on earth, and call space into the reckoning as well.

Given this context, questions about the 'educational' use of the media should not be posed in too narrow or conventional terms. We are clearly not dealing simply with the impact of education by television on existing forms of adult education but with basic questions both of educational technology and of education, about learning and teaching. We are inevitably involved in discussions of values as well as discussions of techniques, just as we were involved in such discussions in the early years of the industrial revolution, when new ways of working changed the pattern of feeling as well as the pattern of working. What, if any, is the relationship between the experience of that first industrial revolution, which set the mould of our lives here in Leeds, and the communications revolution of our own time? Is it true, as Denys Thompson puts it, that 'the nineteenth century maimed and enslaved the worker's body; perhaps in the twentieth century it is his mind that is maintained in servile contentment'.

Before I try to deal with any of these questions, I hope that what I have said already, will have goaded you (in the best traditions of the Workers' Educational Association) into asking a number of your own. Do people really communicate through the mass media? Are we not talking essentially about transmission? Is exchange the right word to describe some of the processes I have been describing? Do not many messages come to us as gifts by kind permission of advertising agencies? Even if we welcome the media, is not mass communication the wrong term? Can we communicate with masses as distinct from individuals? How can we relate the exchange of scientific data, a transforming agency in our understanding of the world and our power to control it, to the trivial content of much mass communication? What about 'candyfloss', and, where the trivial is avoided, what about preoccupation with the safe? As for money and power, is not one basic facet of the new instruments of communication that they cost a great deal of money to make and to run – a big newspaper, for instance, or an international film – and that they will automatically pass more and more within the orbit of great business interests dominating mass markets, including the mass entertainment market? Will they be anything more than instruments, consolidating what is already dominant in our society? What will be the role of the State?

I will not have time to try to answer more than a few of these questions tonight, but I hope to provide some material which will enable you to try to answer them for yourselves. I must begin by saying, however, that I do not agree with Denys Thompson, even when he inserts the word 'perhaps' before his argument. Many of the effects of the media seem to me to involve the very opposite of enslavement. They quicken, liberate, add to awareness, change the size and interplay of minorities as well as influence mass reactions. I have spent a great deal of time myself on the detail of broadcasting history because I am suspicious of easy generalizations about very complex social processes. The reason why I have studied the media is not because I am frightened of them but because I am interested in them. I believe, too, that in relation to communications technology we are in those fascinating early stages when breakthroughs are beginning to take place, the first of many. I suspect that more and more people will become interested in them, both inside universities and outside.

My own approach to the range of questions I have outlined is conditioned by the fact that I am a social historian rather than a technologist or a philosopher. The period with which I shall mainly be concerned in this lecture is roughly that of the last 180 years from the industrial revolution to the present. In the beginning was the steam engine. It is useful, however, at least to begin by going back further in time to the introduction of printing and the intellectual and social changes printing carried with it, in order not only to set more recent trends in perspective but to compare sequences and consequences.

I want to make only a few main points about the long period between the invention of printing and the invention of the steam engine, a period when only a small proportion of the population were taught to read and to write and when literary communication was essentially minority communication. First, printing made possible what Francis Bacon called 'the advancement of learning'. Without it there could have been only a limited spread of learning – in breadth and depth – based on intermittent and arduous communication between scholars. Second, it made possible many other changes as well as the advancement of learning: it became a medium of entertainment as well as a medium of instruction. Some of the entertainment was good, some bad. Third, because only a limited number of the population was taught to read and write, some of the unprivileged were moved by a deep longing for literacy. Fourth, throughout this period, other forms of communication continued in an age of printing. Folklore coexisted with book learning, the oral tradition with the literary tradition. Much of that folklore was both traditional and localised. The units of communication were small, intimate and personal, yet, to take the other side of the picture, stratified, hierarchical and sometimes closed. Fifth, in retrospect, we can see that the shift from pre-literate to literate societies provides breakthroughs comparable in significance to those created by the shift from pre-industrial to industrial societies. Experience of our own history enables us to understand more fully certain aspects of other people's twentieth-century experience. Sixth, in the age of printing we can trace the emergence of a number of key issues of control which have been posed once again in more recent communications history – issues, for example, of monopoly, of licensing and of censorship. Seventh, much of the most interesting development in relation to printing, economic, social and cultural, has followed the invention of the steam engine. The rise of the press (steam printing was introduced in 1814), the spread of literacy, the paperback revolution – all these are phenomena stretching into our own times, into the period of the bigger communications revolution.

Our appetite for received communications has more than kept pace with the supply. One medium may displace another, as talkies displaced silent films, but one medium may reinforce another or swallow it up, as television swallows up films. In terms of technology alone, some of the most interesting aspects of current research and development relate to printing – photocomposition of newspapers, for example, instead of use of raised type, simultaneous re-setting and printing of several editions of newspapers miles apart, and so on. All these changes continue to affect our conceptions of time and place, and we are by no means at the end of the story. Sir Gerald Barry has written recently, indeed, that 'twenty years from now there will have been accomplished a technical revolution in both the printing and production of news comparable to the revolution caused by the revolution in printing itself. A newspaper distributed by van or pushed through the letter box will have become a preposterous anachronism.'

If the story of printing leads back to the fifteenth century and ends in the present, there are more recent developments in communications which enable us to understand further not only how one aspect of communications history is related to another, but how intricate and complex is the relationship between technological and social history. With the steam engine not in the background but in the very foreground of the picture, the first great change in nineteenth-century communications was the invention of the railway. This change in physical communications was thought of by many contemporaries as a great divide in human history. As Thackeray put it,

> it was only yesterday, but what a gulf between now and then. *Then* was the old world. Stage coaches, horses, highwaymen, Druids, Ancient Britons . . . all these belong to the old period. I will concede a halt in the midst of it and allow that gunpowder and printing tended to modernize the world. But your railroad starts a new era . . . We who lived before railways and survive out of the ancient world, are like Father Noah and his family out of the Ark.

Railways and telegraphs, the first nineteenth-century invention dealing with the communication of messages, were directly related to each other. There was, indeed, a continuing link between physical and electrical communication, well illustrated in the dramatic story of the laying of the great international cables. The cross-Channel cable of 1851 and the trans-Atlantic cable of 1866 were thought of as stepping stones to international interdependence. Just as many of the inventions were international, so it was hoped that the organisations to develop and control them would be international. The International Telecommunications Union, founded in 1865, had this objective. It was brought into existence at a time when the full significance of what was happening in relation to communications was not apparent to contemporaries. The transitional state of affairs was well expressed in the fact that one of the delegations which assembled in Paris to found the new organisation, the Turkish delegation, had to travel part of the way on horseback.

I have not time to show in detail how the history of the telegraph was related to the history of newspapers as well as to the history of railways. More important to note are a consistent range and a regular sequence of human reactions to each successive new innovation in communications technology. There was in the beginning an initial sense of wonder, accompanied by fear; fear about organization, sometimes the very specific fear of threatened vested interests, along with fear about impact, a general fear, bound up with failure to see where it was all leading. Only through conflict did routine come to be accepted. There was also considerable concern about what we would now call the content of the media. Newspapers challenged existing authority. Railway literature debased men's minds. As for telegraphs, it is recorded that when Emerson was told how wonderful it was that somebody could send a message from New York and have an immediate reply from London, he asked, 'But will he have anything to say?'

The difficulties of predicting future social trends were clearly illustrated in relation to the history of the telephone and radio. Some observers believed that one of the main uses of the telephone (1876) would be to permit mistresses of households to communicate more effectively with domestic servants in the basement than by speaking tube. In the case of wireless, the very name suggests that it was thought of essentially as a substitute for communication by wire. The broadcasting possibilities of radio figured in this context as a positive disadvantage. Messages could be picked up by strangers. There was another element of irony in the prophecy that wireless would be most useful in poor and undeveloped countries where the cost of laying landline would be prohibitive.

Some, though not all, of the difficulties of prediction sprang from ignorance of the social *milieu* within which a new technology would develop. To understand the history of communications at the threshold of our own times, it is necessary to turn from the work of a few scientists and inventors and of those businessmen with an eye to innovation – from Edison's laboratory or Marconi's workshop – to the kind of society which would provide them with their market. The 1890s formed a critical decade in English social history, as we can see in retrospect. The demand for efficient business communications grew every year with the growth of office staffs: typewriters as well as telephones were basic products. The demand for popular entertainment was growing too as the cities grew, as consumer purchasing power increased and some of the dividends of the industrial revolution and British overseas expansion began to be realised, and as enterprising businessmen turned to retail distribution; an extended interest in advertising was merely one response to this situation.

In retrospect, 1896 looks like a quite peculiarly critical year.* The first motor show was held in London; this was to usher in quite a new phase in the history of physical communication. The *Daily Mail* was launched by Alfred Harmsworth; this was the beginning of a remarkable development of the popular press. Both these two events were signs that the balance between local and national was changing. The motor car brought with it unprecedented mobility; the new national newspapers undermined the nineteenth-century power of the local and provincial press. In the same year, the first regular cinema show was held in the West End of London, Marconi arrived in London to try to exploit his wireless patent, and the Post Office reached an agreement with the National Telephone Company to take over the main telephone trunk lines. The cinema was to change the balance not only of local and national life, but of national and international life; the wireless was to disturb the balance between home and outside as much as any development since the emergence of the factory system; and the telephone was to revolutionise personal communication.

Yet none of the implications of these changes, which we now see as related changes, were apparent in the 1890s. Motor cars were for the few, symbols of luxury and status. The popular press did not spring into existence overnight. Wireless was not thought of as a medium of entertainment or of education, and new inventions – particularly, the thermionic valve – were necessary before it could become one. Hollywood or any other 'dream factory' was not conceived of, and in England, at least, telephones were almost as much badges of social status as motor cars – with no prospect of an English Postmaster General playing the part of Henry Ford. Again ironically, one of the most modern-looking quotations of the 1890s relates to one element in the communications complex about which I have said nothing – the gramophone (this name is, of course, as out-of-date now as the name

* In making this further reference to 1896 (see above, pp. 33, 42) I have now added the automobile to the 1896 list of firsts, the kind of list that might have made its way into the *Guiness Book of Records* which first appeared in 1900.

wireless), and it concerns for once a development which did not come off – advertising by gramophone (see above, p. 44).

In relation to the exploitation of the inventions of the 1890s and of the backroom decades that led up to them, the years between the two world wars were of basic importance. It was then that the motor car, the wireless set, the telephone, the daily newspaper and the cinema came into their own. Interestingly enough, however, different societies controlled what had become a universal communications technology in different ways. The difference can be brought out in relation to the history of the motor car as much as in relation to the history of radio. More than economic considerations were involved. The foundation of the BBC, for example, in 1922 cannot be explained simply in economic terms, and its policies after 1922 often ran counter to what the Americans thought of as the basic philosophy of the mass communications revolution, the same as that of the retail revolution – 'giving the people what they want'.

During the 1930s radio became an instrument of business in the United States and an instrument of totalitarian government in Germany. In relation to other media also, communications technology served different societies in different ways. To explain divergences in the pattern is a difficult task for any historian. Why, for example, were the Americans more prepared to accept shared private telephones than the British? Why did the British accept the telephone far more willingly as an instrument of business communication than of personal communication?

It may be, however, that these national differences were merely short-lived manifestations of cultural and social traditions which were bound to be eroded by an increasingly universal communications organization as well as a universal technology – that, in other words, there was a time lag. Again there is evidence to support this view. During the years between the wars words like 'mass culture' and 'mass communication' made their way into the language. The phenomena were thought to be international. Hollywood, in particular, represented international direction of one of the biggest industries, film-making, and other countries, while sometimes retaining national styles in film, were all influenced by Hollywood. The United States, as the most highly-developed consumer economy, with the most dynamic advertising industry, was placed in a very special position in relation to what was being increasingly thought of as an international mass market for entertainment. Although Britian led the way in introducing regular television programmes – through the BBC – in 1936, within a few years there were far-sighted *entrepreneurs* who realised that the cheapest way of running television would be on a diet of films just as the cheapest way of running sound radio (as it came to be called) would be on a diet of discs.

During the period since 1945 tendencies which were apparent before 1939 have all accelerated dramatically. Many of the statistical indicators can be plotted on curves which soar to heaven. The number of telephones – 40 millions in 1939 – had reached over 100 millions in 1956, and is now on the way to doubling yet again. The number of telex calls going out from London beyond Europe was less than a million in 1952; it is now ten millions. There were 14,560 television licences in Britain in 1947; now, there are over 12 million. The Buchanan Report has presented staggering but completely convincing statistics about likely increase in motor car ownership between now and the end of the century.

Nor are these statistics the whole of the story of change. Qualitative changes have been even more remarkable. The international record business has boomed beyond belief. Eurovision was merely the first stage in the internationalisation of television which had hitherto, unlike sound radio, stopped at set boundaries. *Telstar, Early Bird* and the like offer technical possibilities of televising the world to the world. The computer industry, as we saw at the beginning of this lecture, has established itself as a key industry, and laboratories have been set up to measure human behaviour in detecting signals, making decisions and predicting future action. In the background, therefore, of the movement of the mass communications graphs, there have always been more fundamental graphs about the growth of scientific knowledge. Business organisation has come to depend more and more on highly skilled people in research fields, and prophets of cybernetics, like Norbert Wiener, have warned us, much as Robert Owen warned us in the early years of the factory system, that 'one of the great future problems we must face is that of the relationship between man and the machine, of the functions which should properly be assigned to these two agencies . . . The hour is very late, and the choice between good and evil knocks at our door.'

Yet there is little doubt that what has happened so far in relation to the communications revolution is no more than a transitional prelude. Future developments – with lasers, for instance, and electromagnetic wave guides – will produce results which will make the present state of the communications industry seem primitive. The visiphone already exists, and it is already being questioned whether mere physical presence will any longer be necessary in 1984! In assessing likely trends in the future, we must relate technological to other factors, bearing in mind how wrong some of our predecessors have been in getting these relationships clear. Three points stand out. First, economic factors set the pace of development as much as technical factors, and the economic organisation of the industries I have been talking about, particularly at the mass entertainment level, displays a high degree of concentration. There are powerful interlocking interests, some of them international, in the Press, the film, television, the record industry and so on. In relation to computers and almost all other categories of electronic capital goods the United States has a pronounced world lead. Second, every communications technique carries with it an invitation to convert it into an art, and every art carries with it the potential to change ways of seeing and feeling. Unless we take note of the general impact of the new communications network, we will be producing out-of-date prescriptions about what to do with particular bits and pieces of it, including the educational 'pieces'. Third, social and cultural implications remain mysterious and controversial, and it is difficult to answer the biggest question of all – and the simplest – about the effect of the communications revolution on the quality of living. We tend to fall back on set stances, sometimes even to become nostalgic, rather than to scrutinise our own values.

When I turn, therefore, in the second part of my lecture from the bearings and perspective of development in communications to what we can and cannot do in relation to them, I am supremely conscious of the difficulties in the way. Nearly everyone who has written about this field of change has been far more firm in description than in prescription. This has been particularly true of literary critics, but it has also been true of sociologists and psychologists. Those of us involved in adult education are similarly placed. We are well aware, too, that we speak in terms of very limited numbers and even more limited resources, and that, in many cases, our own problems do not seem to touch some of the bigger problems I have been talking about. At the same time, we fully appreciate that 'mass communications' not only raise specific educational questions, for example about 'the University of the Air', but do much to shape the general cultural environment within which we work.

The impact of the communications revolution depends on four elements – ourselves; the philosophy and tactics of the providers; the media themselves (not, I would suggest, neutral, as is often thought and said); and our children. Before we can look in detail, however, at its impact on any of the four elements, we must clear our minds. First we must separate out the effects of the communications revolution from other social influences – changes in work habits, for instance (independent of automation, which in one sense is part of the communications revolution); in the income and styles of teenagers; or in the scope and power of the national system of education. It is never easy to separate out, particularly when the evidence is historical, the influence of one social variable or set of variables from another. I have never found this easy in broadcasting history – and it has inhibited me from making a number of what have seemed to other people obvious generalisations – nor has it proved easy in relation to pressing contemporary problems, like, for example, the effects of television on crime.

Another initial difficulty in making assessments is that we tend, often implicitly, to idealise situations before the variables begin to operate, just as many people idealised the social situation before the advent of the industrial revolution. Before condemning the average television viewer for spending thirteen-and-a-half hours a week watching television, it is wise to ask what he did with that time before. Displacement effects may be less important than they are sometimes thought to be. A third difficulty springs from seeing other people as just like ourselves. This has long been a difficulty in England, when class differences have been so great that it has been all too easy for one class to impose its norms on another: in such circumstances observation itself becomes suspect.

Given the difficulties, the impact made by the media is affected by the expectations which we bring to their reception, by our previous experience and education, and, above all by our power to discriminate and to cut off. An output theory of television is not enough to explain impact. It is not difficult to see where we can extend personal control. Discrimination, nourished by literary culture, will have to be extended into the world of impressions, fragments, images. The power to cut off is even more vital, because, while we can always be over-fed by the media, in a balanced world the diet provided by all the mass media taken together will never be sufficiently sustaining to the active, creative individual. So far, any rate, evidence collected from research suggests that the media reinforce rather than change values and that they do little to touch values that are deep-set or strongly held.

We need a great deal more research, however, along the lines followed by Joseph Trenaman, whom Leeds was fortunate to attract as its first Granada Television Fellow. Dr Trenaman, whom I was proud to count as a friend, showed how limited – so far – was the impact of television on politics. But he would have emphasised the 'so far' and stressed the need to find out more about the long-term effects of television on attitudes as well as opinions. He was always interested in the philosophy of the providers, and would have agreed with those recent writers on the media who have emphasised that in the long run the best defence of the recipient lies not in administration or policy making, important though these are, but in the creative power and honesty of vision of the producer. 'The task I am trying to achieve,' wrote film pioneer D. W. Griffith in 1913, 'is above all to make you see.' Independent of all philosophies of control or modes of presentation, the media themselves, as media, have definite and obvious effects – cutting down, for instance, the life of songs and jokes, altering our conceptions of amateur and professional, accustoming us to a flow of images and sounds, changing our approach to the world while we are still at school and even before we are at school.

At this point, the children come in. We know less about what television and other media will do in the long run to new generations than what they will do to those of us who are older, nor need we be completely convinced in this case by evidence that it all depends on what kind of children they are and from what kinds of homes they come. I suspect that a world pulled together by a more elaborate, more expensive, more cohesive communications network will be a very different kind of world to grow old in – look at future patterns both of old age and leisure – than the world which most of us know.

In adult education, we should be willing to spend more time in our studies on all these themes – on delving into the cultural aspects of technology; on learning about the relationship of media with each other; on developing discrimination, even if this leads into quite new areas of adult education; on discussing the problems of control; on pursuing boundary problems of economics, aesthetics, psychology and sociology; on looking more fully at future leisure patterns (not merely at adult education problems) within a world of mass communication and on planning strategies to help with them; on laying stress not only on the individual who knows how to choose but on the community which knows how to act.

Just as the minority's small-group activities of a personal or a socially purposive kind, which we organise and encourage, are likely to retain their appeal in an age of large scattered audiences sharing mass programmes, so there is every likelihood that, precisely because of the existence and stimulus of the media, we can make these groups grow in size, if we have the drive and organisation to do so. We can also emphasise the role that such groups can play in initiating enterprise, in arguing about social priorities, in looking to social needs and purposes.

To turn more specifically from the educative role of the media and the part we can play to questions of educational method and organisation posed by the communications revolution, I regret that these questions are often narrowed in scope to cover only the educational effects of television or the University of the Air. What is happening in educational television – not only through the mass media but through limited experiments of a closed-circuit kind – is part of a set of changes in educational technology, all of them associated with the bigger communications revolution. Yet, largely for cost reasons, there has been only a limited breakthrough in this country, and the same kind of vague, pervasive fear is still expressed that was expressed when other technological changes were being propounded in the past. Indeed the fact that this is an *educational* technology, that it is concerned with men's minds, adds very considerably to the fear.

It is right that those of us engaged in adult education should be especially sensitive to the dangers of gimmickry – that we should point out, for instance, that there are basically worthwhile forms of education that cannot be dealt with by teaching machines, and that we should reveal the irony of a community willing to contemplate spending millions of pounds on a University of the Air without being willing to spend a few thousand pounds on viable forms of existing adult education. At the same time, we would be foolish to ignore the fact that the educational possibilities of the communications revolution are greater than any other of its possibilities and we would be timid if we left the development of this set of possibilities to a quite new set of people.

In terms of fundamental knowledge, we are offered new insights into the process of human learning, a strategic subject about which we know far too little, and we are given new opportunities of examining the structure and logic of the subjects we teach. In terms of applied knowledge, by making the most effective use of new instruments of educational technology to teach those subjects for which they are obviously suited, we can release our best tutors to deal with those subjects for which tutorials or tutorial classes ought to be the proper educational media. We can draw out the distinctive elements in our own kind of adult education and make the most of them – the unravelling of the complex argument through discussion; the exchanging of experience and the relating of experience to knowledge derived from other sources; the engagement in argument about controversial issues. In our own limited world we have always been dealing with our own very difficult problems of communication – between tutors and students, between students and students, between writers and readers, between experts and laymen. All these attempts at communication, particularly the last, are of continuing relevance in a society where a communications revolution is taking place but where there are large and at first sight intractable areas of exploration which the media can never fully explore.

In conclusion, I would like to lay emphasis on the point that we have been discussing throughout this lecture. We are living in a society where a communications revolution is taking place, not a society where it has taken place or will take place. The revolution is likely to go on, and it will affect different sections of society – even different parts of the country – in different ways. We will be dealing, in our life times, therefore, as the people born in the early nineteenth century were, with old and new in coexistence, with contrasts of circumstances, with mixed reactions and ambivalent values, some looking backwards and some forwards. I like the account given of educational technology in the brochure produced to inaugurate the educational magazine *New Education*:

> A technology is not a collection of hardware. It is a social activity, involving people and ideas, methods and machines, dynamic structure, communications, and interacting systems, values and tools. But always people. Its objective is to achieve an efficient and rational division of labour, subject to human control, between people and the system they evolve, to amplify human creativity not to replace it, to expand the opportunity for human concern and tenderness, not to restrict it . . . And its creation is essentially the work and the responsibility of those who practise in its field.

Quite apart from the stress on responsibility in this statement, the reference to 'expanding the opportunity for human concern and tenderness' surely points to what could be the most significant by-product of the communications revolution. Increasing interdependence inevitably means increasing involvement. The men of the nineteenth century may have been over-optimistic when they believed that the setting up of bodies like the International Telecommunications Union pointed the way to the unity in peace of all mankind, yet there is a sense in which the international revolution about which I have been talking – and I have restricted almost all my attention to Britain – should pull us closer together. In order that it may do so, we should try to get rid of the manipulative word 'mass', while retaining the sense of a revolution. As in the classical revolutions of the past, we *are* overturning established views of authority, we *are* creating new groupings, we *are* seeing the world in a new way. We have only ourselves to blame – and our education – if we believe that 'our productive powers have acquired a life of their own and run away with us'.

5 The Pleasure Telephone: A Chapter in the Pre-history of the Media*

The telephone was neither the first nor the last invention to be thought of as a toy. Although Thomas Edison objected to coin-in-the-slot phonographs on the grounds that they would give his new invention 'the appearance of being nothing more than a mere toy', he himself conceived at first of his kinetoscope, 'a peepshow viewing machine', as little more.

The sense of pleasure in playing with a new toy – perhaps a necessary part of the inventive process itself – persisted with telephone users until novelty gave way to routine. The pleasure in this case was usually private, although there were *entrepreneurs* who set out to exploit public possibilities instead. Just as Queen Victoria had enjoyed playing with telegraphs at the Great Exhibition of 1851, Lady Sackville amused herself contentedly with her father's first telephone forty years later. Indeed, Queen Victoria herself, having had Alexander Graham Bell presented to her in 1876, listened attentively to Kate Field singing 'Comin Through the Rye', on the model telephone that Bell had brought with him. She found this first telephone 'most extraordinary', a favourite adjective of hers, and installed one as early as 1879.

Guests at Hatfield, the ancestral home of Lord Salisbury, Queen Victoria's last nineteenth-century prime minister, were amazed when sitting in their rooms, 'as they thought alone', to hear their host's 'spectral voice' reciting nursery rhymes from 'a mysterious instrument on a neighbouring table':

> Hey diddle diddle
> The Cat and the Fiddle
> The Cow jumped over the Moon.

Salisbury, one of the great patrons of electrical devices of every kind, was testing his telephone in much the same way as the physicist, Lord Kelvin, who used the same nursery rhyme in his own demonstrations. Meanwhile, Edison tried out the possibilities of his kinetoscope with the aid of a performing dog, a trained bear and a strong man.

* This essay is based on a paper delivered at the Massachusetts Institute of Technology on the occasion of the centenary of the telephone, 1976.

Salisbury's guests would perhaps have been more alarmed than amazed had not some of them already got used to his earlier pioneering experiments with electric lighting at Hatfield, when he used naked, uninsulated wires. At first, these must have been at least as thrilling to spectators as watching sequences of looping the loops were to be during the toy phase of the aeroplane. Yet Salisbury saw beyond the play: he identified and acclaimed a new 'age of electricity' that would follow the 'age of steam'.

> You have by the action of the electric telegraph combined together almost at one moment, and acting at one moment upon the agencies which govern mankind, the opinions of the whole intelligent world with respect to everything that is passing at that time upon the face of the globe.

This was only one of Salisbury's many public messages about electricity.

'Intelligence' was one thing, entertainment another. Salisbury's nursery rhymes, like Bell's own '*Yankee Doodle*', were not messages of the kind that he received by telegraph in his office every day. An element of skill in performances, as in the later case of flying, could turn private diversions into public pleasures, and this was to be one of the necessary links between the toy and the medium. It was not only instantaneous knowledge that could be shared – and shared ubiquitously – but instantaneous entertainment programmes. And the history of the silent cinema was to prove this before the 'golden age of wireless' proved it for sound.

A conscious element of entertainment was present, indeed, in the first public 'demonstrations' of new inventions of many kinds, and for this reason, when *The Electrician* reported the not very exciting occasion when Sir Oliver Lodge demonstrated 'Hertzian waves' at the Royal Institution in 1895, it greatly regretted the absence of mystery or of drama: 'a mixed gathering requires its doses of science to be dashed with theatrical effect'. The showmanship mattered. When Sir William Preece of the British Post Office appeared at the Royal Institution in 1897 to exhibit and explain Marconi's wireless patents, 'the impressive delivery of the lecture', in contrast to Lodge's performance two years earlier, was said to be 'in keeping with the "wizard-like" nature of the experiments': 'electric bells' had been 'placed inside galvanised iron dustbins and completely isolated from the outside world, ringing merrily in response to Mr. Marconi's commands from the cellar below'. Later in life, Sir Oliver himself had well learnt the lesson.

The American business leader, William Orton, President of the Western Union Telegraph Company, might contemptuously reject Bell's offer of all rights in the new telephone for his powerful company on the grounds that the telephone was merely 'an electrical toy', but other businessmen were immediately impressed by Bell's propositions. His *Hamlet* soliloquy at the 1876 Centennial Exhibition in Philadelphia, like the smell of 'Salem witchcraft' in the air, was not merely an incidental of the telephone story. Users, as well as businessmen, were titillated too. It is interesting, indeed, to note that some of the first telephone users were said to be suffering from 'stage fright', an anticipation of microphone and television nerves. In an early circular of 1877, Bell had to advise possible subscribers that 'conversation can be carried on after slight practice and with occasional repetition of a word or a sentence'.

Showmanship, followed through by advice, was even more necessary for the retailers of new products than for their inventors or their sponsors. In Quebec, for example, a jeweller who was anxious to prove in 1878 that he had 'perfected some new and certainly wonderful improvements in the original telephone of Professor Bell', presented 'singers over the wire' to people visiting his shop. And before long, 'brisk young men in hard bowler hats, with handle-bar moustaches and broad check suits' were promoting 'telephone concerts', during which young ladies might recite or sing 'Lord Ullwin's Daughter' or 'Kathleen Mavourneen' into a telephone for the benefit of 'audiences' either in private homes or in 'central premises', some of them in other cities. The repertoire was limited and conventional, but if 'Home Sweet Home' and 'Auld Lang Syne' were popular favourites, there was a place also for the two superbly apposite numbers – 'Thou Art So Near and Yet So Far' and 'I'll Listen to Thy Voice, Thy Face I Never See'.

Appeals to an 'audience' carried the experience of the telephone beyond confined circles of sisters and brothers, hosts and guests or Queen and subjects. The existence of the telephone, therefore, was felt to represent more than a marvel of science, an unprecedented extension of ear and voice. It began to raise questions of a social and cultural kind, which were to become very familiar during the twentieth century, among them questions concerning 'content' and 'performance'.

Once sound was transmitted along telephone wires in both directions – a very early achievement, accomplished in 1876 itself – the telephone was to establish itself mainly as an instrument of person-to-person or organisation-to-organisation communication rather than of broadcast communication. And this was to take time, with different countries, for different reasons, following their own chronologies. Yet during the brief period before its two-way capabilities were fully appreciated, the telephone was publicised on both sides of the Atlantic as a device to

transmit music and news as much as or more than speech; and long
after its multiple private and organisational uses had been exploited, it
continued to offer the prospect of shared entertainment, information
and instruction.

The periodical *Nature* seemed to be pointing the way ahead from
London with its forecast in August 1876 that 'by paying a subscription
to an enterprising individual who will, no doubt, come forward to
work this vein, we can have from him a waltz, a quadrille, or a galop
just as we desire'. And soon similar forecasts were made and 'experiments' conducted in widely scattered contexts, particularly after so-
called 'improved' telephones made use of more up-to-date technology.
In Paris, for example, long queues gathered at the International Electrical Exhibition of 1881 to listen by telephone to music transmitted a
mile away, and a few years later 'theatrephones' were placed in the
Parisian boulevards from which anyone could be 'put in communication' with theatres for 'five minutes for five pence'. There were similar
instruments in Bordeaux.

In the United States, news was added to the agenda during the
Presidential election of 1896, when there was a systematic telephonic
relay of election returns, a revelation not only to the public and to the
great telegraph and news-gathering associations, but at least to one of
the candidates, McKinley, who talked from his Ohio home by telephone to campaign managers in thirty-eight states. (There had been a
telephone in the White House since 1878.) The 'elasticity' of the telephone as an instrument of communication now began to be pointed
out. It was capable, wrote the *Electrical Review*, of 'manipulation by
everyone, except they be deaf or dumb'. 'Thousands transmitted the
vote of the country townships that had never operated a telephone, and
thousands sat with their ear glued to the receiver the whole night long,
hypnotised by the possibilities unfolded to them for the first time.'

If there is an intimation of the excitement of the first televised elections in this contemporary comment, there was more rhetoric than
evaluation in the remarks of Vice-President E. J. Hall of the American
Telephone and Telegraph Company at a Detroit convention of the
telephone industry in 1890.

> More wonderful still [he told his audience] is a scheme which we now have
> on foot, which looks to providing music on tap at certain times every day,
> especially at meal times. The scheme is to have a fine band perform the
> choicest music, gather up the sound waves, and distribute them to any
> number of subscribers. Thus a family, club or hotel may be regaled with the
> choicest airs from their favourite operas while enjoying the evening meal,
> and the effect will be as real and enjoyable as though the performers were
> actually present in the apartment.

Next, however, came two qualifications. The first of them, in Hall's own words, was that the 'audience' he was contemplating was limited: he had attracted 'over a hundred subscribers, or rather persons who have certified to their anxiety to be subscribers'. The second was that the proper means of technical transmission were inadequate. The telephone could not successfully distinguish between the notes of a harp and of a piano or among reed, wood and brass tones.

Perhaps, some enthusiasts felt, the Russians had found the answer in the same year. A Russian scientist, Kildischevski, was said to have invented a new form of telephone 'of remarkable superiority'. It was not necessary to place the ear near the receiver, thereby avoiding the dangers of 'telephone ear', as serious a complaint as 'the electric light eye'; and there was adequate amplification. Speech, songs and music, *Science Siftings* reported in 1890, could be heard in places as distant as Moscow and Rostow on Don. Such gossip sounded far more promising than factual information about the existing telephone link-ups with events in Madison Square Gardens.

Americans persevered, however, and in 1890 the Editorial Association in Boston listened over hand telephones in the parlour of the Boston Press Club to a cornet and piano performance of 'Little Annie Rooney' and other popular songs, and later 'made connection to the Broadway Theater and the Casino, New York'. 'Snatches of popular opera' were said to have been 'heard as distinctly as the cornet and piano music had been'. Three years earlier, the *Sun* had reported two ladies waltzing in the parlour of Thomas Eckert, the General Manager of Western Union. They held a telephone close to their ears and from time to time reversed their steps to prevent themselves becoming tangled in the wires. They were waltzing to music provided by the West End Hotel which offered concerts every day at noon.

If this was 'progress', it was in London and Budapest that general questions were raised about 'telephone' systems, questions which were not to be raised again in such clear-cut fashion until after the development of radio broadcasting thirty or forty years later. In London, what ultimately proved to be an unsuccessful 'electrophone' service was offering relays of music in the 1880s, but in Budapest there was a relatively successful regular service, which captured considerable public interest inside and outside Hungary.

The framework within which the general questions were raised, as well as the answers given to them, reflected contrasting social and cultural features in British and Hungarian society and culture. If telephonic fare were to be offered to subscribers, the Hungarians asked, what items should be transmitted? Should there be a balance between entertainment, information and instruction? How should news, which had already been revolutionised by the telegraph, be handled on the telephone? And to move from the topical to the eternal, what should be the place of religion in the service? What about standards of perform-ance once you were past the testing phase? How much advertising should there be, in what styles, and when?

Given the very limited use of the 'pleasure telephone' – still a relatively costly object to install and employ – and the many technical inadequacies and limitations always associated with it, it is remarkable just how many pivotal questions were asked. As in the later case of radio broadcasting, a technology common to different countries was being utilised in different ways in different societies. In Britain there was a tendency, continuing into the twentieth century, to treat tele-phones as luxury objects; and at first, for all the excitement that the invention generated, it was not thought of even in those limited terms. A correspondent to *The Times* in 1877 thought that it might perhaps 'come into use practically' across the Atlantic, but that in Britain, 'with most of the telegraph wires already overweighted', it was 'hardly likely to become more than an electrical toy, or a drawing-room telegraph, or at most a kind of electrical speaking tube'.

The classic British statement of the situation around the turn of the century came not from a letter but from a leader in *The Times* itself:

> When all is said and done, the telephone is not an affair of the million. It is a convenience for the well-to-do and a trade appliance for persons who can afford to pay for it . . . For those who use it merely to save themselves trouble or add to the diversions of life it is a luxury. An overwhelming majority of the population do not use it and are not likely to use it at all, except perhaps to the extent of an occasional message from a private station.

The weakest part of a weak leader was its opening words 'When all is said and done'. Yet in its assessment of underlying British trends *The Times* was realistic. As late as 1928, one year after the British Broad-casting Corporation was founded, there was only one telephone per thirty-five persons in Britain.

In the United States, by contrast, there was then one per seven persons. From the start, while Britain was arguing about ownership and control, the United States pushed development, placing emphasis both on potential 'mass' involvement and on individual choice, the emphasis varying according to the source. In the early years, however, 'pleasure' uses were listed on both sides of the Atlantic, and what was actually then possible in each society was projected through imaginat-ive extension into the future.

One of the most famous forecasters of the future, Edward Bellamy, read avidly in Britain as well as in the United States, had spoken in 1891 of staying at home and sending 'your eyes and ears abroad for you' while taking your 'choice of the public entertainments given that day in every city of the earth'. Three years earlier, in his most famous book, *Looking Backward* (1888), Bellamy had talked of 'co-operation' in music as in 'everything else', whereby people in their homes could hear music relayed from central halls 'to suit all tastes and moods'.

There were many reasons of a non-technological kind why future forecasts and key questions, including questions of choice, came to the forefront in different countries during the late-1880s and 1890s – the growth of urban populations, a dramatic growth in the United States as the immigrants flowed in; the rise in consumer incomes, marked not only in the United States but in Britain, where real wages rose during the 1870s and 1880s; the increase in 'leisure time', with workers everywhere demanding a shorter working day; and the demand for more 'entertainment', not just as a 'sometimes' thing but as an integrated element in daily life. Everything converged. Arthur Schlesinger Sr quotes a contemporary who said that 'vaudeville belongs to the era of the department store and the short story'.

In such circumstances, there was no shortage of 'enterprising individuals', as *Nature* had called them, who were prepared to see opportunities in 'mass audiences' both for home entertainment and for new forms of the written word – popular magazines at one end of the spectrum, specialist weeklies at the other; 'mass' newspapers; and 'books for the millions' of different kinds, from short stories to bulky works of reference. The newspapers and periodicals which prophesied what the future of communications would be like were themselves part of the same complex within which electronic communications were changing.

'We take it', one of the many new specialist periodicals, *Electrical World*, wrote in 1884, 'that everything which can knit a community together and which can cause a rapid interchange of sentiment and ideas, annihilate distance, isolation and prejudice, is of the greatest happiness to the greatest number.' Bentham was being put to topical use.

In considering the history of 'the pleasure telephone', therefore, it is necessary, first, to study it in the light of a far longer history of communications and, second, to relate it to a cluster of other inventions patented during the last quarter of the nineteenth century. The first line of investigation means looking backwards to the 1830s and 1840s to railways (themselves very soon used for pleasure – 'excursions' – as well as for freight) and to telegraphs (themselves concerned with private as well as with official or business communication).

The two were very closely associated, not least by reason of the policies followed by governments towards them, but in looking with hindsight at the history of 'pleasure', it is other connections which catch attention. Very early the feeling was expressed that telegraphy was 'too good a thing to be confined to public use' and that it should be introduced not only into the office but into 'the domestic circle'. The idea of the 'singing telegram' has a long history. 'It appears that songs and pieces of music are now sent from Boston to New York by electric telepgraph', *Punch* reported in 1848, adding that 'it must be delightful for a party at Boston to be able to call upon a gentleman in New York for a song.'

The thought implications could be – and were – pushed much further. 'If "popular vocalists" could sing in four or five places at once, might not their incomes be trebled or quintupled?' 'Our own Jenny Lind, for example, who seems to be wanted everywhere at the same time, will have the opportunity of gratifying the subscribers to Her Majesty's Theatre and a couple of audiences many hundred miles off at the same moment.' Note that although the idea of ubiquity was not as yet fully developed, the conception of instantaneity was already present. In 1858, we read of how 'electricity is now fairly taking the circuit of the entire globe . . . We do not see what there is to prevent a pianist, who holds this electric accomplishment at his finger's ends, from performing in every capital of Europe at the same time.'

There were other interesting thoughts in 1858. With the advent of a house telegraph, there would be a perpetual *tête-à-tête*. 'We should all be always in company . . . The bliss of ignorance would be at an end.' Yet it was not 'ignorance' alone that might be shattered. Truth might be in serious jeopardy also. Long before the adjective 'phoney' was coined, *Punch* complained of telegraphic 'fibs':

> What horrid fibs by that electric wire
> Are flashed about! What falsehoods are its shocks!
> Oh! rather let us have the fact that creeps
> Comparatively by the Post so slow
> Than the quick fudge which like the lightning leaps
> And makes us credit that which is not so.

Instantaneity was being described as 'quick fudge', of course, not because of the inherent characteristics of the telegraph, but because of the system of reporting. In other words, one of the questions concerning the control of 'content', which was to be forced to the forefront in later phases of communications history, was already being posed at the beginning of the story. So, too, was the question of triviality. After the installation of the Trans-Atlantic Cable, Emerson is said to have remarked when told that it would in future be possible for someone in London to speak to someone in New York, 'But will he have anything to say?'

Considering the history of the 'pleasure telephone' means not only looking backwards to those absorbing early days, but looking forwards also to the 1920s and to the 1950s, the critical decades, separated by a generation, in the history of sound broadcasting and of television. It was then that the idea of what the perceptive American writer Gilbert Seldes called 'the great audience' took shape – with more concentration, as in the case of the cinema, on the size of the audience than on individual choice.

The second line of investigation of 'the pleasure telephone' involves relating 'pleasure telephony' to the phonograph and to the kinetoscope, as the London *Times* related them in 1878. While 'not many weeks have passed since we were startled by the announcement that we could converse audibly with each other, although hundreds of miles apart, by means of so many miles of wire wound round a magnet', *The Times* explained, another wonder was 'now promised us'. This was an invention, 'purely mechanical in nature', by means of which 'words spoken by the human voice can be, so to speak, stored up and reproduced at will'. 'What shall be said of a machine', *The Times* asked, 'by means of which the old familiar voice of one who is no longer with us on earth can be heard speaking to us in the very tones and measures to which our ears were once accustomed?'

Such connections reveal different preoccupations in the nineteenth and twentieth centuries, and it took even more time for the 'pleasure' uses of the phonograph to be fully appreciated than the pleasure uses of the kinetoscope. As far as radio broadcasting was concerned, there was to be a still longer gestation period, during which necessary technical development took place, before Marconi's inventions of the 1890s became the basis of a 'medium'; for as long as wireless broadcasting was in Morse code few people gave much thought to 'radio', except as a 'miracle' that might help in times of war or disaster.

Just as the great inventions of the late eighteenth century transformed factory production only in the nineteenth century, so the new inventions cluster of the late nineteenth century radically transformed home life styles only in the twentieth century – through a sequence of thirty-year cycles. Yet the contemporary reading public of the late nineteenth century, specialised or unsophisticated, tended to think from the start of the cluster of inventions as 'marvels' or 'miracles', closely related to each other. Even X-rays came into the same picture during the 1890s.

In 1889 a reviewer of Oliver Lodge's *Modern Views of Electricity* had already written confidently in the centenary year of the French Revolution that 'progress is a thing of months and weeks, almost of days. The long line of isolated ripples of past discovery seems blending into a mighty wave, on the crest of which one begins to discern some oncoming magnificent generalisation.'

It is through such reactions as well as through the history of technology itself that change is registered. And such comments were not just reactions, 'impact effects' following the introduction and diffusion of an invention: they carried with them apprehensions of promise or threat. Moreover, it was before the invention of new devices to produce 'signals in time and signals in space' that the first significant changes in attitudes towards time and space had revealed themselves. Regular hours of work preceded regular hours of entertainment; a railway system reducing distance preceded a system of telegraphy which promised to annihilate distance; the global system of telegraphy preceded the global system of radio without wires; transportation metaphors preceded metaphors of electrical nervous systems.

'Magnificent generalisations', therefore, were less new revelations than up-to-date glosses on years of both technical and social evolution. And there were many of them. It could be claimed in the *Electrical World* in 1884, for example, that 'the world now lives like a lumbering whale whose nerve centres and brain are slow to tell him that he has been harpooned, but all the members respond to influences exerted to any one of them with the sensitiveness and promptitude of the most highly wrought organisms.'

Continuities between late-nineteenth-century and twentieth-century communications history were to be emphasised more than contrasts by John Logie Baird, the pioneer of television. When from the vantage point of the 1920s he first advertised his 'televisor' in 1926, he began his long and somewhat flamboyant advertisement with a reference not to Marconi, with whom he has often rightly been compared, but to his fellow Scotsman, Bell. A few 'wags', he said, had claimed in 1876 that 'seeing by telephone' would follow naturally from hearing by telephone. Now, Baird proudly maintained, the claim had been justified. It had been done.

Ignoring all the rejected alternatives of communications history – and the 'pleasure telephone' by then was one of them – and ignoring all the blocked paths in the way of specific technical advances, Baird concentrated on the essentials. In directly linking what he himself was doing with what his predecessors had done, he was proud to advance a kind of Whig interpretation of communications history with a dose of prophecy and a dose of the history of entertainment thrown in, ingredients not usually found in Whig political history.

Baird did not point to the fact that 1922, the year of Bell's death, was also the year of the founding of the BBC, not because he did not like the BBC – which he did not – but because he himself had completely skipped the sound radio phase; he was thinking of systematising vision at a time when the BBC was still seeking to systematise sound.

Less prophetic figures than Baird fitted sound radio into the story of communications development as a natural development from telephony. Thus, his friend Frank Gill, who was the Engineer-in-Chief of the National Telephone Company from 1902 to 1913 and later of the International Western Electric Company, treated 'radio telephony' as one branch of telephone history in his preface to Baldwin's *History of the Telephone in the United Kingdom*, published in 1925 (see above, p. 45). It could either be clothed with privacy and given to one individual only, or it could be broadcast to millions simultaneously.

Gill, a President of the Royal Institution of Electrical Engineers, was one of the many European telephone engineers who bemoaned the slow development of the telephone system in Europe before 1922, attributing it to the predominance on this side of the Atlantic of public rather than private ownership; he was also, however, one of the participants in the crucial talks on broadcasting that were arranged by the British Post Office in 1922 and that led to the foundation of the BBC. When he surveyed the future of communications in Britain, he put his trust (rightly as it turned out) in a very rapid increase not in the number of telephone users but in the number of owners of wireless sets.

Another writer on communications, Archibald Williams, noted in his book *Telegraphy and Telephony*, published a little later in 1928, how 'hundreds of thousands of people who had never even heard speech over telephone wires now donned headpieces and found themselves linked magically with voices and sounds in some far-away station studio'. The 'enormous number' of wireless licences issued, he added, was 'perhaps the best proof that, to use the language of the advertisements, it meets a long-felt want'.

Williams was seeking to summarise half a century of unfinished communications history, as were Baird and Gill, both with practical ends in view. And unlike Williams, neither Baird nor Gill drew a sharp contrast at that particular moment in the 1920s between 'messages' and 'programmes' or between television exchanges with switchboards and broadcasting studios with microphones. Even Williams with his talk of 'headpieces' had not fully adjusted either to what was soon to be called 'an age of broadcasting'.

This term, like the term 'medium of communication', soon emerged, yet even before the development of the telephone there was clearly a sense of there being 'media', both printed and electrical. What the development of the 'pleasure telephone', the phonograph and other inventions of the late nineteenth century had done was to extend, to enrich and to complicate this sense.

Within a long continuum, the history of the Budapest Messenger or Gazette (*Telephon Hirmondo*) is exceptional but revealing. It was more than an experiment, for it worked regularly over many years, increasing the number of its subscribers (including hotels) and offering them a genuine telephonic programme service. Ultimately it was to be swallowed up in Hungarian radio. Its 'inventor', Theodore Puskas, who had worked for Edison at Menlo Park, was present at the International Exhibition of Electricity in Paris in 1881 and in the same year obtained exclusive rights to develop the telephone in Hungary. Nikola Tesla, a pioneer and prophet of electricity, was hired to take charge of the construction; he was a friend of the family.

Thereafter, Theodore Puskas publicised his own way of developing telephonic services at a large number of international conferences. The word *Hirmondo* means 'town crier', but the message Puskas proclaimed was for the world not for the town. His company started regular 'broadcasting operations' in the city of Budapest in 1893, and within five years it was said to be making use of 220 miles of wire and to have attracted 6000 subscribers. But by then Theodore Puskas was dead – he died only a few weeks after the start of the *Telephon Hirmondo* service – and the control of the system had passed out of the hands of the Puskas family. By 1900 the new company was employing over 150 people in its office in 'one of the finest' avenues in Budapest.

It was in relation to the operations of Puskas and his successors that the description 'the Pleasure Telephone' was coined. 'The Pleasure Telephone', we read in an article by Arthur Mee in the *Strand Magazine* in 1898, opened out 'a vista of infinite charm which few prophets of today have dreamed of.' 'In future, no element in our social life would be unprovided for.' 'Who will dare to say', Mee concluded, 'that in twenty years the electric miracle will not bring all the corners of the earth to our own fireside?'

Baird would certainly have approved of this particular prophet, who was to establish his twentieth-century fame as editor of the *Children's Newspaper*. 'If as it is said to be not unlikely in the near future, that the principle of sight is applied to the telephone as well as that of sound', Mee had maintained in 1893, 'earth will be in truth a paradise, and distance will lose its enchantment by being abolished altogether.'

Mee also foresaw the broadcasting of football and cricket, sport, politics and religion at a time when some of these forms of broadcasting were already being developed in Budapest. The city then had a population of 500,000, and *Telephon Hirmondo* divided it into thirty circuits, each connecting 200–300 subscribers. Within each house, 'long flexible wires' made it possible 'to carry the receiver to the bed or to any part of the room'. The receiving apparatus occupied a space of five inches square and included two tubes so that two members of the family might listen at the same time. Subscribers could not talk to each other 'on their own account' and remain connected to the system, 'thus ruling out private communication'; and the company installing the apparatus, which by-passed the regular telephone network, had the right to introduce it into any house in the city without the landlord being required to give his permission.

Each day there was a schedule or a programme which was announced to the subscribers. (The magazine *Invention* called it a 'programme', Mee called it a 'time table', the established railway term.) The day began with a news bulletin and with summaries of the newspapers. In the mid-morning there were summaries of stock exchange prices, repeated at regular intervals while the Exchange was open. There were then hourly news summaries for those who had missed the earlier bulletins, and at noon there was a report on proceedings in Parliament. During the afternoon, 'short, entertaining stories' were read, 'sporting intelligence' was transmitted, and there were 'filler items' of various kinds. In the evening, there were theatrical offerings, 'visits to the opera', poetry readings, concerts and lectures – including repeats of Academy lectures by well-known literary figures.

There was also a weekly children's programme, along with 'linguistic lessons' in English, Italian and French which were hailed 'as a great benefit to the young generation'. ('Each telephone subscriber who cares to listen holds a copy of the book before him, and the teacher speaks into the double telephone transmitter at the central office.') At that office – and note that it was still not called a studio – there were over forty 'reporters and literary men' in addition to 'the ten men with strong voices and clear enunciation', as the *Scientific American* called them, who 'actually speak to or transmit the news to the subscribers'.

The very language, stilted though it now sounds, anticipates the language of sound broadcasting by radio. Yet during the 1890s the terms which were felt to describe most closely the wide-ranging operation were 'telephonic messenger' or 'gazette' or 'newspaper' – admittedly, it was stated in 1898, 'for want of a better name'. The nomenclature must be related, of course, to the changing format and role of newspapers themselves during the 1890s. They were becoming more explicitly 'entertaining', were priding themselves on their 'scoops', were extending their advertising, and were appealing frankly to 'mass audiences'.

To experienced British observers, like the editor of the *Newspaper Owner and Manager*, the Budapest service 'completely fulfilled the functions of the daily paper' – from the leading article to stock exchange news, 'from the agony column to the advertisement of the latest panacea'. It constituted 'a spoken instead of a printed record of the world's doings'. Yet the parallels were not complete. The 'listener', if he wished, could 'spend the whole day at the telephone', and he could end by lulling himself to sleep by 'the latest music of Strauss' if he and the programme-makers so chose.

No newspaper, however new, could offer such distractions. Moreover – and it was an essential qualification – the Budapest 'telephone messenger' was a newspaper not for the masses but for an elite. So, indeed, had been a London service provided by Electrophone Ltd. As the magazine *Lightning* put it in 1893, electrophone parties were for the idle rich, not for the idle poor. In Budapest the prime minister, Baron Bánffy, was a subscriber in 1897, along with all the members of his cabinet. There were then 6000 subscribers in all.

Most foregin commentaries on the Budapest service concentrated on the news it supplied rather than on the music, and certainly the handling of the news was very sophisticated. It was collected during the day and night, edited before being transmitted, brought up to date in as many as twenty-eight editions a day, presented in a telegraphic style that was 'clear, condensed and precise', and summarised in short bulletins. Special 'flashes' brought news to subscribers long before they could read it in the newspapers. And there was a wide range of reference. Foreign news was presented in the late evening, but there were also detailed city reports. Since subscribers often found themselves 'lying in wait for the news', ways and means were suggested to record it for them in their homes. A phonograph transmitter was to be fixed to the telephone receiver 'in such a way that the first sound over the wire would start the phonograph, which would then record the news, and make it available for the subscriber at his convenience'.

When British observers tried to explain why London could not do 'bigger and better' what Budapest was doing, the first answer given was economic – higher costs. Legal reasons were suggested also – the law did not confer the same rights of access – along with social explanations. Budapest was 'a city of pleasure'; in London, 'time was everything', and 'a man could not sit the whole day with the apparatus to his ear waiting for some particular news or exchange prices'. It may well be, however, that the Budapest service was promoted with relative success because it was not possible in that city to develop the telephone system along 'American lines' quickly. The very first mention of Puskas in the *Scientific American* in 1881 refers also to the visit to Hungary of D. H. Washburn, who was trying to introduce the telephone into the country.

Far from appreciating the flexibility of Hungarian law, Washburn stressed its restrictiveness. Before a man could subscribe to the 'telephone exchange', in Budapest his name and business had to be sent to four different government offices. Budapest might be a city of pleasure, but it was also a city of bureaucracy. The telephone company, Washburn added, had to report to the authorities what everything cost and what every employee received by way of wages. In fact, he concluded comprehensively, 'everyone that lives here is but a slave of the government'. Not surprisingly, *Telephon Hirmondo* abandoned the regular telephone system for what we would now call its own 'cables'.

By 1910, Herbert Webb, reporting on the development of the telephone in Europe, rightly did not mention *Telephon Hirmondo*. His summary of the condition of the telephone industry in Hungary was admirably concise.

> Outside of Budapest there is little development of the telephone, and the development of the whole country is somewhat lower than that of Austria, and only slightly exceeds that of Italy, where the telephone is practically non-existent. In Budapest the telephone service was originally started by a company, but the State purchased the system after a few years and assumed the monopoly of telephone work. The system was reconstructed in 1903 . . . The low development and the slow progress of the telephone in Hungary are principally due to lack of capital, absence of commercial policy, and to the retention of the old flat rate tariff.

None the less, there were still as many subscribers to *Telephon Hirmondo* in 1910 as there had been in 1897. They paid an installation fee (said to be about twenty-five shillings or five dollars) and an annual rental of thirty shillings. In addition, the company derived revenue from advertising. In defiance of American experience, this was already a deterrent in the Britain of the 1890s as it was to be in the Britain of the 1920s and the early-1950s. It was doubtless easy to be disdainful about advertising in a decade when there were innumerable innovatory advertising schemes, including 'signs upon the clouds', 'celestial advertising'. There was even an anti-advertising society in London, supported by William Morris.

The role of advertising in the development of the media was a matter of debate long before the question arose during the 1920s of how best to finance radio programs. It was certainly a matter of debate within the Harmsworth Press empire, and it also affected the development of the 'cinematograph' which, according to *Invention*, was being 'vulgarized' like the phonograph.

> Nestlés, of condensed milk renown, and Levers, of soap ditto, have put
> their hands and purses together . . . and have put up free machines behind
> hoardings in various parts of the town . . . If the experiment is a success, i.e.
> if a marked increase in the business transactions of Mr. Lever and Nestlé
> reasonably attributable to the cinematograph takes place, it will be con-
> tinued on an increasing scale.

It is interesting to note that both Lever's (in the form of Unilever)
and Nestlé's were to be staunch supporters of commercial television
in Britain fifty years later. In the sphere of advertising, therefore,
there was as much of a continuum as there was in technology, and it
goes back well before the 1890s to the development of consumer
goods industries and new systems of retailing earlier in the century.
There are links with entertainment there too. Thus, the British provincial firm of David Lewis, which deliberately set out to imitate the
methods of P. T. Barnum's circus, had as its most active manager
between the two world wars Lord Woolton, who was to play a major
part as a politician in the successful politics of British commercial
television.

That was in the distant future. The 'electrophone' venture in Britain
that parallelled *Telephon Hirmondo*, the Electrophone Company,
never had powerful commercial backing. Nor, of course, did it attract
interest on the part of the State. By the end of the first year of its
operations it had only forty-six subscribers, and by the end of ten years
only sixty. This was at best minute communication within a minority
communication set-up. Yet there were highlights, for example in 1892,
when concert performances in Birmingham, Liverpool, Manchester
and other cities were transmitted 'with entire success' to audiences
gathered at an Electrical Exhibition in the Crystal Palace, a completely
appropriate link across time with the Great Exhibition of 1851. It was
appropriate, too, that the links, like the economic and social links of
1851, were between the provinces and London.

It was appropriate, too, that there was to be a royal link. Queen
Victoria heard the electrophone for the first time just before the end of
the century in 1899, when she listened at Windsor Castle to boys from
naval and military schools singing 'God Save the Queen' and later to a
concert from St James's Hall.

What was said about the Electrophone Company is more revealing
for the historian than what the Company actually did. Thus, the phras-
ing of its own prospectus is interesting when it is stated that its object
was 'the hiring out of an instrument designed to enable subscribers to

hear at their own homes or at central offices [an interesting concept] the performances at theatres, concert halls etc.'. An article in *Answers* in 1897 is memorable because it went much further in defining the Electrophone Company's purpose than the Company's own prospectus had done. The electrophone, according to *Answers*, was

> an invention by which persons may have laid on in their houses, with the water, the gas and the other usual accessories, a regular supply of the most up-to-date music, the most recent plays, the latest *cause célèbre*, or the best passages from a sermon by one of the most eminent divines.

The concept of 'the wired city' was already being formulated, and there was great stress on topicality, not just on the up-to-date but on 'the most up-to-date'. For this reason, contemporary cable companies, though inevitably more interested in the future – and in the present – than in the past, should trace their pedigree back to the Electrophone Company, as Paul Adorian, pioneer of pre-war radio cable, often did. In 1945 he wrote an extremely interesting article on 'Wire Broadcasting' in the *Journal of the Royal Society of Arts*. It was always stimulating to discuss the subject with him at a time when television was the major national preoccupation.

There was one remarkable half-ancient, half-modern journalistic note in an article of 1892 on the 'dangers' of a 'laid-on-service'. 'It seems to us', wrote the *Electrician*

> that we are getting perilously near the ideal of the modern Utopian [back to Bellamy] when life is to consist of sitting in armchairs and pressing a button. It is not a desirable prospect; we shall have no wants, no money, no ambition, no youth, no desires, no individuality, no names and nothing wise about us.

The *Electrical World* had been even more uneasy when it commented on E. J. Hall's remarks in 1890.

> With the success of the first telephonic musical association there will spring into being rival organisations, the very names of which would make incipient deafness bliss. Imagine the awful devastation that would be wrought by 'The Organ Grinders' Telephonic Manual'. Fancy the horrors of having one's disposition wrecked by a 'popular programme' headed by . . . [x].

The omission of the name left readers free to fill it in, and they doubtless had many choices. It was, however, the omission of news from the London service that was the biggest and most significant contrast with Budapest. Newspaper interests, re-forming during the 1890s, were exceptionally strong in Britain – as was the well-entrenched telegraphic interest – and they were to remain strong enough during the 1920s and

1930s to prevent the BBC developing a news service of its own before the Second World War. In Budapest a solution was found which was to be found only in the Britain of the 1940s and 1950s. 'The newspapers of Budapest persistently boycotted the invention on its introduction', wrote Arthur Mee, 'but they recognise now that, instead of being taken as a substitute for a newspaper, its effect is to whet the appetite of the public for events announced briefly through the telephone.'

The presentation of music and drama posed fewer such problems, for the Budapest theatres realised that 'to give the public a snatch or two from a favourite opera *gratis*' would not adversely affect their receipts. They knew, too, that if they did not cooperate, *Telephon Hirmondo* could always 'organise concerts and entertainment in the editorial office'. There might be some difficulties concerning performing rights, as there had been in Paris, where there was also an electrophone service, which deserves a history in itself, if only because Paris was a city where there was a high level of 'electrical consciousness'. The most serious difficulties, however, were technical, not legal, as they also were in Paris and London. The technique of transmission did not favour the transmission of music. One early injunction speaks for itself. 'The transmitters should not be fitted in close proximity to the bass drums or the trombones of the orchestra.'

Religion always figured prominently in the bill of fare, as it was to figure prominently in the first bill of fare of the BBC after 1922. Thus, as early as the late 1870s the enterprising Halifax carpet manufacturer, Louis Crossley, installed telephones not only to communicate with his friend Sir Titus Salt in Saltaire but to link his home with the Congregational Tabernacle where he worshipped. Around the same time, a short story writer in an Australian magazine, *The Australian* – it might have appeared first in Britain – had contemplated a telephone line being installed back in the 'mother country' between Abney Hall and the village church of Mortham 'so that the Hall people could have the benefit of Mr. Earle's pulpit oratory without going outside their own doors'. Mr Earle was not very pleased, but he would doubtless have been less pleased had the hall people decided to link up with a fashionable church in London.

This was the theme of a later dialogue.

> 'I hope this cold weather agrees with you, Mr. Meteor', said the vicar to me the other day. 'No', I replied, 'I have the service laid on by electrophone from St. Margaret's, Westminster to my study.' The vicar looked very grave and his pretty daughter turned her head to hide a smile. Then I began to realise that my £5 for installing the instruments and £10 per annum for using them was quite thrown away. Neither the vicar nor Mrs. Grundy would be satisfied with this substitute for personal attendance.

Mr Meteor, the editorial *nom-de-plume* of the editor of *Lightning*, remained convinced, however, of the advantages of the telephone for this purpose. 'You could listen to just as much of the service as you felt inclined for, and put the tube down when you'd had enough.' Meteor knew also, of course, that it was precisely this 'convenience' to which the vicar was objecting. 'It is only too easy to salve one's conscience by the reflection that you can't really afford to suffer from "telephone ear" [back to the diseases again]. And besides there's the collection to consider.'

Of course, such religious 'broadcasts' would be of special value, it was felt, to the infirm – an argument to be made many times in the future, when the 'consoling power' of broadcasting was to be stressed. Budapest was praised also because its programmes reached the hospitals, and it may have been with this example in mind that the Electrophone Company supplied its apparatus 'gratuitously' to London hospitals on Hospital Sunday so that patients could listen to sermons. Arthur Mee tried to find his own right balance, a word that was to be endowed with special significance in the early years of broadcasting. 'It may be objected, perhaps', he conceded, 'that religious worship by telephone is not calculated to inspire reverence or inculcate virtue, but at any rate the system is an inestimable boon to the aged and infirm, the patients in hospitals, and the women who are unable to leave their houses.'

Some doubt was expressed as to whether people would want 'only to *listen*' to concerts, operas and sermons. Would they not want to *see* what was going on as well? It was convenient, of course, that chronologically the phonograph, offering sound alone, pointed in the right initial direction long before the advent of sound broadcasting. Music need not be seen, and it might not be thought desirable to see Parliament debating, even if it was right to hear it. None the less, seeing was very quickly brought into the reckoning as well as sound. 'What if Edison and his followers advance so far as to bring out newspapers whose moving illustrations furnish their own descriptions . . . when readers might see . . . every detail and action?' asked the *Referee* in 1896, inspired by a cinematograph show in Paris.

The properties of selenium had been known since the 1880s – they were very well-known to Bell, who produced his own photophone – and it did not require special gifts of imagination for a writer in *Lightening* in 1893 to forecast that

> before the next century shall expire, the grandsons of the present generation will see one another across the Atlantic, and the great ceremonial events of the world as they pass before the eyes of the camera will be enacted at the same instant before all mankind . . . The theoretical possibilities are far beyond the reach of the wildest dreams of the imaginations

of the most visionary of such quasi-scientists as Flaumarion and Jules Verne. What are we coming to? At this rate is there any necessity for limiting ourselves to such a mere bagatelle as space? Inter-planetary communication will be carried on at fixed rates.

This last forecast was conceived of as a fun prophecy with a gentle touch of satire. Yet it makes it easy to understand why within this cultural *milieu* Marconi's wireless inventions of 1896 did not create quite the surprise that they might have done. One year before Marconi arrived in London, a writer in the *Electrical Engineer*, not given to wild speculation, had summed up the situation very concisely.

> Telephones are daily becoming more and more used, and hence more and more useful. The future for them should mean still further usefulness by reason of more perfect service. In future, too, we may hope to have communications by telephone without wires. Shall we also see by electricity without wires?

Paradoxically, there was less talk between 1900 and 1920 about wireless providing the opportunities for a new 'medium of communication' than there had been in relation to the telephone before 1900. It was thought of at first mainly as a substitute for line telegraphy, and the 'broadcasting' element in it was underplayed, not least by Marconi himself. It was only after the invention of the thermionic valve that wireless telephony became possible, and even thereafter, despite the work of Fleming, Fessenden and de Forest, the idea of a regular 'programme service' was slow to take shape.

Business interests were less interested in broadcasting by 'wireless telephone', or by other means, than a growing group of radio amateurs; and although by 1914 the world of 'amateur wireless' was a world of lively activity, it was certainly not controlled by entrepreneurs. The 'enterprising individuals', willing 'to work the vein', whose existence had been taken for granted by *Nature* in 1876, had not then appeared. There were, after all, other veins for such entrepreneurs to work, very profitable ones, like the cinema and the Press.

It was left to a publisher who was in close touch with the newly-founded London Wireless Club to launch the magazine *Wireless Age* in 1913, the same year that the *Yearbook of Wireless Telegraphy and Telephony* was published. Yet even then, despite its title, it had little to say about telephony. It was only on the eve of the founding of the BBC that the Wireless Society of London, the re-named London Wireless Club, changed its name yet again to the Radio Society of Britain. The story of its own contribution to the development of broadcasting I have set out in my book *The BBC, the first Fifty Years*.

Meanwhile, the telephone industry had developed in Britain far more slowly than in the United States – on the basis of a service to private and business customers – taken over in 1912 by the State. By then, much of the early talk about theatrephones and electrophones had been forgotten, buried in a recent but rejected past. Fortunately, however, the idea of 'the pleasure telephone' never completely disappeared. James Joyce's imaginary newspaper headline in *Finnegan's Wake* (1939) 'Television kills Telephony in Brothers Broil' was bad prediction, for with the coming of television there was to be a huge parallel increase in the number of telephone subscribers. And as the business uses of the telephone had become obvious, advertisers made more and more reference, as they still do, to the possible private uses of the telephone for 'pleasure' – for social chit-chat; for family drama; for ordering tickets for entertainment; for dialling a joke or a prayer.

Telephone culture, more lush in the United States and Canada than in Europe, had long ago caught all the moods, particularly in popular music, with the moods ranging from 'All Alone by the Telephone, All Alone Feeling Blue' and 'Find My Baby's Number' to 'Hello Central, Give Me Heaven'.

6   Prediction and Control: Historical Reflections on Early Broadcasting Seen in Perspective*

'The impact of sound broadcasting in the second half of the century', a commentator on the impact of broadcasting wrote in *The Round Table* in 1960, 'could almost have been predicted from its origins in the twenties.' The remark was made with the benefit of hindsight, two years before the fortieth anniversary of the BBC.

In fact, there was great uncertainty during the early 1920s about the future of broadcasting. Many of the key inventions which made broadcasting possible had been in existence for decades, yet for long there was less recognition of the possible social role of broadcasting than there had been in the early years of the telephone. The fact that wireless messages could be picked up by third parties, thereby making point-to-point communication insecure, was stressed far more than any other factor in early discussions. Ferdinand Braun, who developed the induction transmitter, wrote not untypically in 1900:

> There are enough coasts, islands adjacent to one another, sparsely populated regions where a cable connection is not worth while or when telegraphic communication by wires is threatened by storms, by wild animals or by ignorant human beings . . . The problem of making it impossible for an unauthorised person to pick up a message . . . is not hopeless although its solution has not yet been achieved. The best wishes are laid in a child's cradle, and there is joy if he develops accordingly. But who can say with certainty even five years hence what sort of man he will become?

The possibilities of broadcasting as a medium were first grasped in the United States, but even there only by a minority of men with a shrewd business sense, with more knowledge about the market than about the inventions. Harry P. Davis, the Vice-President of the Westinghouse Company, wrote confidently in the spring of 1920 – his

*This essay has its origins in an article I wrote for the *Sociological Review Monograph* (1959), 'Prediction and Control' and in an article written in the same year for the *Twentieth Century*, 'The Image and the Voice'. In this version I have added no points that I did not make in 1959 and have inserted no new references.

views were anticipated by David Sarnoff, the first commercial manager of the Radio Corporation of America, founded in 1919 – that 'efforts . . . to develop radio telephony as a confidential means of communications were, he believed, wrong, and instead its field is really one of wide publicity, in fact, the only means of instantaneous collective communication ever devised . . . Here was an idea of limitless opportunity, if it could be "put across" . . . The natural fascination of its mystery, coupled with its ability to annihilate distance, would attract, interest, and open many avenues to bring happiness into human lives.'

By 1929 radio had boomed in the United States. Two years after Davis had seen the significance of a shift of direction towards the public in 1920, it was reported that

> the rate of increase in the number of people who spend at least a part of their evening in listening in is almost incomprehensible . . . It seems quite likely that before the movement has reached its height . . . there will be at least five million receiving sets in this country.

The report suggested, as did many other reports of the period, that radio was a fad. The statistical projection also was wildly wrong, for by 1928 there were forty million receiving sets in use in the United States.

In Britain also, where the financing, organisation and programming of radio were in quite different hands, there was the same boom in sets. The number of licence holders increased from just under 600,000 at the end of 1923, the first year of BBC operations, to almost 2,500,000 in March 1929. C. A. Lewis, one of the first BBC staff to be appointed, had compared the first broadcasters to Columbus's crew. 'This is a book about a new thing', he wrote in his *Broadcasting from Within* (1923), 'a thing that has never been done before.' And he added that he and his colleagues had been appointed 'guardians and attendants of the most voracious creature ever created by man – a microphone – which clamoured daily to be fed'.

The exploratory phase soon ended, however, and soon, too, did the often wild speculation about the likely social and cultural effects of broadcasting. By 1926, indeed, before the British Broadcasting Company was converted into a public corporation, the Archbishop of Canterbury remarked that

> broadcasting is now a well-assured factor in our national life – a uniquely widespread influence. The fact that upwards of two million people in this country hold wireless licences means, I suppose, that several more millions of people are constantly listening to the broadcast programmes. There is no stratum in our social life, no place of recreation, no educational centre into which the influence of broadcasting does not already penetrate.

It was still possible, none the less, for the Archbishop, writing in the *Radio Times*, to revert to the surprise of it all. 'We woke, so to speak, to find it in our presence and affecting us all.' A. R. Burrows, the BBC's first Director of Programmes, who had an international career, based on Geneva, rather than a national career ahead of him, had chosen more spiritual langauge in his *The Story of Broadcasting* (1924), the first chapter of which was called 'Towards the Infinite', although it is true that his tenth chapter was called 'The Fun Begins'.

Who were the communicators during this first period of hectic growth? Some had moved from engineering into broadcasting, some from journalism. There were other men, too, who had acquired a practical knowledge of wireless during the First World War and realised after the War that it could become more than a hobby. Others were essentially salesmen. The paths, of course, criss-crossed. Peter Eckersley, the first Chief Engineer of the BBC, provides an excellent example of the first group. He was experimenting with wireless while he was a boy at Bedales before 1914, became an electrical engineer in a Manchester factory, served as a Wireless Equipment officer during the First World War, joined the Marconi Company after the War, and ran the first regular British wireless programmes from the experimental station at Writtle. 'We always maintained', he wrote in 1941 in his lively book *The Power Behind the Microphone*, 'that we started the idea, if not the form, of many features which are now part of a broadcasting day.' Yet, also in his own words, 'we failed to take ourselves seriously, and broadcasting, as we saw it, was nothing more or less than an entertainment, for us as much as for the listeners'.

Other early communicators came from the stage and some from the ranks of the middle-class unemployed. There was only a small working-class intake. Eric Maschwitz, for a time editor of the *Radio Times* and later in charge of BBC light entertainment, has described them as 'a mixed Bohemian flock' with Reith as a shepherd, strange but kindly. 'He had under his aegis a bevy of ex-soldiers, ex-actors, ex-adventurers, which a Carton de Wiart, a C. B. Cochran, even a Dartmoor Prison Governor might have found some difficulty in controlling.' Maurice Gorham, another former editor of the *Radio Times*, who for a period after the Second World War was to head British television, described them as

> a mixture of enthusiasts who believed in the possibilities of radio, pioneers who loved any new enterprise, ready-made specialists like musicians, actors and journalists, and a proportion of people who just wanted a job and found it hard to get one in the conditions that followed the First World War. Some of them were geniuses, some were unable to grow with their jobs, some were misfits.

Both these pictures stress the 'mixture'; both suggest that a framework of organisation was necessary. Reith was impressed, above all, by the potential of his recruits, given, of course, the right kind of Reithian leadership.

> The Broadcasters [he had written in 1924 (note the capital B)] are mostly young men. From the nature of things in the beginning this was, I think, to be expected; in view of the arduous and diverse nature of their labours, it is probably fortunate. They are rather shadowy personalities to the average man; they are aloof and mysterious. You will probably not find them at garden parties or social functions; their names may not figure among the distinguished ones present, even if they do go . . . [yet] they are personages of much importance in the land, although this so far may not yet be recognised.

There is more of the observer than of the observed in this last picture which certainly could not have been painted convincingly in this manner by any other organiser of broadcasting in any other country. Yet even in the United States, where unfortunately there has been no study of the initial process of recruitment, anonymous broadcasters soon gave way to recognisable persons. 'Each announcer', Norman Brokenshire wrote of the years 1924 and 1925, 'knew in his heart that he was God's gift to radio.' Which British announcer would have written in this way? There seems to have been less of a sense of team in the early American set-up than in Britain and far more sense of pressure on the individual, a pressure that was to increase on both sides of the Atlantic in the television age. Again, we have no statistics of drop-out rate, very low indeed in the BBC.

There are more details of ownership. In Detroit Thomas F. Clark, who ran an electrical appliance goods store, began by broadcasting music on a telephone receiver for people travelling on lake steamers, and gave invaluable advice to James E. Scripps, founder and owner of the *Detroit News*, who with his son William launched WWJ, a historic American station in 1920. This was the first station opened by a newspaper, and the *Detroit News* was also the first newspaper to start a radio column. Like the other early American newspaper stations (WMAQ, Chicago, and WDAF, Kansas City), it neither sold radio time nor planned to do so. The Scripps family was fascinated by the prospects of wireless. At a different level, H. V. Kaltenborn of WEAF, which did sell time and which set high standards of technical excellence, evolved into one of the first radio commentators straight from journalism; like Eckersley, however, he was also a radio enthusiast who liked playing with crystal sets.

Owen D. Young, founder and first President in 1919 of the powerful

Radio Corporation of America, did not have broadcasting in mind when he dominated the discussions leading up to it and went on to stipulate that only United States citizens might be Directors or officers. Writing later in 1929, when giant companies like RCA were under attack, Young was to generalise that men like himself had worked 'less for luxury than for power'. Their aim was primarily 'achievement'. They might give their money away, but 'the power to embark on great enterprises' they would never give away.

David Sarnoff, born in Russia in 1891, thought in somewhat different terms. He was above all else a salesman who calculated how much money could be spent on broadcasting in terms of sales of wireless sets:

> It is not possible [he had written as early as 1915 of his first broadcasting plan] to estimate the total amount of business obtainable with this plan until it has been developed and actually tried out; but there are about 15 million families in the United States alone, and if only 7 per cent of the total families thought well of the idea, it would, at the figure mentioned, mean a gross business of about $75 million which should yield considerable revenue. Aside from the profit to be derived from the proposition, the possibilities of advertising for the company are tremendous, for its name would ultimately receive national and universal attention.

Sarnoff was to establish his reputation essentially as a top executive. What counted in the first days, however, was his vision. He saw beyond the crystal set age to the almost unlimited possibilities of a 'communications revolution'. When he was explaining to Owen D. Young, then of the General Electric Company, the stringent finances of the American Marconi Company in the early years of broadcasting, he told Young that 'the greatest of our assets doesn't even show up'. This, he went on, was 'the vast ignorance about electronics'. 'The ignorance is what remains to be explored and conquered – because that's where we have unlimited potentials for industry, in fact, for many industries, that are still in their infancy or unborn.'

The record as set out by Sarnoff was both a public and a personal record of forecast and performance, and the personal side of it was unique. So, too, was John Reith's record on this side of the Atlantic, although it was far shorter and, I believe, less exciting. When Reith became first general manager of the British Broadcasting Company in 1922, he had not been a wireless enthusiast, as Sarnoff had been. Indeed, he knew nothing of what broadcasting meant. He was an engineer, however, and he combined vision of his own, unique vision too, with enterprise, a vision of radio as a 'national service', set out clearly in his first book *Broadcast over Britain* (1924). There was nothing of Young in Reith – he would have disliked him strongly – but at this stage Sarnoff himself was not far removed from Reith in outlook as might be believed, and later on they were to get on well together. 'Broadcasting', he wrote in June 1922, 'should be distinctly regarded as a public service'. He thought, indeed, of broadcasting by endowment, 'similar to that enjoyed by libraries, museums and educational institutions'.

Sarnoff's vision was apparent also during the 1930s, when he threw his by now substantial weight behind television. He had met the young Westinghouse television engineer, Vladimir Zworykin, as early as 1927, when sound radio was still in its first phases, and he immediately committed RCA funds to its development. Twenty years later, he had not convinced most of the businessmen whose stake in sound broadcasting constituted a vested interest of the future of television; and in a remarkable speech of September 1947, delivered to the National Association of Broadcasters in Atlantic City he summed up his own long-term role in the communications revolution before urging his audience 'to enter the field of television beyond the point where you yourself think that it is good business for you to do so'.

I have lived through several periods of development in the fields of communication and entertainment. I remember the day when wireless as a service of transoceanic communication was regarded by some as a joke . . . I lived through the day when the Victor Talking Machine Company – and they did a great job in their day – could not understand how people would sit at home and listen to music that someone else decided they should hear. And so they felt that the 'radio music box' and the radio broadcasting were a toy and would be a passing fancy. What was the result? Not many years after their fatal dream, RCA acquired the Victor Talking Machine Company, and the little dog changed its master.

I saw the same thing happen in the field of talking motion pictures. It was urged by many that people would not go to a movie that made a lot of noise and bellowed through an amplifier and disturbed the slumber of those who enjoyed the silent movie. That, they said, was a preposterous idea! The very virtue of a silent movie, they contended, was its silence. And then – in 1927 – came Warner Brothers with 'The Jazz Singer' and Al Jolson. Almost overnight a new industry was born. The silent actor became vocal, and the silent pictures was given an electronic tongue. Today, who goes to a silent movie?

Now, I should like to impress upon those of you engaged in radio, that for the first time in its history, radio has a stake in the present. It must be careful not to act like the cable companies, which looked upon the new children of science as ghosts of obsolescence that might affect their established businesses. In their desire to perpetuate and to protect their existing businesses, some of them stubbornly resisted change and progress. Finally, they suffered the penalty of extinction, or were acquired by more progressive newcomers.

> Let me assure you, my friends, after more than forty years of experience
> in this field of communications and entertainment, I have never seen any
> protection in merely standing still.

Sarnoff has entered mythology as well as history. There were some
pioneers, however, whose names have not appeared in the history
books and who deserve to find a place there.

In Britain, John Scott Taggart, in his own words 'a passionate and
obsessive communicator', knew about broadcasting in 1922 when
Reith did not. A radio engineer and barrister, and a member of the
Radio Society of Great Britain, he had written thirteen articles on
valves, which Sir Ambrose Fleming considered 'excellent', and he had
also invented radio equipment – there were thirty patents to his name
– and had advised radio manufacturers. He had fought for 'the
rights of the amateur', too, and – through his work with and for
'amateurs' – 'hams' as they came to be known – he had also taken
an interest in the likely content and arts of broadcasting. The public
for broadcasting, he was to write later, was created not by the BBC
but by the ready-made 30,000 listeners who were amateur technicians.
And he pointed to the strategic role of the same group in the United
States.

Scott Taggart was involved not in the organising of broadcasting
but, rather, in talking about it. *Popular Wireless*, published by the
Amalgamated Press, the first of the popular periodicals created by
broadcasting, had appeared in the middle of 1922 before Reith took up
his assignment, and Scott Taggart wrote for it before founding his own
more authoritative and in his own word 'sober' periodical *Modern
Wireless* in January 1923 and his *Wireless Weekly* in April of the same
year. He also wrote weekly articles in the *Daily Express* and produced a
sixpenny monthly, *The Wireless Constructor*. In the winter of 1926–7,
when the British Broadcasting Corporation came into existence, he
sold out his periodicals to the Amalgamated Press, while remaining
a regular contributor. Ironically, he turned from radio journalism to
the journalism of aviation, anticipating the similar move by Reith to
Imperial Airways ten years later. For him Reith was not a genius but a
man who always got in the way.

A study of the first period in the history of broadcasting must bring
in the 'radio societies' which, Scott Taggart recognised, ceased to be
important 'after 1923 and 1924, when their "big men" either died off or
returned to their professional and business activities'. The 'enthusiastic
coterie' to which he had belonged ceased 'to mean anything' when
hundreds of thousands of people were now making wireless sets 'without the aid of a society'. 'The mystique had vanished'. It is through

meeting Scott Taggart that I have come to believe that the historian of broadcasting must begin by putting the mystique back in.

Four kinds of research can illuminate this early period and subsequent periods. First, detailed histories of individual countries can bring out the relationship between the chronology of broadcasting, including broadcasting for 'amateurs', very much an international community after organised broadcasting began, and other aspects of social change. Before the age of television, when broadcasting was based on national broadcasting authorities, the distribution of wireless sets was very uneven throughout Europe, not to speak of the world. What were the factors that encouraged and limited growth? How far were the policies and the programmes of the communicators themselves relevant? How did broadcasting change after the Second World War in the age of transistors, which swept the Middle East? Second, studies concerned with the organisation of radio production – and later of television production – preferably with a comparative dimension, can reveal and possibly explain the substantially different creative responses in different societies to what was essentially the same basic technology. And in this second context the experience both of Asian and of Latin American broadcasting is relevant.

The divergence between systems took place very early – as Reith put it in 1924, 'early days are crucial ones in either individual existence or corporate organisations' – and it is possible to trace already by the late 1920s three broad types of broadcasting system – those geared to business; those geared to government; and those which followed, never completely faithfully, the British pattern of independent management, coupled with financing by licence. A fourth type, broadcasting for development, was to come much later.

Third, studies of the background, recruitment, training and attitudes of staff – in a depth not so far very much attempted – can be related to the second type of study, as they can also be related to the fourth – studies dealing with the impact of particular programmes on particular places or on particular social groups. These can illuminate limited processes of change (e.g. schools broadcasting in Britain or the growth of an audience for 'classical music'), where the evidence is adequate and where it was collected by the communicators themselves.

Most often, of course, there is no material, since the communicators were far too busy communicating. In consequence, the first comments on the impact of broadcasting were often as general and wild as some of the first prophecies about the uses of radio during the 1890s. This kind of literature, spilling over into science fiction, always has its interest in relation to any kind of invention, and it is interesting to

compare what was being said in the 1920s about sound radio with what
was being said in the 1940s about television or, for that matter, what
was being said in the 1840s about railways.

Broadcasting, it was claimed, would not only keep people away
from concerts but would stop them reading. It would encourage contentment with superficiality. Little attempt was made, however, to
note how people were actually spending their time on the eve of the
advent of broadcasting, so that there was little precision in any account
of radio's displacement effects. 'Instead of solitary thought', the headmaster of Rugby complained, 'people would listen in to what was
said to millions of people, which could not be the best things.' Reith
certainly would not have agreed.

Every assertion led to counter assertion. People would read more.
There would be less passivity as 'minds were opened and horizons
widened'. 'In five years' time the general musical public of these islands
will be treble or quadruple its present size.' The commonsense middle
view was well expressed by Lord Riddell, a Press magnate, who knew
that most of his colleagues feared broadcasting as a competitor of vast
potential:

> What effect is radio going to have on life? (By the way I do not like the
> description 'wireless': why describe a thing as a negation?) Are people
> going to read less? Are they going to talk less? Are they going to be better
> or worse informed? Are they going to go to the theatre and music less? Are
> those who reside in rural districts going to be more or less satisfied: Who
> can tell? . . . So far as the present generation is concerned I believe that
> those accustomed to read and who like reading will continue to read
> whether they use the radio or not. But what about the next generation
> brought up on radio? Are they going to prefer information through the
> medium of the ear to that of through the medium of the eye?'

The same distinction between first and second generations has been
made in relation to television. It was not until the mid-1920s, however, that 'background' listening, as distinct from 'deliberate' listening,
became a regular feature of listener behaviour; and by then, as crystal
sets were giving way to valve sets, the first talk of television was already
making it far less certain that Lord Riddell's last question meant much
at all.

Later questioning about television could be as comprehensive as that
of Riddell. Would it too threaten book sales? Would it wipe out talk?
Would it reduce audiences in cinemas, theatres, churches and chapels,
or football and sports stadiums? Was viewing plays a form of day-
dreaming? Would disasters be trivialised?

In the posing of such questions and in the attempts to answer them it
was relevant that sound broadcasting had come first in time, and that

for many observers, used to such questions and answers, 'talk about the social and cultural power of sound radio is high hat pontification', as Kenneth Baily, then television critic of the *Evening Standard* and associate editor of *Television*, put it in 1949. 'Those who cannot remember the days before wireless find it difficult to realise that their mental processes and cultural tastes have been influenced by radio, despite its quite ordinary and normal place in the house.' Baily's conclusion, an abdication of judgement, suggested that the questions and answers were out of place:

> Thousands of people, and then people in millions, are going to become subject, to some degree, to their household screen. What will it mean to them? Good or ill? With this new power there are unlikely to be half-measures; it will choose its way, and then do what it cannot stop itself from doing.

Such determinism attaches far too much importance to the technology. It does not look closely enough at the component elements in an audience. It deliberately ignores sociology.

The development of audience research, first about listeners, then about viewers, sprang from the attempt on the part of organised communicators assembled in the new broadcasting organisations to discover necessary facts about their audience either for marketing or for programming purposes or for both. They were not interested in speculation. The first American service was devised in 1930 after competitive American radio companies had been fully commercialised. 'Co-operative Analysis of Broadcasting', organised in that year by the Association of National Advertisers, carried out telephone interviews with a small population sample to provide the basis for CAB or 'Crossley ratings': its task, *Radio Broadcast* had suggested earlier, would be 'equivalent to determining the number of crickets chirping at any instance in a swamp on a foggy summer evening'. In Britain in the same year, two experienced BBC communicators, Charles Siepmann, concerned with 'talks' and with education, and Val Gielgud, concerned with entertainment, both pressed for a 'salaried investigator' to help them to assess audience reactions.

Reith himself was uneasy about the dangerous uses of ratings, and though he never referred to 'crickets in a swamp', he believed that to base broadcasting on ratings would be equivalent to listening to crickets. None the less, a 'listener research service' was eventually started by the BBC in 1936. It distinguished between (a) research into listeners' habits; (b) research into the efficiency of broadcasting techniques; (c) research into listeners' preferences; and (d) research into 'reactions of a type which are of more direct interest to the psychologist or to the sociologist than to the BBC' – for example, on the subject of whether the coming of wireless had tended to strengthen family life. There was still ample scope for speculation there.

Indeed, on this side of the Atlantic very general speculation remained in vogue even after Paul Lazarsfeld and others had used more sophisticated survey techniques, some of which had already been developed in the world of market research, a world which still lacks its historian. The first book referred to in Joseph Klapper's *The Effects of Mass Communication* (1960) was published in 1942, and Patricia Kendall's *Radio Listening in America* did not appear until 1948, the same year as Lazarsfeld along with Harry Field produced *The People Look at Radio* and a year after W. S. Robinson had written an article on 'Radio Audience Measurement and its Limitations'. Yet by 1948 much interesting and carefully conceived work had already been carried out by the BBC through Robert Silvey's Listener Research Organisation, and many war-time studies of propaganda had been published, resting on a closer study than had ever been made before the War of the social psychology of broadcasting. The subject was, of course, of great interest to the Germans, but that is another story, still to be told.

As the War progressed, there was a far more profound understanding of the differences between the different broadcasting systems which had grown up in such a short space of time. Content analysis, statistical techniques of measurement and 'impact studies' were coming into their own. None the less, when the BBC celebrated its twenty-first birthday in 1943. the main article written for the occasion by Sir Ernest Barker lacked any kind of sociological sophistication and concluded with statements which were as general and imprecise as any which had been made in 1922. 'The end of the matter' for Barker was that 'broadcasting has done the nation good and is essentially (as the writers of *1066 and All That* would say) a "Good Thing". The BBC has been free from the taint of advertising: it has not been too pedagogic: it has mixed the grave with the gay and the *utile* with the *dolce* in a happy combination.'

One thing that Barker could not entirely ignore was the fact that by 1943 'institutionalisation' had completely transformed the organisation of the communicators. Indeed, the pioneer stage had already given way to a 'routine stage' by the late 1920s, when people were joining the BBC not as a new venture but as an established institution. The move from Savoy Hill to Broadcasting House in 1932 symbolised the change. *Punch* described it well:

Ten years ago we hailed the new invention
Just as a curious scientific freak . . .
Those were the days of cramped accommodation
For workers on the hillside of Savoy –
A Company, not yet a Corporation
Who spent laborious days with little joy
And hasty meals, in long negotiation
Before they gained permission to employ
Artists and actors, and allayed suspicion
Of any undermining competition.

Now in 1932, while the BBC was 'not a bed of roses', it could be said that it

well has earned and well deserved its Wreath;
For here at last we safely can applaud
One thing we manage better than abroad.

After the move to Broadcasting House and during the 'routine' phases of the 1930s – a misnomer, in fact, given that these were 'the golden years of wireless', when all kinds of experiments with the medium were being tried out, particularly in Britain and Europe – efforts were made to distinguish between 'creative' communicators and administrators, a distinction drawn by Peter Eckersley's brother Roger as a fact of human nature, although he widened the term 'administrative' to read 'political'. This distinction became the basis, indeed, of a thorough structural reorganisation of the BBC in 1933, with separation its declared object. 'The transferred administrative staff', it was formally laid down, 'will work, under their administrative chief, to the requirements of the creative staff, who will be relieved of all immediate and direct responsibility in administrative matters.' Engineers were still separate. The latter separation persisted. The former did not survive the Second World War.

In the United States, a different distinction, which was to enter Britain only after 1955 with the development of commercial television, was made between sales staff and production staff, each with their own techniques, and each responsible to 'top management'. Some of that management could be very remote, but when occasion demanded it could be brutal. To the Americans the British pattern seemed 'stiff and bureaucratic'. To the British – at least, to the British officials of the BBC – the American pattern seemed casual, loose and ultimately irresponsible. In both countries, however – and again the phenomenon has not been properly charted – there was increasing 'professionalisation'. 'The professional identity of the broadcaster, whether as controller or as producer' was being established.

The Second World War complicated the story. First, it held back television, an exciting career for a new generation of young men. Second, it forced communicators to organise broadcasting for overseas as well as for home-based audiences. Third, it led to a great expansion of staff, particularly in Britain, many of them with no previous experience of broadcasting, some of them, none the less, the key figures of the future. Fourth, with shortages of newsprint, it gave sound broadcasting temporary advantages over other media of communication. It strengthened the demand for rapid news.

On the third of these points, the change in scale involved something of a complete transformation. BBC staff rose from nearly 4000 in 1939 to over 12,000 in 1945, the great majority 'unestablished', three-quarters of them women. The proportion of engineers remained constant at two-fifths of the whole, a necessary constant, but numbers in other groups moved upwards and downwards according to immediate needs. In these circumstances, some of the communicators were forced also into new areas of political persuasion and propaganda of the kind which the Germans, pioneers of the third system of broadcasting, had specialised in since 1933. The Americans, too, entered the game, with less success than the British.

The organisation of German broadcasting is a subject in itself, a neglected subject, but it is interesting to note that the 'Nazi élite' who managed the radio propaganda machine of the 1930s were also young men, most of whom had been only eighteen years old at the outbreak of the First World War. They were, indeed, on average, about ten years younger than the 'Nazi élite' as a whole. More than a half of them had attended a university as compared with only one-quarter of the Nazi administrators. They were certainly as much of a 'mixture' as the first BBC mixture described by Maschwitz and Gorham, and one out of five of them had been without a job during the days of the Weimar Republic.

The Germans, like the British, were swamped with new recruits during the Second World War, while the Americans were faced with the more intractable problem of trying to create an institutional framework within which their Office of War Information could ensure that broadcasting, commercial in orientation, would carry out certain agreed national tasks. The BBC maintained continuity, and while it is possible to write its history during this period in terms of the defeat of an 'old guard' at the hands of 'new men', it responded to its war-time tasks more effectively than any other broadcasting organisation in the world, and as it approached its twenty-first birthday party in 1943, looked back to its beginnings. Meanwhile, the Press made the same points that it had been making since the 1920s. 'It may be that British broadcasting would have gained in entertainment value', wrote the *Yorkshire Post*, 'if it had been developed on the American model with sponsored programmes, but we believe that it would have suffered greatly as a public service.'

We are already further away in time from 1943 than Barker was from the birth of broadcasting in 1943. Yet our studies of the effects of television – in its origins and its development still a young man's service, posing the same problems of growth and development as sound radio had done – remain patchy and of varied quality. William Belson's *The Impact of Television* (1967) has a valuable bibliography listing work that has already been carried out. It reveals the gaps and brings out, incidentally, how little of the work has any comparative dimension.

Four points stand out in recent years in so far as our understanding of historical perspectives are concerned. First, we have begun to relate both radio and television, which are linked together, to a 'communications revolution' which is seen as part of a 'long revolution' with different phases. Some comparisons have now been drawn between two phases, but they are very incomplete. Second, sociological work is becoming much more specialised and is being increasingly cut off from history. More attention is being paid to the functional relationships within the communications set-up between controllers, salesmen, planners, producers and performers, as they actually are now, rather than with the relationships as they have developed. At the same time, organisational theory is being brought into the institutional analysis.

Third, 'problem' or 'opportunity' areas are being identified more closely in the communications process, and work is being carried out not only to report or analyse what has happened but specifically to induce change, particularly in education. *Television and the Child* (1958) by Hilda Himmelweit was a pioneer study of international importance. It has been followed by other studies, British and American, many of them sponsored.

Fourth, the compass of studies is widening as increased attention is being paid to problems of development. Wilbur Schramm's *Mass Media and National Development* (1964) was a great landmark. Since then we have begun to examine appropriate radio 'strategies'. None of them operate in a vacuum, and fortunately, it is possible to carry out certain kinds of research, both of communications and of impact, in areas where broadcasting, including sound and television broadcasting, is still a new force.

In general, there is more talk at the present time about the future

than about the past. The possibilities of new developments in communications receive more attention than previous failures. There is
some loss in this. Yet at the same time what is happening now enables
us, if we choose, to look at some aspects of the past in different perspectives from those of Riddell or Barker. We may have exaggerated
somewhat the distinctiveness of the British broadcasting system. It is
obviously different from the French system, with its dependence on
government, and the American system, with its almost total reliance on
business. What would once have seemed a fundamental difference,
however, now seems, in places at least, to be a time lag.

Moreover, we may have been prone to exaggerate the difference
between the BBC sector and the 'independent' sector, brought into
existence as a result of the one big, new structural change in the history
of British broadcasting since the advent of television. At the time of the
Television Act of 1954, as during the struggle that preceded it, emphasis
was placed on the incompatibility of two different approaches to
television, one commercial and one traditionally 'British'. Yet, as
Professor George Wedell has recently suggested,

> one has only to put side by side the documents governing the conduct of
> the two British broadcasting organisations, the Charter and Licence of the
> BBC and the Television Acts under which the ITA operates, in order to be
> struck forcibly by the essentially *unitary* character of the broadcasting
> system in the United Kingdom. The same point has been made by Burton
> Paulu in his valuable studies of broadcasting and television in the United
> Kingdom.

We in Britain have never fully studied the effects of competition on
the position (and salaries and career prospects) of the communicators,
but we are far clearer, if not fully clear, about the relationships between
one *medium* and another, a way of looking at communications which
was not common before 1939. Indeed, what we have discovered about
communications today has led us to re-examine the printing revolution, the rise of the Press and the rise and fall of the mass cinema; and
we have been drawn into a brief, fashionable debate about Marshall
McLuhan's approach to the role of communications, a debate which
on this side of the Atlantic has petered out, characteristically, before it
has had time to move much below the surface.

So much is happening at the present that it provides us with no very
secure vantage point from which to survey radio history, yet there is an
urgent need to do so while many of the broadcasters who took key
decisions are still alive and while it is possible to catch and interpret
philosophies which are no longer current and styles which are no
longer congenial. There are prospects of a history of German radio,

post-War as well as pre-War, which will be particularly interesting in its European context, and there has recently been a growth of interest across the Atlantic in the history of American radio.

In my own historical work on the BBC, I have tried to write in sufficient detail to avoid premature generalisation, to provide a narrative which will be sufficiently definitive for other scholars to take it as a frame, to identify problems, some of which I hope can be tackled in detailed monographs, and to avoid forming easy judgements about past decisions and policies in the light of what is being said in the very ephemeral present. The work will only be complete, however, when it is given a genuine international dimension.

7 Problems and Possibilities in the Writing of Broadcasting History*

Scattered throughout the four volumes of my *History of Broadcasting in the United Kingdom* are various general observations on the scope, methodology and objectives of broadcasting history.† Some of these observations represent initial assumptions on which the whole (and as yet unfinished) history has been based; some are the by-products of the experience of research and writing; and some reflect the impact of the work of other scholars concerned with communications, not necessarily historians, since the publicaton of the first volume in 1961.

The twenty years which have elapsed since the beginnings of this project have been strategically significant but often difficult years in the history of broadcasting. They cover, for example, what Peter Black in his book *The Biggest Aspidistra in the World* (1972) has called 'the forced retreat' of sound broadcasting in face of television; fierce competition for audience ratings between the BBC and the commercial companies, particularly in the late-1960s and early-1970s; the rise and fall of more 'permissive' broadcasting, including satirical broadcasting, associated with the Director-Generalship of Sir Hugh Greene; the launching of BBC 2; the beginnings of local radio; the controversies surrounding perhaps the most controversial report that the BBC has ever produced, *Broadcasting in the Seventies*; two major outside reports on all aspects of broadcasting by the Pilkington (1962) and Annan (1977) Committees; the rise of trade unions; and the tangled and always shifting networks of relationships with successive governments and public opinion. Sir Ian Jacob, who was Director-General when work on the *History* began, was understating the extent of change when he wrote in the spring of 1979 that 'governing the BBC is a very greatly more difficult job than it was in my comparatively peaceful days'.

Such a list of changes in the history of the BBC, long though it is, still does not cover adequately either the history of commercial television

*This article first appeared in *Media, Culture and Society* (1980).
†*A History of Broadcasting in the United Kingdom*, 4 vols.; *The Birth of Broadcasting* (1961); *The Golden Age of Wireless* (1965); *The War of Words* (1970); and *Sound and Vision* (1979).

and the IBA since 1955 nor the advent and subsequent development of commercial local sound broadcasting. There are different, if sometimes converging, themes in this second, parallel history; and if a volume five of my *History* were to be produced within the general framework of the present title, *A History of Broadcasting in the United Kingdom*, it would also have to include at least an outline history of the commercial companies. Such a volume would also have to include the 'radio pirates' of the 1960s. Given such an extension of coverage, different problems and possibilities from those considered in this article would inevitably be raised.

None the less, throughout the period covered in the four volumes that have already been published, the history of broadcasting in the United Kingdom was, as some historians have already forgotten, the history of the BBC; and this is true although there were some early private broadcasting ventures to take into the reckoning before the BBC secured its monopoly in 1922, the monopoly that it held until 1955. It is also true that since 1927 many British listeners have always chosen to listen to programmes from overseas, some of them specially designed for them, and that BBC policies were not unaffected during the 1930s by Radio Luxembourg and by Radio Normandie, commercial ventures, a large part of the profits of which depended on an audience on this side of the Channel.

There is one interesting feature of the time span already covered in the existing four volumes. Work on the first of them began very soon after the period of history covered in the last of them had ended. Present research for a fifth volume is beginning with a period of history that began very soon after my initial contract to write the *History* had been signed. In other words, history is catching up with contractual obligation. Indeed, the BBC's decision to commission a history must be related to its own growing concern in the mid-1950s to get its history straight both for itself and for the public. There had been talk of 'a book' in BBC circles for a considerable time before it appeared.

In considering time spans, it is essential to take account not only of changes in broadcasting itself but of changes in the approach to broadcasting issues of those writers, including scholarly writers, who for various reasons have turned to the subject. In 1961 there were few general histories of broadcasting in any country with the exception of that of Maurice Gorham for Britain, *Broadcasting and Television since 1900* (1972), and that of G. L. Archer, *History of Radio to 1926* (1938), for the United States: Erik Barnouw did not publish the first volume of his three-volume trilogy on American broadcasting, the first volume of which had the delightful title *A Tower of Babel*, until 1966. Burton Paulu's *British Broadcasting: Radio and Television in the United*

Kingdom (1956) and his *British Broadcasting in Transition* (1961) were genuinely pioneering general works.

Several books on broadcasting procedures and institutions had already appeared, however, some of which included brief historical sections, and many autobiographies of leading personalities concerned with broadcasting – a genre in themselves – had been produced along with a few biographies. There were few attempts at synthesis, however, and, as far as sociological, as distinct from historical, research was concerned, there were huge gaps. Of the 222 items cited in Elihu Katz's *Social Research on Broadcasting* (1977), an admittedly incomplete and highly selective list, only nineteen were published before 1960, with five of the nineteen by the American Professor, Paul Lazarsfeld and his co-operators.

J. T. Klapper's *The Effects of Mass Communication* did not appear until 1960 and Marshal McLuhan's *The Gutenberg Galaxy* until 1962. A historian looking in the late 1950s for outside reinforcements had to make do, therefore, with R. H. Coase, a solitary pioneer, not mentioned by Katz (and with Coase's economics, then somewhat out of fashion), and with Harold Innis, an original, but completely unsystematic, thinker who ranged over the centuries – back to the ancient world – in his book *The Bias of Communication* (1951). The work of the Frankfurt School was little known in Britain, and Raymond Williams did not write *Communications*, the first of his several books on the subject, until 1962. It is significant, however, that before the now familiar term 'communications revolution' had come into regular use, Williams had used the term 'long revolution' as the title of his book which appeared in 1961, bringing the Press as well as broadcasting into his survey. Publishing remained strangely neglected.

To complete the picture, it is necessary to recall that, whatever the academic *lacunae*, an intimidating mass of largely neglected contemporary social comment on sound broadcasting and on television was buried away in newspapers and periodicals, a few of the latter specialising in content as the listening audience grew during the 1920s and 1930s and the viewing audience during the 1950s and 1960s. Moreover, there had been bitter debates in Parliament during the early 1950s about broadcasting policy, debates that were stirred up again after the first two years of competition. *Hansard* is an indispensable source.

My own work on broadcasting history, which preceded my decision to write a commissioned history, grew out of the cultural concerns of the period from 1956 to 1962, when, as Williams wrote in retrospect in his *Britain in the Sixties* volume on *Communications*, there was such an 'intense development of ideas in the field of culture and communications' that 'by the time of the Pilkington Report (1962) this had reached the level of open and conventional politics'.

The scattered literature with which I was familiar when I started my *History* already covered the battles to break the BBC's monopoly, but these battles had centred on 'commercialism' more than on the role of 'the media', while much of the 'output' literature concerned not questions of how what was seen on the television screen was produced or controlled, but rather the shift from sound to vision, from words to images.

It was the existence of this second kind of literature which, years later, was to influence the choice of title for my Volume IV – *Sound and Vision* – although by then I had in view long-term perspectives which included the invention and diffusion of printing, the development of publishing, the rise of the daily Press, photography and the cinema, and the growth of the entertainment industry. I had become interested in voices and in pictures, noting that what had been written about the former during the 1920s and 1930s had already passed into oblivion.

Little attention had been paid by reviewers of books on broadcasting to the significance of shifts of interest in research; and when they dealt with the controversial present, as they usually did, they had concentrated instead on the pressure group theme. Even in relation to this theme, a theme that roused strong emotions, J. D. Stewart's *British Pressure Groups*, the first British book systematically to use the concept of 'pressure group', appeared as late as 1958, and the American political scientist H. H. Wilson's influential book, *Pressure Group: The Campaign for Commercial Television*, appeared even later (very conveniently on the eve of Pilkington) in 1961.

Given this list of relevant publication dates, it should be clear that Volume I of my *History* was planned and written very much on its own. There were no outside influences on the way that I approached it or on what I had to say. As Reith remarked of broadcasting as a whole in the 1920s in his *Broadcast over Britain* (1924), 'there were no sealed orders to open; the commission was of the scantiest nature'.

When I was invited by Jacob to write the *History*, it was an invitation that surprised me, but it was because I was already interested in communications history that I accepted it. In particular, I was interested in the role of 'the image', a subject which I had already discussed with Daniel Boorstin, whose book with that title was to appear in 1961. Yet, in accepting the commission I was influenced too by a quite different consideration – my conviction that if the history of the Press had been tackled in the nineteenth century in the way that I then wished to tackle the history of broadcasting, our knowledge of the nineteenth century would have greatly increased. In consequence, we would have been in a far stronger position as historians to contemplate the present and future of 'the media'. I already saw these as grouped, sometimes operating together, sometimes in competition.

In general terms, the first problem in writing broadcasting history seemed to me to be the same as that faced in the writing of all recent history – that of securing access to every kind of material, public or private, whether in the form of documents, ephemera or visual evidence, or through oral interviews. Yet I knew that there would be special difficulties in writing such a history because of the huge bulk of broadcast output, a term already in use, and its transient nature; not until after the development of sound and visual recording, which was to be one of the major subjects in my *History*, but which has never been touched on by any reviewer of my volumes, did the bulk of it become accessible to the historian. I knew also that to listen to and to view even limited examples of broadcast 'output' would take up a disproportionate amount of time. There was no easy equivalent to browsing through a newspaper.

I knew, too, that much essential 'recall' as far as the early years were concerned – recall relating to 'control' as well as 'output' – depended more on John Reith than on those of his managers and producers who still survived. Yet I was aware that Reith's own relations with the BBC were then at their worst. He told me, indeed, when I first approached him for help, that if I had written to ask him for it on BBC notepaper he would have thrown my letter into the wastepaper basket. As it was, after protracted and penetrating discussion, Reith gave me full access to everything he had – and what he had was unique. I knew, of course, the limits of documentary evidence. Vital documents – including, for example, the documents relating to the choice of Reith as General Manager of the British Broadcasting Company in 1922 and to the choice of the first BBC staff – might be missing, and they were. I knew also that what evidence survived obviously had to be interpreted in the light of other evidence, 'unofficial' as well as 'official'. It might have survived for a purpose. In consequence, I knew that past gossip would matter.

As far as 'oral history' was concerned – and this itself was still one of the terms of the future during the late 1950s – little note had been taken of its use in 'history from below', a phrase also not yet used, although a few business historians, including Alan Nevins across the Atlantic, whom I knew as a friend, had become interested in its possibilities. My own introduction to its methodology was through unrecorded interviews, but I added one innovation of my own – bringing together a group of people to talk through old arguments and to recreate old atmospheres. The newly invented tape recorder was an invaluable ally.

Reith, however, did not want to play such games; he had to be dealt with on his own, complete, of course, with his diaries which no one had then seen and which he made freely available to me.

Any historian choosing to discuss the development of broadcasting in Britain would have had to consider as a preliminary task Reith and his distinctive contribution to British broadcasting before considering anyone else. As I stated in Volume I (p. 4), 'during the four years with which this volume is concerned (1922 to 1926) there is a strong element of personal history . . . Reith did not make broadcasting but he did make the BBC.' None the less, I called the introduction to Volume I 'Broadcasting and Society', demonstrating that I was as interested in social history then as I was to be later. From the start I wanted to write what I then thought of as 'total history', not personal nor, for that matter, purely institutional history. I had worked in this way earlier on my *History of Birmingham* (1952).

I went on to write a shorter but more analytical account of 'Broadcasting and Society' with this title for BBC Talks, subsequently reprinted in *The Listener* (November 1962), by which time I had developed a number of further ideas about cultural history. Having long been interested in the relationshp between sociology and history – could sociology, I often asked, provide for social history what economics provided for economic history? – I now wanted from the start to relate 'culture' to both social and economic history. I felt that this meant getting inside the language systems of the past and not reading back into the past current fashions of description and explanation. Yet I did not wish to draw a line across the past, separating it from the present. This approach meant that BBC archives would provide only one source, if the most important, for my reconstruction of the past. I should add that in Volumes II, III and IV I was more explicit in recognising the need for studying a far wider range of sources than BBC archives than I had been in my introduction to Volume I. By then I knew what the archives left out.

When I began Volume I, I was particularly concerned about the dangers of 'official history'. There had been a lively post-war debate on these dangers between 1945 and 1955, centring largely on the departmental war histories that had been produced by a team of scholars under the general editorial direction of Professor Keith Hancock. I had read the contributions to this debate of scholars as different as A. J. P. Taylor, a foe to all 'official' history, and Herbert Butterfield, another foe, who none the less – and entirely in character – pressed me to write the history of the BBC. He told the BBC that I should write it, although I only learned this later. So also did Alan Bullock.

In the light of the post-war argument, while I welcomed access to what were then often unsorted archives, I was anxious to avoid the term 'official history' in relation to my own future product, and I have never subsequently used the term myself; indeed, I preferred my volumes to be called *A History of Broadcasting* rather than *The History*. I should add that since accepting the commission from Jacob, the BBC as an institution has never interfered in any way with any sentence I have written, although for what I believe to be good reasons, *pace* Andrew Boyle, whose biography of Reith appeared many years later in 1972, I have not been able to use personal files for my last two volumes. The fact that I was able to use them in the first two undoubtedly added to the interest of the text.

I wanted my *History*, above all else, to be definitive – that is to say, to be as accurate and as well backed by *all* available evidence as possible, consistently and comprehensively referred to in footnotes which I have not used in many of my books. I had later scholars in mind when I did this, scholars whom I hoped would write the kind of monographs on broadcasting which I wished could have been available to me. I also wanted to quote at length from original sources, even though this was not then very fashionable among historians, first because I hoped to capture lost modes of expression as well as lost moods and, second, because I wished to enable scholars who might draw different conclusions from myself to have before them not only footnote references but the necessary amount of published evidence to draw to their attention themes that they might otherwise have missed.

I strongly disapproved of the selective and tendentious way in which Lytton Strachey had used evidence, and I knew from my own work on Victorian England – and now know better than ever – that Lytton Strachey was neither unique among historians nor the last of them to proceed in this manner. An intelligent debate about public broadcasting must begin on the basis of accepted facts. I have never believed, like some programme-makers, that there are no facts and I have never been happy about programmes that blur distinctions between fact and fiction.

When I started my *History*, the three major decisions that I had to take concerned scale, chronology and range of content. Yet I could take none of these decisions until I had explored what was available in the form of 'official' and 'unofficial' evidence. In 1960 care of the BBC archives was not formally separated from the Registry, and before I could start work on the *History* it was necessary to produce a hand list of relevant materials in the possession of the BBC, a 'Brief Guide to Documents' which included both documents and a useful collection of Press cuttings. Subsequently, catalogue volumes were produced for me on the Second World War and on a 'Select List of

Material, 1947–1954'. Perhaps the most important by-product of my *History* has been that the BBC has begun to put its own archives in order and has appreciated their national as well as their institutional importance.

The foundations of the archives had been laid in 1927, when the Central Registry was formed, but it was not until 1970 that the archives, now clearly separated from the Registry, were moved from central London to Caversham. By then, Volume III was at an advanced stage of preparation. There were bigger problems in relation to archival material for Volume IV (particularly for the history of the external services) than there had been in relation to Volumes I, II and III, but I had already become aware myself of all the archival issues when I was writing Volume I: no fewer than 6500 items in the BBC's archives, some of them bulky, were concerned with the period which ended with the foundation of the Corporation in January 1927. Erik Barnouw has had no comparable archival evidence at his disposal in the writing of the history of American broadcasting, and this accounts in part at least for the difference in the organisation and layout, if not the style, of our two histories.

It was difficult to settle questions of scale even after 'measuring' the volume of available archival evidence. There were two reasons for this – first, the lack of a basic chronology of broadcasting dates (the nearest approach to one was in the BBC *Yearbooks*) and, second, uncertainty about how much detail would be necessary to elucidate major themes. In working on chronology it became clear very quickly that the period from the founding of the Company to the founding of the Corporation possessed a tidy unity of its own, even though there was considerable continuity before and after 1927, represented in the perpetuation of the same initials, BBC.

The alternative would have been to have taken the Reith years as one period and to have ended my first volume in 1938, when Reith dramatically left Broadcasting House, but if I had done this, I would have ignored some of the striking contrasts between the 1920s and 1930s. I would also have had to cut out much significant detail and I might have magnified the importance of Reith's personal contribution to the history of the BBC, particularly in the later stages, after a much pondered and far-reaching reorganisation of the Corporation in 1933. After that, Reith had become bored with his duties. He did not feel 'fully stretched'. By 1936 he was writing in his diary, 'Very disgusted with everything and feeling that I cannot stand things longer in the BBC.'

My title for Volume II, *The Golden Age of Wireless*, a nostalgic title for some readers, might well have been used in relation to the history of broadcasting in other countries where there was no Reith to guide or dictate; and I had come to the conclusion by 1960 that I wanted to consider British broadcasting within an international frame. In my view, during the 1930s the medium became more important and interesting than the man. As far as the period of Volume III was concerned, however, there was no choice. *The War of Words* has as much unity as Volume I, and covers roughly the same period of time. In writing it, I appreciated fully that the war years, when the BBC's reputation abroad was at its height, deserved detailed monographic treatment. And I had to become a war historian in the process.

I had originally thought of three volumes in all, but I did not then know where I would end my story, and once I looked beyond 1945 there was a further choice of possible titles and ending points. In retrospect, however, there was something inevitable as well as artistically satisfying in my ending Volume IV with the first night of commercial television. That, of course, had broader significance also. The year 1956 stands out in retrospect as a year of almost as many 'new things' as the year 1896, when Marconi brought his wireless patents to London. Research on my fourth volume was difficult. The evidence at times seemed limitless. There were far too many people who were still alive.

The length of each volume has been determined not only by the volume of available material, but by the identification for each period of major elements in the story which seemed to demand full treatment. Volume IV would have been much shorter had I not included a chapter of almost three hundred pages, Chapter VI, called 'Sounds, Words and Pictures', in which I tried to show how the shift from sound to vision affected the approach to the broadcasting of news and views, of politics, of drama, of features and variety, of music, of religion, of education and of sport.

This chapter is in effect a collection of short monographs within a monograph, each of which might have been placed in a separate volume. They were written at the right time, however, since many of the people described in the chapter to whom I turned for vital evidence are now dead. The chapter will be useful to other historians, although it somewhat breaks the continuity of Volume IV. I might have been wiser to include the different sections of it in a separate volume or as detailed appendices.

It was in Volume IV that I made explicit a number of points about historical method that I had touched on only lightly in my earlier volumes. First, the relationship of broadcasting to society as presented in my *History* is never one of foreground to background. I have always felt it essential to consider, however difficult it may be to do so, the extent to which broadcasting registers experience and perception and the extent to which it has influenced them. This can only be done if the historian of broadcasting is a social and cultural historian interested in other forces in society besides broadcasting, including technology, and how such forces have operated.

Second, hindsight can mislead. If I had written Volume I with the Pilkington Committee in mind, as Sir Hugh Greene almost expected me to do, and with the kind of broadcasting issues which were then in the air at the very front of my mind, Volume I would now look very dated. It would have been equally precarious, of course, to have written Volume IV with the Annan Committee in mind. Reviewers of books on the history of broadcasting are naturally concerned with current issues – they know about these and they know that their readers know about them – and they have these in mind when they review what is said about the past. By contrast and in defiance of reviewers – I chose to eschew hindsight and to concentrate on what people had in mind at the time I was describing and, when necessary, to explain in each volume how and why what they had in mind had changed. The reviews of my volumes are now far more dated than the volumes themselves.

Third, my mode of proceeding meant leaving open a number of questions, answers to which would be offered only in a later volume. 'Competition will be deathly', wrote the BBC's Head of Television, George Barnes, in 1955. Only a later volume, still unwritten, could deal with competitive television as it actually worked out. I noted, however, in the 'monographic' chapters of Volume IV those tensions in relation to the broadcasting of news and of political and religious programmes which were already present in 1955 and which were to provide a special opportunity for the new 'competitor'.

I have not yet described historical attitudes towards local and regional broadcasting in terms of the period since *Broadcasting in the Seventies*. This adds to, I believe rather than subtracts from, interest in what I say about pre-war local and regional broadcasting in my volumes written in 1961 and 1965, before *Broadcasting in the Seventies* was conceived of. It will doubtless add, too, to the interest of a possible Volume V when local broadcasting was formally introduced.

Fourth, in dealing with social attitudes, political opinions and 'moral standards', it is essential to begin by recognising that whatever structural relationships persist in British (including Scottish and Welsh) social and cultural history, there are always specific situational relationships to consider – 'snapshot' relationships – within each period under review. As we look back in time, the snapshots fade. There is abundant evidence also of public or private attitudes that now seem obsolete or even repugnant.

This does not mean, however, that the attitudes should not be analysed (at least initially) in terms of the period when they were held or expressed. I am aware that a study of what was 'repressed' – or constrained – through self-censorship, the latter of great importance in the history of the BBC, can be as revealing as a study of what was actually transmitted through the microphone or the camera. From such angles, the Greene period in the history of broadcasting stands out as exceptional. To discuss it will be a formidable task.

Fifth, accepted explanations of policy changes should never go un-challenged. It is too simple, for example, in seeking to explain the end of the BBC's monopoly to write exclusively in terms of manoeuvres of a pressure group as H. H. Wilson did in 1962. The internal politics of the Conservative party during the early 1950s cannot be speedily dis-posed of in this way. Nor can the ultimate compromises written into the Television Act of 1954. Likewise, the 'public service' arguments which for many years had sustained the BBC's monopoly require to be related to something more than Reith's personal philosophy. The adjective 'Reithian' often conceals more than it elucidates. We have to look at shifting balances of political and commercial forces, at webs rather than at conspiracies.

I made one further general observation in the introduction to Volume II, an observation that covers one of the most important questions in writing institutional history, never in my view just 'house history' even if old members of the institution will read it with special interest and with inside knowledge. What you thought of the BBC in the 1930s, if you were a member of it, depended not only on your tempera-ment, character, experience and outlook – and the conditions and date at which you entered the Corporation – but on the place which you occupied within the system. Your perspective would often change as you moved upwards, downwards, or across.

> The historian, freed from such a framework [I suggested] has less difficulty in interpreting the institution than in interpreting the society in which it developed. He has the advantage of being able to look at the scene from more than one angle, to take into account evidence which was hidden from partial viewers at the time, and 'to trace complex sequences of cause and consequence'. He has a certain disinterest which is invaluable in discussing not only personalities but problems.

Long after these words were written, the reception given to Tom Burns's interesting socio-psychological study *The BBC, Public Institu-tion, Private World* (1977) showed that, whatever may be true of historians, non-historians may have more difficulty in interpreting an institution than I suggested. Burns's references to 'professionalism', 'managerialism' and 'mission orientation' provoked argument inside the BBC as well as outside, along similar lines of argument to those provoked by *Broadcasting in the Seventies*, and the argument still continues, not least among the professionals.

There is no surviving evidence relating to the 1930s comparable to the evidence Burns collected 'from within' the BBC in more recent years, and what autobiographical evidence there is requires to be treated with some caution. I noted in an adjacent passage in Volume II that most of the accounts of the BBC during these earlier years, covered in my Volume II, were written by 'rebels', by people who were forced to leave the BBC either because they did not like its ethos or because they criticised its organisation.

I now believe that I should have paid more attention in Volume II to what such rebels had to say, but I also believe that had I done so I would still have been required to judge – and sometimes to condemn – the tone and content of their criticisms in the light of my general observation about experience and status within the organisation and within the society. It is fascinating to note that Reith himself ended by being a rebel. Of course, 'official' voices need to be treated just as critically as rebel voices. Oral testimony from established insiders that relates to early years in the Corporation is often tilted by later, 'successful' experience within the hierarchy.

If I were writing a single volume on the history of British broad-casting – and I intend to do so* – it would not be an abridgement of the existing four volumes, if only because I would want to get rid of some of the self-denying ordinances that I had imposed on myself in the four published volumes. I would want, in particular, first to concern myself more fully with controversial issues both in the institution and in the society, now taking for granted the chronicling element; second, to chase 'complex sequences' across different periods, avoiding bound-aries and looking for tendencies, trends, continuities, contrasts and configurations which are not merely 'period' configurations; third, to consider the British experience of broadcasting comparatively along-side experience in other countries; fourth, to continue to make use of new or newly accessible evidence – 'official' evidence, for example, which was previously inaccessible because of the thirty-year rule – and 'unofficial' evidence, derived for example, from magazines, which I used far too little in Volume I in particular; and, fifth, to lengthen my perspectives in relation both to broadcasting and to the economic, social and cultural factors that influenced its evolution, both by looking

---

* I wrote such a volume in 1985, *The BBC: The First Fifty Years*. My approach is clearly set out in my *Preface*. By 1985 I had had access to many new sources, particularly for the pre-history of broadcasting, and for the years after 1945.

backwards to pre-broadcasting years and forwards to years when new technological possibilities and new social options emerged that force us to review the past.

I would want to go beyond the time limits of Volume IV, therefore, into the Greene era and beyond that era through the 'crisis' of the 1970s, down at least to the re-summoning in 1974 of an Annan Committee (with surprising speed) by a new Labour government. The first of these objectives would mean taking a closer look at the limitations on British broadcasting during the 'golden age of wireless', studying what was left out of its scope as well as what was put in. The second would mean relating the attitudes of advertising interests towards Press and radio and television during the 1930s and during the 1950s and re-examining the Act of 1954 in the light of what came afterwards, when 'commercial television' did not take the shape that both its friends and its enemies had forecast.

The third objective would mean pursuing further the contrasts between American and British broadcasting – there are already many side glances of the relationship in the fourth volume – and the perceptions each had of the other, a topic of perennial interest to me. The fourth would mean studying more carefully war-time patterns of broadcasting, war-time official papers relating to post-war broadcasting and the role of propaganda in the various types of programming. The fifth would mean probing more deeply into local, regional and national relationships and the pre-broadcasting history of the curious British dichotomy between education and entertainment, the political economy of both, and the range of changing conceptions of 'culture', an ambiguous, awkward, but much used, term in Britain (not least by Reith).

French writers have analysed 'culture' more searchingly than British writers, and foreign scholars are now beginning to produce interesting work on the BBC, most of it still unpublished. When Leo Lowenthal, called 'popular culture' a concept common to the humanities and to sociology, he was pointing to a whole area which the social and cultural historian must explore, an area far bigger than 'popular culture' itself, however defined. It was one of the few areas, indeed, which was already beginning to be cultivated when I first began to write my *History*.

As a historian, I have been involved in work in two areas of social history which have subsequently 'boomed' – urban history and labour history. I have also turned to 'leisure history', a lively field and a possible boom area of the future, which it is always important to relate to other fields of history. There are few signs so far of broadcasting history booming, although there are now more monographs in preparation than ever before, more revision is being undertaken of work already produced, more national histories of broadcasting systems are being written, often by teams, and more comparative studies are being undertaken of communications structures and policies in different countries. The archives of the BBC are being used by more scholars than ever before, and there is more contact between them. As the possibilities begin to be more widely realised, there will be scope for a more systematic discussion of a wide range of problems than has so far taken place. This article has been written to help discussion to proceed more easily.

8 John Logie Baird: Fifty Years On*

It is just fifty years since John Logie Baird gave his first formal demonstration of television in January 1926 to a rather startled group of members of the Royal Institution, all of them in full evening dress. They had had to climb a rickety staircase in Soho to see what was being shown to them there. Within three years, Baird went on to send signals by landline from London to Glasgow.

Baird had been a student here at the 'Tech' in Glasgow before the First World War, and after five years he took his associateship in electrical engineering in 1914. By a coincidence that was to have consequences long afterwards, he was a fellow student of John Reith, who was to play the dominant role in the making of the BBC. There was, however, little contact between them. Neither seemed a particularly promising scholar.

Strathclyde, which has incorporated the old Andersonian Institution, first commemorated its association with Baird by naming one of its halls of residence after him. Now, as Baird himself would have liked, it has planned a superb exhibition of Baird materials, collected with great assiduity, some of them associated with forgotten phases of Baird's life. My lecture is complementary to the exhibition. Baird believed that pictures should go with words.

The photographs of him in this exhibition tell us something of him – at school he was President of the Photographic Society at a time when photography still presented a technical challenge – as do the various pieces of equipment that he invented a little later in his life. Their names and the advertisements describing them are sometimes just as revealing as the objects themselves, like the original advertisement for 'the Televisor', Baird's first marketable receiving apparatus, which claimed that the 'jesting words' of 'wags of Bell's day, who had said "we shall be seeing over a wire next",' had 'now been made true'.

There is no photograph of the 1926 demonstration, and the words that *The Times* used on that historic occasion were cautious. The

---

* Based on a Memorial Lecture delivered at the University of Strathclyde, 1976, and on an article by me in *Futures* (1977), 'From Prophecy to Prediction: Towards an "Age of Television".'

picture on the screen was described as 'faint and blurred', and the report concluded that it was yet 'to be seen to what extent further developments will carry Mr. Baird's system towards practical use'. Baird himself had been 'thrilled', however, a few months earlier when in the first week of October 1925, after weeks of steady progress, he had observed on his receiving screen the ventriloquist dummy's head that he was using for experimental purposes 'not as a black and white effect but as a real image'.

Baird's next experiment, carried out immediately, led to a seeming setback, for when the first 'living object' that he could find for screening, William Taynton, the office boy from the office below his workshop, replaced the dummy's head, the screen went blank and 'no effort of tuning' could produce any results. Yet the setback did not last long, for once Baird, 'puzzled and very disappointed', had gone back to the transmitter, the cause of failure was immediately apparent to him. 'The boy, scared by the intensely bright light, had backed a yard or so away from the transmitter.' Baird in a brainwave decided to give Taynton a half-a-crown to appear in the bright light, and this time his head was clearly visible on the screen. 'It is curious to consider', Baird stated, 'that the first person in the world to be televised should have required a bribe in order to accept the invitation.'

The way Baird told this story revealed him at his most engaging. For every important turning point in the story of his life he always found an anecdote. And others who were involved with him, like Victor Mills, an early wireless enthusiast, usually found one too. When Mills's hand had been successfully televised two years earlier, Baird himself is said to have called out 'It's here, it's here.' There are many anecdotes in Baird's unpublished autobiography.* One great event of May 1927 was to be the transmission of pictures of himself from London to Glasgow over 438 miles of telephone line, an event backed by the *Daily Mail*. When three months earlier he had visited Glasgow to give a lecture, the Duke of Montrose, in the Chair, had compared him with James Watt. 'Even Papa was impressed', Baird noted.

I have a special interest of my own in some of the anecdotes about the young Baird, since they relate not to Scotland but to Sussex, where Baird was to die – at Bexhill – in 1946. When in 1922, on the advice of his doctor and an old Glasgow friend, 'Mephy', Guy Fullarton Robertson, Baird moved to Hastings – as far south as he could go – this was not the first time that he had travelled so far: some of his first experiments in television before 1914 had been carried out in Brighton.

*The autobiography, *Sermons, Soap and Television*, described as 'autobiographical notes', was to be published in 1988 by the Royal Television Society.

Now, in 1922, a Hastings attic over a seaside flower shop in Queens Arcade (now Queens Avenue) in the centre of the town was the setting where he carried out the crucial, but always hastily improvised, television experiments that led up to the 1926 demonstration.

Baird made his first disc out of an old hat box, used a darning needle as a spindle, housed his first projection lamp in an empty biscuit tin, and bought his first bull's eye lens for fourpence in a bicycle shop. But there was another first too. It was in Hastings that he put his first advertisement in a newspaper, *The Times*, in June 1923:

> Seeing by wireless. Inventor of apparatus wishes to hear from someone who will assist (not financially) in making working model. Write Box S.686.

Perhaps not surprisingly, the advertisement raised no money. None the less, it evoked some interest, for example, from the then Chairman of Odhams Press, W. J. Odhams, a member of the family that by a coincidence also produced John Reith's wife, Muriel. There were some Hastings folk who gave Baird encouragement, too, including Mills, who ran a wireless business, and William le Queux, novelist and writer of features and short stories, some focused on the future.

A year later, Baird finally decided to devote his inventive talents solely to television and not to something else, and he took out his first patent for a 'System of transmitting Views, Portraits, Scenes by Telegraphy or Wireless Telegraphy' in May 1924. It was in Hastings in 1924 that he first demonstrated on the screen the shadow of a small Maltese cross, made by a local schoolboy, transmitted over a distance of a few feet, one of his first practical demonstrations. As early as 1929, a plaque was to be placed in Hastings over the shop above which Baird experimented: it bears the inscription 'Television first demonstrated by John Logie Baird from experiments started here in 1924'.

Hastings was already proud of Baird before television had established itself, but he had had to leave the town hastily, early in 1925, after the Press had reported an explosion in his attic. Already he had amazed local dealers by ordering several hundred torch batteries. Now his experiments were thought to be dangerous, particularly by his landlord. He had to get out.

After his flight from Hastings, Baird took refuge in an even more Bohemian setting, an attic room in 22 Frith Street, Soho, the place with the rickety staircase that members of the Royal Institution had to climb to see his now famous experiment in 1926. There is now a plaque, too, at this address in London where, except for worries about money, he worked in peace.

It was at this stage of his life that Baird won his first real backer, the retailer Gordon Selfridge, who saw the publicity value of Baird's work just as a few years earlier he had seen the publicity value of wireless and had arranged a broadcast by Dame Alice Melba. Selfridge's advertisement of 'the first public demonstration of television by Baird' still survives. 'Television is to light what telephony is to sound', the advertisement read:

> The apparatus here demonstrated is, of course, absolutely 'in the rough' . . . But it does, undoubtedly, transmit an instantaneous picture. The picture is flickering and defective, and at present only simple pictures can be sent successfully; but Edison's phonograph announced that 'Mary had a little lamb' in a way that only hearers who were 'in the secret' could understand – and yet, from that first result, has developed the gramophone of today.

Selfridge described Baird as 'the sole inventor and owner of the patent rights' and added that 'we should perhaps explain that we are in no way financially interested in this remarkable invention'. Selfridge was, in fact, paying Baird, who valued the publicity, £20 a week for three weeks. The money was useful too: Baird had never been paid so much before for a week's work.

Publicity in itself is a major theme in the Baird story, although we do not get to the heart of the story either from advertisements or from anecdotes, however memorable or colourful. It is necessary to examine the context, economic and technological, of Baird's work; to relate the publicity that he coveted and attracted to the technology that he employed; to consider how both publicity and technology influenced the economics of his usually precarious business enterprise, the success of which depended on a motley collection of characters; to draw contrasts between his inventive work and achievement and those of others, particularly those of inventors, unlike himself, who were using electronic rather than mechanical scanning; and, finally, to trace connections between one television invention and another in a communications world explicable less in terms of cause and effect than of intricate and persistent interactions.

As early as 1880, it had been noted in *Nature* that the idea of 'seeing by telegraph' or 'by electricity' belonged to a number of men not to one single individual; and that was twenty years before the word 'television' was apparently used for the first time in French. Its first use in English, independently, may have been in 1909, when Hugo Gernsback, later to pioneer early science fiction magazines, used it in the periodical *Modern Electronics*. Baird took the word for granted, although he invented many others.

The technology provides in some ways the simplest element in what was a long story, for there was to be a winner here – and it was not Baird. The story went back to Edmond Becquerel's discovery of the electro-chemical effects of light in 1839, followed in 1873 by the recognition of the photo-sensitive properties of selenium, the 'moon' element (first isolated in 1816), when exposed to light. A glut of schemes for exploiting these properties followed during the 1880s. It was then that scanning techniques, essential to all television systems, began to be studied. Pictures to be shown on the screen are treated as arrays of small picture elements, and are transmitted in sequence. The receiver of the signals, however, is conscious only of a single continuous image.

The mechanical approach that Baird followed in his experimenting with scanning down to the late-1930s led back to Paul Nipkow's rotating disc, spirally perforated with small holes through which a strong light shone. It was devised in Germany in 1884, but Nipkow never actually constructed a prototype. This approach to television was not to prove as effective in the long run as that through 'electronics', a word which passed into common usage only after Baird's death. There had already been one English pioneer of the second approach, however, before Baird started to experiment. Alan A. Campbell Swinton, born a quarter of a century before Baird, had set out his first ideas on the subject in an article published in *Nature* in 1908 while Baird was still at school.

Campbell Swinton, a founder member of the Wireless Society of London, later the Radio Society of Great Britain, could no more convert into practical inventions his ideas on what he then called 'distant electric vision' than Nipkow had been able to do. Twenty years later, however, when Baird, who loved to produce prototypes, had shown that his mechanical television worked, Campbell Swinton reiterated his initial opinion, based on considerable technical knowledge, that the future lay not with 'mechanical devices' but with 'new promising methods in which the only moving parts are electrons'. 'The only way television can ever be accomplished', he believed, is by using the vastly superior agency of electrons.' Campbell Swinton was not content, however, with such a general statement. Baird, he believed, was 'a rogue', like his backers, and their advertising of the merits of his mechanical system was 'impudent'.

One well-known intellectual was even less sanguine than Campbell Swinton. When told in 1928 that 'sets capable of receiving pictures' were to be shown at a London radio exhibition, Bertrand Russell urged that 'a word of warning' rather than a word of encouragement should be addressed to the public:

There is undoubtedly apparatus capable of transmitting more or less recognisable pictures of still life objects such as a drawing, a page of writing or a stationary illuminated face, but there does not exist, nor, as far as one can see, is there likely to exist in the near future, any apparatus capable of transmitting a real life moving picture such as the Boat Race or the Derby. Even with such transmission as is now possible it is very difficult to see how anything like the broadcasting of pictures can effectively take place. The wavelength band required would be very wide, and it is doubtful if the Post Office would sanction it. The apparatus required in the home would be complicated and delicate, and very likely to get out of adjustment. In fact, the public would be well advised to discount heavily the flamboyant anticipations that have appeared in the non-technical press on this subject.

Not surprisingly, the science fiction author, Arthur Clarke, picked out this passage as one of the silliest predictions made by a distinguished intellectual.

Given such sentiments, so forcefully expressed, it is obviously necessary in paying tribute to Baird to look backwards as well as forwards, particularly as far as the technology is concerned. As early as the 1860s, Sir William Crookes, who figures prominently in the prehistory of broadcasting, had drawn attention to 'cathode rays' and had described what came to be called 'Crookes tubes'; and, a generation later in 1897, one year after Marconi had arrived in London with his bundle of radio patents, Sir J. J. Thomson, Professor of Physics at Cambridge, had confirmed the existence of the electron and had experimented successfully with electric charges.

The crucial further new developments, as far as television was concerned, had been the invention of the diode, 'the Fleming valve', by another Professor of Physics, Sir John Ambrose Fleming (1849–1945), who had been retained as an adviser by the Marconi Wireless Company, and the invention in 1906 of the triode by the American, Lee de Forest (1893–1961), whose approach, like that of Baird – or Marconi – was essentially non-academic. De Forest had three hundred patents to his credit, but in 1906 he did not know how his triode worked. There were bitter patent disputes – some involving Fleming and de Forest – before the formation of the Radio Corporation of America – and the pooling of patents – in 1920. (See above, p. 54.)

The story had been an international story from the beginning. One early pioneer, Ferdinand Braun, was German; another, Boris Rosing, who filed his first patent in 1908, was Russian. Later experimenters included another Russian, Boris Grabovsky, a Hungarian, Von Mihaly, and a Japanese, Kenjiro Takayanagi. After Thomson had confirmed the existence of the electron, the American Robert Millikan had measured its charge. Parallel to the work of RCA, laboratory work went on in England in the factory of EMI, Electrical and Musical Industries Ltd, a 1931 merger between the Gramophone Company, founded in 1898, and other interests. There were links across the Atlantic, however, for some of these interests were American, and after 1934 there were further links with the Marconi Company. Indeed, David Sarnoff and Marconi now sat on the EMI Board. Baird himself had crossed the Atlantic for the first time in 1931 where he was welcomed as a hero.

Developments in electronics were inevitably to become a matter of highly organised international research – as Marconi himself had clearly recognised long before the founding of RCA which had been deliberately designed to check him; and the EMI research team included the Russian-born Isaac Shoenberg, who had joined the Marconi Company in 1914. Among the other members were A. D. Blumlein, G. E. Condliffe, C. O. Browne, J. D. McGee and E. L C. White. They presented their first demonstration to the BBC in 1932, six years after Baird had presented the first of his. They had no more doubt about the advantages of their own approach than did another Russian-born inventor working across the Atlantic, Vladimir Zworykin, who in 1932 produced his first effective 'iconoscope', a charge-storage type of transmitting tube. The British team was to name their similar device the Emitron Camera.

There was one lone American inventor, Charles Francis Jenkins, who followed the mechanical approach, as Baird did, and who succeeded in demonstrating the transmission by television of photographs and maps in 1922 and 1923. His public demonstration of 1925 attracted as much attention across the Atlantic as Baird's British demonstrations. Like Baird, Jenkins was thrilled by publicity: like Baird, too, he was troubled by illness. Eleven years older than Baird, he died, a disappointed man, in 1934. Meanwhile, another lone American, Philo T. Farnworth, born on an Idaho farm, had tried to develop electronic television on his own; he, unlike Jenkins, secured backers and did not entirely fail either on the technical or the business side. Indeed, in 1933 Baird was to borrow from him an electronic camera, a patented 'image dissector', less effective, however, than Zworykin's iconoscope or the Emitron.

It is tempting in dealing with the technical history of television to rest content with broad contrasts between inventors like Baird and Jenkins, who through their publicity put television on the map, and inventors, like Zworykin, who worked quietly inside corporate organisations to make television more perfect. Yet as W. J. Baker recognised in his *History of the Marconi Company* (1970), while it seemed 'ironic that Baird, who contributed not a single invention to television as we know it today, should be regarded by the general public as its father figure, while the names of those who were truly responsible should be known only in electronic circles', it would be wrong 'to begrudge Baird his niche in the public mind'. 'He was, after all, the first man to produce true television pictures, even though his success led many along the blind alley of mechanical scanning.'

In any case, to focus on one single kind of contrast would be as inadequate for an understanding of Baird as to rely only on anecdotes. The first and still most relevant contrast remains that between Baird and Reith, although it is a contrast that has little to do with either technology or economics. Born at Helensburgh in 1888, one year before Reith, Baird died in 1946, a quarter of a century before him. There was an initial similarity, however, as well as a contrast. Like Reith, Baird was the son of a Presbyterian minister, if not the son of a manse, for Helensburgh did not possess a manse: it had a lodge instead, where his father lived, albeit in far more humble circumstances than the Very Reverend George Reith D. D. Baird's father, large, black-bearded and in Baird's own word 'impressive', was 47 years old when Baird was born and he wanted him to go into the Church. Electrical engineering was his own choice. Reith's career pattern was less definite.

There was a physical difference, too, between Baird and Reith. Reith towered and Baird looked frail. Reith had piercing eyes and bushy eyebrows. Baird had weak eyes, eyes that never served him very well. It was ironic that a journalist as early as 1924 produced the headline 'Young Scotsman's Magic Eye' and that in time television was to be called 'the universal eye'.

That, of course, was in the years after Baird's death when the concept of a 'communications revolution' had become widely current. I should emphasise, however, that neither Baird nor Reith would have talked much of 'media'. Reith once or twice did, but more frequently he preferred to talk of public service, while Baird, who talked little of public service, certainly did not conceive of the work that he was carrying out as being the creation of a new medium of communication. He conceived of the new techniques that he was developing in relatively simple terms, moving on from one technique to another before he had perfected the preceding one. For all his determination Baird lived by improvisation.

Reith frequently complained from the mid-1930s onwards that he was not 'fully stretched': Baird was often over-stretched, not least in his first paid job as Superintendent Engineer of the Clyde Valley Power Company. By then, however, he was already inventing. One of his first ventures was marketing 'Baird Undersocks' which kept him warm while he visited Clyde Valley power plant. And next, before turning back to television, which he had played with before 1914, he tried jam, chutney and 'Baird's Speedy Cleaner'. The year when his health broke and he moved to Hastings was the year when Reith became first General Manager of the British Broadcasting Company, discerning the hand of God in his appointment.

The inability of Reith and Baird to get on well was not based entirely, however, on personal incompatibility. The BBC was the first of a number of great organisations which Baird encountered, and it was not only a monopolistic agency, but an institution with a distinctive aura of authority. Not surprisingly, it was the one institution against which Baird thought that he was perpetually pitted. Reith's greatest achievement was to create an institution. Baird's greatest failure was not knowing how to work with one. From the start, he was determined to follow his own course. He refused to obey any set rules. Even late in life, he refused ever to become an organisation man. In no circumstances could he ever have fitted into a team, like the EMI team, and when he found himself dealing with businessmen, as he so often had to do, he was frequently impatient or bored.

Reith could be impatient and bored in dealing with businessmen, too, but he would never have expressed his impatience and boredom in the same way as Baird, who on one occasion, after he had been to the Board meeting of one of the many television companies set up to promote and sell his wares, exclaimed revealingly,

> I was busy with wheels and pulleys most of the time, and I soon came to regard going to board meetings as analogous to going to church, functions to be slept through. Sometimes I woke with a start at the proceedings at these meetings, but after a few questions I relapsed again into dreams of further permutations and combinations of wire and mirror drums and lumps.

Baird was not as practical as this *cri de coeur* suggested. One of the key words in the passage was 'dream'. When he was at school he had read H. G. Wells with great pleasure. Indeed, his delight in Wells's stories continued for all his life until he actually met him, and then it wore a little thin.

Some journalists who believed in dreams – or, at least, claimed that they did – picked out from the start Jules Verne rather than Wells. 'In our laboratories ', one of them wrote in 1926, 'there exists a need for men who can combine the imagination of a Verne with the cold, deliberate work of the men of science.' Baird was neither cold nor deliberate, and he admitted once, when he was talking about the powerful forces which he had had to take account of during the late 1920s and the 1930s, that his own temperament had proved a handicap.

'To face the world single-handed' had been 'sheer insanity.' 'We had against us the whole resources of the United States', including General Electric, Westinghouse and later 'the vast Radio Corporation of America'. They were allied too, with 'the great Telefunken Company in Germany and a host of other European companies'. 'If only we had been able to join the Marconi Company', Baird reluctantly concluded with hindsight, 'we could have been able to meet this combine and not to fight against it.'

It was a special kind of 'sheer insanity' that Baird came best to represent, and it now looks more attractive perhaps, than it did in the 1920s and 1930s. There was a time, not very long ago, when it was fashionable to praise organisation men more than lone individuals. They conformed and they prospered. I have the feeling now, however, that Baird as a quintessential individual appeals to the present generation more than he would have appealed to the intermediate generation of the late 1940s or the early 1950s. The fact that an eccentric genius, surrounded by bits and pieces of wire and every kind of Heath Robinson contraption, was pitting his ideas and his beliefs against a vast concentration of highly organised economic and social forces now seems appealing. So also does the fact that he combined single-mindedness of purpose with a strong sense of humour.

The scientist Sir Edward Appleton, much in demand as a consultant and assessor, and Secretary of the Department of Industrial and Scientific Research in the year when Baird died, described him as a man of engaging simplicity of character, who got as much pain as pleasure out of his inventions, but never lost faith in them or in his own role as inventor. 'Above all, he was a real visionary.' Appleton was himself a radio pioneer and President of the International Scientific Radio Union. He was later to become Principal of Edinburgh University and was a Nobel prizewinner in 1947.

Baird had less to do with academic establishments than with big business – he never got an honorary degree – whereas John Reith was to take immense pride in being elected Rector of Glasgow University. None the less, one phase in Baird's life Reith missed. Baird followed up his time at 'the Tech' with six happy months at Glasgow University. There was one decisive phase in Reith's life, however, that Baird missed. He was never a soldier. The reason was medical unfitness. It was not just that Baird died long before Reith; because of bad health throughout his life he was physically incapable of doing just what he wanted to do.

Reith was not the only person inside the BBC who was suspicious of Baird. It was a very different BBC figure from Reith, Peter Eckersley, its brilliant first Chief Engineer, who stated in a memorandum of 1926 that 'the Baird apparatus not only does not deserve a public trial, but also has reached the limit of its development owing to the basic limitations of the method employed'. Two years later, after the BBC had staged a demonstration on the suggestion of the Post Office, another BBC official, who was equally different from Reith and who even had links with Baird, Gladstone Murray, Assistant Controller in charge of public relations, wrote that 'yesterday's demonstration would be merely ludicrous if its final implications did not make it sinister'.

I have told the story of the subsequent strains and tensions between Baird and the BBC – and the occasional moments of cooperation – in my *Golden Age of Wireless*. They culminated sadly in 1936 when in the contest between Baird's mechanical system and the first British all-electronic system, devised by the team of researchers in EMI, Baird lost. It was a contest called for not by the BBC but by an official committee, the Selsdon Committee, and Baird was shattered by the result. 'To be thrown out by the BBC, after all these years of pioneer work', he wrote later, 'to be displaced by newcomers, was to me a bitter blow.' On this, for him tragic, occasion it did not help that his own financial backers did not seem to him to appreciate just what had been at stake: they thought that he should be content to make and sell television sets.

It so happens that by a series of coincidences, this year is not only the centenary of Bell's invention of the telephone, but also the fortieth anniversary of the first BBC regular television service and the thirtieth anniversary of the resumption of British television after the end of the War, when the screens flickered into life again after a war-time blackout. Ironically, 'the Sleeping Beauty' awoke in the month in which Baird died.

Baird had been hurt on the very day of the official opening of the new television service, 2 November 1936, even though he had won the toss – with a sovereign – and his own transmission system had been allowed the first chance in the race between the rivals. Nobody paid much attention to him, he thought. He did not speak – nor did Reith – and not having been invited to the platform, he had had to sit 'in considerable anger and disgust in the body of the hall among the rank of file'. This was a day when emotion ran high. The announcer, Leslie Mitchell, famed for his presentation of Gaumont British newsreels, was struck by 'sheer, absolute terror'; Gerald Cock, recently appointed BBC Director of Television, who had known nothing about television when he was appointed, was unsure whether anything would work and had a breakdown microphone ready; Jim Mollison, the aviator, who was interviewed as part of the opening programmes, was breathless and ill-at-ease.

The language used by the Vice-Chairman of the Governors of the BBC was apposite enough, however: he spoke of the day as 'historic', 'not less momentous' than the first day of sound broadcasting, fourteen years before, from Marconi House. Meanwhile, the language used by the Baird Company might well have been chosen specially to appeal to viewers in Glasgow had there then been any:

> The whole installation, with typical British thoroughness, is built as solidly as a battleship and is a masterpiece of technical efficiency and engineering ability.

Baird himself might well have employed different imagery.

The Press praised the first day's regular television as it had praised a makeshift, pre-official opening day at Radiolympia earlier in the year, but it cannot have escaped Baird's attention before he lost his place in the race that television performers had not wished to be televised on those occasions in the alternating broadcasting schedule when his own system was in use. 'Don't put us on in the Baird week' they had entreated. There was a further blow, too, in the intervening period. The Baird workshop at the Crystal Palace (what more appropriate setting?) was burnt down and destroyed.

Ten years later, Sir William Haley, one of Reith's successors as Director-General of the BBC, was in charge when post-war television resumed in 1946; and although he was a reluctant promoter of television and was to say far more critical things about it than most people connected with the BBC have ever done, he had, none the less, forecast in October 1945, just after the end of the Second World War, that when 'vision was added to sound' and 'the pictures' had been 'made complete', nations would start exchanging the pictures daily. 'After that', he went on, 'the world will never be quite the same place again.'

Haley's forecast, which focused on news rather than on entertainment, provides a kind of text for the second part of my lecture; indeed, it would have been a suitable text to quote at Baird's memorial service. The social and cultural history of television, like the business history, is more complex than the technical history. An American writer, R. E. Lee, stated in 1944 that 'you don't have to be a Bachelor of Science to operate the modern television receiver'. Yet it is almost necessary to be a Bachelor of Economics to understand the business history of television, and to major in Sociology to examine the role of television in society.

Forecasts of the likely role of television predated the advent of effective technology. They even predated the use of the word. Some of the forecasts were visual, like a Du Maurier cartoon in a *Punch Almanac* in 1879, or the remarkable 1882 sketches of the French artist Albert Robida, whose 'pictures on the wall' were cannily, almost eerily, predictive. The *Punch* cartoon of 1879, published in 1936, showed a picture of the mother and the father of a family sitting with an Edison 'telephonoscope' over their bedroom mantlepiece. The caption read 'Every evening they gladden their eyes with the sight of their children in the Antipodes, and gaily converse with them through the wire.' The picture on the screen showed young men and women dressed in formal style playing a curious looking game that might have been a variation of badminton. In the foreground was a very large dog.

On the facing page in *Punch* in the week of re-publication in 1936 there was an E. H. Shephard cartoon depicting Mr Punch looking gravely at a terrestrial globe on which a small television screen had been inserted. The caption ran 'The Televisionary: I don't care how long it takes me, I'm going to turn and turn until I get a sight of peace.'

A writer in *Chambers' Journal* in 1893 had been more pleading than predictive:

> What is really wanted is the means of doing for the eye what the telephone and the phonograph have accomplished for the ear. Such an instrument does not seem to be outside the range of possibilities, but it will need a genius to work it out.

This statement should be compared with a statement made in 1935 by Captain Robinson in a book called *Televiewing*:

> We must expect swift changes in the manners and customs of the young once television is firmly established. And these changes will react on the whole community. Of course, the changes will depend upon the establishment of television heroes and heroines. The supply of music, drama, information and education in the home parallel to the supply of water, gas and electricity, is a remarkable scientific and commercial achievement. It would seem that there is only needed a world language to bring about a much closer knitting of peoples in understanding. Pictures can provide such a world language in the future. In an intimate house atmosphere the influence of television will begin by providing topics of conversation for us all. For pictures are stimulating to the imagination. From the home this influence will extend to the office and to the works. We may suppose that this new method of presenting ideas will not as much affect the educated and well-read person. It may and will affect those who take all their ideas from the picture papers and the sensational press. Its major influence must be by suggestion. The type of suggestion will depend on

those who provide the programmes. In this country we will be mercifully free from any commercial bias in the matter of programmes as far ahead as we can see.

There was no reviewer of Robinson who was prepared to take him up.

Baird seldom concerned himself with long-term social forecasting. Indeed, he seems to have been somewhat insensitive to major social and political changes. An early article on him, written for the *Kinematography Weekly* even before the demonstration of January 1926, compared him not with Bell but with Edison, the pioneer of the phonograph and the cinema. And this, too, is a strictly relevant comparison. As Baird's wife, Margaret, daughter of a Johannesburg diamond merchant, whom he married in New York in 1931, put it memorably, 'ideas came so fast that he hardly knew which of them to develop first'.*

Already by 1928, Baird had offered to the world along with television 'junior kits', the 'phonovisor', quickly dropped, 'Noctovision' (seeing in darkness by the use of infra-red rays, 'the searchlight that can't be seen'), a television transmission to a ship in the Atlantic, cinematic television and colour television. He had also successfully sent a transAtlantic television transmission from London to New York. The world, in fact, was his parish, in his marketing as much as in his inventions, and he looked to Germany among other countries (until 1933), and to Australia, South Africa and the United States as promising markets overseas. In his own words, 'in the first flush of success we decided to form companies in every country in the world'.

Baird was also interested, like Wells, in the fact that inventions, including those with which he himself was concerned, carried with them a potential both for good and for evil. And, like Wells, he brought war into the picture as well as peace. Thus, his Noctovision experiments of the late 1920s, not in any way precursors of radar, none the less tried to deal technically with the same kind of problems that radar was to deal with – ultimately in wartime.

As far back as December 1926, his friend Captain Hutchinson, who was very closely associated with him, wrote:

> It is difficult to estimate what may be the importance in war of television. It becomes feasible to follow an enemy's movements when he believes himself to be in darkness. Attacking airplanes approaching under cover of night will be disclosed to the defending headquarters. They will be followed

*I had the benefit of reading Margaret Baird's useful account of her husband only after I had delivered my Glasgow Lecture, and I have added this reference.

by searchlights emitting invisible rays, and as these rays will be unseen by them they will continue to approach until without warning they are brought down by the guns of defence.

Hutchinson was thinking only of military 'war uses'. The political and social effect of television on war was to be demonstrated only decades later, long after the Second World War was over.

My subject tonight is television rather than warfare, but you can see from Hutchinson's note how attitudes to television during the 1920s and the 1930s were related to themes that have been examined systematically by a Strathclyde literary scholar, I. F. Clarke, whose work I greatly admire, in his important book *Voices Prophesying War*.

The themes became action themes also in 1939, when more than fifty of the engineers and the staff who had been operating the pre-war television system, including four or five of them who had worked with Baird before they had gone into the BBC, almost immediately found themselves in government research establishments concerned with radar. That was a real as well as an imaginative link. And in the autumn of 1945, many of the people who had been involved with radar during the War moved back again to 'Ally Pally' (Alexandra Palace) ready for the resumption of post-war television. Two of the EMI team were not among them. Blumlein and Browne had been killed in a war-time aeroplane crash.

Baird's business experiences, like his 'private life', went through many phases in peace and war, not many of them happy. The *dramatis personae* changed more than once, but the problems persisted. No-one else spoke Baird's language, and funds were almost always low.

His first backer, Will Day, was a co-patentee. He soon got out. Hutchinson, an Irishman, who had met and dealt with Baird when he was engaged in the soap business before moving to Hastings, stayed longer, becoming Baird's business manager in 1926. In a newly formed Baird Television Ltd he was made a co-director also. All too soon, however, there were quarrels, including a quarrel about the name of a second new company, the Baird Television Development Company, registered in April 1926: Hutchinson wanted to substitute 'British' for 'Baird'.

It was Hutchinson who was responsible for carrying out many of Baird's early negotiations with the BBC and with the Post Office, but he lacked both the patience and the skill to make up for Baird's own deficiencies as a negotiator. He also lacked the know-how to deal adequately with the affairs of a third company, Baird International

Television Ltd, set up in 1928 with an over-subscribed capital of £700,000. This was a large sum – the first capitalisation of the British Broadcasting Company had been £100,000 – but, while Hutchinson was always looking for a 'big deal', the company, now chaired by Lord Ampthill, was never in the same league as the American Telephone and Telegraph Company, RCA or EMI. In 1931, after an unsuccessful trip to the United States, Hutchinson quarrelled with his own Board and resigned. Soon afterwards Sydney Moseley, a journalist, took his place.

The first chairman of the Baird Television Development Company, had been Sir Edward Manville, who was also Chairman of the Daimler Company, and his connection with television was more tenuous than his connection with cars. He had also disturbed Baird by booming at him 'through a cloud of cigar smoke'. There was nothing tenuous, however, about Moseley's interest in television. A wide-awake observer, who described himself as 'Britain's first radio critic', Moseley survived many changes of regime after meeting Baird for the first time at Radiolympia in August 1928. Indeed, he was to become Baird's closest friend and main publicist and biographer (1952) – and the main publicist of television. Unfortunately, he was to prove also to be at least as controversial a figure as Hutchinson.

I owe a debt to Moseley myself, for it was he who provided me with invaluable oral and printed material when I was writing about television in *The Golden Age of Wireless*. I was aware, however, in talking to him of how and why his publicity skills had sometimes turned into handicaps. He had personal links with the BBC, which he knew how to exploit, but he made a great mistake in always dramatising Baird's relationship with it. 'Hostilities' was one of his favourite words. 'The struggle to put Baird over with the BBC', he was to write in his biography, 'is more or less a *guerre à mort*, no holds barred.'

Baird's own delight in publicity was fuelled, not controlled, by Moseley. He arranged some striking *coups*, like the gift of a television set to the prime minister, Ramsey MacDonald in 1930, a gift that elicited a personal letter for Baird, which included the words 'what a marvellous discovery you have made! when I look at the transmission I feel that the most wonderful miracle is being done under my eye'. Yet for every such Moseley *coup*, there was an ill-timed publicity leak, calculated to irritate the BBC. Its officials studied Press comment – and Baird without any help always attracted this – with what in retrospect was undue sensitivity.

Not all the sensitivity was undue. When after one such leak in 1928, on the eve of the BBC's first television trials, *The People* described 'the attitude of the BBC in regard to this amazing British invention' as 'absolutely incomprehensible' the BBC was rightly annoyed, as it was three days later, when after the *Financial Times* had reported a *rapprochement* between the Baird Television Development Company and the BBC, the Company's shares rose, as Baird International shares were to do more than once on rumours of foreign deals. There was ample room for sensitivity on this score, and not surprisingly, when Reith first met Hutchinson, he began by asking him about the financial pattern of Baird interests. Meanwhile, the popular Press, cultivated by Baird, did not speak with one voice. *Titbits*, widely read, once described 'television fever as a sure symptom of the silly season'.

Baird was unfortunate in the timing of his inventions, a point made by few of his biographers, who leave the economics out. The Wall Street crash of 1929 shattered many business hopes; and 1931, a year of national financial and political crisis in London, when Baird incongruously succeeded in televising the Derby, was an economic crisis year for him too. He sold out to the Ostrer brothers of Gaumont-British Ltd, millionaires who wished to exploit big screen television in cinemas. Moseley remained as Director of Programmes, but in 1932 Isidore Ostrer formally took over as Chairman, bringing with him two of his own nominees, one of whom, Sir Harry Greer, was to appear on the platform at BBC Television's opening in 1936.

Baird, for all his dislike of giant companies, would have preferred at this stage to have linked up with the Marconi Company, but he and two of his supporters on the Board, Moseley and Captain A. G. D. West, formerly Chief Research Engineer in the BBC, were outvoted. Instead, Marconi linked up with EMI, a move that jeopardised Baird's future far more than Reith could have done. Another Baird financial move that failed was a possible link between the Baird Company and General Electric. The result on this occasion was that Moseley, much to Baird's chagrin, was forced off the Board.

There were bursts of publicity during these difficult years, not all of them – or most of them – concerned with finance. Thus there was an impressive new Selfridge demonstration in 1932, and in July of the same year a big screen television appearance of the comedian George Robey, the politician Herbert Morrison and the Chief Scout, Lord Baden-Powell, at the Coliseum. In 1936 there was a further demonstration at the Dominion Theatre in Tottenham Court Road – this time of colour television. Unfortunately for Baird, no demonstrations, however dramatic, could by then make up for failure on other fronts, particularly failure in the BBC trials.

When the Board tried to place its main emphasis on the sale of Baird television receivers after that failure, Ostrer backed Baird, and it was at his suggestion, and not that of Baird, that Moseley returned to the Board. And yet another new company was founded, Cinema-Television Limited, which with its large nominal capital of £250,000 could control the older Baird Television Ltd. Baird himself became President of the new company, which did not bear his name – Edison had had the same experience – and Moseley became a Director. Greer, however, remained as Chairman of Baird Television Ltd, hardly a recipe for success. Despite considerable evidence of new drive, demanded by Ostrer, neither the new nor the old ventures were successful, and soon 'the house was as divided' as 'Manville's house' had been.

This was not the nadir of Baird's fortunes. The outbreak of the War in 1939 was an even bigger blow for him than his failure to win the BBC's race three years earlier. He was now ill once again and desperately short of money, this time not just money for business but money on which to live, although he rejected various invitations from Moseley, who had moved to the United States, to leave the country and to join him there. He continued with his experiments, strongly supported by his wife. But he only just survived the War.

The story of Baird as I have told it has more than one sub-plot. To my mind the best summing up of his historical significance is still that which was made by the first Chief Engineer of the BBC, Peter Eckersley, himself a controversial character, who wanted to do justice to him. Eckersley had been one of the Writtle boys, working at Chelmsford with the Marconi Company before the BBC came into existence, and, like Baird, he enjoyed improvising and doing things in his own highly individualistic way. But Eckersley did not like Baird and was very suspicious of some of the claims that Baird made:

> The world which enjoys today's television [he wrote] is indebted to Baird for calling attention in 1927 to the fact that the existence of the valve and the light cell converted television from the theoretical concept it had long been into a practical possibility. Baird is to be honoured, therefore, among those who see past immediate technical difficulties to an eventual technical achievement. Marconi did much the same with radio. Neither Baird nor Marconi were primarily scientists or physicists, they had, however, that flair for picking about on the scrap heap of unrelated discoveries and assembling the bits and pieces to make something out of them, to make something work, and so to reveal possibilities which had not been understood before.

Eckersley had little to say about the EMI team. Neither it, nor Baird, he concluded, 'nor anyone else invented television: no one can invent a principle, protection is only given to a process of manufacture'.

If Eckersley's summing up focuses on the most important aspect of Baird's personality as well as of his achievement, there are, none the less, complexities that affect any summing up. It was not only that the particular television technology which eventually triumphed and served as the basis of a regular television service was not that which Baird himself had invented or which he was seeking to perfect. It was that Baird's own attitude towards cathode tubes, basic to the rival system, was never entirely consistent. On several occasions during the early 1930s he stated that the kind of system that was ultimately worked out by EMI could not be perfected. Yet by the end of the 1930s he himself was producing televisors with tubes, and during the course of the Second World War he was actively experimenting to try to perfect what was essentially someone else's system. How much he himself knew about electronics is in doubt. There is no evidence that he ever studied the relevant literature. In fact, the duality of the two systems in the 1920s and 1930s had already been anticipated by 1914. There were already two ways of looking into the future before Baird effectively started his successful television experiments in 1923 and 1924.

A further complexity in any summing up relates not to technology but to institutional structures. For Baird to have been successful in making use of his inventions, he would have had to depend on the BBC with which he had the oddest of relationships. He could not ignore the BBC, although he must have been greatly tempted at times to do so. Instead, he had to work through it – and there were many BBC people, all committed to sound broadcasting, involved in the protracted process of negotiation – because the BBC had a monopoly, granted it by the State, to provide broadcast programmes. It was not surprising that many of Baird's backers, who would have felt easier in the United States, tried to persuade him to put all his efforts into producing receiving sets and to forget about the production and transmission of programmes. Fortunately or unfortunately, Baird never looked at television or at business so single-mindedly. He moved on from one invention to another, never perfecting any single one of them.

Baird was never given any backing by government despite the flattering letter from Ramsay MacDonald. No national honours came his way. He had to rest content with the Honorary Fellowship of the Royal Society of Edinburgh. Yet ultimately, as Reith recognised more clearly than Baird, the BBC's television policy was strongly influenced by, if not dictated by, Post Office and Treasury; and it was the government, not the BBC, that insisted on the trial of the two television systems which ended far more quickly than Baird had expected. The BBC's revenues accrued not from market operations but from licence fees, and successive governments were not prepared to make separate subventions for television.

The victors in the trial had reiterated quietly time and time again that they would not present any results for anybody, including the BBC and government, until they were satisfied that their new devices would work, and they knew that there was a great deal of money at stake. Meanwhile, the BBC knew more about EMI than it was allowed to say, and this inevitably produced some of the misunderstandings with Baird. As for the government, EMI's electronic solution was a more interesting one than Baird's. It seemed likely to have greater spin-off.

The scientists were on the side of EMI when they knew about it. Thus, the Professor of Physics at Trinity College, Dublin, John Walton, who shared a Nobel Prize with Sir John Cockcroft, argued as early as 1930 that 'if television is to be done successfully, it must be by using cathode ray tubes. All the mechanical systems are doomed to failure.' Like Bertrand Russell, however, the scientists had their limitations. Walton made his remarks about the future of cathode tube television to a future member of Shoenberg's team, J. D. McGee, who was then a nuclear physics research student in the Cavendish Laboratory. McGee was looking for a job, and when he said that he was going to take one with EMI in order to develop television, the comment of another Nobel Prizewinner, Professor James Chadwick, was short, if not sweet – 'Oh well, McGee you'd better take it, I doubt if this television will ever amount to much, but at any rate it will keep you going until we can get you a proper job.' Obviously, there were scientists as well as sound broadcasters who did not believe that television was a serious pursuit.

9 John Reith: A Centenary Profile*

Eighteen years separate us from the death of John Charles Walsham Reith, first Baron Reith of Stonehaven and architect, and many have said father, of the BBC. He was born at Stonehaven, near Aberdeen, on 20 July 1889, the fifth son of a distinguished minister and later Moderator of the United Free Church of Scotland.

In the words of an obituary leader in the *Daily Telegraph* in 1971, Reith was 'a huge bear of a man, who defended strict standards of morality and taste with courage, arrogance and often ferocity'. And so he was – a great authority figure, known as such to a huge public before and after he left the BBC. 'The Tsar of the BBC' was one of the many non-official titles bestowed on him. Another, better remembered, was 'Wuthering Heights'. Lord Hill called him 'a man and a half'. Others drew comparisons with Moses and Elijah. The *Daily Telegraph*, having focused on the personality, ended its leader with a plea for the maintenance of the BBC as a 'public service'. 'Though it has changed greatly, it is on his well-designed foundations that it has been re-fashioned. It has retained the independence for which Reith fought.'

During the eighteen years since 1971 we have moved further and further away from what came to be called in Reith's own lifetime 'Reithian' conceptions of public service broadcasting. Yet as long ago as 1958 when as a young historian I was asked to write 'a history of broadcasting in the United Kingdom', Reith was doubtful about the Reithian credentials of the BBC as it then was. When I invited him to lunch to enlist his support – very necessary support – for the venture, he told me as he left that had I written my letter of invitation to him on BBC notepaper he would have 'cast it at once into the flames'.

The words linger in my mind as does the recollection of his towering physical presence. Over 6 feet 6 inches in height, he was a giant whom few men could look at face to face until John Freeman with his

---

*This paper is based on an article in the *Daily Telegraph*, 15 July 1990, although it is greatly extended and draws on an earlier article of mine on Reith in *The Listener* and a paper on 'Authority' delivered at a symposium on broadcasting at Leeds Castle in 1980 and subsequently published in R. Hoggart and J. Morgan (eds.), *The Future of Broadcasting* (1982).

television cameras looked at him face-to-face sitting down. One who could literally stand up to Reith was Sir Hugh Greene, who became Director-General of the BBC, a very different Director-General from Reith, two years after I started writing my history. Greene confessed no 'awe' of him, and even succeeded for a time, but only for a time, in tempting Reith back within the portals of Broadcasting House. The two of them not only on one occasion discussed current BBC programmes, a difficult topic of discussion in the early 1960s, given that one of the programmes was *That Was The Week That Was*, but once took part in a game of 'rough croquet' with 'another pair of giants' at the BBC's management training school at Uplands.

That was the high point. Thereafter, misunderstandings multiplied, and after an awkward telephone call – and Reith loved the telephone – the two men never spoke again. In an earlier telephone call to a wartime Director-General R. W. Foot, a call that came to him out of the blue on the first day he had entered his frighteningly empty office, Reith told him that he should never have been appointed. The longest telephone call I have ever had in my own life was with Reith. He rang me to tell me that he was going to destroy the diaries that he had laboriously kept day by day. I knew that he never would do so, but I had to pretend that he might. It was like arguing with a man who says he is going to jump from a tower. The next time I saw Lady Reith she said that if her husband had destroyed them it would have made a mockery of the whole of their life together, for after any visit to the theatre or dinner party he had rushed to his diary as soon as he returned home.

I quickly lost my own awe of Reith as I met him frequently, and I was allowed access to all his papers, including his most private, and to all his diaries, then unpublished. I was given what he called the freedom of Lollards Tower, his apartment, appositely named, in Lambeth Palace. The setting was old, but I soon learned how interested Reith was in new things. That was what had appealed to him most when he became first General Manager of the British Broadcasting Company, the commercial progenitor of the BBC, in 1922, when it had a tiny staff of three (there were less than 35,000 wireless licences then), and little sense of direction. He was himself only 33 years old. I was engaged myself after 1961 in building up the new University of Sussex, and Reith once wrote to me that it must be 'fun' to be starting it. In 1923, when the new BBC acquired its first notepaper, he had written proudly to his mother that the letter was 'the first sheet of paper with my name on it'.

'There were no sealed orders to open', Reith wrote soon after he was appointed. 'The commission was of the scantiest nature', he went on.

'Very few knew what broadcasting meant; none knew what it might become.' Long before 1938, when he left the BBC, the term 'age of broadcasting' had become familiar and there was little doubt that he personally presided over it. Since 1927, the BBC had been a public corporation, a natural institution and not a business company. Its authority – and it was a word that Reith liked – rested on a Royal Charter, not on an Act of Parliament; and its operational *rationale* as a non-profit-making public corporation was defined by Reith himself and not by the government.

It had 'Governors', a carefully chosen word, not members of a committee, and it enjoyed a monopoly which long outlasted Reith's leaving the Corporation and which he continued to defend long after he had left it. He never hesitated to justify the 'brute force' that went with it, force that enabled it to maintain standards and defy a cultural Gresham's law that entailed the bad driving out the good. Reith, thinking of himself essentially as a public (not a civil) servant, spoke also of 'the public interest'. That counted for him more than the distinctive mode of finance of British broadcasting – by income derived from nationally levied licence fees.

Reith extolled the merits of this system of broadcasting wherever he travelled at home or abroad, and he succeeded in persuading some countries in the British Empire (and that is how he thought of it) to adopt versions of it themselves. As a result, people all over the world, including Americans, were in no doubt what *British* broadcasting meant. British meant Reithian. By 1938 the BBC had a staff of 4000, and there were over six and-a-half million wireless licences.

Seven years earlier, the then fashionable novelist Gilbert Frankau had written an interesting profile of Reith for the *Strand Magazine* in which he dwelt primarily on Reith's authority.

> I, for one [he began] am always a little amazed at realising him five years younger than myself. For not only is his appearance one of authority: but when he speaks – and he is one of the very few after-dinner speakers in London worth listening to – his voice, no less than what he says, confirms the impression that here at any rate, in an age of almost universal flabbiness is a leader, a man of forthright competence, who both understands and means to carry on with his job.

A later generation, less drawn to the idea of leadership, would have chosen the word 'professional' to capture this sense of competence; and it was a word that was to dominate much of the discussion of broadcasting during the 1960s and 1970s. Yet the sources of Reith's authority lay outside rather than inside the daily routines of broadcasting, and people could like him – or dislike him – irrespective of whether or not they approved of this or that radio programme or even of the whole balance of British broadcasting. 'Authority' for Reith – and the monopoly that went with it – were necessary not just on technical grounds but on grounds of values, and ultimately these were inner values, more complex than most people realised. The private Reith was hidden from view, and the occasional glimpses outsiders had of him were contradictory.

It would be a mistake, none the less, to focus exclusively on 'authority', a word with an aura around it. Reith's view of broadcasting rested on the responsibility of broadcasters to give thousands of people access to purposes – and pleasures – that had hitherto been confined to the few; and most broadcasters, though not all, responded to the challenge. 'We were on trial against the measure of our ambitions', Peter Eckersley wrote, 'and so we never became complacent.'

Access meant as much to Reith as responsibility, and one of the most striking passages in his early *Broadcast Over Britain* (1924) reads:

> Till the advent of this universal and extraordinarily cheap medium of communication a very large proportion of the people were shut off from first-hand knowledge of the events which make history. They did not share in the interests and diversions of those with fortune's twin gifts – leisure and money. They could not gain access to the great men of the day, and these men could deliver their messages to a limited number only. Today all this has changed.

In another chapter Reith wrote of access to music as well as to words. He believed that music could appeal to far more people than the limited numbers of existing 'music lovers' who took it for granted.

Reith wrote a foreword to Percy Scholes's *Everybody's Guide to Broadcast Music* (1925) in which Scholes prophesied that

> in five years time the general musical public of these islands will be treble or quadruple its present size. And the next generation, instead of regarding a symphony as a mysterious contrivance of concerted boredom, will accept the great symphonies of the world as part of its regular daily or weekly pleasures.

As Nicholas Kenyon has pointed out in his admirable book *The BBC Symphony Orchestra, 1930–1980* (1981), it did not help when Sir Thomas Beecham, as large a character as Reith, could write in a provincial newspaper in 1928 that 'there has been committed against the unfortunate art of music every imaginable sin of commission and omission, but all previous crimes and stupidities pale before the latest attack on its fair name – broadcasting it by means of wireless'.

That is only one example, if a particularly memorable one, of the kind of nonsense the young Reith had to take note of, not just from musicians but from some, but fortunately not all, owners of news-papers, theatre managers, sports promoters – and canons of cathedrals. It was a source of necessary encouragement when anyone agreed with him that what was being said was nonsense. Often, however, he was driven by frustration to dispose of it in silence in his diary.

When Reith left the BBC in 1938, many of the public assessments of his work as Director-General had the quality of obituary notices. 'Sir John Reith's resignation closes the first chapter in the history of broadcasting in these islands' was a characteristic judgement. 'What might have happened had it been someone else?' was a characteristic question. Reith himself had felt from the start that he had been called upon and entrusted to carry out 'great work', and later on he was to maintain that the Almighty had helped him 'materially all through' his years at the BBC. 'He was there in my receiving that job and was there in the execution of the job.'

At the time, others were there, too, notably from 1923 to 1938 his henchman, Rear-Admiral Carpendale, a man of very different quali-ties. And at the start or before the start, Reith himself had owed much to the politician Sir William Bull, a small-firm Director of the original British Broadcasting Company, who mentioned Reith's name in the right places. Reith himself had made the most of his place of birth when in 1922 he had applied for the position of first General Manager. He had posted his application for the job in the letter box of his club without knowing anything of Sir William Noble, Chairman of the Company, to whom the letter had to be addressed. Aware of possible opportunities – and dangers – he consulted *Who's Who* and discovered that Noble was an Aberdonian. Resourcefully he extricated his letter from the box, not without difficulty, and added to it the words 'No doubt you know my people in Aberdeen.'

Reith got the job although he knew nothing of broadcasting, less than the first listeners, and all that *Wireless Weekly* could say about him then was 'A high broadcasting official – Mr. J. C. W. Reith – is six feet six inches in height.' Yet within two years he produced at great speed the most remarkable of his books, *Broadcast Over Britain*, far more interesting than his somewhat bleak autobiography *Into the Wind* (1949), a book 'written mostly by night' that he felt 'had to be done'. His first book, a study of great vision which could have been written by nobody else revealed that he by then knew everything about broad-casting. It revealed also how much attention he paid to 'public service'. 'The Company is not out to make money for the sake of making money', he emphasised, 'Indeed, by its constitution – [and this was five years before it was converted into a public corporation] – it was debarred from doing so.'

'I think it will be admitted by all', Reith added with vigour in a passage that has been quoted many times and has made its way even into general history books, 'that to have exploited so great a scientific invention for the purpose and pursuit of "entertainment" alone would have been a prostitution of its powers and an insult to the character and intelligence of the people.'

There would be no centenary articles about Reith had he not created a national broadcasting institution based on a conception of public service and an ethical approach to 'the best' in 'culture'. 'Broadcasting is a servant of culture, and culture has been called the study of perfection.' Not surprisingly, therefore, for years the BBC was thought of in some quarters as a model, and Reith himself looked back longingly to it after he had ceased to be Director-General in 1938. It had been 'stupendous folly', he wrote in a postscript to *Into the Wind*, 'to have left one of the most responsible and rewarding posts in all the world'. None the less, had Reith not been an extraordinary character, an unforgettable personality, like Montagu Norman, the Governor of the Bank of England, whom he knew well and with whom he was often compared, such centenary articles would have lacked savour. So, too, would they have done if everyone had agreed with him. One person who did not was Virginia Woolf. She called the BBC 'the Betwixt and Between Company': it claimed to serve as 'a broker between high and low culture without understanding either'.

The fact that Reith was controversial in his own time, and that the controversy started inside the BBC, where most people looked up to him, must be the starting point for any centenary appraisal, though it is a fact that has been implicitly denied by writers who claim that the Reithian BBC was more a child of its time than a child of Reith.

During the 1920s he was ill at ease with his own Governors, many of whom he despised and vilified – 'damn silly' he called them, with an extra grudge against Mrs Philip Snowden whom he described 'as a truly terrible creature, ignorant, stupid and horrid'; while during the 1930s his 'dictatorial' staffing policies – the dictatorship started at the interview stage – were called into question, sometimes inside Parliament. Many of his staff defended him, knowing he left them with ample discretion, but there were some who dreamed of a change of regime.

Reith himself was unrepentant about his judgements, and towards the end of his life he warned Glasgow students in a stirring and thoroughly unorthodox Rectorial Address that in life they would come up against 'almost incredible inefficiency, incapacity, stupidity, unreliability and indifference'. It was a *cri de coeur*, followed by the De Gaullian phrase *C'est moi qui parle*.

In *Who's Who* Reith did not choose to insert his exact day of birth,

yet he had as strong and as distinctive a sense of destiny as the man with
whom he was so often to clash, in a different way 'a huge bear of a man'
also, Winston Churchill. It was Churchill who described the tone of
Reith's BBC as 'pontifical mugwumpery'. Reith once described him in
simpler language as 'a bloody shit'.

Trained narrowly as an engineer – and he deeply regretted, even
resented, the narrowness – Reith might well have been killed by a
sniper's bullet in 1915, when he was in France, a soldier 'wearing
spurs'; and the 'escape' left him not only with a conspicuous scar but
with a brooding sense that he might then, like so many others, have
disappeared from history. War, face-to-face war, was more at the heart
of his own experience than it was even of Churchill's. Why, he complained to me after Freeman's *Face to Face* interview, had Freeman not
asked him about the scar? Reith felt no tranquillity in recollection.
A man of memories and fantasies, which influenced the national
institution that he created almost as much as his philosophy did, he
was always something more and something less than the BBC.

The sixteen years when he was in charge of its fortunes were, indeed,
only a short period in a long life, shorter than the twenty-five years
of his early life which he had spent in Glasgow. Nor was broadcasting
Reith's only interest. He dreamed at times of being Minister of Defence,
Ambassador to the United States, Viceroy of India, Governor General
of the Central African Federation and even, though he was always
deeply suspicious of politicians, Prime Minister. 'Party allegiance is, to
the country's loss, more horizontal than vertical, more social than
moral.' One of the most striking things about him was that, unlike
most public figures, he exposed such 'ambitions' in public. They
figured prominently in *Into the Wind* (1949), and they dominated large
sections of his voluminous diaries which, when published in 1975,
endangered or, for some, destroyed his reputation. 'I could scarcely
believe my eyes', wrote one critic, 'as I found myself reading tirades
of violent unreasoning abuse and catalogues of self praise.' Reith's
impulse to destroy them may have been right, although his will to do
so was lacking.

There are brutal passages in the diaries that still shock, although they
were never a place for what Reith would have deemed considered
judgements, and my own personal judgement on them differs sharply
from some of the reviewers of Charles Stuart's selected edition of 1975.
Reith used diaries to let off steam as well as to leave a record. Interspersed with a terse catalogue of engagements there is an indulgent
re-creation in often ill-chosen words both of dreams and of nightmares. Some comments have more than a touch of absurdity. Thus,
when Reith actually did achieve one old ambition, that of being Lord

High Commissioner to the Church of Scotland, he wrote simply in his diary 'extraordinary how completely naturally I have slipped into vice-regality'.

'I am obsessed by my own fate,' he wrote on another occasion, 'and by a desire for revenge for my treatment, by a sense of injury', adding that he had 'no ordinary kindness or tolerance', a judgement that would have been contradicted by many of his friends, at least as far as the 'kindness' was concerned. Indeed, in outlining his 'ethic' to Malcolm Muggeridge in remarkable televised interviews in 1967 – more remarkable than the Freeman interview – Reith chose to put 'kindness' second among virtues after 'truth in oneself and in one's actions and in one's believing'. 'That's a quality which one doesn't find as much of as in the past.'

Nearly twenty years before interviewing Reith, Muggeridge had referred in 1949 to 'his gaunt angular spirit' which continued 'to brood over Broadcasting House', an image which persists. Yet the 1967 interviews, like Andrew Boyle's biography of Reith that appeared, with his blessing in 1972, showed convincingly that this image was incomplete. It left out his snobbery, a thoroughly unattractive quality, but it left out his smile too, a smile that for those who knew him was more impressive than his frown. I had no doubts that Reith and Muggeridge would get on well when they met, and told Reith so when he expressed his own doubt to me as to whether he should see him. And this, I knew, would have little to do with the established image or with the image of the Reithian BBC that had been one of the main objects of a younger Muggeridge's scorn, although the element of despair in Reith would be a matter for more than polite conversation.

Unfortunately Reith never disposed of the image that he himself had done so much to create. The fact that he died proclaiming in public as well as in private that his life had not been a success, but a failure – he had seldom been fully 'stretched', his favourite word – was embarrassing to his listeners, friends as well as enemies. So, too, were comments like 'output factor from February 1942 to November 1947 about 30 per cent; for the last two years of this period 15 per cent', a sentence solemnly written into the postscript to *Into the Wind*.

On his death in 1971, there was a surfeit of obituaries, many of them written by people who had never met him, let alone known him, and one obituary leader in a provincial newspaper was headed 'Man who was sure'. No headline could have been less true. Doubtless, most centenary assessments will concentrate on the changes in a society and culture – perhaps politics – since 1938 or since 1971 that have made him look like a figure from the distant past and that have encouraged – or forced – the BBC to cast off its Reithian aura. The consensus summary will surely be – and I have done something myself elsewhere to formulate it – that given the changing times it had no choice.

Reith himself, however, wanted to be outside time, and would have been sceptical of centenaries. He once told me that his favourite quotation ran 'We must wait till time is exhausted, and we can look back on these scenes of struggle from the realms of security where friendship is everlasting, where the only change is an increase of love, and the only rivalry that of benevolence.'

10   Local and Regional: The Story of Broadcasting in the North of England*

This essay was completed on the day when Radio Trent, a Nottingham-based commercial radio station, first went on the air – 3 July 1975. The coincidence in timing is interesting not only because of the theme of the paper – local and regional sound broadcasting – but because for centuries the River Trent has figured in English historical geography – and, indeed, in popular advertising – as a 'natural' dividing line between North and South. This was so long before southerners felt that 'anything beyond the Trent' was 'a mass of cobblestones, fog and industry'.

During its early formative years in Leeds, the Northern History Group, which I helped to create, spent much of its time discussing where 'the North' and where 'the South' might be said to begin, and in those discussions the role of the River Trent figured inevitably – and prominently. Yet even the most cursory study demonstrated that the river is not a divide and that its role as a boundary between regions is and has been far more complex than bridges over the Trent suggest. Similar complexities apply in attempts to define the area of what is now called 'the minor conurbation' of the 'East Midlands' with its Northern and Midlands affiliations and with its Eastern ramifications. By comparison, Leeds is unequivocally 'Northern', distant though it is in miles and in outlook from the historic 'North Country' in the North-East and along the Border, country well described in relation to the eighteenth century by Professor Edward Hughes in his *North Country Life in the Eighteenth Century* (1952).

While the Northern Group was discussing regional characteristics, the BBC, which from the mid-1920s had been concerned with them in practice, was taking decisions. Doubts were often expressed during the late 1940s as to whether Nottingham and Nottinghamshire should fall within the BBC's North Region with its capital in Manchester or the Midland Region with its capital in Birmingham, and it was not until 1950 that an East Midlands Representative began to be based on Nottingham within the Corporation's well-established but often controversial regional structure. (A talks studio in Lincoln belonged to the

*Based on an article 'Local and Regional in Northern Sound Broadcasting' in *Northern History*, vol. x (1975).

North.) Within the same regional structure Leeds had always enjoyed separate facilities from those provided in Manchester, and it was gaining in importance within the regional pattern in the immediate post-war years, linking areas – agricultural as well as industrial – within the North Region which from other points of view were distinct, even 'separatist'.

In 1975 broadcasting has quite different patterns and perspectives. The creation of Radio Trent, following in the wake of the BBC's own Radio Nottingham, the fourth of a series of BBC 'experimental' radio stations to open in January 1968, represents a topical triumph of 'local' over 'regional' interests, and both the BBC and commercial interests have been at pains to distinguish between the two. 'Once the area served becomes larger than a single community', Radio Leeds told the Leeds Junior Chamber of Commerce in February 1969, when the latter asked why regional services were not being expanded, 'time on the air to each local population grouping has to be rationed with the result that listeners would lose all sense of local appeal.' On similar lines, a Bow Group Report of 1970, advocating the further expansion of local commercial radio, actually picked out Leeds as an example to bring out the difference between 'local' and 'regional' in broadcasting. 'The BBC station for Leeds', it said, 'is local radio. But a BBC station for the West Riding would not be local radio. The area covered would be too wide, the population too varied: it would be regional radio writ small.'

The contrast in pattern and perspective is already a matter for historical study, and it is interesting to note that the claims of the 'local' in broadcasting have been propounded more and more eloquently during a period when the claims of the 'regional' in government, administration and planning have been advanced with authority. This is a second contrast (or reaction) which would deserve a paper in itself. This essay is concerned exclusively, however, with aspects of the relationship between 'local' and 'regional' in sound broadcasting.

There are good reasons for concentrating on somewhat neglected areas of cultural history rather than extending or deepening what is already known in general terms at least about 'local' and 'regional' aspects of economic history, including transport history, or about urban spheres of influence in surrounding areas. There are, of course, parallels between the history of physical communications and of broadcasting – and some of the same techniques employed by geographers can be used in analysing 'networks' in both – just as there are useful ideas and concepts and techniques to be borrowed by historians of broadcasting from those geographers who are concerned with urban dominance and dependence.

There are good reasons of a different kind, too, for concentrating on the cultural content, realised or potential, of 'local' and 'regional' broadcasting, given that in most current public debate about 'regionalism' in England (although not in Scotland and Wales), emphasis is usually placed almost exclusively on the powers and responsibilities of government and administration at a 'regional level' intermediate between the 'local' and the 'national'. Here again, however, it is useful to borrow from the recent constitutional debate, recognising that the term 'local' at first sight seems highly simple and straightforward, particularly in a North of England which has been riddled historically with local rivalries. Meanwhile, the term 'regional' remains 'versatile' or even vague.

The theme of the essay is interesting to pursue for a further reason. When the BBC moved deliberately from regional patterns of organisation to 'local radio in the public interest', some BBC administrators at least, tended to assume that 'the traditional English regions were artificially created by the BBC' during the 1920s and the early 1930s and that 'the concept "region" now so familiar to us in connection with British Rail, Economic Planning, the Gas Board and so on – was practically unheard of before the BBC introduced it'. This is an exaggeration, for fifty years earlier than the assumption was made, C. B. Fawcett, in his *Provinces of England* had considered most of the issues which confronted the young BBC. He even compared Leeds and Nottingham as 'provincial capitals' at the northern and the southern end of a great coalfield, the development of which had already transformed English economic geography. 'At the northern end is Leeds', he wrote. 'At its southern end is Nottingham, out of the lowland, a bridge-town on the Trent and a node of more numerous but less definite and important natural routes than Leeds.' It was as a result of his analysis that Fawcett identified an East Midlands Region – he called it 'Trent' at first – adding that 'the central position of Nottingham would probably enable it to unify the life of the province; but it is not likely to be able to dominate that life to any great extent'.

The BBC's 'North Region' was far bigger than any of Fawcett's 'regions' or 'provinces'. It accounted, indeed, for one-third of England, and included not only some of the most dense concentrations of industry in Europe but also large agricultural areas. It represented 'history' and 'progress', and there were many internal contrasts within it. Even its four large cities – four out of the six largest in the country – were themselves conscious not only of historical difference but of current rivalry. In the North was Fawcett's 'North England' province, which incorporated not only Hughes's 'Old North' but part of Yorkshire's North Riding. In the South were parts of his 'Peakdom' and of his East Midlands. In the West were portions of Staffordshire as well as

Cheshire. This 'region' was not created by one single great act of policy, Reithian or otherwise. It took shape gradually, and as it took shape the BBC was forced at almost every critical point in the story to consider the relationship between the 'local' and the 'regional', not simply in terms of 'devolution', the terms in which it is often thought of in current debates about government and administration, but in terms of cultural identity and activity. It had to take account, therefore, of forces working 'from below' as much as of decisions arrived at in broadcasting offices. 'It will be our aim', one of the chain of North Regional Directors put it in 1945 – and he was speaking for those who came before and after him – 'to represent the North in its modern aspect – its cultural, musical, sporting, intellectual, and industrial life . . . I believe the North will, once again, emerge as the great originator of experiment.'

Such terms did not merely place 'the North' in an older context of London versus 'the provinces', a familiar theme in English history, cultural and otherwise. They directed attention to the relationship between 'localities' and 'regions'. Reith was surprised no less as a Scotsman than as General Manager of the BBC to learn in the earliest days of broadcasting that Sheffield preferred to be linked as a local radio station with London rather than with Manchester. This was before the 'North Region' was created, and during the period of creation the BBC had no choice but to ask difficult questions not only about 'the industrial North as a nation within a nation' but about the relationship between Leeds and Nottingham, Manchester and Shef-field, and Newcastle and Durham, not to speak of York and Lancaster, Liverpool and Preston, Hull and Middlesbrough, or even Brighouse and Ramsbottom.

Somewhat similar questions have had to be asked again – in reverse – during the implementation period following the publication of the important White Paper of 1966 giving government approval to the opening of a chain of 'experimental' local radio stations and the decision of the Conservative government in 1971 to provide 'an alternative system of local radio financed by advertisements'. The whole idea behind 'local radio', BBC or commercial, was that 'local' community interests and pressures count and should count in the daily pattern of British broadcasting, and that in consequence 'regional' structures would have had to be transformed.

My essay goes back in time to the beginnings of broadcasting, and although for reasons of space it is highly selective in what it picks out in the later story, it rounds off the story in the present. Five phases can be separated out. In the beginning – and this comes as a surprise even to students of the history of broadcasting – there was genuinely local radio. This was a curious first phase which came to an end primarily for reasons of technology. The second phase is associated with the creation of the BBC's 'regional scheme', a major achievement in broadcasting history. There was always far more agreement about technology than about programme content or initiation, and many of the difficulties of making a regional pattern work were already apparent before 1939. The third phase – the Second World War – requires relatively little attention, for because of the forced limitation of wavelengths during the War 'regional broadcasting', as it had existed before 1939, came to an end. The most interesting aspects of the third phase concern the pressures to restore 'regionalism' after the War was over, and among those pressures those from the North were the strongest. The fourth phase from 1945 to 1966, by far the longest phase, is best described as one of regional renewal. The Beveridge Committee on the future of broadcasting, appointed in 1949, advocated a substantial expansion of regional broadcasting, and for a time after the publication of the Beveridge Committee's Report early in 1951 'regionalism' (particularly, however, in relation to the so-called 'national regions' of Scotland, Wales and Northern Ireland) was the main topic of the day. Yet television dominated public debate after 1951 and the issues raised by the Beveridge Committee lost their urgency. It was mainly inside the BBC that the battles about 'national', 'regional' and 'local' were fought.

The fifth and still incomplete phase centres on the growth of local radio. Lessons have already been drawn from the 'experiments', but it is by no means certain that the existing pattern of ownership and provision will last. The change to local radio, as this paper will show, was influenced very strongly, like the 'regional scheme' of the inter-war years, by technical factors – in this case, the development of VHF broadcasting – yet, it also was advocated by an official committee. The Pilkington Committee, appointed in 1960 and reporting in 1962, gave its blessing to the idea of 'local radio' dealing with material that 'would for a sufficient part of the day be of particular interest to the locality served by the station rather than to the other localities'.

When Radio Sheffield, the first of the Northern local radio stations, went on to the air on 15 November 1967 (one week after the first local radio station at Leicester), the wheel may be said to have come full circle, for Sheffield had been the first of the low-power relay stations constructed by the BBC and was opened on 16 November 1923. The inhabitants of Sheffield may well have preferred London to Manchester, as has been noted, but their first preference, of course, was for 'a local programme of our own'. Reith was prepared to generalize.

'It appears that no city counted sufficiently important to have a relay station could listen to the programmes of any station other than London without loss of dignity.'

A few local broadcasting stations preceded the founding of the British Broadcasting Company in the autumn of 1922 – among them 2ZY in Manchester – but it was only after Sheffield had led the way that the great proliferation of low-power local relay stations began. The selection of the cities to be equipped with relays depended on 'such considerations as their population, civic importance, distance from existing stations, and some technical elements such as geographical "shielding" or "jamming" [a word which was later to acquire a very different significance] by other stations'.

Leeds/Bradford, 2LS, with its unromantic-looking headquarters in Cabinet Chambers, Basinghall Street, did not come into existence until 8 July 1924, the first 'dual station' in the world, it was claimed, and the thirteenth local station to be opened by the BBC. 'Good morning, Bradford' was the beginning of the first test message from Leeds Town Hall, making it clear which city was first in the act. The first staff consisted of Philip Fox as Station Director, Lionel Harvey as Engineer-in-Charge, four assistant engineers and a lady clerk. Within two years the numbers had risen to eighteen.

Opening Night from Leeds Town Hall was said to have been presented with 'fine flourish'. Walter Widdop the tenor, Elsie Suddaby the soprano, * and the band of the Grenadier Guards were the entertainers, and among the speechmakers, making speeches 'short, but pregnant' with a sense of the making of history, were the Lord Mayors of Bradford and Leeds, the Pro-Vice Chancellor of the University, Professor J. Kay Jamieson, and Reith. 'There were many visions abroad', said Jamieson, who was in more prophetic mood than Reith. 'His students had visions of being able in the future to lie back in their easy chairs after breakfast and listen in peace and comfort to the professor speaking at a microphone.' Everyone who listened may not have shared the opinion that the evening was a 'qualified success', but there was certainly plenty of excitement and some wit. A householder in Manningham Lane in Bradford who put a loudspeaker in his window was one of the people, along with the wireless-dealers – all hoping for 'forests of aerials' – who gathered the crowds. 'It was amusing', wrote the *Yorkshire Observer*, 'to see the way in which passers-by stayed their steps when they heard the majestic strains of the band or the clear notes of the singers. Puzzled gentlemen gazed round in bewilderment,

---

* 'As an artist who gives more thought to the music she is interpreting than to her own glorification', wrote the *Yorkshire Post* (19 July 1920), 'she is ideal for broadcasting, where one is heard and not seen.'

expecting perhaps, some great procession to make its appearance.' The Vicar of Leeds, who was in London on opening night, said how nice it was that two lovers like Leeds and Bradford should share a relay station.

During its first year of operations, 2LS transmitted a total of 2860 hours of programmes – with only 364 minutes of breakdowns, usually described as 'technical hitches'. It overlapped with other Yorkshire stations, Hull and Sheffield, posing difficulties for listeners in fringe areas, but it maintained remarkable continuity even when its first aerial in Claypit Lane was struck by lightning. Although many of the basic programmes were relayed from London, and it had to rely for news not on reporters but on agency reports, it showed a good deal of ingenuity in programming. Thus, it was the first station to broadcast from the bottom of a coalmine (with the Whitwood Collieries Silver Prize Band), the first to organise a Charity Wireless Concert to raise funds to provide 'ailing Leeds children with a holiday', and the first to make a financial appeal for a University, 'Yorkshire's own'. It also broadcast services from York Minster, even in its first year. Its critics included Scarborough Sabbatarian objectors to 'jazz' after the *Messiah* – a surprisingly unReithian piece of programming – and populist critics of Friday evening concerts, which were hailed by the BBC as a lively expression of West Riding musical culture. There was little sign as yet, however, of the argument, which was later to twist its way through all regional broadcasting, that regional standards were necessarily lower than metropolitan standards. The blend of 'simultaneous' broadcasting from London and local broadcasting seemed just about right to local licence holders – over 30,000 of them in Leeds alone in mid-1925, contributing, it was stated very precisely, £15,822 10s. 1d. to BBC coffers. There were also large numbers of listeners who paid no licence fees. They were already called 'pirates' and they did not consist exclusively of impecunious owners of crystal sets.

The atmosphere of 2LS, like that of London's famous 2LO, was remarkably informal, and several graphic accounts survive of the padded studio and the warning notices designed to keep all visitors silent. There are testimonies, too, to the fears of the first local broadcasters and the enthusiasm of the first professional staff. The birthday party at the end of the first year was obviously hilarious. The professional staff had to turn themselves daily, like their colleagues in the other local relay stations, into 'uncles' and 'aunties' for 'Kiddies' Corner', the children's audience, the needs of which were kept very much to the forefront. 'Uncle Bob' (R. D. Green, M.A., as he was more formally described) and 'Aunt Doll' (Doris Nichols) were soon only two out of a sizeable family. Meanwhile, Philip Fox followed many local trails, as his later colleagues of Radio Leeds were to do during the late 1960s and early 1970s. He addressed large numbers of local bodies and communicated much of his own belief in the future of the medium to often sceptical Yorkshire audiences. There was room for 'stunts' also – in which the local radio trade often participated – like a great open-air demonstration in a Huddersfield park. Sometimes scepticism was accompanied by hostility. Thus, Harrogate Corporation passed a resolution in June 1923 before the station opened refusing to allow broadcasting from the Royal Hall. The resolution was maintained after challenge the following year and not rescinded until 1925.

Mention of Huddersfield and Harrogate, two communities with their own identities and styles – not to speak of Bradford – makes it plain that 2LS was not quite an anticipation of the kind of 'local radio station' that the BBC was to proclaim during the 1960s. From near the start, indeed, there was talk of it serving as a distribution centre for a large area, and even before the British Broadcasting Company was transformed into a Corporation in 1927, it was being described as a likely 'pivot to serve the North of England'. Yet there was much precocious local initiative, including broadcasting to schools in Bradford – there were Bradford critics who called the educational programmes too 'amusing' and not 'educational' enough – and experiments with drama. There was even a sort of Works Wonder programme from the Rowntree Cocoa Works in York.

In Leeds, at least, the station was thought of as 'a mouth, so to speak, through which Leeds can speak to the world', a point made at the time of the celebrations of the three hundredth anniversary of the granting of the City Charter. Should not plays being broadcast be Leeds plays, it was being asked, and the history Leeds history? The local pride was strong enough to survive shocks. When E. J. Turner was preparing a series of broadcast talks on Leeds, 'its history, changes and developments', he wrote to George Bernard Shaw whether he repented remarks he had made earlier about wishing to see Leeds burned. Was it not only particular parts which ought to be destroyed? The characteristic Shavian reply on a characteristic Shavian postcard (the BBC in London was a recipient of many such cards) was given full publicity by 2LS and the Leeds Press. 'The whole d . . . d place, more or less.'

Although on the eve of the changeover fears were being expressed in Leeds and Bradford about the effects of 'public control' on the impromptu life of the studio, the end of the 'localism' of 2LS was brought about less by the change from Broadcasting Company to Broadcasting Corporation than by the gradual development of the regional scheme which involved 'scrapping practically all the existing one-programme relay transmitters' and relying on five high-power twin-wave stations. This development started before 1 January 1927. Indeed, Eckersley had prepared a 'paper plan' on regionalism even before the Leeds/Bradford station was opened. It was modified in the light of official discussions and controlled experiments, one of the first of which took place after midnight, high up in the Pennines when the normal broadcasting services had closed. The object then was to test common facilities and shared wavelengths for Leeds/Bradford and Sheffield. It was on those same Pennine moors that the great new high-power transmitter was to be built at Moorside Edge near Pole Moor above Slaithwaite – with Huddersfield as the nearest town. The transmitter was not opened until 12 July 1931, but long before that the local studios in the North of England had lost a great deal of their independence.

The title of 'North Regional Director' was first used as early as 1928, a sign that E. G. D. Liveing, the Manchester Station Director, had established a position of primacy in the North which was never lost. Liveing thought in these 'almost medieval' terms, but he had been encouraged to do so by Reith and the BBC's Control Board in London. In September 1927 he had been told 'gradually and tactfully' to acquire 'ascendancy over the smaller stations in his area as E. R. Appleton had done over Swansea with a view to easier transference to the Regional Scheme'; and while the BBC's *Handbook* for 1928 still described the activities of the different Northern stations separately, that for 1929 explained how 'a regional administration of the various stations in the area was [now] centred at Manchester'. In October 1929 the BBC in Manchester moved to new Headquarters in Piccadilly. It ceased then to have 'local station' functions.

The unity of the North of England was now stressed as it never had been before. It was appropriate, the publicity began, that new regional transmitters would be based on the Pennines, the 'backbone of England', which 'runs almost imperceptibly, from the Derbyshire hills till it meets the Cheviot Hills on the borders of Scotland'. Geography came before sociology. 'Sufficient progress' had been made by July 1929, however, 'to show listeners the advantages of linking the various stations with each other. Civic, athletic, and other events in our part of the North [Manchester] became available to listeners on both sides of the Pennines.' To reinforce 'Northernism', a series of talks on the history and industrial growth of the North was broadcast in 1929, 'each talk delivered by a well-known representative of each city, the speaker broadcasting from the station nearest at hand'. 'The talks', it was claimed, 'have given a comprehensive survey of northern characteristics and the evolution of industry; they have shown the importance of

each city not only as an individual entity, but also as a member of a
great commonwealth'.

If it looks at first sight that the 'great commonwealth' in question
was the North of England, it must be remembered that Reith was
already thinking in imperial fashion. He had no sympathy with what
seemed to him 'parochial' ways, and he started with 'the Region'.
Thus, he encouraged Liveing to replace 'local' news by 'regional' news
in November 1928 and 'regional' education services for 'local' education
services then and during the following year. At the same time, he
pressed forward with 'centralisation' alongside 'regionalisation', generating many discontents in the process. The reactions of Leeds/
Bradford are not known, but the first Midland Regional Director in
Birmingham told Reith forcefully in February 1929 that 'the ever
growing policy of centralisation in London has clearly gone a good
deal further and more rapidly than public opinion here is prepared to
accept'.

One of the sharpest critics of the Reithian approach was Eckersley,
the architect of the regional scheme, who, following his divorce, left his
post in the BBC for personal reasons in 1929. He had believed, in the
very earliest days of 'paper planning', that a place should be left for
'local' news, local education and local debates in regional programming – Reith had questioned his assumptions then – and in retrospect
he was to write bluntly 'I designed the scheme technically and the BBC
used it stupidly.' Before he left the Corporation in 1929 he was even
advising the Regional Directors to demand a 'Declaration of Independence'. He wanted them to tell Head Office 'Give us the money and we
will do the rest. Hang your continued interference, give us a broad
policy and trust us that, within a loose framework, we will make
interesting and individual programmes.'

There were some inconsistencies in Eckersley's stance, and, in retrospect, he may have had a tendency to rewrite some of the earliest
BBC history. There is no doubt, however, that he hated bureaucracy,
believed in competition and had a natural liking for the informal and
the impromptu. His main reason, however, for introducing 'regionalism' was to provide listeners with an alternative programme, not
to buttress regional cultures. A first key date in his timetable was
the opening of a new high-power station at Daventry in July 1925
which made it possible for 94 per cent of the population of Britain to
receive a 'National' programme. A second was October 1934 when a
new high-power station was opened at Droitwich. The 'Regional'
programmes were first thought of as alternatives and later as 'feeders'
into a Home Service. From the beginning Eckersley believed, however, that Regional programmes should include 'Regional programmes

of any sort reflecting a definite character of the Region they serve. His own tastes were 'metropolitan'.

The new argument which lay behind almost all discussions of 'regionalism' during the 1930s was whether or not London 'standards' were 'better' than those of the North or, indeed, of any other 'Region', including Scotland and Wales. Accent came into the reckoning too. As early as 1589, the author of *The Arte of English Poesie* had advised poets never to use 'any speech' save 'our Southern English'. The BBC during the 1930s was in a far stronger position than a sixteenth-century writer to drive home the advice with sanctions.

It would be wrong to underestimate the volume and quality of much of the 'Northern' material produced during the 1930s, including that produced in Leeds, and it would be wrong also to minimise the substantial as well as the symbolic importance of the move in 1933 (opening day was 3 May) to larger, completely re-designed premises in Woodhouse Lane. The studios, control room and other offices in what had been the old Society of Friends' Meeting House, offered facilities, particularly for brass bands and for certain kinds of drama superior to those in Manchester.* A Yorkshire architect, J. C. Procter, who had worked on University buildings and laboratories, was responsible for the changes along with M. T. Tudsbery, the BBC's Civil Engineer.

There was no shortage of Yorkshire material in 1933, the year when the studios were opened. It included two plays, *Luck* and *Peace and Comfort*, performed by the Yorkshire Comedy Players, a Heckmondwike Lecture relayed from the Upper Independent Chapel, Heckmondwike, and the Wilberforce Centenary Service from Holy Trinity Church, Hull.

At the same time, all this material was now part of a bulky, general Northern package. Newcastle had by now been fully integrated into the Northern broadcasting context, and there were arguments about the fate of the Potteries, as distinctive an area as Tyneside. For Charles Siepmann, senior BBC administrator, who prepared the first comprehensive report on the Regions in 1936, the Potteries properly belonged to the North and were cut off from the Midlands by the agricultural belt just south of them, but 'as the North Region is already larger than is convenient', it was more sensible 'to consider them part of the Midlands'. 'Convenience' may also have dictated that Nottinghamshire was divided between Midlands and North, although the division was not between East and West Midlands but between south and north.

Siepmann criticised 'the short-sightedness' of the centralisation

---

* I was to employ a brass band there myself in 1946 for the broadcast of a feature programme written by me for the centenary of the repeal of the corn laws.

policy which had been pursued with increasing vigour – and rigour – during the early 1930s. 'The provinces', he maintained – and his own outlook was the very opposite of 'provincial' – 'are the seed ground of talent and the ultimate source of supply of our London programmes.' He went much further, however, when he argued that 'most London material' was 'out-of-tune to Northern and Western ears' and that the Regional Directors should offer further opportunities for expression of 'the differential pace and tone of life and feeling in the provinces'. They had been too slow to adapt their services, too uniform in their output.

> It is appropriate that National services should achieve as high a standard of excellence as possible, but the purist's concern for artistic integrity can be carried too far, and the case for Regional broadcasting cannot be measured by this single yardstick of artistic achievement . . . The patronage of all the arts, the representation of local life and local interests are limiting factors from a Head Office point of view, but need to be carefully weighed in the balance of advantage in considering the purpose on which our Regional policy depends.

The Governors accepted the main points in Siepmann's Report, relating it to other aspects of life and policy during the 1930s that fall outside the scope of this essay. They recognised 'the general tendency outside broadcasting towards centralisation in the metropolis' and described it as 'a bad tendency, which broadcasting can counter by representing the local point of view and encouraging local talent'. Yet their very use of the word 'local' does not inspire confidence in their appreciation of the problems, and they did little, particularly on the financial side, to encourage greater 'autonomy'. Nor was there very much freedom, let alone 'autonomy', *within* the huge North Region. E. A. F. Harding, Programme Director of the North Region in Manchester from 1933 to 1936, was extremely successful in hitching Northern broadcasting to the creative groups in Northern society and culture, but it was acknowledged almost without comment in 1937 that Leeds 'acts in almost all things directly under instructions from Manchester'.

The very success of Harding, whose motto was 'Anything London can do, we can do better', was not calculated to foster 'local' broadcasting. He enjoyed a unique power – in the absence not only of the Arts Council but of almost all other forms of cultural regionalism – to employ Northern artists, writers and producers, but he could not fail to note the divisions between Lancashire and Yorkshire at the very core of the region. Indeed, his Regional Controller, John Coatman, perhaps the most passionate supporter of Regional claims within the

Corporation, who had been sent to Manchester in 1937, wrote in 1943 that 'each of the great cities of the North thinks that it should have been chosen for the Regional headquarters, and old passions in respect of this still burn'.

Coatman's Memorandum was prepared as part of a series of solicited memoranda when the BBC was more immediately concerned with resistance movements in Europe then with the post-war North. It still stands out however as the most powerful single statement of a 'regional' as distinct from a 'local' case. There had been an inevitable centralisation of BBC programming during the War, when through national policy only one and later two wave lengths were available for Home listeners. The Regions still contributed to national programming – as they had contributed to a pre-war network of programming – and the North Region, which acquired a new underground studio in Manchester before the war-time bombing started, was a major contributor. Yet as many fears were expressed during the War about the future role of Northern broadcasting as complaints about its limited scope in the present. Early in 1943, the Ministry of Information's Regional Advisory Committee was demanding 'the full restoration of Regional broadcasting as early as possible', and a year later Coatman himself was criticising the fact – to the Director-General – that 'the characteristic activities of the North of England hardly enter into our programmes'. By the end of the War, the Director-General, now Sir William Haley, a Channel Islander, who had Mancunian connections through the *Manchester Guardian*, was involved in a keen national debate – in public rather than in private – about what would happen to the Regions with the return to peace.

For Coatman, who wished to write a large-scale book on post-war broadcasting, 'the initiative and control' of British broadcasting was deemed best to lie with the Regions – he proposed three, North, Midland and South, leaving out the West which was in fact, to prove the most innovatory of the Regions – for it was in the Regions that 'people live'. 'Broadcasting must be side by side with the people, must be animated by the pulse of their life, and feed itself directly from their thoughts and doings.' 'The divorce of broadcasting from the intimate life of the Regions has led to a decreasing interest in broadcasting as a whole.' There was no doubt, in his opinion, about the integrity of the North. When he had served as a young man on the North-West Frontier of India, 'the words "The North Country" had touched a much deeper layer of feeling than even the word England because they referred to my England'. 'Even those who are not North Countrymen will agree when I say that the North of England is now the outstanding example of regional individuality in England, known in common speech throughout our history as the "North Country". In literature, in

Parliament, in journalism, in politics, and in sport, the North Country is a recognised entity.' Differences inside the North were complementary, not hostile. 'The differences even between Tyneside and Lancashire are no greater than those between North and South Wales.' There would be no difficulty in securing superb broadcasting material from the North, 'not "kail-yard stuff" only, but the best'. 'The very essence of my conception of the Regions is that they shall be power-units of broadcasting.' Their boundaries did not need to be those of the pre-war Regional scheme which had been drawn up with engineering considerations in mind. They were properly thought of as cultural. Thus, the North would include the whole of Lincolnshire and the whole of Derbyshire for cultural reasons. If South Derbyshire were taken away, the people of that area would 'resent expulsion from the North'.

All these comments were deeply felt, although after he retired from the BBC in 1949 ironically to take up an academic post in St Andrews, Coatman who wrote four articles on 'Broadcasting in the North' in 1949 in the *Manchester Evening Chronicle*, admitted that 'none of the other Regions would have been in quite the same position as the North': 'the simple fact is that for broadcasting purposes the North is more than a region. It is, literally, the "other half" of England'.

Regional broadcasting after 1945 flourished for a time as it had not done for many years. It had a new ingredient – five-minute bulletins of Regional news – and a larger current affairs output; and it developed not only new forms of 'participation programmes' (like 'The Mike goes to the People') and broadcast discussions (like The Fifty-One Society) which expressed much of the 'local' (as distinct from the 'regional') feeling of particular places, but new forms of entertainment, the most striking of some of them described in the autobiography of Wilfred Pickles, *Between You and Me* (1949). Pickles was prominent, as he had been during the War, in drawing attention to Yorkshire dialect, for although dialect plays were a feature of Northern broadcasting after 1945, the Yorkshire Dialect Society was protesting as late as 1949 that the BBC was moving too slowly.

There were some serious problems in the new Regional pattern when viewed nationally – the linkage of East Anglia with Birmingham, for example, or the linkage of Brighton with Penzance or in the 'old North' the sharing of the same wavelength between Newcastle and the North-East and Northern Ireland – but there was a strengthening of local loyalties to the Regions. 'How do you like your BBC these days?' John White asked the readers of the *Yorkshire Evening News* late in 1945. 'This re-regionalised radio, I mean, with its local colour, dialect, brass bands and general emphasis on the North.'

It seemed appropriate that John Salt, a great-great grandson of Sir Titus Salt, the founder of Saltaire, was first post-War North Regional Programme Director; and certainly his successor, Robert Stead, made a point, as did Coatman's successor, Donald Stephenson, of looking out beyond Manchester to the whole region. When Manchester celebrated its first centenary as a city in 1953 – compare Leeds's tercentenary – Stephenson wrote as a Manchester man that while he shared the local pride in Manchester, as North Region Controller 'we have also very important and energetic bases at Leeds and Newcastle'. 'Even this', he added, 'is only part of the picture. If we did not devote as much time as we do to outside broadcasts and to the exploitation of local talent in a dozen other cities, and twenty times that number of important towns and boroughs, we should be failing miserably in our job.'

Recalling this period, a senior BBC official in the North Region claimed that 'we knew our Region in those days in a way we've never known since . . . In those days it was our *mission* to get out and put people on the air . . . You went all round the Region, you stayed a week here and there; you made recordings, you met people. And one really knew something about the North of England.' The Beveridge Committee, which made much of the claims of Scotland and Wales to a special place in the structure of British broadcasting, might have found rather less interest in 'regional autonomy' in the English Regions, but in practice there was a strong emphasis on 'independence' of judgement, at least in the North.

'The BBC bosses in London are watching with some astonishment the turn of events at Leeds studios', wrote the *Yorkshire Evening News*, for example, in 1951 – when television was beginning to pose a threat to sound radio – 'where the drama department is upsetting official notions about radio plays.' More than twice as many people were listening each week than had been expected. In the same year, 'a new suite of super-studios' was brought into use in Manchester and Lincoln, and Liverpool also was given new studios. It was surely a sign that the policy of 'getting side by side with the people' was working that there were complaints – very 'Northern' in feeling – about programmes 'misrepresenting' Liverpool and, for that matter, Brighouse and Southport. The Town Clerk of Brighouse complained to the BBC, and a Southport Councillor (facing considerable local opposition) called a broadcast from his town 'tripe'. In 1953 it was said that Southport was talking of buying programme time on Radio Luxembourg.

The sharing of the same wavelength between Newcastle and Belfast continued sharply to irritate:

'We know full well the microphone
Can link Korea with Ceylon,
Sub-tropic to sub-Arctic zone
When linking up is bent upon –

Surely an even simpler course
Is to arrange for a divorce
That severs that unholy tie
Binding us fast to Northern I.'

The failure (or inability) of the BBC to give to 'the people of Newcastle'
Stagshaw, the Northumberland broadcasting transmitter – which had
been built in 1937 – seemed to suggest that 'the unity of the North' was
being taken lightly, and two years after his retirement Coatman was
pressing Northerners to make representations to Members of Parliament with as much noise as possible. 'Fight for N.E. Radio urges
ex-BBC Chief' was one newspaper headline.

Not everyone in the North of England shared the Northern philosophy propounded at its most eloquent pitch by Coatman; and in a
fascinating correspondence in *Time and Tide* in 1946 one listener,
writing from Wetherby, objected to the idea that *Tales from the Dales*
or *Rambles up the Coast of Yorkshire* was what Northerners wanted.
'We are assumed by those who arrange our programmes to be passionately devoted to sport, especially boxing, brass bands, and curiously to
hearing about ourselves', but the assumption merely led to a lot of
unwanted material being 'rammed down our throats'. What Northerners wanted, other correspondents added, was what everyone else
in Britain wanted – 'the best' – and this was most easily dispensed
through a 'national' programme.

This argument, however, was counter-balanced, like most arguments
in broadcasting, by an equally strong argument in the North from
the opposite side. If the Wetherby listener thought that the BBC was
doing too much 'regional' broadcasting, there were always people who
thought it was doing too little. Thus, in 1954, a group of Northern
Labour MPs met the Regional Controller and the BBC's high-sounding
Director of the Spoken Word in London to press for far more 'regional'
programmes. There should be more political and parliamentary news,
they urged, and a special North of England Home Service Report on
Parliament. They even complained of a lack of Northern non-political
features, although Stephenson could retaliate properly that 'virtually
everything we do is redolent of the character of the region. Our Music,
Drama, Religion, Stories, Pageantry, Agriculture, Humour, Industry
and Commerce, are all essentially Northern and of the North.'

Stephenson had written earlier – before he left the General Overseas

Service for Manchester – that 'regional broadcasting is a vital and permanent part of our reason for existence' but that 'the creation of a network of "parish hall" broadcasting stations would be an even worse evil than the total abolition of the Regions'. How did the outcome to which he objected so strongly and which he put in such fierce language actually come about? It became technically possible with the development of VHF – the first field trials had been arranged even before the end of the War – but it was less the development of technology than a new set of attitudes towards sound broadcasting in an age of television which influenced policy-making. At a BBC General Advisory Council meeting in 1950 Principal Nicholson of Hull University College, an eager participant on such occasions, had then expressed the prevailing Northern 'orthodoxy' that 'the springs of spontaneity are in danger unless there is more devolution and still more freedom for the Regions', adding that 'Regions are not parochial, they are concerned with matters of vital importance.' It would not have entered his head to ask for a local broadcasting station for Hull.

The biggest single non-technical factor making for a change in outlook and policy was a new emphasis on 'topicality' in broadcasting, what Frank Gillard, one of the chief architects of the new policy, called 'telling the running daily story of local life'. Many of the upholders of the older orthodoxy were educationists who were suspicious of too much preoccupation with the Day and the events thereof in broadcasting, while the supporters of the new approach were journalists fascinated by the immediate or even the conjectural or the anticipated. The switch from 'regional' to 'local' radio, therefore, implied a different approach to Time as well as to Place. The heart of the matter was put very clearly in the BBC's pamphlet *This is Local Radio* (which perhaps as a sign of the shift from longer to shorter perspectives has no date on it):

> The listener wants more news about local sport, weather, police information, traffic, lost children and pets, escaped prisoners, what happened at the Council meeting, what's on next week at the Townswomen's Guild, and how to join an amateur dramatic society. What did the local M.P. say in the Commons.

It is too early for the historian to evaluate the cultural significance of the great change, but it is very important to chronicle it before the detail is forgotten. We are obviously concerned when we turn to broadcasting history both with reflections of social trends and with influences upon them. Historians should beware premature sociological generalisation. They are interested in maps – 'mental' as well as physical or economic – and in contours. Whatever happens to Radio Leeds or Radio Nottingham or Radio Trent, the River Trent is still there.

11   International

I   The BBC in World Perspective*

The publication of the Annan Report is only weeks away, and for all the necessary and laudable efforts to open up a debate *before* publication day on some of the issues that the Report is likely to raise, most of the initial reactions will be immediate reactions stimulated less by previous thought than by Press headlines.

This is unfortunate, for the issues are profound as well as topical, and they go beyond questions of institutional rearrangements to questions of values, the answers to which will have long-term implications. They cannot be provided effectively, however governments approach them, in the light of short-term calculations.

There is another danger too. It seems probable that the debate *after* publication day will be nation-centred or – to use a more forbidding term – culture-bound. Certainly the parallel 'great debate' on education, suggested by the prime minister, James Callaghan, in so far as it has really begun at all, has already taken that turn, a comfortable turn even when the controversy is sharpest; and it will be even easier for a debate on communications to concentrate on what we actually see and hear directly day-to-day in our own homes. Most of us have little opportunity to judge otherwise. Yet broadcasting is likely to become more global than national, and already, even within our restricted national system, a significant part of what we see on our screens comes from the United States.

The purpose of my Lecture today is to try to widen the perspectives. After all, the Annan Report is only one of a number of reports of its kind being produced in all parts of the world: in some countries, indeed, like Australia, a report – in this case the Green Report – has already made drastic proposals, some of which have already been modified by government, a government of a different complexion from that which commissioned it. There, as in a number of other countries, what were designed to be completed packages of proposals have been split up into acceptable and non-acceptable items, but one major revision remains – a new control body for the whole system.

*Based on a BBC Lunchtime Lecture, delivered on 8 March 1977 and subsequently published by the BBC.

174

In other countries, major changes in broadcasting policy are in the course of actually being carried out: the report stage, the debate stage and the legislation stage are all past. Thus, in France the changes associated with the end of ORTF have already produced both anticipated and unanticipated results. Finally, in countries where so far there has been no review of a systematic kind, there are pressures to start one. Thus, in the United States, there is talk of amending the Communications Act of 1934, a landmark in American history with no precise British parallel. It was passed at a time when no one on either side of the Atlantic had begun to think in terms of a continuing 'communications revolution'.

There have been times when it has seemed as if American television patterns were so immutable that no one could ever shake them. Yet there are many signs now of a demand for new thinking, general rethinking, for, as one American group has put it:

> the peculiar strains to which established values and old institutions are today subjected represent, both in kind and intensity, a new challenge to which a fresh and timely response is required. Otherwise, the accelerating pace of change could well outstrip the governing process and leave us with an information society that is neither efficient nor harmonious nor free.

The manifesto left out entertainment, but somewhat similar points might be made about that also.

My first reason, therefore, for trying briefly today to widen the perspectives before the publication of the Annan Report is that it is useful to examine to what extent we can or should expect common answers to be formulated. As Charles Siepmann, ex-BBC official and later American professor, put it in his book *Radio, Television and Society* (1950), 'to any one interested in broadcasting' knowledge of what other systems are doing, how far their practices resemble ours, and how far they differ is extremely important. 'We may discover in other systems practices and techniques that we might emulate.' Of course, that is only part of the interest. We may discover in other systems practices and techniques that we should *not* emulate, but rather shun. The BBC, which over the years has sent large numbers of its officials over to America, some of whom have produced fascinating reports on American broadcasting (more interesting in some cases than those which the Americans have produced themselves), has always been exceptionally good at shunning.

In 1950 Siepmann noted that when we make comparisons we are not merely looking at 'practices and techniques' in isolation, some of which we can choose and some of which we can reject. We are looking at systems which can only be fully explained if we relate broadcasting to other aspects of society – to political systems, for example, and to cultural traditons – and if we pass from structural comparison to dynamic processes.

In 1976 we realise this far more clearly than anyone did in 1950, when there was very little talk of 'the media', even less of communications history as a clue to general history. Who would have thought that the time was not far distant when there would be talk not only of deregulating but of de-institutionalising broadcasting or at least of extending the communications range to include not only 'citizens' band' radio, now winning adherents in Italy and Germany as well as in the United States – a totally de-institutionalised form of personal communication – but all kinds of new visual devices designed through recording to offer individual choice? The rapid expansion of the video market means that individuals, rather than institutions, become programme selectors and compilers.

Given the spirit of enquiry in the air and the unwillingness to take 'established values and old institutions' for granted, as the Americans put it, there are two ways of looking at broadcasting structures and processes when they are subjected to careful review either by committees or by individuals. The first – and perhaps the most immediately appealing – is to consider them functionally in terms of activities and relationships – the selection and production of programmes; the determination of the mix of different constituents of output; the development and exploitation of the relevant technologies; the modes of management and finance; influences on the system from outside, competing or complementary; impact; and accountability. The attraction of this approach is that it seeks the logic rather than turns to experience. There are, of course, versions of the approach which allow a place for informalities in a system and point to gaps between expectation and performance that characterise all systems. Whatever the version, however, the object of the exercise is to blueprint a new system which will be better than the existing system.

The alternative approach is to take an existing broadcasting system, survey its operations, judge it on its record, and when necessary suggest modifications and improvements. The system itself is then recognised to be a historical product in the course of continuing change, understandable only after grasping how things came to be as they were and how, if at all, they had come to be criticised. On the whole, this is how most reviews of the BBC in the past have been carried out – on the basis of the record. There has always been a danger of complacency in this approach, and one day it may be abandoned. At present, indeed, it may push possible alternatives out of view and underestimate technological potential. None the less, there is an under-lying realism in such an approach. Existing assets and advantages are not to be bartered for hypothetical gains. Changing a system to achieve the ideal may produce something worse.

The second approach is congenial to me as a historian, for in order to understand where we are I want to know the route by which we have arrived here. I also want specific details of the route and of the people who have trodden it, as well as general guidelines. I am sharpening the distinction between the two approaches, of course, for I also believe that in order to study any single broadcasting system it is helpful to discover when we are travelling on other people's routes and where we diverge. I am fortified, notwithstanding, by a recent generalisation of a philosopher that it has always been a mistake to identify rationality with logicality – to assume, that is, that 'the rational ambitions of any historically developing activity can be undertood entirely in terms of the propositional or conceptual systems in which its intellectual content may be expressed at one or another time'.

To understand how the BBC works, we have to understand more than the functional relationships at particular snapshot moments of time. We have to look at personalities, traditions, generational lags, con-tinuities, discontinuities, innovations and reactions. And as soon as we look at the BBC this way – and the same would apply to IBA and the programme contracting companies – we can best avoid the besetting dangers of insularity and complacency by placing the British activity within an international context.

It used to be said that within the international context there were three kinds of broadcasting structures – those with a set of commer-cial incentives, profits linked to selling goods, marked-based if not always market-orientated; those which were governmentally control-led, linked to the making of propaganda, carrying purposive messages, if not all the time; and those which were neither controlled by govern-ment nor underpinned by business. American broadcasting represented the first; pre-1939 German broadcasting and Russian broadcasting the second; and the BBC the third. Each of these major systems had its derivatives and its variants, with the BBC being used as a model for a large number of other broadcasting institutions, mainly in the English-speaking world. Moreover, even when it was not used as a model, it was often thought of as a model, not least in Europe.

This simple picture of three types of structure was, broadly speaking, true of the 1920s and 1930s, although even then there were examples of rather different approaches to the organisation of broadcasting. The Netherlands, for example, built up its broadcasting system on the initiative neither of the government nor of business, but on that of private independent groups – a Protestant Association, a Socialist Party Association, a Catholic Foundation and a Protestant Christian Association. There was no body like the BBC. Likewise, in Sweden Swedish Radio was neither given the independent legal status of the BBC, laid down by Charter, nor made part of the national administration. Swedish radio, ABR, was established in 1924 as a non-profit making corporation, a limited company in which the radio industry held one-third of the shares, the Press one-third, and the Swedish News Agency (TT) the rest. There were, however, government representatives on the Board; and the government representation was increased in 1933 when it was decided not to nationalise the company.

In both these countries it is impossible to understand the present without looking back at traditions which have been perpetuated. In the Netherlands, a ninety-eight page note on mass media policy presented in 1975 to the States General by the Minister of Culture, Recreation and Social Work stood by the concept of 'pluriformity'. In Sweden, a report is being prepared for publication this year on the basis of a brief not dissimilar from that of Annan. The answers in it will be no more totally detached from Swedish historical experience than those likely to be provided in Britain. A comparison between the two reports, indeed, will be a *must* for the growing number of people, still a small minority, who are interested in the evolution of broadcasting policy. They will look to see what ideas are really new in either of them.

For many years, however, the pre-war threefold model has ceased to correspond faithfully to the structures actually in operation. This is partly because television after the Second World War introduced new problems of scale, finance, organisation and control; and because the pedigree of television was more diverse than that of sound broadcasting, with the cinema as part of it. It is partly because more diverse 'mixed systems' not only took shape, but began to be thought of as having special advantages of their own. It is partly also because of the enormous expansion of broadcasting in the Third World, where there were many breaks with pre-war traditions as new countries, some of them determined to distance themselves from 'colonialism', took charge of their own broadcasting policies. There were changes which in some cases were gradual, almost, at first imperceptible, but there were other changes that were deliberately sudden and dramatic.

The BBC model did not survive social and political change in Africa, including South Africa, and Asia. But neither did it survive social and political change in Britain itself. Ironically, however, the effect of change in Africa and Asia was usually to protect monopoly, whereas in Britain the BBC's monopoly was destroyed after protracted debate, a debate that sometimes cut across party lines and that revealed more about society and culture than any post-war debate on any other subject.

There were 'mixed systems' in Australia and in Canada before there were in Britain, but for one brief moment in 1954 and 1955 the lime-light was focused on Britain as the BBC's monopoly was broken and a commercial sector began to operate. The new sector was financed and managed, however, quite differently from the American system, although there was an obvious pressure for profit, and advertising was the key to it. In retrospect and in terms of international, not domestic, perspectives, the post-1955 system has seemed to stand out as being more unitary than dual, with Professor George Wedell arguing in his useful study *Broadcasting and Public Policy* (1968) 'one has only to put side by side the documents governing the conduct of the two British broadcasting organisations, the Charter and Licence of the BBC and the Television Acts under which the ITA (now the IBA) operates, to be struck forcibly by the essentially *unitary* character of the broadcasting system in the United Kingdom'.

By contrast, as public broadcasting has gained in confidence and in ambition in recent years in the United States – financed and managed very differently from the BBC in Britain – a new, if limited, element of genuine duality is present across the Atlantic, and there are programme links, too, between Public Service Broadcasting (PBS) and the BBC.

The existence of 'mixed systems' both in the Third World (where in some countries there are commercial as well as public sectors) and the more developed world blurs some of the distinctions, which were there before 1939. It is now possible to claim, indeed, as Herbert S. Schlosser, President of NBC, did in a lunchtime lecture here last year, that while the British and American systems differ in structure, finance and the approach to many of their obligations, 'they both exist in free societies. They retain a large degree of independence from Government. And in this they are different from most of the broadcasting systems of the world.'

Certainly the number of directly government-run systems has in-creased since 1960, and the number of government interventions in the operations of non-directly government-run systems has increased still more. Yet, while there are remarkable 'mixed systems' in some countries, not all of them small ex-colonial territories, where directly-run government broadcasting coexists with commercial broadcasting, there is no mixed system, to my knowledge, where directly-run government broadcasting coexists with broadcasting by an independ-ent public corporation. Commercial competition is deemed safer than competition with an organisation which has its own sense of autonomy and responsibility. It is for these qualities, expressed in its external as well as in its domestic services, that the BBC is still renowned in different parts of the world.

Within any range of models now extant a place should be given to a 'development model'. The BBC conceives of itself as a public service, commercial broadcasting conceives of itself as a profit-making activity, propaganda broadcasting conceives of itself as seeking to reach set, if moving, targets. There is an element of the first and third in 'development model' broadcasting – even an element of salesmanship derived from the second. Above all, however, there is an emphasis on a single-minded social need. A so-called communications component or dimension is introduced into national development plans, realistic or utopian, that have defined purposes such as national integration or socio-economic change. And broadcasting can be deployed tactically in relation to particular development projects or strategically in relation to a national plan as a whole.

In consequence, it is possible to talk of a 'communications policy' which incorporates telecommunications as well as broadcasting within its ranges. In the most sophisticated plans, an attempt is made to cost new forms of electronic communications technology against other more traditional forms of communications, even against transportation. In the most sophisticated of the plans there is a feedback loop, too, whereby public reactions to the plan can influence its development. Of course, there can be an element of propaganda in all this – and sometimes this is preponderant and obvious – just as there can be propaganda – and little else – in some plans conceived of as a whole.

There was nothing quite like this before the 1950s, and somewhat surprisingly at first sight it was American commentators, products of a totally different broadcasting system from ours, who were the first to try to assess it in such books as Wilbur Schramm's pioneering *Mass Media and National Development* (1964). Yet, however surprising, there is nothing paradoxical about this. First, much of the language of the first planners was sociological, and communications research in the United States, a major academic industry, was sociologically, not historically, philosophically or institutionally geared. Second, the first plans made much of 'modernisation', a concept which rang more bells in the United States than it did in the so-called developing countries themselves.

More recently, however, as talk of one single general theory of development has been abandoned and the talk has switched to so-called 'paths of development', the American involvement has been challenged. There has also been a challenge in Third World countries themselves to simple notions of 'modernisation' resting on advanced technology and urban and industrial growth. There is now a marked difference between communications development strategy as urged, for example, in Iran and in Malaysia. Meanwhile, there has always been a Marxist model in those Third World countries that look to Moscow for guidance, and their broadcasting systems follow guidelines that were set for the most part before 1939.

The International Institute of Communications, of which I am a Trustee, is producing a series of short case studies on broadcasting systems which deliberately choose examples of contrasting situations. Each study is written, whenever possible, by a citizen of the country concerned. A study of Malaysia, just published, shows how far removed from the kind of considerations which must interest the Annan Committee are the objectives of Malaysia's 'government mass media activities' as they are defined in their own rules and regulations. These, not untypically, are coordinated by a Minister of Information with two main divisions – a Department of Broadcasting and a Department of Information. It is the Ministry which lays down guidelines for government communicators and broadcasters. There are five of them:

> to explain in depth and with the widest possible coverage government policies and programmes to ensure maximum public understanding; to stimulate public interest and opinion to achieve its desired changes; to assist in promoting civic consciousness and fostering the development of Malaysian arts and culture; to provide suitable elements of popular education, general information and entertainment; and to promote national unity by using the national language in a multi-racial society towards the propagation of a Malaysian culture and identity.

I need hardly point out that such a conception of broadcasting and mass media policy – note how the two interlock, with telecommunications brought in, as they often are in developing countries – is far removed from mere regulation. It is nationally based, however, and usually has little in common with the outward-bound propaganda activities of the 1930s. In a country like ours with a plurality of interests and opinions and domestic channels for expressing them, the conceptions which shape such development not only seem to threaten freedom, but to close frontiers. Yet it is easy to see why 'social need communications' models have been felt to be desirable, even necessary, in other kinds of society. One distinguished African writer, a professor, has gone so far as to argue that all development is communication.

If a collection of case studies should ultimately lead to a general comparative analysis, it is already clear, whether one is concerned with Britain and the BBC or Malaysia and RTM, Radio Television Malaysia, that the future of broadcasting, like its past, does not depend on technological development alone. There are many exciting new communications technologies, some of them pointing the way forward from an age of mass communication into an age of greater individual choice, but the speed and scope of their development will be determined by social, economic, political and cultural factors as well as by the technologies themselves and their inherent potential.

Past experience shows, moreover, that the same technology has been employed in different countries in quite different ways. Sometimes there are only a few control devices imposed by governments or by professional or trade-union groups. Often there are many. And usually, as has been and will be the case in Britain, it is governments that decide whether or not to talk about 'communications policies'. For this reason alone, it is necessary to understand the general history of a country in order to understand what it has done and what it is doing with communications whether or not it professes to have a communications policy. The point is immediately apparent if one turns to the differences either between Britain and the United States, to which I have already referred, or to the differences between Britain and France. It would have been possible as early as the last years of the seventeenth century, I dare to suggest, to predict what differences there might be in Britain and France in the way that they would handle developing communications systems.

As for the United States, only a 'people of plenty', as Professor Potter has called them, could concentrate boldly and optimistically – with inevitable minority dissent, now turned either into a monologue or a dialogue – on 'the technology push' and 'the new electronic abundance'. Yet the first stages of technological development are often left to others, and the subsequent pace of development depends on an internal market, held back by entrenched existing interests, and on caution or lack of imagination on the part of entrepreneurs. The BBC has always been well ahead in the development of new technology – in the provision of a regular television service, and more recently the development of CEEFAX. And Japan is showing signs of forging ahead of every other country, including Britain.

The BBC operates in a society where there is increasing fear of technological change and where there have never been the same opportunities of scale that existed in the United States. There have always had to be priorities in capital investment, with timetables determined not by the market but by the government; and the size of the retained licence fee that the government has chosen to fix – an important lever in an age of inflation – is now as capable of inhibiting development as much as government-imposed physical controls inhibited the development of television broadcasting before 1955.

I have no time to expand further my first reason for trying to place the BBC within a world scene – that of examining through case studies the extent to which we can determine whether or not we are talking about common problems in different countries when we review and plan, and whether common answers can be formulated. I have two other reasons, however, both of which have links with the first. For all the attempts at national planning, electronic communications are by their nature trans-national and cross-cultural. We are not dealing with parallel but with related systems, and for all the barriers which still separate societies and cultures – and some are becoming less easily rather than more easily surmountable – there are elements of the communications system which we can call 'global' or at least incipiently global, 'girdles round the earth'. For more than a hundred years – indeed, from the age of the telegraph – prophets of the 'communications revolution' have been proclaiming the gospel not just of interdependence but of shared benefits – 'everyone, everywhere', more recently 'everyone, everywhere, all at one time'.

It is because of recent progress in technology, notably the use of satellites, that more attention has recently been paid to the social and cultural significance of global communications and the gaps and so-called biases or imbalances within the global system.

Arguments about the implications of the free or controlled flow of communications from one part of the globe to another raise fundamental and still highly controversial issues which go beyond those raised nationally in enquiries like those of Annan; and Finns and Swedes have been prominent in research. As early as 1953, a study of the International Press Institute, *The Flow of the News*, concluded that in the American Press 'the picture of other countries is generally objective, but spotty and incomplete, lacking in continuity and uninterpreted', and since then attention has passed from Press to radio and television and from the role of information in the so-called advanced countries to its role in the Third World. UNESCO is a forum.

We know far too little about the geography of flow to have at our current disposal all the basic weather charts setting out clearly what is happening, but we do know that the BBC itself plays an important part, an increasingly important, if, because of government, a vulnerable part, in the pattern. We know also that the economics of flow are of the utmost importance, too, for they influence both programme output and news presentation.

The BBC's links with the United States within the developing global system have made possible a number of exciting programme ventures designed for audiences on both sides of the Atlantic, while its links with Europe, represented in the European Broadcasting Union, have always been close, not least through BBC Director-Generals who have always taken a lively interest in the Union. The important, but little studied, regional Broadcasting Unions – and the EBU with thirty-four active members in thirty-one countries celebrated its silver jubilee in 1975 – operate between the national and the global, and encompass both developing countries and countries with sophisticated economic and communications systems. They deserve very full study. 'Where others debate the political merits of the free exchange of information', Sir Charles Curran, the EBU's President, wrote in 1975, 'for us broadcasters it is a simple programme and engineering requirement, and our contacts and broadcasting practices must facilitate this free exchange.'

The United States, which has been accused, not least by Americans, of 'communications imperialism', does not belong to any of these great regional Unions, but statistics relating to its role, particularly in Latin America, have received far more attention than those relating to the BBC. 'Cultural imperialism' is more than a slogan. It is against this background that the IIC, which has been deeply concerned since its creation with the problems of flow, is planning to start a major enquiry into the structure and direction of international flows, starting with the Arab States, and continuing, it is hoped, with Europe. The first object will be to establish a sound quantitative data base, now not there; the second will be to interpret data. Much of the interpretation already available rests on the basis of inadequate data. It starts with slogans and it decorates them. There is need for a more sophisticated approach which draws on new approaches to social geography. The Arabs themselves are interested in this.

The quality of what flows is obviously of more importance to the future of world communications than mere quantities of flow. In news, what is needed, above all else, is accuracy: in entertainment creativity and liveliness of performance. And within any system of international flows the BBC has the undoubted advantage of having established a reputation both for accuracy and creativity. The reputation has not been easily won and it is always assailable, but it would be difficult to explain it solely in terms of broadcasting structures. My third and final reason for choosing to talk about the BBC in World Perspective is that I thought it would be useful at this particular moment to reflect on the quality question.

Historically there are landmarks. Before 1939 the insistence of J. B. (later Sir Beresford) Clark on news accuracy in external broadcasting still seems to me to be of pivotal importance. I have been so impressed by it that I dedicated to him the third volume of my *History of Broadcasting*, 'The War of Words'. What could be more decisive than Clark's simple sentence 'the *omission* of unwelcome *facts* of News and the consequent suppression of truth runs counter to the Corporation's policy as laid down by appropriate authority'? This sentence was penned in January 1938 in relation to the young Arabic Service of the BBC after the Arabic Service's sub-editor, with a Foreign Office background, had suggested tentatively that 'there should be such selection and omission of items as to give a favourable impression of this country to an Arab audience'.

Clark's view prevailed in all pre-war external broadcasting, limited though that was; and it emerged, sometimes a little battered, but always unscathed, from the Second World War itself, a period when even Britain found it necessary to have a Minister of Information. In consequence – and it owes nothing to government – the World Service of the BBC is one of the country's most distinctive achievements because of the standards which uphold it.

Clark was to become successively Controller first of the Overseas and then of the European Services of the BBC during the Second World War, and one of his distinguished successors, Gerard Mansell, now Managing Director of BBC External Services, described the subsequent history of the development of the service in a Lunch-time Lecture last year in which he related technology to what he called features 'inherent in the nature of the society from which we draw our professional and corporate substance'.

As far as the technology was concerned, the post-war transistor revolution had been accompanied by a revolution in short-wave broadcasting 'which was losing its specialised image and becoming accessible even to the poorest of Third World peasants'. In twenty years, the number of radio receivers in black Africa had grown from under half-a-million to twenty-two-and-a-half millions; in India it had increased from one million to eighty millions. Pre-war audiences had been tiny minority audiences. Now there were unprecedented opportunities provided that standards were maintained.

As far as 'professional and corporate substance' was concerned, Britain, according to Mansell, was seen outside these islands not as 'the confused, disputatious, dissatisfied, disorientated society which we imagine ourselves to be [and he might have added, the Annan Committee may imagine us to be] but a country in which reigns tolerance, justice, sanity and democracy'.

Mansell also pointed out how the BBC's World Service, originally the Empire Service, had acquired faithful devotees in Britain as well as abroad. 'MPs late home from the House have found the midnight news . . . on the World Service a useful way of catching up with the day's events.'

The story of the BBC's handling of news broadcasting as a whole has had many vicissitudes at home and abroad, and the complexity of the personal and public issues that have been involved contrasts sharply with the simplicity of Clark's memorable pre-war sentence. There have been protracted arguments, often fierce, about the proper relationship between BBC news and Agency news, world news and domestic news, television news and sound news, news of all kinds and current affairs, news of strikes and news of Northern Ireland. Some, at least, of the arguments still continue, and there have been new ones as the issues thrown up by the news have themselves changed. Yet the basic attitudes were right as they were expounded at a point in time when it would have been far easier for them to be wrong. It was obviously of the utmost importance that they were clarified within the context of external broadcasting at a time when the war of words had already begun to rage, with many of the words being directed at – and not from within – the Arab World.

I have always believed that the BBC's place within an international family of broadcasting institutions would never have been the same had its external activities – not part of the Annan remit – been hived off or, worse, left to government spokesmen. I believe, too, that within those external services the most difficult battles were fought at the beginning. The point was emphasised most recently in an important article in the *Washington Post* which traced back the strength of the BBC's external services to distant times. It was trying to urge on the Carter regime the urgent need for institutional changes in United States external broadcasting which had had an often unattractive record. A market economy and a pluralistic society had depended all too often on crude political propaganda in transmitting programmes abroad.

More recent phases in the story of news and of its relationship to domestic political broadcasting are well covered in Grace Wyndham Goldie's *Facing the Nation*, a book which will appear before the Annan Report and which characteristically does not shirk any of the main issues. Incidentally, it will be the first book published in this country to deal in depth with the relationships between politicians, journalists and broadcasters. It is especially illuminating because it deals with real people and with specific issues, with experience and not with logic, to go back to my two initial approaches. It would have gained even more in power, I believe, if it had more fully compared the BBC's ways of doing things with the way they were – and are being done – in other countries.

On the question of quality of television programmes of other kinds – entertainment programmes, feature programmes and drama of various sorts – there are a few simple sentences almost as revealing as that of Clark on the news. Thus, when Norman Collins took over television at Alexandra Palace in 1947, Sir William Haley wrote him a memorable order of the day about quality. Even though Haley had deep misgivings, which he never hid, about the nature and likely impact of the new medium, he told Collins 'Give television a sense of adventure, give television a sense of style, get it into the heads of the Staff that it is quality that counts.' Translated into action terms by Cecil McGivern, who was a pioneer in television programme making, this read 'We must aim at making every programme a good programme.'

There is certainly no guarantee of this in any television structure. Indeed, Professor Potter, whom I have already identified as the author of *The People of Plenty*, stated in a talk in America in 1966 on the historical perspectives of television that 'democratic public regulation would gravitate politically to the level of the mass society just as market-orientated programming also gravitates economically to the level of the mass society'. He put his faith only in the ultimate breakdown, perhaps an imminent breakdown, of the 'monolithic' bulk of a vast audience. Some more recent American writers see the means for achieving this in new communications technologies which will 'put broadcasting in its place'.

Huw Weldon more than any other person in the history of the BBC has explained why faith in quality need not be apocalyptic. 'Quality is all', he concluded in his Lunchtime Lecture of February 1975, 'and it is necessary as a statement of intention, and without reservation across the whole wide range of programmes; in variety programmes no less than in Elizabethan tragedies; in current affairs no less than in programmes for children; in song contests no less than in the coverage of golf.' Weldon found the explanation of quality less in structures than in the personal dispositions and gifts of programme-makers and in group traditions – the tradition, for example, of employing script writers with names, and not just relying on formulae; the willingness on the part of administrators, bound to involve tensions, to leave a high degree of creative freedom to producers; the sense that lay behind both the tradition and the recognition that broadcasting was drawing on older traditions in national life, including a long literary tradition. In the international scene the role of the BBC can only be properly understood when such elements are taken into the reckoning. Doubtless the Annan Committee will take up some of these themes, not least in relation to the operation of a fourth television channel, which, if given the right remit, could prove a landmark in the history of British broadcasting.

Meanwhile no picture of the international scene would be complete if it left out the production in some countries by commercial organisations of cheap programmes for Third World countries, programmes of the lowest possible quality; of political give-aways; and of dumping procedures which by their very nature entail the distribution of the worst – and the most stale, not the best or even the mediocre. It would be healthy if we could encourage a flow of the best, and for me the study of the conditions of encouraging such a flow has to be part of the survey being carried out by IIC. Under its first name, the International Broadcast Institute, it came into existence to encourage quality.

This Lecture, which has touched briefly on many themes, should end, perhaps, with a reference to de-institutionalisation, a process which has not yet found its Ilych, but which has found a large number of observers and commentators. Huw Wheldon made much of institutions, and certainly the BBC itself emerged very quickly not only as an organisation, but as a national institution. It had done so, indeed, before it changed from Company to Corporation on 1 January 1927. The institutionalisation, which carried great advantages in that decade, also carried with it longer-term dangers, some of which influenced public attitudes after the BBC's institutional status had been immensely enhanced, and further enhanced in the eyes of the British public and of people abroad during the Second World War.

I shall have something to say of the changes in public attitudes, then, in my fourth volume of the *History of Broadcasting* which takes the story down to 1955 and which will appear later this year. The image of 'Auntie' BBC was born at that time. Yet the biggest dangers were to become apparent later still, particularly during the 1960s and early 1970s, when it seemed as if all institutions were under threat – economic, political, religious, educational and cultural. And – as before and since – there was confusion in the minds of some critics between the conception of the BBC as an over-large organisation and and the BBC as an over-powerful institution.

The largeness implied the linking of activities that might have been kept separate and were kept separate in some foreign countries, and it has meant at times that one bit of the BBC has not known what another is doing. There have been worlds within worlds. Yet it had and has had advantages too. The linkage of Sound and Television makes certain 'combinations' possible, even if it has never guaranteed them, while the movement of people from External Services to Television became a recognised route which persons of talent could travel. Many foreign countries envy these linkages, which have to be deliberately contrived, it is important to remember, when broadcasting is conceived of in terms of a development model. Given the BBC's history – and there have been times when the linkages have not been effective – something more is needed than structural contrivance.

De-institutionalisation is best expressed in 1977 by Citizens' Band Radio – person to person or network talk without supervision or control – almost at the opposite pole from the BBC. Yet the idea of it preceded Marconi's wireless patents. When, in a well-known passage, Sir William Crookes forecast in 1892 'the bewildering possibility of telegraphy without wires, posts, cables of any of our present costly appliances', he went on to prophesy that 'any two friends living within the radius of sensibility of their receiving instruments, having first decided on their special wavelength and attuned their respective instruments and mutual receptivity, could thus communicate as long and as often as they pleased'.

The California truck drivers made this dream come true in 1973, using radio for purposes which would never have been permitted in any institutionalised system – organising traffic blockades on state highroads, for example, to protest against speed limit regulations which were costing them time and wages. There was an outlaw element in the first network (as there had been with Britain's radio pirates) before the fun – and the weather forecasts, the best in the state – came in. The folklore followed, some of it encapsulated in best-selling magazines which combine the severely technical with the culturally outrageous. In a sense we are back in the world of radio hams before the BBC or any of its opposite numbers came into existence during the 1920s. Yet it is a different kind of world in its ethos and its language . . . not surprisingly, given the huge social and cultural shifts since the 1920s. One American observer has written tellingly, 'I have yet to hear what may be characterised as a "well bred" voice or a highly articulate conversation such as one hears in the "ham" bands.'

I do not believe that this phenomenon should be ignored. Indeed, it is important to ask why it has emerged as well as how. For all the tendencies that make for increased order and global system, there are counter-tendencies which, I believe, are already becoming apparent in the video world as well. The old frameworks will creak. The Annan Report will come out too soon for such tendencies and counter-tendencies to become clearly identifiable, and they will work themselves out differently in different countries. What is legal in Sweden may be illegal in Denmark and *vice versa*. What can be done in the United States will not necessarily be copied everywhere. But at some point between now and the end of this century the BBC, like all broadcasting organisations and institutions, will have to take account of a new communications ecology. That, however, is a theme for quite a different lecture.

II   Europe: Words and Images*

Image and word have often been pitted against each other in the history of Europe, most dramatically during the Reformation. Yet over the centuries the sense of Europe has been conveyed both by images and by words – cathedral sculptures and papal encyclicals; castles and charters; the sights of Renaissance Rome and anti-Roman sermons about how lurid they were; seventeenth-century paintings and seventeenth-century tracts; eighteenth-century grand tours and Enlightenment encyclopedias. The nineteenth century, an age of paper that began with popular struggles for literacy, used words as much as flags to assert national identities. Yet it produced the camera and ended with the moving picture. In the early twentieth century the sights of Europe began to be associated with picture postcards, and there was a brief period during the 1920s when new modes of electronic communication offered people pictures without words ('silent') and spoken words without pictures (wireless). Yet it did not require special gifts of prophecy to forecast that there would be an age of television before the century ended.

The new medium of television was already a significant force in Europe when the continent was last surveyed by *Daedalus*. By 1965 the great breakthrough had already taken place. There were over thirteen million television sets in use in Britain and over eleven million in the Federal Republic of Germany. France, with less than six-and-a-half million sets, and Italy, with just over six million, lagged somewhat behind. Britain, outside the European Community, had led the way in the development of the new medium, and as early as 1953, when Britain had nearly three million television sets and the rest of Western Europe only a hundred thousand, the English diarist, man-of-letters, and sound broadcaster Harold Nicolson called television the *deinotatos*, 'the most powerful force ever invented'. He suggested that it would not only replace books, newspapers and the cinema, but also sound broadcasting, the stage, and reading. Despite the lag in French development, by the mid-1960s there was a similar recognition there that a new force

* Based on an article with this title in *Daedalus* (Spring, 1979) 'The European Predicament'.

190

had entered the society. In the aftermath of 1968, a prominent French broadcaster wrote as comprehensively as Nicolson had done that 'once each home had its television set, our civilization was no longer the same. From then on, citizen and society had a means of direct contact which could be used to initiate action as much as to diffuse information.'

The year 1953 saw the first assembling of European television links, although the scope of the new medium, at least in its infancy, was national, not European. Apart from overlap areas which were to grow in importance – particularly at the periphery of Western Europe, where values and systems clashed (the two Germanies, for example, and Italy/Yugoslavia) – television transmission and reception systems were national. Indeed, the occasion for assembling the first European links in 1953 was a national, even imperial, event: the Coronation of the Queen of England. During the crisis year of 1968 – which prompted the reflection that television was actually changing the course of history, not merely reflecting it – many European, as distinct from national, images were widely circulated – particularly that of a European students' revolt. But the argument about the relationship of television to history-making soon passed back from the European to the national level.

What was certain by 1970 was that television had become the mass medium everywhere and that exposure to it was taking up more of people's time than all the other media put together. By 1970, Britain had 293 television sets per one thousand people, the Federal Republic of Germany 272, France 216, and Italy 181. Critical opinion was divided, however, as to whether the main influence of television on society was diversionary, through the trivialising effect of much of its entertainment – this was one of the themes of the Pilkington Report in Britain in 1962 – or action initiating, through the potency of instant images, whether or not they were accompanied by associated verbal messages.

After almost a decade of further exposure, it remains equally difficult to assess the impact of television, not simply because of the impossibility of completely separating out its influence on social, political, and cultural change from that of other forces, but because impact is itself related to those other forces. 'The individual viewer is receiving impressions and images which are manufactured precisely to satisfy his own anticipated needs and beliefs and his supposed powers of comprehension; they may end up either by confirming them or disturbing them.' Television has had different impacts in different places, therefore, and at different times, and on different people in the same place at the same time.

Within the processes of transmission and reception, the political messages carried by television – and they are necessarily selective and limited in range – depend for their effectiveness on factors that may have nothing at all to do with television as such. The medium is not the message, although there are distinctive facets of the medium which have influenced political styles. Seeing how a politician performs on television (which includes how he looks) has become part of the political testing process in all the Western European countries, although it is not the whole of the process. When Alec Home became leader of the Conservative Party – and Prime Minister – in 1963 television had nothing to do with the choice, although it may have had some influence on his defeat at the next election. Between election times, however, as well as during elections, a new forum had now been created. And just because television is daily *and* selective, it has done much to set the political agenda and to diffuse information and images about the different items on the agenda in an order of its own choosing.

The study of the effects of television both on people and on the other media was slower to take shape in Europe than in the United States, and one of the first American writers on political images, Daniel Boorstin, was the 1976 Reith lecturer, one of the BBC's most prestigious appointments. There was an existing base for media studies in the Marxist analysis of the Frankfurt School, however, a base that was to be exploited lavishly during the late 1960s and 1970s, while pragmatic British studies of elections were widely commented upon and were to be copied in other countries. The main influence of Marshall McLuhan, whose writings peppered the 1960s, was to encourage those European intellectuals who did not read sociology to speculate about the characteristics of the different media as 'extensions of man' and about their changing role in history. Yet 'man' seemed far too generic a term on the European side of the Atlantic. Europe was obviously not a village, and the diversity of historical experience in different European countries made it difficult for students of communication to accept theories relating to television that omitted examination of the frameworks of control and of detailed content analysis.

There was a further and equally obvious contrast between what was happening in Western Europe and the United States by the early 1970s. On both sides of the Atlantic about 1 per cent of national income was being spent on the purchase or hiring of television sets and on the provision of television programmes and some of the most popular programmes were trans-Atlantic. Yet in Europe government played a far bigger role than business in the development of television. It was government that dictated the frameworks of control, following inquiry and legislation, and it was government, too, in Britain that decided on the level of fees for television licences and thereby determined both the communication, however, about what they have been trying to do, and this has duplicated effort and wasted time.

In some other programmes, of course, producers have had an open field, and programme-makers like Stephen Peet, who is here at this Conference, have made the best use of it. They have tapped memory through an oral rather than through a literary tradition, creating their own archives in the process. I, too, now have a substantial private archive of my own, and I am sure that the number of such archives will increase. Anthropologists love them even more than do historians.

During the last few months, a Contemporary Archives Unit has been set up within BBC Documentary Features Television, which is considering possible programmes and programme series for the European as well as the British public. A team of producers is being recruited, and the themes in which the Unit is interested are both foreign, including the history of Eastern Europe, suddenly opened up, and domestic, still in the course of revision. For its Executive Producer, Jeremy Bennett, who earlier in his life wrote a detailed study of BBC war-time broadcasting to Denmark, making use of sound and written archives, the work of his new Unit, 'begins with yesterday's news'.

In parallel, Radio Features, Arts and Documentaries have recently transformed their approach to sound archives, switching from the whimsical or the idiosyncratic selection of sound items by presenters largely for entertainment purposes to more serious archive-based programmes.

Turning in the second part of my address to the linked question of what problems arise in selecting and making available for wider access broadcast records, the BBC, as far as sound archives are concerned, has for long categorised 'stock' as it did when giving evidence to the Advisory Committee on Archives in terms of 'events', 'voices', 'social history', 'linguistic', 'drama and light entertainment', 'music', 'natural history', 'sound effects and documentary sound' and 'miscellaneous material for documentary', the last including accounts of first-hand experiences and of 'oddities'.

As far as television is concerned, categorisation, now rather more comprehensive than it was in 1979, is directly related to selection. An Archive Selector, working initially on a week-to-week basis, subject to review, follows guidelines designed to ensure the retention of visual material for the BBC's 'own long-term purposes and as a comprehensive record of its output'. The Archive Selector is responsible to the Head of Film and Videotape Library.

There are eleven specified categories of material, two of which, Categories B and F, are directly geared to the BBC's own 'long-term

pace of development – it could control the timetable for building transmitters also – and (an equally important power, particularly in periods
of inflation) the amount of money available for programming.

The European advance of television, therefore, was thought of less
as a means of opening up new markets for consumer goods than as a
natural extension of the existing audiences for sound broadcasting. The
conception of an 'audience' carried with it the older conception of a
'public' or series of publics. Existing organizations concerned with
sound broadcasting and deriving their income from listeners' licence
fees took over the new medium of television usually without question
and usually with the full blessing of the different National Post Offices
– important, if often bureaucratic, institutions in Europe, each with a
long history. And when commercial television broadcasting was introduced, dependent on advertising, as it was in Britain in 1954, it was
subject to far tighter controls than would have been acceptable in the
United States.

The serious study of commercial television in Europe has concentrated at least as much on structures of national control – and their
influence on the range and quality of programming – as on market
research concerning the efficiency of the advertising and selling operations. (Given the attractiveness of television as a medium to advertisers
– and the great growth of advertising agencies – there has been no
European counterpart to Vance Packard's *Hidden Persuaders*, and
no published study of the influence of television advertising on the
Europeanisation of national name-brand products). One of the main
problems on which attention has been focused has been the extent to
which commercial interests controlling older media – cinema, the Press
and publishing – have been able to acquire a stake in the new media.
Indeed, it is at this point in the analysis that Marxist models of concentration and influence have been most influential.

The difficulty of any kind of analysis, Marxist or otherwise, is that in
different Western European countries the same advancing television
technology has been employed within quite different frameworks of
national control. The West European broadcasting organisations have
been linked since 1950 in EBU, the European Broadcasting Union, a
union with no United States counterpart, and since 1954 the union
has developed 'Eurovision' – retransmitted or shared programs among
the different countries of the West with each country following its
own path. The creation of the Union followed an East/West rift that
had broken up an older European organisation, but it has had little significance in relation to the development of the European Community.
Wider in its coverage than the Community or even Western Europe, it
began with twenty-three countries as members and now has thirty-one.

Its programs of exchange have focused far more on sport – and on popular entertainment – than on politics. There has been no suggestion of a common communications policy, although its programme committee has concentrated since 1964 on 'areas in which, by effective international cooperation, enrichment and, not infrequently, economy, can be achieved in the national programs of EBU members'. It was a sign of the shape of things to come that the first Eurovision programs in 1954 were Charpentier's *Te Deum* and live coverage of the Narcissus Festival in Montreux.

Within EBU, national patterns of development have sometimes converged, but more often they have diverged. For that reason, it is necessary to proceed by way of national case studies, relating new development to national traditions as well as to current economic, social, political, and cultural patterns. Tracing the patterns of convergence and divergence is a far more complex task than charting the few moves made toward European integration.

In Britain, the BBC, founded in 1927 as a public corporation, has continued to pride itself both on its freedom from government – at all levels, including the managerial – and on the balanced nature of its programming. It exerted a powerful influence in Euro... during the Second World War, when it hosted broadcasters from ... cupied countries and encouraged the growth of a European resist...ce, but on the insistence of government, it drastically reduced its European operations after 1945 and since then it has never tried to maintain or to create any sense of Europe through its external sound broadcasting. If it has had any active policy, it has been to project Britain and to spread accurate news in Central and Eastern Europe. The Russian Service, which began in 1946, has acquired a wide audience. The funding of the service has depended entirely on government grants-in-aid, and successive governments did not find it easy to accept the BBC's view that external broadcasting was a very cheap, cost effective way of sustaining Britain's influence abroad. They were increasingly sensitive, too, to domestic BBC programmes which they did not like.

In France, the Office de la Radiodiffusion et Télévision Française, ORTF (renamed after 1959), was far closer to the State than the BBC in 1964, and it remained so throughout the whole period of its existence down to 1976, when it was broken up. A 1964 reform, the first of many, created an administrative council as a buffer between government and ORTF – with the tasks of establishing general lines of action; deliberating on how to control the budget; evaluating the 'quality and morality' of the programmes; watching over the 'objectivity and accuracy' of the news; and ensuring that 'the principal tendencies of thought were expressed on the media. Yet half the members of its council were controlled by the government, and the government could give orders to and remove from office ORTF staff, including the most senior members. It is not surprising, therefore, that one of the most complex of the *évènements* of 1968 was a strike of ORTF workers which began in May and lasted for eleven weeks. It was led by some of the best-known television personalities in France and had widespread repercussions, immediate and deferred. The results of the reforms of 1976, involving the disappearance of ORTF, have so far not lived up to the hopes of the most ardent reformers.

In Germany, where the machinery of broadcasting was remodelled under the Allied occupation, nine deliberately decentralised Chartered Broadcasting Companies, each based on a *Land*, came together in 1950 in a federal union, the Arbeitsgemeinschaft öffentlich-rechtlichen Rundfunkanstalten der Bundesrepublik, ARD. The new union was not subject to federal government control, though each of the different *Länder* governments evolved its own pattern of appointments and organisation, and in each case the patterns involved recognition of *Proporz*, 'the sharing of broadcasting appointments according to a formula based on the balance of political affiliations within the *Land* parliament'. The different ARD companies also shared a common policy code, according to which they would not denigrate the post-war German state nor the basic institutions of marriage and the family, would not stir up religious controversy, and would not disturb the mutual respect of social groups, nationalities and cultures. None the less, there have been frequent controversies in Germany, not least because the political situation in the different *Länder* varied considerably.

It was because of history that the clauses in the German common policy code of 1950 were so explicit. In Britain, the conventions that sustained the treasured autonomy of the BBC as a public corporation were tacit, although they were increasingly difficult to keep tacit during the 1970s, while in France the political forces keeping ORTF under constant scrutiny throughout the Gaullist and Pompidou regimes were powerful enough – and widely enough recognised – to require no spelling out. It is interesting to note, however, that in Germany an attempt by Konrad Adenauer (who disliked television criticism) to set up a central commercial radio network failed after a challenge in the courts. Instead, the *Länder* set up their own federal commercial network, Zweites Deutsches Fernsehen (ZDF), and insisted that it follow the ARD code.

Such an account of formal broadcasting history in three countries can and should be extended to cover the history of RAI, the Italian national broadcasting authority set up in 1946, and the history of broadcasting systems in some of the smaller broadcasting networks inside and outside the European Community. Of these, the Dutch and the Swedish are perhaps the most interesting. From the 1920s onward the Dutch had allowed air time to be shared by religious–political organisations, each carrying out its own programming. Each paid its own way, and was not dependent on revenue derived from licence fees. The system was revived after the German occupation, and applied (with significant modifications) to television. (The most important modification was that the new Television Foundation retained 40 per cent of broadcasting time for itself.) Divisions over broadcasting policy in 1965 brought down the Dutch coalition government, the first to fall on such issues; and thereafter new measures were introduced which, while linking sound broadcasting and television, ensuring a sizeable proportion of 'common time' and deriving revenue for common programming from a licence fee, still permitted most broadcasting in Holland to be organised by voluntary groups. In Sweden, also, considerable emphasis was placed on pluralism. Swedish Radio was a private company, of which 20 per cent of the stock was held by the radio and television manufacturing industry, 40 per cent by the Press and 40 per cent by a wide range of voluntary organisations. The government, however, appointed the Director-General and five members of the Board, and could outvote the stock owners. It also owned the transmitters. A code of practice drawn up during the 1960s set out to protect the interests of controversial minorities as well as to guarantee strict political impartiality, and in 1967 a broadcasting council was set up to supervise the working of the code and of a prior agreement between Swedish Radio and the government that had been drawn up in 1959. The Council consisted of seven independent individuals appointed by the government and drawn from the ranks of professional, occupational, and intellectual groups.

Formal accounts of political settlements and of constitutional powers do not cover adequately the dynamics of broadcasting nor the kind of issues which the Swedish Broadcasting Council had to consider. Nor do they centre precisely enough either on the challenge that television, in particular, seemed to present to government during the 1960s and 1970s or on the tensions that were experienced inside the broadcasting organisations themselves. Although they were national challenges and tensions, they were fairly reported in foreign countries and by 1970 seemed increasingly to form a consistent pattern.

Since the early 1960s, European politicians, whether in government or in opposition, had become increasingly aware of the political importance of television not only at election times but as a running commentary on politics in between. They were aware, too, of the importance of their own access (and that of others) to the medium. Meanwhile, television broadcasters, like Press journalists before them, became more professionalised, more enterprising and more competitive in their operations – a subject of sharp criticism, particularly in West Germany – more confident in their techniques, and more sure of their news values. Whatever the divergences between different countries, there was ample scope everywhere for conflict among producers, broadcasters, and politicians, both in government and the opposition. In Britain, it was the Labour opposition that stirred up one of the controversies that directly brought in the public as well – that following a BBC program *Yesterday's Men* in 1971. In such circumstances, intermediate bodies, like the governors of the BBC, have been placed in a difficult position, seeking at the same time to monitor the most controversial programs prepared by their own producers and to maintain the autonomy of their organisations *vis-à-vis* governments.

It is significant that in the latest phases of European television history there has been far less public discussion of the likely implications of technological change than there has been in the United States. The term 'information society' is little used, except in France, although there are many branches of communications technology in which Europe more than holds its own with the United States. The convergence of communications techniques, that bring together broadcasting, sound and visual: person-to-person communication, sound, and, if desired, visual; and data communication and control through computerisation, has received little attention; and even less attention has been paid to its social and cultural implications, ranging from a possible widening of individual freedom of choice to tightly controlled systems of comprehensive communication. Two of the most recent European inquiries into broadcasting, the Annan Committee in Britain and its Swedish counterpart, whose reports appeared within days of each other in 1977, were sceptical about many such techniques, when they considered them at all, and cautious about the timetable. The Annan Committee recognised that at some unspecified date in the future 'formidable changes in constitutional arrangements' would be necessary to meet the challenge of a new 'era of multiplicity of communications service'. Yet there was something almost plaintive in its conclusion that 'eventually governments will have to face the problem of communications policy'. Even foundation-sponsored reports have rested content with generalisations like, 'the technology we possess but have as yet not fully employed will become more and more active and produce a greater and greater impression on the life of society and the individual'.

The same note is apparent in the Report of the Committee on the Post Office in Britain, chaired by Sir Charles Carter, and the 1976 report of a powerful German committee on telecommunications. While recognising that there would have to be a communications strategy, the Carter Committee did not choose to identify alternatives, but rather left this task to a citizens' advisory council, and it conceded that 'as between government and Post Office there is no clear and agreed understanding about those policy matters in which it may be appropriate for government to intervene and those executive management matters in which it is not appropriate'. Although the British Post Office is perhaps the most innovative and lively of all European post offices on its technological side, the Committee did not believe 'that the widespread use of new methods of message transmission which use *both* postal and telecommunications facilities is likely within a period that should affect thought about organisation'. The German committee, while acknowledging the realities of what it called 'technical transmission integration' and while admitting the inadequacy of existing structures to cope with technical change, stated that any reforms would raise political issues on which it did not wish to offer advice.

It is clear, therefore, that at the national level the notion of a long-term communications policy is either embryonic or suspect. It is embryonic in so far as such a policy might encompass television and new electronic technologies, sound broadcasting, private and public communication (hitherto largely kept apart), data transmission, including viewdata, and computer development and use. It is suspect in so far as such a policy might include within its scope the media of the word, book publishing, and the press – there are strong traditions of non-intervention by democratic government in this area – and even of the cinema as a medium of images. There are many people involved in the operations of both old and new media, indeed, for whom the very term 'communications policy' is anathema. Yet there is resistance in Europe also to freeing the whole complex to achieve 'electronic abundance' or individual freedom of choice.

The position in Austria, as described by a recent writer, is not untypical. 'It is still too early to speak of a coherent system of communications policy in Austria. As a branch of public activity, communications policy is a novelty. But it has had an increasingly significant impact on the evolution of the Austrian media since the early 1970s.' In most countries, there is little public knowledge about the ingredients of such a policy. Thus, in the recent wave of Press and television interest in microelectronics, the main focus of interest has been less on communications policy than on fear of unemployment. The main theme in communications remains the adaptation, often for immediate or short-term reasons, of inherited structures.

Above all, there are few signs of any desire to evolve a Western European or European Community communications policy as distinct from national policies. As Roy Pryce, formerly Head of the Brussels Directorate for Information, pointed out in 1976, while Europeans are surrounded at every moment of their lives by the visible symbols of the nation state (and of the local authority) – banknotes, coins, stamps, identity cards, passports, car licenses and number plates, and so on, not to speak of flags – the Community itself is 'virtually invisible to the great mass of its citizens'. In a period when national – and local – images have multiplied, there is a dearth of Community images, although several countries inside and outside the Community have issued 'Europe stamps'. Brussels, moreover, is far away from most people's homes and lines of travel, and is associated with long verbal wrangles and bureaucratic forms rather than with images that inform, entertain, or educate. The Belgian ex-Prime Minister, Leo Tindemans, has often shown how well aware he is of the problem, and has stressed persistently that the 'will of the national governments' is not enough to ensure that Europe will draw 'close to its citizens. . . . The need for it must be perceived by everyone.' Yet even Tindemans has spelt out an educational and cultural policy, so far largely unimplemented, rather than a communications policy.

One limited attempt to make a start with sound broadcasting has already foundered. A 1973 proposal by the BBC's External Broadcasting Service to inaugurate a European (not a BBC) news service, broadcasting three news bulletins of thirty to forty-five minutes a day in English, French, German, and Italian, has not been implemented, even though it had won the support of a number of political leaders, including Raymond Barre; and its sponsors were frank in admitting that television, the major medium, was 'by its nature too expensive and too technically complex for day-to-day, on-the-spot purposes'. Radio Europe, the sponsors of the scheme pointed out, would have had political as well as cultural importance.

> There is remarkably little understanding among the general public in the nine member countries of the European Community either of the Community decision-making processes or of the nature of the compromise solutions required in order to achieve progress towards the common goal. Such understanding exists, broadly speaking, only among experts: political leaders, parliamentary representatives and officials of individual governments or the Commission. The rest of the public still tends to take a narrower, purely nationally-based view and to judge common decisions by their local material effects.

One recent development in national communications history – the growth of community radio and television – has given an even narrower significance to the term 'local'. In Italy, where far-reaching, if in some cases transient, changes in the structures of broadcasting have been introduced – not as a result of carefully considered policy-making but of (unforeseen) judgements in the courts – the shift to the local and the fragmented has been most striking. Yet there have been changes in Sweden and cautious, but significant, changes in Britain, which now has a wide span of local radio stations, BBC and commercial.

A series of mid-1970s free speech decisions by the Supreme Constitutional Court in Rome, the first of them in 1974, broke the authority of Radiotelevisione Italiana (RAI) and led to the creation of dozens of small local radio and television stations. At a time when the concentration of Press and publishing interests in Italy was being intensified, both sound broadcasting and television passed into the hands of a wide variety of agencies – some 70 per cent directly involved with newspaper and magazine groups, local radio traders, or other commercial interests; some 20 per cent cultural; and a small but active 10 per cent minority political.

So-called alternative media have emerged on the left-wing fringe, often drawing on disgruntled journalists of the word. Thus, Radio Città in Bologna was set up by a group of professional journalists who had failed to sustain an alternative newspaper to compete with a well-established rival. Offering regular access to minority movements, such as the women's liberation organisations; keeping Sunday as an open day for phone-ins, individual and group requests, and unscheduled use of the studio; and running an alternative news agency with the aim of 'voicing reality,' such a station diverged sharply from older European models. Another station, Radio Alice, which was closed by security forces in March 1977, but continued in various forms, set out quite deliberately 'to go to the other side of the mirror: . . . we did not want to have a fixed schedule for the public, because we didn't believe in the public'. These were 'way-out' examples of local radio. Television was freed, too, when RAI lost its monopoly, although because of the problem of financing, of the 200 television stations existing in 1977 a sizeable proportion were simply televising still images in order to register their wavelength position.

The anarchy continues, even though RAI was reformed by a law of 1975, which placed its control in the hands of a forty-member parliamentary commission representing different political groups and a sixteen-member board with ten of its members chosen by the commission. Although supporters of public broadcasting argue powerfully that a large number of broadcasting stations inevitably results in splitting up the public into reduced, isolated groups, without ensuring that any of these groups has access to real pluralism of information, the confusion appeals to both the Left and the Right. And the reformed RAI constitution is hardly a recipe for effective broadcasting.

Throughout Europe, the development of local broadcasting raises many interesting questions about the dimensions of social, political, and cultural involvement. The Italian Minister of Posts has defined local operations as those within a fifteen-kilometer radius and with a coverage of no more than one hundred thousand viewers or listeners. This is a narrower definition of 'local' – at least as far as coverage is concerned – than the British definition, which allows for local broadcasting to millions of Londoners. Yet although British local stations are owned, managed, and operated in a quite different way from the Italian stations – and place more emphasis on community issues and light entertainment than on 'class' or ideology – they also split up the public. 'Local radio has quite a different kind of relationship with its community', the Annan Committee reported, 'and the community has, or should have, an almost proprietary feeling about its local station that it cannot have about a national network.'

Whatever the rationale of local radio – closeness to local opinion and interests; involvement in community affairs (although not to the extent of some of the United States or Canadian cable stations); access to the microphone and to participation in management (Radio Città had a general assembly); or immediacy of comment – within a European context its further development (strongly recommended by official committees in Britain and Sweden) may well divert attention from European to parochial issues. Indeed, it will reinforce the tendency already apparent in the Europe of the last seven or eight years to pick up local grievances and concerns as the raw material of politics. The range of issues is thus affected, as well as the style. There can, of course, be local attachments and alliances across the dividing lines of nation states, ranging from 'town twinning', an innocuous activity, rarely with much depth, to joint action in 'green' environmental politics or occasionally in shared educational projects. It is not only politics that are affected. The quest for local culture sometimes leads in the name of participation and creativity to (a not necessarily lamented) decline in artistic standards, a deliberate cutting off from the metropolitan and even the large provincial centres of culture. At this point, issues raised in policy-making for the arts overlap with issues raised in the making of communications policies.

There is, of course, an intermediate tier in Europe between the locality and the nation state – the region – and a considerable amount of effort, little of it successful, has been devoted during the last seven or eight years to discussing, deciding upon, and implementing European regional policies. Paradoxically, regionalisation in broadcasting has declined in significance – though not broadcasting for or by submerged nationalisms – as localism has increased. If 'regions' were to be given more than economic meaning in the Europe of the Nine, there would have to be far more emphasis on communications policies within and between regions. This would be a necessary part of any evolution of the European Community beyond collaboration between states or beyond the further growth of a 'harmonising' bureaucracy.

The only attempt by the Press to pass beyond sport, entertainment, and culture in dealing with Europe is the monthly newspaper *Europe*, drawing on the editorial resources of *Le Monde*, *The Times* (London), *Die Welt*, and *La Stampa*. Yet clearly the forthcoming European elections will bring in the different media, including television, and will reveal to what extent local, regional, national, and European issues will interpenetrate. An important research project is being planned by the International Institute of Communications to cover the elections, to compare the use of the media in different countries, and to assess their impact. The elections will indeed offer an unprecedented opportunity to study the relative role of images and words in a Europe that has so far passed through only the first phases of its communications revolution.

So far, television has influenced but not destroyed other media, including the media of the written and the spoken word. 'Minister blames illiteracy on too much TV' was a recent, not untypical headline in *The Times*, where it was pointed out that two-thirds of British children between the ages of nine and twelve were spending up to thirty-five hours a week watching television. Yet the actual story is far more complicated than such headlines suggest. The media of the word have had a complex history of their own during the 1960s and 1970s, with inherited structures and processes posing difficult problems, some common to all European countries, some distinctive. The distinctiveness, moreover, can only be explained in terms of traditions that began long before the twentieth century.

Five general points stand out. First, television has not yet destroyed the book, although there have been changes in the appearence of books. The 'crisis of the book' that occurred in the mid-1970s involved pricing problems rather than competition from another medium. Second, the newspaper has undergone a genuine and continuing crisis which is only partly related to the growth of television. Rises in costs and breaks in production during often bitter industrial disputes have

allowed television to strengthen its hold. Although, of course, television, like the Press, has been increasingly unionised, breaks in production have not had the same consequences, notably reduction of
individual freedom of choice to buy a particular product. Third, the
incomplete 'communications revolution' – and this is a term that has
stuck in Europe – carries with it a whole cluster of still unresolved
choices, some of which will be made within the market, some within
the political process. Fourth, sound broadcasting has not lost its importance, as many prophets predicted it would in an 'age of television'.
It has re-established itself as something more than an inferior or out-
dated medium, 'steam radio'. Fifth – and in the long run perhaps the
most important – some of the concepts and procedures associated with
the new media are being applied to the old media and vice versa.

The survival of the book during the 1960s and early 1970s can best
be illustrated from Britain; here a 1973 symposium 'Do books still
matter?' not surprisingly reached the conclusion that they did: a
message from McLuhan to the symposium hailed them as 'the only
available means of developing habits of private initiative and private
goals and objectives in the electronic age', and George Steiner, pointing
to the 'lone effort' of reading them, found it a matter of praise that
they 'silently exclude'. Britain has a long-established tradition of printing and publishing, going back to Caxton – the Oxford University
Press celebrated its 500th anniversary in 1978 – and there are large
numbers both of bookshops dealing in new and old books and of
public libraries. (Only 4–5 per cent of the French population is
estimated to use a public library as against 20–30 per cent in Britain.)
Between 1946 and 1972 the annual number of new book titles in Britain
rose from thirteen thousand to over thirty thousand and the turnover
of the trade from £27 million to £200 million. Television seemed to be
encouraging people to buy books, while increased leisure (and travel)
were giving them time to read them. Pictures were not driving out
words; in fact the allure of books was increasing. Far more attention
was being paid to graphics and there was even talk of a new literary
form – 'the mook', half-magazine and half-book.

Yet Britain illustrates also the books crisis of the mid-1970s. Following rises in printing and paper costs, greater than in any previous
period of history, book prices soared. Pressure on publishers' profits
heightened at the same time as sales resistance, including the resistance
of libraries, particularly hard hit by inflation, thereby pushing up
prices still further. There was talk of a vicious circle affecting sales of all
but the most popular books. 'They're not burning our books,' the
Guardian complained in 1976, 'they're freezing them out.' A lively
correspondence in *The Times* in late April and May 1978 followed the

publication of a controversial article by Ian Bradley dealing with one limited category of books, but a category always prestigious and usually profitable in Britain – history books. It raised important questions about the organisation of publishing – there had already been big changes since 1964, including greater concentration – and about the policy of publishers, many of whom had come to rely more and more not on accepting manuscripts offered to them but on commissioning titles.

The correspondence touched also on the relationship between domestic and foreign sales, in the European as well as the American market, but it did not touch on the relationship between publishing interests and the ownership of the electronic media, a major issue in the United States and one that will doubtless become a more important issue in Europe. If words and images are controlled by the same groups – or persons – this could have a profound effect on Europe and on attitudes to the relationship between Europe and the United States in a new global context.

Sweden has been one of a number of European countries – France another – that offered governmental aid to the newspaper – in the name not of control, but of democratic pluralism. Newspaper sales had reached unprecedented heights in many European countries during the immediate post-war years. Even in France, where there had been talk of a newspaper crisis as long ago as the late 1930s, there was a brief golden age between 1945 and 1950. The position deteriorated in the 1960s and 1970s as a result of increasing costs and labour disputes – some of which centred on the authority of the editor or on the respective roles of editor and proprietor – and deteriorated still further when efforts were made to apply new electronic technologies designed to save labour and to speed up production. Resistance was strong in a number of different European countries, including Britain and the Federal Republic, and strongest of all, perhaps, in Denmark, where one of Copenhagen's oldest and best-selling newspapers, the conservative *Berlinske Tidende*, went out of action altogether for several months.

Given fears for the survival of well-established newspapers, different European countries have reacted in different ways. France, where there were far-reaching structural changes, was merely following an older policy when it resorted to governmental subsidies. In Italy, where a smaller number of newspapers are sold to a smaller segment of the population than in any other Western European country (99 per thousand in 1974 as against 441 per thousand in Britain), subventions from government have coexisted uneasily with retail price fixing.

Is it the idea [*Corriere della Sera* asked in October 1976] to invite the newspaper to commit suicide in order to avoid the cost of living index rising by one point? . . . We are against the public financing of newspapers. But they must be able to pay their way by being allowed to operate at a price which corresponds to the cost of production. . . . If the publishing companies collapse, so, too, will the freedom of the Press which we are only just beginning to enjoy.

In Britain, where resistance to official subsidies has been greatest, with the possible exception of Denmark, the Press benefits from exemption from Value Added Tax (VAT), and has expressed itself willing to accept official support to pay for the retirement and retraining of workers made redundant by new technology.

The situation of the Press in Britain remains highly competitive and was the subject of an official inquiry, quite separate, though parallel, to that of the Annan Committee. It recommended a bigger public voice in the Press Council, which reviews individual and institutional complaints and which had operated in this increasingly difficult field since 1952. (In West Germany there is a *Press-rat* and in Sweden a Press Ombudsman). As long ago as 1964 the British Trades Union Congress had sold its shares in Britain's only official Labour party newspaper, the *Daily Herald*. The *Herald* duly went out of circulation that year, to be replaced by the commercial *Sun*, which under later ownership became an aggressive, popular tabloid. Important issues were raised then which have never been settled. The images of society – and of Europe – as presented in the popular Press (separated everywhere from a 'quality' Press) do not in any country reflect the political situation. In Denmark, for example, where the Social Democratic party is the largest in the country, the old Social Democratic Press, product of the late nineteenth century, commands only 6 per cent of newspaper readers.

As the newspaper crisis continues – and it raises many other issues, including those of editorial as well as of ownership control – it has been argued just as strongly of the newspaper as it was argued earlier of the book that it is not one single product. It fulfills different needs – like television, for entertainment as well as for the supply of information, or, unlike television, offering material in perspective and in depth for rereading as well as reading, or even for keeping. It is certainly read and used by different readers in different ways (for home or for travel literature, for instance). Its role as an advertising medium, threatened by television and at the community level by local sound broadcasting, is of critical importance to its economics. As long ago as 1962 a British High Court judge said of books that they should never be compared with eggs or oranges. A new book cannot be recognised as something that will certainly satisfy some known public appetite or need as easily as can an orange or egg.' The same might be said of the newspaper.

It is because the Press is one of the oldest forms of mass communication and has had to struggle throughout its long history for the right to be free, that efforts have been made to encourage self-regulation rather than direct government intervention. Yet the latest struggle – to cope with new technology – is more controversial than any previous struggle within the newspaper industry itself. Electronic text editing and photocomposition are merely the first developments in a traditionally labour-intensive industry, and already there are signs of blurring of printers' and journalists' traditional roles. Electronic distribution is not science fiction; it is a step in the present logic, although Europe is still some distance away from finding an economically viable substitute for the printed page. There are three systems of teletext already in operation in Britain, however. While the BBC has developed CEEFAX and the Independent Broadcasting Authority ORACLE, the British Post Office is testing VIEWDATA, linking television receivers through the telephone systems to information stores in computers, a genuine example of 'compunications' at work.

Who should control such development – and the extent to which they should be controlled at all – is a matter of debate. The German Press is anxious to carry out pilot teletext projects using broadband communications, while the British Press tried to persuade the Annan Committee – it was unsuccessful in its efforts – either to proclaim a moratorium on new developments (a not unfamiliar Press tactic in the earlier history of innovation in communications techniques) or to grant newspaper publishers the prescriptive right to participate in the ownership and management of teletext systems. Meanwhile, the British Post Office, far more liberal in its attitudes toward the operations of VIEWDATA than it was to the diffusion of the older technologies of cable radio and television, will permit any individual or institution – including newspapers – to become either information providers or recipients, even entrepreneurs, leasing telephone lines from the Post Office and serving the public directly. The common carrier issue is assuming new importance.

Such technical developments remain competitive in Europe, as does the often hectic, but so far unexploited, business in video-cassettes and video-discs, where analogies are usually drawn not from the radio or telephone business but from the phonograph record, cassette, and tape recorder industry. While rival systems pour money into research and development – and there is a strong European stake – the relationship between hardware and software is still receiving inadequate attention. New technologies offer the possibility of far greater individual choice than ever before, but they might lead alternatively to new linkages and systematisation.

The sense of system has never been absent in Europe since the development of railways, telegraphs, telephones, and telex, and it has been pushed much further since 1964 in the growth of computer networks in banking (credit cards) and transport (particularly aviation). In 1979 the computer network Euronet will go into full operation, linking not only the Europe of the Nine, but Scandinavia, Spain, and Austria. There will be four main computers – Paris, London, Frankfurt, and Rome – and second-level computers in Amsterdam, Brussels, Copenhagen, Dublin, and Luxembourg. Users will be able to connect to the network either via direct access circuits or the public switchboard telephone network. Existing public data transmission networks, like that of the European Space Agency, will be brought in. Given Europe's history, the operational rules will appropriately enough be called 'Protocol', although we seem far from the Europe of history. Two dangers have already been pointed out – loss of individual privacy (and several European countries, including the Federal Republic and Sweden, have taken public steps to protect this, the latter prohibiting transborder transmissions of personal data that is not accorded equivalent privacy safeguards in foreign storage or processing) and information overload. 'On the one hand, the communications systems offer an increased output and a greater variety of choice; on the other, the psychological demands inherent in these choices require initiative and active effort. How can these demands be met, when the human nervous system responds to an excessive input by loss of initiative and loss of involvement?'

This is not a specifically European question, although it has been asked with particular force within Europe, where it is being considered along with a cluster of questions concerning work, unemployment, leisure, and apathy. These are thought to be directly related. The question of integration tends to be considered quite separately. The same is true of physical travel. The 1960s and early 1970s saw the great European boom in packaged tours, yet non-packaged intra-European travel remains both expensive and inconvenient and little or no research has been carried out on the effects, if any, of tourism on integration. Sometimes there is the minimum exchange of words and an exchange only of the most stereotyped images. *Coelum non animam mutant qui trans mare current*: 'those who cross the sea change their skies but not their natures'. In relation to intra-European travel, nature (sun, sea, mountain, lake) counts for as much as culture. It is interesting indeed to note that in 1970 two countries at the periphery of Europe headed one relevant league table and came at the foot of another. Sweden had the fewest tourists (0.4 per cent) and the most television sets per thousand of the population, 312. Spain had the most tourists (21 per cent of the total number for Europe) and the fewest television sets, 124. Since then there have been interesting changes in the table, with Britain's dramatic increase in the number of tourists having far more to do with the attractions of relatively low prices than with membership in the European Community.

The fourth and fifth of the general points about the position of other media in an age of television raise different issues. The continued existence of sound broadcasting had more to do with music than with words or images. It has much also to do with mobility and the popularisation of car radios. The transistor radio evolution hit the beaches of Europe during the 1960s at the same time as it hit the cities, often carrying the same pop music to different parts of Europe. There are significant differences in tastes, revealed in the Eurovision Song Contest, which has become one of the main events or pseudo-events in the calendar; and American influence has been reduced since 1964, though not extinguished. Meanwhile, VHF and stereo have strengthened the capacity of sound broadcasting to meet the needs of lovers of classical music. In the twentieth century more than the nineteenth, when music was often an instrument of nationalism, music has held Europe (sometimes West and East) together when images and words have failed. Sound broadcasting has one other major use, education. Television is a far more expensive medium for educational purposes, and although it is used for both school and adult education programmes, sound broadcasting remains the major medium.

There are many interactions between the different media. Teamwork in newspaper journalism and graphics in book production both owe much to the world of television. Meanwhile, the concept of 'publishing' has been carried over into that world. The breakup of ORTF in France was designed in part, it was stated, to allow independent producers to 'publish', and the same theme runs through the Annan Committee's proposals to grant control of a fourth new television channel in Britain neither to the BBC nor to the IBA, but to a new organisation, the Open Broadcasting Authority, which would have a publishing, not governing, function: it would commission programmes from 'independents', not make them. It has recently been argued that the main challenge to government in Europe as the controller of the shape of broadcasting systems will come less from the liberation of market forces than from the assertion of older traditions of free publishing. It has also been argued, however, that debates about television news presentation and impact have strengthened demands for a more responsible Press journalism.

All this is unfinished business. Moreover, in any assessment of the changing relationships between word and image in Europe, global as well as local factors have to be taken into the reckoning along with the national and European factors. Communications technology is universal and the potential of the media is global. In any study, therefore, of news flows, of culture contacts, or of technological transfers, a broader framework than Europe is necessary. It should be added that two of the main international news agencies (Reuters and France-Presse) have their headquarters in Europe; that Europe shaped the pattern of culture contacts during the colonial age; and that several European countries have a major stake in the communications industry.

The division of Europe into East and West is an essential feature of the situation also. It is a division that defies history at many points. Nor has it lost any of its force since the Helsinki Agreements of 1977 asserted that the thirty-five signatories would 'make it their aim to facilitate the freer and wider dissemination of information of all kinds', an unqualified aim. The interaction of Western European and Eastern European media is intermittent and limited. The images are often stereotypes, and the words do not usually flow. If they were to flow, Europe would change.

12   The First Broadcasting Critics*

'There is still very little serious criticism of broadcasting', wrote Geoffrey Tandy in T. S. Eliot's prestigious quarterly, *The Criterion*, in October 1935. 'Most of that which appears in that guise consists of grumbles at the BBC for not conforming more closely to comic-paper standards of entertainment.' The general position was not improved with the advent of regular television programmes, what was described as a 'service', from Alexandra Palace in November 1936. Indeed, *The Criterion* itself, firmly set in a literary tradition, was uneasy about the prospects of an age of television. The main note in it was usually defensive, like Tandy's comment in October 1936 that 'it is to be hoped that the coming of television will not hinder the due development of radio drama'.

One of the few serious critics in 1935 and 1936, Grace Wyndham Goldie, remarkable among her colleagues in going on to graduate from criticism to television production and management, had started with radio drama. Her first piece of criticism, 'At the Broadcast Play', appeared in *The Listener* in May 1935. 'How am I to criticise radio plays', she began disarmingly, 'when I know little or nothing about broadcasting?' The freshness of the question, not uncommon at that time, did not save her from criticism by Tandy who objected in April 1936 to the way she had dealt with T. S. Eliot's *Murder in the Cathedral*, described by the broadcasting critic of *The Sunday Times* as 'a jewel among microphone plays'. Yet from the start there was something distinctively fresh in Grace Wyndham Goldie's approach.

'I cannot believe in criticism', she wrote in her very first article, 'which is based on ignorance of the conditions of work . . . The physical limitations imposed upon any art by the material through which it works determines its form, and it is impossible to criticise without knowing what they are.' Given this approach, Wyndham Goldie was

*This essay is based on a number of pieces that I have written for *The Listener*, particularly 'The First TV Critics' (30 October 1986) and 'Still Listening' (18 January 1979), where I suggested that 'historians of the last fifty years will turn to *The Listener* not only in order to retrieve a record of radio in action, but to catch something of the intimacy of lost times and the range of preoccupations associated with old climates of opinion'.

210

a forthright critic, unimpressed by authority, literary or otherwise, when regular programming began in November 1936. 'I always suspect', she wrote in September 1937, 'that the "Golden Age of Radio Drama" was a myth.' Three months later, she maintained resolutely that

> the most exciting thing of the whole year has been the development of television drama from a curiosity to current entertainment. And the most exciting news of the week is that on the fourth of January viewers will be able, for the first time, to see an entertainment televised directly from the place where it is being performed to the public. In other words they will be able to sit at home and see the Circus at Olympia.

Gracie Wyndham Goldie was ready for television in a way that very few other people, including R. S. Lambert, the first editor of *The Listener*, were. Indeed, in her own words, she had to pull strings and to get him to pull strings in order to be present in Studio A at Alexandra Palace in August 1936 to see the experimental television transmissions being broadcast from there to Radio Olympia. 'All right', he told her, 'but you're not to write about them. Television won't matter in your life-time or mine.' It was a commonly held view. Reith would have agreed with him.

The experimental television programmes were not covered by Grace Wyndham Goldie, and her only piece on television in *The Listener* in 1936 posed the question raised defensively by Tandy one month later, 'What is television going to do to radio drama?' she asked, at once giving her own answers, 'Change it. Obviously. Revolutionise it? Probably. Kill it altogether? No.' Her own approach to television, which she was to describe years later in 1948, after the Second World War, as 'the bomb about to burst', was from the start positive. 'Television is more advanced than broadcasting was when we first heard it', she wrote in September 1936. Moreover, it had an appeal of its own which was 'quite different' from that of the cinema.

Much of her criticism was specific, related to her view that physical possibilities and limitations had to be taken into account in judging any particular programme from *East End* to *Cyrano de Bergerac*, but she made many important general points as her criticism moved from plays to the circus, to other outside broadcasts, to Cecil Madden's *Picture Page*, and, not least, to the news. She was always interested in the relationship between 'intimacy' and 'reality' in television, and while she considered that the 'trump card' of television was its 'immediacy in time' – 'it can let you see the thing *now*, while it is actually happening' – she felt that it had many other more surprising cards to play. 'The latest and exciting news about television', she wrote in February 1938, 'is that television is going to be strong just where broadcast drama is weak. That is in comedy.'

Grace Wyndham Goldie continued as drama critic of *The Listener* until April 1939, although she occasionally devoted her column to television, and between March 1938, when *The Listener* grouped its critics under the collective title *Critic on the Hearth*, and April 1939 she swapped roles from time to time with Peter Purbeck, who now became a television critic. By then, *The Listener*, which was celebrating its tenth anniversary, was proud of all its criticism: as the editor stated on that occasion in January 1939, 'we have aimed at building up, with the aid of several regular contributors and of our occasional correspondents, a system of intelligent criticism of current programmes, which has often, we believe been of interest to listeners and of service to our colleagues who arrange the programmes'.

That had not been conceived of as its first purpose. Indeed, the first conception of *The Listener*, as propounded by Sir Henry Hadow, musician and educationist, had been that it would be an educational journal, 'a stately sixpenny', serving as a supplement to 'aids to study'. Fortunately, after a battle of memoranda, characteristic of the BBC, 'a properly wide view of education' had been taken that, in the words of the high-ranking BBC administrator Basil Nicholls, was not just concerned with 'members of study groups or tutorial classes'. Nicholls's view prevailed, although to win the battle he had had to invoke the image of 'an invalid who requires new interests or learns to listen intelligently to music or to poetry'.

At the moment of celebration in 1939, Sir Denison Ross called *The Listener* 'the best three-pennyworth [half the sixpenny] ever offered the public', and the New College historian, H. A. L. Fisher, who was a Governor of the BBC, forecast that 'the bulky volumes of *The Listener* will be invaluable to the historian, not only as illustrating the ultimate development of the use of the spoken word since the inception of the BBC, but as a guide to the multiple and changing interests and activities of the age'.

Surprisingly, perhaps, T. S. Eliot would have agreed. He had told its then Literary Editor, Janet Adam Smith, in the summer of 1933, while television was still experimental, that *The Listener* was aiming at a public 'which is curious and avid for information about the latest facts, ideas and discoveries in contemporary art and thought'; 'at the very least', he went on, it would serve 'as a document upon the time'.

Fisher did not mention television at *The Listener*'s tenth birthday party, but F. W. Ogilvie, Reith's successor as Director-General of the BBC, did. After referring to the 'amazing imageries which could come through the ear', not a promising start, he expressed the hope – what would Grace Wyndham Goldie have made of it? – that television would never rival *The Listener*. Lambert did not comment, although he wrote in 1940, one year after he left *The Listener*, in his book *Ariel and All His Quality*, that his years as its editor had proved to him that 'there is a fundamental antithesis between officialdom and journalism'. In 1939 statistics backed Ogilvie. *The Listener* had 49,642 readers: the number of television owners was then between 20,000 and 25,000, almost all of them in the London area.

The first regular daily television critic, Marsland Gander of the *Daily Telegraph*, presented his own well-informed but thoroughly unofficial journalistic account of what was happening on the television screen, well briefed both from Alexandra Palace and Broadcasting House. Most television set owners were probably also his readers. Marsland Gander, too, had been present at Radiolympia in August 1936, along with 'the wireless correspondent' of *The Times*, who was content to dwell on the flaws in 'this new entertainment' – a tendency 'to flicker, which it shares with most of the old silent films, and a curious and uneasy shifting of parts within the image which is peculiar to itself'.

Marsland Gander also directed attention to the deficiencies, while encouraging development. 'That drama had improved out of all recognition', he said, and 'enormous strides had been made in outside broadcasts', a field in which television was coming into its own 'above every other'. Most important of all, the BBC was the only organisation in the world that had 'tackled the problems of television programme technique and made a really successful attempt to find out what type of material is most suitable for a television programme'.

None the less, even for Marsland Gander, the achievement was precarious, and he could raise a laugh in this connection when he addressed the Television Society in December 1938. After quoting the BBC's Chief Engineer, Sir Noel Ashbridge, who had said that there were 'a hundred times as many things to go wrong in a television station as there were in a broadcasting station', there were laughs when he added, 'In practice his words proved correct.' At that time, Ashbridge, who occasionally gave the public advice about television, was more preoccupied with a Broadcasting in Wartime Committee which had first met in October 1937. Television, it was soon clear, would eventually in case of war come to an abrupt halt.

Marsland Gander's was a knowledgeable voice at a time when the *Daily Express* was running headlines like 'Mouse in Cables delays Television' and the *Evening News* was announcing 'Thrills on a Bright Screen and a Traffic Snag: Set "Picks Up" Passing Motor Cars'. Even the *Daily Telegraph*, however, had reported in August 1936 that one of the biggest differences between Alexandra Palace and Broadcasting House was that while the latter remained 'strictly dry', the former was providing for the first time refreshments that were not teetotal. Labour's *Daily Herald* had had longer vistas in view when it had warned its readers as early as January 1935, 'Television and the BBC: Radio Sets Not Obsolete: Non-Visual Service for Years.'

There were few signs in September 1939 that the 'non-visual service' was losing ground, although at the opening of the 1939 Radiolympia Sir Stephen Tallents, the BBC's Controller of Public Relations, prophesied that BBC Television would be 'a world winner'. In fact, 'Black Friday', was only a week away, for television programmes came to an abrupt end in the middle of a Mickey Mouse cartoon on 1 September 1939, two days before War was declared. Most of the sets had been bought by 'viewers' – the term was not yet established – since the Munich crisis of 1938, when Chamberlain had been televised on his return to London from Germany. More sets had been sold between early October 1938 and Christmas 1938 than the total number of sets sold before that time. There was no separate television licence, and the cheapest sets cost as little as 21 guineas. Meanwhile, the total cost of the television programming was £450,000, which was paid for by listeners, not viewers. The favourite advertising slogan to attract new viewers was 'Television is here. You can't shut your eyes to it.'

Very few of the first viewers can have been regular readers of the *Daily Herald*, for the television set was a status symbol which, if it did not 'automatically give you access to Ascot's Royal Enclosure', could at least ensure that you were 'in the swim with the best people'. A *Men Only* cartoon of 1939 showed an immaculate frock-coated sales assistant telling the potential customer of a huge television set, 'When selling this model, Sir, we require an assurance that it is going to a suitable home.'

'Would we all be viewers if we could?' Grace Wyndham Goldie had asked in September 1937. 'In other words, if we could sell the radio, the cat, the dog and the piano to buy a television set, would we?' She was not prepared to offer a single-word answer, but suggested instead that television was already providing enough 'fun' to encourage the sacrifice. At the same time, she noted that while television was still a new baby, the more sophisticated members of the public were not asking whether 'the dear child could lisp "Mama" prettily today' but 'whether the important little brat is likely to have either brains or imagination when it grows up'.

This was the language of *Punch* which, in different vein, was predicting a not-so-distant time when television would be perfected and when we would complete 'our present slavery . . . to that series of strange boxes to which we are already, like monkeys to barrel-organs, very largely bound . . . There will be no need to see any real person, nor look at any real thing, nor move, nor think, nor read at all'.

There was no danger that pre-war television would kill social life, however, since the evening programmes lasted for only one hour. The fare might consist of light piano music, a cookery demonstration, a Movietone newsreel and a cabaret. Lack of funding limited the service, but it was thought in any case that long hours were inadvisable because of the 'high degree of concentration required for viewing'. Occasional direct broadcasts from the theatre enabled the BBC to boast that private sitting rooms were becoming 'part of an immense theatrical auditorium'.

The viewers were far from being 'ideal types', and *Punch* reflected their concerns more faithfully than Grace Wyndham Goldie. Their tastes were lowbrow. They did not like 'morbid, sordid and horrific plays' and they were sceptical about ballet and foreign cabaret. They liked the Boon–Danahar fight of February 1939, as I did. Between that month and the last pre-war programme, viewers' opinions, collected and analysed by audience research, showed that nearly 60 per cent of viewers thought that the programmes were satisfactory and only 6 per cent that they were not. Moreover, nearly 80 per cent believed that the programmes were getting better.

Turn back to the pages not of *The Listener* but of the *Radio Times*, and it is all there – down to what proved to be the last weeks of peace. Grace Wyndham Goldie began her piece in the first week of July with 'Who'll deny that we're getting our money's worth these days?' A week earlier, she had been to a 'television tea-party' in Broadcasting House, a very different place from Alexandra Palace, 'so impressive, so organised, so aloof a place, however nonchalantly one has learnt to walk in and out of its doors'. The overwhelming impression left by the party was not the impressiveness or the organisation, but the 'friendliness', of pre-war television. For Grace Wyndham Goldie the viewers' own hope of the future was, none the less, impressive enough. 'They don't want it just to be a means of transmission. They are prepared to see it become a new medium.' In retrospect, it is clear that the one who was most prepared was herself.

There were bets in 1939 between British and American radio manufacturers as to which country would have most television sets in use by the end of 1939. The losers were to pay for a dinner in Paris in the spring of 1940, a dinner which would be televised. Other events intervened besides the blackout of the screens.

The British radio manufacturers in 1939 believed that whether or not they would win the bet depended not only on themselves but on the government, a point ignored by the critics who were mainly interested in 'output'. In fact, behind the scenes there was keen argument about the economic future of television.

In 1935, the Selsdon Committee, headed by an ex-Postmaster General, had been appointed to consider the future development of television; and there had been little enthusiasm in Broadcasting House. In his capacity as Postmaster-General when the BBC came into existence as a Corporation, Selsdon, according to Reith, had so mismanaged matters that sound radio had been given the most inauspicious of starts. The unimpressive twenty-eight-page report on television, Cmd 4793 (1935), authorised regular programming, but left open all the crucial questions of finance. 'We have not budgeted', Selsdon stated, 'for a programme comparable in duration, variety or quality with existing sound programmes.'

Direct advertising was not to be permitted, but sponsored programmes, 'for which the broadcasting authority neither makes nor receives payment', were deemed acceptable. Reith himself had recognised, as had Ashbridge, that during an 'experimental period' such sponsoring might be necessary, but between 1935 and 1939 opinion had hardened inside the Corporation, and during the spring and summer of 1939 there was to be deadlock in long negotiations about the finance of further television development between Corporation, Treasury and Post Office. During the last months of pre-war television Ogilvie wrote as gloomily as Reith would have done that 'the arguments against sponsoring such as they are (independence, artistry, the attitude of the Press, etc.) are hardly likely to appeal to the Treasury'.

The intermediary body between BBC and government, the Television Advisory Committee, which had been set up in 1935, acquired a new Chairman in March 1939, Lord Cadman. A respected businessman, who had served on the Selsdon Committee, Cadman a year earlier had also been Chairman of a small committee on civil aviation which reported just before Reith became Director of Imperial Airways after leaving the BBC. (Interestingly, the Civil Aviation Committee included F. J. Marquis, the future Lord Woolton, a strong post-war supporter of commercial television.) Cadman, anxious that the television service should be extended to the Birmingham area as quickly as possible, came to the conclusion that sponsored programmes were the answer to the BBC's difficulties and advised the Treasury that if the BBC wished to give a 'really stirring and immediate impetus to television', as the Press was demanding, sponsored programmes should be introduced at once.

When the BBC continued to resist, the Postmaster-General, Major J. C. Tryon, passed on the Treasury view that it was 'difficult to understand' the BBC's reluctance 'to adopt the measure which is, of all measures, most calculated to secure this result'; and on the eve of the War the Television Advisory Committee went even further. 'In view of the great difficulty of financing the television service and providing for its extension to the provinces', it told the government, 'we consider that the inclusion of sponsored programmes and even direct advertising in that service would be fully justified.'

The three words 'even direct advertising' were as ominous for the BBC as was to be Selwyn Lloyd's minority statement appended to the Beveridge Report on Broadcasting in 1951. He was to refer then to 'a public service non-commercial programme financed by a licence fee and alongside it one or more agencies financed commercially'. There was a chink there which others were to turn into a hole.

The Television Advisory Committee pointed also in 1939 to other means of securing extra finance – the introduction of a special licence, covering both sound and television at an initial charge of £1 a year, twice the wireless licence – and the imposition of a special charge for large screen reproduction of television in cinemas. The BBC strongly favoured the idea of a special licence – and this was to be the way ahead – but it was disturbed that the cinema industry might get some kind of special footing in the television world. For Ogilvie and his colleagues, 'the delivery of the television service in any shape or form to cinema interests' seemed to it to be the ultimate disaster.

This was a solution, none the less, which was being openly advocated, in 1939, if not in the pages of *The Listener*. An article in *Wireless World* bore what for the BBC was the ominous title, 'A Partnership with the Cinema'. And during the War, when the screens were blank, there were many meetings behind the scenes, when a partnership pattern was strongly canvassed. Enthusiasts for television, including cinema viewers, continued to believe that a large part of its success in the future would depend on public showing of programmes in cinemas. Private viewing, which some enthusiasts believed would be subsidiary, might be financed, they continued to claim, by the proceeds of public viewing. Thus, at a meeting in 1943 held at the Institution of Electrical Engineers, when the problems of post-war television were being examined seriously, the main speaker directed attention to schemes whereby a considerable proportion of the cost of television would be borne by the cinema industry 'which has already established an incomparable distribution system'.

Grace Wyndham Goldie before and after 1939 was interested in the future of television not in the cinema, but in the home, and so, too, was the first post-war magazine on the subject, *Television*, which appeared in 1947 a few months after the restoration (still for the London area only) of regular BBC television programming. The first so-called post-war receivers then on offer were 'improved 1939 models', although by 1947 Pye was producing two 'entirely new models', one with the unglamorous name of DI6T, and Murphy one – with a range of about fifty miles. The DI6T model, a console set, cost £45, plus purchase tax; the cheapest table model £35, plus purchase tax of £7. 17s. 3d. The most expensive set was a Ferranti Floor Model Television Receiver at £98 10s., plus purchase tax of £20 25.

'Purchase tax is no longer necessary', a *Television* leader of Spring 1949 was to read. 'It should have been removed from television receivers before now. It restricts trade, adds an unnecessary burden to the already over-taxed population and hampers the industry's efforts to capture export markets.' Yet the television manufacturing industry had been optimistic after the reintroduction of regular programming in 1947. 'Next year', we read in the second number of *Television* in February 1947, 'it is anticipated that Birmingham will have a television station and, no doubt, other regional stations will follow more rapidly. Yes, television is the coming thing. You'll see.'

The issue of monopoly *versus* competition had been raised in the very first number – according to one reader 'squarely joined' – but there was more in the pages of the new journal about 'output' than about modes of finance or control. These remained shadowy, for the war-time Hankey Committee, which in 1945 reported that 'television has come to stay', dodged all the issues, as the Selsdon Committee had done, when it wrote that 'until the television service is well developed, commercial interests would not be willing to incur large expenditure for [development] owing, for example, to the limited audience served . . . In these circumstances, and without prejudicing the matter for the future, we feel it would be premature to come to a conclusion on this question.'

In dealing with the less intractable question not of development or of control but of output, *Television* still stressed the virtues of 'intimacy and informality' which were said to run through John Irwin's *Kaleidoscope*, a term later to be expropriated by sound radio, 'like a peal of bells'. In the same number, a set of notes by Richard Hubell would have been thoroughly approved of by Grace Wyndham Goldie: they bore the heading 'Inside Information: An Outline of the Technique of Production', and they argued, as she always had done, that no criticism was credible if it ignored 'conditions of work'. This was not the only theme, however, in the discussions of output. One article in the second number of *Television* was called 'Are we to have Soap Operas?'; the writer, W. W. Weal, concluded that since 'advertising by television can't happen here, we shall not see soap operas'.

By the Spring of 1949, when there were now 400,000 viewers, we read 'Television is growing up. It must become more professional in its approach, less easy going. Viewers are being critical, they resent too frequent repeat programming, especially of those items which hardly justify a single viewing.' And *Television* had helped to make sure of them becoming still more critical, for example by including a long-running series called 'Focus on the Producer'. 'Months of Mediocre Programmes' was the heading of a long article by Isabel Winthrope, one of a series that covered plays, features, music, talks, outside broadcasts – and equipment.

An insider-type article by the Irishman Maurice Gorham, an ex-editor of the *Radio Times*, who had run the BBC's revived television service until his resignation at the end of 1947, explained that while the service was now costing £700,000 a year it would not

> be possible to go on at the present level for long. A pioneer service, with all its limitations of content and coverage, might be worth running ten years ago, but before long it will be obvious that something more must be done if a lot of money and a lot of skill is not to be frittered away . . . We cannot live for ever on the prestige of the post-war service or what we did in 1946. Even successful experts depend on a live market here. Britain glories in a lot of quaint survivals, but we don't want our television service to become one of them.

Gorham had reached television *via* not only the *Radio Times*, but the Light Programme, and there were many people inside the BBC, including its first post-war Director-General, Sir William Haley, who somewhat condescendingly believed that that was the right route. Yet there were others inside the BBC, men and women who were actually writing, producing and presenting television programmes, who welcomed more searching criticism. With hindsight, there was one remarkably prescient passage in Isabel Winthrope's article:

> I am looking forward to seeing more programmes produced by Mrs. Wyndham Goldie, who is new to television, but whose *Authors in Focus* showed originality and an awareness that cameras can give the viewer vanity in a talk.

This was modest criticism, and Grace Wyndham Goldie was more trenchant when she became Television Talks Producer in 1948. She had abandoned criticism for the Board of Trade during the War, and when she moved to her new post she saw faces 'grey with fatigue' and offices that were 'dirty and overcrowded'.

She had big thoughts, however, as did another writer in the same number of *Television* in which Isabel Winthrope's article appeared. A piece called 'A Power of the Hearthside' concluded with the rolling words – 'when the eyes confirm what the ears hear, the mind is easily won'.

13   The Final Edit: Selecting and Rejecting the Broadcast Record*

The term 'the final edit' in the title of the opening session of this symposium, *Documents that Move and Speak*, carries with it echoes of the still more formidable term 'the last judgement'. The questions that follow the title, and that relate to the control and safeguarding of archives are not, however, the questions that we are likely to be asked at the last judgement. These will surely relate less to archives, import-ant though we judge them, but to the actual content of the broadcast record, to the motives and talents of those who have prepared and presented it, and to the role that they have played within institutional structures of profit and power.

There is nothing 'final' in my own introductory remarks' which fall into three sections – first, how as a historian I came to be concerned with broadcasting archives and with what results; second, what prob-lems arise in selecting and making available for wider access broadcast records; and, third, how does a historian as distinct from a programme-maker approach and utilise broadcast records as evidence?

The most difficult and, I believe, the most profound issues relate to the third section of these remarks, and these undoubtedly do have bearings on the questions that we are likely to be asked at the last judgement. Like the archivist, on whom he depends, the historian selects and rejects too, but, having selected and rejected according to criteria which may not be the same as those of the archivist, he goes on to analyse, to synthesise and, most important of all, to assess and to judge. Equally important, he is always revising past judgements so that for him there is no 'final edit'.

For most periods of history – that is, for all periods of history before the nineteenth century, there was no photographic record, and only since the 1920s has the historian had any broadcast record available to him. What difference has the very existence of the broadcast record made to the work of the practising historian? Is it more than a running commentary? It obviously is, if only because it is a record that lends

* A version of this paper was read at the opening session of a symposium organised by the National Archives of Canada in Ottawa in April 1990. The topic of the symposium was 'Documents that Move and Speak'.

itself to interpretations different from those of the people who made the record. And we can hear and see things in it that they did not see. We can rearrange it, too, in far more subtle ways than shuffling a pack.

It was because I was convinced that the broadcast record is full of treasures that I became interested in broadcasting history a generation ago and accepted an invitation to write the history of the BBC. I wanted to write 'total history', history that dealt with all aspects of society and culture, but in addition I felt that if some historian had written the history of the Press in the nineteenth century we would have had available for us a first-hand account, drawing on recent experience, that would have enabled us to relate the transmitted facts of nineteenth-century history to nineteenth-century perceptions, selections and rejections of fact. We would have known more about the dynamics, too – particularly about the formation of opinion and of taste and about the influence of what were then novel mediatory processes. We would have been in a position to relate them to older mediatory influences, both social – particularly through the family and through religion – and educational, through the school and the university.

The nineteenth-century print media available then included the ephemeral, 'today's newspaper', and the 'everlasting', religious treatises and books of sermons – with periodicals and reviews between. Yet historians may find more of interest today in the ephemera than in the 'everlasting'. Valuations change, as vantage points change. For the twentieth century, broadcasting archives will reveal this, for broadcasting now is – although it may not always be – central to the media system. The other relevant nineteenth-century strand is the history of photography, and the radical shift from stills to movement.

When I accepted the invitation to write the history of the BBC, the first thing that I had to do was to ensure that the compilation and organisation of its archives were adequate to enable me to write it. The most important by-product of my own work, I believe, was a drive to ensure that the *written* archives of the BBC, a superb documentary archive, were put into good shape. I started with papers about broadcasting output and the framework in which it was produced rather than the output itself. In a multimedia age documents still count.

It is said that Miss Edwin, the Secretary of Reith's adjutant, Admiral Carpendale, was the first person in the BBC to start collecting archives – in the 1920s. It was not until 1970, however, that the BBC Written Archive Centre was opened at Caversham, in future open not only to me but to what were called in a document prepared for the Director-General, '*bona fide* researchers' interested in 'a fascinating and perhaps unique record of contemporary social history'. Even then, the documents to be placed there – which included scripts of 'programmes as broadcast', material leading up to them, details of audience reactions, and, not least, Press cuttings – stopped at 1954. And conditions at Caversham soon became cramped. Three decades of history were crammed into 5000 square feet.

The Programme Archive was limited too. Indeed, in 1975, Paul Thompson, pioneer of oral history in Britain, writing in the second number of *Oral History*, then described as 'An Occasional News Sheet', compared it unfavourably with newspaper archives. 'It is a strange and disturbing fact', Thompson wrote that

> while virtually evey page of the first mass media, the newspapers of the years before 1914, have been preserved in the national collection at Colindale, scarcely any early recordings of broadcasts exist, and, even now, when a far larger audience hear radio and television than ever read the *Daily Mirror* or the *Daily Express*, we are only preserving a mere fraction of this material in a private archive.

It was for technical reasons, of course, that there were few early recordings: they were cumbrous to make and expensive to collect and preserve. After the post-war development of sound and video recording, however – and this fascinating chapter in technical history is still neglected – costs of recording fell and conservation began to be taken seriously. And by then the concept of an 'archives policy' had emerged.

There were concomitant changes on the demand side, for during the 1970s there was a great increase in the number of 'contemporary historians' who were interested, above all, in the twentieth century, and more of them than ever before who wished to go to Caversham. It became a kind of Mecca. The range of curiosity of historians was widening, and with it a more sophisticated sense of what constituted evidence. Three other sets of BBC archives – sound archives; visual archives; and music archives – were becoming increasingly relevant, too, and the pressure on these archives was to increase to such an extent that in 1975 the BBC decided to set up an Advisory Committee on Archives which I was asked to chair.

It held its first meeting in 1976 and reported in April 1979 after a thorough enquiry, probably the most thorough in the history of any broadcasting organisation. The Committee was wide-ranging: it included the biographer, Michael Holroyd, Professor Randolph (later Sir Randolph) Quirk, authority on the English language and a future President of the British Academy, Professor Kenneth Charlton, Professor of Education at King's College, London, the historian, Professor Margaret Gowing, author of the official history of atomic power in Britain and a future member of the Duncan Committee on the Public

Records, the actors Marius Goring and Donald Sindon, Peter Morley, freelance film and television producer, Benny Green, freelance writer and broadcaster, Anthony Hobson, specialist in bibliography, David Francis, Curator of the National Film Archive, Richard Coward, Director-General of the Bibliographic Services of the British Division of the British Library, David Jenkins, Librarian of the National Library of Wales and Professor Michael Tilmouth, Professor of Music at Edinburgh University. The Secretary was the historian Norman Longmate, then an official of the BBC, a distinguished old member of Worcester College.

The Committee met ten times, and its Report set out more than eighty recommendations, most of which, though not all, have subsequently been implemented by the BBC. One recommendation, constitutional, was that any future Charter of the BBC, unlike previous Charters, should include a reference to the archives, and I conveyed this reference myself to the then Home Secretary, Mervyn Rees, who accepted it. One other recommendation related to the extended use of the archives – 'We recommend that as soon as adequate facilities are available to cater for an increased number of enquiries, publicity should be given to the range of archives available to outside users.'

The main reason, though not the only reason, why all eighty recommendations have not subsequently been implemented has been finance – and this limiting factor, which was recognised by the Advisory Committee itself, was singled out in an immediate BBC comment welcoming the Report. 'Ultimately,' the statement read:

> the BBC's Archives depend, like everything else, on the BBC's income . . . Nine-tenths of the value of the Archives must necessarily not be obvious to the ordinary viewer or listener, who is only aware of them when a programme draws specifically upon past files or programme material – or conspicuously fails to include actuality of material about some past event, because the item concerned was not preserved. The Archives Committee very properly drew attention to the cost of its proposals and though the amounts involved are not large in relation to the BBC's total budget, financing some of them is likely, in present circumstances to prove difficult.

This immediate BBC reaction in 1979 makes points that have become even more relevant since 1979. BBC financing, like the financing of most public broadcasting institutions, has become more, rather than less, difficult. Meanwhile, however, the preparation of programmes drawing specifically upon past files or old programme materials has greatly increased, for a number of reasons, among them anniversaries; and the 'entertainment' value of vintage materials, including materials to be used completely outside the context in which they were first broadcast, has been increasingly prized too. Most important of all, however, use has grown because the relative cost of making totally new programmes has greatly increased.

Television has been at the centre of the story, since there has been increasing recognition, too, of the extent of loss when visual materials, varied in age and character, have not been preserved. This is because historians, among others, have developed during the ten years since 1979 a greater interest in the visual dimension of history – and that for reasons broader than their increasing recognition of the significance of television. Meanwhile, television itself has become more interested in developing its own memory.

The last words in the BBC statement of 1979 were carefully measured:

> The Report, in the BBC's view, if not everywhere representing a blue-print for immediate action, does provide a valuable long-term plan and one for which future generations of archive-users and indeed of ordinary listeners and viewers who will be its ultimate beneficiaries will have cause to be grateful.

Eleven years later, given the uncertainties of the present, the question of what would now constitute a long-term plan for the BBC's archives is more open than it was in 1979. One unit of the then archives in 1976, the *Radio Times* Hulton Library, consisting largely of still photographs, of great interest, particularly to contemporary historians has already been sold. The BBC's local and regional archives remain scattered – and fragmented. The products of competitors in broadcasting have multiplied. The British Film Institute has enhanced its role, and the British Library is moving to a new home. The British Institute of Recorded Sound, at present a part of the British Library, has continued to flourish and has widened its own interests. It receives copies of most recordings added to the sound archives and, in addition to being permitted to record programmes off air, has supplemented its collection of BBC programmes with other sound material. Meanwhile, cable and satellite television have been introduced – with no archival responsibilities.

The last time I came to a symposium on archives in Ottawa was almost ten years ago – in October 1980, during the third General Assembly of IFTA/FIAT, when I opened a discussion at the third general session, presided over by Sam Kula, on 'Access to Television Archives'. Only three years before that, the British Universities Film Council had produced a Working Party Report on the registering of film archives, the value of which as historical sources had been appreciated even before the end of the nineteenth century. It was said that there was still great uncertainty about the future.

Access was then a key question, closely related to finance, and there were few broadcasting organisations which would have found themselves able to choose as a slogan that chosen by the Essex Public Record Office, '*Archives for All*'. The position has improved greatly since 1970, although there are still problems, and technical progress has slowed down also in relation to storage, transfer and compatibility of formats. Documents that move are, as always, more expensive to maintain for wide use than documents that simply speak.

For me as a historian of broadcasting, my own problem is more one of time, however, than of finance. Documentary materials, the kind that in the BBC are filed at Caversham, just about to open new premises, take less time to study and to assess than past television – or sound – programmes. I can examine all the extant files on a large number of subjects; I can only sample television – and sound – programmes, turning back later to associated documents which reveal the origins and the process of that particular piece of programme-making. Only rarely – indeed, only when I deem it necessary – have I tried to examine output material that was not used in broadcast versions.

When I came to Ottawa in 1980, I was lucky that the second speaker in my session was Eric Barnouw, historian of American broadcasting. Then and since, we have been able to compare not only organisational structures and processes concerning archives in Britain and in the United States, but the way in which we as historians of broadcasting have used broadcasting archives in our own work. Barnouw was seldom able to make use of substantial written archives – they did not exist – and this has added a special dimension to my account of the development of the BBC as an institution. Yet, just because of this gap, he made somewhat greater use than I have of actual broadcast material – the output of broadcasting – and of current comment on it.

Both of us have recognised fully, however, that simply because of time limitations there is a need for specialised monographs – the kind of monographs on which we would have liked to have been able to draw in our own work, but which had not then been written – and we have both concluded that such monographs will be based in far greater measure than our own work on the direct use of television – or sound – as broadcast. Technical as well as general skills will be required in the research process.

I am aware, too, that some BBC television scriptwriters, researchers and producers have been able in preparing programmes for public viewing, even programmes on aspects of the history of the BBC itself, to make far richer in-house use of specific BBC television archives than I have done in my *History*. There has been far too little

purposes'. Category B relates specifically to 'material of significance in the history and development of television', including new television techniques and outstanding examples of existing techniques and programmes or items about television itself. Category F covers 'programmes or series which reflect the output of BBC television and the work of individual contributors, including producers, direction, writers, performers, etc.'.

The most general category is H – 'material of general historic interest, including material on current events, of historic significance, and documentary material on historic subjects'. News bulletins are included in this broad category. The three main daily BBC News bulletins are recorded off-air for the use of the Current Affairs department rather than for – or as well as for – posterity, and they can, therefore, be immediately designated for preservation. The edited news stories and original materials are initially the responsibility of News Library, although all material later transferred to the Film and Television Library will be preserved (in the case of transmitted items) or considered for preservation in the case of unedited material which is sifted later. Judgement is certainly called for in relation to this last, extremely important, task.

Less judgement is required in relation to so-called 'outside events', although such events, when they recur, are themselves treated selectively. For example, the ceremony of Trooping the Colour is considered 'much the same every year': only when a member of the crowd fires a gun is an intrusive element introduced that is deemed worthy of special record. In selection attention is always paid, however, to what are thought to be significant changes in presentation – for example, in religious broadcasting, highly distinctive in Britain – and circumscribed – or in weather forecasting, where styles, often uneasy, have changed as much as the weather itself is said to have done.

In some cases, all programmes are preserved – for example single documentaries and documentary series and viewer access programmes. In recent years 'light entertainment' in the form of comedy shows has moved towards total retention also, not so much because future historians may try to judge a society or a culture by its jokes as because light entertainment programmes have 'enormous repeat potential'. All music and arts programmes are archived too – with a substantial amount of unused interview and performance material being preserved, usually on film but increasingly on video-cassette formats. In this connection, the performer has less to fear than he had in the past. He cannot be so easily wiped out.

The ramifications of a selector system by categories, designed to be flexible, not rigid, are obvious. There are two other points of importance relating both to organisation and to procedures. First, no material on film or on videotape can be destroyed or wiped out 'without consultation with the originating department'. Second, 'responses to BBC television output will be taken into consideration in the assessment of material for archival retention'. This includes 'critical responses, audience ratings, awards, controversies, etc.', a diverse, but challenging, list.

I should add – and this leads me to the third, and, for reasons of time, inevitably the shortest – section of my introduction, that for the historian some of the most interesting questions about archive use are raised not by Category E, 'events', although this category is obviously important, but by Category C, 'material of sociological interest, giving examples of contemporary life and attitudes'. 'This Category', a BBC note adds, 'includes material from all forms of output, including current affairs, documentaries, drama and light entertainment.' To me as a social historian, who has written about British social history before and after the advent of broadcasting – and television – this is the category that requires the closest examination.

Historians, influenced by French historiography, that has increasingly separated the history of structures – and 'mentalities' – from the history of events, will find that evidence acquired through broadcasting archives will be of particular relevance to them. Moreover, it will be not least relevant when it is indirect evidence not specifically related to the purposes of programme-makers and their presenters. As I have already suggested, they will often see more in programmes than they did.

As historians they will have to learn, however, how to interpret such evidence through a critical understanding not only of content but of form – in this case the modes of programme-making and of presentation. They will not be able to take broadcast evidence simply as raw material. Modes change in terms of technology as well as of art and style – and in a continuing communications revolution they will continue to change. Historians do not need to be told that in all programming there will always be an element of contrivance that can properly be called fiction or that evidence cannot be separated from its specific context in time and place. They know that they themselves can never escape from time.

Because what will be left behind for the historian depends on archival policies of selection and rejection, I favour in the absence of costly total retention the preservation of complete time slices of broadcast material, chosen, perhaps best, at random, from each particular year. The study of such random slices, consisting of much that we consider ephemera, may enable people in the distant future to learn far more about us than we have consciously chosen to tell them. It will be easier for them to plug in, a term they may well continue to understand. The material they tap will be complementary material to that deliberately placed – and selected by conscious choice – in real or imaginary time capsules, the kind of capsules that attract the twentieth-century mind in the dawn of the space age.

When I was writing about Victorian England, I came across a fascinating passage in an obscure journal *Mental Science*, written in 1851. I quoted it in my recent book *Victorian Things* which is more concerned with archaeology than with archives.

> Suppose [the author of the article wrote] that a modern drawing room, with its sumptuous velvet, silk, glass, gold, china and rosewood were to be hermetically sealed up and consigned to the inspection of our descendants in two thousand years to come they would scarcely understand its paraphernalia . . . Their minds would be discordant from ours and the material substances upon which they employed themselves or by which they signified their wishes or wants would in the process of time become so completely new and foreign that *we* could not understand them nor they us.

Broadcasting, almost unthought of in 1851, could help over time to narrow the artefact gap, which in the year of the Great Exhibition, a year of the artefact, greatly concerned the writer, just as it can narrow, as we well know, the twentieth-century gap between cultures. And that must be my last thought at an international symposium.

I do not just want the preservation of random broadcasting slices from Britain. I would like to see the task accomplished in different countries, each with its own broadcasting system, before satellites, key instruments of the space-age, change the whole story. It is already a global story, as recent events in central and Eastern Europe have made plain, and the archival – and historical – significance of what has already happened is not the least important item on our agenda. 'Tomorrow is already here.'

14   Select and Reject: Aspects of the Study of the History of Education*

The study of the history of education is best considered as part of the wider study of the history of society, social history broadly interpreted – with the politics, the economics and, it is necessary to add, the religion put in. Yet for long the study was either neglected or left to a small and scattered group of specialists, largely working in isolation, some of whom were unaware of the broad trends of historical scholarship. As late as 1966 Brian Simon could talk about their 'traditional concerns' in terms of 'a flat record of acts and ordinances punctuated by accounts of the theories of great educators who entertained ideas "in advance of their time"'.

During recent years, however, changes both in education and in the study of history have altered the picture. Education has once more become a major social, political and economic issue, and it has seemed natural in such circumstances that there should be a reinterpretation of old issues and the struggles surrounding them. We are already far removed, in consequence, from the attitudes eloquently expressed by J. L. Garvin in his biography of Joseph Chamberlain. 'No Ezekiel's wind', Garvin exclaimed, 'can make dry bones live in some valleys. Nothing seems more dead and gone today than the educational battles of the early seventies in the Victorian age.'

A year after the centenary of the Education Act of 1870, which itself stimulated the production of large numbers of local studies based on the examintion of source materials which had long been buried and forgotten, the mood of the times is a very different one. It is easy in the light of our own contemporary campaigns to understand why the 'battles' of the nineteenth century were so fiercely contested, and my next essay will be concerned specifically with one of them, the battle for the Education Act of 1870 itself.

* This essay is based on a talk to the History of Education Society, given at the London Institute of Education on 22 May 1971. The Society then had 410 members. It produced its first *Bulletin*, appropriately in retrospect, in Spring 1968. I have not changed the content of this talk in the light of more recent work on the history of education, much of it substantial, although for the sake of completeness I have referred in my revised version to some work published in and before 1971 that I had not specifically noted in my talk.

As for changes in the study of history, which have been as influential as events in the shaping of attitudes, these have been sufficiently comprehensive for slogans like 'the new history' to be bandied around not only in academic circles but in adult education groups and in the media. Several of these are of special interest and importance to historians of education, and this paper is particularly concerned with six of them.

The first is a new approach to local history, a far more sophisticated version of local history than that common in the past. The study has cast off the shackles of antiquarianism, has moved from a rural to an urban ambience, and has begun to take account not only of institutions and of personalities but of structures and processes. At its best, such study does not divide the past into convenient periods: it searches across the centuries for continuities and discontinuities. Moreover, as it broadens out, it ceases to involve an exercise in illustrating what is already known about national history from local examples and becomes a means of constructing national history afresh from local materials. We can already trace the breaking down of set interpretations of national history and the building up of new interpretations in their place.

The second, less fully developed, is a new approach to comparative history, a natural sequel to the rediscovery of the variety of experience embedded in local, regional and national sub-cultures. Comparative studies pivot on the discovery of what was common between and what was distinctive to different societies. 'When an analyst cannot experiment with his subject matter through replication, establishment of controls and the manipulation of variables', an American historian, R. F. Berkhover, has observed recently, 'then he resorts to the comparative method in the hope of achieving the explanatory results.' Whatever the difficulties in establishing categories and definitions – and to establish them is essential if historians are to ask similar questions of similar materials – the approach implies both greater interest in theory, and greater care for methodology in research and greater analytical power.

The third is the study of quantitative history, 'Cliometrics', as some Americans have christened it. What began with 'new' economic history has subsequently been paralleled in the writing of social history, with historical demography playing a strategic part in the development of scholarship. There are dangers in a commitment to quantitative approaches which excludes other approaches and in a multiplication of quantitative studies at a low level of historical analysis. Yet given a critical frame of mind, not least concerning the reliability and comprehensiveness of the available data, and the ability to ask relevant questions, quantitative studies, assisted by statistical techniques and supported when necessary by computers, can point to fascinating and sometimes unexpected conclusions.

In one respect they are particularly important. 'A quantitative discrepancy between theory and observation', Professor T. S. Kuhn has written, 'is obtrusive. No crisis is so hard to suppress as that which derives from a quantitative anomaly that has resisted all the usual efforts at reconciliation.' Moreover, the analysis of bodies of data which were often collected for strictly limited immediate purposes, very different from the purposes of the historian, can in itself stimulate the asking of new questions. As Schumpeter put it, 'we need statistics not only for explaining things but in order to know precisely what there is to be explained'.

Quantitative history has attracted many able, pioneering minds. So, too, has the 'new social history', 'history from below', which is still in the process of articulation and development. This, indeed, is the fourth approach which deserves to be identified. Such history makes use of concepts derived from sociology, anthropology and psychology without being imprisoned (at least when it is at its best) in borrowed social science categories. It also directs attention to people whose names never figured in the older history books, the people who were deprived or neglected in their own time and whose participation in government was minimal or non-existent and whose attitudes towards 'authority' could be deferential or resentful, passive or hostile. The study of 'history from below' often creates a greater sense of understanding along with a recovery of immediacy. It quickens the curiosity of the historian and leads him into the examination of related patterns of work and 'leisure', of 'participation' and 'apathy'.

The fifth change in the study of history – at the opposite end of the spectrum – has been the development of a more analytical kind of political history, with attention moving from particular pieces of legislation, although it is still important to study these within a different frame, to cumulative administrative processes, to the making of critical decisions, to their resource implications, and to the changing scale and role of organisation. A consequent re-scrutiny of administrative history is also in process, carrying with it useful controversy. It involves less concentration on the 'landmarks' and more on the interplay of people and problems. It will eventually produce a new synthesis, particularly in relation, perhaps, to the way in which social policies were forged.

The sixth change relates to intellectual and cultural history. The history of ideas is beginning to come into its own – not merely the history of the ideas of 'great thinkers', particularly those who were 'in advance of their time', but the history of chains of ideas and their modes of communication through different 'media', of the shifting relationships between 'minority' and 'mass' communication, of the significance of 'language' and of the development of varied forms of 'control'. The new history of ideas has been associated with a re-examination of such crucial changes as the invention and development of printing, the subsequent history of literacy, and the more recently identified 'communications revolution'. Yet it has encouraged new tendencies within political and social history also. The kind of interpretation advanced by A. V. Dicey in his still influential *Law and Public Opinion in the Nineteenth Century*, first published in 1905, has been challenged without so far being fully replaced. Although Dicey had very little specifically to say about education, his approach to the broad subject of the making of social policy has done much to influence writers of every kind, many of whom have sharply questioned his assumptions and conclusions.

It is the main argument of this paper that each of these new approaches – and they are related to each other – needs to be studied carefully by historians of education. To some extent they all reflect current preoccupations, as most historiographical change has always reflected them. To some extent, they are made possible by the availability of new materials and techniques, although techniques (including oral interviews) are, of course, instrumental and depend for their success on the quality of the questions asked as much as on the skills of the questioner. Most important, the new approaches represent a somewhat new balance between specialisation and generalisation. Historical study must involve specialisation if it is to advance, but the old barriers between the different sub-branches of history are breaking down and new efforts at synthesis are being made.

The study of the history of education will not, in my view, be adequately furthered if there is to be new departmentalisation, with a new sub-branch of history, 'the history of education', being increasingly separated out from the rest. There may be something to learn in this connection from recent developments in the study of labour history, of urban history, and of the social history of medicine. In each of these cases, groups of interested historians have been created in this country in recent years, each with its own meetings and its own system of scholarly communication. The wisest among the labour, urban and medical historians have recognised that critical issues in the history of labour and of cities cannot be studied in isolation from other branches of history, but unfortunately there are always historians who are more aware of their separate identity as specialists, even of their status, than of the potential contribution which they can make to the study of history as a whole.

Against this background, the History of Education Society, founded in 1967, is poised at a particularly interesting moment of its short life. There are so many questions to ask about educational history (curriculum as well as policy) that it is essential that they should be placed in their general context and that the answers should be related, when possible, to the kind of answers which social historians are seeking to provide.

Although the six developments outlined in this paper are 'new', less new perhaps than some of their practitioners realise, there are old guides in the history of education who point in the same direction. One of the most stimulating of them was R. H. Tawney, who was always looking for a synthesis. In an essay written as long ago as 1914 in the *Political Quarterly* and recently reprinted in Rita Hinden's *The Radical Tradition* (1964), he argued that 'educational problems cannot be considered in isolation' and that in every period of history – he himself was mainly concerned with pre-industrial periods – 'educational policy reflects its conceptions of human society'.

Much of the later Tawney is forecast in this early statement. In one of the key passages in *Equality* (1931), he emphasised that in considering the place of education in English society it is always necessary to bear in mind that the English social system has been shaped by pre-industrial as well as industrial influences, that it is marked not by a single set of class relations but by two. 'It is at once as businesslike as Manchester and as gentlemanly as Eton; if its hands can be as rough as those of Esau, its voice is as mellifluous as that of Jacob.'

The remark, which should be examined alongside W. G. Runciman's *Relative Deprivation and Social Justice* (1966), has often been overlooked by those writers who have generalised too simply about English experience, and it reminds us that historians of education must concern themselves not only with 'crises' or 'struggles' of a dramatic kind but with long-term influences and trends. Tawney also reminds us perpetually that society in the first and last resort must be looked at not in terms of categories, however valuable they may be, but in terms of people. He was willing to look for evidence in every kind of place from 'high literature' to 'common experience'.

Another writer who drew on all kinds of material was Michael (later Sir Michael) Sadler, who was an active figure on the educational scene during the 1890s, a somewhat neglected decade, long before he became Vice-Chancellor of Leeds University in 1911 and later Master of University College, Oxford. I have long been interested in him, and I am glad that Dr J. H. Higginson is preparing a selection of his lectures, essays and papers on education. Among his last papers his son found what he described as a 'sad little slip', dated 11 December 1940. The fifth of a list of items which he called 'Things I should like to finish' was 'Sketch of the history of Education in England'.*

Each of the six approaches that I have outlined above is relevant to the study of the history of education in this country. The first, indeed, is basic. The new approach to local history and its relationship to national history must be grasped because of the 'localism' of the English educational pattern. It was from the periphery not from the centre that English education developed. As Sir Joshua Fitch, for thirty-six years a leading HMI (Inspector of Schools), put it in a magisterial article in the 'new volumes' of the *Encyclopedia Britannica* (1902), which deserves to be reprinted, educational provision in England was

> not the product of any theory or plan formulated beforehand by statesmen or philosophers. It has come into existence through a long course of experiments, compromises, traditions, successes, failures and religious controversies. What has been done in this department of public policy is the resultant of many diverse forces, and of slow evolution and growth rather than of clear purpose and well-defined national aims.

If it is necessary to turn to foreign writers, like de Tocqueville, to grasp the significance of 'localism' and 'de-centralisation' when viewed in international terms, it is equally necessary to explore local economic, social (including religious) and political structures, to understand why initiatives and activities in education varied as much as they did before the passing of the Education Act of 1870.

It is illuminating to examine in this way bodies like the Lancashire Public School Association which, like the Anti-Corn Law League, to which it owed much, professed itself a 'national' body in 1850, and the National Education League, founded in Birmingham nearly twenty years later, which heralded Birmingham's Liberal caucus. The contrast between Manchester and Birmingham, about which so much has recently been written in relation to nineteenth-century history as a whole, has its significance in relation to the history of education, and given the interest of Cobden and Chamberlain's views on education, integrated into their general philosophy, it is obvious that we are not just dealing with 'events' when we examine the background of the Education Act of 1870. We have to be careful about words too. It is obviously not sufficient in discussing what happened in English education before 1870 to talk in simple terms of differences between 'rural' and 'urban' areas. A far more intensive survey and analysis of particular places is necessary.

---

* Dr Higginson's book *Selections from Michael Sadler, Studies in World Citizenship*, to which I wrote a foreword, appeared in October 1979.

After 1870, though the administrative framework changed, the same kind of survey and analysis remains necessary, with one additional point to consider – the relationship between 'national' pressures and local provision. The fact that between 1870 and 1902 the first development of a deliberately organised pattern of national primary education was left to locally based 'School Boards' is of major importance, as is, of course, the role of the local education authorities since 1902, a subject covered in Brian Egglesham's *From School Board to Local Authority* (1956) and in A. Kazamias, *Politics, Society and Secondary Education in England*, published ten years later.

The best contemporary national source for the work of the Boards is the *School Board Chronicle*, and there is a useful account of the pattern of their activities in M. Sturt, *The Education of the People* (1967). Several histories of individual Boards have been written, often in the form of theses, but few of them move into the kind of comparative local history which is most rewarding.

There were more than 2000 Boards in 1902, and there are some interesting aspects of their distribution. Yorkshire, for example, had 280 Boards; Lancashire with a population nearly a million larger had only around fifty. The contrast here is worth studying, as is the contrast between Lancashire and Yorkshire in other matters of education, including technical education. Within Yorkshire it would be interesting to compare Leeds and Bradford. Fortunately, a number of works like J. Lawson's *A Town Grammar School through Six Centuries* (1963) and D. Wardle's *Education in Nineteenth-Century Nottingham* (1971) relate local history to national history, and there is excellent advice to would-be local researchers in M. Seaborne's *Recent Education from Local Sources* (1967).

Turning to comparative national histories, we still lack studies of the way in which primary education was developed 'on the ground' – say in a British and a French or a German city or in two agricultural areas in different parts of Europe. The next stage in our understanding of nineteenth-century English history as a whole may well be to follow up the local breakdown of structures and processes within England by comparing across national boundaries.

In this connection, it is useful to turn back again to the important article by Fitch in the *Encyclopedia Britannica* which was written at the time of the debate on the Education Act of that year and which remains a good starting point for further exploration. Fitch went out of his way to outline developments in other countries, drawing out what seemed to him the relevant comparisons and contrasts, and there is a revealing article about him in J. Leese, *Personalities and Power in English Education* (1950). The same approach had been followed in a more limited way by Francis Adams in the last decades of the nineteenth century when he preceded his important book on *The Elementary School Contest* (1882) with an earlier study of *The Free School System of the United States* (1875).

Such 'anatomisation' had been pursued even earlier by Bulwer Lytton in his still valuable book (one of the first nineteenth-century examples of a *genre* which has led up to Anthony Sampson), *England and the English* (1834, reprinted in 1874 in the aftermath of the Education Act). It included chapters on 'the education of the higher classes', 'the state of education among the middling classes', and 'popular education'. The very division itself is illuminating. Books of this kind have been used far too little by historians of education, yet backed by contemporary evidence they help us to understand (i) the place of 'voluntarism' within the English context (ii) the lateness of 'national development', and (iii) the lack of 'system'. It is important to note that none of these points can be explored adequately in terms of the history of education narrowly interpreted.

There is a further way in which comparative approaches are useful. It is interesting to compare the successive *Encyclopedia Britannica* articles on education with each other, going back to James Mill's famous essay for the fifth edition, in this century reprinted on its own. Fitch, perceptive as always, showed how the approach had changed. In particular, he drew attention to the contrast between his own article and that of Oscar Browning, the famous Eton master, which had been printed in the main volumes of the ninth edition. Browning, writing very much in dilettante style, had been concerned with 'the ideals which have prevailed from time to time' in education (going back to the ancient world); Fitch concentrated on tracing 'the gradual growth of what may be called the English system, the forces of which have controlled it, and the results it effected during the last quarter of the nineteenth century'. It is interesting that the parallel article to that of Fitch – 'education in the United States' – was written by Dr Nicholas Murray Butler, President of Columbia University.

The third new approach to the writing of history – the use of quantitative techniques – sharpens discussions of a comparative character. It was always evident in the nineteenth century, at least from the time of the foundation of the local statistical societies in the 1830s, that the case for educational reform was buttressed by if not grounded in the exposition of statistics; and, in particular, comparative statistics from Britain and the United States were often set out side-by-side. The Act of 1870 was itself preceded by the major local statistical inquiries of the 1860s, some of which were deliberately comparative in character, and Lawrence Stone, ranging further back in time and extending the study of educational history to the study of more general questions of literacy, has published two important articles on literacy levels that are based not on impressions but on quantitative evidence.

The huge mass of nineteenth-century material is worth sifting as it stands, yet it is worth noting that far more can be done with it than was done in the nineteenth century itself. Increased statistical sophistication has already influenced the way in which educational issues are being presented in the twentieth century, and more attention is being paid in current debate to the 'economics of education', the subject of a valuable book by Mark Blaug, *An Introduction to the Economics of Education* (1971). The subject covers claims on national resources; shares of national income devoted to education; modes of financing numbers, buildings and equipment. The reason for the increased attention has doubtless been the growing volume of public educational expenditure and the need to identify priorities. At the same time, quantitative methods have been applied to educational sociology also, with reference both to class differentials and mobility.

So far, these increasingly fashionable approaches have had little impact on historical studies, although one interesting article in the *Economic History Review* (1970) by E. G. West, who has been actively involved in current debate, is of a pioneering kind, if not the last word. On the basis of rigorous quantitative analysis West questions a number of accepted assumptions about relative educational provision in England and Scotland in the early nineteenth century. The article has been followed up by his book *Education and the State* (1970).

The contrast between England and Scotland is one which must be explored by all students of British educational history, and there is as much scope for assessing quantitatively the economic limitations to the expansion of voluntary primary education in England in the nineteenth century (and its social limitations) as there is for examining comparable aspects of public provision in the 1970s. We know far too little about the economics of voluntary effort in every field of social policy and the financial and manpower 'crises' which were a feature of the 'system' both locally and nationally. It is perhaps important to bear in mind also that the Education Act of 1870, which shifted the locus of finance, was passed in a year of exceptional business prosperity.

The fourth of the new approaches to the study of history – the emergence of a new kind of social history – has such obvious bearings on the study of educational history that it is not necessary to do more than identify a number of key issues and to point to a number of books, like J. F. C. Harrison's *Learning and Living* (1961) and R. Lowe's 'occasional publication' of the History of Education Society, *New Approaches to the Study of Popular Education* (1979). As far as the relationship between social history and sociology is concerned (terminology, methodologies, boundary questions), there has already been one paper in the *Bulletin* of the History of Education Society, and one textbook, P. W. Musgrave's *Society and Education in England since 1800* (1968), draws fully on sociological analysis. So, too, does Olive Banks in her valuable study *Parity and Prestige in English Secondary Education* (1955), essential reading for all scholars concerned with access.

It is important to bear in mind that in any partnership between historian and sociologist (even in the case of the most manageable of partnerships, that where historian and sociologist are the same person), the role of the historian is not simply to supply facts and to correct errors. As D. S. Landes has put it,

> History has always been a borrower from other disciplines, and in that sense socio-scientific history is just another example of a time-honoured process; but history has always been a lender, and all the social sciences would be immeasurably poorer without knowledge of the historical record. The social sciences are not a self-contained system, one of whose boundaries lies in some fringe area of the historical sciences. Rather the study of man is a continuum, and socio-scientific history is a bridge between the social sciences and the humanities.

It would be unfortunate if there were to be boundary disputes in relation to the history and sociology of education, given the need of both for each other, a need clearly recognised by Harold Silver, who with J. Ryder published *Modern English Society; History and Structure* in 1970. The history of education must obviously be related to changes within the family, the economy and the social-class system, and the historian of education must be interested in such matters as 'education' through agencies outside the school and relative 'mobility' through education and routes other than the school (a basic theme in nineteenth-century social history), even if these are not his primary focus of interest. It is absurdly restrictive to argue that the history of education is primarily the history of teaching, interesting though that history can be, as R. W. Selleck has shown in *The New Education* (1968). Some of the relevant materials have been collected in P. H. J. Gosden's *How they were taught* (1967).

At every point in the history of education, institutions and motivations, facts and values must be considered together. Take any key passage from the past relating to educational provision and it immediately provokes questions. In 1851, for example, Nathaniel Woodard, founder of the Woodard schools, had this to say:

It is the glory of a Christian State that it regards all its children with an eye of equal love and our institutions place no impassible barriers between the cottage and the front of the throne; but still parity of rights does not imply equality of power or capacities, of natural or accidental advantages. Common sense forbids that we should lavish our care on those least able to profit from it while we withhold it from those by whom it would be largely repaid. The class compelled to give the greater part of each day to the toilsome earning of its daily bread may be as richly endowed as that which is exempt from this necessity but it is manifest that those who are subject to such a pressure must, as a body, enjoy less opportunities of cultivating their natural endowments.

Whenever the historian of education comes across terms like 'common sense' or 'it is manifest that', he must begin to probe deeply. Indeed, he must be sensitive at every stage to the language of the past (vocabulary, tone, rhetoric).

It is important to bear in mind that in the middle years of the nineteenth century, to which this passage belongs, the relationship between education and social class was posed most frequently within the context of relations between the 'middle classes' and the aristocracy and gentry, and that the history of the public schools is as relevant, therefore, as the history of other schools. The leading voices were Tawney's two voices of Eton and Manchester, not those to whom we have become accustomed in twentieth-century dialogue. The Taunton Commission, which does not figure in Eric Midwinter's useful booklet in 'seminar studies on history' called *Nineteenth-Century Education*, is an essential source.

It needed an unorthodox thinker like Lytton to get away from mid-Victorian 'common sense' about education and society. 'One great advantage of diffusing knowledge among the lower classes', he wrote provocatively, 'is the necessity thus imposed on the higher of increasing knowledge among themselves. I suspect that the new modes and systems of education which succeed the most among the people will ultimately be adopted by the gentry.' Of recent books on educational history that will last I would suggest that David Newshome's *Godliness and Good Learning* (1961) will certainly be one. It should be considered within the context of J. Bamford's *The Rise of the Public Schools* (1967). There will certainly be many more books in this field.

During the last two decades of the nineteenth century attitudes towards education and society changed as much as attitudes towards other aspects of organisation and policy, with H. G. Wells, emerging from a radically different social background from Lytton, playing a prominent part in shifting the terms of the debate about education and class to middle-class/working-class relationships. The Education Act of 1870 was for him 'an act to educate the lower classes for employment on lower class lines, and with specially trained inferior teachers'.

At this point, 'history from below' comes into its own, as Brian Simon has shown in *Education and the Labour Movement* (1965), the beginning rather than the end of an analysis. Since the Act of 1870 owed little to working-class pressure and since aspects of its implementation were often bitterly resented in working-class areas – the 'school bobby' could scarcely be a popular figure – it is essential to examine what happened after 1870 from the vantage point of those who were 'receiving' education, particularly after it became compulsory, in 1876 and 1880, as well as from the vantage point of those who were 'supplying' it or causing it to be supplied. (Half-timers are particularly interesting.) Recently it has been clearly realised also that the same kind of examination is necessary even for the period of voluntary provision before 1870 when there were many varieties of provision of varying quality and when there were already many educational reformers who conceived of education as an instrument of social control.

It was difficult for those engaged in promoting education fully to understand the attitudes of those *for* whom they were promoting it, as was frankly recognised by Henry Moseley (a scientist as well as a clergyman), one of the first HMIs. 'The fact is', he wrote in a minute of 1845, 'that the inner life of the classes below us in society is never penetrated by us. We are profoundly ignorant of the springs of public opinion, the elements of thought and the principles of action among them – those things which we recognise at once as constituting our own social life, in all the moral features which give it thought and substance.' The same kind of point has been made about social policy as a whole in the nineteenth and early twentieth centuries by R. B. Titmuss:

> The poor law, with its quasi-disciplinary functions, rested on assumptions about how people ought to behave . . . Valuations about the nature of man were written into the social legislation of the day. They informed the means of policy. Derived, as they commonly were, from the norms of behaviour expected by one class from another, and founded on outer rather than inner observation . . . their application to social questions led the new services to treat manifestations of disorder in the individual rather than the underlying causes in the family or social group.

In examining the detailed history of schools it is essential, therefore, to look critically at 'behaviour' and 'discipline' as well as at curricula and methods of teaching. What can we make of such comments as that of the Rotherham School Board Inspector who wrote in a log book of 1890 'found boys and girls in the same playground. Witnessed much indecent behaviour'? The relationship between discipline and 'drill' is well brought out in many late nineteenth-century log books, including that of the head teacher of another infant school in Rotherham who hired a drill sergeant to visit school every Tuesday afternoon after being criticised by an inspector. Logbooks and diaries are particularly useful sources, but we have to penetrate beneath the surface to some of the fundamental problems of language and communication which were as crucial in the nineteenth century as they are today.

To understand what was 'going on' in a school it is necessary to take account of complex systems of personal and social interaction. How were the experience, language and values which children brought into the school from their own (sometimes contrasting) neighbourhoods related to information and ideas imparted by their teachers, some but not all of whom came from their own local social backgrounds?

Questions of curriculum and methods of teaching, including questions of quality, are best examined when these social complexities are properly understood. The success of the sixth new approach to the study of history, identified earlier in this paper depends, therefore, like the fourth, on insights as much as techniques, although there is much to be gained from the work of anthropologists and of social psychologists. One possible seminal article has already appeared in *Past and Present* (1970), Richard Johnson's 'Educational Policy and Social Control in early Victorian England'.

I am uneasy myself, however, about relying too much on the word 'control'. The situations it covers seem to me to be so different. Indeed, I like to approach the history of education through the sources and not through the concepts, valuable, often indispensable, though these become at a later stage.

The fifth approach to the history of education that I have identified is worth very full consideration in relation to the whole field of educational policy-making, since too often the history of educational legislation is treated in functional terms of a general kind as a necessary adaptation to new sets of economic or political circumstances. The difficulty is that similar circumstances produced different kinds of results in a different order in other societies.

To understand what happened in each particular case we have to look at the intricate interplay of individuals and groups, ideas and interests, and pressures and restraints. The point was well made by John Rex in his *Key Problems of Sociological Theory* (1962) when, after urging 'the reshaping of sociological theory so that it is built around

the notions of conflict, imperative coordination and balance of power',
he went on to take the Education Act of 1902 as his example:

> Some sections of the ruling classes were opposed to the ideas of secondary
> education altogether. Those who were in favour of it vied with each other
> about controlling it because they had different ideas about the content of
> education. And the working classes demanded it either in the hope that
> their children would 'get on' in the existing order, or because they recog-
> nised that such education would help them in the establishment of a new
> social system. The resulting educational system was the outcome of a
> compromise between these competing pressures. It is not a system which
> can in any way be explained in terms of orthodox functionalist theory. But
> the manner of its development and the eventual compromise is exactly
> what we would have expected from a conflict model.

Rex dwelt on 'conflict', and conflict models are fashionable. The
historian, however, must always take account also of 'consensus',
when it was there.

Unlike many other countries, notably the United States, England
has never been a society where there was a powerful built-in pressure
either in the society (or in Parliament) for the extension of education.
There have been long periods in the history of education when little
has happened at the centre, and these must be explained along with
the 'emergencies', 'campaigns' and 'crises' when conflict was always
apparent, as it was in 1869 and 1870 and again in 1902. When Butler
raised the question of education with Churchill in 1941 he was told by
the Prime Minister that instead of thinking of new legislation, which
would be bound to create a row, he should get on with his main task of
getting the schools working as well as possible under all the difficulties
of wartime.

Oliver MacDonagh's emphasis in a genuinely seminal article of 1958
in the *Historical Journal* on 'The Nineteenth-Century Revolution in
Government', which traces cumulative administrative processes of a
self-generating kind, is directly relevant, therefore, to the historian of
education. None the less, attention must be paid also to the forces that
created a sense of emergency at particular times, to the way in which
opinion was then mobilised, and to an assessment of what were the
practical results. Educational change has come in fits and starts, and we
have to look at moments of crisis as well as at administrative processes
or social trends. This means going further, of course, than examining
particular pieces of legislation.

Given that England accepted the notion of an educational 'system'
only imperfectly and falteringly – even Rex's use of the term in relation
to the Act of 1902 must be qualified – we have to find a different kind of
driving force during many periods of history to that of system-building.

The most interesting suggestion for such an alternative was made by John Morley, who, moving away from August Comte, became profoundly suspicious of 'systems' and who was yet at the same time wary about leaving everything to local initiative. As early as 1867 he was writing of the need to develop a 'collective national impulse', and by 1873 he had formulated the idea of reform through the identification of single great 'national issues', among which education was then paramount. His biographer speaks of Morley 'focalising'. It may well be that the interpretation of the history of education in this country during the nineteenth and twentieth centuries would be strengthened if this concept were incorporated within the analysis.

15   Struggle: Fighting for the Education Act, 1870*

Buried away in the Birmingham Reference Library are two massive folios containing letters, papers, reports and bulletins of the National Education League which was founded in Birmingham in 1869. There is nothing private in either of the two folios. There was a private history of the League, a history of personal ambition and of rivalry, but it is not recorded in that place. It is only the essential materials for the public record that are present there, although these are substantial enough, and it was largely on the basis of them that Francis Adams wrote his interesting and informative *History of the Elementary School Contest* in 1882, five years after the League was dissolved. It remains the most useful single monograph on the subject, a book that no historian of English education in the nineteenth century can afford to neglect.

Adams's use of the Birmingham materials may be compared with the use William Lovett, the Chartist leader, made of a similar bundle of Chartist papers which are also assembled in bulky folios in the Lovett Collection in the same Birmingham Library. Lovett, too, wanted to get the record of 'struggle' straight: the word 'struggle' came naturally to him, as it did to Adams. He, too, was always interested in history in the making. Yet he was interested also in the social significance of his own autobiography and in the external forces which had helped make him what he was, and he called the autobiographical volume which he published in 1876 *The Life and Struggles of William Lovett*.

Lovett was a self-made working man, proud of his own self-education. Adams, a solicitor by occupation, was far more self-effacing. He almost writes himself out of the story. We know very little about him except that he was a solicitor, that his office was in Temple Street in the heart of the city, and that he lived in Bristol Road, that soon after the formation of the League in 1869 he became its secretary (which also had an honorary secretary who was far better known than himself), and that after two changes of residence first to Yardley

*This essay follows for the most part of the text of my introduction (1972) to Francis Adam's *History of the Elementary School Context in England* and John Mosley's *The Struggle for National Education*. It does not draw on histories of education published since 1972.

and then to West Croydon in Sussex he died in 1891 at the early age of fifty.

His *History of the Elementary School Contest* has very little to say about the personalities who gave the League its particular 'Brummagem' flavour and who determined the tactics, sometimes devious, ultimately unsuccessful, which it pursued – the most remarkable personality, Joseph Chamberlain, who supplied a large share of its founding capital, perhaps significantly, never springs to life – but it directs attention to all the relevant educational and political issues, local and national, and seeks to place them in historical perspective. It can be supplemented by a number of other works by Adams, including a sketch of Brougham, one of the early-nineteenth-century pioneers of education, and a lively public lecture on education delivered at Huntingdon in 1870. In this lecture Adams stated something of his own philosophy:

> Let me say that the members of the League were not anxious to make this question one of political warfare. It would have been a pleasure to them if for once in the history of this country a great work, having for its object the benefit of the multitude, had been suffered to proceed on its way undisturbed by the bitterness of party conflicts. But, sir, this has not been permitted. Our old enemies – the enemies of free-trade, of religious liberty, and popular government – the old obstructive party – ever on the watch for an opportunity to impede – has risen up against us to prevent, if possible, the accomplishment of our object. Though we did not seek it – though we would gladly have avoided it – we accept the situation which has been forced upon us, if not without regret, at any rate without despair . . . We are charged with seeking to revolutionise the country. We hope so. There is nothing we desire more than to effect a revolution; but it will be a bloodless one – one which will put into the hands of the people no weapons but those of peace and industry, one which will break down no barriers except those which impede the way to a higher civilisation.

Adams anticipated the idea of 'the silent social revolution' associated with long-term educational advance, but like so many of the Birmingham 'crusaders' of the 1870s he was anxious to carry his message into the heart of the enemy's camp. The honorary secretary of the League, Jesse Collings, shared the same philosophy: he was always more active in the countryside than he was in Birmingham itself.

The *History of the Elementary School Contest* is concerned almost as much with the perennial battle between 'the progressives' and 'the old obstructive party' as it is with education itself. Not surprisingly he starts with the middle ages. The Dissenters, whose cause he propounded, always looked back through time, particularly to the seventeenth century, which they saw as the critical century in the battle for civil freedom. As a recent historian, John Vincent, author of *The Formation of the Liberal Party* (1966), has remarked, 'the real corpus of thought uniting the middle class, or the Liberal section of it, was not a Benthamite, utilitarian, or natural-law view of the world, not American or economical principles, but something of a different order: a view or recollection of English history.'

Within that view of history persecution (trial by ordeal) played an important, even crucial, part: 'These persecutions tested the vitality and strengthened the determination of English nonconformity, and became powerful stimulants to the growth of the civil and religious freedom they were designed to crush.' So, too, did the sense of progress with the great material advances of the recent past deriving from earlier victories:

> The foundation of all that has been achieved since then [the 1770s] – the social progress, the material comforts, the diffusion of wealth, the advancement of science and mechanics, the development of industry, the improvement in morals, and the stride in religious and political freedom was strengthened and firmly established in this early period [before the 1770s]; and in the struggle between the democratic and aristocratic principle, the former took definite form and asserted itself with all the consciousness and confidence of ultimate triumph.

In the nineteenth century the battle against Church rates had been the militant culmination of many old battles. It ended significantly enough on the eve of the articulation of the Education issue in 1868, when Gladstone's new Liberal government carried its Compulsory Church Rates Abolition Bill.

Adams considered all questions of education in broad evolutionary terms within a long time span: 'The history of education is a part of this wider history of the progress of society, and in its completeness is only to be found in connection with the general advance which has taken place during the last two centuries.' Turning back to the seventeenth century, he stated categorically that 'it was during this period that the great struggle for intellectual, political and religious freedoms was proceeding, the triumph of which could alone render a state system of education tolerable or desirable'.

This approach explains the at-first-sight curious balance of his book. Four chapters out of nine deal with the period before the League was formed. They outline the reasons why England, unlike several far less economically developed countries in Europe, failed to develop an effective 'national system' of education. They also describe the activities both of voluntary societies, religious and non-religious, on which English educational provision long depended, and of pressure groups which demanded reform. Adams had little use for 'voluntaryist' arguments which had captivated large numbers of nonconformists: 'It was evident the Voluntaryists did not rely upon the law of supply and demand, but on sectarian and party rivalry and zeal which is quite a different thing.' Anglican 'realists' might have argued that the voluntary provision of education was 'the only scheme that could have been introduced into our free, tolerant, dissentient and jealous country' and have extolled 'the most gigantic effort ever made by private charity to perform a public duty', but Adams was quite unimpressed: 'The voluntary movement was beaten by the irresistible logic of facts, which no easy improvisation of first principles, no versatility in the arrangement of statistics, and indeed no generosity of purse and service should successfully encounter.'

Adams believed that only the State could act effectively and continuously in matters of education, but that before it would ever be prepared to act it was necessary for public opinion to be mobilised. He emphasised, therefore, 'the necessity of combined action out of Parliament to secure that pressure of public opinion which is the only guarantee of useful legislation'. It is not surprising, that one of his heroes was Richard Cobden, who had devoted his energies after the repeal of the corn laws to a number of other causes amongst which education figured prominently. He presents a useful account of the activities of the National Public School Association which had its origins, like the Anti-Corn Law League, in the city of Manchester. It was this Association, guided by Cobden which, according to Adams, propounded 'the first comprehensive and elaborate scheme put forward for securing national education; based on the principle that the cost should be thrown on property, that the management should be confided to local representatives, and that the people should be taught to regard education, not as a bone of contention between churches and sects, but as the right of free citizens'.

Unlike most Birmingham men, Adams was unusually appreciative of initiatives coming out of Manchester. Indeed, when he came to the founding of the League in 1869, he pointed out that George Dixon, MP for Birmingham and mayor of the city in 1866–7, approached people in Manchester to take a lead. He quotes Dixon as saying: 'Had my suggestions been favourably received by the gentlemen to whom they were made, Birmingham would not have originated the League, but would have followed Manchester, which in my opinion ought to have headed, and was entitled to lead a national movement.' It is doubtful if Chamberlain would ever have assented to this proposition. Yet the Manchester Education Aid Society, founded in 1864, which developed into an Education Bill Committee, was the model for the Birmingham

Education Aid Society founded three years later; it is interesting to note that after the League had been formed, its critics chose Manchester as the centre of the rival National Education Union.

While Adams insisted upon 'agitation' as a necessary element in educational advance, he was aware also that over long periods of time change often took place quietly behind the scenes. He noted, for example, that the increase in educational funding by the State in the 1850s owed little either to debate in Parliament or to pressure from outside it: 'The capitation grant was a conspicuous feature in the new plans of the Government [in 1853], and the way in which it was adopted is a curious illustration of the manner in which the power of the Education Department was capable of extension, almost without the exercise of parliamentary authority and supervision.' He obviously recognised what recent historians of nineteenth-century administration, in the wake of Oliver MacDonagh, have identified as 'cumulative' pressures from within the system making for change without the stimulus of political agitation.

Adams was unimpressed, however, by Sir James Kay-Shuttleworth, whose indefatigable activities, often well out of public view, have been praised by most subsequent historians of education: for the secretary of the League, the compromises which had been forced upon Kay-Shuttleworth seemed far too much like those propounded by W. E. Forster, who introduced the Education Bill of 1870. Adams did not know that Kay-Shuttleworth wrote to Forster in 1870 advising him to remain calm. 'You will have to do what I have done over and over again in this cause, you will have to disappoint some of your friends in order that the education of the people may not be indefinitely postponed.'

By contrast, Adams was exceptionally kind to Robert Lowe, Vice-President of the Committee of the Council for Education from 1859 to 1864 and author of the revised code of 1862 that introduced 'payment by results' into elementary education. Lowe's attitudes towards education have been criticised even more sharply during the twentieth century than they were at the time. Yet Adams called Lowe 'the most able Minister who has yet held the post of Vice-President', and praised his stolid unwillingness to be 'taken in' by the 'propaganda' of the voluntary societies, his relentless scepticism about 'proprietary rights' in school ownership and management, and his genuine concern for the quality of education. Adams went on explicitly to compare Forster unfavourably with Lowe. For his part, Forster, like his brother-in-law Matthew Arnold, strongly disliked Lowe's 'twice revised code'. Indeed, he disliked the whole tenor of Lowe's approach to education.

When he reached the critical point in time when education became a major issue in English politics, the late 1860s, Adams had relatively little to offer by way of analysis of the reasons for the 'crisis' and for the 'advance'. Like Bagehot before him – and many other commentators – Adams referred to the death of Lord Palmerston in 1865. Walter Bagehot had gone further than Adams and had spoken of a change of generation. Adams mentioned, none the less, albeit briefly, some of the statistical enquiries in the provinces which brought to light the extent of the educational problem, particularly in the great cities, and the inadequacy of the voluntary agencies to cope with it. He also made reference to the comparative position in England and in other countries, a subject to which he was to return in 1875 in his book *The Free School System of the United States*. He did not seek, however, to draw a direct causal connection between the passing of the Reform Act of 1867, which granted the vote to large sections of the urban working classes, and the introduction and passing of an education act.

Much has subsequently been written about these two measures as cause and effect, with certain key passages serving as texts in the argument, notably Lowe's 'I believe it will be absolutely necessary to compel our future masters to learn their letters.' In fact, Lowe was convinced of the need for public-provided elementary education *before* 1867 as were most Liberals of a 'progressive' cast of mind, including many who were to be bitterly opposed to the activities of the League, and some Conservatives, like Sir John Pakington, MP for Worcester, who had raised the education issue as long ago as 1855. Adams was right to emphasise the continuities; indeed, he anticipated the verdict of a recent historian, Gillian Sutherland, that 'the impulse to action on popular education and the impulse towards parliamentary reform seem to have had common roots'.

This was certainly true of Birmingham, where Dixon, for example, had 'long taken a great interest in the subject' of education. The Society of 1867 preceded the passing of the Reform Act, and Chamberlain was writing to the United States for information about the American school system before Birmingham working men were enfranchised. A local essay prizewinner, A. B. Greenwood, stated in 1868 that 'national education is not only desirable, but it is a necessity. That question has passed beyond the region of controversy . . . The problem is what kind of measure will be best in present circumstances.'

It is interesting also to note that Adams makes nothing of economic arguments in accounting for the timing of the new agitation in the late 1860s. All his emphasis is on the momentum of popular Liberalism. In his Huntingdon lecture he referred to 'the position of England in industrial competition', quoting the scientist Lyon Playfair, but he did not develop the point. He stressed rather as the leading question 'how and where shall the children of the masses be trained in streets, gutters, kennels and hovels, encompassed by misery, vice, dirt, poverty and crime . . . or in properly appointed and conducted schools, and subject to the influence of law, order, self-restraint, cleanliness and know-ledge'.

There is ample evidence from Adams's book that he believed that education was necessary for the simplest of reasons, well put by one of the first working-men members of parliament, Thomas Burt, 'We say educate a man, not simply because he has got political power, and simply to make him a good workman; but educate him because he is a man.' This view, rooted in a tradition which went back to the eighteenth century, may well have been more widespread during the late 1860s than some historians of education have implied.

Certainly the element of 'economic necessity' behind the 1870 Act has often been exaggerated. Trade was exceptionally good and com-petition was less evident than it had been at the time of the Paris Universal Exhibition of 1867 and was to be later in the 1870s. More-over, many of the supporters of educational advance believed (for political and social reasons) that it was even more urgently necessary to introduce public provided education in the agricultural areas than in the large industrial cities. This was the view of Henry Fawcett, MP and economist, for example, who was briefly to be associated, as a radical, with the activities of the League. Government could do little to help the 'neglected' agricultural labourers except through the extension of education. Fawcett has been described (misleadingly) as 'an educa-tionalist pure and simple': the vital question for him was 'universal compulsion'.

Unsophisticated 'functionalist' approaches to nineteenth-century educational history which relate provision to 'social need', do not help us much with problems of the timing either of agitation or of legis-lation. Nor do they help us to explain the differences in chronology and patterns of provision between England and other countries. They are at once too comprehensive and too vague. It is more profitable, perhaps, to examine the dynamics of agitation, the motives of cabinet ministers and the conflicts and compromises embedded in legislation.

There was a time when the conflicts seemed archaic and dull and when the compromises were passed over complacently as expressions of a distinctive English genius for institutional adaptation. Now, in the aftermath of the celebrations of the centenary of the Education Act, when there is no shortage of educational topics for current debate, perspectives have shifted. It is for this reason alone that Adams's account of the activities of the League has acquired a new kind of interest. Because he was personally involved in all the affairs of the League he is a witness as well as a historian, an actor, indeed, as well as an observer. Yet given his self-effacing temperament, which has already been noted, he never places himself in the centre of the picture. Nor did he ever resort to 'sensationalism'. As has been noted, he devotes four of his nine chapters to the period before the advent of the League and three to the period of excitement after the passing of Forster's Act.

He begins his account of the League with the briefest reference to an historic conversation between George Dixon and Jesse Collings. Yet he does not quote what Collings is reputed to have said to Dixon, 'If we could have an Education Society on the right lines, the very stones in the street would rise and join us.' The exact date of this conversation is not known, and Adams does not give us the date of the first meeting held at Dixon's house, The Dales, on 7 January 1869, when many of the leading figures in the later history of the League were already present. Already, before the League was founded, there had been evidence of differences of approach, some of them doubtless temperamental. Dixon had an established position in Birmingham. Born in 1820, he had arrived in Birmingham in 1838 and had first joined the Town Council in 1863; he was Mayor in 1866, and in 1869 was said to be 'probably the most popular man' in the city. Yet he was a less strong personality than he appeared to be: in 1843 Charlotte Brontë, who met him in Brussels, had described him unkindly as 'a pretty-looking and pretty-behaved young man, apparently constructed without a backbone'.

No one could ever have described Joseph Chamberlain in these terms. He had arrived in Birmingham sixteen years after Dixon, when he was eighteen years old, and from the start he was intensely ambitious. As a friend wrote of him long afterwards, 'He far surpassed in ability any previous local leaders . . . I remember him appearing at a meeting in a seal-skin top-coat. This made people gasp. A man daring enough to dress thus must be a Caesar or a Napoleon.' Chamberlain was to clash swords with Dixon in 1876, when he replaced Dixon as MP for the city, and he was to engage in even more bitter argument with him in 1878 when Dixon, who had always been uneasy about the power of the formidable Liberal caucus, stated in public that it was nonsense to argue that 'Chamberlain is Birmingham or Birmingham Chamberlain'. The rift was healed, and Dixon followed Chamberlain in opposition to Irish home rule in 1886, becoming treasurer of Chamberlain's new National Radical Union, but there was an obvious contrast of spirit, purpose and ability. Dixon was an Anglican, deeply interested in education for its own sake and was to serve continuously on the Birmingham School Board from 1870 to the time of his death in 1898, the year when he was made a Freeman of the City.

Chamberlain, chairman of the League's Executive Committee, was undoubtedly interested in education, but he was also interested in militant nonconformist campaigning of the political kind expounded by the Liberation Society, launched in 1853 on the foundations of the earlier (1844) British Anti-State Church Association. He was already a master of political calculation, and in a letter to Dixon after Forster introduced his Education Bill he expressed attitudes which Dixon never shared:

> I wish our side would fight like the Conservatives – the Bill would then have been doomed long ago. The Tories are never afraid of being factious and it is a great advantage to them . . . It [the bill] is not National Education at all – it is a trick to strengthen the Church of England against the Liberation Society . . . I would rather see a Tory Ministry in power than a Liberal Government truckling to Tory prejudices.

This letter should be compared with Dixon's comments at the opening of the third annual meeting of the League over which he presided in October 1871:

> Some of our opponents consider the League a discredited and defeated party. But what are the facts? Every one of the six means by which we have proposed to secure the education of the children of this country were vehemently denounced by our opponents . . . Yet when I again read them to you, you will be unable to resist the conclusion that all the measures we proposed have either been carried, or that we have secured in the Education Act of 1870 a lever, by the wise use of which their adoption has become merely a question of time.

Before turning to the 'six means' and to the 'objects' of the League, which were set out in its first public circular, reprinted by Adams, a little more should be said of the mix of other personalities.

Collings was a Chamberlain man through and through, a *confidant* and a henchman rather than an independent political personality in his own right. William Harris, the Chairman of the Parliamentary Committee, was a very different kind of person. Far from borrowing his ideas from Chamberlain there is considerable evidence that he implanted his own ideas in the mind of the budding politician. He had been the organiser of the Liberal victory at the general election of 1868 and, long after the controversial idea of the 'caucus' had been perfected, Chamberlain wrote that 'the whole credit of having initiated and carried out this new machinery belongs to my friend, Mr. Harris'. J. T. Bunce, the chairman of the Publications Committee of the League, was editor of the influential *Birmingham Daily Post* for which Wright wrote articles. He was an enterprising and hard-working journalist with whom Chamberlain remained in regular contact throughout his life; he was also a lively historian of the city which he believed had 'a living personality' peculiar to itself. R. F. Martineau, chairman of the Branches Committee, belonged to one of the small group of local families, interconnected by marriage, who constituted something of a ruling class in Birmingham. George Dawson, a member of the Executive, was a renowned independent preacher, 'the prophet' of the 'civic gospel' for which Birmingham became famous.

The other great Birmingham nonconformist, Dr. R. W. Dale, minister of Carrs Lane Chapel, however, stood aloof at first. 'It was painful for him', his biographer writes, 'to stand apart from Mr. Dixon, Mr. Chamberlain, Mr. Collings and other friends with whom he had worked for public ends; but he could not accept the fundamental principle of the League that the schools aided by local rates should be free.' In this he was at one with his influential fellow Congregationalist, Samuel Morley, MP for Bristol. None the less, Dale joined the League later in 1869 and thereafter 'took his share of the fighting', something of an understatement.

In such company Adams was doubtless a servant rather than a maker of policy, and he was never listed in the impressive catalogues of subscribers to the League, some of whom gave it large sums of money: there were no fewer than sixteen donors of £1000. Yet Adams was close to Dixon, and through his editorship of the *Monthly Paper* of the League, first published in December 1869, he was in regular communication with Bunce. He was also active in places outside Birmingham. By the time of the first issue of the *Monthly Paper*, forty-three branches of the League had been created, including one in Oxford University, with Kenelm Digby as its secretary, and Adams knew something of most of them. He was a key figure, too, in all contacts with working-class associations to which the League attached the utmost importance from the start. Chamberlain was not alone in boasting that 'directly or indirectly, from 800,000 to 1,000,000 working men have, at their meetings in Birmingham, given their support to the platform of the League'.

Robert Applegarth, the trade-union leader, whom I have described at length in *Victorian People*, was a member of the Executive Committee of the League, W. R. Cremer, a future Nobel Peace Prize Winner, was a stirring campaigner, and George Howell, one of Adams's regular correspondents, suggested a membership card that would give status to the small subscribers. Many of the trade unionists came into the League straight from the Reform League which had just been dissolved. The word 'League' was itself a link. Yet it was the aggressive middle-class leadership of the League rather than the working-class presence which was most sharply criticised by contemporaries.

The efficiency of the apparatus frightened many people, including

Liberals outside Birmingham, and provoked more opposition inside Birmingham itself than Adams implied in his History. It needed an aristocrat to try to put Birmingham in its place. 'There is nothing that *riles* mankind so much', Lord Houghton (formerly Richard Monckton Milnes) wrote to Forster in 1869, 'as seeing the objects they desire accomplished by other means than their own. Thus, the Radicals are as indignant at popular education being brought about with Conservative assistance as Mazzini and Garibaldi at the unity of Italy being brought about by Victor Emmanuel. But the Mialls of England and Italy must submit to their lot. *Sic vos non vobis* is the law of the world.'

Edward Miall, one of the most uncompromising of the militant dissenters and editor of the *Nonconformist*, was Forster's colleague as MP for Bradford – he had secured the seat in 1869 only after the winning candidate had been unseated on petition – and they had already found it difficult to work easily together as colleagues. Yet it was to Birmingham rather than to Bradford that 'the Mialls of England', the targets of Matthew Arnold's criticism, looked in 1869 and 1870; and Forster's biographer, J. Wemyss Reid, rightly heads his chapter on education in 1870 'The Struggle with the Birmingham League'. Unfortunately after the publication of his biography Forster's widow destroyed the papers on which the biography had been based.

It is a mistake, none the less, to believe that in 1869 and 1870 the advancement of the cause of education depended solely on the League and on people who shared its philosophy. The real issue was much more complicated. Education had been mentioned in the Queen's speech of 1868, and there were many Tories who were anxious for national legislation. Nor could the Leaguers themselves avoid the intricacies and complications of educational policy. Whereas the Anti-Corn Law League earlier in the century had been able to carry out its crusades on the basis of the simplest of formulae – and that a negative one – the repeal of the Corn Laws, the League, when it tried to take the initiative, was forced to draft an outline of a comprehensive educational scheme, not all parts of which would appeal even to its own adherents. Thus, Fawcett was very unhappy as a doctrinaire political economist about the idea of *free* education, and many Nonconformists, even those who had abandoned any lingering belief in voluntaryism, were never happy about the term *secular* education.

Whatever compromises Forster was forced to make from inside Parliament and these deserve a fuller treatment than any historian has yet devoted to them – the League also had to pick its way warily with the public, particularly at the beginning. Adams does not quote the first draft plan of the League which is to be found in the Birmingham Collection, placed immediately after Dixon's invitation to the first

Provisional Committee meeting. Interestingly enough, this draft does not use the adjective 'unsectarian' which was incorporated in the first published circular of the League which Adams prints (not quite in full). Instead of clause 4 of the circular it had employed the words 'in all schools aided by local rates and under the management of local authorities, theology peculiar to any religious denomination shall form no part of the school teaching'. This might have been a better formula than that which was eventually adopted. What is most significant, however, was the refusal of the League at the start to use the word 'secular' in its propaganda, even though Dixon himself had used it in inviting the little group of people to his home to found the League. In his own words nearly two years later, 'it was decided' at the first meeting 'that the word "secular" did not represent the views we entertained, and "unsectarian" was inserted in the programme without a single dissentient voice'.

Earlier in the century Cobden had recognised the political difficulties in using the adjective 'secular' even if it was made clear that it carried with it no anti-religious bias, and his biographer, John Morley, quotes him as telling a friend that 'if you propose to leave out religion, they denounce you as an atheist, and then reason and argument might as well be addressed to the clouds'.

The League's use of the word 'unsectarian', however, may have caused at least as many political difficulties for it as the word 'secular' would have done. What exactly did it mean? Adams says nothing in his book of the origins of this problem, but he, as much as his colleagues, had to deal with its ramifications in his letters and speeches. Inside the League, there was always a strong group which would have preferred the term 'secular'. It was particularly strong in London and included most of the working-class leaders whom both Dixon and Chamberlain were anxious to attract. Miall was at one with them on this issue:

> There can be no doubt that the desire of its [the League's] members is compulsory secular education. Then why not say so? Only on the ground that education is secular can compulsion be justified. Even the reading of the Bible without comment, or the employment of the Lord's prayer would be an injustice . . . necessitating for its relief that clumsy and invidious device 'a conscience clause'.

The Times was to note later in October 1870 that at the conference of the League it was 'the secular party' which got most cheers. Yet in their effort to move cautiously on this issue the leaders of the League settled for an uneasy compromise.

After Fawcett had stated at the first national conference of the League in October 1869 that Bible reading might be permissible in public elementary schools, Dixon and Collings replied that the League had no intention of interfering in religion, but wished to leave it to local educational authorities to decide whether to keep the Bible in such schools provided that in all circumstances it would be read 'without note or comment'. Adams himself, like the radical MP Sir Charles Dilke, questioned the soundness of this decision:

> As events proved, it might have been wiser to have gone at first for the absolute separation on all points, of religious and secular teaching. Bible reading was satisfactory to no considerable party; and the permissive use of the Bible did not prevent the members of the League from being denounced on Church and Tory platforms as the enemies of religion, of Government and of morals.

That this compromise did not impress some members of the League even in Birmingham itself was already clear by January 1870 when a group of working men asked that it should be set aside. They were only too well aware that it did not impress the League's opponents in Birmingham. A satirical verse published by a leading local Tory, Sebastian Evans, in the *Birmingham Gazette*, depicted the new public elementary school as a bleak, godless place. In a nightmare of the future he caught a glimpse of:

> A dismal house which I knew was a school . . .
> The one word 'League' grim lettered in black.
> 'Twas the dismallest house the world ever saw
> Where to pray to God was to break the law.

In London and in the countryside there was even more criticism, not always set out so politely in conventional verse.

There was another compromise – or rather evasion – which complicated the approach of the League in 1869, when it urged the building of rate-aided schools, but left vague its attitude to the finance of the existing voluntary schools. It talked of 'supplementing' such schools, but it often seemed to be arguing that they should be superseded. The evasion was irritating to many members of the League, particularly in Wales, where feeling against the Church was extremely strong, and a matter for challenge from the opponents of the League in whatever part of the country they were. Indeed, it was on this point above all others that the rival organisation, the National Education Union, brought into existence in November 1869, chose to fight.

After George Dawson, drawing on all his eloquence as a preacher, had told the first general meeting of the League in October that if its plans were adopted 'the existing system must go by a slow, sure, and, I hope, painless extinction', his words were eagerly seized upon as a declaration of the true intent of the League. Dixon himself, though he accepted the existence of Church schools, argued that in time they would be superseded by (not supplemented by) rate-aided schools because rate-aided schools would offer better teaching. Similar points were made by Adams in his Huntingdon speech where he cited Lowe in support of his view that the voluntary schools provided inferior teaching. He went further in pooh-poohing the idea that the 'due influence' of religion should rest on the control of the very young. 'We do not believe that the due influence of religion is to be secured with the incongruous mixture of its most solemn truths with the childish rudiments of letters.'

There was a third problem which checked the momentum of the League as the year 1869 drew to a close – the problem of time-tabling. At its general meeting in October a drafting Committee had been appointed to prepare a Bill. Adams says little about it, although the motion proposing it was introduced by Fawcett and seconded by Thorold Rogers, the radical Oxford don, associated with Worcester College, who in later life was to edit the speeches of Bright. The reason why he does not discuss it is not simply because the Committee got swallowed up in bigger problems after Forster had introduced his official Bill in Parliament in February 1870, but because the Committee very quickly ran into difficulties inside itself, with feelings sometimes running high. Amendments to the first draft of the League's Bill, prepared in November, were invited from members of the Executive Committee, with the correspondence being kept secret, and although the headings of the Bill were published later in December, some of the controversial details were left out.

It became clear during the following month that many of them were not acceptable to some of the leading members of the League. Before Forster fully realised the perils of carrying an Education Bill through the House of Commons, the League itself knew how difficult it was to relate principle to practice in a public campaign. In its case, it relied more and more on militant Nonconformity – with a continuing drive for labour support – and in January 1870, before Forster introduced his Bill it summoned separately a meeting of working men and a conference of Nonconformist ministers. In this respect it was following in the footsteps of the Anti-Corn Law League, but it was also inaugurating a burst of pressure-group politics which was to destroy not 'the obstructive party' but Gladstone's Liberal government.

It is important to examine side by side the chronology of League activities in the autumn and early winter of 1869–70 and the chronology of official government initiative in relation to an Education Bill, for at a critical point in the story the League instead of pressing for legislation began to demand its postponement. The first reference to an Education Bill in Forster's diary was on 10 October 1869, but Forster had been anxious to proceed even earlier – there was also a pre-history of Cabinet interest – and Gladstone had written to Lord de Grey (afterwards the Marquis of Ripon), President of the Council, a committed believer in educational advance, eight days before Forster's reference, stating that 'it would be very desirable that we should avail ourselves of some early occasion on our gathering in London to lay the foundation stone of our Education measure for England'. Forster was not a member of the Cabinet, and during the next few days he had to take soundings about the prospects for immediate progress at a time when the general political situation was not entirely propitious. He wanted to move quickly and decisively, and his main moves were being prepared when the League held its first general meeting one day later in October and started to plan, as Adams says, in terms of an agitation which might last for ten years.

Forster's important Memorandum of 21 October – Gladstone described it as 'able' – took a completely different approach from the outset to that of the League. The object of the League, as stated in its first circular, was 'the establishment of a system which shall secure the education of every child in England and Wales'. Forster stated as his object – 'to supplement the present voluntary system – that is to fill up its gaps at least cost of public money, with least loss of voluntary cooperation, and with most aid from the parents'. He explicitly condemned the League:

> The complete logical machinery of the Birmingham League would quickly undermine the existing schools, would relieve the parents of all payment, would entail upon the country an enormous expense and – a far more dangerous loss than that of money – would drive out of the field most of those who care for education, and oblige the Government to make use solely of official or municipal agency.

Whether all the leaders of the League would have approved of the accuracy of the assessment – the word 'solely' was a far more explicit statement than any of them chose to make – there was evidently the widest of gulfs between Forster and the League.

Yet it would be a mistake to believe that Forster was doing anything more than state the position as accurately as he saw it. When he wrote, there was no rival body to the League in the country, although a few days later the National Education Union held its inaugural meeting in Manchester on 3 and 4 November. The object of the Union – that of 'judiciously supplementing the present system of denominational education' – seemed to be nearer to Forster's object than that of the

League. Forster, none the less, had not been strongly influenced by the kind of thinking (or feeling) subsequently represented in the Union, and according to A. J. Mundella, the radical MP for Sheffield, who was seeing a lot of Forster around this time, 'ridiculed' the Union when it came into existence. He went ahead with his own planning, consulting Mundella, who had attended the first meeting of the League and had accepted membership of it with marked reservations, and even Applegarth with whom he had been in correspondence earlier.

Mundella, who disliked the 'secularists' and what they stood for, had himself been associated earlier with Applegarth and the trade unionists on labour questions, and he was delighted to be of any assistance he could to Forster. He was told by Forster on 5 December that he hoped the education question would 'be settled this year', that is to say, within the current parliamentary session. The cabinet had accepted Forster's memorandum as the basis for legislation on 24 November.

When Forster told Mundella of his hope, rumours were circulating in London that the government was not going to rush the measure. These rumours were reported in the newspapers at the end of November and during the first few days of December, along with commentary on the likely reasons for delay – not cabinet procrastination on an urgent social question, but the preference of some members of the cabinet for a comprehensive measure on League lines:

> The Chancellor of the Exchequer [Lowe] and those who concur with him in the view that immediate legislation is not expedient are understood to be, on the whole, favourable to the scheme of the National Education League, and we are informed that one of the considerations by which they are influenced is the probability that if further time is allowed for discussion it will be made evident that the preponderance of public opinion is in the direction of the Birmingham plan.

The rumours appeared in *The Times*, which quoted a *Manchester Guardian* correspondent.

Forster was worried by the rumours and wrote to the Liberal whip, George Grenfell Glyn, for an assurance that his Bill would be introduced as quickly as possible: 'we shall gain nothing, but lose much, by departing from the true ground, that the conditions of the education problem are different in Ireland [a source of cabinet dissension] and England'. He also corrected the substance of the rumours: 'There was no specially ridiculous *canard* that Lowe urges delay, whereas he, as well as Bruce, have with me the strongest possible opinion that we ought to make up our kinds to prepare a bill and carry it.'

Glyn refused to give a 'specific engagement'. At the same time, he pointed out that *'two big questions* can't go on at the *same time* in the House, and that land [the Irish Land Bill] is No. 1.' Bright, whose reaction to Forster's moves was somewhat ambiguous, was one of the members of the Cabinet who favoured delay, and he was the member most in touch with the League: in a public speech a few weeks later (just before illness removed him at a critical time, as it so often did in his career, from the public scene) he put the matter more vividly than Glyn, 'You cannot easily drive six omnibuses abreast through Temple Bar.'

Bright was not speaking just for himself. A new voice in English politics – that of Chamberlain – was also heard. If the government Bill was to be a compromise, he told a Birmingham breakfast meeting in January 1870, in the presence of Bright, it should be held over. 'Half-measures' would delay a solution 'perhaps for another decade and until it would be too late to overtake the progress which more enlightened nations would make in the meantime'. Meanwhile, the League would mobilise opinion for a more comprehensive measure. Chamberlain was backed by Nonconformist journals and was obviously speaking for the League Executive.

Adams says little of this development, nor does he deal with Forster's public *riposte* – a speech in his own constituency at Bradford on 17 January. Referring directly to Bright's metaphor, Forster expressed the hope that when the Irish land omnibus had passed through Temple Bar, Lord de Grey and he would be allowed to drive the education bus through. The religious difficulty, he added, in another transport metaphor, which he was never to be allowed to forget, would be 'cantered over': 'Almost everybody in the country sees the importance of the end we are aiming at and almost all are convinced that the end must be attained at once.'

On 4 February Forster was given the green light. 'The bill is through – compulsion and all', de Grey wrote to him, 'to be brought in as at present advised on Thursday the 17th. This is first-rate. On the 8th he gave notice of the Bill, and on the 17th, as planned, he introduced it.

Instead of dealing with this sequence of events – not all of which, of course, was known to him – Adams dwelt on the struggle in the provinces between the League and the Union. He was on familiar ground. This was not the first time in nineteenth-century political history when two rival organisations, each professing the need for change, had been pitted against each other: 'The contest between the rival societies was conducted with much animation, and before the assembling of Parliament there was not a town of any importance in England where meetings or conferences had not been held.'

Only a few years earlier, the Reform League, many of whose

members, as we have seen, joined the National Education League; it and the Reform Union, different in composition and outlook, had both been engaged in the fight for the extension of the franchise. Their activities had had a complementary as well as a competitive element. There was no novelty in 1869 and 1870, therefore, in the League and the Union vying with each other in holding of mass meetings, presenting star speakers and circulating propagandist literature. Yet there was a fundamental difference in the situation. The League was genuinely reformist: it went out on the offensive as the Anti-Corn Law League before it. It could not afford to do otherwise. The Union, however, was socially respectable and, for the most part, politically conservative. Its reform ideas were limited and strongly tinged with paternalism as well as with residual voluntaryism: it considered the 'education of the poor' within a traditionalist context. It did not need to attack.

This is not to say that its leaders believed that education was an issue which was lacking in urgency. They thought the time was ripe for action and that reform should not be postponed. Two years earlier, T. H. Huxley, prominent among secularists, had rightly identified among the 'classes of men' who favoured an expansion of education sections of the clergy 'seeking to stem infidelity'; and there were many Anglicans, like Sir John Pakington, who had been long interested in education for broader reasons than this.

Given that the Union included those Nonconformists, led by Edward Baines, the Leeds newspaper proprietor, who were opposed to the abolition or erosion of denominational education, it was perhaps an exaggeration for Adams to argue at Huntingdon in language he never employed in his book that

> The Union would have slumbered for ever in the womb of obscurity, had not the League been founded. It was then that the supporters of the Union hastened to the walls to array themselves once more, as the party of which they are composed has so often done before, against the just demands of the people! Their object is the supremacy of class interests, the perpetuation of priestly interference in national concerns and the conservation of the spirit of servility and dependence.

Yet such remarks bring out the obvious social differences between the Union and the League which Adams insisted upon even when he was recollecting in comparative tranquillity: 'Their lists were wholly uncontaminated by any agitation with popular institutions, or their representatives.'

The Union had two archbishops, five dukes, one marquess, eighteen earls, twenty-one bishops and twenty-one barons among its sponsors. It also won the support from the sidelines of the venerable Lord

Shaftesbury. It might follow the League in seeking the glamour of mass meetings, but more important in its calculations was the knowledge that it could rely on the steady backing of established power in every constituency. It had no need to emulate the League's policy of central-ising business from a head office in Birmingham in the same way as the Anti-Corn Law League had centralised business from its headquarters in Manchester. In the last resort, if operations in the constituencies proved inadequate it looked not to Manchester but to Canterbury, York, Oxford, Cambridge and Westminster. Not surprisingly, it did not need to try to draft an Education Bill of its own: it concentrated on other people's Education Bills which it did not like. One source of support in London was *Punch*.

Not surprisingly, too, the Leaguers were afraid of the Union's influence, not least on a Liberal government which included a sub-stantial majority of Anglicans and a sizeable number of Whigs.

> We do *not* assume that Forster will bring in a rotten bill [Dixon had written at the end of October 1869 to George Melly, the Liberal member of Parliament for Stoke] but what I do assume is this, that exactly in proportion to Forster's estimate of the strength of the League, will be the liberal colouring of the Bill. He will be afraid of the Churches until we convince him that we are stronger. He is not yet so convinced. He thinks that the Manchester Union will grow faster than the Birmingham League.

It is doubtful whether Forster ever thought in these terms, but the letter tells us a great deal about Dixon and the League.

Once Forster had produced his proposals in February 1870, all the pent-up fears were unleashed. Thereafter, the Leaguers depicted Forster as a weak man who could easily be knocked off his balance by social as well as by political pressure. It was sometimes suggested, indeed, that he preferred Conservatives to Liberals. In Adams's view 'From the beginning of the parliamentary discussion he was adopted as the *protégé* and instrument of the tories and the clergy, a position which ought not to have been a comfortable one for a strong Liberal statesman.'

The fact that many Liberals were put off by language of this kind never stopped it from being uttered. Indeed, Chamberlain eventually extended his indictment to many other Liberals besides Forster, for example in the *Fortnightly Review*, where in an 1873 article on 'The Liberal Party and its Leaders' he complained that 'many Liberals act as if the possession of political power were itself the end, instead of the means by which it is to be secured'. It is a complaint that has frequently been echoed by radicals in the twentieth century.

In 1870 there was, however, a brief calm before the storm. When

Forster first introduced his Bill he was received with great respect in the House. As an experienced parliamentary reporter put it: 'So interesting was the subject, so clearly did Mr. Forster unfold his scheme, that whilst he was speaking we took no note of time, not even to mark its flight; nor did any one else that we observed, for the attention of the House during all that long space was close and unbroken.' Although in the light of what happened later it may be significant that the same reporter quoted an old Conservative member as saying 'I like to listen to Forster because there is no nonsense about him', even the Leaguers in Parliament were sufficiently impressed not to challenge him at once.

To put Forster's speech into perspective – and Adams does not do justice to it – it is important to bear in mind first that it undermined all the Union's favourite arguments by concentrating even in the title of the Bill, on 'national education' and not on 'the education of the poor'; second, that it paid a tribute to the pressure of public opinion; third, that Dixon as well as Mundella was praised; fourth, that the issue was deliberately raised above party politics; fifth that it was explicitly stated that 'the Government has not brought forward this measure with any notion of a compromise'. The 'sanguine' views of Forster's Conservative predecessor, Lord Robert Montagu, were dismissed, and there were many telling phrases, like the terse summary of the situation as Forster saw it, 'much imperfect education and much absolute ignorance'. The relationship between the extension of the franchise and education was put in its proper context: 'I am one of those who would not wait until the people were educated before I would trust them with political power. If we had thus waited we might have waited long for education; but now that we have given them political power we must not wait any longer to give them education.' Even the international dimension was introduced: 'Civilised communities throughout the world are massing themselves together, each mass being measured by its force; and if we are to hold our position among men of our own race or among the nations of the world we must make up the smallness of our numbers by increasing the intellectual force of the individual.' The speech was a speech with broad horizons in view. It asked for confidence: 'We think it will be supported by both those who wish to protect the present system of education and those who wish to change it.'

There was, in fact, immediate praise from all sides. George Melly, MP for Stoke, wished the bill 'God speed as it went down into the country, as one of the noblest messages of peace and goodwill to all classes'; Sir John Pakington said that he had never listened to a speech 'with more heartfelt satisfaction' than to the speech Forster had just delivered; W. F. Cowper-Temple, Liberal MP for Hertfordshire and Anglican chairman of the Union, who is remembered in history for an amendment which he was subsequently to propose, said how gratified he had been with the spirit in which the plan had been introduced. 'The spirit was one of tolerance and comprehensiveness.' Only the last speaker, G. H. Whalley, MP for Peterborough, struck a discordant note, and he was not a Leaguer but an opponent of education, who believed, he said, that the experience 'of conferring education upon children irrespective of their parents had not been satisfactory'. 'The result was not the diminution of crime or pauperism; there did not follow any of the effects which we desired to achieve by a national system of education.'

The atmosphere of 'tolerance and comprehensiveness' was dissipated by the time the Bill was read a second time. What went down well at Westminster did not go down well in Birmingham. Adams briefly mentions the deputation which went to see Gladstone on 9 March. In the context of the later personal and political relationship between Gladstone and Chamberlain the interview has a special interest of its own, and at the time Mundella was not happy about what happened. But Chamberlain revealed some of the political qualities which were to ensure his subsequent, if always controversial, political success. One admirer present at the meeting noted how he was able to secure 'the earnest and rapt attention of Mr. Gladstone while purposely ruffling the temper of Mr. Forster'.

We know now that Gladstone had many reservations, some of them fundamental, about Forster's Bill and the fact that he had been willing to find a place for it in a crowded session was more perhaps on account of his 'especial commitment to the strenuous prosecution of government business' than 'because he was keenly interested in teaching children to write or read'. He would have preferred a simpler solution to that of Forster – with school boards being given a 'free discretion with regard to denominational education'. As a Churchman, he may also have believed that there was a better chance for the continuation of Church-sponsored education in 1870 than there was likely to be later, and it may well be that, for this reason – as well as for reasons of pressure on him of business relating to other issues – he raised no objections to what de Grey and Forster were proposing. Yet he did not share the objection, which he thought Forster 'entertained', 'to a law which should permit a strict limitation of the State-aided as well as of the rate-aided teaching to secular instruction. His responsibility in 1870, he wrote later, was one of concurrence rather than of authorship. But there was a touch of ruthlessness in his summing up: 'Forster undoubtedly . . . became in some sense the scapegoat of the Government. I do not know that I personally can relieve him from much of his responsibility.'

We miss in this daunting statement the kind of human concern for education which characterised Forster – even the human concern for politicians. Forster made his own position quite clear on 1 April 1870 to Charles Kingsley, who had been a member of the League and had wrongly had his name quoted as being present on the deputation: 'I still fully believe that I shall get my bill through this year, but I wish parsons, Church and *other*, would all remember as much as you do that children are growing into savages while they are trying to prevent one another from helping them.' Forster had an acute sense that his bill dealt only with the rudiments of education and that in order to get the rudiments provided there would have to be, if not compromise, friendly give-and-take. He would have agreed with G. M. Young that education was 'the great Victorian omission'.

It was after the deputation to Gladstone that the League took the decision, an unusual step, to oppose the second reading of the Bill which was scheduled for 14 March. By then a Central Nonconformist Committee had been set up in Birmingham on 3 March with Dale and the Rev. H. W Crosskey, minister of the Unitarian Church of the Messiah, Birmingham, as honorary secretaries. Adams's opposite number as operating secretary was Francis Schnadhorst, 'the spectacled, sallow, sombre' Birmingham draper, who within a short period of time was to establish himself through the Birmingham Liberal caucus as one of the most brilliant organisers in the country. Mundella had been right when he wrote to Leader after Gladstone had received the League's deputation that 'the secularists in the League are pushing the Nonconformists into antagonism about the religious question'. The antagonism was to persist and grow between 1870 and 1873, and Chamberlain was already clear in March 1870 that there was the possibility of pressing for 'the disestablishment of the English Church'. Indeed, once thought of in these terms, 'the ruinous question' was to influence the whole shape of national – as distinct from educational – politics. Meanwhile, with Forster's bill on its agenda, the League set aside its own. It gained a new momentum in the provinces, where it now had 113 branches, and it had prepared a special publication, one of nineteen publications in all on its list, which dealt with 'regulations' for forming branches and conducting business.

The amendment on the second reading of the bill was proposed by Dixon and seconded by Alfred Illingworth, MP for Knaresborough, who lived in Forster's own constituency. The debate on the amendment is described by Adams. Dixon's could not be said to have been a good speech, but it sounded warnings about future agitation and directed the attention of parliament to what was happening out-of-doors:

Already the tocsin had been sounded and the forces were mustering; and it would be found that the Churches were on one side, and the Nonconformist bodies on the other. Which would be likely to prevail? If they consulted history, they would not be left in much doubt; and behind these armies there stood an enfranchised people, and, the people had always given their votes in favour of equality.

In reply, Forster made it clear that he had already received notice of a number of other amendments which would be put later and carefully considered, but he did not succeed this time in winning the same kind of support as he had received less than a month earlier. Mundella and Lowe both backed him from the Liberal benches, but Henry Winterbotham, MP for Stroud, who because of early death soon disappeared from the political scene, urged postponement just because more time was needed in order to rouse a popular agitation: 'A year is not a long time in a nation's life. It is long enough in the present circumstances for public opinion to be formed; and the nation which has tarried so long might well have ensured another year's beneficent delay.' He quoted a comment of Brougham in 1825 that 'the people themselves must be the great agents in accomplishing the work of their own instruction'. Miall was, as always, intransigent:

> Everyone knew that when they got into Committee, questions of principle were usually frittered away, and they thought, therefore, it was better for them to state fully, fairly, and impressively before the House the fault they found in the Bill, and that they could not do, unless they raised the question on the second reading.

It was only after Gladstone, who said that it had been 'a most animated and interesting debate', had promised that there should be further examination by the government of some of the issues raised, that Dixon withdrew his amendment.

During the course of the debate Vernon Harcourt, MP for Oxford, who supported Dixon's amendment, coined the term 'the Irreconcilables' to refer to the Nonconformist opponents of the Bill. Yet he and those like him who vociferously objected to the fact that there were Conservatives who were supporting Forster were given short shrift by the prime minister:

> We surely do not think it necessary . . . to regard Gentlemen opposite as our natural enemies . . . We are here, no doubt, for the purpose of arguing manfully and stoutly our own particular principles; but, if without compromising those principles, we find occasions arise when, whatever the circumstances, we are in harmony with Gentlemen who sit on the opposite side of the House, and there is an approximation to oneness of mind, that I think is no subject for regret, but a matter for satisfaction.

Adams passes over this observation and turns to the debate on the different clauses of the bill as amended by the government which were laid on the table on 26 May.

It is not necessary to add to his account of what happened in Birmingham and the provinces during the intervening weeks when 'public feeling' was deliberately whipped up as much as possible. The most important single event was a second deputation to see Gladstone, this time a deputation from the Central Nonconformist Committee, on 11 April. Meanwhile Bradford Leaguers were putting the maximum amount of local pressure on Forster. For reasons set out by Adams, the changes proposed by the government were thought to be 'imperfect' and the League went on to mobilise additional funds, to hold mass meetings and to summon its Council on 16 June. Gladstone was at last beginning to be fully aware of the wide range of problems associated with educational legislation. In one of the very few references to education in his correspondence with his colleague and friend Lord Granville we find him writing in a letter of 30 May asking him to read a paper: 'I am loath to trouble you with a quarter of an hour's reading but the subject of Education is so important & so arduous in regard to the "religious difficulty" that I am perhaps justified in attempting this infliction.' Granville replied very diplomatically, 'I like your plan, always subject of course to its being acceptable to your House.'

The House went into committee on 16 June several months after it had first been planned to do so, and by then a formidable battery of amendments had been assembled. 'The natural interest, warming into eagerness, which the House and the country feel with reference to the measure', the Prime Minister began his introduction to the debate, 'has caused the Notice Paper to be charged and loaded with a number of motions, all of which express alternative and different methods of proceeding with regard to questions bearing upon religion, but all of which it is not possible, according to the forms of the House, to bring under consideration upon equal terms.' 'Nothing except a general disposition to make sacrifices of cherished principles', he went on, 'for the purpose of arriving at a common result, can enable us to go through a work so difficult as that before us.'

Immediately, however, Gladstone fired the flames of the Nonconformist revolt by accepting on behalf of the government an amendment from Cowper-Temple, a Whig back bencher and an Evangelical Churchman, who proposed first that no catechism or other distinctive religious formulary should be taught in a Board School, *and* second that voluntary schools should receive no assistance from the rates. In accepting this amendment Gladstone, on his own initiative, pledged an increase in annual government aid to the denominational schools from one-third to one-half of the total cost. He also proposed to discontinue the building grant to these schools after a period of grace to which the Nonconformists had already objected. Yet such discontinuation was not based on principle but on pragmatism: 'The building of schools is the easiest of all the efforts made by the promoters. Their great difficulty is the maintenance of the schools; and when we give liberal assistance to the maintenance, I think we may fairly leave to the locality the cost of the building.'

One of the best speeches in the subsequent debate was that of Disraeli who described Gladstone's speech as introducing 'an entirely new bill', a subject with which he was familiar enough in the light of his own manoeuvres with the Reform Bill in 1867. Thereafter, Disraeli could enjoy the spectacle of Liberal dissension – and the Nonconformists themselves were divided – reasonably uninterrupted. He saw the issue as it faced Gladstone in straight political terms; he had written earlier: 'Gladstone, I apprehend, is prepared to secularise, if he were only convinced he could keep his majority together by that process. But the elements of the calculation are various and discordant, and every possible result, therefore, doubtful.'

During the debates on the various amendments the elements of the calculation were always doubtful, and there was as much strange cross-voting as there had been in the Reform Bill divisions of 1867. Yet the fact that the Conservatives either supported Forster or abstained (except on the question of the use of the ballot in school board elections) and that there was a solid group of Liberals always prepared to support the government ensured that there would always be a government majority. It also ensured, of course, that the Leaguers and their friends would be in a perpetual minority, and it was for this reason that Miall complained in a famous passage in the concluding debate on the third reading that he and his supporters had been made to pass through the Valley of Humiliation.

Miall's remark was prompted by a comment of Cowper-Temple that the Nonconformists had failed to secure any of their main objectives. 'They laughed who won', said Miall bitterly. 'All the desires of the Church had been met, at least all the desires which it was thought could be conveniently put forward by the Church.' As a 'fair moiety of the party now in power', the Nonconformists had not been dealt with 'considerately': 'Once bit, twice shy'. It was this colloquialism rather than Miall's oblique reference to the Old Testament which roused Gladstone to reply in an equally famous passage:

> I hope my hon. Friend will not continue [that] support to the Government one moment longer than he deems it consistent with his sense of duty and

right . . . So long as my hon. Friend thinks fit to give us his support we will cooperate with my hon. Friend for every purpose we have in common; but when we think his opinions and demands exacting, when we think he looks too much to that section of the community he adorns, and too little to the interests of the people at large, we must then recollect that we are the Government of the Queen.

Glastone was saying no more on this occasion than he had said at the beginning of the long debates, debates which are well worth reading in full for the light they throw not only on nineteenth-century attitudes to politics and the role of government but on attitudes to religion in a period of transition. He also went back in his last speech to a defence of the continuation of voluntary schools which must have been anathema to the League:

> It was with us an absolute necessity – a necessity of honour and a necessity of policy – to respect and to favour the educational establishments and machinery we found existing in the country. It was impossible for us to join in the language or to adopt the tone which was so conscientiously and consistently taken by some Members of the House who look upon these voluntary schools, having generally a denominational character, as admirable passing expedients . . .

There was clearly as big a gulf between the League and Gladstone – not to speak of Forster – at the end of the debates as there had been at the beginning, and it was natural that Dixon should open his own brief speech by giving notice that during the next session he would move for leave to bring in a bill to amend the Elementary Education Act of 1870. To measure the gulf we should place alongside Gladstone's declaration of faith the statement of principle enunciated by Henry Richard, the Liberal MP for Merthyr:

> If he knew anything of the principles of Nonconformity, one of the most fundamental and universally acknowledged of them was this – that it was not right to take money received from the general taxation of the country, and apply it to purposes of religious instruction and worship . . . For if they claimed the right to compel one man to pay for the support of another man's religion, and to enforce that by law, they passed at once into the region of religious persecution.

Once more we are back in the seventeenth century.

One man who at the end of the debates had both feet planted firmly in the nineteenth century was Melly. He had some witty things to say, as usual, though he chose to say them outside Parliament: 'This bill contained immense probabilities of good and great possibilities of evil. The Liberals accepted it because of its probable good and the Tories because of its possible evil.' Inside Parliament, he appealed for

conciliation even between Gladstone and Miall. While confessing his
mixed feelings, he joined hands with Sir John Pakington in urging
'bygones to be bygones', adding that 'he would rather look forward
than backward in relation to this great measure of popular education.'
He valued the object 'above the means of attaining' and the education
of their children above "a religious difficulty" or "party ties"'. Thereafter, Melly did his best to make the Act work.

We can see after a century that the Act was a great landmark in
educational history, although we have rightly been warned by Eric
Midwinter in his book *Nineteenth Century Education* (1970) against
studying educational history 'as a series of legislative enactments, with
its students jumping from one Act of Parliament to another, like
mountain goats from peak to peak'. Few people came straight down
from the mountain in the summer of 1870. The Act received the royal
assent on 29 August, but as Adams says the irritation remained and
grew. Leaguer feeling was reinforced by strong expressions of dissatis-
faction with the Bill on the part of intellectual leaders. Adams quotes
John Stuart Mill, who believed that 'a more effectual plan could have
scarcely been devised by the strongest champion of ecclesiastical
ascendancy, for enabling the clergy to educate the children of the
greater part of England and Wales in their own religion at the expense
of the public'. A different kind of political philosopher, T. H. Green,
an active member of the Oxford branch of the Education League,
shared the same sentiments. He objected to the voluntary schools
being given a 'needless term of grace' and pressed for compulsory
attendance, a subject on which Mundella had always felt strongly: he
even went so far as to suggest that it should have been the sole plank in
the League platform, like the repeal of the corn laws between 1839 and
1846.

Yet very soon after the Act had become a *fait accompli* it began to be
put into operation with Leaguers working hard to make the most of it
while continuing to demand amendment in the future. School Boards
were quickly set up in the League strongholds – Birmingham and
Leeds founded their Boards on the same day – and even outside the big
towns it was often the districts with a large proportion of Nonconformists which were the most zealous in creating Boards. Adams gives
a good account both of this educational activity and of the continuing
political pressure which the League was seeking further to increase. He
describes, for example, the Nonconformist Conference in Birmingham held at Dale's chapel on 19 October and the second annual
meeting of the League held six days later at the Queen's Hotel. At the
first of these meetings the Central Nonconformist Committee decided
to ask for all grants of money for denominational education to be

withdrawn: Dale had already been preaching this programme, which had the full support of Chamberlain, and he followed up the Birmingham meeting by visiting Manchester towards the end of November when the audience in a packed Free Trade Hall heard him speak on 'The Politics of Nonconformity'. If the government did not concede Nonconformist demands, he thundered, 'let the Liberal party be broken in pieces and forever destroyed'.

At the third annual meeting of the League, held a year later, equally strong language could still be heard. C. Dilke, for example, argued that

> every gathering of Liberals in the kingdom is a meeting for the denunciation of the Liberal ministry . . . If the Liberal party breaks up, it will be from the want of ecclesiastical Liberalism on the part of the Government. The only means by which that can be prevented is by such Parliamentary action as will enable us to out-number and beat the Government, and will enable us, if strong enough, to know who are our friends and who are our foes.

From speeches of this kind we can conclude that the emotional temperature of the League rose sharply after Forster's 1870 Act had passed. 'Let a few hundreds throughout the country refuse to pay the new education rates', Joseph Cowen of Newcastle told the Conference, 'and the obstinacy of the Vice-Prsident of the Education Department would have to give way. He would find behind him a force he could not control . . . Their battle should be short, sharp and decisive; and the sooner they went into the strife, the sooner it would be over.' By then, the League had 315 branches.

Six points should be made about the period of fierce agitation which was further intensified in 1872. First, the League, with strictly limited support in Parliament and hampered by continuing divisions among Nonconformists, deliberately polarised opinion outside Parliament, taking up a more extreme position in January 1872 than it ever had done before, casting aside the Bible-reading compromise and demanding the universal introduction of School Boards to control all existing schools and to provide secular instruction, with denominations being left to service religious instruction in out-of-school hours. Second, the League began to make preparations for intervention at elections. Chamberlain collected notes on the political situation in different constituencies, and along with other League speakers invaded the strongholds of those Liberals who were unwilling to accept the League programme in its entirety. Rejecting appeals for Liberal unity, he asked plainly 'What matters it to education – what matters it to the welfare and prosperity of the nation – whether a Tory government sits on the

Cabinet benches or a Liberal government passing Tory measures?' In another speech later in the year he described himself as 'one of that little knot of fanatics, one of those much abused beings, a political dissenter', adding that he 'gloried in it'.

Third, there were enough 'fanatics' in different parts of the country to further and seek martyrdom by refusing to pay the education rates. One of the noisiest centres of this extreme movement was Sheffield, where the peak of the agitation was not reached until late 1872 and early 1873; and it was Sheffield which Chamberlain was to contest unsuccessfully at the general election of 1874. He was to stand then on an extreme anti-Church programme, about which the radical Mundella, one of the sitting members – and himself passionately interested in education – had grave reservations; and he even went so far as to argue that 'education should be made free by the simple expedient of utilising the revenue of the established church', a proposition which alienated even some Liberals who accepted the League programme. *The Times* was to attribute his defeat to 'the unpopularity of his educational principles'.

Fourth, even in places where there was not quite so much party political drama, the life of the new School Boards, as Adams shows, was often characterised by fierce political and religious strife. Birmingham itself, where the 'denominationlists', showing considerable political skills, won an at first sight surprising majority on the first School Board through the operation of the controversial cumulative vote, was one of the great storm centres. 'The fortnightly meetings of the Board were looked forward to with the greatest interest and zest, partly because of the principles at stake, though no doubt also because of the intellectual enjoyment they afforded.' With considerable skill the Liberal town council was to keep the Board in check.

Fifth, though the problems of the Boards and the debates inside them ranged widely over a broad span of problems, including the control of property and the quality of education, the ideological conflict with which the League was preoccupied (if never exclusively) centred on clause 25 of the Act which empowered Boards in those cases where the parents' poverty could be proved to pay fees at any public elementary school whether the school was a Board School or not. This clause had been allowed to pass the Commons without any amendment and without a division, and a few Boards began to pay fees to denominational schools before building schools of their own. Manchester was one of them. 'This injustice – so palpable, so unforeseen', writes Dale's biographer, 'roused the indignation of Nonconformists, even if they had been lukewarm before.' Any Board which paid such fees, Adams concluded sharply, was 'in fact merely a relief agency for the denominational managers'. The sums of money paid out by Boards under this heading were remarkably small, but, as Disraeli recognised, they had a quite disproportionate symbolic significance. Adams put it briefly: 'the 25th clause was merely the key of a position, chosen upon which to fight the issue, whether the country was prepared to accept in perpetutity the system of sectarian schools supported by public rates'. Just because there were echoes of the earlier nineteenth-century struggle about Church rates, battles about this particular question were never to lose their punch.

Sixth – and it is much the most important point of all – militant Non-conformists were always in danger of over-playing their hand in 1872 and 1873. However much they or their local and national leaders campaigned against the clause 25, they were demonstrating as a minority rather than communicating politically with the majority, even the majority within their own party. The political effect of their strident campaign was essentially destructive, for, as the *Economist* had put it during the year 1870 itself, 'a broad and symmetrical plan with a revolutionary tendency' never appealed to 'any large mass of English electors'. The Leaguers made a great deal of noise, which was fully reported in the Press, and they intervened, often causing great local bitterness, in a number of by-elections, but, as H. J. Hanham in his *Elections and Party Management* (1959) has written, they made comparatively little impression on the ordinary Liberal voter 'unless he were already thinking of voting Conservative or abstaining', in which cases League activities confirmed him in his intention. 'The ordinary nonconformist (even), and particularly the ordinary Wesleyan, had no wish to be an agitator except perhaps for better living conditions.'

This kind of hard evaluation is missing from Adams's account. Nor, of course, was Adams in a position to know (from unpublished private sources) how, at least from the beginning of 1872, Chamberlain and a number of other prominent Leaguers, like Dilke, had become convinced that the education question by itself was of limited interest to the electorate. Of course, they may well have been aware of this from the start. Certainly, by January 1872 Bright, who throughout his life was afraid of splits in the Liberal Party, told Dale that the working classes, who in his view and that of many other politicians, played a strategic role in post-Reform Act politics, had 'little real interest' in a dispute between 'Church Parsons and Dissenting Parsons'. His own reaction to this line of argument was the opposite of Chamberlain's. Although he stated in public that the 1870 Act was 'the worst Act passed by a Liberal Government since 1832', he re-joined Gladstone's weakening government in August 1873 after Gladstone had tempted him by pointing to other and in his opinion more popular issues than education, like the repeal of the income tax. Harcourt, one of the fiercest critics of the Act, also joined the government in the autumn of 1873.

Chamberlain, by contrast, wished not to make peace but to broaden the front of Liberal opposition to the government by raising other issues than education – among them 'Free Land' and 'Free Labour' – outside the House of Commons. He was quite prepared to face the consequence that the Liberal government, in relation to which he was a young, provincial outsider, might lose the next general election. In particular, he believed that working-class support for a full, radical programme depended on what he called 'an extension of the argument'. Though there were to be many criticisms later that the Education Act of 1870 was designed to keep the working classes in order, Chamberlain was anxious at the time to keep them in movement. He expressed his views with characteristic frankness in a letter to John Morley months before the dissolution of Parliament: 'I have long felt that there is not force in the Education question to make it the sole fighting issue for our friends. From the commencement it has failed to evoke any great popular enthusiasm . . . The assistance of the working classes is not to be looked for without much extension of the argument.'

In the curious political circumstances of 1873, when the Liberal government, faced what Adams called a 'creeping process of disintegration', education was no longer, for all the virulence of the League, the issue with the most popular potential. The failure of the League – and ultimately its abolition – was clinched by Gladstone's timing of the general election. Disraeli had made it clear during the course of 1873 that he was utterly uninterested in profiting from persistent Liberal divisions to throw the government out and form a minority Conservative government. With improved constituency organisation to back him he had his eye on winning full power at a general election after Liberal disintegration had crept even further. Yet when in January 1874 Gladstone announced a general election a month later he could not have chosen a worse time. Thinking of everything except education and particularly of abolishing the income tax, the issue with which he had baited Bright, he took all his supporters by surprise. The League in particular was unprepared. For all the attention it had devoted in 1872 to electoral organisation and its efficient financing, it found it difficult to discuss such matters publicly in the autumn of 1873 because of 'uncertainty respecting ministerial intentions'. For the first time in its brief history, therefore, its annual meeting in 1873 was 'of a formal character'. When Gladstone's announcement came, 'members and candidates were scattered abroad; constituencies were unprepared; plans were not matured, and differences were unreconciled'.

Adams claims that out of 425 Liberal candidates 300 were pledged to the repeal of Clause 25, but there is little evidence that this issue swayed the electorate. 'The prominent members of the League had various fortunes.' The Liberals as a whole suffered a disastrous defeat. In England the Conservatives won sixty-five seats, in Scotland twelve and even in Wales three. There was evidence of substantial Nonconformist abstentions from the polling, though, as the Webbs wrote later, 'it will be a question for the historian of British politics whether the un-expected rout of the Liberal party . . . was not due more to the active hostility of the Trade Unionists than to the sullen abstention of the Nonconformists.' The rout was far less unexpected than the timing of the election, and the most recent political historian of the period, Trevor Lloyd, concludes that leaving issues on one side there was 'widespread relief' in 1874 that 'politics would become less exciting'. In other words, the whole tactics of the League had been wrong.

None the less, after the Liberal defeat it was by no means certain that the League would be dissolved. It was possible to argue in 1874 that with a Conservative government in power it would and should begin a new lease of life, and Adams himself talked of the defeat not being 'an unmixed evil' since it 'prepared the way for the reunion of the party on a more liberal basis'. In fact, however, the League, which was not formerly dissolved until 1877, was doomed for two reasons. First, the return of a Conservative government did not check educational advance. Lord Sandon's educational code of 1875 came to Adams as 'a surprise' and though he was shocked by the spectacle of Whitehall being 'crowded by clerical wirepullers and friars of all colours' (prob-ably the most colourful passage in the whole of his book), he could not deny that with compulsion in 1876 (free education was not to follow until 1891), 'the object for which the League was established was now guaranteed by legislation'. Second, however, the leaders of the League – or at least the most politically ambitious of them – were beginning to think of the League as redundant. They were moving away from a conception of pressure politics towards a novel conception of party politics, eventually to be expressed in the foundation in 1877 of the National Liberal Federation. Education was merely to be one item, and a not very prominent item, in the new 'popular' Liberal agenda.

Adams does not tell us how he viewed this shift of attitudes which he may well have known about only after the main moves had been made. What is clear, however, from the last pages of his book is that, whatever may have been the motives or actions of the League's leaders before and after it was dissolved, he himself remained passionately devoted to the cause of education. He was one of the small minority of Englishmen devoted consistently and continuously to education whether or not it was in the forefront of national politics. He had little use for 'the amiable philosophy of optimism' which prevailed after the dissolution of the League. England still lagged behind the United States, but in the United States, for all the progress, people were healthily 'not satisfied with the results they have obtained'. Even Adams did not realise, however, just how many obstacles stood in the way of educational advance after 1873.

John Morley, whose lengthy pamphlet *The Struggle for National Education* was published in 1873, did. While he conceived of the struggle for national education, as Adams did, as part of a bigger and longer struggle, Morley's perspectives and philosophies were different. He believed that the country, like other European countries, was passing through a critical period of transition in which ideas and institutions were being tested. In the aftermath of the Reform Act of 1867, which had opened the way to the emergence of a 'new ruling class', his own term, what was most needed was the unifying vision of a 'national cause' which would transcend interest and class and mobilise large-scale moral as well as political support. Education was such an issue, 'the most serious of national concerns', as the repeal of the Corn Laws, which he was to deal with fully in his *Life of Cobden* (1881) had been during the 1840s.

'It is above all things desirable to remove the task of national instruction as far as possible from the region of philanthropy into the drier climate of business and public duty,' Morley maintained. Yet before it could be so removed there would have to be the heat of argument. He did not mind opposition. 'Every reform', he had written in 1865, 'has been carried out in spite of hostile public opinion.' He saw himself consequentially as a leading opinion-maker, the *Fortnightly Review* as the major organ of communication with 'the respectable middle classes', and education as an issue raising a cluster of related national themes of urgent importance – the improvement of the working classes, the abolition of privilege and the extension of local self-government, all subjects which had long interested him. 'True statesmanship', he maintained, 'lies in the right discernment of the progressive forces of a given society, in strenuous development of them, and in courageous reliance upon them.'

There were Positivist undertones in such a statement. Yet in a sensitive probing of Morley's motives D. A. Hamer has illuminated his attitudes more clearly. Morley had moved away from Positivism before he met Chamberlain and had already found in the idea of a 'collective national impulse', generating the articulation and mobilisation of a 'national cause', a substitute for a belief in 'systems'. He had come to consider it to be the duty of opinion-makers and politicians working together to present great issues to the electorate, taking each question singly in order to avoid confusion and to maximise involvement. Hamer, borrowing one of Morley's own words from a different context calls this process 'focalising'.

Hamer's analysis is particularly interesting for the historian of English educational politics for two reasons. First, we cannot understand what has happened in terms of 'system'. There never has been a 'system' of education in England as there was in Prussia, and in order to sort out problems both of substance and of chronology it is essential to trace policy as 'the resultant of many diverse forces'. Second, there has been no built-in pressure in England, as there has been in the United States (or parts of it), to expand educational opportunities. When J. A. Roebuck, influenced by James Mill raised the educational issue in 1833 he apologised for taking up the time of the House of Commons on such an uninteresting topic. Decades later in 1891, half-way through the debate on the first reading of the government's proposals to provide free education, the House was counted out to make sure that forty members were present. Against this background the 'focalising' periods in the history of English education stand out dramatically, posing fundamental questions about conflict and consensus in our society and our capacity to change it. They still do.

The late-1860s and 1870s were one of those periods, and Morley, whose tastes and purposes were more than polemical, gives a more convincing explanation of why this was so than Adams does. Indeed, he takes up eloquently, if superficially, the main economic and political 'reasons' for educational advance which have been set out in the context of the recent discussions centred on the centenary of the 1870 Act while also underlining religious reasons (on the part of the Church) which have been neglected recently or overlooked.

His central question is familiar enough. 'Will rude vigour, undisciplined by intellectual training, undirected by intellectual skill, uninformed by knowledge, suffice for England in the conditions of modern society?' he asks. Unfortunately, this question is crudely functionalist, and Morley himself was the first to admit that primary education by itself could not be expected to achieve more than limited results. 'Skill in reading and counting will not protect its possessor against the mischief that is wrought by overcrowding, by exhausting labour in childhood and youth, by unbounded temptations to get drunk, by inveterate traditions and class habits of self-indulgence.' Morley had no clear view, however, of the relationship between primary education and later stages of education as a continuing process. Indeed, he did not believe that the State should supply higher education free. 'The ground of state interference in education is the expediency, not of having citizens who know Latin and history and drawing, but of making sure that every child shall have a chance of acquiring mastery over the essential instruments of knowledge.

The conclusion of another writer, Dr Rigg, that, given 1870, eventually there would follow logically 'national provision of elementary schools, and grammar schools, and high schools', he dismissed as 'this bubble of an argument' which 'barely needs puncturing'. In an address which he gave in 1876 and which he chose to reprint he argued the interesting thesis that it was of 'questionable expediency to invite the cleverest members of any class to leave it – instead of making their abilities available in it, and so raising the whole class along with, and by means of their own rise'.

In the light of the next 'focalising' period in educational history – the late 1890s and early 1900s – Morley's perspectives in 1873 seemed confined and outmoded and his book a document with little abiding interest. Yet his concept of 'focalising' applied as much to this new period, which culminated in the Education Act of 1902, as it had done to the old, and the arguments then raised, some of them going back to 1870, some pointing to the future, were just as bitter. Nonconformists raised old issues: believers in the importance of 'national efficiency' raised new ones.

Educational policy continued to rouse differences when the debate passed from primary to secondary and then to higher education, with the social argument intertwined with the educational and the political; and even though in retrospect later 'focalising' periods during the First and Second World Wars seemed to involve consensus rather than conflict, the fear of controversy remained strong.

'Focalising' periods have been followed, of course, by longer periods of administrative implementation, worthy in themselves of detailed study, and during these periods there has usually been a lull in public opinion along with a quiet consolidation of resistance to further change on the part of existing interests. Relatively little has been written about this process. Why does the earlier excitement evaporate? Is there a pattern here? Morley, thinking of his own experience during the 1870s, would have explained the evaporation in political rather than in social – or economic – terms. After Chamberlain had ceased to believe for political reasons that the education issue should be pressed on its own, Morley stuck to his belief in politicians raising one issue and one only at a time. 'Shall we not fight with most effect', he asked Chamberlain in August 1873, 'by stirring the Nonconformists and leaving other people alone?' He never became converted to Chamberlain's views on 'party' and 'programmes' even after the formation of the National Liberal Federation in 1877. None the less, he dropped the issue of education himself in 1874 and in 1875 in favour of the bigger issue, as he had then come to see it, of Disestablishment of the Church of England, and later he dropped that too.

Curiously, it was Forster who influenced him most in dropping the latter issue by warning him that the outcome of pressing it might be the opposite of that which he intended. Moreover, Morley had come to recognise himself, through experience, that the enthusiasts for Disestablishment were people 'who live in exclusively dissenting circles, or have no opportunity for surveying our society widely in its varied strata'. This was a very different kind of conclusion from that which a reader of *The Struggle for National Education* might have expected. 'Dissent', Morley wrote then, 'offers little that touches the fastidious and sentimental love, which is so much in fashion in our times, for the picturesque, the gorgeous, the romantic, the sweetly reasonable', and yet 'it possesses a heroic political record. It has little in the way of splendour and state, but it has a consistent legend of civil enlightenment. It may lack majesty, but it has always shown honest instincts.'

At various places in *The Struggle for National Education* Morley was more willing to deal in personalities than Adams, and in this connection it is fascinating to read a future biographer of Gladstone comparing unfavourably the Prime Minister's attitudes at the time of the passing of the Education Act of 1870 with the attitudes of Disraeli at the time of the passing of the Reform Act of 1867

> Mr. Disraeli had the satisfaction of dishing the Whigs who were his enemies. Mr. Gladstone, on the other hand, dished the dissenters who were his friends. Unfortunately he omitted one element of prime importance in these rather naive transactions. He forgot to educate his party. The result of this one slight oversight has been a serious disaster.

The judgement confirms Morley's considerable admiration for Disraeli's 'realism'. Morley also compared Gladstone unfavourably with Bright, whom he was later to accuse of 'an unlimited self-confidence which amounted to a corruption of the soul': Morley believed in 1873 that at a time when anti-clerical forces were triumphing in continental Europe, where political leaders were 'fully aware that the priests had too much power', 'it was left for Liberal leaders in England to find out that priests had too little power and straightway hasten to make it greater'. This was a remarkable statement for a future biographer of Gladstone to make.

It was memorable passages like this in Morley's pamphlet which were seized upon at the time, and there was one equally memorable passage of a different kind towards the end. After saying that he could not admit that the owners of the sectarian schools had the shadow of a vested interest, Morley plunged on boldly in a direction which would have shocked Gladstone even more than his personal remarks about him:

> It is simply monstrous to urge that these volunteers are for ever to stop the way to the formation of a national force. The owners of the schools only provided half the original cost of the buildings, and they have always provided a great deal less than half of the cost of the maintenance of the school. On what principle does this constitute an eternal right to the everlasting control of our educational system, and an inexpugnable claim to exclude all other schools from their parishes?

And in his very last sentence he was in the front line with Chamberlain:

> if we are to impose a heavier burden on the country for the sake of providing gratuitous instruction, people may begin to look around them and ask, whether after all the whole of the endowments of the National Church are at present put to the most wise, just and useful purposes that the electors can think of.

It is Morley the politician and commentator, not Morley the historian or the educationist, who lives through his pamphlet, despite the fact that he devoted so much space to talking about the quality of education. And the final questions which he leaves in our mind are ones well put by Adams. Would there have been a better education act than that Forster introduced in 1870 if the education issue had been 'focalised' more in public before a national act was introduced? Was it better, rather as Forster wished, to get any act on the statute book as soon as possible? Adams had no doubt:

> Looking back on half a century of procrastination and trifling, it may seem paradoxical to hold that the Act of 1870 was introduced prematurely, yet there are grounds for the belief that a stronger and more liberal measure, and one which in an educational sense would have been economy of time, could have been passed if legislation had been delayed for another year.

Looking back after a century of massive, if uneven, educational change, probably few historians today would argue that it was unwise to make a start in 1870, which was after all, a very belated start. They are more concerned with the effects of education on class groupings and opportunities, the subject which Morley and Chamberlain broached as outsiders to the working class, than they are with the battle between Nonconformists and Church of England which neither side was able to win. In dealing with the developing educational system after 1870, therefore, they will have a different agenda from either Adams or Morley. They will wish to trace the association between education, work and poor laws, to assess the effects of compulsion, to trace the effects educationally of the continuing routine operation of the

Revised Code before and after 1870, and to explore in detail (as some of the local case studies have already begun to explore for particular places) the role of schools in their neighbourhoods, the attitudes not only of children but of parents, and the recruitment and education of the teaching profession.

16   Demand and Response: The Development of Higher Education in the United Kingdom*

It is only during the course of the last few years that it has become possible to talk meaningfully – if, even then, somewhat uncertainly – about a 'system' of higher education in Britain. 'There can be no serious doubt', it was stated in 1944, 'that there is a great need to rethink and replan our university system, if it may be called a system'; and although the first pages of the Robbins Report on Higher Education (1963) refer specifically to 'a system of higher education,' the Report states flatly that

> even today it would be a misnomer to speak of a system of higher education in this country, if by system is meant a consciously coordinated organiza- tion . . . Higher education has not been planned as a whole or developed within a framework consciously devised to promote harmonious evolu- tion. What system there is has come about as the result of a series of particular initiatives, concerned with particular needs and situations, and there is no way of dealing conveniently with all the problems common to higher education as a whole.

Most changes in British history have to be explained in this way, although attention has recently been paid – rightly – not only to 'particular initiatives', separated in time, but to cumulative and self- generating processes within the history of administration itself. In the history of British universities since the early nineteenth century, it is necessary to separate out four related aspects of history – first, changes within the universities themselves, mainly, though not solely, the product of inner forces, some intellectual, some organisational, some personal; second, changes within society affecting the demand for university places, with women coming late into the story; third, changes within society affecting attitudes to universities and other institutions of higher education and ideas about them; and, fourth,

*This paper is an extended version of a paper read at a Quail Roost, North Carolina, seminar in December 1968. It was published in its earlier form, with footnotes, in W. R. Niblett (ed.), *Higher Education: Demand and Response* (1969).

changes in the pattern of resources, institutional and governmental, upon which universities can draw.

Each of these aspects of history can be treated separately, and each aspect has its own complexity. Thus, for example, it is not always easy in examining the internal history of universities to plot the relationship between intellectual changes and organisational changes. The key to understanding is to examine the role of individuals and groups, the succession and interplay of generations and the modes of intellectual and social transmission as yesterday's students became today's teachers and administrators. Likewise, a study of the demand for university places leads at the same time to a study of other educational institutions – schools in particular – and to a study of professions and graduate occupations, in other words to a study of input and outflow. The number of related variables is immense, although the story began relatively simply with the clergy.

At the same time, generalisation is never easy because of the diversity within the pattern. Oxford and Cambridge for centuries prided themselves on their differences rather than on their similarities, while within each of them different colleges emphasised their own identity. One of them, indeed, Balliol, through its famous Master, Benjamin Jowett, made the bold claim on one occasion that 'if we had a little more money we could absorb the university'.

The later world of 'Redbrick', superficially much the same everywhere, reveals, on a closer examination, at least as much variation, and variation in far more than style. The very term itself, popularised by 'Bruce Truscott', Professor E. Alison Peers, in his *Red Brick University* (1943), is suspect. British cities in the nineteenth century, out of which Redbrick institutions emerged, were strikingly different from each other in social structure and in cultural drive; and although during the twentieth century there have been many tendencies making for increasing standardisation, even the most casual visitor to the Universities of Nottingham and Leicester, for example, is struck with the differences between them.

Taking the United Kingdom as a whole, the Scottish tradition in education, that of what has been called 'the democratic intellect', is different from that of England; and although persistent efforts were made during the nineteenth century to narrow the differences and to assimilate the Scottish tradition – with its rich European background – within the English tradition, it emerged, if not unscathed, at least not destroyed. In its turn, the Scottish tradition has influenced, usually obliquely, some features of twentieth-century English university history. Wales, too, has traditions – and problems – of its own.

There is no adequate single narrative account in existence of the development of English universities during the nineteenth and twentieth centuries, and most general histories of England covering this period include few references to them. Were there such an account, it would probably concentrate on a number of episodes widely separated in time, 'the particular initiatives' that are mentioned in the Robbins Report.

Among them, the first of the landmarks that stand out is the founding of University College, London in 1826, 'the radical infidel college' which broke the centuries-old duopoly, reinforced by religious tests, of Oxford and Cambridge. With King's College following in 1829 ('a Counter Reformation') the country's capital city was provided for the first time in English history with the beginnings of what was to become by British standards a quite exceptionally large and complicated 'imperial' university.

Henry Brougham, who was one of the most active of the founders of University College, believed not in one new university, but in several – to make higher education more accessible, or, in his own characteristic words, 'come-at-able by the middle classes of society'. Progress was slow, however, and it was not until later in the nineteenth century that the newly-chartered civic universities – the term was coined by R. B. Haldane – came into existence. Their origins can be traced back to the founding of Owen's College in Manchester, in Richard Cobden's old house, in 1851, the year of the Great Exhibition. (The first Principal came from University College, London.) Leaving in the background, Durham, a university of clerical foundation, which secured its degree-granting Charter in 1837, each of these ventures was an initiative of private enterprise – and the grants of charters to them (the Victoria University, Manchester, led the way in 1880) followed sustained local pressure on the Privy Council.

The ideal behind the nineteenth-century civic university was unmistakably Victorian, and, like the ideal of the Victorian city itself, it was best expressed by Joseph Chamberlain. 'To place a university in the middle of a great industrial and manufacturing population', he proclaimed at the first meeting of the Court of Mason University College, Birmingham in 1898, 'is to do something to leaven the whole mass with higher aims and higher intellectual ambitions than would otherwise be possible to people engaged entirely in trading and commercial pursuits.' Ideal and reality were thus placed in uneasy relationship to each other.

Nine years before this declaration, however, the government had taken what in retrospect seems to be just as important a step as the local sponsors of new university institutions had taken in Manchester,

Birmingham, Liverpool, and Leeds. The Salisbury Government decided in 1889 to distribute £15,000 per annum from Treasury funds to the civic universities and appointed a committee to advise on the disbursement of the grant; Manchester received, incidentally, £1800 from it. In 1904, the total grant, which then stood at £27,000, was doubled, again by a Conservative government, and its allocation was delegated to a committee of four, who included R. B. Haldane. Once the decision to make such government grants was taken, there could be no going back.

In 1919, when the University Grants Committee (UGC) was formally established, Oxford and Cambridge for the first time accepted grants. The task of the new UGC, which included a majority of academics and was made directly responsible no longer to the Board of Education but to the Treasury, was that of 'enquiring into the financial needs of university education in the United Kingdom and advising the Government as to the application of any grants that may be made by Parliament towards meeting them'.

From 1915 onwards, four years before the setting up of the UGC, there were other government grants which extended the range of public provision, for in the heat of the First World War it had been decided – Haldane was involved behind the scenes in the making of this decision also – to set up the Department of Industrial and Scientific Research (DSIR) with an initial grant of £25,000. The same man, Sir William McCormick, was part-time Chairman after 1919 both of the new UGC and of DSIR: already for ten years he had been Chairman of the Committee advising the Board of Education on the distribution of university grants, a Committee which on the eve of the First World War was already visiting English universities and, incidentally, meeting with resentment from some of them concerning its modes of inspection. There was one new name in 1919, however. The Secretary of the UGC was a civil servant from the Board of Education. A. H. Kidd.

The next landmark in the story was 1935, when Sir Walter Moberly, former Vice-Chancellor at Manchester University, a philosopher of education more than an administrator, became full-time Chairman of the UGC: he was to stay in the post until 1949, spanning the Second World War. By then, Parliament was granting slightly over £2 million each year to the universities, a figure determined, in effect, by government. It was a figure, moreover, which remained more or less the same throughout the inter-war years and during the Second World War, when there were never more than 50,000 full-time university students in the country. In 1945, after a further burst of pressure for university expansion during the War – as one of many expressions of a greater pressure for post-war social reconstruction – the current grant, soon to be called a recurrent grant, was greatly increased until it reached £6.9

million in 1946–7. The UGC itself hailed the increase as 'initiating a new era' in the financial relations between the universities and the State.

It is interesting to note how in 1947 the UGC chose to express in words the relationship between what was happening in the universities and what was happening in society:

> The contributions which the universities were able to make in many fields of war-time activity won for them a new prestige and a place in the national esteem which it will be their ambition to retain in the period of reconstruction which has just now begun. Within the academic sphere itself, the intermingling of institutions of contrasting types brought advantages which went some way to counterbalance the inconveniences of evacuation.

The UGC was encouraged in its plans for expansion not only by the record of the immediate past, however, but by projections of the future, which began to play an increasingly important part in university history, and particularly by the recommendations of the Barlow Committee, which had been appointed in December 1945 to examine problems of scientific manpower and its use. This Committee reported the willingness of the civic universities to increase their numbers by 86 per cent in ten years – it described this figure as 'an appreciable underestimate of what could be done' – and while stating firmly that it was in the national interest to double the output of graduates in science and technology, in addition – and this was important – it urged an increase in the number of graduates in arts and social studies.

The UGC referred to the Barlow Report, therefore, as giving 'authoritative expression . . . to the demand for university expansion' and set a target of 90,000 students in 1948–9, asking all universities in the light of this recommendation to revise their estimates of possible expansion and to ignore financial considerations. As a result, the total offered rose to a revised 88,000. The UGC admitted that 'these recommendations involve changes at the universities which can only be described as revolutionary'.

It should be clear even from this very brief history of a few landmarks that by 1947 the UGC had already changed its role. Beginning as a distributor of funds, it was becoming an agent of planning, even if the planning to which it was turning was of the simplest kind – essentially collecting estimates from universities, comparing them with 'targets' set out in official papers, and offering 'guidance'. Things moved much faster than was anticipated, however, and the doubling of numbers of students in science and technology was reached in two years rather than in the ten years envisaged by the Barlow Committee. The problem of the divergence between projection and outcome – the accomplishment being determined by hundreds of 'micro-decisions' in particular universities – was henceforth to become of major importance in university history.

The UGC, not surprisingly, had its terms of reference widened in 1946 to read

> to inquire into the financial needs of university education in Britain; to advise the Government as to the application of any grants made by Parliament towards meeting them; to collect, examine and make available information on matters relating to university education at home and abroad; and to assist, in consultation with the universities and other bodies concerned, the preparation and execution of such plans for the development of the universities as may from time to time be required in order to ensure that they are fully adequate to national needs.

Sir Keith Murray, later Lord Murray of Newhaven, who was to serve as Chairman of the UGC from 1953 to 1963, has described this statement as 'the first open recognition that national needs should be a factor in the development of universities' in Britain.

When the UGC went on in 1947 to make its first non-recurrent grants to universities to meet their capital requirements and their demands for scientific equipment, it had no architects of its own to 'vet' the building plans submitted by universities and no experts inside its own office to 'vet' other proposals about equipment. It had to rely on outside consultants. None the less, its power had increased significantly, and it was soon to develop its own distinctive apparatus. Its first officials were essentially financial officers operating a system of quinquennial grants under the aegis of the Treasury. Gradually, what came to be a new bureaucracy was brought into existence.

With little thought for the consequences, the Vice-Chancellors' Committee, a body which had first come into existence very informally in 1918, welcomed the new dispensation.

> The universities entirely accept the view that the Government has not only the right, but the duty to satisfy itself that every field of study which in the national interest ought to be cultivated in Great Britain is in fact being cultivated in the university system and that the resources which are placed at the disposal of the universities are being used with full regard both to efficiency and to economy.

We seem to be very near to our own times with this statement which includes the word 'system'. Yet it is doubtful whether it would have been subscribed to in 1947 by most academics other than Vice-Chancellors – few academics were interested in university finance – or even whether at that time most Vice-Chancellors would have regarded it as more than a concession to expediency. Moreover, the firmness of the statement concealed some doubt as to its exact meaning. Before the Second World War no university was receiving as much as a half of its income from the State through the UGC. What was the government now prepared to offer by way of 'resources'? And how could the 'national interest' be interpreted?

Our own times seem so different from those of Moberly that at the recent jubilee dinner of the Vice-Chancellor's Committee, a substantially re-modelled body, it was rightly said that the last ten years had seen bigger changes than the previous forty. Moreover, Sir John Wolfenden, the present Chairman of the UGC, remarked recently that

> if Moberly came to Park Crescent [the present HQ of the UGC] tomorrow morning, he would quite simply – for all his great wisdom and experience – not have a clue. The UGC has changed a good deal over the past twenty years and, indeed, over the past ten or five. It has changed, not because there was anything wrong about the way it did its job, but because the job has changed, in size and in complexity if in no other ways.

In this most recent period, statistics and the trends they indicate have seemed to count for more than landmarks. The number of full-time university students increased in Britain from 77,000 in 1947 to over 94,000 in 1957 and to 169,486 in 1965–6. At the same time, government expenditure on recurrent grants to universities rose from £7 million in 1946–7 to £28 million in 1956–7 and £122 million in 1965–6. Non-recurrent grants rose sharply from £28 million in 1961–2 to nearly £80 million in 1965–6. These figures spoke for themselves, or at least appeared to do so to governments: in consequence, marginal items of expenditure in particular universities now became politically significant, posing questions both of absolute scale and of priorities within the educational system as it was beginning to be conceived.

None the less, there have been several landmarks too – or, at least, what seemed at the time to be landmarks – in the recent history of universities. The first genuine innovation was the setting-up in 1949 at Keele of the new University College of North Staffordshire, an institution which deliberately set out itself to innovate: for example, it offered four-year, not three-year degrees and it had a 'foundation year' in which a number of subjects were studied. The second was the granting of charters of independence to a group of university colleges which had previously been attached to London University: this was a slow process, starting with Nottingham in 1948 and ending, after discussions inside the UGC in 1955, with Hull, Exeter and Leicester. The third was another long sequence of decisions, first taken this time within the Ministry of Education in 1953, which led in 1956 to the designation as Colleges of Advanced Technology (CATS) of a number of local technical colleges of high standing, financed from 1962 onwards not only by local authorities but by direct Ministry of Education grant. They were to be granted charters as full universities from 1964 onwards, thereby both broadening the base of the community of universities and widening the scope of the UGC.

The fourth was the decision taken by the UGC in 1958 to sponsor seven brand-new universities, not upgraded institutions nor institutions subjected, like North Staffordshire, to an initial period of tutelage, but autonomous and free. It is the implications of this decision that have received most public attention. One new university would have been incremental, as North Staffordshire was. Seven changed the dynamics of the system, indeed, helped to foster the sense of a system. It was a decision taken in steps without a debate in Parliament five years *before* the Robbins Report on higher education – and taken essentially on the same basis, to begin with, as the decision taken to increase university numbers after the Barlow Committee had reported in 1946.

The Barlow Committee, indeed, had itself recommended the foundation of at least one new university and several university colleges, and it was only after the UGC had found in 1946 and 1947 that existing universities were able more or less to meet the need as defined by Barlow that it had decided not to pursue this particular recommendation. The language remained cautious, even if the argument was somewhat general:

> It is clear that the situation contemplated by the Barlow Committee does not immediately arise. In these circumstances the establishment of new institutions could no longer be regarded as a necessary means to the policy of expansion, and we have acted on the opinion that, in present circumstances, with shortages of qualified staff and with restrictions on building, greater progress can be made by concentrating the limited men and materials upon the development of existing institutions than by scattering them over a wider field.

Meanwhile, before 1958 there were a number of approaches to the UGC, some of them tentative, about possible places for new universities, and in 1955 a UGC paper listed some of them – Brighton, Bury St Edmunds, Canterbury, Carlisle, Coventry, Leicester, Norwich, Salisbury and York.

Of these, Brighton (1947), York (1947) and Norwich (1949) were taken with 'some seriousness' by the UGC, and deputations were received even in Moberly's time. It was possible, therefore, in 1954 and 1955, when the UGC began to consider a shift in its policy, to go back to the word 'immediately' in the first sentence of the Barlow statement and use it, in a way familiar to all members of committees, as a link word across time. The argument in 1957–8 for creating new universities looked simple. Existing universities could not meet – or were not willing to meet – the demand for additional university places by 1970, 'irrespective of questions of finance'. It was assumed without much questioning that they were institutionally quite free to determine, each separately, what their maximum rates of growth and maximum future targets would be, just as it was also assumed by 1957–8 that it was right that the UGC as a national body should assess future total demand for university places.

The national assessment was based on demographic factors – 'Bulge' – and socio-educational factors – 'Trend' – and the demand for action was quickened when it became clear that the government itself was disturbed that unless more university places were provided, a sizeable number of those qualified to go to university on current standards would not have a chance of securing a place. According to Sir Edward Boyle, then the minister in charge of higher education, the fact that 'the English sense of fairness came into play' was of considerable importance in changing the government's opinion. Meanwhile, spokesmen of secondary education on the UGC pressed the same point. From 1954 onwards, therefore, there was protracted debate inside the UGC (a very English debate) about the quantitative estimates of 'Bulge' and 'Trend', about what lines of action to pursue in order to speed up expansion, and about just how speedy expansion should be.

Even as late as 1956, when it was decided to support proposals being made locally in Sussex for a new university to be located in Brighton and to encourage its planning, there was no commitment to a whole cluster of new universities. By then, however, the Association of University Teachers was suggesting six or seven new institutions; *The Times* and *The Economist* were pressing the claims of Coventry and Norwich; and Gloucester, Cheltenham, Stamford and the Isle of Man had thrown their hats into the ring. Yet it was not until 1960 that York and Norwich were also accepted as new university sites, and the Treasury was informed that three or four more new universities would be necessary if a new target of 170,000 was to be reached.

The setting-up of a UGC Sub-Committee on New Universities in April 1959 enabled the UGC to examine and choose between local bids for universities: there was some discussion before it was set up on the basis of a paper prepared for members of the UGC:

> The officers have considered whether there might not be advantages in approaching an 'outside' sub-committee like the Gater Committee [which had dealt with the capital requirements of universities], but they have come to the conclusion that the problem to be studied is so near to the heart of the

Committee's financial responsibilities to the Chancellor that the Committee should not divest itself, even temporarily, of their own responsibility in this matter. Furthermore, the appointment of a sub-committee of that kind, would almost inevitably call for a *published* report, which might be a source of considerable embarrassment to the Committee and the Government.

The Committee concurred with the advice of its officers and restricted membership to its own members. At the same time, it noted the increase in public interest, particularly local interest, 'partly no doubt because of the Sussex project, but mainly because of the growing public concern about the need to find more places in universities in order to cope with the growing number of qualified students coming forward from the schools'. The emphasis had now clearly shifted to the demand side.

A UGC paper of March 1960 tried to place such changes in longer-term perspective:

At the present the picture is very different from what it was in the Nineteenth Century, when most of the provincial Universities were founded, and even from what it was in the early years of the Twentieth Century. Universities now cost more, the number of private benefactors is smaller [a contention that had not been fully tested] and the Government contribution is very much larger [indubitable]. Nevertheless we assume that it would be the view of the Government that, generally speaking, local interest and effort are essential preconditions to the establishment of a new institution and that it should be for those concerned in the given area, not the Government, to take the effective steps to that end.

There was, therefore, to be no central map with little flags placed upon it by government decree. From the start, the UGC attached great importance to local enthusiasm and interest, and all claims were considered, even if some of them were quickly disposed of. In May 1961 Essex, Kent, and Warwick were approved as university centres, with Lancaster following in November.

The act of choosing sites took the UGC outside the realm of applied mathematics. So too did a concern for innovation both in teaching and in research which was already beginning to be expressed in many other circles. Yet one other point must be made about the mathematics behind the critical decision, since it has never been entirely clear to a certain number of commentators in Britain itself. It was assumed that in the short run there could be only limited growth in the new universities and that the main thrust of immediate expansion should be met in the existing universities, some of which, notably the old university colleges of Hull and Leicester, had grown rapidly since 1945

(Hull 800 per cent by 1958, Leicester 1100 per cent). 'We did not face a choice between expansion of the existing universities and creation of new ones', the UGC reported faithfully in 1964. 'It was clear to us that both were needed.' This was the last bit of mathematics, and qualitative as well as quantitative questions now quickly entered into the argument: indeed, they were part of the texture of the argument inside the UGC itself. 'We also had in mind the need for experimentation.'

After Southampton, Hull, Exeter, and Leicester had passed from somewhat ambiguous university-college status under London tutelage to full university status between 1952 and 1957, ending a long dialogue between metropolis and provinces, the UGC recognised that an epoch had ended, and that any new universities brought into existence ought to start freer than North Staffordshire had done. The 'newness' of the institutions and the fact that they were not upgraded institutions with a history were now deemed to be of their very essence. 'New institutions, starting without traditions with which the innovator must come to terms, are more favourably situated for such experimentation than established institutions.'

The formula that was devised for the creation of new universities – local initiative; competitive bidding to the UGC; formulation of academic plans by UGC-appointed Academic Planning Committees; granting of Charters through the Privy-Council – encouraged not only innovation but diversity, although the Charters tended to be standardised. Each new university appointed its own faculty, devised its own curriculum, its own approach to teaching methods, its own governmental organisation, although the Privy Council (*via* the UGC) had to approve of their charters and the UGC itself could influence the 'mix' of subjects they taught and their rate of growth. The diversity was accentuated by the fact that from the start the new universities never worked together as a *bloc* or attempted to bargain together to strengthen their position *vis-à-vis* older universities. Between 1961 and 1968 they moved on separate lines, although they obviously had common problems and sometimes, at least, produced common solutions.

The fourth recent landmark was the Robbins Report on Higher Education, which appeared in 1963. The Robbins Committee, a Committee, not a Royal Commission, had been appointed in February 1961

> to review the pattern of full-time higher education in Great Britain and in the light of national needs and resources to advise her Majesty's Government on what principles its long-term development should be based. In particular, to advise, in the light of these principles, whether there should be any changes in that pattern, whether any new types of institution are desirable and whether any modifications should be made in the present

arrangements for planning and coordinating the development of various types of institution.

This was the first occasion on which universities had been reviewed along with other institutions of higher education in Britain, institutions that had their own separate histories and their own group status.

The range was wide, including as it did colleges for the education and training of teachers, started originally in the nineteenth century by voluntary bodies, mainly religious, but expanded in numbers by local education authorities, which were responsible in 1963 for 98 out of 146 institutions; local, area, and regional technical colleges; colleges of advanced technology; colleges of further education, a group with a future, not yet clear to them; agricultural colleges; colleges and schools of art, a group to be very much under review, as they often had been; and a small number of other institutions.

Perhaps more important than the review of institutions, however, was the collection and analysis of statistics, a task delegated by Robbins to a research team headed by Claus (later Sir Claus) Moser, who was seconded from the London School of Economics, where he was then Reader in Social Statistics. The systematic use of statistics in the Report and in the final recommendations was rare in the history of British education.

The Report recommended that there should be some changes in the previous pattern, including the conversion of the CATs into new universities, and the creation of an augmented Grants Commission, dealing with the needs of all 'autonomous institutions of higher education', including non-university institutions. It also recommended, however – and it obviously attached great importance to this – that on the basis of statistical projections, there should be sufficient expansion of numbers of students to permit 'courses of higher education to be available for all those who are qualified by ability and attainment to pursue them and who wish to do so'. This was a new kind of statement in the history of higher education in Britain. The stress on autonomy of institutions was not.

The Report, which reflected and to some extent stimulated greater interest in higher education than had ever been shown before, was clearly concerned more with student demand than with 'national need', and R. A. Butler, architect of the war-time Education Act, saw it 'as a kind of follow-up in higher education to what we did for secondary education in 1944'. He, it was, who according to his own account recommended Robbins as Chairman of the Committee. None the less, perhaps because of this emphasis, the Report produced fewer results than had been anticipated. While it was being prepared, there were serious strains in the relationships between the UGC and the government, and by the time that it reported the Prime Minister who had appointed it, Harold Macmillan, had disappeared from the stage.

No new universities were created in its aftermath, nor was a new Grants Committee, although in February 1964 the UGC was transferred from the Treasury to the Department of Education and Science. Medical education, which then accounted for around a quarter of all university expenditure, was not directly affected. Teachers' Training Colleges were renamed Colleges of Education, and subsequently B.Ed. degrees were introduced, but the colleges were not transferred directly into the university sector.

It was partly as a result of the Robbins Report that in 1965, when a Labour Government had come into power, there was now as much talk of sectors as there was of systems, and a confused public argument had started (and is still in progress intermittently) concerning a so-called 'binary system', involving the existence side by side of a university sector and a non-university or 'public' sector.

The new Labour Secretary of State for Education, Anthony Crosland, gave a speech on the subject at Woolwich in April 1965 which is in its way something of a landmark; it was followed in May 1966 by the publication of a White Paper (Cmnd. 3006), vague in language and uncertain in intention, but proposing the designation of twenty-seven institutions as polytechnics, very much *not* to be in the university sector. In April 1967, the twenty-seven became twenty-eight, and the green light was flashed: the work in them was to lead to the granting of degrees and to other national qualifications, administered not by particular universities, but by a recently founded (September 1964) Council for National Academic Awards (CNAA).

Public debate about the 'binary system' has been confused for three reasons. First, it was never made clear whether the 'system' was considered to be an 'ideal' system, aiming at diversity, or something to be accepted as a *fait accompli*, largely for economic reasons, and involving the 'systematisation' of what had hitherto been unsystematic dualism or polycentrism in higher education. Second, the bare economics of the systematisation were never clearly set out: there was no public presentation of relative costs, for example, in universities and polytechnics. Third, the implementation of policy was determined largely by civil servants in discussions with local authorities and others, and much that was happening was hidden from public view. Although a higher education planning group was set up within the Department of Education to consider the relation between the different parts of the system, its work has been confidential and its statistics have never been published.

The Robbins Report had stated that the Committee initiated its own statistical inquiries and surveys because of 'the paucity of information on higher education in general' and that it hoped that the 'information here assembled will serve as the foundation for further observation and analysis'. Yet, while research was given a boost, there seems to have been a retreat not an advance on this front after the Robbins Report was pubished. The Robbins projections are becoming increasingly out-of-date, and there have been no open moves towards 'ten-year planning' as the Committee recommended.

At this point in the history of higher education, which for the first time is beginning to be considered as a whole, the economic determinants of global expenditure on university expansion and the development of other educational institutions have obviously begun to be treated as imperatives. Controls have been tightened, and for economic reasons there has been little preparation for what Robbins anticipated would be a new wave of expansion during the mid-1970s. Indeed, it was specifically stated in February 1965 that no further universities would be created during the next ten years,* and all recent official statements have suggested not increases in but curbs on university expenditure.

The gap between aspirations and achievements has consequently widened. The controls, some of which have been inevitable given the increased scale of expenditure, have taken different forms – UGC costing exercises; establishment of building and equipment 'norms'; limited rationalisation of courses; and, in July 1967, the government's decision to give the Comptroller and Auditor-General power to inspect university accounts and to report back to the Public Accounts Committee, which had been seeking tighter control as early as 1951–2, before the expansion began.

The Committee of Vice-Chancellors and Principals has in the meantime been seeking to carry out what internal reforms it can within the 'university sector'. It has recognised that while there is now a greater measure of State involvement in university provision than any Victorian, radical or conservative, could ever have contemplated, universities in Britain have retained to the present day a substantial measure of autonomy and that, as the two English universities of 1800 have given way to the thirty-six of today, universities and government have seldom come into direct confrontration with each other. Between the government and them as a group – and they are a disparate group – there still stands the UGC.

---

*One was created after the first seven – Stirling in Scotland. Northern Ireland was to acquire a new one also – Coleraine.

They know, of course, as Wolfenden has stated, that the UGC is a changing UGC and that if the present is cloudy the future is not clear.

> It is not easy [Wolfenden has also stated] to combine the proper autonomies of the universities with the proper attention to effective use of scarce national resources. It could well turn out that the degree of success with which the UGC and the universities conduct this (delicate) operation over the next few years will determine their whole future.

The arrangements depend on 'the continued observance of conventions', on 'reciprocal good will', and, not least, in my view, on the role of particular personalities at crucial stages.

The issues have little to do with party politics, which have themselves changed completely during the period since 1889, although they have much to do with opinion. Constitutional history and social history cannot be realistically studied in separation from each other, just as social issues cannot be divorced from economic issues, much as we should like to divorce them.

A number of points emerge from this bare outline of the story. First, the history of university development has been one of fits and starts, with much of the *élan* concentrated into short sharp bursts. 'University education', Sir Richard Livingstone remarked in 1948 in *Some Thoughts on University Education* 'has grown up in the casual English way. It has never been viewed, much less planned, as a whole. A cynic might give a book on the subject the title of *Drift*.' And while there has been much more 'planning' – a difficult term to apply to university policy-making – and much more 'system' since 1948, an educational journalist, R. Bourne, could write in *The Guardian* in 1969 – on the occasion of the retirement of Wolfenden as Chairman of the UGC – that his successor would find the task 'unenviable': he would confront 'higher education in turmoil':

> Stop-go economics for the universities, confusion of purposes as universities, polytechnics and even the Open University expand in directions that only cohere in some sublime pigeon-hole in the Department of Education, and revolting students will buffet him from all sides. Not the least of his problems is the inexorable rise in demand; a rise which, unless some new methods of financing are developed, is going to make higher education one of the Exchequer's biggest headaches in the 1980s.

After an anxious search for the right man, Sir Kenneth Berrill, a very different character from Wolfendon, sharper and more down-to-earth, was appointed.

Second, the pattern of higher education as it has emerged, down to the current question marks, is very similar to other patterns in English history – to that of the social services, in general, for example. In other words, the outline of university history is not unique within the general web of history. Development has owed much to particular individuals; it has been characterised so far by remarkable continuities more than by sudden reversals; it has depended on delicate conventions that have obviated frontal conflict; in Whitehall, the Chairman and Secretary of the UGC have been in behind-the-stairs or in-the-corridor contact with their 'opposite numbers', civil servants not ministers; and on the periphery considerable margins of choice have been left to Vice-Chancellors, each with his own academic diocese.

Each university remains a separate unit, therefore, as universities were in the nineteenth century, but the UGC has developed a common system of financial provision and control which affects all universities, including Oxford and Cambridge, which to a limited extent retain a greater measure of autonomy than other universities because of their college endowments and their more independent financial arrangements, totally obscured from public gaze. The element of competition within the 'system' has been curbed, therefore, as it has in all other sub-systems of English society.

There are more or less common pay scales in all universities – Americans are always surprised by this – and in all subjects (except medicine), and common formulae have been devised for dealing with building costs and services ('norms'). Diversity, therefore, which was such a conspicuous feature of the British solution to the problem of university expansion during the 1960s, is diversity within set limits; and there is always a danger that *micro*-planning within the particular university will be handicapped or frustrated by *macro*-planning – or the lack of it – in the Department of Education and Science or in the UGC.

Third, although the number of university students has increased sharply during the period, the proportion of the age-group attending a university institution (or a polytechnic) in Britain remains small, by both American and European standards. Indeed, as a well-publicised UNESCO chart of 1957 showed, in the provision of university places per head Britain's parsimony was surpassed in Europe only by that of Ireland, Turkey and Norway. There were always arguments about the validity of such comparative statistics, but there was little argument about the ultimate merits of the institutional tradition. Thus, the Robbins Committee, members of which visited several overseas countries, including the United States, the Soviet Union, France, Germany, Sweden and Switzerland, came out firmly in favour of the British tradition:

> In our travels abroad we have seen much that is admirable and much from which this country might well learn. But in this respect [the relationship between the State and institutions] we have seen nothing that has induced envy of the position of the other systems and much that has led us to prefer the British.

The passage might have been written by Sir Michael Sadler, a pioneer in the study of comparative higher education.

'The significance of any plan or system of education', Sadler once wrote, 'lies in its presuppositions. The inner life of it is to be found in the social and moral ideal which it attempts to express.' The British presuppositions, strongly held, usually without argument, were first that universities were free and autonomous corporations, holding property and administering their own affairs, and second that the numbers of *university* students would necessarily be limited: they constituted some kind of elite. There were differences of opinion, however, about what kind of an elite and how it should be selected.

The presuppositions rested on social foundations which in their time were as strong as the economic and social foundations of twentieth-century theories of 'national need'. 'Obligation is a strong word in reference to going to college at any age', F. D. Maurice wrote in 1837, 'but I do conceive that those who are destined by their property or birth to anything above the middle station in society, and intended to live in England, are bound to show cause why they do not put themselves in the best position for becoming what Coleridge calls the *Clerisy* of the land.'

The main effect of the direct, although strictly limited, intervention of the State in the mid-Victorian affairs of Oxford and Cambridge was to stimulate a movement for internal reform which had gained ground before the State decided in what ways to intervene. Colleges revived their community ideal and re-stated it in Victorian language, emphasising its relevance to moral education and the formation of character. British universities were compared with German institutions, and serious, if inadequate, attention was paid to the implications of an increase in the number of professors and in the scale of research.

Reformers inside Oxford and Cambridge in this key period were never in complete agreement with each other – nor were the academic reformers within the University of London or within new civic universities, particularly the latter, where views on the purposes of education were often expressed that had much in common with those of Oxford from which some of the professors came. It was a London graduate, however, the first Principal of Owen's College, who most eloquently stressed the need to combine research and teaching in the interests of the student. 'He who learns from one occupied in learning drinks from a living stream. He who learns from one who has learned all he is to teach, drinks "the green mantle of the stagnant pool".'

The Victorian debate inside universities, a far more sophisticated debate than that conducted between radicals and conservatives in Parliament, touched on every relevant issue – the curriculum, which was transformed and extended; modes of teaching and examining; college and university organisation; attitudes to the community outside the universities; and university 'extension', which meant in the first instance university expansion. In the often painful process of debate, when the theory of the elite was being given a new form, balances were struck in Oxford and Cambridge themselves. Colleges strengthened their tutorial system: more university professors were appointed. A new breed of 'dons' emerged, but they were still dons.

Many of them, not least Mark Pattison, whose views have been admirable discussed in John Sparrow's little book *Mark Pattison and the Idea of a University* (1965), were disillusioned with the domestic effects of reform, but others, whether they thought of themselves as public servants or as social reformers, were proud of the influence of the universities in public life. Moreover, their own influence as dons, along with their status, was magnified by the influence of their pupils, and by the pull of the university within the minority communications system of the day.

We find, therefore, a whole variety of responses in the nineteenth-century debate about the university, which all too often is discussed only in terms of Newman's *Idea of a University*, the acknowledged classic which appeared in 1852. Alongside Pattison's intellectual uneasiness we have to set Jowett's worldliness; we have also to take account of what was called in the 1880s, when the debates were beginning to shift yet again and a new generation was emerging that did not remember Newman, 'the new Oxford movement'. This was a movement, I believe, that developed, I think for the first time, an overall though limited, view of the relationship between the university and society as a whole:

> The most living interest in Oxford [is] now that in social questions. Yes! Oxford has turned from playing at the Middle Ages in churches, or at a Re-Renaissance in cupboards; and a new faith, with Professor Green as its founder, Arnold Toynbee as its martyr, and various societies for its propaganda is alive among us.

Throughout the late-nineteenth century debate, however, university education remained an education for an elite, a social elite living alongside an educational elite. There might be 'outreach', as it would now be called, into Whitechapel or Sheffield, but dons did not expect unusual or sudden changes in social structure in Oxford (or Cambridge) themselves; and, as Sheldon Rothblatt has put in in his illuminating study *The Revolution of the Dons* (1968), none occurred, at least none that can support 'a causal explanation of reform': what statistical evidence there is points to 'a remarkable continuity in the social background of undergraduates'. It was not merely a matter of working-class exclusion: industrial and commercial wealth was not represented significantly either.

Even in the industrial cities, where there was access to new wealth, new institutions languished for want of recruits. During the late 1860s, when Oxford and Cambrige were in the midst of spontaneous reform, Queen's College, Birmingham was in debt to the extent of £10,000 and its Charter was repealed, while Owen's College was fighting against what was called 'half-hearted sympathy and openly expressed contempt'. In 1885, James Bryce, who had spent six years as a lecturer at Manchester between 1868 and 1874, before taking his Chair in Oxford, pointed out that Germany, with a population of 45 millions, had 24,187 university places, while England, with a population of 26 millions, had only 5500. 'Nothing', he asserted, 'could so clearly illustrate the failure of the English system to reach and serve all classes.'

Pattison in Oxford and Seeley in Cambridge were only two of the distinguished 'Oxbridge' men who were shocked by this state of affairs, yet essentially it persisted despite the emergence of new institutions in the late nineteenth and early twentieth centuries. It may be said, indeed, that throughout the nineteenth century the universities were influenced relatively little by the economic and social changes which were transforming the country industrially, that many people inside them thought that they stood for a way of life superior to that involved in 'the pursuit of wealth by industrious competition', and that outside opinion, curious or critical, in relation to the universities, except for that of their own graduates, had only an extremely limited influence upon them. While there were some reformers who wanted to introduce more scientists into the elite or to widen the basis of its social recruitment, there was little challenge to the conception of the university as a place where an extended 'clerisy' was not 'trained' but 'educated'.

In 1810, Edward Copleston of Oriel College, Oxford, who was often involved in controversies that have curious modern overtones, had told his readers never to believe that

> the improvement of chemical arts [among which he also included industrial arts], however, much it may tend to the augmentation of the national riches, can supersede the use of that intellectual laboratory, where the sages of Greece explored the hidden elements of which man consists and faithfully recorded all their discoveries.

And the attitude behind this statement survived a great improvement in the chemical arts, an even greater augmentation of the national riches, and the decline of the classics. There was certainly little desire in the British university tradition to be too much in line with the current 'spirit of the age'. Indeed, it was a very different thinker from Coplestone, John Stuart Mill, who wrote a generation after him that universities had

> the especial duty . . . to counteract the debilitating influence of the circum-stances of the age upon individual character, and to send forth into society a succession of minds, not the creatures of their age, but capable of being its improvers and regenerators.

This approach to university education – and it was broad enough to encourage research as well as teaching, that is to say the discovery of new knowledge as much as the transmission of existing knowledge – permitted or rather stimulated belief in a 'high' conception of the university as a special kind of institution within the constellation of educational institutions, the rest thought of not only as different but as inferior. The learner, it was maintained, should become an explorer as well as a critic. He should actually be changed as a result of his experience.

This vision of learning was put most clearly by Mark Pattison when he exclaimed in a college sermon – note again how close the relation-ship still was to religion – that the university student should be placed in a position where

> his intelligence is not only the passive recipient of forms from without, a mere mirror in which the increasing crowd of images confuse and threaten to obliterate each other; it becomes active and throws itself out upon phenomena with a native force, combining or analysing them – anyhow altering them, imposing itself upon them.

'The point in time in our mental progress at which this change takes place', Pattison went on,

> cannot be precisely marked: it is a result gradually reached, as every form of life is developed by insensible transition out of a lower. [And science broke in at this point.] As physical life passes into psychical life by a succession of steps in which there is no break, so does psychical life into spiritual. This is the life that the higher education aspires to promote, this is the power which it cherishes and cultivates, this is the faculty to which it appeals.

There were also community as well as individual implications in all this. 'The University must be the intellectual capital of the country, attracting to itself not all the talent, but all the speculative intellect.'

Such a statement of a philosophy of higher education is clearly very different from those familiar twentieth-century statements about higher education, that are primarily 'organisational' or quantitative in character. Yet it has echoed and still echoes through much twentieth-century writing in Britain, and it has influenced much English thinking within what may be called, not purely rhetorically, the English tradition. It lies behind the mathematics of the English staff–student ratios, and it has influenced some at least, of the pioneers of new universities in a quite different phase of twentieth-century educational expansion. It has survived first the fragmentation of the clerisy, and then the loss of the sense of a clerisy and, finally, departmentalisation of the academic community into different peer groups linked professionally between universities and with links outside them in the world of media.

It is important to bear in mind, however, that Pattison and many men who thought like him envisaged what they regarded as the central experience of the university student in a broad context. Pattison, in particular, wanted 'the national mind' to work and live as its 'proper organisation' in the university. He was concerned deeply about the state of the nation, going back again to the idea of 'system'. 'We have no system in anything', he complained, 'our affairs go on by dint of our practical sense, a stupid precedent implying in all cases the want of method'. He wanted universities to provide something more, however, than a response to the practical needs of the times. The national challenge was to transcend the practical sense, so much in evidence, through the creation of an intelligent, highly-motivated elite. For him there was to be no under-writing of social privileges. The future would not rest on that.

So long, however, as the social composition of the Oxford and Cambridge colleges remained unchanged and the role of the civic universities remained subordinate, limited, and, in their own judgement, inferior, the Victorian debate was very different from the twentieth-century debate as we know it. At first, the other universities were made to feel inferior. 'Anyone educated in Manchester', wrote the *Saturday Review*, 'would certainly be dull and probably vicious.' Later, inferiority became acceptable. 'The teachers at modern universities have no need to worry unduly about the tendency of the best students to go to Oxford and Cambridge', wrote G. L. Brook in his book *The Modern University* as late as 1965.

For a quite different view of the universities at the end of the nineteenth century, this time a view from outside, it is revealing to turn to George Bernard Shaw's *Socialism for Millionaires* (1901), in which he warned millionaires against endowing universities:

Be careful, [he exclaimed], university men are especially ignorant and ill-informed. An intelligent millionaire, unless he is frankly an enemy of the human race, will do nothing to extend the method of caste initiation practised under the mask of education at Oxford and Cambridge. Experiments in educational method and new subjects of technical education are . . . abhorrent to university dons and are outside the scope of public elementary education, and these are the departments in which the millionaire interested in education can really make his gold fruitful . . . It is the struggles of society to adapt itself to new conditions which every decade of industrial development springs on us that really need help. The old institutions, in the interests of that routine, are but too well supported already.

This seems to me to be an appropriate text on which to pin much of the experience of the twentieth century, the main landmarks of which I have already tried to describe. There were, indeed, more university and college teachers in the United States when Shaw wrote (24,000) than there were university and college students in England; and the American story, in which real millionaires were among the characters, had already diverged sharply from that of Britain.

The Shavian approach – and characteristically it was stated more basically, with less irony and with more crudity, by H. G. Wells – has become a key factor in twentieth-century English experience for four main reasons – first, a fundamental change in the provision of school education, elementary and secondary, influencing aspirations, expectations, and the possibility of realizing them, for girls as well as boys; second, growth in the demand for graduates – not surprisingly, the Cambridge Appointments Service was founded in 1899 (it became a Board, with full university provision three years later); third, a rise of scale and organisation in business, industry, and government, each of which made demands on the universities as science institutions; and, fourth, an increasing expenditure on scientific and technological research, already discernable before DSIR started with its first small grants during the First World War.

Given these four factors by themselves, the consequent growth both in student numbers and in university expenditures and the increasing involvement of the State in the process have had about them an air of social inevitability, although in English history, at least, there have always been as many brakes as accelerators. The nineteenth-century echoes seemed to provide as many alarms as inspirations. 'Those who know our universities best', Ernest Barker, then Principal of King's College, London, wrote in 1932 – and he was a university man who spent much of his academic life in Oxford and Cambridge as well as London – 'are haunted by the fear that a democratic enthusiasm, as genuine as it is ill-informed, may result in an attempt to increase the quantity of education at the expense of its quality.' 'One cannot but deprecate the attempts that are being made to found universities up and down the country', another writer on the civic universities, what were then called 'the new universities', had remarked four years before:

> If matters continue as they are at present we are promised a spate of new universities. They will either lower the standard of education in the universities that are already in being, and widen further the breach which exists between the old and the new, or else they will form a new and surely unnecessary type, perhaps most like the American small town colleges.

'Narrow the gates of entry', the Vice-Chancellor of Birmingham warned his colleagues in 1930, telling them that the percentage of really good students was lower than 'indulgent universities' cared to assume.

Although during the 1960s new voices were raised, stressing the importance of broader access to universities, the older line of argument was never broken. 'More means worse' was a familiar cry when the latest batch of new universities was brought into existence during the early 1960s, mercifully free from constitutional dependence on other universities. A few weeks ago, a Fellow of a Cambridge college generalised boldly that recent student unrest was explicable mainly in terms of quantitative expansion by itself. 'Any community that grew at a rate beyond its normal growth [whatever that was] was in danger of losing its characteristic ethos.'

It would be easy to end the story here were it not for the students themselves and for the changing communications system which not only influences in quite different university situations the scale of student activity across national frontiers (the wind sometimes blows across the Atlantic and sometimes across the Channel) but also influences public attitudes towards universities – to an exceptional extent perhaps in England – through the attitudes of the non-university population towards students. Because they are a minority – and seem to be a privileged minority – students are particularly vulnerable to majority attack.

The anti-student movement is strong, and public reactions, particularly local reactions, to relatively minor forms of student disturbances, particularly in places where new universities have been created as a result of the local pressure of which the UGC approved, have been disproportionate and undiscriminating. Issues have been oversimplified in terms of discipline and authority, and local Press reporting, if that is the correct term, has made for misunderstanding rather than greater knowledge of the central issues of university expansion.

If the universities were to be left in these circumstances to the mercy of local pressures – and there are signs that behind the scenes there has been a trend in this direction for some time – then we are in for a very tough fight indeed during the course of the next twenty or thirty years.

Given the limited resources available for British universities and given the relatively generous overall national and local support for students through grants – these are not administered through the UGC, but directly by local authorities – any increase in misunderstandings between the public as citizens and taxpayers and the universities as bodies dependent for 80 per cent of their income on the State could jeopardise further university expansion. It could also jeopardize the precarious 'system' in so far as it exists and the equally precarious traditions – particularly the teaching traditions – which survive in Britain and, in some cases, have been recently revitalised. It could also influence the course of discussions not only about university finance – and the student grant system – but about the still unsettled relationships between universities and other institutions of higher education.

The balances on which the English 'system' depend are as delicate as the individual universities themselves are fragile. As Karl Jaspers put it a few years ago, 'complex relationships are not resolved but destroyed by simple solutions, such as separating research from teaching institutes, liberal education from specialized training, the instruction of the best from that of the many'. All this points to the fact that the year 1968, with its compressed, if occasionally dramatic, debates, does not provide a very satisfactory vantage point for the historian who wishes to survey either the future or the past.

17 Tradition and Innovation in British Universities, 1860–1960*

'It has been truly remarked', wrote Herbert Spencer at the beginning of his essay on Education, published in 1861, 'that in order of time decoration precedes dress.'

This was a characteristic beginning to a Spencer essay which, like most of his essays, was lacking in specific examples. Perhaps the most revealing point about the essay is that there was virtually nothing in it about universities. Almost as revealing is the fact that what little was said was wholly unfavourable. Spencer would not even admit, as many contemporary critics of universities did, that what was taught in them represented tradition, however ossified. 'If we inquire what is the real motive for . . . a classical education', he claimed,

> we find it to be simply conformity to public opinion. Men dress their children's minds as they do their bodies, in the prevailing fashion. As the Orinoco Indian puts on paint before leaving his hut, not with a view to any direct benefit, but because he would be ashamed to be seen without it, so a boy's drilling in Latin and Greek is insisted on, not because of their intrinsic value, but that he may not be disgraced by being found ignorant of them – that he may have the 'education of a gentleman' – the badge marking a certain social position, and bringing a consequent respect.

Spencer was one of the great majority of Victorian Englishmen who had no university education, but in his case he stayed out not of necessity but of choice. His father was a schoolmaster, and his uncle, a clergyman, offered to send him to Cambridge. He refused. What higher education he received, therefore, was largely the result of his own reading. So, too, of course, was John Stuart Mill's. And while Mill, who had published his essay on Liberty two years before Spencer's essay on Education, was more sensitive to the significance of tradition, even of tradition of which he disapproved, he was just as hostile as Spencer was to endowed universities. 'Unfortunately', he had written in 1852 in a dismissive article on Dr Whewell, the Master of Trinity College, Cambridge,

*This paper is based on a paper read at an Edinburgh Conference on 'University, Society and the Future', to celebrate the 400th anniversary of the University of Edinburgh in 1983. It was published, with footnotes, in N. Phillipson (ed.), *Universities, Society and the Future* (1983).

it is not in the nature of bodies constituted like the English universities, even when stirred up into anything like mental activity, to send forth thought of any but one description. There have been universities (those of France and Germany have at some periods been practically conducted on this principle) which brought together into a body the most vigorous thinkers and the ablest teachers, whatever the conclusions to which their thinking might have led them. But in the English universities no thought can find place, except that which can reconcile itself with orthodoxy.'

Pusey would have been an even better target for Mill than Whewell, although it was Whewell's attack on Bentham which most disturbed Mill. Two years after Mill's article, Pusey, in the wake of Newman, had written explicitly that 'the problem and special work of a university' was 'not how to advance science, not how to make discoveries, not how to form new schools of mental philosophy, not to invent new modes of analysis, not to produce works in Medicine, Jurisprudence, or even Theology, but to form minds religiously, morally, intellectually, which shall discharge aright whatever duties God, in his providence, shall appoint to them'. There was more abundant evidence of a dislike of what was new in this forthright statement than there was of an appeal to an older tradition or traditions.

Yet there was something new in the tone of Pusey's statement itself. When fifteen-year old Bentham had been made a Senior Commoner at Queen's College, Oxford, Queen's was certainly not like that, as Bentham's often amusing letters show. He was not an easy conformist, and in one of his first letters home tells how after intending to fast in order to prepare for the Sacrament, 'it would not do, for I began to grow sick for want of victuals; and so was forced to eat a bit of breakfast with Mr. Cooper'. He was also prepared to show far more spirit than Spencer would have done in the same position. Hoping to see the transit of Venus in 1761, he broke college rules to gain access to a telescope which the Fellows had appropriated to themselves:

> Whatever belongs to the College far from being for the free use of all the individuals belongs only to the Fellows. Instead therefore of letting the undergraduates have the use of the telescope, the Fellows had it only to themselves, so that we had no hopes of seeing this remarkable Phaenomenon which it was almost impossible we should ever have an opportunity of seeing again in our lives as it will not happen again this 160 years or more. But I and two others of my acquaintance, thinking it unreasonable that we should not see it . . . stole up the commonroom stairs and marched up to the leads where the Fellows had brought the telescope for the convenience of observing the Phaenomenon. There we found only Dr. Dixon and a Master of Arts of his hall, by good luck as the Fellows were gone to prayers, who very obligingly offered to show it to us, but unluckily the sun

just then happened to pop his head under a cloud, and we could not get to
see it again 'till the senior Fellow Mr. Knaile came up thither, who seeing us
there behaved civilly enough, as he could not then very well turn us out
again.

This anecdote relating to a year just one century before the date in my
title is worth telling if only because it brings out the important point
that, whatever the state of universities and their attitudes towards
innovation and tradition, there are ways round the system for the
bright and active. Edward Gibbon, with his talk of 'idle monks',
should not always have the last word on eighteenth-century Oxford.

There were, of course, great changes in the university scene both
in England and in Scotland between 1761 and 1861, notably the setting
up of the 'godless College' in Gower Street, London, with which
Brougham had much to do. (Bentham does not seem to have subscribed money to its foundation, though he bequeathed it a skeleton,
wax head and clothes). The influence of Scotland on the new institution was greater than the influence of Bentham, since many of its most
important sponsors, like Brougham, had studied at Edinburgh, as had
most of the new Professors. There was not a single graduate of Oxford.
As the historian of University College, Professor Hale Bellot, has put
it 'the extended range of the subjects of university study, the lecture
system, the non-residence of the students, their admission to single
courses, the absence of religious tests, the dependence of the professors
upon fees and the democratic character of the institution, were all
deliberate imitations of Scottish practice'.
    Within England, this was real innovation, innovation through con-
trast. And texts from Scotland, like George Jardine's *Outlines of a
Philosophical Education* (1818), were employed in the defence of
innovation. 'We do not in this part of the Kingdom', Jardine wrote,
'attach to classical learning that high and almost exclusive degree of
importance which is ascribed to it elsewhere, thinking it of greater
consequence to the student to receive instruction in the elements of
science both physical and mental, than to acquire even the most
accurate knowledge of the ancient tongues.'
    When this approach, a main theme of the *Edinburgh Review*, was
challenged in Scotland itself in 1826, Francis Jeffrey offered the second
basic argument in favour of the Scottish tradition. While admitting that
'our knowledge, though more general, is more superficial than with
our neighbours', Jeffrey claimed that this was a 'great good on the
whole, because it enables relatively large numbers of people to get . . .
that knowledge which tends to liberalize and make intelligent the mass
of our population'.

The story of Edinburgh and other Scottish universities between 1826 and the Universities (Scotland) Act of 1858 raises almost every issue related to tradition, innovation and decline. Of the many issues, the increasing power of the State is a major one, but in general talk of the role of the State seems to have been used neither to support tradition nor to encourage innovation but rather to tighten order. Sir William Hamilton suggested, indeed, that the proposals of the State-appointed Commissioners left unreformed those things which should have been reformed and reformed those things that ought not to have been reformed.

Whatever may be said of the domestic management of arts or medicine at Edinburgh – no new Chair was founded in arts between 1761 and 1861 – it was certainly an odd governmental decision to abolish the Chair of Military Surgery in 1856 just when the need for such a Chair had been demonstrated amid considerable publicity during the Crimean War.

When John Stuart Mill gave his famous Inaugural Address at St. Andrews in 1867, he argued less in terms either of distinctive tradition or of deliberate innovation than in terms of what was coming to be a kind of conventional wisdom that transcended boundaries:

> The proper function of a university in national education is tolerably well understood [he began]. At least, there is a tolerably general agreement about what a University is not. It is not a place of professional education. Universities are not intended to teach the knowledge required to fit men for some special mode of gaining their livelihood. Their object is not to make skilful lawyers, or physicians, or engineers, but capable and cultivated human beings . . . Men are men before they are lawyers, or physicians or merchants, or manufacturers; and if you make them capable and sensible men, they will make themselves capable and sensible lawyers or physicians.

And by 1867 this was an acceptable approach to many people not only in St Andrews or in Edinburgh, but in Oxford and Cambridge also.

In England, when the reform issue had been raised during the early 1850s, the argument inside universities was at least as interesting as the public debate in Parliament. Nor had conventional wisdom hardened. The decade was opened with the important Examination Statute of 1850 in Oxford, which raised the whole question of college tuition and ultimately of professorial tuition (the two were, of course, to be forced into contrast), as well as of the reform of the curriculum. And on this occasion, at least, the claims of innovation and tradition were deliberately pitted against each other.

The historian E. A. Freeman, for example, opposed the setting up of a new History School on the grounds that it was impossible to combine the traditional education offered in Oxford with the specialisation demanded in the Statute, while the reforming Master of Pembroke, Francis Jeune, wanted to go further and bring in political economy. 'Political economy we greatly desire', he wrote to the Professor of History, 'and have urged on the Board but have always been scornfully refused. Now even Adam Smith stinks in their nostril I fear he must be adjourned.' Eventually, a revised Statute was carried creating the School of History and Jurisprudence and including a paper on Adam Smith. Compulsory classics was the price of compromise. And all this preceded the setting up of the Royal Commission to inquire into the state, discipline, studies and revenue of the University of Oxford.

The subsequent interplay of internal and external opinion, to a limited extent public opinion as well as opinion in the Royal Commission or in Parliament, demands detailed examination. Three points stand out, however. First, there was a continuing difference of opinion within the University, often expressed in pamphlet wars. There were not only 'liberal' Fellows and 'conservative' Fellows, but 'liberal' Colleges and 'conservative' Colleges. Second, the Press, particularly the periodical Press, increasing in range and in influence during the 1850s and 1860s, spotlighted what it took to be the main issues. So, too, did newspapers: the *Morning Post*, for instance, dismissed the curriculum as a collection of odds and ends swept together 'for no better reason than that there was no room for them elsewhere'. Third, it was not only Benthamites who were suspicious of endowed colleges. Walter Bagehot, for example, wrote of Oxford in the same year as Mill was criticising Cambridge (1852) that 'badly as the University has observed her statutes, her very laxity seems scrupulous when compared with the scandalous evasions of her Colleges'.

Bagehot, educated at London, was not in general unfriendly to Oxford – or Cambridge – as places but, strongly influenced by critics like the Mancunian, James Heywood, he noted acutely that the kind of education offered there was even in its ideal form unsuited for more than a few people and that the social role of the university was not easy to defend for this reason. 'The canon law is gone by, the medieval theology is food for the inferior animals', he wrote of the curriculum *after* the first reforms:

> The finer classic – the lighter thoughts – the more delicate fancies – the most evanescent shades of meaning and of language, these are what we now call scholarship. We cannot expect to train any great number of persons in any age to spend their lives on these.

Praising Oxford men for their 'thoughtfulness', he criticised them for 'their overcaution of understanding'. In his own way, Bagehot was as damning as Spencer when he dissected Arthur Hugh Clough's ironical argument that 'universities are and ought to be, and must be, mere finishing schools for the higher classes'.

He was even more sarcastic about Robert Lowe's opinion (ironical?) that they should prepare undergraduates for going to Australia.

> The gentlemen of England are educated at many schools; they come to College for a year or two to learn one another's faces and names . . . and derive from the society of one another – from wine parties – from the common *et ceteras* of college life – a certain cultivation, certain friendships, certain manners, which are a step in advance of what in each kind they previously possessed, and give them besides an excellent start in English life. The gentry of England are thus, it is said, 'finished'. They take the social type which is to last them for life. But surely this is hardly a sufficient reason for so great colleges. Scarcely a sufficient account of such large structures and such enormous revenues.

He admitted that some colleges tried to promote change, but too much should not be made of this. 'Even the fellows of All Souls decline, we observe, to maintain explicitly that the object of a university is exactly to do nothing.'

Bagehot held that 'the object of a university education is to train intellectual men for the pursuit of an intellectual life', as, indeed, did Mill and defenders of the old Scottish system. And Mill would have agreed also with Bagehot's proposition that by contrast – and it may have been too sharp a contrast – 'the real education for every practical pursuit is specific'.

Neither writer would have been much impressed, however, by Carlyle's dictum that 'the true university of today is a collection of books'. Both of them thought that reforms of university structure, if not of curriculum, would have to come from outside the universities, and both of them were convinced that change was inevitable. As Bagehot put it succinctly, 'the University is a part of the nation; it has changed, is changing, and will change, with the nation'.

None the less, Bagehot, if not Mill, was aware of the fact, as he put it years later in an essay on 'Matthew Arnold and London University', that since he himself was an outsider to Oxford, he was dealing in images as much as in facts, in what Arnold called 'unreal words', and that he was missing 'shades and touches' – and perhaps much else which could only be known from within. Few critics who shared his general stance would have been so generous. The point had been made earlier in the century, however, in 1831, when Sir William Hamilton, himself a distinguished philosopher – and a Balliol graduate – had attacked the Oxford system in the *Edinburgh Review* and elsewhere.

From within, the university picture in Oxford becomes more rather than less complex during the 1860s as groups of reformers emerged with a variety of motives and philosophies, their outlook in every case radically different from that of Pusey. Some, indeed, were directly influenced by Mill, a few by Comte. And while it now began to be possible inside the university either to advance a 'high' view of college tutorial teaching or to mobilise strong pressure for a German-style professoriate in the name of a 'community of scholars', it also began to be possible, at least for radicals, to look outside the University altogether and to dream of a new alliance between brains and numbers in order to secure political change.

By the time of the passing of the Reform Bill of 1867, the case was being regularly (and eloquently) presented that an enlightened university elite was a necessary agency in the making of democracy, not antithetical to it. This was a totally different conception from that of the Scottish 'democratic intellect', deeply rooted in the past, and that of Clough's finishing school, loosely rooted in the present. In John Morley's words, 'the extreme advanced party is likely for the future to have on its side the most highly cultivated intellect in the nation, and the contest will lie between brains and numbers on the one side, and wealth, rank, vested interest, possession in short on the other'.

The picture in Cambridge was not dissimilar, although there were fewer links with the outside world of politics. 'A new group of dons emerged there during the twenty years preceding the statutory reforms of 1882', Sheldon Rothblatt has written, 'who placed more emphasis on scholarship, more on teaching as a career, much on the "idea of the College"'. Indeed, the death in 1866 of Whewell, Master of Trinity College, marked the end of a generation, and within a few months Henry Sidgwick, a key figure in the new generation of the 1860s, was writing that 'we are in a considerable state of agitation here, as all sorts of projects of reform are coming to the surface, partly in consequence of our having a new Master – people begin to stretch themselves and feel a certain freedom and independence'. For Sidgwick, innovation was a cultural phenomenon out of which a new tradition could emerge, an interesting and pertinent conclusion if only because much of the sense of 'traditional' Cambridge in the twentieth century can be traced back only to Sidgwick.

By the beginning of the twentieth century, however, many national reforms had been realised that had long-run implications for the development of higher education in the twentieth century. First, the Test Acts went in 1871, opening up all teaching posts in Oxford and Cambridge regardless of religion. Second, the marriage of dons narrowed the gap between dons and the rest of the population, while changing the nature of the colleges as social institutions. Third, an extension movement developed which took both Oxford and Cambridge into industrial towns and cities, widening contacts, if not extending access: this was based on the idea of a 'peripatetic university'. Fourth, the higher education of women had been begun – significantly in a wide range of very different institutions and with different motivations, still to be fully explored by historians.

Fifth, school education had been grasped as a national issue and compulsion, difficult to envisage before this date, had been introduced at the elementary level. Sixth, there had been pressure for secondary education, and in some places much had been achieved *before* the Education Act of 1902. Seventh, the Technical Education Act of 1889 had at least identified new national purposes. Eighth, new university institutions had emerged which incorporated science and technology into their curriculum. Ninth, there was a great expansion of professional education, with a proliferation of examinations and diplomas: 'professional society' was coming into its own. Tenth, an embryonic University Grants Committee came into existence in 1889.

Each item in this list could be singled out for detailed treatment. In particular, however, the new 'civic universities', as they came to be called, must obviously figure even in the briefest account of innovation and tradition. Owen's College, Manchester, founded in 1851, had a difficult early history, though it quickly established an *ethos*, if not a tradition, of its own, closely bound up with the life and work of a lively industrial city. The kind of idea behind it had been expressed a quarter of a century earlier in industrial Leeds, where Yorkshire College was to be founded in 1874, for it was in 1826 that John Marshall, President of the Leeds Philosophical and Literary Society, had put forward a scheme for a university with no religious tests, which would teach 'the whole circle of literature, the sciences and the arts', and which would conceive of higher education not as a finishing school but as 'a preparation for active life'.

There would have been few quarrels with this approach in any of the new institutions which emerged late, not early, in the history of English industrialisation, during the critical decades of the 1870s and 1880s – University College, Bristol (1876), Mason College, Birmingham (1880) and University College, Liverpool (1881). Yet in all of these places there was as much emphasis on continuing tradition as there was on innovation.

The detailed histories of individual 'Redbrick' universities, as they came to be called somewhat misleadingly, have much in common, although the differences between them are as illuminating as the differences between Oxford and Cambridge Colleges. In general, however, they were drawn into innovation only in piecemeal fashion at the departmental level; and after the first pioneering years were over, they became very departmentalised. They also seem to have made few experiments in modes of teaching.

Their relatonships with Oxford and Cambridge remained import-ant, for while they drew a significant proportion of their staff from them – James Bryce, for example, taught at Manchester for six years – they were conscious of the fact – too conscious, indeed – that they seemed unprepossessing when compared with Oxford and Cambridge Colleges. Their sense of themselves was a cultural matter, therefore, inextricably bound up with the sense of the cities to which they belonged and with the texture of the whole industrial environment. My book *Victorian Cities* was an attempt to explore just how that environment was perceived.

The extent to which new universities – as they were often called – had established their own traditions by the 1920s is well brought out in a popular book of 1928 with that title, *The New Universities*. It begins not with the Senate Chamber, but with the Union, has much to say about 'home and vacation' and, while it recognises defensively that 'the civic university loses because it is not detached', adds more positively that 'the very life of the city brings life to the university'. It goes on to suggest, first, that relationships between academics and students are wrong and, second, that they cannot be improved.

> The student very often regards the lecturer as a schoolboy regards his master or as a workman looks upon his employer. They do not often feel as partners in a common adventure for the discovery of knowledge.

Throughout, there are glances back to 'Oxbridge', usually to a highly idealised version of it. A dose of Hamilton would have been salutary.

Innovation at the departmental level in the 'new universities' is difficult to ferret out, though there are many examples of innovation in research, with no immediate cultural connotations. An excellent example comes from the University of Leeds. The first lecturer in textile physics, appointed in 1928, W. T. Astbury, was concerned with the fine structure of the wool fibre, a subject of direct economic importance in the West Riding of Yorkshire, and by 1933 a skeleton structure of the wool molecule had been established. But textiles were then left behind as Astbury and his colleagues concerned themselves with other proteins, and in 1945 Astbury became Professor of Bio-molecular Structure. What had started as applied science in a field covered in only a few different civic universities had passed, therefore, into pure science and into applied science in quite different fields.

Yet tradition had a part in this story too, for it was a London Livery

Company, the Clothworkers, great benefactors of Leeds University, that provided the first funds for Astbury's research. The State did not figure in the picture at all. Before a Royal Commission of 1881 that enquired into the City companies made them consider their public role, twelve companies had already set up the City and Guilds Institute in 1878. It was as traditional bodies, however – with their traditions backed by wealth – that the City companies moved into the twentieth century.

Well-off members of the local communities in which the civic universities were created could prove more substantial benefactors than the companies or, indeed, any of the benefactors to Oxford and Cambridge. Thus, in Leeds, Sir Edward Brotherton endowed a new library; and at Nottingham and Bristol, Jesse Boot and the Wills family were generous benefactors. In turn, the civic universities were willing to try to meet local interests. Birmingham, for example, developed brewing, Leeds leather studies, and Reading an active department of agriculture, which as early as 1907 included horticulture.

The University College at Leicester, founded in 1927, was perhaps the best example of what W. H. G. Armytage has called civic universities as 'community service stations'. The last clause in the articles of association produced by its promoters read

> to co-operate with and receive grants from and make arrangements with County Councils, City and Borough Councils, Educational Societies and Committees, Railway Companies and other public bodies, with a view to promoting and forwarding all or any of the objects of the Association.

None the less, such local service – or enterprise – did not make the pre-war universities into fully accepted social institutions. As a German observer, William Dibelius, put it in a book on England published in 1930:

> From the purely academic point of view, the new universities may beat the old on this or that point. It makes no difference . . . If a post is to be filled, the academic qualifications of the M.A. of Liverpool or Leeds will not prevail against the social status of the Oxford B.A., which bears no mark of coal dust and the fumes of the brewing vats.

It was only after the Second World War that the position changed, and then never completely. Even then there were limits. When the new University College of North Staffordshire was set up in 1949, the innovation was again Oxford-based. Lord Lindsay, Master of Balliol College, was the main influence, and he carried with him from Balliol to Keele a rich, if seldom for him totally rewarding, experience of Oxford life and ways. Keele genuinely proved innovatory; after a gap in its wake the UGC encouraged the new universities that followed to be even more innovatory – even going to the extent of neglecting the interests of Keele, a small institution which felt itself deprived in relation not to the oldest but to the newest.

The decision that the UGC took in 1958 to sponsor seven brand-new universities falls just within the limits of my period and although on this occasion innovation was being pressed for from the centre in the interests of the State – as it was in relation to a number of courses, for example in Russian, in existing universities – the way that the UGC operated encouraged innovation at the periphery too. The seven new universities were not to be upgraded institutions nor institutions subjected, like North Staffordshire, to an initial period of tutelage, but from the start autonomous and free. The fact that there were to be seven was crucial. One new university would have been incremental, as North Staffordshire was; seven changed the dynamics of the system, indeed, helped to foster the sense of a system.

The mode of creation which I have described elsewhere* fostered innovation in the siting of universities as well as in their curricula. 'Bids' were invited from what would now be called 'action groups' in places that wished to have a university. Some of the action groups had been in action for years, others were hastily mobilised. All were expected to put forward a 'case' that the UGC could consider. Some of the prospectuses that were produced were elaborately thought out; a few of them were just 'glossy'. They would, if put together, provide the basis of an interesting exhibition. A few stressed novelty for novelty's sake. Most made much of their sites, some of them located in England's most traditional places, like York, Coventry, Canterbury and Colchester. The names were often names like Essex, Kent and Warwick. Satirists fitted them all too easily into Shakesperian scenarios.

The first academic staff for all these institutions had already been appointed or were being appointed in 1961, and it was they who provided the most important link between tradition and innovation. Coming as they did from existing universities – although there was a healthy infusion of a few people from outside universities altogether – they were often reacting either against Oxbridge or Redbrick or sometimes both. Yet there were some of them who were inspired also, as the founders of London University had been in the early nineteenth century, by the example of Edinburgh. And some of the first – and later – intakes actually arrived from Edinburgh University. They felt that they had more open-ness of opportunity, academic and social, in a new university setting.

* In a paper given at Quail Roost, North Carolina in 1969, reprinted in this volume pp. 284–307.

A detailed Namierite study of the first academics – and, indeed, of the first administrators – would be of great value to future historians of higher education in Britain. And so, too, would be a detailed study of the motives of the first students who went there, motives that were very different from the motives of the first students who went to London University in the nineteenth century. There is ample primary material on which to base such studies.

Already, however, through hindsight, university experience since 1961 colours the interpretation of the new universities in their very first phase. Moreover, Walter Bagehot's mid-nineteenth century warning still holds – if you have not attended a university what you say about it is often limited to images. Not surprisingly, it was the images of the new universities rather than the facts about them that already gripped the public imagination in 1961 itself. How things have actually worked out since is a theme for a quite different paper.

18   Cerberus and the Sphinx: Modern Greats in Oxford*

There is no more distinctive Oxford product than the Honour School of Philosophy, Politics and Economics, Modern Greats. Its foundation in 1921 was a sign that the social studies had arrived; it was also a sign that Oxford was determined to take an interest in them.

Nearly a hundred years earlier, an Oxford don had remarked that 'before long political economists of some sort or other must govern the world': by 1919, when a formal request was made to Hebdomadal Council to set up a new final Honours School, the claims were a little more modest. Emphasis was placed on 'the expectation of foreign students, especially from America, of finding in Oxford a complete apparatus of systematic training in social studies'. It was also stressed, however, that in the future there would be 'a strong wish of British students for some planned courses suitable as equipment for entry to and pursuit of careers like the Civil Service, or the administrative and legislative work of citizens or the conduct of commercial and industrial enterprise'. The satisfaction of these wants, the petitioners stated, using proper economic language, 'can be given without sacrifice of breadth by such a final Honour School'.

Since 1921, many of these claims have been justified. American students, among them some of the brightest Rhodes Scholars, have rushed to Oxford in the hope of finding a complete apparatus of systematic training, while PPE graduates from Britain have flocked into the City and into the administrative class of the civil service. Some moved – unfortunately how many is not clear – into industry. Within the University, the School has established itself, and is now generally accepted as a natural component in a balanced range of undergraduate degree courses. There is no college without a PPE tutor, and there is no college without a substantial number of undergraduates studying the three subjects. Two new colleges – Nuffield and St Antony's – have set out to cater for the needs of graduate students mainly in the field of PPE. There has even been a start through vacation courses in

*Based on a paper read to the Cerberus Society in Balliol College and an article with this title in *The Twentieth Century* (1952).

320

management education. The mystic three letters PPE have become as well known to educationists in Iraq or in Hong Kong as they are in the Rochdale WEA or in the Ministry of Education.

Yet it would be idle to pretend that feelings about PPE have reached a state of complacent tranquillity. If criticism from other Faculties, including the older Greats, and from outside the University has declined, introspection has increased, PPE, it is often claimed, more often with pride than with alarm, disintegrates into P., P. and E. Recent developments both in philosophy and economics have led to an intense specialisation which makes effective intercommunication difficult. It is even frowned upon. Politics, by contrast (despite the emergence of the psephologists), remains a happy hunting ground for non-specialists, a field still to be defined rather than a private preserve of a group of experts called 'political scientists' or politicians'. Even when philosophers and economists, murmuring words like 'welfare', occasionally shake hands intellectually, politicians are left out in the cold. Sometimes their preference for the company of historians shifts the academic groupings.

It is natural that robust subjects like philosophy, endowed with great prestige in Oxford, and economics, caught up in the web of its own controversies, should occasionally seek to carve out their own territories and to retreat – without too much fuss – from the empire of PPE. None the less, to those who believe, like myself, in the particular combination of subjects which Oxford has made its own, even the quietest retreats appear a little ominous. Mild scepticism about the effectiveness of PPE as an over-all education about the modern world leads all too easily not into the search for a more integrated curriculum but into gentle pressure to tilt the general balance. It would be paradoxical if the ultimate defence of PPE had to come from those who were not directly engaged in the teaching of it. I have no confidence that even its immediate defence can be left to professors of different social sciences.

In one of the Oxford colleges, Balliol, a college with an established teaching reputation, particularly in PPE, there is a recently founded society, typical of a wide range of such undergraduate societies, organised, from below, to satisfy the intellectual interests of PPE students. It is called the Cerberus Society, presumably on the grounds that although Cerberus may originally have had fifty heads, in the period of his greatest influence he was endowed with only three. Honey cakes are thrown to the Cerberus Society by economists, philosophers and politicians alike, and it is a pleasure to address them. Most of the propitiators are unaware that Cerberus and the Sphinx were both strange children of the same parents, yet both creatures are appropriate symbols. Cerberus may explain the contemporary status of PPE in Oxford; but it is the Sphinx that guards the future.

An attempt to interpret the riddle involves both an intellectual and an institutional calculation. Intellectually one of the main achievements of recent Oxford history has been the emergence of an influential school of philosophy, too much of one piece perhaps, but all the more effectual for that. In economics there has been no such school. The Institute of Statistics has directed attention to particular branches of practical investigation and has developed a distinctive flavour of its own, but it is by no means representative of the variety of economic thinking in Oxford. The two Professors represent not only different experience and knowledge but radically different attitudes to all major questions.

A post-war publication edited by David Worswick and Peter Ady, *The British Economy*, 1945–50, one chapter of which I have written myself, gives a fuller picture of the diversity of Oxford economists at the College level. By and large, as one American writer has put it, 'the authors fall, in the British spectrum, a little left of Centre, if any substance is still to be accorded that means of designation', but there are sufficient exceptions to the classification to make it an imperfect one. The emergence of a 'school' of philosophy has had some effects on the development of economics. Ian Little's *Critique of Welfare Economics*, for example, sought to discover acceptable philosophical and logical grounds for his economic analysis; his book could scarcely have appeared in any other university but Oxford.

It is doubtful, however, whether the link between the two subjects is as close as it was either in the early nineteenth century or in the early twentieth century. When in 1800 the First Examination Statute prescribed the teaching of logic, political economy was soon used to demonstrate the technique and problem of precise definition, and according to Richard Whately, an academic with the keenest of minds, 'the principal share of our attention in Political Economy, strictly so-called, must be the reasoning process: – the accurate and dextrous application of logical principles' (1832). Economics and philosophy grew up side by side, therefore, with the blessing of theologians as well as logicians. As Nassau Senior, the first Henry Drummond Professor of Political Economy, put it, 'if there be a place where political economy would be kept in order, and would not be suffered to leave the high-road and ride across the pastures and the gardens dedicated to other studies, it is the University of Oxford'

In the early twentieth century, the union between fashionable political and social philosophies and current economic thinking was likewise very close. In the PPE examination papers for 1924, for example, philosophy candidates were asked to discuss the ethical basis of the institution of private property, while economics candidates were asked a little shamefacedly, 'What is your opinion of the value of the analytical methods of modern economic theory?' A bright PPE-er in 1924 would have found no difficulty in linking his philosophical and economic studies together.

Contemporary tutors in philosophy and economics are less willing to pose big questions, to provide ready-made answers, even to discuss the approaches to big questions. There is no religion of PPE in 1955, and there are very few tutors left who teach more than one branch of the syllabus. Even within the subjects there is greater and greater specialisation. Undergraduates studying banking and currency are often sent out to other colleges: so, too, are those reading industrial or development economics. Philosophers are perhaps less specialised, but the same tendencies are at work in philosophy. Kant is hived off by many college tutors. Only G. D. H. Cole tries to pull everything together.

Perhaps the most hopeful sign for continued integration between subjects is the increase, small though it is, in the number of interdisciplinary seminars and 'circuses' (as series of lectures given by different lecturers in the University have come to be called), but these are mainly for postgraduates. (There are, of course, revision classes, but these tend to be in one subject only.) Unfortunately, an alternative hopeful sign – the increasing number of young PPE tutors who have studied PPE themselves – looks less hopeful on closer examination. For reasons of time, if not of interest, and with career considerations in mind, peer-group considerations, most of them very quickly become specialists, and only co-operate fully with their colleagues in other branches of the curriculum when they appear red-and-black hooded and white-tied at the examination table. The best students can dare to be very specialised indeed and to get away with it when they get to the Examination Schools.

The place of politics in the intellectual arena of Oxford deserves closer attention. Very few colleges have full-time politics tutors, and the interests of those tutors that there are tend to separate themselves out into particular branches of the subject. These branches are as far apart as public administration and international affairs, the history of political thinking from Hobbes to the present day and the structure of local government. Clever undergraduates may be expected to wrestle with such contrasting problems, but can tutors? Most do not try.

Yet in the field of politics also there are some hopeful signs in Oxford. Three of them stand out – the variety and vitality of politics seminars, including many which draw upon the services of distinguished 'outsiders', including some people actually involved in the pursuit of politics; the association of the University with many new or little-developed research projects in politics, particularly in the field of election studies and recent international history; and the impact on history itself, an over-powerful neighbour, of disciplines borrowed *via* PPE from other social studies. In particular, the revival of interest in nineteenth-century history, which is as much a feature of historical studies in Oxford today as was interest in the seventeenth century against the background of the 1930s, has been strongly influenced by PPE. And no one in Oxford, with a side glance at PPE, would ever define social history as history with the politics left out.

From this sketchy survey of the intellectual adventures of contemporary PPE tutors it is clear that the future of PPE will not be jeopardised for want of ideas. The students may be harassed by them, but the tutors will thrive. The institutional structure, however, must also be taken into account. The growth of social studies in Oxford has always depended upon an academic sub-structure and super-structure. The sub-structure, as represented by sub-faculties, is extremely interesting. They have become more and more self-contained.

Before the advent of PPE, there existed a Diploma in Economics and Political Science. The Diploma was of great interest to a large number of extra-mural organisations with their roots in the labour movement rather than in academic life. No account of the place of Oxford in English history is complete without attention being paid to the special contribution of the university to workers' education both through the Delegacy of Extramural Studies and the WEA and in Oxford itself through Ruskin College. Some post-war intellectual developments in Oxford – *pace* G. D. H. Cole – have widened the gap between Oxford and England rather than narrowed it, although it is still true that the sub-structure counts for much in Oxford life and that some parts of it, like the Delegacy for Social Training, have recently been reinforced.

The super-structure has grown in importance with the years as Oxford since 1945 has moved far along the road to becoming a graduate as well as an undergraduate university. The provision of new degrees in social studies, such as the degree in PPP (Philosophy, Physiology and Psychology) and the B.Phil., taken in one only of the three PPE subjects, along with a growth in the number of D.Phil. and B.Litt. students, has greatly augmented the graduate population. In the process, teaching responsibilities have moved increasingly from colleges to the university. These graduate developments have in turn influenced PPE. Indeed, there is a danger that most of the intellectual energy of some professors and tutors may be diverted to the welfare of the graduate rather than to that of the PPE undergraduate population, to very special requirements rather than to the needs of the majority.

There may be another long-term danger, too, that the postgraduate colleges will want to handle all the research in social sciences rather than leave a substantial part of it to well qualified College tutors. There has even been talk outside, particularly in Cambridge, of Oxford and Cambridge becoming graduate universities.

The most effective organisation of the super-structure has yet to be discovered. In the case of colonial studies, for example, arrangements have not yet been made which are as efficient as those which were made, for example, in social policy, designed when the organisation of the sub-structure was transferred to representative 'delegacies', consisting of elected and appointed representatives. The expansion of colonial studies is one outstanding feature of post-war Oxford, but so far there has been no investigation of its implications which is as stimulating or as searching as the pioneer report *Oxford and Working Class Education* of 1907.

As was the case in the demand for extra-mural education, the demand for education by overseas students from colonial territories is 'not the outcome of merely fugitive conditions, but has behind it a mass of experience derived from attempts made in the past, sometimes unsuccessfully, sometimes with moderate success, to organise higher education suitable to their needs'.

Adequate organisation is very much a concern of the active PPE-er, for colonial studies fall naturally into the range of social studies and cannot properly be studied apart. The problems demand insights from different disciplines. It is significant that since 1945 philosophers, economists and politicians in Oxford have all written and lectured on this subject. Their interest springs not only from intellectual curiosity but from a sense of social involvement. The extent of the involvement is far greater than even the involved are sometimes prepared to admit.

Perhaps the answer to the riddle of the Sphinx is a simple one, and a modern Oedipus – an appropriate PPE figure, although regrettably there is no psychology in the PPE mix – or for that matter no sociology – could find a quick answer. What, seems more likely is that a hundred answers will be given, more or less satisfactory. One of the fascinations of PPE is its lack of finality: along with sub-structure and super-structure, it must be refashioned each generation to meet changes in the world as well as changes in the university. It will be affected, for example, far more by changes in the colonies (or in the labour movement) than by changes in academic approaches to colonial studies (or to the study of the labour movement).

It is characteristic of Oxford that its problems are rarely brooded over, and serious purposes are interspersed with lighter reflections. PPE in its short life has not only produced front-rank politicians, higher civil servants, successful businessmen and overseas potentates; but has also produced fourth leaders in *The Times*, a rare distinction among academic subjects.

The greatest tribute to it is that it cannot be copied. Every university may have its department of economics or philosophy or politics or sociology, but only Oxford – with or without sociology – has PPE. The School may not always fit people to solve problems that have economic, philosophical and political dimensions, but it should at least enable them to know what those problems are. Whether it can deal with its own problems I am less sure.

19   The Sussex Experience

I   In Prospect: The Map of Learning*

In accepting the invitation to deliver the first of the Research Students' Lectures at the Australian National University I was deeply aware both of the privilege and the perils. Although my subject is 'The Map of Learning', my lecture in an obvious sense is a journey without maps. I shall call on a host of witnesses, but not one of them will be the most familiar kind of witness to whom pious reference is made in all annual lectures – the lecturer of the previous year. My subject, moreover, even though it is a subject of my own choice, is of an alarmingly general kind, and its title is almost as cryptic as 'The Tree of Life'. This at least can be said of the themes that I shall cover – that they fit neatly within the rubric drafted by the Research Students' Association: 'each lecture in this series will be concerned with the general topic of "University Education"'.

In deciding with more vigour than prudence to discuss 'the map of learning' – a title which will make some of my specialist colleagues shiver before the lecture and doubtless quarrel with me sharply after it – I felt that I would inevitably be in the position of one of those now almost forgotten Victorian preachers who occasionally regaled their congregations with sermons entitled 'If I had only *one* sermon to preach'. Into a period of considerably more than fifty minutes, my allotted span, they would cram their ideas and their experience. They would spend most of their preparation in finding the right text, usually an unfamiliar and arresting text, and they would seek to illuminate their timeless themes with the most timely contemporary allusions. Above all, they would seek to frame their generalisations in such a manner that they would convey a compelling personal message to every single individual in their congregation.

I hope that the parallels between my lecture tonight and one of these Victorian sermons will not be too close, but the components of what I have to say will be very similar – a grounding in the scriptures, in my case in the rich, illuminating but neglected classic literature about

---

*A lecture delivered at the Australian National University, Canberra, November 1960. It takes up some themes of my Leeds inaugural lecture (1955), 'History and its Neighbours'.

universities and about learning, a literature which inspires humility
and dispels all desire for novelty for novelty's sake; a reasonable span
of experience, in my case in two quite different kinds of British
university – 'Oxbridge' and 'Redbrick' – along with some acquaintance with universities outside Britain, including the giant universities
of the United States and a brief but already rewarding membership of
the British University Grants Committee; a number of ideas, some of
which I shall try to implement in a new university at Brighton, a
university still without students, one of the scores of new universities
throughout the world which are being created in the middle of the
twentieth century, a boom period in university building; and a number
of topical allusions of which this is the first – a recent paragraph in
an Australian newspaper describing the athlete Herb Elliott's likely
education at Cambridge: 'Lectures are not compulsory, but each week
students are closely "quizzed" by tutors at "supervision" sessions on
what they have learnt during the previous week.'

I shall be sustained throughout by a powerful underlying conviction
that whether or not I can convey a compelling personal message to
every single individual in this audience, university education is only
really effective if it does entail an individual quest during the course of
which other people's knowledge becomes personal knowledge. As
Michael Polanyi has put it (with proper and persuasive explanations),
'the personal contribution by which the knower shapes his own knowledge manifestly predominates both at the lowest levels of knowing
and in the loftiest achievements of the human intelligence'.

Last, but not least, I have a text. Francis Bacon, who was one of the
first great writers to compare intellectual exploration with physical
exploration, is the obvious source, but his writings are so generally
forgotten that almost any text out of them would be unfamiliar. I take
this one – a rather long one – from Book I of *The Advancement of
Learning* (1605), where Bacon is discussing what he calls 'errors and
vanities which have intervened amongst the studies of the learned'.

> Another error [he writes] is in the manner of the tradition and delivery of
> knowledge, which is for the most part magistral and peremptory, and not
> ingenuous and faithful; in a sort as may be soonest believed, and not easiest
> examined . . . In the true handling of knowledge, men ought . . . to pro-
> pound things sincerely with more or less asseveration, as they stand in a
> man's own judgement proved more or less.

Bacon was writing in the light of the far-reaching changes in the
organisation of the 'map of learning' in the fifteenth and sixteenth
centuries, changes to which historians have attached the phrase 'the
new learning'. Bacon himself looked forward to still more far-reaching

changes in the future. He wished to carry the spirit of the exploration of the earth into the exploration of the whole universe of nature, believing that time would show 'that the new-found world of land was not a greater addition to the ancient continent' than the new world of the mind that promised inventions and sciences as yet unknown'. Bacon concerned himself as much with society as with nature, and devoted parts of his treatises to history and to poetry as much as to science. He was interested, moreover, not only in the content of learning, but in the institutions where learning was pursued and in the kinds of people who were pursuing it.

He made many provocative comments about universities. Four of them are very pertinent. The universities were all 'dedicated to professions', he complained, 'and none were left free for the study of the arts and sciences at large'. This was a grave weakness which held back not only the advancement of learning but social action also. They were slow to reform their curricula, failing to consider honestly whether old courses might be 'profitably kept up, or whether we should rather abolish them and substitute better'. They needed to strengthen their international associations, for there had to be 'a closer connexion and relationship between all the different universities of Europe than there now is'. Last, and to him and to us doubtless not least, university teachers deserved more pay and the cost of university equipment needed to be more generously subsidised by the government:

> It is necessary to the progression of sciences that readers be of the most able and sufficient men ... This cannot be, except their condition of endowment be such as may content the ablest man to appropriate his whole labour and continue his whole age in that function and attendance ... If you will have sciences flourish, you must observe David's military law, which was, *That those which staid with the carriage should have equal part with those which were in the action*; else will the carriages be ill attended.

More men required more money: laboratories required more equipment – 'spheres, globes, astrolabes, maps, and the like ... as well as books'. (Bacon rightly thought of books as much as apparatus as essential equipment which should never be stinted.) 'As secretaries and spials of princes and states bring in bills for intelligence, so you must allow the spials and intelligence of nature to bring in their bills; or else you shall be ill advertised.'

So pertinent are these four reflections of Bacon that they can be used as oblique propaganda in our own society in the same style that French *philosophes* of the eighteenth century criticised their own society by referring to Persia, China or the South Sea Islands. I do not wish tonight, however, either to linger in seventeenth-century Britain and Bacon's New Atlantis or to criticise (through the medium of Bacon's eloquent seventeenth-century prose) the Australian bonding system for teachers and the prevalence of pass degrees in Australian universities. I want to stick to the nineteenth and twentieth centuries, centuries with which I am most familiar, and to propound as sincerely as I can a thesis which, while neither particularly subtle nor particularly oblique, is not very often examined today.

Just as Bacon was writing in the light of far-reaching changes in the organisation of learning in his day, so are we. They are changes which are seldom considered in the large: the history of the subjects in our university curriculum and the relations between them is sadly ignored. The new learning of the Renaissance has inspired more studies than the newer learning of the nineteenth and twentieth centuries. The failure was recognised in the nineteenth century. 'Our times too have their New Learning, like the Renascence Age', wrote A. W. Ward in 1878, in a paper with the very pertinent title, 'Is it Expedient to Increase the Number of Universities in England?'

Most of the subjects which figure in the modern university curriculum, including, for example, my own subject, history, are academic products of the last hundred years. Before the reforms of the 1860s at Oxford and Cambridge, the curriculum was largely confined still to classics, mathematics, and theology. History was taken no more seriously than science until the last half of the nineteenth century, and it is instructive to note that the average attendance at the modern history course in Oxford in 1850 was eight. The Regius Professors of Modern History at Cambridge combined with the far from arduous duties of their Chair the responsibilities of poets *ex-officio* to the University, visiting the University 'at decent intervals', as one nineteenth-century writer put it, 'both before and after the French Revolution supplied them with a favourite subject for their courses'.

The limitations of school education were not remedied at the universities until the last forty years of the nineteenth century. In the British public schools which 'fed' Oxford and Cambridge in the middle years of the nineteenth century, T. H. Huxley, proponent of science education, suggested without much exaggeration, most pupils had never had the chance of learning 'that the earth goes round the sun, that England underwent a great revolution in 1688, and France another in 1789, and that there once lived certain notable men called Chaucer, Shakespeare, Milton, Voltaire, Goethe, and Schiller'. Another writer was even more comprehensive. Undergraduates going up to Cambridge in the 1850s, he maintained, 'were wholly ignorant of the world, of society, of literature, of everything'.

The development of new subjects, like history and modern languages (which now look like very old subjects), the proliferation of a number of social studies, among which economics in the twentieth century has established a position of acknowledged pre-eminence after a very shaky and controversial start, the advance of psychology which has revealed, as Bacon would have wished it to reveal, a new world below the surface, and the enormous (if delayed) expansion and specialisation of the natural sciences, are all historical phenomena of a very recent period in university education. So, too, is the virtual disappearance of the classical basis on which the whole of the old educational system rested.

Even the very words which we use are themselves new. The word 'scientist', for example, was not used until after the accession of Queen Victoria; while the word 'expert' has become popular only during the last forty years. Huxley popularised the former word 'scientist', which was used in inverted commas in 1840 by William Whewell, then the Master of Trinity College, Cambridge: 'We need very much', Whewell wrote, 'a name to describe a cultivator of science in general. I should very much incline to call him a "scientist".' Graham Wallas, the somewhat-neglected British social thinker of the early twentieth century, warned his contemporaries about the use of the second of these words, 'expert', in a number of his writings. His critique of 'professionalism' in education (and outside education) – he wanted educated men, he said, not experts – went further than Bacon's, and deserves to be set alongside the famous critique of professionalism by A. N. Whitehead. Wallas did not scruple to probe what he thought were the professional interests and weaknesses of the academic profession itself. Unlike Bacon, however, he admitted that his vision was necessarily limited in his own century. 'Every general survey of our social heritage must start from the vision of a single mind. But no single human mind can see more than a thousandth part of the relevant facts of even a section of that heritage.'

What no single human mind can do in the twentieth century, the collective minds of universities have not attempted to do against the background of the emergence of the 'newer learning'. New subjects have taken their place in the map of learning, but the whole map itself has not been consciously re-drawn. Far too easily universities become 'going concerns' where radical re-thinking is neither encouraged nor welcomed. Many new universities have come into existence during the last hundred years, but the departmental form of organisation which developed in the first of them, a source of strength historically and, in many respects, it is essential to add, of academic independence, has revealed serious weaknesses as the organisational shell has hardened.

Duplication and dispersal of effort, lack of planning and co-ordination, rivalry and occasionally friction, boundary disputes and far from splendid isolation are familiar features, alas, in the twentieth-century university world. It is usually only when new universities are being created in the present phase of university history that re-thinking assumes reasonable proportions. And even now, if such universities are expected to grow in size too fast (as they often are for extraneous reasons), there may be neither the opportunity nor the leisure to contemplate current experience or ultimate purpose. Sometimes indeed the decision to create a new university is taken before adequate thought has been devoted to essential facts, let alone values, particularly facts relating to availability of staff, openings for students with qualifications in the particular subjects which it is hoped to develop, and the local supply of books and equipment. The map of learning may be scanned briefly on these occasions, but it is seldom examined with due care.

This may sound very chilling in an age of university expansion in all parts of the world, when social and political pressures to create new universities (some of the pressures are very laudable) are greater perhaps than they ever have been. Chilling it may be, but it is not intended to be alarmist. The writer in 1878 who asked the pertinent question 'Is it expedient to raise the number of universities in England?' answered it very plainly – 'existing national means in university education are insufficient to meet our existig needs' – but he also said equally plainly, 'a reckless or haphazard increase in the number of universities is inexpedient in any age or country'.

I do not want tonight to discuss organisational issues, such as the proper size of universities, the maintenance of standards, the balance (often tilted) between honours work and pass work, or the relations between universities and the State. The institutional and organisational difficulties mirror more profound academic uncertainties, uncertainties, however, which may perhaps be subjected to more critical and less passionate examination and discussion than the more practical issues. In particular, I wish to discuss two underlying sets of attitudes within universities – the attitude of scholars to their own specialisms and to adjacent and removed disciplines and the attitude of university teachers to the respective calls of teaching and research. I want to talk about the first in detail and the second very briefly.

In discussing the attitude of scholars to their own specialisms and to adjacent and removed disciplines I shall take my examples from history, the subject which I myself profess. They could, of course, be taken from the history and development of any other subject – classics, social studies, or science. And I hope, in the manner of the nineteenth-century preacher, that what I say about history will be applied in your own minds to the subject with which you are most directly concerned. To wander more widely than history would be to lay myself open to charges of arrogance, a charge which incidentally was frequently made against Bacon and occasionally in the nineteenth century against Dr Thomas Arnold, headmaster of Rugby, who was once accused of 'arrogance of tone' in a pamphlet in which he brought to bear his knowledge of modern history and of what he called 'the laws and literature of foreign nations' on the topical question of Catholic Emancipation. Arnold rebutted the charge in a manner worthy of Bacon at his best, stating that he did not consider 'it to be arrogance to assume that I know more of a particular subject, which I have studied eagerly from a child, than those who notoriously do not study it at all'. There is no evidence that his readers were convinced by this bold declaration. For this reason, I shall keep fairly firmly to history tonight.

History as well as science figured prominently in Bacon's scheme. His map of learning comprehended three territories. The jurisdiction of the three territories was related to 'three parts of man's understanding': 'history to the memory, poesy to the imagination, and philosophy to the reason'. Within the boundaries of history there were different kinds of history and different kinds of historian. History was natural, civil, ecclesiastical, or literary. Bacon rightly complained that the fourth – what we would call the history of ideas, including ideas about society – was seriously neglected:

> for no man hath propounded to himself the general state of learning to be described and represented from age to age, as many have done the works of nature, and the state civil and ecclesiastical; without which the history of the world seemeth to me to be as the statue of Polyphemus with his eye out.

The history of nature included for Bacon what we would now call the history of technology, 'nature altered or wrought' – a subject very close to my own heart. This subject also, Bacon complained, was neglected, 'for it is esteemed a kind of dishonour unto learning to descend to inquiry or meditation upon matters mechanical, except they be such as may be thought secrets, rarities and special subtilties'. Civil history, Bacon said, rested on a variety of materials and was concerned with 'a time, or a person, or an action'. The time might be ancient or what we would now call contemporary. Bacon interested himself in both, and put up a very vigorous defence of the study of contemporary history. 'The person', he added – and this was in an age before great biographies had been written – deserved full and comprehensive treatment: 'I do find strange that these times have so little esteemed the virtues of the times, as that the writings of lives should not be more frequent.' 'Actions' or narratives were better written and more frequently written, Bacon said: 'there is no great action but hath some good pen which attends it'. At the same time, 'it is an ability not common to write a good history, as may well appear by the small number of them'.

Bacon saw many weaknesses in the current study of history. It concentrated on 'the pomp of business rather than the true and inward resorts thereof'. It lacked frequently 'true motive and lively presentation'. It might culminate in dull, conventional and educationally useless text books, particularly the abridgements of chronicles, for which Bacon reserved his strongest condemnation.

> As for the corruptions and moths of history, which are epitomes, the use of them deserveth to be banished, as all men of sound judgement have confessed, as those that have fretted and corroded the sound bodies of many excellent histories, and wrought them into base and unprofitable dregs.

This is a comment about text books which would still be echoed by many historians.

Not all Bacon's observations on history and its place in the map of learning are acceptable, but his conception of the scope of the subject and its relation to other subjects was more vast and exciting than 'history teaching by example', the theme of much of the historical writing of his day, or history narrowly confined to courts, cabinets and *haute politique*, the kind of history that established itself in the universities in the nineteenth century once the subject had been recognised as a proper academic discipline. There were other deficiencies then too. The eight undergraduates (if they were undergraduates) who listened to lectures in modern history at Oxford in 1850 were certainly not taught history as Bacon envisaged it. Charles Kingsley, who attracted huge lecture audiences in Cambridge after becoming Professor of Modern History just a hundred years ago in the autumn of 1860, certainly did not succeed by widening and deepening the foundations of his subject as an academic subject, but rather by appealing to the emotions of his young hearers. His theme was heroism, and his object was what we would now call inspirational. His expectation was that he would be able in the course of his lectures to persuade his audience that the heroes whom they were studying were heroes whom they themselves might imitate. He was sufficiently successful, it is said, that the undergraduates often burst into tears at the temporary eclipse of a hero, the apparent defeat of righteousness, and loudly applauded the hero's successes, the triumphs of virtue, righteousness vindicated. Kingsley himself later spoke somewhat cynically of his brief official honeymoon, as he called it, with the Muse of History, a Muse with deceitfully hollow charms.

There have been four main developments in the history of history as an academic subject since Kingsley's arrival in Cambridge, and I want tonight to illustrate what I have to say about the changes in the map of learning by taking as my example history since Kingsley's day. First, history has established itself as an academic subject in all British universities, including Oxford and Cambridge, which led the way, and also as a 'field of learned activity' with journals, societies, conferences, institutes and all the apparatus of learning. When I say that the subject has been established in all universities, I mean, of course, that members of academic staff (including professors) are appointed to teach it; that departments of history have been created (Oxford and Cambridge were content and are still content with professors and tutors: in England it was Manchester which pioneered a separate department for the study of the subject); and, not least, that students are examined in it. The last point, indeed, in many respects – let us be frank – is the foundation of all the rest. Non-examined subjects have very little chance in the modern university curriculum. More students mean more teachers. For this reason the refinement of examination papers is as remarkable in relation to the history of history as an academic subject as the foundation and development of the *English Historical Review*, which first appeared in 1886, or the organisation of the learned societies. Questions set in the 1870s and 1880s in the examination papers at Oxford and Cambridge were of this kind – 'Describe the main events in the history of England between 1640 and 1660', 'Who was Oliver Cromwell?' 'What wars was Britain engaged in during the seventeenth century?'

Some non-historians are still doubtless inclined to believe that questions set in history today are of this kind. The critics of a separate history tripos at Cambridge in the 1860s complained that to examine a man in history was merely to ascertain whether or not he had within a given amount of time crammed or amassed a certain amount of remembered information. In modern terminology, indeed, he was simply being 'quizzed'. Bacon's reference to history as that part of man's understanding related to his memory was being taken very seriously indeed. Although percipient advocates of history replied that historical power lay not only in the accumulation of materials but in the criticism, combination, and explanation of them, 'the reasoning from them directly and by analogy, and the artistic treatment of them so as to meet the demands of true taste', progress in the establishment of history as an accepted academic subject was far from easy.

At both Oxford and Cambridge history was for a time associated with law in a *mariage de convenance*, where 'the equality of conjugal rights was only nominal'. The foundation of the Manchester History Department to which I have referred was something of a landmark, although even there the complicated history of the department reveals how new is the map of learning which now seems so familiar to us. A Chair of History was created at Owen's College, Manchester, in 1854. The first holder of the Chair was R. C. Christie, a close friend and disciple of Mark Pattison, one of the most illuminating, intimidating and provocative of Victorian academics. Soon afterwards Christie was given two other Chairs – one in Political Economy and one in Jurisprudence and Law. He held all three Chairs until 1866, when W. S. Jevons, who had already worked in Australia at the Mint and had written on a range of topics that included the society of Sydney and Melbourne as well as the coal supply of Britain and pure logic, became Professor of Political Economy and Logic and Philosophy in the University of Manchester, and A. W. Ward, a Cambridge man, was appointed Professor of History and of English Language and Literature.

Ward abandoned the teaching of English Language but not of English Literature in 1880. Ten years later, he was succeeded as Professor of History by T. F. Tout who, with his lecturer (and later fellow Professor), James Tait, established the famous Tout–Tait partnership, which promoted history in Manchester as a serious, independent discipline, cut away at last from the other subjects with which it had previously been associated. The two men were often described as 'dual manifestations of a single personality'; in fact, as Professor Powicke has written, 'while Tout took the lead, Tait kept the balance'. Their research and their teaching were not two separate compartments of life, but different aspects of their work as men of learning.

Tout and Tait were among the men who established history as an academic subject in the universities, and you can illustrate what I have said about the process from the history of any other academic subject. The second development in history, which you can likewise trace in the story of other academic subjects, has been the emergence of specialised kinds of history within the framework of the broader subject, each specialised kind with its own practitioners, its own journals, its own societies and 'wherever feasible' its own examination papers. These specialised kinds of history may be called 'sub-histories'. In their early years they were products of a revolt against the preoccupation, the narrow preoccupation, of a number of established historians with formal constitutional, political and diplomatic history, the history of statecraft and the history of foreign policy.

The first new specialised kind of history was social and economic history, deliberately conceived of by rebel historians both as a more fundamental and a more useful kind of history and, moreover, as a saner history based on a richer sense of values – the substitution, as the famous writer J. R. Green put it, of knives and forks for drums and trumpets. The social history was sometimes too colourful, the economic history was sometimes too vague, but the subject, none the less, established itself. 'Social and economic history' or sometimes 'economic and social history' – the order chosen has had considerable, if esoteric, academic significance – still figures in syllabuses and at the head of examination papers. But this is only part of the story of these two influential and leading sub-histories.

The fortunes of social history and economic history have subsequently diverged, and in the divergence there are features which can be traced in the history of other subjects too. Economic history has acquired staff, prestige, journals, concepts (sometimes appropriated from theoretical economists) and rigorous modes of quantitative analysis: social history has languished in universities until recently. It has had very few specialist staff, little prestige – outsiders and some insiders usually dismiss it as the history of everyday things, of knives and forks and of nothing else – few journals and, in England at least, no highly developed sociology to provide it with terms or tools. Although much excellent work has recently been published on social history, using original methods and employing fascinating materials, the best-known writer of the best-selling book on English social history, G. M. Trevelyan, chose very arbitrarily to limit its scope to history with the politics left out. This not only takes the sting out of the subject, but diminishes its attractions. This is my own field, and I myself, if pressed, have always preferred to treat it as economic history with the politics put in.

More broadly, I want historians to devote more time not only to people in society (with proper concern for people) but to the study of the development of societies both in themselves and comparatively. I am bound to recognise, however, that while good and, I believe, better work will continue to be produced in social history, the subject in many respects is torn between pressures to make it either *the* synthetic history, the history that pulls all the other sub-histories together, or one particular sub-history, that concerned with social structures, social institutions and social changes which might otherwise – despite Bacon – receive little attention from other sub-historians.

As the sub-histories develop – and of sub-historians there now seems no end – there is increasing need for synthetic history. Military historians, art historians, intellectual historians, cultural historians,

historians of science, historians of technology, historians of religion and so on, all pursue crafts which tend to separate them not only from other specialists but from each other. In the meantime, the word 'historian' is seldom used by other historians without an adjective, and the general public continues to read biographies.

As the practitioners of the sub-histories have carried history over its old frontiers, there have been interesting changes in the map of learning. In discussing the origins of the Manchester History Department I showed how history as an academic subject was at first part of a cluster of subjects, and how a professor of history could be a professor of languages, literature, law, politics or political economy besides. History was eventually separated out of the cluster, not so much because of the strain on the subject as the strain on the professors. During the last fifty years the development of the sub-histories has drawn back into closer relationship the practitioners of particular sub-histories with specialists in adjacent subjects, some of the subjects, like economics, having become established university subjects rather later than history did.

Sometimes the results of closer association have been rewarding, sometimes they have been very odd. Economic history is perhaps the best example to choose of the oddity. It can be approached via the oceans of history or the canals of economics. The more it depends on a detailed knowledge of theoretical economics, the more it is diverted from history departments into economics departments. There is a further complication – a twist in its history, particularly on the continent of Europe. A fierce battle was waged in the nineteenth and early twentieth centuries within economics itself, particularly in Germany, between those economists who pursued economics as a deductive subject with theory that was held to be universally applicable, and those economists who drew their theory from history and went so far as to see economics itself as a branch of history.

It is of academic importance that the unity of history should continue to be emphasised and incidentally that economic history should be related to other kinds of history as well as to economics. At this point, the weaknesses of rigid departmentalism in universities become apparent. Economic historians in economics departments may know very little about what other historians are doing; they may themselves lack adequate historical education. Likewise, economic historians in history departments may have far too little knowledge of what economists are doing, and their work may lack both discipline and refinement. Two kinds of economic history are being studied, written, and taught today – 'economic history A', with emphasis on 'economic' and 'economic history B', with emphasis on 'history'.

This consequence represents something more than a failure of lines of communication within universities: the failure concerns the advancement of learning itself and the communication of knowledge. It is a failure which also has an element of absurdity about it, for it is often a matter of historical accident whether economic history is taught to undergraduates in an economics department or in a history department. The location of the subject does not usually depend on a deliberate choice made within a university now, but on people who made that choice, for what may be obsolete reasons, ten or twenty years ago. Few universities ever review these old choices unless they pose institutional as well as academic problems.

Given the recognition of an institutional problem, one possible answer – a sort of Parkinson's Law answer – is to create a new department, in this particular case, a department which is neither economics nor history but economic history. Given strong enough pressures, this is the answer which a university will usually choose. Yet in some ways, it is the least satisfactory of all the answers. It does not always serve the advancement of economic history. It multiplies frontiers and divides the interested academic population: it provokes claims and counter-claims. And even if it can be arranged amicably, it does not preclude battles in the next generation. To me the only real answer to this kind of problem which arises in this context is a bold answer – to change departmental structure altogether. Academic reasons should come first; institutional responses second. This is surely the right order.

In many other subjects besides history, problems arise that are similar to those which I have been discussing. The subjects in question have established themselves in the university curriculum, have become specialised from within, and sometimes (often, indeed, quite appropriately, if departmental structure exists) have thrown off new departments. Chemistry provides a good example, and within chemistry the study of biochemistry. There are many examples, however, particularly in the biological sciences. It may be that a historian is particularly favourably placed to see these academic issues in perspective. After all, he likes to think that he understands history, including the history of subjects other than his own, and he is professionally interested in bringing to bear the experience of the past on the experience of the present. The history of history is, not without accident, one of the most thriving of the sub-histories.

The subject matter of the historian, moreover, has many frontiers. Like poetry and music, history is the province of a Muse, and there has long been both a private and a public recognition of the close association between history and literature. At the same time, with the proliferation of social studies, it has been influenced by them and it in turn has influenced them. Indeed, it can be classified simply – as by UNESCO – as a social science. Other links predate the conception of social science. Traditionally and in more subtle forms than Kingsley's muscular Christianity, preached in Cambridge in 1860, philosophy and history have been directly related to each other, and historical questions and moral questions cannot easily be separated. History, moreover, has always been linked with law and the classics, the former link enriching both law and history through the work of men like Maitland and Vinagradoff, the latter link with classics being so strong that the boldest advocates of a separate historical tripos in Cambridge in the nineteenth century were prone to argue that

> the man who has been led by the close study of the classics to the special study of what is called Ancient History is the most promising student of History in general; and it is not those who study, but those who ignore, the history of Greece and Rome who are indifferent to that of their own country and of the modern world in general.

In more recent years, as I have suggested, classical education has been pushed into the background with remarkable but far too seldom considered results. The link between history and scientific education has become more generally established; history has been drawn into association with science, still in my view not close enough, and more recently into association with technology. To examine the historical component of any scientific and technological subject, as scientists and technologists increasingly recognise, requires a knowledge not only of science and technology but of history.

The historian, therefore, is in a strategic position to comment on two of the sharp divides in general university studies at the present time – that between science and the humanities, a divide recently publicised by C. P. Snow and others in the discussion of the 'two cultures', and the less publicised but equally important divide between literature and social studies. In the modern map of learning science and humanities, literature and social studies inhabit separate continents. A few boats pass between them, fewer still on regular service; there are a number of distinguished travellers and a diminishing number of visitors; there is little long-distance migration, either temporary or permanent. Inhabitants know a little of their adjacent territories, but their ideas of what happens in the more distant regions are imprecise, sometimes prejudiced, and often wrong. Government by department diminishes mobility; school education, which increasingly requires that choices between arts and sciences are made far too early and on the basis of inadequate knowledge, fortifies adult provincialism. Occasionally joint voyages of discovery are made by outstanding explorers who care little for local allegiances.

Metaphors are dangerous, and this one certainly can be pressed too far. There are four practical tasks in universities which deserve to receive serious attention, however, in this context. First, the inhibiting influence of departmentalism, particularly on undergraduate education, should be overcome or at least reviewed. Second, care should be given to the problems of general education not as a second-best refuge for the second-rate or worst. Third, the relationship between school and university studies should be a matter of concern to universities and not just to teaching departments or their equivalents. Fourth, research should always be based on a genuine desire to explore (not simply to acquire a qualification) and there should be more exchange of views and experience among graduate students, working in separate fields and sometimes ignorant of each other's approaches and problems. As Professor Tawney has written, 'If research requires a division of forces, a humane education requires a synthesis, however provisional, of the results of their labours.'

When I say that serious attention should be given to these tasks, I mean serious attention. Some stock answers are as unsatisfactory, in my view, as the existing situation. I do not like the words 'tertiary education' applied to university education in an attempt, desirable although the attempt is, to direct attention to the complementarity of school and university education. The concept of 'stages' in education appeals only to administrators, who may know little either of teaching or learning, and universities are only universities if they have their own individual identities. Models may help, but they are never enough. The use of the word 'tertiary' suggests to me also that there might be a further need for a fourth stage, 'quarternary' education, and then I get to 'five' and I cannot continue beyond that point. The very ugliness of these unfamiliar adjectives is almost in itself a strong enough argument against them.

Within the universities themselves, I agree with Sir Eric Ashby that the case against specialisation is often stated more crudely than the case in favour of specialisation, and I agree also with his basic conclusion that 'the path to culture should be through a man's specialism, not by by-passing it'. I have little use for novelty for novelty's sake, particularly with the invention of new-fangled humanities.

My reading of nineteenth-century academic and intellectual history persuades me that many of the themes I have been discussing tonight were dealt with more searchingly and with more understanding then than they are being dealt with today. And if this statement is accepted as true, the stock explanation for it – that the Victorians had more leisure to think than we have and less of a sense of urgency – is far from satisfactory too.

Finally, I do not suggest that with the improvement of academic structures – even with superabundant funding – there would automatically be a great improvement in the advancement of learning. Indeed, the opposite has sometimes been true. The very deficiencies of universities (including structural difficulties) have often encouraged the development and dissemination of new ideas, and the contest of opinions has stimulated collective change just as bad teaching has sometimes stimulated a lively pupil more than good teaching. In general terms, I agree with Polanyi that while the traveller equipped with a detailed map of a region across which he plans his itinerary enjoys a striking intellectual superiority over an explorer who first enters a new region, none the less the explorer's fumbling progress is a much finer educational achievement than the well-briefed traveller's journey:

> Even if we admitted that an exact knowledge of the universe is our supreme mental possession it would still follow that man's most distinguished act of thought consists in producing such knowledge; the human mind is at its greatest when it brings hitherto uncharted domains under its control.

So far I have discussed only two of the four developments in the history of history since Kingsley's time, approaching more general questions through the study of history as a subject. The third development in the study of history since Kingsley's time also has general bearings. Historians have specialised not only in their choice of sub-history but in other ways – by choice of period, for example, or by area, country, region, and continent. In Kingsley's time all history was his concern, however limited his knowledge was of particular parts of it.

The advocates of a Modern History Tripos at Cambridge objected to drawing a break between the ancient world and the modern world at the 'Fall of the Roman Empire' (still the beginning of modern history in Oxford and Cambridge) not on the grounds that modern history began much later than this, but that the historian (both professor and student) should concern himself freely with Greece and Rome as well as with France and Germany. 'What pretence is there', they asked, 'for the assumption that there is a bar at the boundary, and that the study of the life of the world can be cut in twain like a sheet of paper?'

The Manchester History Department was renowned for its great works of discovery in neither ancient nor modern but in mediaeval history, yet Professor Tout until the last nine or ten years of his teaching life at Manchester had to pay more attention as a teacher to modern than to medieval history, and Professor Tait was responsible throughout his whole academic life for most of the teaching in ancient history and a share of the lecturing in modern history. Intense pre-occupation with one period or phase of history both in teaching and in research, the present mood, is a feature of the last few years, and it is a feature which may narrow the association between the historian and other scholars rather than strengthen it. A seventeenth-century his-torian, who cares little about any other century, may be able thereby to enter into a closer partnership with a professor of seventeenth-century literature, but he will lose contact with students of other periods whose information, insights and methods might be more valuable to him.

Already within this broader context medieval history, I would suggest, has suffered by reason of its established discipline and high prestige. And this can happen to other subjects too. Medieval history was regarded as the foundation of all newly developing historical studies in Oxford in the nineteenth century – under the shadow both of German scholarship and the very English Bishop Stubbs whose *Constitutional History* was published in 1878, to be followed a year later by Freeman's *Norman Conquest*. The same was true also of Cambridge (with Maitland) and Manchester. Discovering the world of the middle ages provided a sense of excitement to the men of the nineteenth century as well as a sense of direct political relevance.

This sense both of excitement and discovery was communicated even to new societies of which Australia was one. John Woolley in his inaugural oration at the opening of the University of Sydney in 1852 referred to 'the spirit of Alfred the Great' as the spirit which he hoped would inspire the new university: Charles Pearson, who was appointed lecturer in history at the University of Melbourne in 1873 and who later for four years was Minister of Public Instruction in the Gillies-Deakin administration in Victoria, had crossed swords with the formid-able Professor Freeman in England and had made his reputation with books on medieval history. He collected enthusiastic 'amateur' audiences for lectures on medieval English history in Adelaide in the early 1870s, although as one South Australian lady disarmingly put it 'he coversed with us as if we were the cleverest people in the world, and his love of banter and repartee made us quite forget that he had written a History of the Middle Ages'.

Professor F. M. Powicke, who moved from Manchester to an Oxford professorship, has been one of the most eloquent twentieth-century interpreters of this powerful medieval tradition within history, de-fending it not because it offers 'a picturesque invitation to the dormant historical faculty, but by reason of its austere disciplinary value and its penetrating ever-present influence on our modern life'. Certainly, in the twentieth century, there is value in African and Asian studies in employing the knowledge, the insights and the methods of the medieval scholar to reinforce those of the modern European historian, and European studies, where the traditions of the medieval historian, once so rich and rewarding, have tended to stultify, there can be value too. As Geoffrey Barraclough has explained, an understanding of remote experience may be as relevant to an understanding of the present as understanding of very recent experience.

Many medieval historians have become so preoccupied with the minutiae of textual exegesis, however, that they cannot seize the opportunities of taking part in new historical ventures. The link between medievalists and anthropologists is far less strong than it deserves to be just at the time when anthropologists are becoming seriously and increasingly interested in history. In my view the salvation of the medievalists will lie in breaking down the barrier (a European barrier) between medieval and modern history – the barrier, if you like of the Renaissance and the Reformation (European phenomena) – with more vigour than Cambridge historians in the 1860s demanded the breaking down of the barrier between ancient and modern.

Area or regional studies in history, another kind of historical specialisation, raise somewhat different questions. Most historians have chosen their own country as the 'proper subject of mankind', sometimes but not necessarily for nationalist reasons, perhaps more often because of familiarity with language and records and easier opportunities of travel. The extension of their range of interest has tended to move in one of two directions – towards their continent – Europe, America, Africa or Asia – or, if their countries are homelands of empire, towards the empires and the rivalries between them. Both extensions of interest may be illustrated from the development of history in nineteenth-century universities. J. R. Seeley, who succeeded Kingsley in Cambridge, refused to study Britain in isolation from the Empire: the first edition of the *Cambridge History of Modern Europe* (and unfortunately to some extent the second edition of the *Cambridge History of Modern Europe*) are monuments to a tradition of scholarship which in its due time and season had raised history to perhaps the most scholarly of all the academic disciplines and the humanities.

Both these kinds of regional history must now be seen in new perspectives. The facts of empire are only relevant when they are related to arguments about empire: the centre of concern of the historian is switching from the centre to the periphery, from government to the governed, from authority to the battle against authority. Writing the history of Africa or India in these new terms requires an even greater labour than the pioneer imperial historians of the past devoted to their half-practical, half-academic studies, many of them great works of scholarship. Once again in its new tasks history has anthropology as its neighbour, and anthropology and sociology and political science are thus being forced into new relationships.

The study of history by continents – of Europe, for example – is still exciting (in some ways increasingly so), but any outlines of that history which will satisfy or stimulate Europeans are not necessarily the outlines which will satisfy or stimulate Africans or for that matter Australians, and the problems of research in European history which Europeans examine will not necessarily be of the same kind as the problems which people from outside Europe will choose to tackle.

Any new regional studies depend upon a close association between the study of language and literature and the study of history, but in the modern map of learning, just when regional studies are being pushed into prominence, this association, alas, cannot be taken for granted. The decline in the knowledge of Latin and Greek has not been followed by any substantial improvement in the working knowledge of modern languages. Nor have improved facilities for travel had much effect as yet on the development of these branches of history. Much historical research in consequence (in Britain and in Australia, for example) is tending to become insular just at the point in time when insularity in practical life is showing signs of breaking down. The new learning of the Renaissance was based on a new curiosity about language; traditionally, indeed it has been thought of, if inadequately, as based on the discovery of old texts. When Freeman and his colleagues proclaimed the newer learning of the nineteenth century, they were also far more ambitious than many scholars today about the place of languages in their study.

> . . . the student of history or of language [wrote Freeman] – and he who is a student of either must be in no small degree a student of the other – must take in all history and all language within his range. The degrees of his knowledge of various languages, of various branches of history, will vary infinitely. Of some branches he must know everything, but of every branch he must know something.

Freeman's words represent an ideal which few historians would dare to expect to realise in practice in the twentieth century. Language departments and history departments have become increasingly separated from each other; the former, indeed, often include historians who have no formal links (and often very few informal ones) with their colleagues in history departments.

The most encouraging field to which to turn is no longer European history, as in Freeman's time, but Asian history, and there are signs that under great pressures Oriental Studies (of language and literature and history together) will be transformed in this century from the interest of a small minority of scholars to a university subject with both popular and public appeal. If this is so, a completely different conception of the map of learning, with which many people in Canberra, but alas, not I, are thoroughly familiar, will become a part of the province of students in universities in all parts of the world.

There are several practical conclusions which arise out of an examination of the relationship of history by region to the study of languages. The schools have a major responsibility for disciplined teaching of languages, including their basic grammar. At the same time teaching a language both in schools and universities means teaching a social subject as well as a linguistic discipline. Third, both the teaching of history in universities and research in history can be most fruitful when materials are used in a different language from that of the student or professor. Fourth, to teach about a foreign society means first knowing one's own – social studies flourish on comparisons. And in this sense, too, there is a very close connection between work in languages and work in history.

I have very little time to deal with the fourth development in history since Kingsley's time – its continued growth as a popular as well as an academic subject. History books are not only studied for instruction or understanding: they are (or rather may be) read for pleasure. This is not only because of the intrinsic interest of the subject – the spell of the past or the desire through the past to understand the present – but because a great deal of history is still written in plain language and some of it in powerful and appealing language. The neighbours of the historian include not only experts in other subjects but the general public. The practical implications of this are many. The historian is forced to do what Gunnar Myrdal advises the economist and the sociologist to do, to talk in two ways – one with his academic colleagues, one with the public – not, of course, saying two different sets of things but saying them in different ways.

'*Vulgarisation*', as the French call it, is a necessary feature in the diffusion of learning. The academic map of learning is thereby brought into close relationship with the popular map of learning, the university with adult education. Nor are the gains one-sided. It is not by accident that certain kinds of history – economic history, for example – established themselves in adult education in Britain before they established themselves in universities. Adult education in my view will never live up to its own highest possibilities if it simply copies the organisation of learning in universities or rests content with drawing adults into examination courses for part-time university degrees. Like university education, it should offer access to the best, and unlike school and university education it should use its greatest single advantage, the fact that it does not need to depend upon examination papers.

I thus return in conclusion – and as I explained at the start of my lecture – perforce very briefly to my text and to the other set of attitudes which must be understood if we wish to shape or to direct universities, new or old, in the twentieth century – the attitude of university teachers to the respective calls of teaching and research. I also return to the newspaper comment on the education of Herb Elliott. Teaching and research are not substitutes for each other in a university but two aspects of the advancement of learning. The pursuit of knowledge and its communication to others are of equal importance in any institution meriting the name of university.

What I have said of history in this connection is true of every other university subject: it can be reinforced, particularly, indeed, in relation to science subjects where 'pure theory' is the foundation of all applied knowledge. If pure theory is not undertaken in universities, it will probably be unduly neglected in other places. Scholars in different subjects in a university (scientists, social scientists, historians, men of letters) should still continue to constitute in some sense – a different sense, perhaps, from that of the middle ages or the age of Bacon – a community. Likewise, the students or undergraduates are themselves not simply numbers to be taught, even in an age which may talk of tertiary education, but individuals who in their formative years in universities learn for themselves not only through their formal teaching but through their reading, their arguments, their broader experience and above all through the choices which they themselves freely make. The mere production of graduates is only the formal and quantitatively measurable aspect of a university's function, although in modern societies where universities tend to be thought of increasingly as institutions supported by the public to meet specific social needs this formal aspect is too easily confused with the whole.

I hope and trust that Herb Elliott will not be 'quizzed' by tutors at supervision sessions in Cambridge on what he has learnt during the previous week, but rather that he will argue and discuss with them problems which are of mutual interest to them both and where they can both learn in the process. Undergraduate teaching is basically no different from postgraduate teaching in this respect: it can no more be disposed of by true–false tests than writing a Ph.D. thesis can. I say this with force, as Bacon would have said it with force, just because Bacon, as we saw, related the study of history in particular to the memory and just because in the nineteenth century, of which I have said so much, Lord Granville used to amuse guests in his castle by winding up any conversation which left any political, historical or other problem unsolved with the remark 'We will ask Johnny Acton.' This was a forceful tribute more to the great Lord Acton's memory than to his judgment.

In the public debate on universities, the voice of the universities themselves should be heard. There may be sharp differences of opinion within them – there should be – and there is room for wide differences between them – differences in size and in structure, for example – but there is need surely for an agreement on certain basic values. To those who argue the shallow view that because of the 'rush and push' of modern life a university is merely a public service institution training the cream of the nation for particular tasks it must always be pointed out, as Bacon pointed out to his contemporaries, that the worst kind of professors are those who instead of devoting themselves to making some 'addition to their science', 'convert their labours to aspire to certain second prizes'.

Bacon's words gain in force because he did not sharply separate the advancement of learning on the one side and the advancement of society on the other. He was not living in an ivory tower nor was he a stubborn and traditionalist professor of the humanities. He was rather one of the greatest prophets of the new technology and one of the most vigorous advocates of science and of social control. 'The commandment of knowledge', he said, 'is yet higher than the commandment over the will: for it is a commandment over the reason, belief, and understanding of man, which is the highest part of the mind, and giveth law to the will itself.'

II In Action: Drawing a New Map of Learning*

The foundation of a new university provides an unparalleled opportunity to fashion a whole curriculum – to prepare a new map of learning rather than to talk about it. It is still possible from old letters to catch the distant excitement of the founders of University College, London, in 1826, with Sir James Mackintosh enthusiastically drawing up 'a kind of prospectus' and Henry Brougham warning a political colleague that, however great the enthusiasm, 'the digesting of a proper plan for the course of instruction must be the work of some time'. More recently, the founders of the London School of Economics and of the University of Keele have enjoyed the intellectual excitement of arranging studies in new patterns, not because they believed in novelty for novelty's sake, but because they were sure that their pattern was academically preferable to those which already existed.

Not all universities, however, have been able to enjoy a full measure of academic freedom during the early stages of their growth. British university colleges, graduating to full university status, have usually been tied initially by the syllabuses of the University of London. Overseas universities have usually found themselves even more tied, their pattern of work being determined from outside as a result of educational and social pressures alien to their own society. From the start, however, Sussex, like Keele, has been thought of as a centre of innovation. If it has followed different lines from Keele, it respects the zeal which has been demonstrated there, particularly in its first-year foundation courses. In turn, it has benefited greatly in a practical way from the radical approach to the curriculum. The freedom to work along new lines and the power to plan new combinations of subjects and new curricula have proved great attractions in recruiting academics from universities where curricula can be changed only with the greatest difficulty. There has also been far greater flexibility – and co-operation – in the deployment of specialist academic skills. Lastly there has been exceptional interest in new countries overseas because Sussex seems to

*A version of this essay was published in D. Daiches (ed.), *The Idea of a New University* (1962).

349

stand for the kind of structural reorganisation of studies which overseas universities demand when they are free to take their own initiative.

By the end of its first year of active existence, the University of
Sussex had drawn up its second prospectus, a full and comprehensive
document of sixty pages, which contrasts significantly with the first
prospectus of twenty-six pages published in 1961 before either academics or undergraduates had come into residence. The broad outline
remained the same, but what had been tentative, vague and incomplete
in 1961 had become bold, precise and far less incomplete in 1962.
The third prospectus of 1963 extended and completed rather than
modified. The changes, which register the intellectual development of
the university, were the result of regular and sustained discussion,
the 'digesting', as Brougham called it, of ideas which had first been
formulated by the Joint Committee and the Academic Advisory
Commitee.

These initial ideas were, in themselves, exciting. From the start, the
idea of a School of European Studies had loomed large in the minds of
the sponsors of a university in Brighton. So, too, had the idea of
breaking free from 'excessive specialisation'. Multi-subject honours
courses were proposed, with history, languages and philosophy being
studied in close association with each other. In the sciences also it was
suggested that the curriculum should include a study of the social
context and application of science. Specialised knowledge was to be
acquired in such a way that the boundaries of subjects were to be
explored – and crossed – as well as the central territories. The unit of
university organisation and planning was not to be the single subject
Department but the multi-subject School.

A range of Schools was suggested, of which European Studies,
English Studies and Social Studies were to be the first three. Each
School was to have a curriculum which would combine in different
proportions – the proportions varying according to the student's own
choice – subjects which would normally, except in general degrees, be
kept apart in existing universities. The position in relation to the study
of sciences was at first much less certain. Indeed, it was not clearly
envisaged in the early discussions, before the arrival of the first
academics, that science departments would be abolished and replaced
by Schools; the most that was hoped was that there would be fewer
departments.

As soon as the first academics were chosen, they were drawn into a
searching discussion of this provisional outline of the curriculum of a
new university. They had to give it both content and organisational
shape. They did not await their formal appointment in October 1961
before seeking to define what they meant by a 'School' or by the

'integration' of studies. Interesting memoranda were prepared by the Deans-elect on the work of their Schools and by the Professor of Philosophy on the role of philosophy as an element in the work of all the Schools. These memoranda were exchanged and discussed by post before two crucial meetings were held in April and June 1961 at which the details of the first curriculum were worked out. It was at these two meetings that the material was agreed upon which subsequently was printed in the first prospectus of 1961. The ideas which had already been in the air before the first academic appointments were made were already considerably clarified. In their new form they were given expression in a number of articles and in a talk by the Vice-Chancellor to a conference of the University Teachers' Group at Oxford in the summer of 1961. They were subsequently approved by the Academic Planning Committee.

It is interesting to note what form the clarification took. First, greater stress was laid on the *linked* nature of the undergraduate curriculum. In each of the Schools undergraduates were to combine study of a specialism in depth with common studies in which all the different specialists within the School would share. The specialism was to be the major subject: the common subjects were designed to set the different specialisms in their intellectual frame and to relate them to each other. In the language of the early discussions the specialism was thought of as the 'core' and the common subjects as the 'context'.

Second, the Schools were envisaged not as super-departments, to which 'subjects' were attached, but as centres of linked studies, some of which would be shared with other Schools. Certain subjects – for example, history – could be studied as major subjects within the different contextual frames of different Schools. Certain contextual papers would be common to more than one School.

Third, the work of the first Schools was more clearly defined, and a plan for a number of new Schools was agreed upon. The title of the School of English Studies was changed into the School of English and American Studies, and it was decided that the work of the School of European Studies should be complemented by a new School of African and Asian Studies. A School of Educational Studies was also envisaged, although it was agreed that its foundation should follow rather than precede the first two years of undergraduate build-up. The *timing* of academic development was very fully discussed. Indeed, the whole question of priorities assumed great importance from this date onwards. It was recognised realistically that what might be very desirable or even necessary might have to wait until after the first phase of growth.

The basic pattern, however, was clear enough. The familiar antithesis between 'specialised' and 'general' education was rejected:

both specialisation and general education were seen as essential parts of a balanced university education. An undergraduate would be expected not to study a multitude of unrelated subjects side by side or one after the other, but continuously to relate his specialised study to impinging and overlapping studies. Thereby, it was felt, he would become not only an educated person but potentially, at least, a better specialist. He would know about the bearings of his specialism as well as about its content. The contextual studies which would be common to different specialists in particular Schools would always include a critical evaluation of concepts and procedures, preferably comparatively, an examination of historical perspectives, and an exploration of contemporary issues and problems. In the School of English and American Studies and the School of European Studies emphasis would be placed on the unity of a civilisation: in the School of Social Studies emphasis would be placed on the inter-dependence of different social studies in the contemporary world.

It followed from this conception of 'general education' that the degree structure would be the same for all undergraduates. There would be no internal status distinctions. A Sussex graduate, whatever his School, would be given the kind of education in three years which would make it possible for him to compare, to relate and to judge. It would be a broader education than he would have received had he followed a conventional single-subject course or even a combined subjects course. At the same time, those graduates, necessarily a minority, who wished to go forward to research or to academic life would have been well grounded in their specialisms and well prepared to pursue them further. Within the teaching of the major subjects it was agreed that there was to be as little reliance as possible on sweeping survey work and as much as possible on learning 'in depth' how to use the skills of the specialist. It was envisaged from the start that there would have to be fourth-year work, mainly of a specialist kind, for a larger number of students than had been conventional in the past. The development of such fourth-year work would not imply, however, that the three-year curriculum was less 'complete' in itself than any other three-year undergraduate curriculum of a more conventional kind in other universities.

Subsequent discussions in 1961 and 1962 turned on the form and content both of the contextual papers and the core papers. It was decided in the autumn of 1961 that at least four-ninths of the curriculum should be concerned with contextual subjects and that certain of these contextual subjects, for example Contemporary Britain and the Modern European Mind, should be common to more than one School. It was also decided how much of the major work should be work in depth. In history, for example, it was laid down that two of the final papers in the history major examination in any School should be devoted to the detailed examination of a Special Subject. Coverage was sacrificed to depth, although there was to be plenty of choice of period and problems. It was decided finally that two papers on Contemporary Europe – one concerned with economic, social and political history since 1945 and the other concerned with the economics of integration – could form an option within both the economics major and the politics and sociology major and that the papers could be studied both in the School of Social Studies and in the School of European Studies.*

Two other conclusions followed naturally from the lines of argument which were being followed. First, a Sussex BA would not offer any kind of 'soft option'. It would demand good students and test the very best. It was also felt that it would attract the best. The first academics at Brighton believed, with due humility, that they were not simply feeding the insatiable appetite of Bulge and Trend by organising one more university. Rather, they were creating the best kind of university that they could envisage. In colloquial language, they had no chips on their shoulders, no sense of inferiority to anywhere else. Coming from quite different academic backgrounds – Oxford, Cambridge, London, provincial and overseas universities – they were pooling their experience in searching discussions of a kind and range which seldom take place when universities are 'going concerns'. Second, they recognised that experience was not enough. The new curriculum being planned demanded rethinking at every point, not only about content but about methods of teaching and learning. Even given good students, it would not be enough to leave them to the tender mercy of large anonymous lecture classes. Nor could the university afford the congestion of a lecture time table which would make individual tutorial teaching and, even more important, ample time for individual reading difficult or impossible.

It was decided, therefore, at the meetings of April and June 1961 that lectures in the University of Sussex would be ancillary and voluntary. The first two terms of university life – terms which fix the way of work of the undergraduate – would be used for 'foundation studies' which would establish the central significance within the University of the tutorial system, based on guided individual reading, the writing of weekly essays and regular encounters with a tutor. During the second and third years tutorials and lectures would be augmented by seminars, some of which would be 'interdisciplinary'. As the three years went

*I wrote articles on 'European Studies in a New University' in *Progress* (1962) and the *Journal of Common Market Studies*, Vol. I (1962).

by, the student would become as 'independent' as he was prepared to be.

The tutorial system was in no sense considered as a panacea. It was no more 'copied' from Oxford or Cambridge than the curriculum was copied from any other university. It was recognised that it would have to be augmented, modified, treated experimentally, tested frequently, and supplemented by new kinds of teaching. Its main importance was in relation to the content of the curriculum. Tutorials would guarantee that the undergraduate spent a great deal of his time thinking, arguing and writing. In other words there would be an active and personal element in the acquisition of knowledge. The university was to provide the outline map of learning which the undergraduate would then fill in for himself.

There were both practical and theoretical considerations which supported this approach. On the one hand there were the needs of 'new students'. On the other there was the recognition that a university education involves not merely the acceptance of information or ideas, but a personal quest which, if entered upon with zest, continues far beyond the three years of undergraduate study. Just because the University of Sussex was daring to lay down a pattern of related studies – in an age when talk of the 'unity of knowledge' is greeted with some scepticism – there was a strong argument for leaving scope not only for tutorial argument but for individual initiative.

Being explorers ourselves in a new university, explorers with ample maps of other universities but with none of our own, we wanted to make our students into explorers also, to encourage them to find relations between subjects where we did not see them ourselves, and to dispute some of our own conceptions. Given the huge changes which are taking place both in the formulation of new knowledge and in the world of action where the knowledge is being applied, we did not want to be confined to our own original territory even though the boundaries within it were being knocked down. We recognised that we would also have to move into outer space.

The main interest was in planning not for present change but for future change. There are likely to be immense rearrangements in the map of learning during the next fifty years – in the biological sciences, for example, where there is remarkable intellectual vitality, or in such fields of study as Asian history and civilization, which will pass from the domain of a small intellectual *élite* to a far broader section of the academic population. There is also likely to be a revolution in communications which will make the changes in the communications system over the last fifty years seem like prelude. We knew, therefore, that a university curriculum which did not allow for far-reaching future growth and change would be doomed from the start. We also recognised our own limitations as surveyors of the intellectual world. If only for this reason, we were more interested in establishing conditions for growth than in preparing a complete atlas.

It is remarkable how many times the geographical metaphor recurs in current discussions on learning, just as it recurred time and time again during and after the age of discovery, particularly in the writings of Francis Bacon. When I moved to Sussex, I had already talked and written both about Bacon and about maps and had argued strongly, with my own subject, history, in mind, that specialist single-subject honours courses that now dominate most university curricular – at least for the best students – need far more critical study from both intellectual and social historians than they have so far received. History, however, was not the starting point for most of the academics who agreed, unanimously and enthusiastically, in 1961 that Sussex should develop a curriculum which would offer the 'benefits' both of specialised and of general education. Coming from different backgrounds, different academics employed converging arguments to support the same conclusions.

Some of them have written about the reasons why they came to think as they did. The Vice-Chancellor, for instance, has referred both to Scotland and to Classical Greats and Modern Greats at Oxford; he has also written, in more practical and instrumental terms, of the needs of 'new students' and the demand from outside universities for new kinds of graduates. It was in nineteenth-century Scotland that a defender of traditional Scottish education wrote that 'speciality need not be inconsistent with unity of learning'. It was in twentieth-century Oxford that philosophy, politics and economics were brought together in a curriculum designed to illuminate the modern world. In his address to the University Teachers' Group in the summer of 1961 the Vice-Chancellor explained his own approach:

Multi-subject courses may be of different kinds. I suppose that a course in say embroidery, horticulture and Albanian language and literature would be a multi-subject course of a certain kind, a kind which deserves criticism. But Classical Greats at Oxford is a multi-subject course also. It is a study of the language and literature, the philosophy and the history of one civilization in the Mediterranean basin within a given span of time; the literature, the philosophy and the history are held together by the unity of the civilization. Modern Greats at Oxford is a multi-subject honours course in which three aspects of civilization – philosophy, politics and economics – are studied together. Here the unity is to be found in their inter-relation and their influence upon one another . . . The Schools we propose at Sussex will have this in common with those older Schools, that the subjects included are intended to have an effect upon one another.

The Sussex Schools were to go much further than this, however, for within an undergraduate's 'major' works at Sussex there were to be papers which would link disciplines under the direction of two tutors from two disciplines. For example, there were to be 'special topics in history and literature', such as 'The Industrial Revolution and the Romantic Movement' or 'The Late-Victorian revolt'. Some contextual papers also were to be shared – 'The Modern European Mind', for example, by undergraduates in the School of European Studies and the School of English Studies and 'Contemporary Britain' by undergraduates in the School of English Studies and the School of Social Studies. Joint seminars with joint tutors would bring both undergraduates and tutors together in 'natural combinations'.

If the contextual papers were designed to set the major work in a frame, the major work itself was designed to illuminate the context. Specialisation was not to be neglected, for however important the claims of 'interdisciplinarity' initial grounding in 'disciplines' is essential.

In the light of this approach, 'general education' at Sussex was thought of in quite different terms from those of universities which have a two-tier system of degrees. The arrangement of major work and contextual work in Sussex may be illustrated in detail from the curriculum of the School of Social Studies which was already settled in outline in 1961. Four contextual papers were planned to pull together the work of the School: five papers in each major subject were designed to provide the necessary skills of the specialist. The first major subjects to be introduced were economics, geography, history, philosophy, and politics and sociology, with international relations, psychology and anthropology to follow as soon as was practicable. Since a proportion of five out of nine final papers represented a greater share for the study of particular specialisms than in many existing universities, there was no fear that a Sussex degree in social studies would involve inadequate specialisation. Specialist skills, indeed, could be employed also in the study of some of the contextual subjects. Economists, for example, could make a distinctive contribution to the study of Contemporary Britain. So, too, could sociologists. Geographers could make a distinctive contribution to the study of 'World Population and Resources'.

Deciding what the four contextual papers should be did not involve long discussion. One of the papers had to be philosophical, extending, as Professor Patrick Corbett, Professor of Philosophy, had envisaged, the specialist interest of the undergraduate by making him more critical. The second, 'Contemporary Britain', was given its first rubric in 1962 – 'Contemporary British culture and society; demographic and social change; social problems and social policies; the instruments of communication and their control; social judgments in contemporary thought and writing; British approaches to the outside world.' Not only was this paper planned to link work in the School of English Studies and the School of Social Studies – a somewhat neglected link, except among journalists – it was also to incorporate within the formal university curriculum topics which, although of great interest to many undergraduates, are usually kept out of the curriculum and discussed loosely and informally in clubs and societies. The reference in the rubric to 'British approaches to the outside world' was not simply an oblique glance at the Common Market, but a recognition of the fact that although undergraduates taking degrees in social studies can most easily approach the problems of society through the society to which most of them belong, many of the most interesting and strategic problems in society can only be studied adequately within a broader framework.

The third common paper was to be specifically concerned with the outside world. A choice was offered between 'international politics' and 'world population and resources'. The international politics paper was to include, with historical orientation, an examination of current problems of strategy, deterrence and disarmament; the 'world population and resources' paper was to bring together economists and geographers and to prepare the way for future co-operation with biologists and engineers. Broad survey techniques were not thought appropriate for either of these papers. For both papers particular cases were to be studied – a post-war dispute, for example, or the geography, economics and politics of a particular commodity, oil, for instance, or sugar. It was envisaged that as the university took shape faculty seminars would discuss fully the scope and method of teaching these and other contextual papers, and that they would revise the field and add to the choices.

The need for continuous faculty discussion was most apparent in relation to the fourth contextual paper called 'Concepts, Methods and Values in the Social Studies', which was designed to be prepared for in seminars towards the end of the undergraduate's three years. By that time the undergraduates would already be familiar with a set of specialist techniques in one social study and ready to compare them with the techniques of others. It was envisaged that in preparing for this paper also the undergraduate would concern himself with a limited number of social 'problems' or 'cases' involving different techniques of identification and analysis and posing different kinds of practical solution. Infant mortality or juvenile delinquency might be examples of one set of problems; disputes, including industrial disputes, examples of another. Philosophers would contribute to the work of these syn-optic seminars, but the seminars would not be primarily 'philosophical'.

To make the seminars effective, clearly there would have to be some additional preparation over the whole three years as well as study in tutorials of the undergraduate's major subject. It was agreed, therefore, that all students in the School of Social Studies would be expected to do at least one term's work on statistics and to become acquainted with the mathematical techniques which in some universities are beginning to command the whole field of the social studies. Operational research, including data processing, would find its place also not so much as a contextual element in the School as an equipping of the undergrad-uate with a set of useful techniques. So too would practical social work, for example in the local community. Undergraduates who wished to pursue social studies with this orientation would have the chance of doing so. It was hoped that by the time that seminars on 'Concepts, Methods and Values' were held, undergraduates would be in a position not only to exchange theories but to compare experiences. The School was to be a School of Social Studies, not of Social Sciences, although such a distinction was considered to be unnecessarily sharp.

The last of the four contextual papers was felt to be at once the most difficult and the most challenging, and the arguments for experi-menting with it were grounded not only in educational theory but in a critical evaluation of the main lines of development of the social studies over the last sixty years. The separate social studies have developed remarkably, though unequally, largely through a process of increasing differentiation. Yet they form a cluster. Their insights and techniques are complementary, and to an increasing extent cer-tain techniques, including mathematical techniques, are common to them all. A knowledge of their historical development depends upon an understanding of comparisons and contrasts, of how both politics and economics, for example, grew out of 'political economy', of how abstractions, like the idea of 'civil society' or 'economic man', served a controversial purpose, or of how nineteenth-century anthro-pology was related to biological and sociological theories of evolution. Similarly the contemporary use of the social studies demands a know-ledge of more than one of them. To debate the Common Market it is necessary to know as much about politics as about economics. To study the tangled problems of economic growth many subjects have to be bestraddled, with history, economics, sociology and psy-chology prominent among them. No single social study by itself provides a proper educational foundation for an understanding of society or for the intelligent exercise of the ability to act and to judge. Specialist honours degrees in economics or sociology which overlook this hardly produce good economists or sociologists, let alone 'educated graduates'.

An education in social studies must necessarily include training in the use of techniques (in politics and sociology as well as in economics), just as an education in European Studies must necessarily include mastery of a language. Yet it must not solely be concerned with this. It must deal also with the contexts within which techniques are employed, and with perspectives and values. It must allow an important place for psychology, but it can benefit from the co-operation of philosophers as well as of psychologists. Indeed, a School of Social Studies will be most effective if it maintains sustained intellectual co-operation.

It is unfortunate that university organisation does not always reflect changes at the frontiers of knowledge. New subjects take their place in the map and become sovereign departments, and the map itself is seldom consciously re-drawn. Biological studies, for example, produce exciting new research which rests on cross-boundary thinking, yet in many universities biology, botany and zoology are controlled by independent potentates. Academic distinctions become confused with status distinctions. Intellectual development is far too often associated with the multiplication of frontiers and the division of people. The Sussex curriculum, based as it is on Schools, which are not super-departments, was deliberately designed to avoid some at least of these dangers.

Both from the point of view of teaching and research, organisation by Schools offers obvious advantages in a period of growth. 'Departmental organisation,' as Sir Alexander Carr-Saunders has written in his *English Universities of Today* (1960), 'often reaches a condition of monstrous hypertrophy, falsifying the academic map, and bringing about the herding of teachers into pens surrounded by fences.' Duplication and dispersal of effort, lack of planning and co-ordination, rivalry and occasionally friction, boundary disputes and far from splendid isolation are familiar features, alas, in the twentieth-century university world. It is usually only when new universities are being created that re-thinking assumes the necessary proportions.

The Sussex plan of a School of Social Studies was based not only on the idea of a linking of academic studies but on the hope of incorporating practical work with the curriculum which is often thought to have no place in the universities at all. Concern for a technical or professional speciality becomes genuinely educational when the full bearings of the speciality are critically examined. Within a philosophical, historical and sociological frame, for example, it seemed to be possible to develop a new approach to 'professionalism'. Two of the five major papers in the undergraduate's major subject could reflect his or her own choices and provide a lead-in to a more practically orientated fourth year for those who wished to become more 'professional'. Within the first three years themselves there could be study of a 'workshop' character.

The crude distinction, all too common among academics, that there is some mysterious difference between all undergraduate and all post-graduate work could also be usefully re-examined in this context. All too often new developments of a promising kind – in management studies, for example, as well as in social work – are held back because of authoritative murmurs that they are 'suitable only for postgraduates'. Obviously most of the work that they entail is best thought of as postgraduate in character, but this does not imply that undergraduate education should necessarily ignore postgraduate interest and commit-ment. The organisation of learning at Sussex pre-supposed a continuity of development from common 'foundation' work in the first two terms to a greater measure of personal choice in the third year and from close tutorial supervision to a greater measure of self-reliance. The optional work within the major subject, provided that it is set in its common frame and associated with basic work in the major subject, can cater for quite different aptitudes and point forward to postgraduate study.

It was of interest in working out this approach to know that within 'practical' social studies, there are interesting parallels to developments within the academic map of learning. In her study *The Boundaries of Case Work* (1959) Jean Snelling has written, for example, of the breaking down of barriers in social case work.

> Ten years ago we might have discussed boundaries in social work. Today the term boundary does not seem right for anything *within* the case work field. A boundary separates off things which are different by nature and centred apart from one another. Where these irreconcilables come most nearly together, there we can draw a boundary line. Now this is not an appropriate concept for us. We can probably think more readily of case work as a figure of . . . interlocking and overlapping circles, each with only a small segment free from its neighbours. I hope that in the next ten years we shall come to feel increasingly certain of the depth and richness and essential rightness of this figure.

Although no attempt was made in the early discussions of 1961 and 1962 to consider fully the implications of 'professional' studies, including the training of teachers, it was believed that the general pattern of university organisation would make it easier to incorporate new developments, possibly in the School of Social Studies, possibly in a new School. It certainly made it easy from the start to em-bark immediately and inexpensively on projects which would even-tually lead to the creation of new Schools. Historians and economists

interested, for example, in African and Asian Studies could be recruited and employed in other Schools before the new School came
into formal existence. They could even constitute a kind of 'shadow
School'. Outside teams, particularly a team of biologists which was
appointed in 1962, could prepare at once for quite distant developments.

In the meantime, the fact that academics were not appointed to
one particular School and could be employed in several Schools after
their arrival meant a widening of teaching experience. Not only did
a number of academics from different disciplines work together to
prepare proper syllabuses for such new papers as 'The Modern
European Mind', but some academics were drawn into the teaching of
more than one 'subject'. There are, of course, dangers in pushing cross-
subject teaching too far, and it was decided in 1962 that no 'subject'
would be introduced into the University unless there was a reasonable
expectation that within five years it would have at least four academic
specialists concerned in the teaching of it.

The study of education, it was agreed, would not be peripheral or
separated by departmental barriers from other parts of the University.
Academic members of the School would usually be members of
another School as well, and university specialists in particular academic
disciplines would be brought directly into the education of teachers.
The School would also concern itself with the evaluation of some of the
experiments in 'higher education' which were being carried out in the
University as a whole. Was the University proving successful in linking
together major subjects and common subjects? Was the tutorial system
producing the results which were expected of it? Such questions would
obviously have to be asked from the start and answered as soon as
adequate evidence was available. They were felt to be appropriate
questions for a School of Educational Studies, particularly when Sussex was the first of seven new universities. Decisions about the shape of
the School of Educational Studies, including the possibility of linking
teacher training and training for social workers, were deferred in 1961
not because the relevant issues were thought to be unimportant or
lacking in urgency, but because they were held to be so important that
they needed the most searching examination.

The same consideration influenced early discussions about the relationship between 'arts' and 'sciences'. In the summer of 1961 the
Dean of the School of Physical Sciences had not yet been appointed,
nor had his colleagues in the various science subjects. The discussions
about the shape of the curriculum within the School of Physical
Sciences, raising remarkably similar questions to those raised in the
arts and social studies discussions, took place a year later. It was felt

that the relationship between 'arts' and 'sciences' could only be examined fully when science had taken its proper place in the University, when there were as many scientists in the academic faculty and the undergraduate body as there were specialists in arts and social studies. As a result of the discussions between members of the science faculty, which also brought in a working party of scientists interested in biological studies, the organisation of the curriculum in the sciences was given a very similar shape to that in the arts and social studies.

Against this background the answer to the question of 'the two cultures' – a question which is often formulated in such a way that the role of the social studies is completely ignored – seemed to be to seek for 'natural links' between arts and sciences and to strengthen them. The Keele pattern, interesting though it is, of expecting all scientists to study one arts or social studies subject and *vice versa*, was explicitly rejected. It was hoped that the same links would be forged between the Schools of Physical Sciences, Biological Sciences and Applied Sciences on the one hand and the Schools of English and American, European, African and Asian and Social Studies on the other hand as were already being forged within and between the Arts and Social Studies Schools.

A number of possible links were examined – the intellectual history of the development of the sciences within the map of learning, how they became separated from each other and how they converge in practice; comparative procedures in natural sciences and social sciences, including the use of hypotheses and of experiments and mathematical model building; the organisation of science, including such topics as the social background and education of scientists, their numbers and remuneration, and how their research is financed; the use of science – or the failure to use it – by government and business, the time lags in the application of new scientific discovery and how they arise, the formulation of scientific policy and what factors, scientific and non-scientific are taken into account in shaping it; and the moral role of scientists, how they conceive of it themselves in a complex society, and how other people conceive of it. Subjects of this kind represent a direct extension of the existing interests of scientists and are, indeed, a proper part of a scientific education. At the same time, they are natural extensions of interest for many arts students also, or perhaps more particularly, of students in the social studies. Other subjects, like linguistics or psychology, provide different links, and it was hoped that they might be added later. Both in the early stages of the scheme and later, it was felt that the undergraduate seminars would have to be supplemented by guided reading and the preparation of individual dissertations, and that, despite the collective nature of the undertaking, some specialists would have to be engaged to deal with some of the 'link subjects'.

Discussions about the long-term future in 1961 and 1962 inevitably became concerned with the logistics of planned growth, and a 'table of growth' was prepared which within a five-year-plan allowed for the necessary element of flexibility. Much that is settled by bargaining power in existing universities was settled quickly with genuine consensus. In the short run, however, the immediate teaching problem pivoted on the needs of first-year undergraduates, and it is not surprising that in 1961 and 1962 as much attention was paid to the 'preliminary work' before an undergraduate began his final work in a particular School as to the future work of the Schools themselves. In both Arts and Social Studies and Physical Sciences the same kind of pattern was agreed upon after careful deliberation. It had something in common with that 'broadly philosophical and historical approach to the languages and the sciences through grounding in first principles', which characterised Scottish education at its best. Yet in other ways it represented a quite new pattern, the logical pattern in relation to what was to follow later.

All undergraduates were to take a preliminary examination after two terms' study, and this examination had to be passed before they could proceed to work for the finals examination within a particular School. Honours would not be awarded in this first examination, a 'foundation' examination, and candidates would be adjudged solely to have passed or failed. Three papers were together to constitute the preliminary examination, and in both the Arts preliminary examination and the Science preliminary two of the three papers would be common to all undergraduates. Again the emphasis was being placed on common elements in university education, the subjects which bind and orientate. The third paper was to be chosen according to the interests of the undergraduate, in the case of the Arts preliminary examination, which was the first to be planned, according to the undergraduate's likely choice of School. There was to be a fourth paper in Translation to be taken only by undergraduates proposing to enter the School of European Studies (whatever their major subject within it).

The two common papers in the Arts and Social Studies preliminary examination were to be 'Language and Values' and 'An Introduction to History'. Both these papers would mark a break with school A-level subjects, and both would be taught tutorially in such a way that they would force the undergraduate to criticise, to argue and to judge. The 'Language and Values' paper required 'a thorough study of the nature and justification of value judgements, especially of moral judgements and judgements about society and policy'. Undergraduates were to be asked 'to examine extracts from current controversial writings in the light of these theories as well as to answer direct questions about them'.

It was clear that this paper demanded tutorial teaching: the way of teaching it was closely bound up with its content.

The same was true also of the second common paper 'An Introduction to History'. This paper was not to be pinned to the study of a particular period, and it was to be attempted, of course, by many undergraduates who had not studied history to A-level at school. It was designed 'to provide an understanding of the historian's craft and of a number of major historical themes which will be useful in all later work at the university'. In the first prospectus the rubric on this paper began 'Historical sources and materials and how the historian uses them; the nature of historical problems; why historians disagree; past, present and future'. In 1962 the rubric was narrowed to read 'With what problems is the historian concerned and how does he define and investigate them? Why do historians disagree in the answers they give?' The narrowing of the rubric was evidence of the influence of experience – and of further thought – on the development of the curriculum.

It was also decided, as broad survey work seemed less and less important as a constituent element in university education, to consider the leading questions about history and historians in terms of two modern historical works. The books initially chosen were R. H. Tawney's *Religion and the Rise of Capitalism* and P. Geyl's *Napoleon, For and Against*, the first concerned with the interpretation of a society and the second with the interpretation of an individual. Together the two books, it was thought, would encourage a probing of values as well as a discussion of ideas. A close study of them would be as beneficial to the non-historian as to other undergraduates, and tutorial arguments about 'Language and Values' and 'An Introduction to History' would naturally converge.

The combination of two common papers and one 'specialist' paper anticipated the combination within the final work of the Schools, although there was to be a difference of proportions. The 'specialist' paper itself was a 'foundation' paper, however, acquainting the undergraduate with tools of analysis which he would employ later on in his studies. In both the School of English and American Studies and the School of European Studies undergraduates were to spend their two preliminary terms in tutorial work on 'Critical Reading', students in the School of English and American Studies concentrating upon 'European Tragedy and Fiction' (back to Sophocles). The close parallelism in the work of the two Schools was achieved not in 1961 but in 1962 when the second prospectus was being drawn up.

Undergraduates intending to join the School of Social Studies were to do a paper on 'The Economic and Social Framework', although it was not finally decided how much of this paper should be devoted to economics and how much to other branches of the social studies. The main emphasis was to be placed on what might be called 'economic reasoning', but the first rubric also mentioned 'economic groups and social groups' and 'the political element in economic decision making'. Full discussion of the content of this paper was to await the very rapid build-up of an economics faculty.

It did not prove difficult to achieve a similar symmetry in the Science preliminary examination. Again there were to be two common papers, one of them, on 'The Structure and Properties of Matter', deviating sharply from A-level work, and the second on 'Mathematics', guaranteeing that all scientists would be adequately grounded in this subject. Interesting discussions took place in 1962 on the possibility of incorporating within the first of these papers the basic biology of the cell as well as the physics of matter, and plans were made to devise an entirely new way of developing this 'lead-in' course. The third science paper was to involve choice, in the first instance between further mathematics and chemistry.

It was one of the features of the curriculum of the preliminary examination that it forced attention on difficult problems which could be reviewed later in the undergraduate's career in the light of finals work. In the School of Social Studies, for example, the probing of value assumptions in the last paper to be studied, 'Concepts, Methods and Values', marked, in some sense, a return in spiral fashion to the problems first posed in two common papers of the preliminary examination. In the Schools of Physical Science and later of Biological Sciences there would be a return at a different level to problems first stated in the preparation for the study of 'The Structure and Properties of Matter'. Although it was realised that only experience would show whether Sussex graduates educated in this fashion would prove particularly qualified to embark upon new branches of research, there was sufficiently widespread interest in the University and its programme for research workers to be attracted to the University both in the School of Physical Sciences and the Schools of Arts and Social Studies.

For all its preoccupation with the education of undergraduates, the University of Sussex recognised from the start that its freedom to grant postgraduate degrees, a freedom which Keele had not enjoyed from the start, was one of its greatest academic assets. A university which is concerned only with the communication of existing knowledge is not really a university at all. The pursuit of new knowledge is a necessary part of its work and a guarantee that it will take its place in the international comity of universities. The first academics at Sussex realised that they would be judged not only by the way in which they planned the work of their undergraduates but by the work that they themselves produced. They wanted to create an environment in which new learning could flourish.

III   In Retrospect: The Years of Plenty?*

Those of us who were living and working in the University of Sussex between 1961 and 1976 were not conscious of the fact that we were experiencing years of plenty, least of all during the very early years. What we were conscious of, however, particularly during those early years in the University's life, was that we were living through an exciting period of unprecedented opportunity. It was unavoidable – and healthy – that we did not usually find it easy to consider what we were doing in historical perspective. There was too much to do. I believe that I was alone in collecting the ephemera of the earliest days on the grounds that they would one day be of historical interest, but as the University grew there was little time even for me to do this. Only seldom did I have time to keep a diary. Outsiders wrote more about the University of Sussex, some of it flattering, some of it nonsense, than we did ourselves.

The term 'plenty' is meaningful only if the 1960s, to which we undoubtedly belonged as a new creation, are contrasted with the 1980s, a bleak decade in British university history. Sussex had its origins, however, in the late 1950s. We were very much a pre-Robbins university. I was a member of the University Grants Committee (and of its New Universities Sub-Committee) during the late 1950s, and I took an active part in crucial pre-Robbins debates about the implications of what were called, sometimes a little pompously, 'Bulge' and 'Trend', the demographic and social forces which, through statistics of the size of school sixth forms, pointed to the need for an increased university population. If the existing universities had responded to the need, there would have been fewer new universities, a solution which later on many of them favoured. As it was, the existing universities failed completely to respond to the challenge – this was not their golden age – and the University Grants Committee had to act. It owed much to its Chairman, Sir Keith Murray, and to the imagination and

*The basic text of this essay was published in R. Blin-Stoyle (ed.), *The Sussex Opportunity, A New University and the Future*, a publication to mark the Silver Jubilee of Sussex University, 1986. The title, which obviously influenced my approach, was not my own. I insisted on the question mark.

drive of a number of its members, and it did not need Robbins to prompt it.

The new universities before and after Robbins never worked as a bloc, although many outsiders believed that they did. Nor did they follow one pattern. This I consider was wise. The tendency to apply formulae to universities during the 1970s and 1980s carries with it many dangers. There were general financial worries about university expansion inside the UGC on the eve of the Robbins Report, however, and it is significant that in 1962, in the second year of the University of Sussex, an uninspired Treasury pruned and pared the university grant suggested by the University Grants Committee.

I shall never forget a well-known highest-rank civil servant coming to the Committee and pompously delivering an elementary economics lesson on this occasion, apparently the first time that such a thing had happened. He had discovered the word 'cost effectiveness', but with us he mainly concentrated on the language of 'sharing the cake'. It was not a good omen. The Robbins Report, accepted with extraordinary speed and with far too little deliberation by the government, to the horror of myself and some other members of the UGC, was never even discussed as such with or by the Committee, which by then was under a far less effective new Chairman, Sir John Wolfenden. None the less, without Robbins the government would never have provided significantly more funds than it had hitherto provided at the behest of the UGC. The cake would have been smaller.

A large share of the increased funds went to universities which had failed to show any initiative during the 1950s, and the physical effects of the so-called 'affluence' of the period are often more visible there today than they are in the new universities. Indeed, at the time, the new universities were given very carefully rationed funds which were more closely scrutinised than those of the older universities. My own private papers reveal the financial difficulties we often faced at Sussex. Fortunately, the Finance Officer of the University, Ray Howard, was extremely able in judging what we could and could not do.

Like other new universities, we had an Academic Advisory Committee to guide us through our first years. It included some distinguished members, some of whom, particularly its Chairman, Sir James Duff, were keenly interested in our progress. Yet while it generated ideas, it sensibly did not seek to go far in shaping the new university. It left planning to the first academics who, despite differences of background, experience and temperament, constituted a formidable team who could sort out complex issues, reach decisions quickly and then speak out clearly with (more or less) one common voice. Very soon, indeed, the Academic Advisory Committee was dissolved.

Those of us now called 'founding fathers', although we never used the term, all felt that Brighton was a good place for the first of Britain's new universities and that, if anything, the timing of its creation had been too long delayed. We all wanted, too, to create a university which would be different. This was not because we were attracted to novelty for novelty's sake (this was anathema to me personally) or because we were preoccupied with image-building (a fashionable term at the time for reasons which had nothing to do with education). We were dissatisfied with aspects of the existing university pattern and keen to innovate. We did not ignore the state of the economy, and this was one reason for our stressing the need for innovation, but we believed, more generally, that innovation was necessary also in the interests of society and of culture. We were strongly motivated people, yet I consider we got the balance right. We felt a sense of privilege in being allowed to build a new university. Our morale was high, and we were sometimes accused outside Sussex of being 'superior' and of inflating our ambition. It would be fairer to say that we refused to think of Sussex as an 'inferior' institution, not least in relation to Oxford and Cambridge, which some of us know well. We were completely free from the status inhibitions of some of our colleagues in other provincial universities. We did not use the term 'morale': we spoke of élan.

The crucial discussions about the shape of the University were 'internal' discussions, and the first, and most crucial of them, were held in the house of John Fulton, the first Vice-Chancellor, then called the Principal, in 1960 and 1961 before the first fifty-two students were admitted, and before any of the handful of academic faculty of the University who were then involved in them were working at Sussex or were on its pay roll. It was then that decisions were taken on the organisation of the University in 'Schools of Studies' rather than in Departments; on the range of the first groups of Schools; on the procedures for choosing students; on modes of teaching (principally tutorials), with a strong emphasis on students' being encouraged to learn for themselves; on the curriculum; and on the sequence of work to be followed by students, beginning with common Preliminary papers to be studied by all Sussex undergraduates. The thinking behind this process was summarised in the 1964 study, edited by David Daiches, *The Idea of a New University*. Most of the thinking remains relevant in the 1980s in completely changed circumstances, although in the short run, largely for employment reasons, there is now a greater demand for very specific single-subject degrees. Some of the thinking the University of Sussex has itself cast on one side in its later phases, not necessarily to its advantage. None the less, we had no desire ourselves to produce tablets of stone.

The idea of this particular new university – and it was very carefully and critically thought out – undoubtedly appealed in 1961 and later to large numbers of sixth-formers, with girls particularly prominent in the first and early intakes. The experience of the first year when the fifty-two pioneering students (chosen by the Vice-Chancellor and the Registrar on the basis of the least detailed of all prospectuses) studied and worked together in two Victorian houses in Brighton remains unforgettable. It was like living in a kibbutz. At a party at the beginning of the second year, when we had moved to the new, largely undeveloped site at Falmer, one first-year girl student said to me rightly that it would never be the same again.

Thereafter, the experience of every year in the first decade was unique – partly because numbers of students and faculty varied immensely; partly because new subjects and Schools were introduced, thereby changing the mix; partly because the physical appearance of the new campus was radically different in different years; partly because the chemistry of the mix – some would call it the sociology – was different; partly because different broad issues were raised outside the University at different times, like relations with the Polytechnic, with the College of Education, with hospitals, doctors and the National Health Service, and, not least, with the local community.

Yet while no two years were like each other, we – not least the students – were deeply concerned about the long run. In the beginning the students, who knew far more about the University and how it worked than students in any other university, had to do without amenities (including sports facilities) that students in other universities could enjoy. There was certainly no plenty for them: nor was there for academic faculty teaching in terrapins. Neither was the University Grants Committee ever able to help us adequately with halls of residence (we all disliked the term) – at first on grounds of principle – and we had to turn to outside sources of finance, difficult to mobilise, in order to develop the campus (one of several American terms we adopted). In what we all thought of as 'laying foundations' (in physical planning, of course, we were not always completely successful) we had to be perpetually resourceful.

From the start we were forced also to attach central importance to the planning process and how best to carry it out. Before I became Vice-Chancellor in 1967 I had been for three years Pro-Vice-Chancellor Planning. It was not an empty title. I knew every member of faculty so that the planning took account of people as well as of numbers. In our early stages we were a highly innovatory university in our creation and development of a Planning Committee that included members of Council as well as academics and in the way in which we related academic planning to resource allocation at every stage of the process.

The key papers for the early years, when our formal constitution resembled that of most other universities and our procedures were already diverging, were the reports of the Buildings Committee – the first of them held at Marlborough House on the Old Steine in Brighton in December 1961 – and the documents headed 'Logistics of Development'. The Buildings Committee meetings, chaired in the first years by Lord Shawcross, later to become second Chancellor of the University, were often dramatic; indeed, they were bound to be with Sir Basil Spence as architect. There was less drama in the academic build-up, but just as much planning. The first of the 'Logistics of Development' papers was dated 22 October 1962, and before the third of them had been accepted it was clear that undergraduate/faculty figures would rise sharply as a result of the government's acceptance of the Robbins Report.

The first Vice-Chancellor had conceived of a university with 3000 students. This was not unrealistic, although some of his fellow Vice-Chancellors thought, perhaps with Keele in mind, that he was inordinately ambitious. The detailed Logistics of Development paper of 23 September 1964 shows how realistic we were at that stage: 'It has become abundantly clear', a paragraph in it read, 'that there would be disadvantages in seeking to expand the University above 3000 in 1967/68 and that the rate of growth will slacken very considerably after 1967/68.' I never believed myself in a target of 3000. I thought in far bigger terms.

The Logistics of Development papers were prepared by myself and Roger Blin-Stoyle, who was appointed as Professor of Physics and Dean of the School of Physical Sciences in 1962. He succeeded me as second Pro-Vice-Chancellor when I became Pro-Vice-Chancellor Planning. I do not believe that any university development exercise was undertaken more systematically. We took into account the total number of undergraduates in arts, social studies and science (in some subjects demand was running at more than twenty applicants per place) and the total number of postgraduate students (from the start we attracted many such students, far more than the Academic Advisory Committee had contemplated, including many from overseas) before calculating the total number of faculty required in each subject: 'The more that we rely on a "table of growth"', we stated, 'the easier it will be to plan appointments for one, two or three years ahead, and this offers great flexibility. Such a table should, as far as possible, be worked out according to agreed criteria rather than on the basis of subject bargaining power.'

Arts, social studies (I preferred this term to 'social sciences' in the School of which I was first Dean) and sciences were kept in balance at Sussex before and after I became Vice-Chancellor. Our ways of working diverged, but planning procedures were common to all. The initial 'agreed criteria' included for arts, where more guidance was given than in the sciences, a standard teaching load of twelve hours of tutorials for each member of faculty, including professors, who were given no special privileges at Sussex in this respect, with lectures excluded from the calculations. (The first faculty included some brilliant lecturers who actually liked to lecture and needed no Logistics of Development papers to lure them to the rostrum.)

An equally important criterion was a minimum complement of four members of faculty for each subject. We did not seek to introduce new subjects – and there was often great pressure to do this – if we were to be understaffed. We also believed – or most of us believed – that it was necessary to exclude from the University curriculum 'subjects where a large number of staff would be required to teach a small number of students' unless such subjects played an 'important part in the overall academic strategy of a School'. We were well ahead of the UGC both in agreeing to do this, and far more sophisticated in arranging how to achieve it.

Given the Sussex arts and social studies curriculum, there had to be agreement also about 'the need for teachers from different subjects to teach common papers', and 'the desirability of cross-subject teaching'. (Some members of faculty were extraordinarily versatile.) Finally, it was stated firmly in the September 1964 paper that 'agreement is necessary well in advance to the start of new Schools or to the introduction of new subjects'.

Since the planning procedures laid down in these papers were in advance of the planning procedures of the UGC of which I remained a member until I became Vice-Chancellor, I was active as a member of that Committee in pressing, along with lively officers, like Richard Griffiths, for a change in the way in which that body planned its increasingly complex and costly estimates. Procedures, of course, are instrumental. The objectives have to be clearly stated. In Sussex, where we stated them very explicitly, we had to stay firmly within the frame of limited public funds, and even before their vulnerability became fully apparent we wanted to get the best value for money.

We were greatly helped by lay members of our Council, notably by its Chairman, Sydney Caffyn. They had as strong a sense of public accountability as any government auditor, but they had imagination too when they helped us to relate resources to objectives. A note of realism ran through all our financial papers between 1961 and 1966.

Thus, we declared firmly in September 1964 that 'we must not over-strain finances this quinquennium'.

The visit of the University Grants Committee on 18 January 1966 was a happy and successful one. We were in step at that time. The last visit which I hosted in November 1975 was less so, largely because the Chairman and some members of the Committee had not fully acquainted themselves with the distinctive pattern of Sussex before they came and, therefore, could not ask knowledgeable and, when necessary, searching questions. We were disappointed with their approach, for they were less willing to learn from such university visits than members of the Committee had been during the 1950s. The decline in the role of the University Grant Committee, which long preceded the Crahorne Report of the 1980s, was not entirely due to governmental pressure. There were weaknesses within.

The whole system of regular visits, usually called in overdignified language visitations, was to break down, of course, under pressure, the pressure first of inflation, then of cuts. Whatever my own views or those of my Sussex colleagues on the fairness of UGC quinquennial allocations – and the issue was to become an important one in the 1980s – we could not have planned and created a new university if there had not been a national planning process. And at its best, when the UGC had less work to do than in the late 1960s and had not devolved an important part of its functions to subject Committees of necessarily varying degrees of knowledge and ability, the quinquennial system provided a good framework for university development. It also allowed for a proper exchange of views.

We told the UGC in a general paper which I wrote on the University in 1966 that 'the decision to establish seven new universities in the 1960s . . . was regarded by all those concerned in the early stages of planning the University of Sussex as a challenge to experiment both boldly and wisely'. By then there were nine Schools, each with a Dean. I was very anxious, having reacted sharply against the departmental system, that they should not become super-departments; in other words, that we should not be exchanging sovereign states for empires, and for this reason we insisted on the importance of students being able to study the same major subject in different Schools within different contextual frames and of academic faculty being allowed to belong to more than one School. There was far greater flexibility within the Sussex Schools system both for students and for academic faculty than there was in the Schools system of most of the other new universities.

It was difficult, none the less, to work out an entirely satisfactory organisational pattern, and, as the University grew, even by 1966, some new members of faculty, despite more 'initiation' into Sussex than in most universities, did not really understand the system. Nor were some of them, particularly specialists concerned with their outside standing in their own subject, necessarily in sympathy with it. Finally, the different Schools did not succeed equally well in establishing themselves as social as well as academic units. The warmth of the departmental system at its best was sometimes missing. So, too, was the intimacy of the college system which was deliberately rejected as a possibility at Sussex in 1960. I knew too much about the atmosphere of Oxford and Cambridge colleges (and of how they were financed) to feel that we could imitate them at Sussex or produce attractive alternative versions of our own. I was forced to recognise, however, by the time I became Vice-Chancellor, that people could get lost at Sussex if the Deans of Schools and a high proportion of members of faculty ignored their social responsibilities.

The first four Schools were Social Studies, European Studies, a pioneering School which having begun as an idea of Brighton's Director of Education, Bill Stone, a member of the Academic Advisory Committee, on the simple grounds that Brighton was geographically near to the Continent, soon acquired a distinctive identity under the Deanship of Martin Wight, English (and American) Studies, and Physical Sciences, with Roger Blin-Stoyle as Dean. The School of African and Asian Studies followed in October 1964: it was based on an idea of my own, and I was fortunate enough to be able to attract Anthony Low as first Dean. I had met him in Australia in 1960 when I was considering at a proper distance and in relative quiet what the Sussex 'map of learning' – my favourite metaphor – would be. I gave what to me was a significant lecture there with this title, and I was deeply impressed by Low's knowledge both of Africa and of Asia.

Educational Studies followed in 1964, later and rightly to broaden its title, and Molecular Sciencies, Biological Sciences, and Applied Sciences in 1965. The relatively late arrival of these three Science Schools was due to the need to build laboratories. Yet there had been important discussions about biological sciences long before the School was started, and the views of the Royal Society on the need to develop interdisciplinary work in the life sciences had strongly influenced my own attitudes towards interdisciplinarity and School rather than a departmental organisation. One distinguished professor who did not come to the University but went instead to the United States, Jim Danielli, played as important a part in these discussions as any of the 'founding fathers' themselves with the exception of John Maynard Smith.

I had to fight hard personally for a School of Applied Sciences, but was fortunate to be backed by one member of the University Grants Committee with whom I always worked closely, Willis Jackson. We owed much to such informed help from outside. It was a difficult fight, however, for there were people in the University Grants Committee, including its then Chairman, who were uneasy about this particular Sussex bid, and I could raise no financial and little moral support from engineering firms in Sussex whose aid I invoked. Industry was not ready, although there was to be creative co-operation with industry further afield during my Vice-Chancellorship.

To me a new university was incomplete unless it had at least one School with a technological base. I was clear in the 1960s about the importance of new technology to the British economy and society and of the importance of electronics, communications technology and materials science. I found, unfortunately, that Toby Weaver, a clever and powerful but, in my view, dangerous influence in the Department of Education and Science, refused dogmatically to believe that an academic like myself, or a university like ours, could or should move in the direction in which I wanted us to move; and I failed to persuade either him or Anthony Crosland, who was much under his influence, that Sussex was the right place to merge or to integrate Polytechnic and University which were geographically close to each other. Department of Education and Science 'solutions' to the problems of the 1980s, which are canvassed as if they are completely new, were very much in our minds in Sussex in the mid-1960s and were turned down then by the DES.

We were to suffer a further blow when the College of Education, which quite deliberately had been sited across the road from the University in order to share in its life, passed by DES decision to the Polytechnic. The memory of the bureaucratic rigidity of at least one key official in the DES on this and similar decisions in other parts of the country – for example, on the issue of the future of Bishop Otter College in Chichester, linked to the University of Sussex – still shocks me. At least Toby Weaver had intelligence. I was not happy either about ministerial will power. Ministers were far too dependent on their officials. They would not use their own brains.

I have bracketed official attitudes to technology and to education together because in both these cases the Department of Education and Science came into the picture as well as the University Grants Committee; and in a period of expansion it was not a Department which inspired great confidence before or after higher education became one of its responsibilities in the aftermath of the Robbins Report. At the top level the first of Secretary of State, Sir David Eccles and a later secretary, Sir Edward Boyle were conspicuously far ahead of their officers in vision and in energy, and in their case they were willing to use their brains and their will. They always had something relevant to say, and they knew how to act. Eccles was present at the first official dinner of the University of Sussex, when we could all assemble – students, faculty and Council – in Brighton Pavilion, and Boyle was a deeply respected Pro-Chancellor of the University of Sussex before he moved to Leeds as Vice-Chancellor. Both Eccles and Boyle had the wisdom to see that the country needed centres of higher education which would be centres of ideas as well as centres of service, and Boyle was particularly interested in the extension of our School of Educational Studies to become a School of Cultural and Community Studies under the same Dean, Boris Ford, in 1971.

It is a convenient fallacy for some recent writers on higher education to claim with hindsight that the makers of the new universities in the 1960s were insensitive to some of the central issues in educational policy which dominate the 1980s. It was the opposition to the idea of Applied Sciences at Sussex, and the apathy on the part of the local people who should have been interested, which stands out most in my mind in retrospect, along with the superficial way of dealing with the problems of teacher education and the development of the Poly-technic. Fortunately the School of Applied Sciences was able to acquire as first Dean, John West, with a very broad approach to the curriculum and with an insider's knowledge of its economic and social implications. Like Anthony Low, John Scott, Michael Thompson and several others, he was to move on to a Vice-Chancellorship.

Education was fortunate also in many of the people associated with it. Manny Eppel, strongly backed by me as Vice-Chancellor, developed a different approach to extramural education, concentrating on con-tinuing education in a community setting before this became fashion-able; and Norman MacKenzie and others devised a new approach also to what came to be called educational technology, a better term than the outmoded but then still current audiovisual aids. There were many problems, but Sussex became a designated national centre, and the work carried out in the University on a battery of new learning methods influenced many other institutions, including the Open University, on whose initial planning group Norman MacKenzie served. There were some members of the faculty who were either uninterested in or hostile to these developments, but they appealed to some of the most influential members of Council, like Leslie Farrer-Brown and Donald Tyerman, and they left their mark.

It is impossible to write university history without referring specific-ally to personalities, although some historians have tried to do so. The School of Molecular Sciences with Colin Eaborn as a highly con-scientious Dean was able to attract chemistry faculty of the highest calibre, including one Nobel Prize winner, John Cornforth, and Ronald Mason, and by the time I left Sussex I was extremely proud of it. The library, which was one of Spence's best buildings, owed much to its first librarian, Denis Cox, who had worked in Leeds when I was a Professor there and who was appointed before any member of the academic faculty, including myself. The beautiful Meeting House had a Congregationalist, Daniel Jenkins, intelligent, sensitive, and highly thoughtful, as its first chaplain. The work of the School of African and Asian Studies was put into a completely different context when, largely as a result of the personal influence of Sir Andrew Cohen, the national Institute of Development Studies was located not in Oxford, but in Sussex. My own personal interest in development studies – and in development education – already there when I went to Brighton – was greatly quickened by my Chairmanship of the IDS. Dudley Seers was a friend, whom I had known for years as well as a colleague.

The reasoning behind the decision to locate IDS in Sussex which, like John Fulton, I pressed for strongly and which I believe to have been the right one, raises different questions, however, from those of personality, just as the development of technology and of education did also. An existing 'centre of excellence' argument was deliberately rejected at the national level in favour of the argument that an institute concerned largely with what was coming to be called the Third World might be less cramped in a new university committed to African and Asian Studies than in an old university where there was then a greater concentration of professional expertise but where African and Asian Studies tended to be peripheral. The decision in 1965 to site the Institute in Sussex, and not in Oxford, was psychologically of the utmost importance and it had wide-ranging implications. Not all of them have been apparent to Cohen's successors in the Overseas Aid Administration, although they have fascinated enterprising businessmen, like Sir Michael Caine, who have served on the Institute's Council.

One broader implication of the decision to site IDS in Sussex was the increasing national recognition that research should not all be in one place; and in the University of Sussex itself there was a strong sense that we should become a genuine research university (with the research, when possible, linked to teaching), where institutes and centres, financed in different ways but only to a limited extent, if at all, by the UGC, would concern themselves with major national and international themes, again where appropriate, in an interdisciplinary way. A Centre for Contemporary European Studies was one of them: it was created at the appropriate time and established close links with a wide range of outside bodies and with European institutions in Brussels and elsewhere. Its first Director, Roy Pryce, was to join the staff of the Commission in Brussels, as was one of my personal assistants as Vice-Chancellor, Hywell Jones, a man of ideas and enthusiasms, totally unbureaucratic, who has subsequently had an influential and distinguished career in the Commission.

I took a personal interest in many of the institutes and centres, some of which were in the field of science, like the Agricultural and Food Research Council-sponsored Unit of Nitrogen Fixation and the Astronomy Centre, which, inspired by William Macrae and Roger Taylor, hosted the most impressive international gathering of my Vice-Chancellorship, the 14th General Assembly of the Astronomical Union in 1970. Mrs Thatcher, then Secretary of State for Education and Science, was a guest on this occasion. I appreciated, however, that such centres might have difficulties in acquiring or maintaining adequate core finance to sustain programmes deriving variable income from projects and that there would inevitably be a high mortality rate. I do not regret the policy. It put Sussex on a different map from the map of learning. For a time through the Centre for Multi-Racial Studies we were even able to have valuable academic links with the West Indies. We had a centre in Barbados.

We were careful to use the simple term 'Centre' rather than the more grand title of 'Institute' when there were possible financial or other hazards, and we sometimes used the term 'Unit' as well. The Unit which I conceived and which was closest to my own heart was the Science Policy Research Unit which was fortunate to attract men of the calibre and character of Christopher Freeman, its first Director, and of Geoffrey Oldham, its second. At that time there was no other unit of this kind in any other university. It has a fascinating history of its own, fascinating enough even in its early phases to attract the beneficence of Reginald M. Phillips, the University's biggest single private benefactor. I had almost weekly tutorials with Phillips throughout my Vice-Chancellorship, some of the most gruelling but fruitful tutorials in my academic experience. He was personally more interested in philately than in science policy – he had presented his famous collection to the nation to found the National Postal Museum – and he also endowed a Philatelic Unit at the University which doubtless raised some academic eyebrows. It brought the University into direct contact, however, with the Post Office and its leading officials, with interesting by-products – just as the Science Policy Research Unit brought it into extremely close contact with the Department of Trade and Industry. There was sometimes a clearer recognition there of how universities can best function in the late twentieth century than there was in the Department of Education and Science.

SPRU, as it was soon called, was associated in my own mind not only with external contacts but with the so-called Arts/Science Scheme inside the University. Much thought went into its structure and content, and although it changed its pattern sometimes in an evolutionary, often in a jerky, fashion, its objectives were plain – to give all arts and social science students in the University some understanding either of a science or of science policy and all students of science some acquaintance with the humanities or with the procedures of the social sciences. The success of the scheme depended on a willing involvement on the part of faculty of the University, and Michael Brown was very closely associated with me in seeking to secure the necessary level of involvement. Like similar innovatory schemes in the early years, Sussex owed nothing to student pressure, and it was not always easy to engage students in its work. Academic innovation during the 1960s was faculty-led, not student-led, despite a burst of student rhetoric in most universities during the last years of the decade. By then, there were faculty-led academic innovations which had not been planned – a sign that the University was a lively community. The most interesting of these were in the field of cognitive studies and linguistics. We were able to attract to Sussex men of the calibre of Christopher Longuet-Higgins and John Lyons. In law, again not part of our original scheme, we brought one of the greatest – and most formidable – characters, Colonel Gerald Draper.

In this brief and necessarily selective account of development during the first years of Sussex I have covered changes before and after I became Vice-Chancellor. There was no sharp break at the time when I took over since John Fulton and I had worked extremely closely together, and most of the developments which I have noted earlier either followed consequently on each other or were the result of initiatives which might have been taken before or after 1967. There were changes in student attitudes and activities, however, after 1967, which demand a study in themselves.

Most of the first students loved the place: a small minority attempted in the late-1960s to turn it into a political theatre. The best of the latter, sometimes, but not always, intelligent, sometimes loved it too, but their often ill-conceived activities diverted local and national attention away from the effective work of the University. Although there was far less disruption of Sussex than there was in almost all of the other new universities and some of the old ones – and little protracted disturbance – 'student protest' at Sussex received a disproportionate share of Press attention and often provoked hasty and prejudiced reactions on the part of people outside the University.

In fact, what was happening at Sussex was part of far bigger inter-national political and cultural patterns, and it was essential for the Vice-Chancellor to try to understand this fact while maintaining the daily flow of university business. Vietnam was never far from my own mind. I had to know exactly what was going on there as well as in my own university, which I was determined should continue to be a serious place of learning.

The most important changes at the beginning of my Vice-Chancellorship in 1967 were organisational and can be explained in terms of the growth of the University as an institution. They were clearly set out in the ninth *Annual Report* of the University, and my views on the reorganisation and on later developments during my Vice-Chancellorship are best traced in the *Annual Reports* which I presented to the University Court. 'It was during the year 1967/68', I wrote, 'that our newness came to matter less than our size.' By then, there were over 3000 students and 197 members of the faculty (including research staff) and rates of growth had slackened. There was necessary realism, too, about financial resources. In the words of my one address to the Court, the University Grants Committee offered the University 'considerably less than we had hoped, and in the light of our budget we had to make substantial changes to the academic plans which we had drawn up, we believed, not unrealistically'.

> There will be relatively little scope from University Grants Committee funds [I went on] for any large-scale new developments between now and 1972. Two consequences follow from this – first, we have to make the very best use of our resources to get full value for money, particuarly in a period of continuing rising prices; second, if we wish to develop – and there is always a far greater desire in this particular University to develop than there is to consolidate – we have to attract development funds from other sources.

The messages of the 1980s were not unknown to the 1960s.

The important constitutional changes which were made in 1967 followed the preparation in the last months of John Fulton's Vice-Chancellorship of an independent report that we had called for from McKinsey and Company.

Covering the government, organisation and procedures of the University, it was the first of its kind in a British university. The report was fully discussed and its recommendations in many respects modified as a result of the discussion. The main changes were agreed upon with little dissent – a streamlining of committees; an increase in participation; a clearer definition of administrative responsibilities; greater devolution; a further strengthening of the planning process; and an improved system of internal communication.

The large number of specialist committees was drastically reduced, and a number of the most important of them, familiar in all British civic universities, disappeared completely, like the Academic Board and the Finance and General Purposes Committee of Council. Business was now to be channelled through four main committees – Arts and Social Studies, Science, Social Policy and Planning – before reaching Senate and Council. The work of each of the first three committees was to be the special concern of a particular university officer. The Planning Committee, which included lay members of the Council and its Chairman, now become *the* key committee. It had no exact parallel in any other British university, and the quality of life in the University depended on its knowledge and drive as well as on its management of resources. The Senate, always a large and sometimes an unwieldy body, acquired student participants through the device of a Senate Committee which saved the University from trying to change its Charter. As a result of devolution, however, much of its business had been settled before its meetings began. This was true of Council meetings also, although it was important to me, as it was to its most able members, that they should not be thought of merely as rubber-stampers. There were too many highly intelligent and experienced people on Council to make that possible, and as questions of industrial relations loomed larger in the late 1960s and early 1970s the experience in this field of some members of Council was invaluable.

As a result of the changes, Barry Supple, my successor as Dean of the School of Social Studies, became Chairman of Arts and Social Studies and Colin Eaborn Chairman of Science. They worked very closely with me, as did their successors. Geoffrey Lockwood became Planning Officer, and for a short time I had a small Vice-Chancellor's Office team to assist me. Brian Smith became involved with social policy and did much to deal with some of the most complex issues of the late 1960s and early 1970s relating to student accommodation, community relations on the campus (we were very much a community ourselves) and with relations with Brighton – very much a distinctive community in its own right and one which I got to know very well. When I left the University in 1976, one of the events that still lingers in my mind was a lunch that Brighton Council gave for me. The extent of my own community involvement would have been impossible in Oxford, where relations between 'town' and 'gown' have traditionally been strained, and it would have been difficult, too, although not impossible, in Leeds. The fact that Brighton had wanted a university mattered. The fact that it was different from the university that most people in Brighton had contemplated mattered too.

I learned as much about politics, local – and international – in Sussex as I did about management, although during the late 1960s I had the sense that I was employing political skills inside the University which would have been more usefully employed outside. I knew that keenly interested as I was in the management of universities, I had to be particularly sensitive to politics at Sussex. There were many people of ability and drive in the University, some in positions of power, who had strong and incompatible views about what mattered most and about how to deal with people who disagreed with them. There was also a strong undertow. There were few people who were completely indifferent. The politics could be tough.

Interesting academic questions had to be asked as the University developed, and each had its political dimension, particularly after 1970. It had been part of the constitutional changes of 1967 that Subject Groups were given formal recognition as well as Schools, and while I did not regard this change as in any way subversive of the Schools system, it clearly influenced discussion on interdisciplinary courses, having a tendency in practice to multiply them rather than to strengthen them. It also strengthened the position of those second-generation academics in the Univesity who had been appointed as subject specialists and who were less interested in the University as a whole than their predecessors. When Deans began to be elected rather than appointed, there was a real danger that 'vision' might be lost. There was also a danger that Arts – never a very satisfactory term – and Science might diverge.

If there was any student pressure at this time, it was for more of an *à la carte* curriculum, which I never favoured, and for changes in the examination system, which on the whole I did. There was also far more ideological talk about the curriculum than there had been in the years from 1961 to 1965: this was a feature of the late-1960s and the early-1970s, and it alienated some of my colleagues, although it never alienated me. I felt that it could be put to creative use. In such circumstances, it was a great help to me as Vice-Chancellor that I continued to do some history teaching and met undergraduates in a different context from that of the Student's Union, the officers of which I met regularly, and some of whom became and remained friends. They were, as was inevitable, a mixed group, but I never felt during my Vice-Chancellorship that I was out of touch with students. They mattered to me most, and they knew it. Many still communicate with me.

Within the small working group of Pro-Vice Chancellors, Arts and Science, I was particularly anxious to continue to affirm my own priorities, academic and social. For example, I was determined to ensure that the School of Biological Sciences, which I regarded as strategically important, was given every encouragement; that work in psychology, which had developed in different Schools and in different guises under powerful influences like those of Stuart Sutherland and Marie Jahoda, should, if possible, be brought closer together and, as an area of strength, be further strengthened; that music should be introduced into the curriculum (the visual arts already had been) even though it was not easy to introduce new subjects at this relatively late stage in the University's early history; and that, if possible, there should be one new science-based school, possibly in environmental studies or in communications studies. In trying to achieve these priorities the main obstacles now were entrenched interests inside the University. It is remarkable how quickly these congeal in a university. Nor do the representatives of those interests usually have much interest in putting forward alternative ideas of their own.

We were not able to create a further new School nor to raise outside funds for a Centre of Communication Studies which, in my view, would have been as attractive in the long run as the Science Policy Research Unit. It was possible, however, with fairly general support, to develop operational research and through Patrick Rivett to establish links with Lancaster University, and entirely on our own to move into linguistic and cognitive studies, this time drawing on additional resources from Edinburgh University. My last academic act as Vice-Chancellor was to chair the Committee which brought John Lyons to Sussex as Professor of Linguistics. Later he was to become Head of a College in Cambridge.

There was one other ambition which took up a great deal of my time and that of my last Pro-Vice-Chancellor, Michael Thompson, subsequently to become Vice-Chancellor of the new University of East Anglia and later of Birmingham (my own choice, with whom I worked very closely indeed and very happily), that of developing medical education at Sussex. We failed there for reasons which had nothing to do with our planning, but we won the enthusiastic support of Tony Trafford and the local medical profession and of several senior professors of medicine outside Sussex.

Throughout my Vice-Chancellorship I used to meet the faculty each term to discuss University development, although it was a sign of the times – and not a happy one – that academic development increasingly figured less than other matters at these meetings during the 1970s. I also helped to initiate and did as much as I could to extend our early leavers' scheme, which brought students, often excellent students, without two A-levels to the University; they were a great new source of strength. I was very proud, too, of the University's Arts Centre which was named after Lyddon Gardner, our benefactor. Indeed, the sudden death of Lyddon Gardner was one of the biggest blows to me as Vice-Chancellor. In time, he would probably have succeeded Sydney Caffyn as Chairman of Council. He enjoyed Sussex, as did Stella Reading, who also died suddenly and bequeathed Swanborough Manor to the University. They always wanted to meet undergraduates as well as members of faculty. Through them and many others the University of Sussex was always more than a University of Brighton. It was related to the whole area and it had a particularly strong impact on Lewes. It was never an ivory tower.

During my last years at Sussex national policy had a bigger impact on the academic pattern and on the mood than local factors. In December 1973 I described the delayed quinquennial settlement as falling short not only of our hopes but of our expectations: it was, I said, very difficult to live with. There were by then over 3500 students (3.9 per cent of them from Commonwealth countries and 8.8 per cent from foreign countries) and we were told that numbers of Science undergraduates should be pegged and numbers of postgraduate students reduced. There were then nearly fourteen applicants for every place in Arts and Social Studies and the research grants for the Science Area of the University totalled nearly £800,000 We had been remarkably successful in raising outside funds for research.

On the eve of the quinquennial visit of the University Grants Committee in November 1975 the latest annual recurrent UGC grant had fallen by 8 per cent in real terms, but the University was still in surplus. New capital monies, we were told on the occasion of the visit, were 'miniscule in relation to needs' – even this was an understatement – and we were asked to set lower targets – under 5000 by 1981–82. 'There is no immediate hope', the Chairman of the University Grants Committee explained, 'of the restoration of the quinquennial system.'

In my last years at Sussex we had to freeze all new appointments and pool whatever posts became available by reason of retirements and resignations. We were forced, therefore, to return from devolution to a greater measure of central allocation of funds. We were forced also to spend more time on trade-union negotiations – these, too, had to be handled centrally – and on counting the cost of our social facilities, like our residential centre at the Isle of Thorns. It was clear that the tasks of a Vice-Chancellor were changing, not only in Sussex but in all universities. The year 1974 was a landmark in national history. It was a year when no one could afford to be complacent.

I did not leave Sussex two years later in 1976 in order to go to Oxford. I had told my closest colleagues and the Chairman of Council, by then a very close friend, that I wanted to cease to be Vice-Chancellor after ten years. I felt that this was the right period. Before the announcement was made, however, I had been invited to return to Worcester College as Provost. I decided to accept the invitation. My last months at Sussex were among my happiest since the exciting beginnings, and a summer conference on interdisciplinary work in arts and social studies, arranged by some of my colleagues, seemed to me exactly the right kind of farewell. However valuable it may be to have heads of universities – or colleges – who are not primarily interested in academic studies, it is important in the national as well as in the local interest that some of them should be. I never stopped writing when I was at Sussex. For me it was not a distraction but a *sine qua non*. And Ashcombe, the Vice-Chancellor's house, sadly – and stupidly – sold by the University since I left, was the perfect place to write – and to think.

20 Towards the Future: The Role of the Open University*

Ritchie Calder would have approved of the title of this lecture, the first in his name, whatever he would have thought of its content. He was always looking towards the future, to what he hoped would be a better age in which science would be generally understood and, in consequence, more wisely developed. He was above all else an interpreter and a communicator.

One of his sons, Nigel, edited two series of *New Scientist* articles which appeared in 1964 under the title 'The World in 1984'. That was seven years before the Open University took in its first students, although Harold Wilson had already envisaged 'A University of the Air' in his historic Glasgow speech of September 1963. It is rather a daunting thought that we are now nearer to the twenty-first century than Nigel Calder's contributors, of whom I was one, were to the world of 1984.

It is now possible to measure the angles of divergence between prediction and actuality in the very diverse pieces which were then produced; and there is special interest in a further book published in 1984 in which some of the writers of 1964 looked back at their own forecasts. Some had been more successful than others. The most optimistic were the least successful.

Certainly, the four writers on 'education' – and I was not one of them – were more optimistic in 1964 than time, so far at least, has proved. 'What I am going to say', wrote René Maheu, the then Director-General of UNESCO, 'rests on the postulate that recent trends will continue.' He was speaking of education within an 'economic and social fabric', and his postulates were wrong. My friend Lord Bowden, then Principal of the Manchester College of Science and Technology, predicted that 'our universities will undoubtedly be much bigger than they are today'. They are not.

What was missing from the 1964 forecasts was as interesting as what

*This lecture, the first Ritchie Calder Memorial Lecture, was reprinted in *Media in Education and Development*, March 1986. On 5 April 1979 I had given an earlier Fleming Memorial Lecture at the Royal Institution, on 'The Open University: the first Ten Years'. It was subsequently reprinted in *Television*.

was put in. No one sketched out the concept of the Open University or mentioned 'distance learning', although René Maheu insisted, in my view rightly, that 'if we are adequately to forecast the education of the future, we have to situate it in the context of the technological revolution', while Lord Bowden, equally rightly, emphasised that 'the most important change in the educational system will come from a general realisation during the next twenty years that education must not finish when a man leaves his school or university but that it should continue for the rest of his life'.

One point which cannot too often be insisted upon is that there is not one future but many. We have options. It is a point that was made forcefully by Nigel Cross, David Elliott and Robin Ray of the Open University when in 1974 they produced their open University Reader *Man-Made Futures, Readings in Society, Technology and Design*. This was an admirable product of the University's pioneering course-team approach – in my view one of its most remarkable achievements. 'Whereas once the direction of technological change seemed to be inevitable', they wrote in their Preface, 'or decided by private interests, there is now a growing belief that alternative directions can and should be the subject of open debate.' I agree without hesitation, adding the words 'and timing' to the word 'direction'. Ritchie Calder would have agreed too.

Ritchie and I were already closely associated with each other in 1964 through the Workers' Educational Association of which I was then President and he a Vice-President; and in 1967 we were both made members of the Planning Committee of the Open University which, under the thoughtful and constructive chairmanship of Sir Peter Venables, spent eighteen months preparing a blueprint. Ritchie was a valuable colleague in the Working Group on Students and curriculum, which I chaired, a group within which, in his words, 'we stripped down the conventional university system to its chassis and examined the essentials'. I should add, of course, that we left it to a still unappointed Vice-Chancellor and to his unknown colleagues actually to build the new model and to make it work. Ours were formative discussions – and exciting ones – and it is a great honour to me today to be giving this first Ritchie Calder Lecture in the presence of his friends, of members of his family, including his wife and his son Angus, who was a postgraduate pupil of mine, as well as of people who did not have the privilege of knowing him.

In 1963 Ritchie had written for the United Nations a characteristic survey, characteristic in its title as much as in its content, *World of Opportunity*. He never ignored problems, but he always saw opportunities, and from the start he conceived of the Open University, as I do, as illuminating and enlarging the world of opportunity for people who had either lacked it earlier in life or who were beginning to appreciate for the first time, later in life, just what was possible for them. We both conceived of the Open University in relation to our own society, not as an experiment but as a necessity, whether viewed from London or Edinburgh; and it was the latter vantage point that mattered very much to Ritchie, as it did to Jennie Lee and to Walter Perry.

Outsiders looking into British society from their own vantage points have often felt the same. They have judged that our complex society, the product of history, needed the Open University. The Open University for them, as for us, has been one major effort to help to get things right, to open access, to help to establish our national direction. Inevitably, too, it has had global implications, and these always interested Ritchie.

Chancellors seldom give lectures on aspects of the universities over which they have the honour to preside. They wisely leave the task to Vice-Chancellors, who are far better informed and who are executively responsible, to Professors, who often think that they can afford to be more contentious than Vice-Chancellors, and to students, who will say what they want anyway. I am giving this lecture today first, of course, because I was invited to do so, but second, because the issues which the future of the Open University raises are national issues that are just as relevant to the 1990s as they were to the 1960s. Indeed, I have found it necessary before and after becoming Chancellor to discuss these issues frequently both at home and abroad. So also did my distinguished predecessor, the first Chancellor, Lord Crowther.

Before I begin to examine the future role – or possible roles – of the Open University, however, I would like to make a number of fundamental points about Open University students, stressing that generalisations do not do justice to the diversity of the group.

First, unlike any other university students, they are a cross-section of the adult population of this country. Second, 70–80 per cent of them are in employment. Third, the median age of new students has for some years been around 32–33 years, an age at which a vast majority of the population could never in the past have contemplated embarking on conventional full-time university courses. Fourth, unsurprisingly, they are very active and deeply motivated people, who make real sacrifices to pursue their studies as do their families, often in conditions of difficulty: they have chosen a hard way to get a degree. Fifth, there are very large numbers of them. The target intake for new undergraduate students in 1986 is 20,000, and there are now near to 70,000 taking undergraduate courses: the scale is of distinctive importance. Sixth, of those who begin degree-level courses, between 65 per cent and 70 per cent gain a pass, a very high success rate in an international context; and since 1971 over 69,000 Open University students from all parts of the country have graduated, with over 10,000 of them taking full honours degrees. Seventh, the Open University now awards nearly 9 per cent of all the BA degrees awarded by British universities.

These statistics identify a significant element in the national population, significant, of course, I believe, in terms of quality as well as of quantity, an animating and also, I believe, a civilising element. They are men and women who at last have been allowed to take their chance in a society (and an economy) which for its own sake, not theirs, cannot afford to neglect talent. And if we project the statistics forward, what I like to call the Open University presence in society is going to gain still further in importance as we move towards the twenty-first century.

The 100,000th graduation should take place, God willing, in either 1989 or 1990. I rather hope that this very special graduation will take place in the first of these two years, because, apart from other grounds, it might distract a little attention from Paris in the year of the bicentenary of the French Revolution.* It would be a manifestation of our own belated revolution of rising expectations. Yet after 1989 or 1990 time will not then stand still. We are dealing with a process, a continuing revolution. By the year 2000, the living Open University graduate population could be well over 150,000. If the career records of our own century and of the last century concerning age and achievement are anything to go by, many of our present graduates will be making their major contribution to national life not in the twentieth but in the twenty-first century.

I should add – and here I come to an extremely important point about my statistics – that the figure of 150,000 rests on the postulate that the Open University will continue to take in around 20,000 to 21,000 degree students annually. Whatever be the implications of demographic trends on other universities – and, in the past, estimates of these have been notoriously unreliable – the size of the cohorts of potential Open University students is continuing to increase. Yet the financial implications of all this do not seem fully to have registered with the authorities. Indeed, there is a terrifying question mark against future Open University numbers on financial grounds. Since 1980, the value of the annual recurrent grants to the Open University (at constant 1983 price levels) has fallen by 11 per cent.

Nor is that the end of the story: there are further institutional cuts in

* In fact, it was to take place in 1990, the 21st anniversary year of the University.

view. The magnitude of such cuts for all universities has just been queried by the National Audit office. In the case of the Open University, we have been conscious not only of erosion but of threat to all that we stand for. It is a matter of deep concern that many of the University's savings have had to be made by cuts in the quality of services offered to students.

What often goes unnoticed, except among unsuccessful applicants, is that there is a growing backlog of unsatisfied demand for undergraduate courses. The Open University in national terms is not a luxury product but an investment, and the level of frustrated demand for Open University places has increased in recent years. In 1985, there was a record number of applications for entry to its undergraduate programmes, 52,612, and it had to turn down over 20,000 applicants. No fewer than 47 per cent of the successful applicants had already applied before. Given such queuing figures, a better case can be made out for starting a second Open University than for reducing the size of the present annual intake. All in all, between 1971 and 1985 there have been well over half a million applications for places, and 230,000 students have been admitted.

The latent demand is far greater still and is likely to grow. At present, the Open University spends only 0.1 per cent of its budget on publicity. What if that figure were to double? There are, of course, restraints imposed by fees which have increased in real terms by 50 per cent since 1980, and there is a wide disparity in the policies of local education authorities in deciding whether or not to provide mandatory grants. Student support is strictly limited. If restraints were to give way to incentives at some point in the future, demand would certainly grow further. It is, of course, this kind of open-endedness that alarms rather than excites governments.

Apart from the fact that there has been no sign of a slackening off in demand since the beginnings of the University – and some critics forecast this – one major hope of the 1960s is now being realised more effectively than it was then, and one new pressure of the 1980s is being responded to with remarkable success. On the one hand, there has been a drop in the average level of previous educational qualifications held by new students at entry: currently 44 per cent of entrants have less than two A levels. Access is more open. On the other hand, a significantly larger proportion of students are now concerned with science and technology than was the case before. Over 50 per cent of graduates during the last five years have taken some or all of their courses in Mathematics, Science or Technology, and among honours graduates this proportion rises to just over 60 per cent.

Given commitment to quality – and to continuing purpose, a purpose explicitly recognised throughout by the State, not least in the Green Paper, Cmd. 9524 – and given such adaptability to changing needs, expressed in the changing mix of students, the Open University should surely not have to spend as much time as it does struggling with what the Vice-Chancellor called in his 1984 *Report* 'crippling reductions, requiring not just efficiency savings or marginal cuts in services but major and long-term reductions in levels of activity and in the quality of student services'. It should be free to concentrate on the more distant future.

There is the will – and the managerial ability – in the Open University to develop a strategy for the years ahead. It would be a strategy in the national interest, but its implementation would require a national commitment to provide adequate resources over a long enough period of time to make the phased strategy work. As the American economist Nathan Rosenberg, outstanding in his field, put it in a different and broader context in a statement on technological change that was included in the Open University book of readings, *Man-Made Futures*, 'technological exploration is intimately linked up with patterns of resource availability'. That applies not least to educational resources.

In a world of increasing uncertainty – sometimes thought to be the major characteristic of the world immediately ahead – there will have to be a greater degree of certainty in the planning of higher education; and as far as the Open University is concerned – and it is directly financed not by the University Grants Committee but by the Department of Education and Science – there are unique implications. It is a national university with an established infrastructure in the regions, and its average costs per student are comparatively low. Furthermore, as it expands, its marginal costs per student fall. It cannot plan in terms of single years and requires by its very nature three-year operational planning cycles. Moreover, it must be conscious of its regional responsibilities in a society where geography counts for so much. Modes of finance as well as levels of finance matter, and there should be no uncertainty here. At present, there is.

Fees are particularly relevant in this context. Whenever the level of student fees has risen markedly above the rate of inflation, there has been an increase in the rate at which applicants offered a place have not accepted it. Moreover, there is evidence that the restraining influence of higher fees is greater in some regions than in others. I need not add that if the regional balance of university enrolment became too tilted – that is, if enrolments from the industrial regions of the North, the Midlands, Scotland and Wales were to decline further in relation to enrolments from other regions, where different, if related, social processes are often at work – then the national purpose of the Open University would suffer. Whatever other sources of its funding may be – and these should be increased – the basic commitment for its basic activities, what the Department of Education and Science now calls 'level funding', must rest with the State.

In considering the role of the Open University in the future I wish that it would have been possible to relate speculation about what may or will happen in the more distant future – or alternative futures – to actual plans which take account of identified needs and the best ways of meeting them. And that was just what the 'Long Term Review Group' of the Senate of the Open University was trying to do after it was set up late in 1983. 'The nature of its work' had to change, however, in the Vice-Chancellor's words, 'from a measured systematic review to a swifter more pragmatic exercise . . . related to a new, restricted financial context'.

Such a pragmatic exercise, necessary though it is, does not provide the foundation for a challenging Ritchie Calder Lecture which should incorporate a long-term vision of the future. We may, of course, feel afraid of aspects of the future, following Ray Bradbury, the science fiction writer, who once wrote 'I don't try to predict the future I try to prevent it.' Yet even when the future looks dark, there is still a strong case for an Open University.

I shall have to touch all too briefly on aspects of the science fiction world in the last part of my lecture, but meanwhile it is possible for me to project forward into the future with some optimism certain features of the Open University, particularly its activities in continuing education which, it is widely recognised, not least in the Green Paper, have already become directly relevant to the making of the technologists of the future. The Open University's non-degree programme now includes 'an extremely wide and varied range of single courses taught at levels both above and below that of a first degree', and I expect the range and the variety further to increase greatly, as more emphasis is placed – and it will be – on the need to revitalise the economy. There will doubtless be a focusing on major areas of change, notably in electronics and communication, possibly moving into the other great acknowledged area of change – bio-technology.

These areas, which are areas of change throughout the world, not least in the United States and Japan, were explored at a conference held in London in April 1984 on *Future Development in Technology, the Year 2000*, which was organised by the Open University with the support of the Engineering Council. The Under-Secretary of State for Industry, John Butcher, in his opening address on that occasion rightly emphasised the need for a long-term view of the future. 'It is natural for government', he declared, 'like most other large organisations, to become preoccupied with the short term. That is why we are devoting more of our resources to the development of longer term thinking in the Department of Trade and Industry' and that was why a Steering Group had been set up to consider them.

The Open University is more than a steering group. It is an action group. And it is more than a service group. It is a centre of ideas. Encouragingly, the Under-Secretary of State praised its work which, he recognised, 'has done so much to revolutionise retraining and post-experience education opportunities for so many people at all stages of their lives'.

Now the continuing education programme of the Open University, important though it is to the nation as well as to the individuals taking part in it, as other Ministers besides Mr Butcher themselves recognise, has to be self-financing; and the introduction of new courses, not least those related directly to identified national need, usually depends on external financial support. Like other universities in other parts of the world, the Open University has had to look increasingly to industry for that financial backing, and some of the strongest supporters of distance learning are now to be found in industry, which recognises its immense potentialities.

There are no dangers in the process of collaboration between industry and the Open University, I believe, provided that two conditions are met. First, schemes must be drawn up in genuine partnership and the terms of the partnership must be mutually understood: they may involve novel arrangements, and that is part of the fascination of the process. Second, the independence of the University and its academics must be recognised. The role of the Open University as a partner was very clearly identified by Derek Roberts, the Joint Managing Director of the General Electric Company (GEC), in a recent article in *The Times*, where he rightly stressed how important it was to have 'enthusiasts' in the University, in business – and in government – if we are to develop modern technology. 'The existence and experience of the Open University – envied abroad – is a foundation', he added, 'on which the response to this challenge can and must be built.'

In this connection, there have been highly significant developments in the Open University during the last few years which point to the future. Thus, in collaboration with the Science and Engineering Research Council (SERC) three new updating courses in science and technology were launched in 1984 – in software engineering, in robotics manufacturing, and in polymer engineering – and seven further courses were planned. Another industrially focused course in Management Education, operating under the banner of the Open

Business School – *Start Up Your Own Business* – was also launched in 1984 in collaboration with Barclays Bank.

These were only some of the constituent items in the range of courses. I have singled them out at this stage because it is clear that the national future depends on development in these fields, linking technology, communications, business and management. It depends also on a broader approach to education than any single industry working alone could provide. I agree with Derek Roberts again when he said that

> we need a better balance between breadth and depth in the undergraduate education of scientists and engineers. Managers must be capable of understanding their colleagues and the technology for which they are responsible. Furthermore, people must expect to change their area of specialisation at least once during their working lives. To achieve this through continuing education and training, they will need to fall back on a solid, broad educational foundation on which they can build their new specialisation. Similarly interdisciplinary teams need interface skills and a common language if they are to work effectively.

The Open University can provide such a balanced approach and the necessary experience to achieve results, and given resources it can respond speedily, more speedily than most university institutions.

As for the educational implications of the study of technology and how to relate it to other studies, I still turn back with enthusiasm myself to a book which has had a great influence on my own ways of thinking about technology, Eric Ashby's *Technology and the Academics*. It was written many years ago (1959), but it should be on the shelf of everyone who is interested in the future.

Past and future meet, as they must, in a recent statement by Brian Oakley of the government-sponsored Alvey Directorate, which is concerned with advanced information technology. Earlier this year he observed that 'when the history books come to be written we will find that the Open University has played *the* vital part in the battle to update and upgrade Britain's manpower'. There are echoes in the observation of battles being won on the playing fields of Eton. Yet I am sure that Brian Oakley would agree first that 'the updating and upgrading of Britain's manpower', a daunting but exciting task, has to be carried out at many different levels, beginning at school, and, second, that there is no final victory. We have to change – and continue to change – a whole population and not just sections of it, and we have to change it in conditions of unemployment and at a time when the morale of the school teaching profession, on which our long-term future in the first instance depends, has been severely battered.

Meanwhile, information technology industries are growing by 20 per cent per annum, but are being slowed down by lack of skilled manpower. And so rapid is new development that updating is required every three or four years. The Open University should continue to play *the* vital part in what are still only early stages of the continuing communications revolution but, as the revolution continues, it will affect all stages of the educational process and will inevitably influence the relationships between schools and universities as much as the relationships between business and the universities.

Whether or not the Open University will play the vital part in the later stages of the revolution will depend on how it responds – or is allowed to respond – to what will, I believe, be an increasing demand in the twenty-first century for every kind of adult education – of a refresher, of a retraining, and, even still, of a remedial type, but also education concerned with life more than with work. More than good management will be necessary in the twenty-first century, essential though good management is and will be. The term 'quality of life' is not rhetorical.

Some of the general issues that are raised under the heading 'education for leisure' are rightly matter for debate, but the word 'leisure', as it is generally used, is too broad. Work – and how to organise it – will influence leisure – and how it is organised. Common influences will be brought to bear on both. The work patterns of twenty-first century society will demand different ways of looking at work in the home as well as at work in the factory, the office, or the plant. And this in turn will create different ways of looking not only at private leisure but at the assets of the community. There will still be public as well as private responsibilities, just as there will still be shared public pleasures as well as increased privatisation of pleasure.

It is easy to oversimplify many of these issues, and I believe that the Open University by its very nature will be a strategic *locus* in relation to sorting them all out. Already its scattered students work in their own homes. They use the media – subject, of course, to severe restrictions – but they are involved in other ways of learning as well. The media count for far less than they did when there was talk of a 'University of the Air'. Students usually treasure their privacy, likely to be a major twenty-first-century preoccupation, but they think of the Open University as *their* university and not just as a distant provider. They turn to it at that point in their lives when they deliberately choose to do so, and thereafter they learn at their own pace. What they choose to learn they also decide entirely for themselves. They use their modular learning for both private and public purposes. That is true open-ness. They help to make the future, not just to respond to it.

I am back to the students again, for it is they as learners who can and will influence the choice of options open to us, including the choice – even in an apocalyptic world – of futures which could be genuinely brighter than the past. 'Making the future work' might well be their motto: it was, in fact, the title of an interesting 1984 report of the Post Office Engineering Union.

To pick out such issues involves peering into the twenty-first century, when we will be able, perhaps, in due time, to place our transient contemporary situation in perspective. We are a long way from there. Nor, as I have already said, are all the possible futures bright. In a recent Charles Carter Lecture, thoughtful and provocative, on the future of the idea of the university, Professor A. H. Halsey was more conscious of nightmares than of dreams, at least during what is likely to be a long and difficult period of social and cultural transition.

> We move, [he said] towards a high technology society with high un-employment. Secure income and employment belong to the educated. Unemployment is the fate of the uneducated and untrained, who are also the least politically mobilisable elements of the population (the young, the women, the blacks). The result a polarized society of two nations – the one a decreasing majority of those with advantaged possession of economic, political and cultural power: the other an increasing minority of marginal people, contained by welfare services and the police. Education in this lurid light, and especially higher education, is the instrument of perpetuating a deeply divided country.

In such a situation – and it would be unstable – the role of the Open University would be of critical importance. It would be keeping access open to uneducated and untrained adults who were seeking education and training later in life than their schooldays – and usually seeking something more. They would not be rejected. It would help to de-polarise not by anaesthetisation but by transformation, and it would thereby limit some, though obviously not most, of the human and social waste that goes both with unemployment and with polarisation. This is how the well-informed American sociologist of higher educa-tion, Martin Trow, views the present role of the Open University, although he is an admirer of its methods as well.

In looking ahead, I myself concentrate on hope as an incentive more than on fear. One of the most interesting brochures produced by the Open University for its would-be-students is called 'Course Choice and Career Planning'. It begins not with shapes of a generalised future but with the actual shapes of individual lives. 'You might like to consider your life in terms of three interrelated threads', it states, with each thread developing at its own pace and along its own lines, but with each one interacting with and influencing the others.

The three threads are family and home, occupation, and leisure pursuits.

> A few minutes reflection [the brochure goes on] will show that the sense of personal worth, satisfaction and challenge which most people crave can (at least in principle) be derived from any one thread individually, or from two or more threads in combination. Additionally, the activities which comprise each thread are constantly evolving and changing, as is the importance of any one thread in the overall picture. For each individual the pattern formed will be unique, but collectively these three threads can be seen as comprising your career. Equating personal satisfaction with career satisfaction in this way may be novel, but clearly suggests that you should look at all three threads equally in assessing what you hope to gain from your Open University studies.

And interestingly enough the brochure talks further of individual alternatives 'in a real world, not an ideal one', along the same lines as I talked about social – and technological – options earlier in this lecture.

It asks very pertinent questions, too, like 'How far do your interests stem from the sense you have of the abilities you can offer to a job?' and 'How far do your interests stem not so much from the intrinsic content of the job but from the extrinsic circumstances in which it has to be done?' 'It may be', the brochure concludes,

> that maximum satisfaction can realistically be anticipated from the traditional solution of qualifying for and obtaining an interesting, stimulating and well-paid job. But alternative solutions may be equally viable and perhaps even more relevant for the individuals concerned, e.g. taking a well-paid but dull job to pay the mortgage and the household bills, but applying your creative energy say to setting up a local poetry magazine, developing new computer software on a home-made computer, researching the effects of pollution on the local community for an environmental pressure group or (men especially!) finding a way to share the daily activities of child rearing equally with your spouse or partner.

It is interesting that in this personalised list one of the most traditional of activities – child rearing – comes last, not first, and that it is associated with the role of the male rather than of the female, and while I think that it was right for the authors of the brochure to pick it out, they did so rather belatedly. Being an Open University student is very much of a family affair. The role of the family is, of course, itself changing controversially, raising questions of values in the process, just as the role of women, who have turned with commitment and enthusiasm to the Open University, is still changing.

It may be that in the twenty-first century changes in the biological sciences, influencing so-called 'life technologies', will affect in practice, though not necessarily all at once, birth, ageing and all the traditional 'rites of passage'. Indeed, they are likely to capture even more attention than changes in information technology from which, of course, they can by no means be completely separated. The genetic code itself is informational.

The main points of the brochure, however, are concerned less with information than with attitudes – with the fostering of an active, rather than a passive, individual approach to the future as well as to the present, and with the provision of a perspective for the future, what every historian has always sought to provide for the past.

In peering into the twenty-first century, now so very near to us in time that it makes all 'personalisation' of centuries seem a questionable activity, we should note, first, that it is only now that we are beginning to see the shape of the twentieth century, our own century, in perspective and, second, that in many ways it has been a very different century from that which our late-Victorian ancestors contemplated a hundred years ago. Some of them prophesied war and revolution, although not holocaust, yet most of them conceived of their own century as a 'wonderful century', the title of a late-nineteenth century book by the biologist A. R. Wallace, and concluded that ours would be 'wonderful' too. For us, the twentieth century, at best, has been a 'troubled century', broken by war, and unlike our late-nineteenth-century ancestors, few people in Britain at least now put education at the top of or near the top of the agenda for the future. The forces of 'unreason' are strong and we will need 'education' in the fullest sense as well as training to cope with them. It is a necessary part of our mission to proclaim this.

I have said more about technology in this lecture than about history, and I shall return to technology in my conclusion. Yet the study of history does help to provide perspectives for an understanding of the future as well as of the past, and historians cast or can cast a critical eye on current attitudes and platitudes. It is remarkable how many writers of science fiction from Arthur C. Clarke to Isaac Asimov include a historian in their *dramatis personae*. Clarke even includes a chapter in one of his novels called 'The History Lesson'. Agatha Christie, too, in a different *genre*, had much of interest to say about history. It was she who wrote that one of the great attractions of history is that different historians say different things.

It is sometimes said – and science fiction writers obviously feel it – that in an age of technology we shall need 'the wisdom of the humanities'. That may be so and it is a reason itself for continuing to support the humanities in higher education and, not least, in the Open University. There is, however, another reason too. I think that we will need not only the wisdom of the humanities but also their daring. They pull across the frontiers of experience and knowledge. They are never just service subjects.

My last word on technology is this. If the Open University is to continue to play a vital role in the teaching and re-teaching of technologies, it must employ the most effective technology itself in its methods of communication. Information technology is an aspect of its own method as well as a subject of courses in its curriculum. The Open University was founded in an age of broadcasting. We have now moved, however, into an age of new communications devices, linking the computer and the satellite and offering the possibilities of many kinds of electronic interchange. This is already the age of the video, too, and continuing education will depend less in the future on broadcast educational programmes.

I do not believe that in the twenty-first century the idea of broadcasting or the practice of it will disappear – that could be the subject of another lecture – but I do believe that more personalised communications, including two-way communications, will become increasingly important. In all this there are financial implications, of course, both for the student and for the provider. Yet the most challenging issues raised by such developments may be that they will enable us to acquire a fuller understanding of the process of learning itself.

Discoveries in this field will be international, and I am sure that during the twenty-first century the Open University will become part of a stronger international network both in Europe and outside. Information technology cannot be confined within boundaries. Nor increasingly can university education. The world may be very competitive for a time – and the strongest claims for more secure resources depend at present on the pressures of international competition – but in the longer run it will have to become more co-operative. There is already far more distance learning in the world than there was when the Open University was founded, and other countries, not least China, look to Milton Keynes. The Green Paper was insular in its approach. In the twenty-first century such insularity will, I hope, become obsolescent. But we have a lot still to learn, as Ritchie Calder never ceased to say.

21   Expanding Educational Opportunities: The Challenge Facing the Commonwealth of Learning*

I am very glad to be back in Barbados again. I have always felt at home here since I first came to this Island in 1963 before the university campus had begun to develop. The last time that I was here was in 1978, and much has happened during the subsequent twelve years.

I had my first chance of looking at Cave Hill, then a development site, after a visit to the University of the West Indies at Mona, and subsequently I came back every year when I was Vice-Chancellor of the University of Sussex from 1967 to 1976 and when we worked closely together to organise the pioneering Centre for Multi-Racial Studies. Since then there has been a break. I am here this time, after a stimulating visit to Jamaica, as part of a Caribbean journey to celebrate the 40th Anniversary of the promulgation of the Charter of the University of the West Indies, and I am going on to Trinidad tomorrow.

Universities in the last years of the twentieth century spend more time talking about their problems than they do in celebrations. Through the centuries, however, university celebrations have given great pleasure to those participating in them, as did the celebrations last year of Europe's oldest university, Bologna. At the same time, celebrations have always offered an opportunity to look forward to the future as well as to recall the past, and appropriately in Jamaica my lecture was one of a series of Vice-Chancellor's Lectures, all of which are concerned with the way in which we will or should move into the twenty-first century. A knowledge of the past, I believe, is a necessary qualification for looking ahead. And for this reason alone, historians are as often asked to talk about the future as about the past on many occasions, not just as occasions of celebration.

If you are a historian, you are bound to be interested first and foremost in human experience and how that experience has been

*This paper is based on a lecture delivered at the University of the West Indies, Barbados, in March 1990. Parallel lectures, each slightly different from the others, were delivered in Jamaica and Trinidad.

shaped, taking into account the institutions which have been created, not always explicitly, to achieve long-term purposes. Being a time traveller, you are bound to be interested also in the relationship at different times and in different places between tradition and innovation, looking at different societies and cultures across time in the same way as when you travel you look at different cultures and societies in space. How is that relationship reflected in institutions and in ways of life? What is continuous in a society and a culture? What do we inherit, and when and why do the breaks come? What is the significance of the breaks, and when we make a break are we still in some sense perpetuating a tradition at the very moment that we make the break? The history of the Caribbean, never a self-contained history, raises all these questions.

There is another reason for calling in historians. If you are a historian, you have to learn how to weigh evidence in order to reach conclusions, recognising that different people reach different conclusions on the basis of the same evidence. Inevitably, therefore, you learn much in the process about the significance of human choice. Weighing up human choices is just as important as weighing up evidence. You inevitably learn much both about human limitations and about human potential – and, not least, human resilience.

Finally, if you are a historian, you learn that there are many things that will surprise you as life goes on. History is often a tale of the unexpected. There is a remarkable degree of unpredictability, as recent events in Eastern Europe have shown. Neither political nor technological determinism holds.

Time itself can play tricks on us, and when I was asked to come to speak as part of the 40th anniversary celebrations, I thought it might be interesting to begin by looking back over the time span since the Charter, a span ten years longer than the usual conception of a generation. My title might have been 'Forty Years On', the name of an old Harrovian song and of a captivating play by Alan Bennett. My vantage point is English. I leave it to you to look back over the same time span from a Caribbean vantage point.

There are comparisons and contrasts. And, of course, there are new connections. The Caribbean region is now related to the rest of the world, including Britain, in a different way from that which might have been expected in 1949, largely through migration on the one hand and tourism on the other. These were among the themes that were always on the agenda of the Centre for Multi-Racial Studies, with the older, and still haunting, underlying themes of slavery and colonialism only just a little further back in time.

Forty years back, we still lived in a world of empires: the term 'Third World' had not been used. Inside Europe, there was an ideological struggle associated with the Cold War, the War that we hope is now over. World War II was still in the background in 1949 – only just finished. Inside Britain, there was no intimation that the country would become a multi-racial society. There was economic austerity, too, with very little sense that we would soon start not only talking about consumer cultures but actually living in them. Nobody talked then about environmentalism either, although the environmental problems were already there. There was little recognition of those global inter-dependencies that now figure prominently in all our minds. Perceptions were as different as facts. So, too, were expectations and moralities.

Television was virtually non-existent: a very small minority was viewing. It was already there in the United States, but it was not until Queen Elizabeth's Coronation in 1953 that television audiences began to increase substantially, turning a minority medium into what is usually called a mass medium. If I were asked to select the one particular factor that has most influenced perceptions, expectations and moralities in all countries – though in varying degrees – reaching a climax in the changes that took place in Eastern Europe during the last year, I would have little choice but to choose television.

The speeding up of the news – a time change – is related to a space change – the sense that events in all parts of the world are instantaneously or soon afterwards accessible on the screen for those people who have television sets; and both changes are now associated not only with national reporting, but with satellites and dishes that are symbols of 'globalisation'. Boundaries have become less relevant. There is scope for argument about the role of television, with the argument often centring not on its positive effects – greater awareness, greater knowledge – but on the trivialisation that goes with it. There is room for argument also as to how much of our imagination and of our energy we devote to the world beyond our boundaries.

Throughout what has come to be called 'the television age' – and there are signs that we are now passing into a new age – I have been deeply concerned myself about whether or not television and other developments in communications technology can have a direct part to play, a positive part, in education. They can clearly have an 'educative' role, indirectly influencing knowledge and attitudes, not always for the best. Can they also have an explicitly 'educational' role – not least in relation to the widening of access to economic, social and cultural development? With such questions very much in mind, I was a member of the Planning Committee of Britain's Open University. More recently, I have been asking similar questions – and seeking to secure answers – in relation not just to Britain but to the whole Commonwealth.

In both ventures I have treated the changing communications technologies as instrumental, not as ends in themselves, and I have learnt much from previous academic experience in contexts where the technology, not thought of as such, was 'traditional'. Thus, before being involved with the Open University I had been one of the founders of the first of a cluster of new universities in Britain created during the 1960s; and while we experimented almost from the start with new techniques such experiment was not part of our remit. We laid more emphasis on our approach to tutorial teaching, although we soon set up a Centre for Educational Technology as well.

When I joined the Planning Committee of the Open University, I inevitably carried with me ideas about 'learning' and experience in developing them, the ideas and experience that brought me out to the West Indies before the possibilities of 'distance learning' had been appreciated in Britain. I already felt then, however, as did some people here, that because of the distances between the islands, the West Indies lend themselves to communications technology.

I knew that links between the islands – before there was talk of Federation – depended not only on cricket but on the broadcasting of cricket, which itself played a crucial part in the development of communications here. I saw, too, on that first visit, when Federation had proved impossible, that 'extra-mural' activity – the adjective takes on new significance in the Caribbean – was a necessary part of the 'mission' of the University of the West Indies.

Some of my reasons for pleasure in being back in the West Indies are personal, but even these are inextricably bound up with the changes that I have already identified. The first Vice-Chancellor of the University, Sir Arthur Lewis, a later Nobel Prizewinner, was one of the minority of economists in the world who had already come to the conclusion by 1949 that economic development is a complex process and that education is crucial to it. His book on development had already left its impact on me, and we had organised a small group of us in Oxford to discuss it. He would, I am sure, understand fully the choice of title for my lecture this evening.

So, also, would Sir Sydney Martin, first Principal of this University College, whom I am delighted to see here in the audience. Sir Roy Marshall, now happily your High Commissioner in London, was a colleague of mine both on the British Committee of Vice-Chancellors and Principals and, more pertinently within the context of this lecture, on the Commonwealth Working Group which produced the report that led to the founding of the Commonwealth of Learning. Finally, among the connections, we were each invited to serve on the Working Group by the present Chancellor of the University of the West Indies, Sir Sridath Ramphal, in his capacity as Secretary-General of the Commonwealth.

It was the Secretary-General, starting with a Caribbean, not a European, perspective, who pressed us to undertake an enquiry into whether we could do something at the Commonwealth level – not just at the national level – to expand educational opportunities. Increased student mobility, which for various reasons was under threat, remained a major Commonwealth preoccupation, but in itself it was not enough. Could 'distance learning' do more? Could it reach people who had been hitherto untouched by 'traditional' universities? Dr Ramphal's imagination, initiative and support were crucial. And it was he who wrote the introduction to our Report.

I am glad that the Report of our Working Group is printed between blue covers, since this suggests not only a blueprint but a blue book. The great blue books in Britain in the nineteenth century dealt with many of the big issues of the time and focused not only on the necessary facts but on the necessary policies, on what needed to be done.

In the introduction to our own blue book the Secretary-General immediately struck the right note:

> It is not often that ideas emerge that stir the imagination and beckon people to work for their fulfilment. This Report contains such an idea. It proposes the creation of a University of the Commonwealth for co-operation in distance learning, itself working closely with and forging an effective partnership between, a wide variety of institutions throughout the Commonwealth. The objective, as the Working Group says boldly, is that 'any learner anywhere in the Commonwealth shall be able to study any distance teaching programme available from any *bona fide* college or university in the Commonwealth'. The technologies for doing so have, of course, been available for some years. The Working Group shows not only how they can be harnessed on a Commonwealth-wide basis, but how teaching materials could be pooled and shared to become a Commonwealth-wide resource, freeing individual learners throughout the Commonwealth from the constraints of distance and the need to study at a pre-set place or time. What more fitting proposal for Commonwealth co-operation could there be as we approach the third millenium? The proposed university would help meet immense and urgent needs. It would also give that international dimension to education and training that the twenty-first century will sorely need.

This very eloquent declaration picks out for special attention the key passage in the Report of the Working Group, the declaration of intent

that draws in not only Commonwealth governments but Commonwealth citizens.

The support of governments was essential, however, if the Commonwealth of Learning were to be brought into existence – and fortunately
they were soon willing to sign a Memorandum of Understanding setting
out the terms of the Commonwealth of Learning, quickly shortened to
COL – but the dream that lay behind COL was non-governmental –
that 'any learner anywhere in the Commonwealth shall be able to
study any distance-teaching programme available from any *bona fide*
college or university in the Commonwealth'. There should be complete freedom of access, genuine open-ness – 'any learner', 'anywhere',
'any programme'. In a world of barriers – and there were barriers
within the Commonwealth itself, not least in relation to the mobility of
students – this was an ideal that modern communications technologies
could at last make feasible.

I would like to pick out a few other phrases in the Secretary-
General's brief foreword to the Report of the Working Party, phrases
that seem to me to be almost as important as the statement of this idea.
He spoke, too, of 'immense and urgent needs'. When we got together
in our small Working Group, we started not by advancing ideas of our
own about what other people should want or need but by collecting an
inventory of defined needs from a wide range of different countries in
the Commonwealth from Canada to Africa, from the Pacific to the
Caribbean.

Many of the countries of the Commonwealth are small islands, and
these have very special needs and very limited resources. But there
were also representatives in our Working Group of large Commonwealth countries too, countries of the size and importance of India and
Nigeria. In making our proposals we had to take account, therefore, of
quite different perspectives, including Caribbean perspectives. The
latter were conveyed to us by Rex Nettlefold, whose educational – and
cultural – activities have been concerned with adults and with the
bringing together of the different Caribbean islands into the common
extra-mural venture that I have already mentioned.

In the inventory of what were thought of as 'immense and urgent
needs' some were very directly related to the field of education,
particularly the need for teacher training. 'Immense and urgent needs'
were also identified, however, in other fields, like health, nursing and
rural development. And these, we felt, would require special attention.
For this reason, having identified the needs, we ourselves had to go on
to identify priorities – in the light of the way in which people themselves thought of their needs – and to make suggestions about a strategy
for implementing our proposals. It was obvious from the outset that

the organisation that we wished to create would have to be directly related to local situations and, above all, that it would have to be flexible in its procedures. It would have to interpret, not to impose. Yet it would also have to be capable of stirring people's imagination.

For these and for other reasons, we decided that what was needed at this first stage – and we deliberately chose to put it that way – was not another new university. That would have been too expensive and would inevitably have involved duplication. Nor would a university necessarily have been equipped to deal with all the issues that mattered most. At the same time, something more was needed, we felt, than a network of existing distance learning institutions. We wanted these to be networked in order that each institution would be in a position to draw on the resources of the whole network with a view to ensuring that the individual learner could eventually be able to do the same. Yet we believed, first, that the network would have to widen and, second, that even if all the existing institutions within an extended network proved willing to work closely together in order to achieve Commonwealth objectives, a very exciting idea, COL itself would still require the power to initiate and to guide as well as to co-ordinate. Above all, it would have to employ an accessible data base, open to learners in every society and culture, the kind of data base, geared to the needs of users, that meets specific and sometimes urgent user demands.

We felt also that COL would have to concern itself directly not only with educational programmes but with technologies – note the plural – including technologies that are still in the process of development. There is undoubtedly an element of excitement in drawing on sophisticated technologies that can triumph over all physical barriers – satellite technologies are the most striking of these – but in education every kind of technology is useful and sometimes it is the simplest materials and methods that are the most effective. Appropriate technology is the right term. There is a need to encourage all ways of learning from oral communication to print, from print to radio, from radio to television, and from television to video. The print must be of the highest standard, usable in itself, not purely ancillary. There is also a place for the telephone, in certain societies an extremely useful medium.

In 1990 we are not at the end of the story of technical development. Indeed, we are moving or have already moved into completely different phases of the communications revolution. Yet the communications revolution, like every revolution, including social and political revolutions, offers hope that may not be fulfilled and introduces elements of contradiction into the picture. Ironically, the possibilities of greatly enhanced individual choice are canvassed most actively by huge multinational companies that are involved also in newspapers, film and in book publishing. Business concentration on a scale and of a kind that we have never known before in the history of culture challenges public broadcasting. How education will fit into this picture is not clear. Can it really play a part in satellite and cable use, or is the provision of entertainment – and separately channelised news – to conquer all else?

Not, I believe, if each individual country confronts massive international business concentration on its own. Other phrases in the passage picked out by the Secretary-General stand out, therefore – 'forging an effective partnership', 'pooled and shared to become a Commonwealth resource', and *in crescendo*, 'What more fitting proposal for Commonwealth co-operation could there be as we approach the third millennium?'

The whole emphasis of our Report was on pooling and sharing. The Commonwealth is a unit of an extraordinary kind. It is scattered in space, it represents all conceivable kinds of development levels, including levels of communication. It is concerned, too, with different traditions and it has its deep political differences. It has one feature, however, which is of vital importance to it. The English language, a rich asset in itself, is a language which is spoken throughout the Commonwealth. In consequence, distance learning becomes practicable.

There is an economic argument for pooling and sharing and saving costs also, and this weighs heavily at a time when individual governments are cutting expenditures, not least in education. Value for money is a universal slogan. Leaving on one side cost arguments in favour of using distance learning rather than other modes of learning inside individual countries, there are obvious possibilities of reducing costs through Commonwealth co-operation. Not every individual country in the Commonwealth need produce distance learning materials of all kinds if it is clear that there are materials which are being produced somewhere else in the Commonwealth that can be tapped. There are, of course, basic questions of adaptation for use, but COL would be in a strong position to help countries to cope with these.

The Working Group was fascinated by the extent of what was already going on in the Commonwealth in terms of distance learning at the university level. The British Open University, a great institution, which from the start has rightly emphasised the importance of quality, has an enrolment of about 90,000 students of various kinds. In India, the Indira Gandhi National Open University, established in 1985, already has more than 40,000 students, and it has bold ambitions of reaching a million. In Canada, there is an impressive open learning network in British Columbia, and several institutions, like Athabasca, have a proven record of achievement. Across the Pacific, there are universities like Massey in New Zealand and Deakin in Australia which have a very sizeable distance learning component in the pattern of their activities. And other countries in the Commonwealth are well advanced in planning more distance education for the future.

Some of the most revealing developments have taken place in Hong Kong, where, first, thanks to the University of East Asia, a lively and enterprising private institution with which I have been personally concerned, and more recently through a government-backed Open Learning Institute, use has been made of course materials from different Commonwealth countries. When OLI was set up, no fewer than 200,000 application forms were asked for, and 60,000 candidates applied for entry. It was only possible to take 4300 of them, selected at random by computer with no effort made to look at previous qualifications. There is no better evidence of pent-up demand, and in Britain, too, the experience of the Open University has shown abundantly that demand is not merely pent-up but continuous. There are frustrations on the part both of would-be users and of providers in not being able to meet it quickly. The queues grow.

Here in the Caribbean, I have been particularly interested in the UWIDITE programme that enables educational links to be made – so far in sound only – not only between the three campuses – Mona, Cave Hill and Trinidad – but between each of the three major university centres and centres in smaller islands like St Lucia and St Vincent. I have already taken part in two UWIDITE programmes since I arrived on this visit, and I feel that they have great potential. So, too, have the satellites that made them possible.

As you go around the Commonwealth, therefore, you can find examples of what distance learning already means in practice, including distance learning work with teachers in training in Nigeria, and other work, of particular interest to COL – there is still not enough of it – in community activity outside the conventional sphere of university education. Outside the Commonwealth, too, the same kind of forces are in operation. In Thailand, for example – and it is a conspicuous example – distance learning has been used on a massive scale, and inside Europe there is now a group of universities that are specifically involved in distance learning: it includes institutions in Belgium, Denmark, France, Ireland, Italy, the Netherlands, Norway, Portugal, Spain and Germany, quite a formidable list of countries. The different units in that system vary in the ways in which they organise their work, but all of them recognise the importance of flexibility. There are five autonomous degree-granting universities, five consortia, a distance teaching unit within a larger institution, and a materials production agency.

Such developments show that across frontiers use is being made at last of the wide range of existing technologies that make genuine open learning possible at all levels, the kind of learning that is not tied by time or space. We have not yet developed, however, the interactive possibilities of distance learning that are already there; and international business, not least the communications business, has sometimes proved more innovative than formalised education in exploring them – for example, in its own closed staff training schemes.

Thus, some of the biggest European producers of communications technology, hardware and software, who are very keen rivals in relation to the running of their own business enterprises, are co-operating together in a scheme called Europace which links a number of companies with a number of European institutions of higher education. It employs methods similar to those of the National Technological University in the United States. (I need hardly stress how important some of the developments in the United States are in this particular field.) The curriculum of Europe consists of courses provided by about twelve universities and research centres, and the programmes are distributed by satellite from Paris and received by select groups both in companies and in universities.

When we reached the conclusion in the Report of our Working Group that there should be Commonwealth co-operation, it was not because we thought that the Commonwealth was in any way a self-sufficient unit. It was in light of what was already going on in many places outside as well as inside it that we proposed 'the creation of a new institution to promote collaboration in distance education throughout the Commonwealth'. 'Its object', we went on, 'will be to widen access to education, to share resources, to raise educational quality and to support the mobility of ideas of teaching, of relevant research and of people.'

In my view, the most important words in that statement are 'to widen access to education', although I would not wish to minimise the importance of improving 'quality'. During the course of the last few years we have fortunately become more conscious of the significance of performance rather than words, and we have recognised more sharply than ever before just how wide quality differentials can be even within the same educational system. Quality must be a criterion when there is a shortage of resources, when the mobility of people and ideas, a key aspect of living in the twentieth century, is restricted, and when user satisfaction is essential.

To me, however, the widening of 'access' remains the most striking message of our century. Ways have to be found to mobilise talent and to generate opportunities. I would not have been interested in the Commonwealth of Learning myself had it not attached fundamental importance to the widening of access. Nor would I have been so enthusiastic about the Open University. For this reason, too, I welcome the approach of a world conference on education recently held in Thailand as set out in a stirring general statement at its close, a World Charter on Education for All. 'Learning', the Charter states unequivocally, 'is the link between the development of the individual and the development of society'.

Our own stress in COL has always been on 'distance *learning*'. Indeed, in my own view, the concept of distance learning is more important than that of distance teaching, although I believe that teaching skills can none the less be usefully taught and that teacher training, itself training in learning, is crucial to development. It is the way in which the individual, including the teacher, learns – and how he learns informally as well as formally – that defines his own perceptions of his place in the world.

The learning process, a life-long process, seems to me to be the key to everything that I am talking about tonight. In the late-twentieth century we have learnt, I hope once and for all, that you do not complete your education when you leave school or university. Indeed, you never complete it at all. The learning process goes on. It is nonsense to think that if you go to a university and obtain a degree you have finished your education. The degree qualification, which matters a great deal – far too much, perhaps – in many parts of the Commonwealth, is in itself incomplete. At best, it is a special kind of visa, although it is a visa that provides income rather than costs money, and that is one major reason why it matters so much.

We have learnt also, sometimes the hard way, that there is much valuable education that is not concerned with degrees, that education to update and to revivify is a vital element in adult education, now rightly thought of as continuing education, and that, above all, education that deliberately draws on experience, not on books, is necessary everywhere. In making our proposals for the Commonwealth of Learning we were interested in co-operation at all levels of technical and professional education, as well as in basic education, remedial education or community education, none of which should ever be neglected.

In his foreword, the Secretary-General wrote of the twenty-first century, thus drawing attention to the necessary future orientation that is present in this Lecture. There are many uncertainties about that century, however, more perhaps than there were about the twentieth century in the decade before it began. What we will make of it depends on adaptability as well as on competence or capability, and both capability and adaptability rest on the qualities of individuals and the aspirations of groups. The groups will need imaginative and forceful leadership. Otherwise, aspirations will be futile.

It was by choice that in our Report we used the word 'people' rather than the words 'human resources' which have now taken over in every country and which are part of the current language both of education and of development. Ultimately, however – and preferably, too, in the first instance – human resources are best thought of as human beings. I do not think of myself as a human resource. I doubt if many of us do. I recognise, of course, that from somebody else's point of view I might well be considered a resource, or possibly a 'resource person'. That impresses me, but it does not satisfy me, much as I hate waste.

It is obviously useful at all times to realise that when we plan any strategy we depend upon human beings to make it work; and I would like to feel that as we develop the strategy of COL it will have meaning not just for governments or, indeed, for administrators of higher educational systems, but for individual people and for their families. (Open learning for adults is usually very much a family matter.) I would like to feel that, as a result of the way in which COL will develop, somewhere in the Commonwealth – in Ghana or in Sri Lanka or in Tonga or in Barbados – there will be some particular person who will himself or herself have access to knowledge that otherwise would not have been available to him.

That was the vision when we drafted our Report. Having completed it, however, we had to have rapid access to people in power, in order that it might be implemented. Happily, our recommendations were transmitted very quickly to the Commonwealth Prime Ministers at their meeting in Vancouver in November 1988, having been presented to a meeting of Ministers of Education in Nairobi earlier in the year. Both meetings accepted it, and the Memorandum of Understanding to which I have already referred was drawn up. This constitutes what is in effect the founding Charter of the Commonwealth of Learning.

I would like to pay a special tribute to the government of Canada for the imaginative way in which it welcomed the idea of a Commonwealth of Learning before the Vancouver and Nairobi meetings. It wanted the headquarters to be located in Canada and it provided funds for this purpose after the Commonwealth Prime Ministers had decided that COL should be located in Vancouver. The Government of British Columbia was extremely interested – and generous too. By being located in Vancouver, we have a window that opens out on to the Pacific. We are the first Commonwealth institution to be located there.

Canada is of interest geographically because, of course, it has windows both on the Atlantic – and through that a window on the Caribbean – and on the Pacific. It looks both ways. Moreover, it has always depended for its own advance on the development of modern communications. Without the opening up of the railway across Canada, the country would not have emerged as it has done. Subsequently, telegraph links were created in close relation to the railway. Broadcasting followed naturally. Not surprisingly, therefore, Canada is a country which has produced more theorists of communciations than any other country in the world. Finally, it has strong interests in assisting the development of Third World countries. Its outlook is global, and it does not seek to impose any one particular point of view.

Other Commonwealth governments made initial pledges – Brunei was one of the first – and some other pledges have been made since. These governments have decided that they will support COL for a period of time, albeit in the first instance a very short period of time; and without their support it would have been impossible either to begin to operate or to plan. The period will not be long enough, however, to test COL's record fully, let alone to assess its potential.

It is on the spot, within the regions, that the activities of COL will be judged. Vancouver will be the centre of COL, but it will not in any sense of the word be at the head of a hierarchy, imposing its will from above. None the less, how strong and active regional centres of COL will be depends in large measure on the resources available to it, and unfortunately it has been plain from the outset that the resources of COL are far too small to cover the demands already being made upon it. Moreover, since some of the pledges are tied, this not only limits what COL can do but diminishes its flexibility. More seriously, if resources remain far too small, there would be a dangerous gap between realities and popular expectations. It would also be difficult to sustain the enthusiasm of the biggest backers and of COL's own staff who have worked as hard as they can to propel COL into action.

The Caribbean expectations of COL are great, as I have learned already in Jamaica. Yet, as things stand, there are limits to what can be done for each particular region, including a region like this which is clearly defined. In the first instance COL is having to work on the basis of a budget and not of a blueprint. As far as the Caribbean is concerned, it is fortunate that the executive Head of the Commonwealth of Learning, its President, is himself a Trinidadian, Dr James Maraj. Fortunately, too, however, his wide-ranging experience, political as well as educational, includes that of having been the Vice-Chancellor of the University of the South Pacific. Possibly for the first time in history, therefore, Caribbean and Pacific experience converges within the Commonwealth in a great meeting of the waters.

In order to look at the specific needs of the Caribbean area, we appointed to the staff in Vancouver, Dennis Irvine, former Vice-Chancellor of the University of Guyana, who has already been involved in detailed regional discussions as to how the Commonwealth of Learning can be helpful here. Plans range from the training of teachers in Jamaica to the development of agricultural technology in Trinidad. There will also be a co-operative network of Caribbean 'centres of technical excellence', linked by distance technology.

When our Board, which includes representatives from many different parts of the Commonwealth, met for our first meeting in 1989 in Vancouver we carefully examined Article 3 of the Memorandum of Understanding, which sets out the 'functions and objectives' of the Commonwealth of Learning as the founding governments saw them:

> assisting the creation and development of institutional capacity in distance education in member countries; facilitating the channelling of resources to projects and programmes in distance education; providing information and consultancy services on any aspect of distance education, including a selection of appropriate technologies; undertaking and supporting staff training in the technique and management of distance education; facilitating inter-institutional communication links; undertaking and supporting evaluation and applied research in distance education; assisting the acquisition and delivery of teaching materials and more generally facilitating access to them; commissioning and promoting the adaptation and development of teaching materials; establishing and maintaining procedures for the recognition of academic credit; assisting in the development of local support services for students; and stimulating and supporting any other activities that fall within the Agency's areas of interest by such means as may be approved by the Board of Governors.

This is a very comprehensive, ambitious list of objectives, and during 1990 we shall have to try to fashion a plan, by its very nature flexible, with price and time tags attached.

Detailed planning is out-of-fashion, but even if it were not, it would be almost impossible to plan in detail in our own changing situation. What we must do, therefore, is to identify options and to establish time tags. The priorities are clear. The most important of our immediate tasks are those of 'providing information and consultancy services on any aspect of distance education, including the selection of appropriate technology' and 'undertaking and supporting staff training'.

These are both 'action objectives', and in the appointment of our own staff, most of them on a short-time basis, these and other action objectives – like the more effective application and diffusion of communications technologies – have determined the pattern of recruitment. As far as the first task is concerned, use will be made of a databank at Milton Keynes, supported by the tied British contribution, and supplemented, when possible or necessary, by information about non-university courses from other sources. With the development of modern technology, the collection, recording and distribution of such necessary information has become possible, but very definite user guidance will be needed about what each individual course offers and how it can best be used. We are not simply drawing up a bibliography. Nor are we interested only in courses leading up to degrees. There is a whole range of courses that present open learning at its best.

We held the second meeting of the Board of COL in Delhi, and there we were brought into direct contact with the Indira Gandhi Open University which operates through twelve regional centres. Just before we went there, it had held its first Convocation, at which the Secretary-General of the Commonwealth received an Honorary Degree. So far, it has put on two sets of courses, one in management studies and one in distance learning itself. And these courses on video and tape are going to be made available directly through COL to all parts of the Commonwealth.

After we had our meeting in Delhi, we then went on to hold our first interdisciplinary symposium in June 1989. Again it is a sign of the wide variety of experience within the Commonwealth that this was held in Malta, one of its smallest countries, an island which has had a fascinating history entirely of its own. The subject was how distance education can be used to meet training needs in marine resource management as identified by island and coastal states. Amongst the participants there were some people from the Caribbean. Out of the symposium the idea emerged of a course on marine resources to be taught at a distance, and in this case, since there was no course already in existence that entirely covered the purposes, the course was to be produced by the COL itself through commission.

The core modules were to include man and the ocean; the physical characteristics of the oceans; the law of the sea; the utilisation and management of living resources through aqua-culture; the utilisation of non-living resources; deep-sea-bed mining; energy from the oceans; navigation; shipping and ports; tourism and recreation; and the protection and preservation of the coastal and marine environment. Some of these modules are obviously of great relevance here in Barbados.

I have stressed 'relevance', sometimes a difficult word in education, even in development education. In conclusion, however, I would like to return to first principles and to draw attention to a statement in the World Charter on Education for All, drawn up in Thailand. 'Basic learning needs', it says, 'refer to the knowledge, skills, values and attitudes necessary for people to survive, to live in dignity, to continue learning, to improve the quality of their own lives and their communities and nations'. The Commonwealth of Learning is testimony to the interest of the Commonwealth as a whole in ensuring that an imaginative collective effort is made to translate such ideals into practice.

22 Plus Ça Change: Back to Keighley: The Largely Forgotten Story of Sir Swire Smith

This is an essay specifically about convergences and coincidences. It deals with them in relation to the town where I was born and to my own experiences in it. Local detail, as my colleague Professor Richard Cobb has shown superbly, can be as rewarding in itself as any generalisations derived from it. Yet there are two generalisations, in particular, in my essay which are related to generalisations made earlier in other essays in this volume. First, it is impossible to deal with the history of education adequately – a history that moves in fits and starts – without dealing with much else. Second, it would be unwise to consider contemporary and educational issues without looking at nineteenth-century educational issues. Little is being said today that is genuinely new either about access or purpose. Technology may change, as it did in the nineteenth century, but the arguments are old.

There is another aspect of the themes dealt with in this essay which should be singled out at the start. My themes relate to strands in school, in higher, in technical and in what we now call further education that have been touched upon but not dealt with fully in my other essays and lectures. Some of them were considered almost a generation ago in M. Argles's *South Kensington to Robbins: An Account of English Technical and Scientific Education since 1851* (1964), a book published in the aftermath of the Robbins Report. Yet neither educational development nor educational controversy since 1964 – nor for that matter political change – has disposed of fundamental uneasiness about a set of persisting English dispositions and structures that seem to hold back the country's economic progress.

Correlli Barnett has regularly drawn attention to them. D. S. L. Cardwell, whom I appointed to a post in the School of History at Leeds years ago, had already referred to them in his important book *The Organisation of Science in England*, which appeared as long ago as 1957. Michael Sanderson wrote an equally important and much quoted book *The Universities and British Industry, 1850–1970* in 1972, which raised many questions, and when G. W. Roderick and M. D. Stephens put their own question mark after the title of their book of readings, *Education and Industry in the Nineteenth Century: The English Disease*? Most of their readers would have felt that the disease had not disappeared in the twentieth century. Their own conclusion was that 'the roots of our problem are mainly to be found in the nineteenth century'. Unfortunately, the disease has almost begun to be taken for granted like the common cold. My essay, which is very personal, and which when it is not personal serves as a contribution to the history of Keighley, is, *malgré moi*, a national case study also.

When I was a boy at Keighley Boys' Grammar School, the names of two of the school houses were Brigg and Smith. There was no family connection between the Briggs and Briggses, though I was naturally placed in Brigg house. I got to know the surviving Brigg brothers, J. J. and W. A. – there had been two other Brigg children – when I was very young and when they seemed very old, and the fact that they were very old twins was not the least fascinating thing about them for me.

I was fascinated too, however, to learn how much both of them were interested in history, particularly local history; and on one memorable occasion, when I was a history undergraduate at Cambridge, I brought back a bundle of articles that they had written on Keighley's history after being entertained by them at their beautiful home, Kildwick Hall, built on a hillside above the River Aire between Keighley and Skipton. They had been at Cambridge, too, and this was another link; and before that they had been sent to Keighley Trade and Grammar School, as it was then called, before going to Giggleswick.

The Briggs and their ancestors, Liberal Nonconformists and mill owners, had played an important part in the development of Victorian Keighley, although the Brigg twins did not seem to know anything about textiles or for that matter about business. In retrospect, that seems significant. It did not seem so at the time. I and they were more interested in the fact that their father, Sir John Brigg, knighted in 1909, had been MP for Keighley from 1895 to 1911. His memory was still fresh in the town when I was a boy.

The Keighley of that time remained essentially a Victorian community, in its attitudes as much as in its appearance. There were few buildings that were out of character, except in the suburbs. My school was in the very centre of the town, housed in a building known locally as 'the Mechanics', an abbreviation of Mechanics' Institute. But the building contained more than classrooms, staircases, and corridors, the second and third of these its chief feature, at least for its daily inhabitants. There was a large 'Municipal Hall' inside it too, a place where lecturers from very different backgrounds addressed more or less the same local audience on a diversity of subjects, political and non-political, and where once every year a round of dances, known in Keighley as 'Cons', were arranged. 'Cons' was short for 'Conversazione'. Most local people did not know that. Nor did they know either just what the Mechanics' Institutes of the nineteenth century had meant to Yorkshire and to Lancashire towns – and to Keighley in particular.

The population of the town – and it was very much a town and not a village or a city – had risen from 5745 in 1801 to 18,258 in 1851, to 21,859 in 1861 and to 41,564 in 1901, and it was actually slightly less big (40,890) when I was a boy than it had been at the beginning of the century. There was already an active bus network, but most of the transport pattern was old. There was a canal just outside the town – the Leeds and Liverpool, begun in 1770 and completed in 1816 – and the town was situated on what had become in stages a main railway line from London to Scotland. It did not seem under threat. Nor did two separate railway links with Bradford and one with Leeds.

The first railway station, a very handsome station, less agreeably rebuilt in 1883, had been opened in 1847, and a new local railway line, the Worth Valley line to Haworth, now restored for railway enthusiasts, had come into use twenty years later. It was in full working order when I was at school, and boys came in to the Grammar School by rail from Haworth just as they came from Cowling on the other side of the town by bus. There was no doubt that these boys were villagers, not townsfolk, and they contributed much to the variety of the School. We all knew, wherever we lived, not only that Haworth was the home of the Brontës but that Cowling was the birth place of the national Labour leader, Philip Snowden.

It seemed quite a long way then from Keighley to Haworth or to Cowling – or for that matter to Kildwick. Indeed, distances in space seemed bigger when I was a boy than distances in time. Memories seemed to stretch back far: geographical horizons contracted. Now, Keighley is part of Bradford. That would have been unthinkable in 1939. It would have been unthinkable, too, that the name West Riding would lose its ancient significance, although Wakefield, its capital, seemed much further away from Keighley than Morecambe, the Lancashire holiday resort to which large numbers of Keighley people went at what was always called, with real echoes of the past, 'the Parish feast'.

The Parish Church by the time of my boyhood was certainly not the centre either of the social or of the spiritual life of the town, and its congregation was only one of many. Nonconformity was strong, and even the Church of England had a congregationalist quality about it.

Yet it was into the Parish Church that we used to file each year as schoolboys for 'Founders' Day services at which we were reminded how much we owed to an eighteenth-century Rector of Keighley, Miles Gale. I knew more about Gale when I was a boy and about Drake and Tonson, early benefactors whose names were then associated with the name of the Girls' Grammar School, than I did about Sir Swire Smith, the subject of this essay. The Girls' Grammar School was a separate, but for the boys a not totally isolated institution, which unfortunately for them – and I believe for the girls, though not for the headmistress – moved further away from the centre of the town during the 1930s.

A monument in the old Parish Church to Miles Gale, who had been born at Farnley Hall, near Leeds, and had been educated at Trinity College, Cambridge, described him as a man who for 'forty-one years lived a life of innocence and peace-making, bearing malice to no man, constant in exhortation'. A surviving pamphlet by Gale, kept in manuscript in the Parish Church, gives a somewhat different impression. Keighley Grammar School, he suggested, had been set up because 'the town of Kighley [sic], having no school, nor any encouragement for promoting humane learning', provided a centre for 'that vile set of Quakers, and . . . that wicked crew of the Anabaptists, to follow false ways of worship'.

Smith, as we shall see, would have agreed neither with such language nor with such sentiments. Nor would John Brigg. I am sad that I never talked to the Brigg twins about Smith, who, as this essay shows, deserves, even for topical reasons, to be remembered. Not all E. P. Thompson's forgotten people had working-class backgrounds. Smith was another of the local mill owners, most of whom, like him, had had little to do with the Parish Church, but much to do with the quality of life in a small Victorian community. The names of Brigg Sr and Smith were bracketed together as frequently in their own time as Drake and Tonson had been earlier and were to be later; and an examination of their achievements, far more varied than those of their bracketed predecessors, is a necessary task for a historian of Victorian England.

Long before Keighley became a parliamentary constituency in 1885, Smith, a life-long bachelor, had forecast that John Brigg, father of six, would be its MP. Long before then, they had joined together in many local causes, and in their later years they had moved beyond the town and its suburbs, now living not far apart – Brigg at Kildwick Hall, a beautiful old building, Smith at Steeton Manor. Despite its name, the latter was a new house that Smith himself had constructed and furnished stage by stage, like the railway. It had a parapet which recalled Haddon

Hall, one of England's oldest and most beautiful country houses in Derbyshire.

In both the Brigg and the Smith houses, the latter a bachelor residence, where Smith lived with his brother, 'plain mannered hospitality' was offered, and both owners were quick to instal that 'new fangled and debatable convenience', the telephone. Smith thought of his house in Biblical terms as being 'firm and sure', designed long to outlast him. 'Five hundred years from now perhaps it will be the only monument that I shall leave to posterity.'

Smith had been born in 1842 in a very different house in central Keighley called Wagon Fold. A general move outwards of Keighley mill owners came later, for the Brigg family too had lived within Keighley or in what were then its nearby suburbs at Guard House. Like other mill owners who produced large quantities of smoke, they soon wanted to get away from it. Was this a 'problem', like the Brigg twins' lack of interest in textiles? I was certainly interested myself in how the Briggs had made their money when I went out to see them at Kildwick, but they never talked about it.

It was much later that I learned, not from them, that Smith had been a central figure in the effort to improve technical education in the nineteenth century, serving on the Royal Commission on Technical Education in 1881 which led to the passing eight years later of the first Technical Education Act. That is his real monument.

There was irony, however, in the fact that State money to develop technical education came not only from a local authorities' penny rate, allowed for in the 1889 Act, but from national customs and excise duties, allowed for in an act passed a year later in 1890, the Local Taxation (Customs and Excise) Act. This was known as 'whisky money', and Smith was a life-long teetotaller, as were many of the leading inhabitants of Keighley.

Later still, Smith, 'pressed by friends and neighbours', was to become MP for the town in 1915, having refused previous invitations to stand. He was then 73 years old, and he had turned down invitations for Skipton also. He was by then well past his prime – and he knew it – but after he became an MP he quickly took to Westminster, so that it could be said of him that 'he never appeared more happy than when entertaining friends in the tea-room or the terrace, or on a more liberal scale in the dining room', entertaining presumably without alcohol.

Much else was said of Smith when he died in 1918. His obituary in the *Keighley News* described his career as 'strenuous', while that in the *Yorkshire Post*, a newspaper which did not share his politics, was sub-titled 'Pioneer of Education'. It ended by noting that the President of the Keighley Conservative Association, another mill owner, James

Ellison Haggas, had stated that the news of Smith's death had been received 'with a feeling almost of consternation in the town, and disquiet, as he had been taken away almost without warning'.

Smith's interest in education, technical and general, remains pertinent because a century later we are still trying to do – with far more than 'whisky money' – what he set out to do – and we are not being very successful in the job. The language of contemporary debate would not have surprised him, but he would have been shocked to discover how little real progress we have made. The term 'contemporary' would have bothered him, too, for it was as long ago as the end of the Second World War that the Percy Report reiterated exactly what he had said at the end of the First World War. 'The position of Great Britain as a leading industrial nation is being endangered by failure to secure the fullest possible application of science to industry and this failure is partly due to deficiencies in education.' *Plus ça change.*

Smith's own interest in education went back far. He is said to have discussed the subject of art education and of technical education for the first time with Samuel Smiles, a point that appealed to me greatly when I first began to be interested in Smiles in the late 1940s. My own personal connection with Smiles, however, had to do with Leeds, not with Keighley. My father's parents had been born in Leeds and had attended the school where Smiles had addressed his first mutual improvement classes on Self Help. That was a coincidence. I had already started to study Smiles before I found it out.

In some ways, Keighley in Smiles's time and in the years of my own boyhood had a closer association with Leeds than with Bradford, and Smith was particularly proud to be involved in the affairs of Leeds University even before it acquired full university status in 1903–4. The honorary doctorate in law, given him in 1914, meant as much to him as his knighthood. He was proud, too, when in the same year he was made Warden of the Worshipful Company of Clothworkers, which he had joined as a Liveryman in 1886. The Clothworkers' Company provided another link with Leeds, for the Company had made substantial benefactions to Leeds education, the first of them in 1874, the foundation year of what was then called the Yorkshire College of Science. The company also gave money to Keighley Technical School, a Smith venture nearer home.

After his death, there was another Smith link with Leeds. Memorial funds were collected from friends and admirers to endow a Smith Fellowship to the University. All this I came to know when I was made a Professor at Leeds in 1955. The Clothworkers' Company were still benefactors. We hear much today of the need for universities to raise private funds. *Déjà vu*. One of the first little books presented to me by Sir Charles Morris, the Vice-Chancellor of Leeds, when I became a Professor was called *The Private Donor in the History of the University of Leeds*.

If all this sounds exclusively local – and personal – Smith himself would have been at pains to point out that neither his interests nor his achievements were restricted by locality or by temperament. He became interested in technical education, as the National Institute of Economic and Social Research has done in recent years, because he felt that Britain was falling behind its competitors, particularly Germany. He was farsighted in appreciating this long before we had actually fallen far behind and long before the number of our competitors had greatly increased. Japan never figured in his vistas.

It had been the Paris Exhibition of 1867 that for Smith and others, like Jacob Behrens in Bradford, had seemed to prove a growing Victorian inadequacy. In the words of his friend Lyon (later Lord) Playfair, a great man about whom I have written elsewhere, particularly in *Victorian People* and *Victorian Things*, 'a singular accordance of opinion prevailed that our country had shown little progress in the peaceful arts of industry' since the Great Exhibition of 1851, when we, at least, proudly proclaimed ourselves 'the workshop of the world'.

Ironically, before 1851, it was the Germans who had argued that 'we are obliged to make up for our lack of money and limited experience by means of intellectual power and scientific insight'. Within only a few years after 1851, however, we in Britain were beginning to say the same – in the same language. The architect of the Education Act of 1870, W. E. Forster, MP for Bradford, said it explicitly, but more with reference to primary than to secondary or what we would now call further education.

On the eve of his Education Act, which dealt only with primary education, the educational statistics of secondary and further education were depressing, as they still are, despite exciting ventures in further education, at present the most interesting educational sector in the country. In 1867, there were only 10,230 pupils studying science in the 212 'schools' – some of them were no more than classes – on the list of the Department of Science and Art in South Kensington, itself a recent by-product of the Great Exhibition – and of these pupils only four-fifths actually took an examination.

Small German cities were spending more on scientific and technical education than Britain. Smith was shocked by this, and a few years later in 1873 wrote a pamphlet on international 'Educational Comparisons'. We would now talk more congenially, but also more anxiously, of a league table.

If there had been no complex of institutions in South Kensington in 1867, the situation would have been even worse. The extraordinary complex there, by no means solely educational in a narrow sense, was dominated by Sir Henry Cole, an even more remarkable man than Playfair, and he, too, figures prominently both in *Victorian People* and in *Victorian Things*. There were other great characters in the South Kensington story, too, notably the scientist T. H. Huxley, 'Darwin's bulldog', who between 1862 and 1884 served on no fewer than ten royal commissions, but even Huxley could never outshine Cole, Secretary of the Department of Science and Art, who is commemorated both in the Albert Hall and in the Victoria and Albert Museum, neither of which would have existed without him.

Smith knew Cole too, but his vision, like his experience, was not the same. Nor was it the same as Huxley's. He first learnt about what was going on in German education from Blue Books, although there were rumours that he had studied at Stuttgart. And if Germany always figured most prominently, by way of comparison, in his dreams of a more efficient system of education in Britain, it was Italy that figured most prominently in his imagination, as it did in the imaginations of many of his fellow-countrymen. To consider Germany without also considering Italy would be to misread the Victorian mental map. The fact that neither country was united until late in the century was registered clearly in 'real' maps in Victorian atlases.

When he was young, Ben Brigg, the Brigg twins' uncle, was Smith's closest friend, and the two of them travelled to Italy together to find out what it was like for themselves, almost as if they were going on a Grand Tour. Like the young Richard Cobden, they were dazzled by Italian 'romance', and when in the late-1860s they were both involved in the building of a new Mechanics' Institute in Keighley, the 'Mechanics' that I knew, they both pressed hard for the tower in the building to bear 'some resemblance to the tower of the Palazzo Vecchio at Florence'.

John Ruskin, who hated Cole, was read avidly by Smith, who took everything that he wrote seriously – if critically. Yet when he travelled abroad, Smith looked beyond Ruskin's vistas just as when he read Huxley he looked beyond his verbal vistas too. The United States interested Smith even more than Europe, and it was what was new there, not what was old, that concerned him most. In particular, he tried to understand what was the secret of *its* economic growth. Was it due, he asked, to its keen interest in education?

Smith approved, also, of the American social system. Was it that which was responsible? 'In America factory girls are described as "factory ladies" – and why not? I have watched them leave wearing veils and gloves with a long line of tram cars drawn up at the gates to take them to their homes.' Our social systems still diverge, not converge, despite changes in fashion that have made veils and gloves as obsolete as steam locomotives.

There was nothing parochial, therefore, about Smith's attitudes or judgements, a fact about him that did not endear him to all Keighlians, particularly those who were nervous and suspicious even about those 'off com'd uns' who came from no further away than Bingley or Skipton. I remember many of these myself in the 1930s long before real 'off com'd uns' transformed Keighley life. None the less, it should be noted at once that there were many Keighlians then, as since, who themselves wanted to think and, not least, to dream in the same non-parochial terms as Smith did. They had a universal hope, the kind of hope that is always necessary to save us from narrowness, at times from despair. In the mid-nineteenth century it was the main local newspaper, the *Keighley News*, founded in 1862, which chose to put the universal claims of art as eloquently as the local claims of industry, stating in 1865 that 'we want to see a large muster of persons desirous of cultivating art, not for the market but for itself.'

In its very first year, the *Keighley News* had reported a local speech by James Ford, which had also placed the case for art education in a completely non-utilitarian frame: the 'manufacturing importance of the question' was overshadowed by 'the moral':

> Truly it [art] has an elevating and ennobling influence; it clears the fog from the imagination, awakens the fancy, discloses beauty in the commonest objects, affords homely amusements, induces a study of nature, the inspirer of true and beautiful thoughts, the source of appreciation and insight into the great and glorious works of the Creator. Therefore, he who cultivates it will be a better workman, a better artist, a better member of society and a better man.

The *Keighley News* also reported a speaker at the School of Art prizegiving in 1866 who told his audience that 'it was necessary to educate the eye until it should not only be a *measurer* of degree in colour, of distance and of form, but also a *connoisseur* of the harmonies in figure and colour'.

Keighley was to provide a Principal of the Royal College of Art in London in 1900 – Augustus Spencer, the son of a blacksmith who had worked as a half-timer in Smith's mill. Smith had caught him painting butterflies and had offered to pay his fees at the Keighley School of Art. He was a good pupil, and he went on to become a good teacher, being appointed in 1885 to the headship of the School of

Art at Coalbrookdale, at the cradle of England's industrial revolution. From there he moved three years later to the headship of the Leicester School of Art before becoming Principal of the RCA.

It is revealing that Spencer came from a family of musicians. The arts interconnected at the earliest stage of his life. And so they could do – and did – in the community too. It is noteworthy that the first Freeman of the Borough of Keighley after its incorporation in 1881 was a musician, John Tiplady Carrodus. Keighley Choral Society had been founded in 1837, the year Queen Victoria came to the throne. Marriner's Brass Band followed seven years later, 'formed for mutual amusement and instruction in music'. There was always music in the town.

Smith, who was interested in music, became Secretary of a new Art Classes Committee in Keighley in 1867, the year of the disturbing Paris Exhibition. Unlike James Ford, he would never have claimed any special insight into the mind of the Creator. Rather he believed that the teaching of art was fundamental for utilitarian as well as for aesthetic reasons. Moreover, he was just as interested in the general evening classes that were being given in the old Mechanics' Institute building as he was in the art classes, and his firm paid half the fees of any workers who cared to attend them. Since 1859 the Department of Science and Art had made possible co-operation with those Mechanics' Institutes, like Keighley, which remained active and innovative.

The lessons learnt by the students there were not confined to reading and arithmetic, and at their prize days, great events in the local year, the speakers that students heard could be just as eloquent as Ford:

> Man should understand that he has a value not as belonging to a community, and working for a good which is distinct from himself; but on his own account. He is not a mere part of a machine. In a machine the separate parts are useless but as conducting to the end of the whole, for which alone they subsist. But it is not so with man. He is not simply a means, but an end that exists for his own sake.

Given all the restraints of the messy and rough local urban environment in Keighley – and given what could be the cramping limitations of local society – this plea for education as a means to the liberation of the individual as well as a means to his self-advancement stands out. Nor was it just rhetoric. In a period, like our own, when the language of education is either threadbare or thick with jargon, it is easy to dismiss as rhetoric sentiments that really mattered not only to the people who heard them uttered but to those who uttered them.

Smith himself was inspired by such talk just as he was when he went into discussion classes in the Mechanics' Institute and heard the members

debating characteristic if not to us immediately captivating social
subjects like 'The Practicability of a Permissive Bill', 'The Utilisation
of Sewage' and 'The Relations of Capital and Labour', three subjects
which he once mentioned specifically. He was inspired, too, when he
met 'eager students of all ages and social ranks, from the Justice of the
Peace and the manufacturer down to the mill operative'. Only the
words 'down to' revealed his social position.

Given that social position, however, his relationship to the changing
society that produced him requires fuller examination. So, too, does
his own approach to education, which was by no means unique. The
millowner, Edward Marriner, a Churchman, who was to become
Mayor of Keighley in 1885 and who had different views on many
subjects, fully shared it. It is clear, none the less, that however many
Keighlians felt like Smith about education, he was in some respects in
a minority. Although a teetotaller in a town where teetotal groups were
strong – as they were in my own boyhood – and although by up-
bringing a Nonconformist in a town where nonconformity was proud
and confident – and it remained so during the 1930s – Smith was
tolerant of 'drinkers' and sufficiently uneasy about the power of the
'dissidence of dissent' that he could once tell a local Nonconformist
minister that he did not think 'that God will shut out the Catholic,
Unitarian or, if you like, Mohammedan any more than the most
evangelical Churchman or the most devout follower of John Wesley'.
On another occasion he wrote, 'I cannot get up any enthusiasm for the
YMCA. In a town like ours it tends to withdraw young men from
educational agencies of far greater value to them.'

Educational agencies were for Smith instruments of refinement as
well as of liberation, for he was less disturbed by the ugliness and
dirtiness of smoky mid-Victorian Keighley – as late as 1900 in the
central place now called the Town Hall Square there was a Corporation rubbish dump – than by the 'rough' and deliberately aggressive
attitudes of some of Keighley's most popular and thoroughly uneducated 'characters'. Meanwhile, however, the majority in the town
seems to have revelled in that particular side of its life, associating it
with 'independence' and 'spirit'.

When I was a boy, there were still many stories in circulation of men
like 'Pie Leech', who made a celebrated speech in the thickest dialect
proposing Keighley's incorporation, 'Professor Hanson', the Barber,
Bill o'th' Hoylus, a local poet, or William Sharp, 'Old Threelaps', who
spent forty-nine years of his life in bed. The town made the most of
eccentricity. So, too, did Haworth or Cowling, as Mrs Gaskell and
Keir Hardie appreciated.

One local character described by Smith's only biographer, Keighley

Snowdon, was, in his own words, an 'old savage' who boasted that he had only one bath in his life. 'He looked it', Snowdon added, but he added also that Keighley backed him in a ten-year fight against public baths which ended in 1876 soon after local educational issues had been settled in what with hindsight seems to have been a rare municipal convergence. Earlier in the century, it had been Turkish baths, not English baths or swimming baths, that had appealed to a significant fraction of the local population, but that was because they figured prominently as an item on the national platform of the radical David Urquhart, who was at least as eccentric as any one ever born in Keighley.

It was Urquhart's view that workingmen must learn for themselves and fend for themselves, and he encouraged his disciples to treat education as a means neither to refinement nor to liberation but to power. All this was reasonable enough, but from that point onwards what we would now call 'paranoia' set in. What needs to be explained is that there is no evidence that Urquhart's Keighley supporters, meeting in his new Turkish Bath in the market, thought that their hero was suffering from anything. Urquhart's voluminous papers are housed in Balliol College library, and I and my wife have worked on them there. You move oddly in them from Mazzini and Marx to Keighley and Bingley, but in the process you learn an immense amount about Victorian England, including popular attitudes to education. Technical education was never deemed to be enough.

Smith must have read the extraordinary 'Chronicles of Keighley', which appeared in the *Keighley News* in 1869 and were subsequently reprinted in pamphlet form. Written in Biblical language, they poured scorn on a wide range of local inhabitants. Their author, granted the licence of a clown to satirise the Bible, obviously remained anonymous. Smith himself was not spared from scurrilous abuse in other publications. In particular, the fact that he never married was made into a point in verses written by his opponents in the local debates about education:

> Dandy Swire went o'er the sea,
> Right away to Germany:
> 'Sure I'm travelled now', quoth he –
> And he was, was Dandy.

> Back he came; chokeful was he
> With a brand-new bright idee.
> 'Now I'll make a noise', said he
> So he did, the Dandy . . .

> Give it up, we don't agree;
> Get a wife to play with thee –
> Or else go live in Germanee,
> Pretty Swire, the Dandy.

SERIOUS PURSUITS

Another fact about Smith – that he liked to sing Victorian ballads – must have given extra point to these chauvinistic verses. His local nickname in 1873 was 'Dandycock'. Snowdon called him 'gay', not realising what the adjective would come to imply.

In advocating educational advance Smith had to take account not only of rough humour but of rough ways, for along with the small bunch of local 'characters' in Keighley who diverted the townsfolk there was also a much larger and at times dangerous 'idle riff-raff in the streets' who alarmed them. It is noteworthy that the Keighley's stocks, located on the site of the old Market Cross, known simply in the nineteenth century as The Cross, did not disappear until 1868. The scale of local prostitution was alarming also. Because of its place on the map the town was described as a 'grand depot' for prostitutes, beggars and criminals.

Whatever may be said about the relationship between crime and poverty, there was no doubt in Keighley that the two coexisted. Ironically, however, it was not the poor but the Guardians of the Poor who drew attention to Keighley's place on the national map in 1874 in a sequence that must have embarrassed Smith. It is not likely that he can have had much sympathy with the eight Keighley Guardians of the Poor who in 1874, a year after local citizens had decided to reject the idea of a School Board, refused to implement a law of 1871 requiring compulsory vaccination. This the Guardians described simply as 'poisoning the blood of children', and they refused to appoint mandatory Vaccination Officers. Fortified by dubious statistics – as well as by local 'public opinion' – they enjoyed the support of a national Anti-Compulsory Vaccination League and a weekly penny periodical, *The Anti-Vaccinator*.

In 1876, seven of the protesters, who had been elected to the Board of Guardians on an anti-vaccination ticket, were to be arrested and taken first to the local Devonshire Hotel, 'the Devonshire' – note the name – and, later, after a day's delay, to York Castle. There had been a serious skirmish in the town the day before, when a rowdy crowd, estimated at 3000 people, unyoked the horses from the High Sheriff's coach that was carrying the prisoners and the men who had come to arrest them; and there was a huge demonstration when the prisoners returned to the town, after being released on bail, to the accompaniment of a brass band which played 'Home Again' with 'great warmth of feeling'. As far away as Cheltenham, another centre of resistance to compulsory vaccination, there were messages of support for 'the Noble Seven of Keighley' and attacks on 'the deaf adder which stoppeth its ears in Downing Street'.

The Keighley protest, which reveals much about what French

historians call *mentalités*, had no long-term results, although years later, in 1962, the *Keighley News* was to praise the Keighley seven for their 'courage in the cause of freedom', claiming that 'such men, and women too, are still needed in Britain if the word 'democracy' is to mean true liberty for the people'. I was not greatly impressed by this comment any more than I was impressed by Urquhart's attacks on the Public Health Act of 1848. Turkish baths for him were fine: drains seemed unnecessary.

In the same centenary supplement of the *Keighley News*, the local newspaper that has survived, I wrote by invitation the lead article 'Looking Back Now, but Preparing for a New Future'. There was no nostalgia in this piece, for I felt and still feel no nostalgia in looking back to the years of my own childhood. I have long since ceased to have any connection with the *Keighley News* or with the *Yorkshire Post* for which I used regularly to write reviews. None the less, I still believe, as I pointed out in the article, that twentieth-century developments, irrespective of the large-scale Asian immigration since the time that I wrote the article, have made Keighley lose 'much of its social compactness and something of its distinctiveness'.

The American historian of cities, Lewis Mumford, had written in his *Culture of Cities* (1938) of the 'insensate nineteenth-century community' on both sides of the Channel and on both sides of the Atlantic. I considered that nonsense when I first read Mumford as an undergraduate on vacation in Keighley, and I have gone on saying so ever since. Whatever else Keighley's Victorians were, they were not 'insensate'. I had written in 1948, fourteen years before I wrote the article and long before I published *Victorian Cities* in 1964, that it was rather the men and women of the twentieth century, who in my view had

> nationalised many things besides railways and fuel. The grey stone which made early industrial Keighley fit into its natural environment has given way to universal brick which might be used anywhere. Many of the great nineteenth-century institutions which won so much loyalty have become extinct or have been threatened. Other institutions have been transformed out of all recognition. They bear the same names but they have changed their functions and even their essence.

That was as near as I could get to the philosophy of the editor of the *Keighley News* in 1962.

The *Keighley News* had had local rivals, notably the nineteenth-century local Conservative paper, the *Keighley Herald*, founded in 1873, which had much to say about education – on the opposite side to Smith – but it disappeared in 1911. Paradoxically – and this has always seemed to me characteristically Keighlian – it had been founded by

Duncan Campbell, a Scottish schoolmaster, who had been brought to Keighley by William Byles, the Liberal owner of the *Bradford Observer*, to become first editor of the *Keighley News*. One of my favourite novelists, Vonnegut, could have devised no better twist.

Byles was a friend of Sir Titus Salt, who built the model town of Saltaire between Bradford and Keighley, and his career spanned Bradford history from Chartism to the beginning of the Independent Labour Party. Moreover, it was one of his many descendants – he had eleven children – who first showed Smith the geography of the House of Commons when he was elected Keighley's MP. Campbell's life followed a very different course. Having abandoned the Liberals for the Conservatives long before the Home Rule split of 1886, he was to die not in Keighley, but in Inverness. Scottish connections, to which I have referred frequently in this book, remained real.

What was said in the *Keighley Herald*, not least in its active and for the historian highly significant correspondence columns, cannot have pleased Smith any more than the scurrilous verses that were written about him. Yet whatever reservations he may have had about elements in the community in which he lived, he belonged unequivocally both to the town and to the north of England. He was proud to claim that his ancestors had fought at Flodden – a very different Scottish connection – and proud too that he was made a Freeman of the borough. On one occasion, when the President of Manchester Technical Society sent him a pamphlet which noted *en passant* that the Northrop loom was the one great invention of the century that was American, Smith replied that Northrop was a Keighley man who still worked with the drawing board, T-square and box of compasses that he had given him when he was a 'night scholar of the Keighley Mechanics' Institute'.

The success of Keighley men always gave Smith great pleasure wherever they were, and he liked to quote T. H. Huxley to back him up. After Dean Huxley had seen more students from Keighley occupying benches in the College of Science at South Kensington than had come from any other town or city in the kingdom, he is reported to have asked the haunting question 'Where is this Keighley?'

I was brought up myself on the memory of that quotation in Keighley Boys' Grammar School, where I learned too of some of the men of the Keighley nineteenth and twentieth century who through education had made their way outside and 'upwards', men like W. H. Watkinson, a Whitworth Scholar, who became a Professor of Engineering of Anderson College in Glasgow, and later a Professor at Liverpool University, Alfred Fowler, and Herbert Butterfield, the last of them a historian. Some successes had been half-timers at elementary school: Butterfield was the son of a mill cashier.

In all that we learned about such men at school we were offered a curious blend of competition and co-operation. We were taught in Smilesian fashion to admire both the drive with which they competed and the work that they did for others. There was also a great stress in school on the continuities of the community in which we were 'reared'. I recall vividly that in 1932, the year of the celebration of the jubilee of Keighley's incorporation my school contributed two *tableaux* to the gala ceremonies – one showing the laying of the foundation stone of the school, the other Sir Richard de Kighley setting out for Agincourt with five men-at-arms and fifty archers. It is only years later and in the light of what has happened since that I note the presence in the brochure, which I still possess, of another tableau, appropriately by the School of Arts and Crafts, that depicted the Keighley squire, the inn-keeper, the blacksmith, the carpenter, the tailor and 'various serfs' paying Richard II's first poll tax – paying it, not refusing it.

Thanks to Smith, as we shall see, Keighley Boys' Grammar School had been called Keighley Trade and Grammar School between 1870 and 1928, and the name still stuck, as did its shorter name 'the Trade School' when I first moved from Eastwood School, now closed, to join it three years later on a Drake and Tonson scholarship. By 1931, however, the school had acquired a new headmaster, W. N. Palmer, a committed Quaker, who was determined, as was his more formidable successor, Neville Hind, one of Nature's Benthamites and, in retrospect, a great headmaster, to preside over a traditional grammar school.

A large section of the local past was now blotted out, even though Hind was a Cambridge historian who encouraged me – the verb is far from strong enough – to follow him to Sidney Sussex College. And whatever I learnt at Cambridge in a college where I was very happy, I learned nothing of that lost history either. I never wrote an essay on English history that covered the period after the passing of the Great Reform Bill of 1832.

The previous headmaster of Keighley Trade and Grammar School, T. P. Watson, had known Smith, and had succeeded in changing times, including years of war, in perpetuating the nineteenth-century tradition that led back to the opening of the new Mechanics' Institute and the Trade and Grammar School in 1870. And he must have conveyed some sense of the tradition to his pupils, for one of the most distinguished of them, Butterfield, who never wrote a line about industry or trade, always stated with unusual consistency that he had been educated at 'the Trade School'. Perhaps that is why he concentrated in his fascinating Cambridge lectures, which I loved to listen to, not on the nineteenth century but on the sixteenth.

As we seek to recover lost Keighley history, we find that while there is an immense amount to be discovered in old newspapers – and as a historian it is essential to immerse oneself in these – there is only one biography of Smith. *The Master Spinner* was written by a Keighley journalist, son of a shopkeeper, James Snowdon, who used the *nom de plume* of Keighley Snowdon. It was published in 1921, the year I was born, only three years after Smith's death. Snowdon was eighteen years younger than Smith and had been a young reporter when Smith first became active in Keighley politics. He also wrote several novels, one of which was called *The Web of an Old Weaver*.

The Master Spinner is an extraordinary book, designed to distil every ounce of romance from Smith's long life rather than critically to evaluate his achievements, and since there is far less about wool spinning in it than there is about education, politics or 'leisure', the title is profoundly misleading. There are a few revealing passages about business, but it is certainly not a book for economic historians. It should not be put on the same shelf as Samuel Smiles.

In retrospect, however, it is particularly informative as a record just because it is not such a book. Smith was a small employer in a small town, the fortunes of which depended on the textiles industry, but it is not because of his business achievements but because of his interest in education that his name will always survive. As far as local business was concerned, it was his cousin, possessed of the unforgettable name of Prince Smith, who was the really big employer in the town. A manufacturer not of textiles but of textile machinery, Prince Smith, like Swire Smith, had been educated – briefly – at Wesley College, Sheffield, but if there had been a Trade and Grammar School in Keighley when they were boys, both would almost certainly have been sent there. Very few boys in Keighley went to public schools.

The great Prince Smith works, the Burlington Sheds, lay near the heart of Keighley, alongside the main railway line and behind what became its leading shopping street, Cavendish Street. Known simply in my childhood as 'The Shed' – or Prince Smith's – the firm had its origins as far back as 1795, and nearly a hundred years later in 1879 it was to be described by John Hodgson in his invaluable study of Keighley's industrial history as 'unrivalled throughout England and the whole world': more than 700 people were then employed there.

During the 1920s and 1930s, time in Keighley was dictated by the sound of Prince Smith's siren or hooter, as I knew well when I was rushing back to school, complete with school bag, after all too short a lunch-time break at home. Short though it was, most workers in the Prince Smith plant would sit by the roadside, ready to go in long before the siren sounded. Most workers were men, whereas women predominated in the mills, and not far from The Sheds were Keighley's most handsome mills, the Dalton Mills – the name Dalton had all the right associations – the owner of which had arranged in 1872 that the functional mill chimney should be encircled by an impressive great tower, 'rising nearly as high as the chimney itself'. 'Distant views' of the town could then be obtained at every level.

The Dalton Mills tower was even bigger than the tower of the Mechanics' Institute, and from it you could see out to the River Worth and the moors beyond. There was much in the foreground that was ugly and confused, not least the River Worth, but in the background, yet still within walking distance, there was 'Nature'. The urban squalor of much of Victorian Keighley must be assessed within this geographical context – mills and moors. I was brought up myself to take long walks out of the town, and you could then quickly get out of it; and it was on such walks with one of my school friends, Leo White, that I first discussed the themes of this essay. We knew the countryside for miles around and could see places where the nineteenth-century industrial frontier had already receded.

Within the town we knew every mill, although we knew few mill owners. Looking back, I appreciate profoundly how by comparison with Prince Smith and his son, also called Prince Smith, or with J. H. Craven, the owner of Dalton Mills, or with the Marriners of Greengate and Hope Mills, Swire Smith was only a small businessman. Nor did he have agricultural interests in the East Riding of Yorkshire as the Prince Smiths did. Yet he got his knighthood thirteen years before Prince Smith got his baronetcy, and he was on closer terms than Prince Smith was with the aristocratic Devonshire family that played an important part both in his own life and in the life of the town. When he became MP for Keighley, one of the first people to express pleasure at his move to Westminster was Lady Frederick Cavendish, who wrote to him 'one word of warm congratulations to you and Keighley – so married to each other that it is indeed a happiness for both parties'.

I have already mentioned the Devonshire Hotel. There was also a Devonshire Street in Keighley, climbing out above the centre of the town, with the biggest local Congregationalist Chapel in it, a chapel attended by a faithful congregation that was far more socially influential than that of the Parish Church. Its foundation stone had been laid by a Brigg in 1855. There was also the 'Cock Church', a Methodist Church with a handsome slim spire and a weathercock on the top. Methodists of different hues came second in the social league table of local nonconformity, with some Methodists still on good terms with the Parish Church. Higher up Devonshire Street, however, there were Christadelphians, and in the next street there were Baptists, if not Anabaptists. There was also a small Quaker community which never proselytised. As a boy I knew all the chapels and churches as well as all the mills. Religion was a guiding influence.

Not far away from all the great chapels was another Devonshire landmark, Devonshire Park, opened in 1887 on nine acres of land given by the seventh Duke of Devonshire. It was situated on what was then the fashionable side of the town, and nearby was Prince Smith's Keighley home. For the Queen's Jubilee of that year 20,000 towns-folk gathered in the park, with Sunday School scholars and teachers prominent amongst them. There had been a problem, however. The town had now been incorporated – in 1882 – and because the Council had decided on Devonshire Park being where it was and not in a different part of the town – the Duke had allowed a choice – there were complaints that the Council had acted 'without consulting the rate-payers'. The result, again ironically, was fortunate. With surprising speed a new park was approved on the rejected site five years later. Near though 'Nature' was, urban parks were necessary.

The reason why there was a Devonshire interest in Keighley went back to the sixteenth century, when the Kighleys, mediaeval lords of the local manor, including the one who marched to Agincourt, had married into the Cavendish family. The marriage was duly registered in the new borough's coat of arms in 1882: it incorporated both the Kighley and the Cavendish arms and crests. The motto, however, was strictly Keighlian, 'By Worth', a pun based on the presence of the River Worth, which joined with the River Aire nearby. There were trout in the Worth in the sixteenth century, even in the eighteenth, but in the middle years of the nineteenth century the local Board of Health observed that an accumulation of rubbish had raised the level of its bed by four or five feet over thirty-five years. When I was a boy, the Aire was appallingly polluted each day by chemicals from a dyeworks.

David Cannadine has outlined both the reasons for and the effects of the Devonshire influence in the nineteenth-century – in towns as much as in countryside. It could, in fact, blur distinctions between the urban and the rural, and the *bourgeois*, a term that I never use in relation to Keighley – or England – and the aristocratic. Yet such distinctions were not the only social distinctions that mattered locally. Outside the Devonshire interest, but equally outside the control of the mill owners, was a flourishing local labour movement, the origins of which lay not in wealth but in poverty. 'Insubordination' and suffering went together, as the local Improvement Commissioners, not always the most sensitive of judges, had noted in 1843: 'this time twelve months', they recorded, the 'labouring population' had been 'aroused to acts of open insubordination' as a result of 'a keen sense of suffering'.

Organisation, difficult though it was both to establish and to maintain through bad and good years, grew out of insubordination. A militant Society of Woolworkers had been formed in Keighley as early as 1812, and by the middle years of the century both working-class unions and friendly societies – the latter in particular – had established a strong local presence. There were important new developments to follow in the last decade of the century, when the idea of a working-class party took shape. The Independent Labour Party – Snowden's party – then became a strong local force also, polling over 3000 votes at the general election of 1906, and in 1922 Keighley was to return its first Labour MP, another Smith, this time an outsider, Hastings Bernard Lees-Smith. The defeated Liberal candidate was one of the Brigg twins – W. A.

A late-Victorian Labour Church survived into my own boyhood, with prayers that took for granted an equality that did not exist in the homes or streets of the town. Nor did it even on community occasions. Keighley Agricultural Show, which began with a pig competition in 1842, had separate sections for 'gentlemen', 'farmers' and 'labouring men'. Victoria Park was a less socially desirable park than Devonshire Park, because it was in a working-class area.

Nearby was Lawkholme Lane, which by the time of my own child-hood had become the name of the ground of the local Rugby League football team, supported in large measure by working-class people. Indeed, social divisions in Keighley were clearly reflected in rugby. The local Rugby Union team was called 'the Keighlians', and it was rugby union football that was taught and played in Keighley Boys' Grammar School. The tough gym instructor of my early childhood, whom I got to like as a 'character', objected to my even watching Rugby League matches, although this did not stop me from going to watch thirteen Keighley Rugby League heroes play at Wembley in 1937. This was the only time they ever got there. Some of the best of them came from Wales.

There were community occasions then and earlier that had a gen-uine working-class flavour. For example, it was working-class people, through their friendly societies, who made the most of the great processions held on annual 'Gala Days' – the first of them in 1871 – to raise funds for the local Cottage Hospital (later called Victoria Hospital) which had been opened a year earlier. The processions ended in Victoria Park, where there was a fun fair, too, and what came to be called 'sports'. It was the Mayor, not the Duke of Devonshire, who graced such occasions, and the first Mayor of the town was a Brigg, Benjamin Septimus, who held office from 1882 to 1883.

There were other social features of Keighley which have not been much commented upon by the few historians of the town. Both mill owners and industrial workers were far more important as social groups in Keighley than professional men, who played an important part in non-industrial towns. Indeed, the professional presence in Keighley was absurdly small by national standards, even if one doctor, Smith's friend, John Milligan, Medical Officer of Health to the Keighley Local Board, was outstanding both locally and nationally. A writer as well as a doctor and a satirist as well as a poet – there were rumours that he had written *The Chronicles of Keighley* – he also had the distinction of rescuing Keighley's old Market Cross from a scrapyard and erecting it in his own garden at Whinburn.

Milligan died in 1876. Five years earlier, at the time of the 1871 decennial Census, there were only six lawyers in the town, five school-masters, and seven doctors. The comparative figures for Halifax, a bigger and more imposing place, but not dissimilar in its economic structure, were 25, 26 and 25. Forty years later, when I was born, the conveniently timed decennial Census of 1921 revealed that the Keighley numbers had risen to 15, 44 and 16, a sign that 'the march of education' had continued. Indeed, I was aware of the professional presence in a way that my mother's father, who moved to Keighley from a moorland farm, never would have been.

One lawyer, whom I got to know well, Harry Wall, disliked local nonconformity and all that it stood for – particularly, perhaps, tem-perance. He was the kind of influence that was largely missing in the nineteenth century. There were, however, two nineteenth-century doctors – George Beck and John Mitchell – who had supported the idea of a Mechanics' Institute in 1825 – and Mitchell was to lecture to its members on 'respiration'. The subject had local as well as universal reference.

There was one remaining – and neglected – occupational feature of the town. No members of the Armed Forces registered their names in Keighley in 1871, and only two did in 1921. That, however, did not stop local volunteers, among them a Marriner, from rallying to join the Aireworth Rifle Corps in 1860 or large numbers of Keighley men from being killed in the First World War. Indeed, the War Memorial in a new Town Hall Square, erected in 1924 and placed in the very centre of the town, opposite the Mechanics' Institute, has become the great local landmark. My earliest childhood memory is of watching the opening ceremony from my father's shoulders. I have learnt since that 25,000 people were present on that occasion.

I do not know who then appeared on the platform, but I feel that the Devonshires were not far away. And other towns, where they were even more prominent than they were in Keighley, included Barrow-in-Furness, where my father was born, and Eastbourne, later to become very much part of my own Sussex University bailiwick. There are co-incidences there too. It was Edward Johnson, 'a Sussex man' – and he was described simply as such at the time – who wrote and illuminated a Borough Roll Call of Honour in memory of the 900 Keighley men who were killed in the First World War. Years later, when I was Vice-Chancellor of the University of Sussex, Dennis Skinner, whom I had never met, once asked me to take the Chair for a debate between him and the then Duke of Devonshire in Eastbourne. I said no, for I had other more pressing debates to attend to, and as far as I know, the Skinner/Devonshire debate never took place.

In Keighley itself, the Devonshire influence was prominent enough in the nineteenth century, beginning with the hereditary right to present to the Rectory of Keighley. But the influence extended from the traditional past to the active present. Thus, the new Mechanics' Institute, of which Smith and Brigg were so proud, was opened by the seventh Duke of Devonshire, whose educational qualifications, at least, seemed impeccable, if at a different level from that of the local inhabitants. He also opened new Owen's College buildings in Manchester in 1873. Had he not been a Duke, it was said of him, he would have been a worthy Professor of Mathematics. He had the rare distinction of being Chancellor first of London University and then of Cambridge, where he inaugurated the Cavendish Laboratory, and the Chancellorship of Victoria University, Manchester was to be thrown in, for good measure, in 1880.

He has another claim to fame, too, within the context of this essay. If the Devonshire influence was prominent in Keighley, the name 'Devonshire Commission' figures no less than nineteen times in the index of Roderick and Stephens' *Education and Industry in the Nineteenth Century*. The seventh Duke was appointed by Gladstone to chair a Royal Commission on Scientific Instruction and the Advancement of Science in 1871. It sat for six years, met eighty times and collected voluminous and highly revealing evidence – most of it subsequently unread – and produced eight reports and four volumes of evidence. When read, the words in the reports – and in the evidence – still echo. The number of science masters was 'totally inadequate'. So, too, were some of their qualifications. 'In the universities the professors' time is so tied up with teaching that it is impossible for them to do more than teach, and in fact not to do that as thoroughly as they would wish.'

Sometimes in the twentieth century complaints have been made the other way round and, as the costs of science have increased, funding problems have increased also. Meanwhile, Devonshire interest in education remained strong, not least in the University of Leeds, where the ninth Duke was to be Chancellor from 1909 to 1938 and the tenth from 1938 to 1950. This was a hereditary succession. The Devonshires do not figure, however, in the impressive list of private donors to the University of Leeds, and the only reference to the family in E. J. Brown's booklet on the subject is to a Cavendish Memorial Chair in Physics, which was endowed not by the family but by public subscription in memory of Lord Frederick Cavendish, the fist President of the Yorkshire College.

Frederick was the seventh Duke's second son, and he was murdered in Phoenix Park, Dublin. He had given away the prizes at the Speech Day of the Keighley School of Art in 1865, and it was his widow who wrote to Smith when he became an MP. The seventh Duke's first son, the Marquis of Hartington, 'Harty Tarty', the Liberal leader who became eighth Duke of Devonshire in 1891, had Keighley connections, too, connections that would have surprised those of his contemporaries who knew him in fashionable London social circles. In particular, he greatly admired Smith's work for technical education, and he it was who successfully put forward Smith's name for a knighthood, which he received from a Conservative Prime Minister, Lord Salisbury, in 1897.

By then the eighth Duke, who had opposed Gladstone on home rule in 1886, had become a Liberal Unionist and an ally of the Conservatives. Smith, however, remained a steadfast Liberal, as did Brigg, and he seems to have had no other aristocratic connections except with the Devonshires. John Bright, while he lived, was the real hero for him: 'outside our own circle, there is no man I love so well, or for whose well being I would make greater sacrifices'. And long after Bright was dead, Smith continued to preach the old gospel of free trade. Indeed, when it seemed threatened in 1903 by Joseph Chamberlain's demand for protection, he made many speeches on the subject. One distinguished correspondent, John Morley, asked him on that occasion to tell him what struck him as 'the salient points in this fiscal controversy', 'You have special experience and knowledge', he went on, 'and you live in a centre where the discussion must be very "actual". Tell me in succinct form, if you have time with what *powers* you would confront the enemy.' Smith obliged.

In terms of Keighley experience, it is notable that Philip Snowden, for all his socialism, was to remain as active in the cause of free trade as Smith had been. As Ramsay MacDonald's Chancellor of the Exchequer, he would not consider any form of protection, and later, too, he was to break with MacDonald's National Government on this old issue. His resignation did not save him, however, from attack in Keighley from his old Labour supporters. One of the most vivid memories of my boyhood is that of being stopped in Cavendish Street by stalwart members of the ILP – one in particular, another Smith – who told me – at length – and I was then a thirteen-year old – just how grave Snowden's betrayal had been in 1931.

The Sir Swire Smith who emerges from Snowdon's biography – and who had emerged, never effortlessly, to become a leader in the town in which he worked – was a man of imagination and vision who, in Snowdon's words, 'could not think of business apart from life'. He made his own way, and this was clear even when he was young. Snowdon concentrates on this period when Smith had stood out as a key figure in a local 'renaissance' that was transforming the town and with it 'the drab morality of church and chapel'. He and the Brigg brothers read poetry together, went to exhibitions, sang glees and admired the work of the Lancashire dialect poet, Edwin Waugh, in Smith's opinion 'most certainly a genius . . . and great company'.

Snowdon quotes, for example, without giving a date, a *Keighley Spectator* article, written about Smith when he was in his twenties:

> We should like to say to some of our young men, 'Be less shy'; to others, 'Be less stiff'; to others again, 'Go on as you have so well begun'. Especially would we say this last to Mr. Swire Smith. His open countenance, his frank and easy manners, and above all his utterances from time to time of vigorous and masterly thought, cause him to stand out as a young man of great promise – an acute and independent thinker.

The long forgotten *Keighley Spectator*, founded in 1868 and described by Snowdon with a mixture of condescension and awe as 'a well meaning little print newly launched by the small band of older *illuminati*', goes on to refer to a speech recently given by Smith at the old Mechanics' Institute.

The Institute had been founded in 1825 in a building which after the completion of an imposing new Mechanics' Institute, planned by Smith, was to house yet another great local institution, the Yorkshire Penny Bank. The physical setting when Smith delivered his speech was said to have been uninspiring. Yet the speech itself, the local *Spectator* added, would 'not have disgraced a second-rate speaker in the National Assembly at St. Stephen's'.

Such a two-edged comment, not intended to be ungraceful, seems to me to be characteristically Keighlian, as characteristically so as the reference to the uninspiring character of the old Mechanics' Institute building itself. In no other town in England, however, can a Mechanics' Institute building have looked quite so prominent as the new building was to be. It was designed by Lockwood and Mawson, who figure in my book *Victorian Cities*, and an imposing sketch of it had appeared in *The*

Builder in 1869. Mabel Tylecote could not resist including a picture of it in her book *The Mechanics Institutes of Lancashire and Yorkshire before 1851* (1957), although it fell far outside her period.

It was a building where I myself have sat through many Speech Days, and it was a sad day for me – and I am sure for the town – when its tower and large parts of the building were destroyed by fire in 1962. It has now vanished from view, as has the imposing United Methodist Free Church, with contrasting spire, that stood next to it. A modern Technical College – of which Smith would surely have approved – now occupies both sites, and who in a secular age now knows just what the United Methodist Free Church stood for? The main Methodist Church in Keighley, solidly Wesleyan, was in a back street that was appropriately named, Temple Street. That, too, has now gone. The idea of *illuminati*, old or young, has also gone – though sociologists now talk of *élites*. Even in the days of the *Keighley Spectator* it came from an older culture than that of the nineteenth-century West Riding or for that matter of Methodism, as of course, did the very idea of a *Keighley Spectator* also.

By contrast, the idea of a Keighley Mechanics's Institute, first mooted in 1824 seemed genuinely new, and it was a matter of pride to the four working men who created it – a reed maker, a painter, a tailor and a joiner – that they were ahead of Bradford. We can see now, however, that even in 1825 the Institute was drawing on older ideas of culture than the 'Scottish ideas' of one of the four, John Farish, whose father was a Scots packman, or of George Birkbeck who linked Glasgow and London. There was a further touch of Keighley pride in the fact, notwithstanding that Birkbeck himself was a Yorkshireman, a 'Craven man', born not far away from the town.

One of the main supporters of the new Institute in Keighley had been the then Rector, the Rev. Theodore Dury, who had arrived in Keighley in 1812 and who ten years later had founded Keighley National School. A Cambridge graduate, Dury was the son of a Coldstream Guards officer and was an old Harrovian. This was a very different inheritance from that of Farish or Birkbeck.

Fortunately for the town, Dury soon proved that his social sympathies were far wider than his background might have suggested. He was on good terms with Nonconformists and with Methodists, particularly the latter, and in 1829 he had founded a children's paper, *The Monthly Teacher*, printed by one of Keighley's booksellers, Robert Aked. After the Mechanics' Institute was founded, whenever he visited London, Dury would order books for its rapidly growing library from London booksellers.

Dury's second wife was the daughter of a local manufacturer, and

Dury himself believed that the Rector of Keighley should count locally in all circles. Was it on his suggestion, therefore, that the following verse was printed on the title page of the 1830 *Annual Report* of the Institute? –

> . . . Serene philosophy
> She springs aloft, with elevated pride
> Above the tangled mass of low desires,
> That bind the fluttering crowd; and, angel-wing'd,
> The heights of science and of virtue gains,
> Where all is calm and clear.

What could be more elevated in sentiment? What could be more remarkable, too, than the fact that the Brontë sisters were among the borrowers of books from the old Mechanics' Institute Library?

A twentieth-century Rector of Keighley, and future Bishop of Wakefield, Canon Eric Treacy, a steam engine enthusiast, as I am, had been in Keighley for three years in 1948, when he persuaded me without much difficulty – as a very young historian – to write a brief history of Keighley for a Parish Church booklet to celebrate the centenary of the new Parish Church building. It was called the Church of St Andrew – another link with Scotland. The foundation stone of the Church had been laid in February 1846, when Dury had been succeeded as Rector by William Busfield.

I like, as I have said, to look for links, and there was another link at that time, too, with Leeds, for the architect was R. D. Chantrell, who had also been responsible for the 'restoration' of Leeds Parish Church. And there was to be yet another Parish Church link, too, with my school, for the Rev. H. J. Longsdon, Rector of Keighley from 1877 to 1888, gave his name to a third House to set alongside those of Brigg and Smith. He had been a pioneer of Church extension, and the motto of the House – how many of its members knew how it had got it? – was *Surge et Fulge*.

The first Parish Church in Keighley dated back to the reign of Henry II – there was real continuity in that – and nearby was Keighley's oldest inn, the Lord Rodney, which before Rodney's naval exploits had been called the Red Lion. One of its innkeepers had been John Drake of what we come to think of erroneously as a partnership, the partnership that had provided the funds for the creation of Keighley Free Grammar School in 1713.

There was contrast, none the less, along with continuity. Pre-industrial Keighley must have been a very different Keighley from Victorian Keighley. When industry was young – as early as 1805 – the Rev. Thomas Dunham Whitaker, a gentleman-historian, with

impeccable eighteenth-century attitudes and equally impeccable Geor-
gian style, had said of Keighley in his impressive *History and Antiquities
of the Deanery of Craven* that there was little in it that could 'interest
the eye, the memory or the imagination'. 'I may therefore be excused if
I betray some anxiety to reach more pleasing scenes, for hard is the fate
of a Topographer while he respires the smoke of manufactures and is
stunned by the din of recent population.'

Back to respiration. There was little that was 'calm and clear' – to use
Dury's words – in Victorian Keighley. Nor was there in the history of
the old Grammar School, which in 1862 was said, not for the first time,
to be infringing 'the benevolent intentions of the founder . . . to the
great detriment of the inhabitants of Keighley'. The feeling was
abroad, again very Keighlian, that the then headmaster, Abraham
Crabtree, was not doing the job for which he had been appointed –
and, more seriously, that he was making too much money out of the
School. By the end of the decade, the School in its old form had gone.

Lord Taunton's Schools Inquiry Commission, set up in 1865, had
surveyed Yorkshire's endowed schools, and had found that Keighley's
free Grammar School was not only old, but 'worn out'. There were
only forty-two boys being taught, including three boarders. The sur-
veyor who made the judgement was Joshua (later Sir Joshua) Fitch,
who has figured, like Birkbeck, in previous essays in this volume. For
him the standard attained seemed to be no higher than that in a
National School. Latin was professed, but not practised. Not one of
the boys was 'far enough advanced to write out from memory the
inflections of a noun'. Nor was arithmetic any better, 'the best boys
being unable to go beyond proportion'.

The income of the school was largely derived from the Drake
benefaction, while income from a Tonson benefaction, managed by a
separate group of Trustees, was used to employ 'an old, incapacitated
and feeble man to teach twenty little children [younger than the
Grammar School boys] in a dilapidated building in the centre of the
town on a payment of 2d. a week'. Nobody, Fitch concluded sharply,
'pretends that this school is of the smallest use'.

Fitch noted, too, how unpopular both institutions were with local
Nonconformists, whether they believed that Latin should or should
not be taught. I did not know any of this when I visited the Briggs as a
boy. Nor did I have any idea either, that Giggleswick, the school to
which they were sent, then a minor public school, was an equally
depressing school at the time of the Taunton visitation: with a rich
endowment, it had only thirty-seven boys. Sedbergh, in my own
childhood a prestigious school – our First Rugby Fifteen used to play

regularly against their Second Fifteen on their notorious pitch – was even worse. How were they to change? Certainly not because of community action.

Fitch's unimpressive biography, written by A. L. Lilley, Vicar of St Mary's, Paddington Green and published as long ago as 1906, tells us nothing of this. Nor does it help us to answer questions. It deals only in generalities, and it has none of the pulsating life of Snowdon's *The Master Spinner*. Indeed, it is just what the history of education should not be. The only clue lies in the advertising blurb which employs an adjective to apply to Fitch which the *Keighley News* had applied to Smith – 'strenuous'. To the end he was 'fighting with his pen'. Individuals counted in creating the new. Trends mattered less.

Whatever may be said of Fitch's role, Smith's role in transforming the old Keighley Grammar School was unmistakably a strenuous one. He was the most active of the local reformers, and it was before the Taunton Commission reported – and not after – that he and his friends, most of them Nonconformists, had planned – on the basis of local evidence, statistical and qualitative – the creation of a new day school to be located inside the new Mechanics' Institute building. It was to be a school that would set aside 'all the old formulas which have made the sum of the education of most lads in the past'.

In the first place, it would have limited objectives – 'to teach what the lads of our district needed to help them to do their work better and easier, and how best to lay out the products of their work in the wisest manner'. Bristol seemed to be a model, but there was cross reference, too, to La Martinière in Lyons and the Turgot Municipal School in Paris. In 1872, Smith was to write an interesting article in *Blackwood's Magazine* about the initiation of his project and what had subsequently happened to it, an article in which he stated rather more broadly, much as the sponsors of new educational institutions might do today, that 'whatever other branches of education they might eventually be able to initiate, their new institution should, at any rate, afford artistic, scientific and technical instruction'.

When the Taunton Committee reported, an unusually complacent *Keighley News* found a measure of satisfaction in the fact that 'Keighley Grammar School . . . if it never rose as high as some of its sister institutions, had not fallen as low as many of them in scale of usefulness.' But by then, thanks to Smith, all the important steps had already been taken radically to change the local educational set-up; and 'with no initiative from the Government' [Smith's own words] an ingenious solution had been found to the problem of how to relate 'the old and worn out' to the new and the challenging. The solution that emerged was somewhat different, doubtless, from that which Fitch himself would have suggested, for it rested on an attempt to get the best out of both worlds.

As the result of the compromise, the new school that had been projected by Smith and his friends was to benefit from a share of the original Drake endowment, so that in a sense it was not to be completely new. But a condition had been attached by the Endowed Schools Commissioners, appointed in 1869 following the report of the Taunton Commission. A 'literary department' was to be added to the school to broaden the scope of the trade education originally envisaged. It was to comprise 'the elements . . . of Latin, English literature, and composition, history and geography'.

Meanwhile, the remaining share of the Drake endowment and the whole of the Tonson endowment were to be used to fund a new Drake and Tonson Grammar School for Girls. The suggested arrangement was bold in that there did not seem to be much enthusiasm for a Girls' Grammar School in Keighley – and a somewhat similar idea was strongly opposed in far-away Gloucester – but the new school was to succeed notwithstanding. There had, indeed, been precedents for action to raise the status of girls in Keighley. There had even been a Female Radical Association in 1839.

Significantly, there was to be no trade element in the curriculum of the Girls' Grammar School, and its first headmistress, Mary Eliza Porter, who arrived in Keighley 'with the highest recommendations', found to her consternation that the first twenty-seven girls who enrolled were 'generally speaking extremely ignorant and unused to any kind of discipline, and very untidy and careless in their work'. It proved 'no easy task to train them into better habits', and she herself only stayed in the new school for one year. What happened next is a topic for a future historian.

The new Mechanics' Institute building, in which the Trade and Grammar School was to be housed, had its official opening in September 1870, and at the opening Brigg stated that the new Trade School might prove to be the most significant element in the new building. He went on, however, to explain just what had happened: there was not

> a gentleman on the committee of the proposed new institution [the Trade School] who had any idea of its having anything to do with the work of the Endowed Schools Commission. They had their scheme well in hand, and their building almost completed when they heard that the Endowed School Commissioners were down upon them, and found that these gentlemen were thinking of doing in the Grammar School what they [Smith's Committee] were intending to do in the Institute.

As a result of hard talking, there were not to be two rival institutions, but one, Keighley Trade and Grammar School. Smith himself was to write in *Blackwood's Magazine* of the 'utilisation of all available resources'. The sponsors of City Technology Colleges – and Sir Cyril Taylor in London – will recognise the language.

The Chairman on the day of the opening of the new Mechanics' Institute in 1870 was Isaac Holden, mill owner pioneer of education, who was to be Keighley's first MP – and its first baronet – and the guests included Lord Frederick Cavendish, Henry Cole, Lord Houghton, and Edmund Baines, owner of the influential *Leeds Mercury* and at that time MP for Leeds. The Duke of Devonshire, as already noted, was the official opener.

Introducing Smith as one of the key speakers, Holden, born thirty-five years before him, not in Keighley but in Glasgow – yet another example of the connection with Scotland – said that he had 'already done a great good for my town and that, as he grew older, the town would be more and more indebted to him'. For Holden, 'labour, the source of all wealth . . . could not be applied without knowledge', and an industrial town with good schools, where 'all the working population could be well and thoroughly taught', would 'win in the race of competition with other towns'. Holden did not refer, however, to competition with other countries, a subject, which as we have seen, had already interested Smith.

For his part, Smith, proud of the fact that while the country had been talking, Keighley had been 'up and doing', explained on this 'auspicious' occasion that Keighley people had at last 'recognised what the wants of an industrial community were'. Emphasising that there were social as well as economic arguments for educational advance, he claimed that 'if a scheme of education' were 'carried into effect, it would be a great boon for the country, and they would save in prisons and workhouses what they expended in schools'. This was a useful but limited argument, generally used in 1870, and fortunately Smith was greatly to extend and deepen it in *Blackwood's Magazine*, when he wrote in broad terms of 'a ladder of learning let down among our struggling poor, whose top reaches the highest realms of culture'.

The extension was called for. Indeed, in 1869 and 1870 there had been critics of the proposed new arrangement in Keighley, who asked whether 'the hobby horse' of technical instruction was 'to be ridden to the exclusion of learning: that is, whether a parent who does not choose to bring up his son to some handicraft will still have to send him out of the town to acquire that knowledge which will fit him for entering the university'. Would 'the highest careers' really be opened up to 'the child of the poorest among us'?

'R.S.', who wrote to this effect in the *Keighley News*, may well have been R. Stansfield, then a curate at the Parish Church. He need not have been worried, however, about the long-term outcome on that score, although the new Head Master, James Spencer, a Member of the College of Preceptors, was not a university graduate, and had arrived in Keighley not from a Grammar School, as Palmer and Hind were to do, but from Worcester Trade and Science School. After all, the object of the new Trade and Grammar School had been advertised in March 1871 as that of supplying both 'a Liberal' and 'a Practical English Education', that was to be 'supplemented by the systematic teaching of such Art and Science subjects as are applicable to the trades of the district', and the first scholarships were advertised as scholarships to 'the Grammar School'. From the start, whatever the fears of R.S. and local people who felt like him, the new school succeeded in providing various kinds of knowledge, 'Liberal' and 'Practical', with sufficient efficiency to ensure that over the years a regular supply of boys was sent to universities, including Oxford and Cambridge.

There were already 200 pupils by 1875 – some of them holders of Drake and Tonson Scholarships, as I was to be – and one of the first old boys, another Smith – T. H. – matriculated with first-class honours from London University in 1876. Already in 1874, when Henry Cole spoke to a meeting of the Yorkshire Union of Mechanics' Institutes at Ripon, he remarked that Keighley was 'a wonderful place . . . a model for the whole of the nation'.

With hindsight, the compromise of 1870 looks sensible, although I am far from sure that in the long run the new institution was as successful in meeting Smith's demand for 'a Practical' education as it was in meeting demands for 'a Liberal English Education'. The 'trade element' became strictly limited, although I learned woodwork and metalwork myself – and the development of a new and separate Technical School after 1902, the Head of which in my childhood was a great antagonist of Neville Hind, Denis Healey's father – seemed to imply that it had not met such local demands. Indeed, in 1871 itself the School is said to have attracted fewer sons of artisans than had been hoped, and to have bridged social gulfs only to a limited extent. Moreover, with the development of local elementary education after 1870, a social as well as an educational gap opened up between different kinds of Keighley schools at the same time as the gap between Keighley Trade and Grammar School and traditional Yorkshire Grammar Schools was narrowing.

The comprehensive school solution that was eventually adopted after the War, had already been talked of before the War began, but it, too, did not solve all the educational or social difficulties. Fewer boys now go to Oxford or Cambridge from the main successor comprehensive school, Oakbank, than used to be the case in my own childhood.

In some ways horizons have narrowed. Why has this been so? I would be less concerned were I satisfied that there was motivated movement to other universities than Oxford and Cambridge or deliberately chosen movement to polytechnics. I am not so satisfied. Nor is Harry Pedley, brother of Robin Pedley, the great advocate of comprehensive schools, who was Keighley's Director of Education, when the town 'went comprehensive'.

Compromises have always been made in educational administration, and essentially, the Keighley compromise was the same compromise as that eventually arrived at in higher education, a fact that has been stressed recently in a carefully researched study by my friend and former colleague, Professor E. P. Hennock, now Professor of History at Liverpool University.

Singling out a number of cases of universities becoming more comprehensive, he started with Manchester. When after 1889 the government, inspired by men like Smith, decided to provide 'whisky money' for technical education, leaving discretion to local authorities in relation to the distribution of available funds, there was a possibility that a well-financed Municipal Technical School in Manchester, based on the old Mechanics' Institute, would receive a large share and consequently find itself in rivalry with Owen's College, the embryonic university institution. The Manchester story, which was to go through many phases, ended with Manchester University teaching both technology and classical and other liberal studies, just as Keighley Grammar School in my boyhood taught both textiles and Latin.

It is not a coincidence that one of the most distinguished Professors at Owen's College, the chemist, Henry Roscoe, who was a close friend and colleague of Smith, threw his weight against the substantial endowment of a German type of *polytechnicum* in Manchester 'alongside a well-equipped university college' on the grounds that it would be 'a waste of educational effort and would almost necessarily lead to hurtful competition'.

At Leeds, too, where the new Yorkshire College of Science opened its doors in rented premises in 1874, there was immediate pressure to develop the arts also. Indeed at the official opening in October 1875, after the Duke of Devonshire, in the Chair yet again, had given what he called the longest speech that he had ever delivered, Forster, in the presence of Playfair and Baines, urged the case, as the Taunton Commission had urged it in Keighley, for the introduction into the new institution of literature. So, too, did the first lecturer in biology, Louis Miall, a friend of Smith who was described at the time as being 'as clear, as honest and as cold as some northern stream'.

The first student to enrol at Leeds was a coalminer – Shadrach

Stephenson, from Methley. He arrived, it is said, well prepared with writing paper, ready to start work immediately. The first full-time paid Principal, not appointed until 1882, Nathan Bodington, was not a scientist, but a Professor of Classics and Philosophy. Michael Sadler, his successor in 1911 as Vice-Chancellor – for in 1904 Leeds had become a full university – had obtained a First in Greats in Oxford, a fact that was as important as the fact that he arrived in Leeds University from Manchester University. Appropriately, the *Manchester Guardian* remarked that 'the University of Leeds has done the best thing possible for itself and the worst possible for Manchester'.

Sadler took it for granted that a complete university required technology, science, the arts and medicine. He took it for granted, too, that the English approach to higher education was superior to the German which he knew at first hand and in detail, and which interested him for the whole of his life. Dr J. H. Higginson has devoted himself to the study of Sadler's work, and in 1979 I wrote an introduction to selections from Sadler's writings which he had very carefully compiled.

Since 1979, the 'hurtful competition' that alarmed Roscoe, and market theories of education that alarmed Sadler, have come to be taken for granted as essential features of the complex – and underfunded – English educational system of the late-twentieth century – if it can even now be called a system. Clearly in the light of this shift, which it is still difficult to view in perspective, nineteenth-century 'solutions' have to be reassessed. There was an obvious case in the late-nineteenth century for developing in this country separate and distinctive technical institutions on German lines, English equivalents of German *technische hochschule*, and for keeping technology out of the universities. That was not, however, to be the English way. Moreover, in the twentieth century, in the capital city itself, Imperial College was to become part of London University and was not to develop as an English version of Charlottenburg in Berlin.

Any twentieth-century debate on the structures of higher education, as Dr Hennock shows, must take account of why an 'English solution' was reached. I myself believe that the case for one, two or a small number of separate well-endowed technical institutions on German lines was – and is – a strong one, although I also believe with Sadler that technology should continue to have a place in universities along with science and the humanities. Such is my own compromise. I would also bring Universities and Polytechnics more closely together. I tried to do that in Sussex, and because of Crosland and his heirs failed.

The debate is not over, and meanwhile the nineteenth-century debate about what elements should be present in the curriculum at the school level continues also. I was fascinated to read a key speech made during the 1870s by John Morley, who believed as passionately in education as his friend Smith did, but who envisaged educational ladders not in terms of clever Keighley boys – or clever boys elsewhere – going to Oxford or Cambridge, but in terms only of their vocational advancement. Indeed – and he made this quite explicit in a Presidential address delivered to the Midland Institute in Birmingham in 1876:

> It is of questionable expediency to invite the cleverest members of any class to leave it – instead of making their abilities available in it, and so raising the whole class along with, and by means of, their own rise . . . I doubt the expediency – and the history of Oxford within the last twenty-five years strikingly confirms this doubt – of giving to a young man of any class what is practically a premium on indolence . . . The best thing that I can think of as happening to a young man is this: that he should have been educated at a day school in his own town, and that he should have opportunities of following also the higher education in his own town; and that at the earliest possible time he should have been taught to earn his own living.

All I can add is that such an approach, which is not without its theoretical attractions, would have been anathema to me as a boy, and that when years later I followed Morley in giving a Presidential Address to the same Institute – I was very proud to be its President – my own approach was completely different. I believe strongly in access – and that not only for the outstandingly clever – and I believe, too, in community imperatives, but I do not believe that any educational system should be limited in the way suggested by Morley. His 'best thing' was far too narrow.

Instead, I strongly approve of remarks made by Canon Robinson, an Endowed Schools Commissioner, when he visited Keighley in 1875 and said:

> There are some principles that they fairly accepted as fundamental – as axioms to which they were bound to adhere. One was that there ought to be no distinctions of education between class and class . . . They must contend for the principle that all should learn . . . and that for each education shall be as free and open as possible. And as there should be no distinction of class, there should be no distinction of sex . . . If it were necessary, by some unhappy law of circumstances, that only one sex shall be educated, it would be more desirable that education should be given to the girls than to the boys.

Both parts of Robinson's statement in my view still stand – and must stand.

And so back to Keighley! The timing of the opening of the new Mechanics' Institute building in 1870 was significant. This was the year of the passing of the first national Education Act, the Forster Act, and while Keighley was introducing a new kind of secondary school it made only a curiously convoluted response to the Act which dealt with primary education. In part, this was because of Nonconformist attitudes – the Birmingham League had many supporters in the town. In part, doubtless, it was because W. E. Forster was an MP for Bradford. The town no more wanted to be told what to do about education than it wanted to be told what to do about vaccination.

Unduly proud of its own educational record, and resenting pressure from Whitehall, Keighley did not choose to set up a School Board until 1875, five years after Bradford; and at the prizegiving of the Art School in 1871, when the distinguished visitor, A. J. Mundella, MP for Sheffield and minister in charge of education in Gladstone's government, suggested that it should, it was John Brigg of all people who said that a Keighley Board was not necessary. Worse still, it would be too expensive also. There have always been economic brakes on educational development, and in this case they were being applied in a period of unprecedented economic prosperity. At first sight, paradoxically, they would be taken off when trade worsened. But the paradox disappears when we realise that it was when trade worsened that Smith's concern about international competition began to be more widely shared.

The independence argument was strongest in 1870–73, when there was unbelievably strong local opposition to any kind of outside interference, an opposition which had been apparent even when the Trade and Grammar School was set up. 'Will there be a local control over the disposition of the endowment in Keighley?', R.S. had asked in 1870. Now such opposition went further. The *Keighley Herald*, the local Conservative newspaper, argued vigorously, but depressingly, in 1873, that 'the fact is whether we be all educated or not, there will always be a greater demand for labourers than managers, and if all be educated, there will be no increased demand for managers, commissioners or prime ministers'.

In a local poll of 1873 there was a majority of three to one against the creation of a School Board, and in the eyes of this majority, by no means a moral majority, Smith, who realised how much the progress of the new Trade and Grammar School might be checked by lack of adequate primary education, was the main villain. By contrast, Smith knew who the real villains were. They were victims, he appreciated, as well as or more than villains. 'Although the school door might be open, there were many neglected children who never went in, but received as their only teaching the pernicious education of the street and the gutter.' His views were confirmed when more people signed with a cross to vote against the creation of a School Board in 1873 – there were 2026 against and only 540 for – 'than with either cross or name' to support it.

The local struggle was rough, and in 1875 Smith claimed that he had actually been threatened with murder in anonymous letters. By then, however, after fierce debates on the platform and in the Press, Keighley had been forced to hold its first elections for a School Board: District Inspector's reports had revealed that it failed to meet minimum requirements. In those stirring elections, in defiance of what had happened earlier, the five Liberals who stood for seats, including Smith, were all elected, along with four others, including the local Roman Catholic priest, the Rev. P. Kiernan. When the Board made a survey of the number of new primary school places that were needed in the town it was discovered that despite claims that everything was well, there was a need for no fewer than 1600 new school places.

Smith saw the provision of adequate primary education as a *sine qua non* for social as well as for educational advance. What would happen to a town where even those who went to school were so ignorant that in one class, as the District Inspector's report had revealed, only one boy was prepared to respond to the question where London was and then put it in Wales? In another class he had discovered that not one child knew the name of his or her county? What would happen to a county where at a 'higher level of education' science students were as difficult to find as needles in a haystack? What would happen to a country if, as was indubitably the case, 'other countries enjoyed both the benefit of a superior system of primary and secondary education', and the opportunities at a later stage for 'the acquirement of technical and scientific knowledge'? The questions might well have been put by Sir Claus Moser.

It was in a dedicated mood that Smith devoted the rest of his life to education, his main contribution being made not during the 1870s but during the 1880s, when he was appointed a member of a Royal Commission presided over by Bernhard Samuelson, one of the greatest of British ironmasters, to study technical instruction as a necessary element in economic progress. The terms were

> to enquire into the Instruction of the Industrial Classes of certain Foreign Countries in technical and other subjects, for the purpose of comparison with that of the corresponding classes in this country; and into the influence of such Instruction on manufacturing and other Industries at home and abroad.

There were seven Commissioners in all, invited by Mundella, who was then Vice-President of the Council – and again in charge of

education – in a new Gladstone Liberal government – and they were all
expected to pay their own expenses in order to save government
money. Mundella knew more about industry than most ministers
concerned with education have done before or since, and the members
of the Commission, like their Chairman, who was Liberal MP for
Banbury, all had substantial foreign experience. Samuelson had been
trained as an engineer by a Swiss firm in Liverpool, had exported
locomotives throughout Europe, had set up an agricultural machinery
business in Orleans, and had made a fortune as an ironmaster on
Tees-side.

The other Commissioners, all well chosen, included Roscoe, Philip
Magnus, founder of the City and Guilds system, John Slagg, who had
accompanied Cobden on his mission to Paris in 1860 to negotiate an
Anglo-French commercial treaty, and William Mather, head of the
great engineering firm of Mather and Platt in Salford, the unpublished
history of which I have written. The Commission's Secretary was
Gilbert Redgrave of the Science and Art Department of South Kensington; Snowdon believed that Matthew Arnold wanted the post.
Smith was in good company, as he knew, and, somewhat surprisingly,
he was paid £100 towards his own expenses by the Bradford Chamber
of Commerce.

The reports of the Commission ran into five massive volumes, and
they reveal not only how far Britain was falling behind in technical
instruction but how, zealous though the seven Commissioners were
in trying to get matters right, it seemed to be difficult to point to
remedies. The links between primary and technical education were
noted, and the Commissioners urged that elementary science – and
drawing – should be taught at the primary school level, but they did
not favour prolonged technical education in separate institutions which
would keep students out of the workshop until the age of 21 or 22. Nor
did they press for radically new structures. They favoured City and
Guilds examinations and the extension of the influence of the Science
and Art Department at South Kensington by the creation of more local
colleges, aided from local sources. Because they were cautious, the
evidence presented to them is more interesting than their own conclusions.

The Commissioners specialised in their tasks. Roscoe dealt with
higher education and research, Magnus with curricula, Smith with
'industry', the broadest of topics. Samuelson edited the entire work,
curbing, it seems, any tendencies to learn too much from abroad –
in Magnus's words 'bringing into prominence the advantage of our
apprentice system and workshop training, whenever any of us ascribed,
in his opinion, too much importance to technical instruction'. John

Bright had taken the same stand in talking to Smith ten years earlier: 'any one wanting to learn the weaving trade of Rochdale, say floor-mats, had best go into the mills, where it must be taught better than in the schools'. And what Samuelson thought and Bright said is still being thought and said today.

Smith, more adventurous, was greatly impressed by what he saw on his four visits to France and Germany, the latter a country which he already knew well, and where he had already used Miall of Leeds University as an interpreter. He also made one visit to the United States. According to Redgrave, he compiled the notes on which the foreign sections of the Report, which Samuelson qualified, were based. Snowdon says little of the actual work of the Royal Commission except that its Report 'made a sensation'. He does not note the significance of the Technical Institution Act of 1889 which followed or of the more important contribution made by the whisky money that came the following year. A more general historian would stress that pressure for action in 1889 had come from a national association, presided over by the Duke of Devonshire, who once said that the object of his association was to induce the country to follow the example of Keighley. The secretaries were Roscoe and A. H. D. Acland MP, a leader amongst the educational reformers of the 1890s.

In John Leese's somewhat curious book *Personalities and Power in English Education* (1950) there is a footnote to the story. In 1895 the Science and Art Department at South Kensington introduced a compulsory literary element into the curriculum of technical and science schools, recognising for grant purposes every subject except classics. There is another footnote in Snowdon. One of the people who wrote to Smith after reading an essay by him on the Technical Instruction Bill was Prince Kropotkin, 'Russian geographer and revolutionary', as his brief biographies quaintly call him. His address then was thoroughly unrevolutionary, Harrow, Middlesex:

> As to technical education [Kropotkin wrote] I noted with the greatest interest the movement which is going on in this country in that direction. But technical education, I am afraid will not help Britain to regain her former position. Everywhere – even in my own country – efforts are made for spreading it. It will be a boon for humanity, not an aim in what they call the struggle for existence.

Smith did not reply.

Snowdon, who himself footnotes this with interest, adding that Kropotkin 'perplexed' Smith, turns with no regrets from Smith's serious pursuit of investigating industry and its needs to trivial verses that seemed to him to catch the mood of the day:

Seven Commissioners Royal are we
Who have gone abroad the schools to see,
To learn how they teach the ABC
And apply it to works of industry,
And all for the sake of our good countree.

Seven Commissioners Royal are we,
Artistic, poetic and literary;
And one can spin in musical tone
An amorous yarn when we're all alone
That awakens no thought of the factory.

The spinner of the 'amorous yarn' was Smith, who years later was to gossip with Redgrave about the romance of their journeys around Europe twenty years before. Between seeing schools and colleges and visiting factories, they had 'shared', as Snowdon inimitably put it in a remarkable oxymoron, 'modest breakfasts in *crêmeries*, and the romantic outlook'.

On one occasion, they had 'run away together' to climb the Brocken at nightfall and, finding no hotel on the summit, had slept badly and briefly between rocks on a 'couch of heather and bracken' – only to discover that, in their absence, the other Commissioners had been entertained by the Empress Frederick at Potsdam. Now, twenty years on, they travelled together to Nuremberg for a centennial exhibition to celebrate 'the freeing of Bavaria' and from there to Serbia and to Budapest.

There is one touch of romance in my own study of Smith which has more to do with coincidence than with educational comparisons, convergences and divergences. Three of the happiest holidays in my own life have been spent in Florida – at Hobe Sound on Jupiter Island – as a guest of my friends Jack and Drue Heinz. The setting was perfect, the company lively. It was only when I was asked to write a brief life of Sir Swire Smith for the *Dictionary of National Biography* that I discovered that he, along with Brigg, was one of the people who had first seen the possibilities of what he called 'a sort of Riviera site' on Jupiter Island.

Smith and Brigg were both shareholders in the Florida Bank, founded in 1889 on the model of the Land Mortgage Bank of Texas, and of the Jupiter Island Indian River Association – as was Sir Isaac Holden – and they dreamed of making more money out of Florida – and its phosphates – than they had ever made out of the mills of the West Riding.

Enterprise at a distance was highly precarious, however, and so, too, was Smith's remark that he looked on Florida as his old-age pension. The Florida venture failed because of irregularities on the spot, and the Bank was liquidated. It had been coincidental that on his way out to the island for the first time Smith had read Robert Louis Stevenson's *Treasure Island*, but there was no coincidence in the brute fact that Florida, while a 'realm of flowers', was not an El Dorado.

None the less, on the way back from Florida there had been one very propitious coincidence for Smith. His fellow travellers included Mr and Mrs Andrew Carnegie, who thereafter became friends for the rest of his life. Smith was often entertained by Carnegie at Skibo Castle, where after listening to the bagpipes – and to Carnegie talking – he would sing some of his own North of England comic songs to entertain him.

For Smith, Carnegie was the most important and interesting man that he had ever met. He spoke 'slowly almost with a drawl', and on the first occasion they encountered each other they discussed Ruskin, electricity, the writing of books and the giving of lectures. The third of these topics was of particular interest to Smith. 'In writing a book', he noted, 'he has the method in his mind, but does not make a skeleton. In preparing a lecture he builds the skeleton – without any jokes in it – and commits it to memory. The jokes grow as the lecture is repeated, and at last it is ready to be given in the big cities.'

Carnegie also told Smith that he believed that the Almighty as revealed in the old Testament was diabolical and that he did not believe in the Trinity. On a different plane he assured Smith that he fully recognised 'the legality and justice' of trade unions. Smith carefully noted all this down.

When Carnegie talked of writing a book, he perhaps did not think too much of the readers of books. Yet he was to establish his fame in many British towns by setting up free public libraries, and it was through Smith's friendship with him that Keighley acquired £10,000 from him to start building the first Carnegie Free Library in England in 1899, yet another Keighley building, 'an early-Renaissance style building', that was to be opened by a Duke of Devonshire – in 1904. Smith saw the Carnegie Free Library in modern terms as a 'continuation school through life, for education ends with life only'. He also made sure that Carnegie was made a Freeman of Keighley. The Freemanship was presented to him in a casket that characteristically had been designed by Carnegie himself.

In the event, the Library cost double the sum budgeted, although all of the original stock of books came from the Mechanics' Institute Library. The Institute also provided it with its first librarian. There was cultural continuity here, just as there had been cultural continuity in 1891 when a new Museum in Victoria Park had been stocked with geological and mineralogical specimens acquired by the Keighley Scientific and Literary Society [note the bracketing] and previously housed in the Mechanics' Institute.

The Museum also contained without any sense of incongruity 'machinery in motion' and an old Egyptian mummy, my own delights as a child. I have been delighted later in my life to serve as President of the Friends of Cliffe Castle, Keighley's present museum. The 'Castle', the home of Isaac Butterfield, deserved its name just as Prince Smith deserved to be called Prince: it was 'a good specimen of the Elizabethan castellated style of architecture'. Just as impressively for me, the bedroom furniture had been Rossini's.

Butterfield provided some of the money that made possible the acquisition of Victoria Park, where the old Museum was located. The twentieth-century benefactor who gave Cliffe Castle to the town was another Smith, Sir Bracewell Smith, Keighley's one and only Lord Mayor of London in 1947. There was certainly romance for the town then, and I felt it myself when I met Sir Bracewell in 1947 in London's Mansion House – and was his guest in the Director's Box at the Arsenal ground, Highbury.

More seriously, the Smith/Carnegie coincidence has affected my own life, for it was in Keighley's Carnegie Library that I first learnt to treasure books. Eventually, too, its Reference Collection incorporated the library of the Labour leader, Philip Snowden, who was made a Freeman of the town in 1925. On this score alone I felt great gratitude to Snowden, whatever local Labour Party dignitaries in Keighley thought about him. Nor was the Snowden Library my only debt to Carnegie. I used to read newspapers in the Library as well as books. The Library has provided Keighley, too, with its leading local historian, Ian Dewhirst, at present Keighley's Librarian, whose brief history of Keighley, now being revised, appeared in 1974, published by the Corporation in the year when the Corporation ceased to exist and when Keighley became a part of Bradford Metropolitan District.

Dewhirst has followed in the footsteps of other local historians, like Clifford Whone, whom it was a pleasure to know, and, indeed, the Briggs themselves. J. J. wrote articles on 'The King's Highway in Craven' and on 'East Riddlesden Hall' and W. A., although a non-Churchman, edited 'The Parish Registers of St. Andrew's'.

While Carnegie was contributing to a new look for Keighley, the Heinzes were helping to change the look of Pittsburgh, the steel city that had actually turned down an offer from Carnegie to endow it with a Carnegie Public Library in 1881. It changed its mind a decade later. There are other links. The American Carnegie Foundation has supported the most detailed twentieth-century study of American higher education ever undertaken, a study for which there has been no British equivalent. Meanwhile, at Hawthornden in Scotland and at Menaggio in Italy, Drue Heinz has been involved in supporting creative writers who need time to think and to work far away from daily chores.

I myself have written part of this essay in Menaggio, which I discover that Smith visited on Easter Monday in 1910. 'Another delicious morning', he wrote, 'Took a small boat for the day . . . Many stories in the hall after dinner.' Through coincidences, circles, fortunately not all of which are vicious, can become curiously complete.

Smith knew this. He also knew that the past is worth studying, although as he studied it, his mood was not the same as mine in writing this book. 'To me', he declared, 'the past is a rich landscape beautiful with flowers and romantic with hills and dales and dells; and, to a sanguine mind, like mine, the future is as a glowing autumn to the year.' To me, as I have explained, there are weeds amongst the flowers and pollution in the hills, dales and dells. Nor do I dream of autumnal futures. I find it difficult to be sanguine.

I prefer Smith in a different and more purposeful mood, as he was when on a visit to the United States just before the First World War, he ended his notes by recording the motto on display in Boston Library, 'The Commonwealth requires the education of the people as the safeguard of order and liberty.' A few years later, after the Great War had begun, he returned to our own national requirement. 'Germany was in a hurry', he told an audience in Manchester after he had become an MP, 'but don't let her murderous threat to the civilisation of the world blind you. Our educational period is the shortest amongst the advanced nations.' The answers to questions still start there.

Index